# Human Computer Interaction: Developing Effective Organizational Information Systems

**Dov Te'eni**
**Jane Carey**
**Ping Zhang**

with a Foreword by Izak Benbasat

John Wiley & Sons, Inc.

| | |
|---|---|
| EXECUTIVE EDITOR | Beth Lang Golub |
| EDITORIAL ASSISTANT | Jennifer Snyder |
| SENIOR PRODUCTION EDITOR | Ken Santor |
| MARKETING MANAGER | Jillian Rice |
| SENIOR DESIGNER | Kevin Murphy |
| COVER PHOTO | Henry Arden / Zefa / Corbis Images |

This book was set in Times Roman by Publication Services and printed and bound by Hamilton Printing Company. The cover and color insert were printed by Phoenix Color Corporation.

This book is printed on acid free paper. ∞

To order books or for customer service please, call 1-800-CALL WILEY (225-5945).

ISBN-13  978-0-471-67765-9
ISBN-10  0-471-67765-5

Printed in the United States of America

10 9 8 7 6 5 4 3 2 1

To m'ladies Mira, Sharon, and Avital
with love and with gratitude
for your unconditional support.
—DT

For my parents, Ruth and Robert Carey
—JC

To Stoney, Cindy, and Melody
who make me happy
—PZ

# Contents

## CONTEXT

### ▶ Chapter 1 Introduction

### ▶ Chapter 2 Organizational and Business Context

## FOUNDATIONS

## ▶ Chapter 3 Interactive Technologies

## ▶ **Chapter 4 Physical Engineering**

## ▶ **Chapter 5 Congnitive Engineering**

## ▶ Chapter 6 Affective Engineering

## APPLICATIONS

## ▶ Chapter 7 Evaluation

## ▶ Chapter 8 Design Principles and Guidelines

## ▶ Chapter 9 Tasks in the Organizational Context

## ▶ Chapter 10 Componential Design

## ▶ Chapter 11 HCI Development Methodology

## ADDITIONAL CONTEXT

## ▶ Chapter 12 Interpersonal Relationships, Collaboration, and Organization

## ▶ Chapter 13 Social and Global Issues

▶ **Chapter 14 Meeting the Changing Needs of IT Development and Use**

# Foreword

This text, written by well-known academics influential in shaping human-computer-interaction (HCI) research in the information systems field, represents a paradigm shift in HCI scholarship. For many years, information systems academics teaching HCI courses in business and information schools faced the challenge of working with textbooks that had a computer-science centric view of HCI. Here at last is a novel, insightful, and comprehensive text that brings HCI knowledge front-and-center into the context of management and organizations. It does a masterful job of integrating the findings of HCI research in information systems with those found in the traditional HCI literature to provide new insights while maintaining the proper balance between theory, methods, and applications to the business context. It is also available just in time for the *Model Curriculum and Guidelines for Graduate Degree Programs in Information Systems* (MSIS 2006), making its implementation more feasible. It is an excellent text for undergraduate and graduate students specializing in information systems in business and information schools, as well as a worthwhile companion for HCI texts used in computer science curricula to provide students with a broader view of the applications of HCI in organizational and decision-making settings.

As one who has been involved in HCI research in management information systems for almost thirty-five years, I would characterize the HCI scholarly communities in computer science and information systems as the two solitudes. They exist in parallel worlds, different publication outlets and conferences, with few connections between them. When I was teaching the first HCI course offered at my university, in partnership with my computer science colleagues, to a group of students from both business and computer science departments, I found the difficulty of bridging the HCI knowledge in these two fields to be significant. Very little, if anything, is found in a typical HCI text about interacting with business systems; for example, how does one design interfaces for decision-support systems, group-support systems, knowledge-based systems, or electronic commerce Web sites? This text does a remarkable job of achieving this goal of knowledge-bridging. The authors have an excellent grasp of the state-of-the-art HCI research in management information systems, of human information processing, of organizations and organizational computing, and of the theories and methods in HCI in general. They skillfully blend this knowledge to deliver this text, which will be of great value in educating future systems analysts, designers, managers, and stakeholders.

HCI research in management information systems, which has played a dominant role in the development of the academic discipline during its emergence, has been experiencing a renaissance in recent years after a period of dormancy. This is partly due to the ubiquitous use of information technologies and partly to the increasing emphasis in the research arena focusing on the design of the information technology artifact, an endeavor to which HCI knowledge is of the utmost importance. The size, strength, and importance of the information systems academic community have increased recently as well due to the formation of the Association of the Information Systems Special Interest Group on HCI, an enterprise that has benefited greatly from the leadership and hard work of the authors of this text, and through the scholarly activities of the members of this interest group. This text, therefore, is published at an opportune time as a conduit to transfer this growing new knowledge generated by information systems HCI researchers to students and future practitioners, and to no lesser degree to the academics teaching HCI topics. The product of this outstanding effort of Te'eni, Carey, and Zhang will play a major role in enhancing the stature of HCI courses in information systems departments and business schools, and among HCI academics in general. I congratulate the authors for this excellent scholarship, and encourage my colleagues to consider the use of this text in their HCI courses.

Izak Benbasat
Canada Research Chair
in Information Technology Management
Sauder School of Business
University of British Columbia

# Preface

This book is about developing interactive information systems that support people at work or when conducting business. Specifically, it emphasizes the need to study and practice the development of HCI for real-world organizations in given contexts. Developing an effective information system means achieving a good fit among the users, their tasks, and the technology within organizational, social, and global contexts. In order to do this, designers need to have a good understanding of important factors that come into play. Designers need to understand why and how people interact with computers in order to accomplish their work and personal goals, what are the physical, cognitive, affective, and behavioral constraints on the users' side, what pleases or annoys them, what makes human–computer interaction a satisfying experience or an experience that users do not want to repeat, and what makes the interaction efficient and effective. This knowledge is the foundation of *human–computer interaction (HCI)* development.

Furthermore, designers of HCI should know how to apply this foundational knowledge by using the tools and methods available for developing interactive information systems. They need to know how to set up the specific goals of effective HCI for a particular organizational information system, how to gather relevant and important data and information to form design decisions, how to evaluate their designs, and how to achieve HCI goals. This application knowledge can guide HCI development in a more structured and disciplined fashion rather than a piecemeal fashion.

In addition, designers need to know how to put the foundational knowledge and its application into contexts. Our position in this book is that one cannot separate people's interaction with computers from the context in which they operate, just as one cannot fully understand what people communicate without knowing the context within which communication is carried out. The immediate context given in the book is organizational, managerial, and business work that dictates a concern with effectiveness of HCI design. Social and global contexts also play an important role in HCI development, especially with the growing global environment within which businesses operate.

The organizational and business context of HCI development is one of the distinctions of our book, compared to several other HCI textbooks. What are information systems in the organizational and business context? These systems support, for example, clerical work by office systems, managerial work by enterprise resource planning systems and project management software, group and individual decision tasks by decision support systems, commerce transactions by business transaction processing systems, information-seeking tasks by online libraries and other online information systems, customer commerce needs by electronic commerce systems, customer relationship by customer relationship management systems, organizational recruiting needs by online recruiting systems, and even business-to-business (B2B) needs by electronic data interchange (EDI) systems. Our concern is HCI development in these systems. This scope excludes a direct treatment of other exciting areas such as HCI in the cockpit, in robotics, on the battlefield, and in entertainment. Yet even with this focused scope, we are still facing a lot of challenges and an opportunity to explore a vast body of knowledge in order to deliver effective and pleasing user interfaces and user experiences. In contrast to several other books on general concerns in HCI, this book goes deeper in the specific organizational context by integrating organizational tasks and user characteristics closely into the development of HCI.

## AUDIENCE

This book is designed primarily as a textbook to meet the needs of students learning HCI for designing organizational information systems. It is intended to meet the teaching and learning challenges of an upper-division undergraduate or graduate course in human–computer interaction within a major in Management Information Systems, Electronic Commerce, Computer Information Systems, Information Studies, Information Management, Library and Information Science, and Instructional Design in Education. The book is designed to have no prerequisites. The book can also be used for other courses such as Interface Design, Human-Centered Information Systems Development, and Information Systems Project Management.

In addition, this book can be used as a professional reference book for those who design and develop real-world interactive information systems. It is intended to provide theoretically informed design principles and guidelines, as well as step-by-step procedures and methodologies for organizational IT professionals who are familiar with daily organizational issues and their impact on designing effective human interactions with organizational information systems.

In recent years, HCI topics have been included in relevant IS curricula such as the Model Curriculum and Guidelines for Graduate Degree Programs in Information Systems (MSIS 2000, MSIS 2006) jointly charged by ACM and AIS, and the Information Systems-Centric Curriculum (ISCC '99). The MSIS 2000 curriculum identifies human factors as a career elective course. Its next version of MSIS curriculum (MSIS 2006) includes HCI materials as IS core courses in both the Analysis, Modeling, and Design part and the Societal Implications part. The ISCC '99 curriculum emphasizes human behavior and computer interaction as an industry-defined attribute of an IS graduate, and HCI as one of the knowledge components. HCI courses have been offered in schools and programs such as E-Commerce, Information Systems, Information Management, Library and Information Science, and Instructional Design; all are non–computer science programs.

The three authors, combined, have been teaching HCI courses at the upper-division undergraduate, graduate, and doctoral levels for many years, both in the United States and in other countries such as Canada, Israel, and England. The students in these courses are often from non–computer science programs as mentioned above. We have been frustrated with our inability to find appropriate textbooks for these courses and have been developing our own teaching materials over the years. We found that most existing textbooks target computer science or computer engineering students and pay less attention to the uniqueness of non–computer science programs. The emphasis of these non–computer science programs tends to be more application-oriented. They take contexts into consideration, pay more attention to the big picture, and pay less attention to the technical or programming details.

## ORGANIZATION

The book has four sections with a total of fourteen (14) chapters:

The Context section provides the environments, context, and business needs. The goal is to motivate students by letting them see the relevance and importance of HCI issues in organizational IS and the bigger picture/context of where HCI issues fit in. Concrete and easy-to-connect-to examples are used.

The Foundation section covers the necessary understanding of basic interactive technologies and human factors. Specifically, we emphasize different and relevant human physical, cognitive, and affective characteristics that affect HCI development. We introduce the current interactive technologies and commonly used interaction styles. This assumes that we use these technologies and interaction styles as building blocks for HCI development. This is where our book is different from traditional HCI or more CS-oriented HCI books where such technologies or styles are the goals of HCI development. This shows that our level of focus or granularity is higher than that of other HCI books.

The Application section emphasizes the processes and deliverables of HCI development. Specifically, we discuss the HCI goals and concerns and how they help form the HCI evaluation metrics. We provide principles and guidelines derived from the Foundation section. We demonstrate how to analyze organizational-level tasks into the lower levels so that they can be supported by human–computer interactions, and how such lower-level tasks can be supported by the specific design options. A human-centered HCI development methodology ties early discussions together to demonstrate the techniques and processes for developing effective HCI for organizational information systems. Many examples are used to illustrate HCI development issues, concerns, and methods. This is the core part of the book, demonstrating the combination of theories (in the Foundation section) and application. It covers what should be considered and how to make it happen when developing HCI for normal/generic and special organizational IS.

The Additional Context section illustrates the need to consider collaborations among users, environmental and organizational changes, and emerging IT development and use changes. It also includes the larger context of society and the global environment. We discuss social issues that are brought about by the information age and interface issues that occur in the development of global software. This coverage indicates the dynamics of the field and challenges of keeping up with HCI development. Sample emerging changes in IT use and impact include ubiquitous computing, social computing, and value-sensitive design. Sample emerging methods for developing IT are open source, component-based software development, and outsourcing.

The following figure depicts the organizing structure of the book as well as the dependencies among the chapters, thus providing a general guide on the order in which the materials in the book are covered. The sequence of chapters begins with the organizational context, follows with the foundation and then the application, and ends with additional context. Although this can be a default way of covering the materials, readers can customize the sequence and content to meet their own needs. Some possible ways of using the book are suggested in the "How to Use the Book" section below.

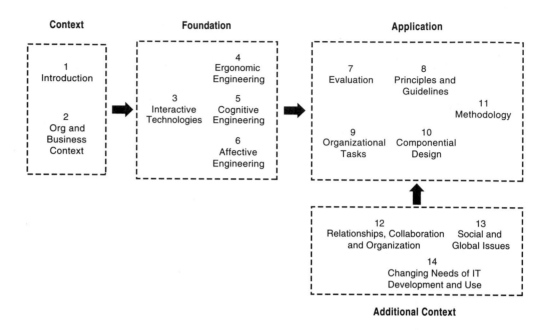

**Figure P.1**   The structure of the book and the dependencies of the chapters.

## DISTINCTIVE FEATURES

1.   Three organizing themes throughout the text: (1) a multilayer description of HCI (task, semantic, syntactic, and lexical), (2) an analysis of the physical, cognitive, affective, and other resources that are needed for the user activities, and (3) a systematic HCI development methodology. These themes help organize the diverse materials in the foundation chapters and later integrate and apply information in the application chapters.

2.   A blend of theory and practice. Although design is not a science, abundant practice failures point out the importance and value of informed design; that is, design ought to be informed by theoretical understanding and empirical research evidence. Thus, our approach is a blend of theory, research, and practice.

3.   Book organization. Materials are organized into three main sections. The Organizational and Business Context section shows the relevance of HCI development in organizations; it serves as a foundation to explain the important factors of human, technology, and tasks. The Application section demonstrates design principles and guidelines, evaluation concerns and methods, and HCI development methodology and techniques. The Additional Context section presents additional organizational, social, and cultural issues. It also forecasts other HCI-related issues resulting from the fast development and deployment of the IT field.

4.   A grounding of HCI development into the typical modern organizational IS architecture. This architecture includes system functionalities, data and information management, Web-based or other platform front ends, and human interface and interaction.

5.   A systematic HCI development methodology. The book provides a human-centered HCI development life cycle methodology that can be incorporated with modern

information systems analysis and design life cycle methodology for designing effective organizational information systems.

6. An international perspective. The international team of authors, with their broad research and teaching experiences, endeavored to ensure an international orientation by demonstrating culturally diverse designs and emphasizing the need to be sensitive to national and cultural idiosyncrasies.

7. Extensive coverage on building readers' various skills. Among these skills, analytical skills are crucial for considering the whole spectrum of organizational information systems by pulling together all relevant aspects and perspectives. In addition, the materials and the nature of HCI development require designers to have organizational and managerial skills, both oral and written communication skills, and collaboration skills, as HCI development is by its nature a collaborative effort involving people with different expertise.

## PEDAGOGICAL FEATURES

1. Road maps: At the beginning of each chapter, a road map shows the entire book structure and the location of the chapter within it. In the Application section, each chapter has an additional road map of HCI development methodology to indicate the role of the chapter in the HCI development process.

2. Learning objectives: These appear at the beginning of each chapter to give instructors and students a clear goal of the chapter.

3. Sidebar boxes: These highlight the important concepts and keywords for easy access.

4. Abundant examples: Examples appear inside each chapter to illustrate ideas and facilitate discussions.

5. Additional information: Scattered throughout the text are boxes containing personal stories, examples, industry reflections, and other information that can be skipped if time is a concern but can add fun for students to read.

6. Summary of key concepts: A summary appears at the end of each chapter for easy review of the material covered.

7. Further readings and references: This section appears at the end of each chapter to provide deeper and broader coverage of the topics, as well as the sources of the main ideas in the chapter.

8. Exercises: Each chapter provides exercises of different types and with various levels of difficulty.

9. Illustrative cases (fictional): Segments of the cases appear throughout the entire book to illustrate the key points and main concepts in each chapter.

10. An instructor resource kit: This provides a full set of lecture presentations in Power-Point, sample solutions to the exercises, sample syllabi for different types of students or emphasis, and teaching suggestions and hints.

11. Companion Web site: This site provides the Web pages for the illustrative cases at various stages of development and testing, launch pages and links to resources and examples, full-color figures (from black-and-white figures in book), and other pedagogical aids.

## HOW TO USE THE BOOK

The book is constructed to fulfill the learning goals of an HCI course for one regular semester (14–15 weeks for three hours/week). However, the book can be customized to fit other scheduling needs. For example, we have used the book for a semester-long course with shorter meetings by leaving Chapters 2 through 6 as guided readings rather than materials covered in class meetings.

Besides the chapter sequence mentioned above, this book can be used in different ways or with different emphases depending on the background and interests of the students. The following are some suggestions.

Chapter 2 (Organizational and Business Context) can be skipped or quickly reviewed for students who have taken courses such as Introduction to Management Information Systems and who thus already know the basic organizational information systems. However, the HCI aspects of the organizational context are emphasized in this chapter and should be pointed out to the students. For other students who have not studied such systems and business context, Chapter 2 is important in order to provide an appropriate context for the rest of the materials in this book.

Some materials in Chapters 4, 5, and 6 can be either skipped or quickly reviewed for students with psychology or human factors backgrounds. Yet, for other students, these materials demonstrate the important human aspect in HCI development.

Chapter 12 can be lessened if a course is designed to focus specifically on developing individual-based interactive systems.

Chapter 13 is important for courses with an emphasis on social, global, and/or ethical considerations. Chapter 14 is about trends and challenges in developing HCI with fast IT development and use. These two chapters can be optional if a class is very specific on a particular type of interactive system, emphasizing hands-on HCI development, or has time constraints and cannot cover the whole book.

For higher-level students (such as some graduate students) and readers who are more interested in theory than practice, we suggest more emphasis on Chapters 3 through 6. For others who are more interested in hands-on applications (such as undergraduate students), we suggest putting more effort into Chapters 7 through 11. Overall, however, we suggest giving exposure to all the chapters to some extent in order to provide a holistic picture of the complexity of HCI development and the importance of each component.

## ACKNOWLEDGMENTS

We are grateful for the following colleagues for their strong encouragement and insightful comments during the preparation of the book: Drs. Dennis Galletta, Jinwoo Kim, and Jane Webster. We thank Drs. Mary Granger (U.S.), Jane Webster (Canada), Jae Yun Moon (Hong Kong), and Radhika Santhanam (U.S.) for testing the textbook in their HCI classes (some are at the undergraduate level, some graduate level). Additional testing of the book has been done by Dov in Israel and Ping in the United States. We want to specially thank Michael Fudge, whose class assignment in Ping's graduate HCI class was adapted as examples in Chapter 7. We would like to recognize Dr. Dawn Gregg, currently at the University of Colorado at Denver, who developed the initial Web site for e'Gourmet for instructional purposes while teaching at Arizona State University at the West campus. We appreciate the following reviewers for providing constructive reviews on the manuscripts:

- Paul Benjamin Lowry, Brigham Young University
- Dennis Galletta, University of Pittsburgh
- Paul Hu, University of Utah
- Jinwoo Kim, Yonsei University
- Adrienne Olnick Kutzschan, Queen's University
- Jae Yun Moon, Hong Kong University of Science and Technology
- Madhu Reddy, University of Missouri Rolla
- Tom Roberts, University of Kansas
- Noam Tractinsky, Ben-Gurion University of the Negev
- Jane Webster, Queen's University

We are especially grateful to Professor Izak Benbasat, who wrote a strong and insightful foreward for this book.

Finally, we are thankful for the strong support and confidence from our editor, Beth Golub at John Wiley and Sons, Inc.

## ABOUT THE AUTHORS

**Dov Te'eni** is a professor in the School of Business at Tel-Aviv University. He received his M.S. and Ph.D. in MIS from Tel-Aviv University and his B.Sc. in Economics and Statistics from the University of London. Dov studies several related areas of information systems in the organizational context: human–computer interaction, computer support for decision making, and systems design. In addition, he is interested in information systems for nonprofit organizations. His research usually combines model building, laboratory and field experiments, and the development of prototype systems such as Spider and kMail. He is currently working on the design of adaptive Web articles and the use of information technology for supporting communication within multinational corporations. Dr. Te'eni publishes widely. He is the winner of the 2001 MISQ Best Paper award. His research has appeared in academic journals such as *MIS Quarterly, Management Science, Organization Science, Decision Sciences, Journal of Organizational Behavior, Information & Management, Journal of AIS, IEEE Transactions on Systems, Man and Cybernetics, International Journal of Human-Computer Studies, Behaviour and Information Technology, Computers in Human Behavior,* and others. Dov is a senior editor for *MIS Quarterly* and serves on the editorial boards of several other journals including *Journal of AIS* and *Internet Research.*

**Jane M. Carey** received her Ph.D. in Business Administration with a major in Organizational Behavior and a minor in Computer Science from the University of Mississippi. Dr. Carey joined the faculty of the School of Business at Arizona State University West in 1988 and is currently an associate professor. Prior to that, she was a faculty member at Texas A&M University. Dr. Carey has research interests in the areas of human–computer interaction, computer access issues (U.S. and international), and Web-based learning. Her work has appeared in journals such as *Communications of the AIS, Journal of Management, Journal of Managerial Issues, Behaviour and Information Technology, Interacting with Computers, Computers in Human Behavior,* and others. Dr. Carey has edited four books on human factors in information systems based on a series of symposia she founded and hosted from 1986 to 1993. Jane's teaching interests include information systems management, systems analysis and design, human–computer interaction, and building e-commerce applications. Dr. Carey spent academic year 1994–95 in the People's Republic of China while on sabbatical from ASU West. She taught a variety of courses in both the Business College and Computer Science Department at Shandong University in Jinan, the capital city of Shandong Province. Jane is the coordinator of the Information Systems Management Concentration in the Global Business Program at ASU West. She has served as president of the ASU West Academic Senate and chair of the ASU West Campus Environment Team (focusing on issues of diversity).

**Ping Zhang** is an associate professor in the School of Information Studies at Syracuse University. She earned her Ph.D. in Information Systems from the University of Texas at Austin and her M.Sc. and B.Sc. in Computer Science from Peking University, Beijing, China. Ping was involved in the development of the very first few management information systems in China in the 1980s for five years. The real-world experience and research inquiries made Ping realize the importance of understanding humans and their interaction with technologies in order to fully utilize the great potential of technologies. She has been conducting research in the broadly defined area of HCI in the past decade. Her research appears in journals such as *Journal of AIS, Communications of AIS, Communications of the ACM, Decision Support Systems, International Journal of Electronic Commerce, Behaviour and Information Technology, International Journal of Human-Computer Studies, Computers in Human Behavior, Journal of the American Society for Information Science and Technology*, and several others. Ping has received a number of Best Paper awards at international conferences, a teaching award from the University of Texas, and an outstanding service award from AIS SIGHCI. She has been teaching HCI, Systems Analysis and Design, and other IT-related courses to a variety of students, at different levels, in different majors, and with different formats. She is coeditor of two research reading volumes entitled *HCI and MIS: Foundations* and *HCI and MIS: Applications*, of the Advances for Management Information Systems series edited by Dr. Vladimir Zwass, both to be published by M.E. Sharpe in 2006. Ping is an associate editor for *IJHCS* (formally *International Journal of Man-Machine Studies*) and *Communications of the AIS* (CAIS) and a guest editor for several special issues in MIS and HCI journals. She was the founding chair of the AIS SIGHCI from 2001 to 2004.

Dov Te'eni, Tel-Aviv, Israel
Jane M. Carey, Phoenix, Arizona, USA
Ping Zhang, Syracuse, New York, USA

March 2006

# 1

# INTRODUCTION

## LEARNING OBJECTIVES

Upon completion of this chapter, students should be able to do the following:

- Explain the terms *human–computer interaction* and *usability*
- Discuss the importance and scope of HCI
- Discuss the main ideas underlying this book: fit, levels of abstraction, human concerns, and context
- Overview the methodology for HCI development
- Describe the overall structure of the book

## SCENARIO

Imagine a large organization that is about to upgrade its computer systems. The company is in a rush to begin development because it feels that the company is too slow in providing services to the clients. And complaints are indeed mounting. The IT department is edgy. The developers are eager to start programming. Imagine that instead of letting the developers begin, management decides to hire human factors experts to observe how workers in the company go about doing their jobs. To do so, the experts spend six whole months observing the workers in their natural work environment, interviewing workers and customers, recording and analyzing their observations, and simulating changes. Then, after six months, the experts get to spend more time developing a prototype of the new system, step-by-step, adding a function, testing it, expanding the functionality, and again testing it, going through 30 such iterations. Sound unreal?

The New York Stock Exchange (NYSE) did so (see the full story in Gibbs, 1997). Two consultant firms worked for six months to develop a comprehensive understanding of traders on the floor. They observed and modeled the way traders behaved in reality. Only then did they propose new technologies that would fit the traders' way of performing their tasks but would allow them to do so more effectively. They introduced new devices such as handheld computers, replacing the current paper cards with more accurate and faster devices, but without disrupting work practices. The workers quickly accepted the technology and learned to take advantage in recording quotes and sales. Have these changes enhanced value for the business? William A. Bautz (vice president for technology) reports, "In two weeks we now process as many shares as we handled each year in the late 1970s" (Gibbs, 1997, p. 88). And at the same time, the error rate has dropped by a factor of 10!

## ▶ 1. HUMAN–COMPUTER INTERACTION: DEFINITION, IMPORTANCE, AND SCOPE

This book is about *human–computer interaction (HCI) in the context of organizational work*. The field of HCI attempts to understand and shape the way people interact with computers: the processes they engage in, the resources they use, and the impact they accomplish. This may seem a very limiting approach to HCI, but it covers the bulk of the field today and we use it to set the scope of this book. We further limit ourselves to HCI in organizations (e.g., clerical work supported by office systems, managerial work supported by Enterprise Resource Planning, project management software and group and individual Decision Support Systems, and professional work supported by an online library). This scope excludes a direct treatment of exciting areas such as HCI in the cockpit, in robotics, on the battlefield, and in entertainment. Yet even with this limited scope, we are still left to explore a vast body of knowledge.

The interactive use of computers is not new. It has been around for several decades, but it has now become an integral, if not dominant, part of work life. What is the state of the art of HCI designs? Are the human–computer interfaces designed well enough to improve work? Improve life? Can they be improved? The cartoon in Figure 1.1, besides being rather amusing in describing the mutual frustration of humans and computers, suggests that there is room for improving the interaction between people and computers.

### 1.1 Quality Human–Computer Interaction

Today, building the human–computer interface consumes 50–70 percent of the systems development effort. The importance of the interface to user acceptance is well understood. The statement that the interface "makes or breaks the system" is generally no exaggeration because users see the system through the human–computer interface. In other words, to users, the interface *is* the system. Users care about what they enter into the system and, more importantly, they care about what they get out of the system and how the entire experience of interaction feels. Given that the system has the functionality to make it useful to the user it is expected to be usable too. Usability is the extent to

**Figure 1.1** Cartoon depicting the failure of HCI effectiveness.

which a system with given functionality can be used efficiently, effectively, and satisfactorily by specified users to achieve specified goals in a specified context of use.

The World Wide Web, which is perhaps the most accessible computer platform to a diversity of users nowadays, may enlighten us about the current practice of HCI design. Recent surveys paint an uneven picture of quality on the Web: some Web sites are highly useful and usable but others are poorly designed. In a recent large-scale survey of Web users (Kehoe, Pitkow, Sutton, Aggarwal, & Rogers, 1999), nearly 75 percent of the respondents reported dissatisfying experiences because of confusing Web sites. Surprisingly, over 50 percent of novice users reported only good experiences with the Web, so capabilities and expectations are probably changing. Nevertheless, the price organizations pay for poor usability is very high as customers abandon them and employees waste precious time. On the other hand, well-designed Web sites seem to make a difference. Consider IBM, for example. IBM decided in the late 1990s to redesign its Web site to boost online sales, creating an IBM Shop that was much easier to navigate. It was simple, cohesive, and easy to search. IBM claims that online store traffic increased by 120 percent and that sales shot up by 400 percent (see report on InfoWorld, April 19, 1999). As in this story, it is usually not the latest gadgets that make the difference. In the report describing the NYSE experience (see scenario above), Gibbs (1997) discusses the disappointing impact of what seemed to be very promising technologies. Speech recognition, wearable computers, videoconferencing, and virtual reality are exciting HCI technologies (described in Chapter 3). They are slowly maturing but have not yet created value in business that can justify their cost. It appears there is still much to do in order to reap the benefits of commonplace HCI technologies.

Thus we can conclude that the current practice of HCI design in many cases is unsatisfactory and that corporations (and users) pay a high price for this unsatisfactory quality of design. With some effort, however, significant improvements can be achieved. There is a need, therefore, for a more systematic treatment of HCI in the development process and a more prominent presence of HCI experts in information systems projects.

This sense that more should and can be done to improve HCI is reflected in a growing field of HCI researchers and practitioners and in innovative HCI technology. Advancements in the technology of human–computer interaction include speech recognition, touch-sensitive screens, virtual reality devices, and devices for the handicapped, among many others. Impressive too is the support for generating human–computer interfaces. Powerful languages, automated analysis and design tools, and built-in interface objects have all served to make the creation of interfaces less tedious. All this activity is not enough, however, to satisfy the ever-growing appetite of the diverse pool of users. Users now expect a standard of usability that was never available before graphical interfaces became the norm.

What constitutes a good user interface? How do we know whether we have a good HCI design? Ben Shneiderman and Catherine Plaisant (Shneiderman & Plaisant, 2005) reproduced the following standard criteria from the U.S. Military Standard for Human Engineering Design Criteria:

- Achieve required performance by operator, control, and maintenance personnel
- Minimize skill and personnel requirements and training time
- Achieve required reliability of person–computer combinations (reliability, availability, security, and data integrity)

**Functionality:** The collection of system operations or services available to users.

- Foster design standardization within and among systems (integration, consistency, portability)

To make things even more concrete, here is a list of common measurable goals for usability (Nielsen, 1993):

- Time to learn how to operate the system
- Speed of performance
- Rate of errors made by users
- User's retention time of information presented
- User's satisfaction with the system

Achievement of these goals is no easy task. In fact, some goals—such as time to learn, speed of performance, and subjective satisfaction—may conflict. The study of HCI is aimed at understanding how the human–computer interface can be designed to further such goals. Yet high-quality HCI is not just about usability or performance. It is also about emotions and about the overall physical and social experience of interacting with computers. Thus a *balanced* view of HCI incorporating many different human concerns is called for.

Consider the two Web pages in Figure 1.2. Both pages are taken from Web sites of online grocery stores (e-stores), and both represent very similar functionality. Thus from the perspective of achieving the goal of purchasing a desired product, the two e-stores are similar. However, their appearance and usability are different. Figure 1.2a is relatively verbal in comparison to the more graphic presentation of Figure 1.2b. The user's

> **Usability**: The extent to which a system with given functionality can be used efficiently, effectively, and satisfactorily by specified users to achieve specified goals in a specified context of use.

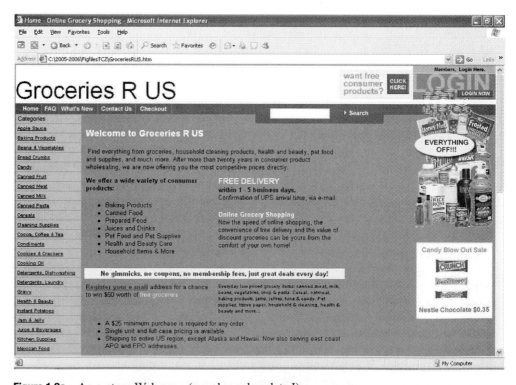

**Figure 1.2a**   An e-store Web page (see also color plate I).

**Figure 1.2.b**  An e-store Web page (see also color plate I).

task is to find a candy bar (say M&M), check its price, and, if reasonable, order it. Chances are that the text-based e-store would be faster. Does this mean that users will prefer the text-based e-store over the graphical one? Not necessarily. People are often drawn to a Web page design based on pleasing aesthetics and a positive user experience. Replicating this positive experience becomes a part of the user's subjective satisfaction when visiting the same site or other sites. We talk about design factors that generate positive affect in the user. Indeed, the designer must understand various design options, understand the pros and cons from a variety of perspectives, and be sensitive to trade-offs among design goals, which can be at both the individual users level and higher or broader levels such as organizational and social goals.

The following section presents how this book is organized to help readers understand and accomplish the broad goals of HCI.

## 1.2  Scope of HCI

The field of HCI is interdisciplinary and requires students of HCI to be familiar with at least some of the relevant reference disciplines. Figure 1.3 shows the wide range of relevant sources of knowledge and inspiration for developing high-quality HCI. It is based on several similar depictions of the field (Booth, 1989; Preece, Rogers, & Sharp, 2002; Zhang & Li, 2004). Each disciplinary source, from computer engineering to art and philosophy, informs parts of the many aspects of HCI development. In this book, which concentrates on HCI in the organizational context, we select a subset of these sources. These include the organizational perspective, the psychological and physiological perspective, the computer perspective, and the broader social perspective.

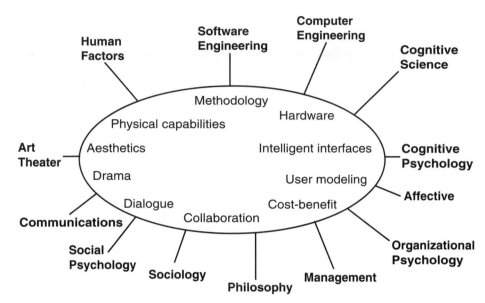

**Figure 1.3** Human–computer interaction is an interdisciplinary field (based on Booth, 1989; Preece et al., 2002; Zhang & Li, 2004).

The organizational perspective brings with it a strong influence of behavioral decision-making and organizational behavior. This perspective is invaluable for understanding how to analyze the way people perform their tasks at work and how technology can support their work. Furthermore, the organizational perspective is tightly related to the psychological perspective of HCI, particularly the cognitive and affective aspects of HCI. Additionally, the computer science perspective builds on software as well as hardware engineering to design interactive technologies, relying heavily on the psychological and physiological sources. Finally, the social and global contexts are also explored to meet the increasingly popular trends of social systems, the expansion of the traditional organization to communities of practice, and systems that are developed and used globally (DeSanctis, 2006). Although this is only a subset of the important sources shown in Figure 1.3 (which itself is probably incomplete), it is sufficient to provide a basis for HCI development and, moreover, to emphasize the need to balance the various contributions. For instance, there is a realization that cognitive and affective psychology complement each other in their implications on HCI design, and similarly, the contributions of sociology and psychology should be balanced. The field as it is represented in its research and publications (see the "Bibliography and Additional Readings" section) reflects well the interdisciplinary nature of the field.

## ▷ 2. THEMES IN HCI UNDERLYING THIS BOOK

This book explains the complex phenomena of HCI by building a view of HCI and then using it to organize the vast and growing body of pertinent knowledge. For some, HCI is an interdisciplinary academic field of applied research. For others, it is a practice of design and implementation. For many of us, it is becoming a productive mixture of both approaches. Accordingly, the book first examines the basic and relevant theories. It then applies the theories to practice by exploring the design of HCI components (such as forms, graphics, and windows) and the design of representative applications (such as an e-store). The last part of the book discusses additional contexts that have important roles in HCI design, as well as the impact of the changing context on HCI development and use. The book presents the theory and practice through some common elements, which are the various concepts and themes to be described in this section.

## 2.1 Fit

HCI should be designed to achieve a *fit* between the (human) user, computer, and task, and it should do so for a given context. This is our underlying design philosophy. Fit is initially defined in reference to task performance so that a better fit is expected to improve performance. Performance reflects both the efficiency of performing the task and the quality of the task product. Measures of performance are selected according to the focus of studying HCI, as we shall see in several chapters that address different performance measures. For example, performance can be measured by the speed and accuracy of operating the computer or the speed and accuracy of preparing a document with a word processor. Subjective satisfaction and other measures are sometimes used as surrogates of task performance when more direct measures are infeasible. Fit, however, is difficult to measure objectively. Fit is sometimes operationalized by measures of performance—for example, the input screen design that leads to the fastest update is said to produce the best fit. Nevertheless, the concept of fit directs the designer's attention to the process of matching the HCI design to the user and the task in a particular context (Te'eni, 2006). If, for example, the order of fields on a screen matches the natural order of receiving information, there can be a high fit between the design and the task. Similarly, if the size of the font adjusts to the user's eyesight, there can be a high fit between the design and the user. In most cases, reducing the effort required by the user leads to higher fit, and conversely, good fit implies less effort than poor fit. Even before measuring performance, a high level of fit would be considered a superior design. Moreover, fit goes beyond performance to indicate a broader human concern with the user's overall well-being. An ill-fitted sitting arrangement may result in backaches and severe health problems. Physical aspects of fit are therefore important in ensuring physical well-being. An ill-fitted interface design may increase users' frustration and stress level, thus affecting users' mental well-being. Figure 1.4 shows the three elements that feed into fit and the link from fit to both performance and well-being.

Using color to discriminate among objects on the screen may be generally effective but may be counterproductive for users who are color-blind (10 percent of the male population is color-blind). This need to consider the diversity of users and the limitations of some of them illustrates the desire to achieve a good fit between the computer and the user.

The example can be taken one step further. Red and blue have traditionally been used in biology textbooks to depict blood vessels carrying blood that is high or low in oxygen content (see Figure 1.5). In fact, in this particular context, any other color combination would be confusing. This convention is considered essential in medical texts. This relationship illustrates the fit between computer, user, and task within context. To accommodate a color-blind user, a technique such as cross-hatching along with the colors (with an explanatory key and/or floating text explaining the color and meaning) may be an additional design feature choice

Note, however, that if the task is to train surgeons rather than teach first-year medical students, the whole concept of symbolic colors may be counterproductive. The training task at advanced stages of practice in the operating room is completely different. The red

**Fit:** The match between the computer design, the user, and the task so as to optimize the human resources needed to accomplish the task.

**Performance** reflects both the efficiency of performing the task and the quality of the task product.

**Well-being** reflects an overall concern with the user's physical and psychological welfare.

Human
Fit
Performance
Well-being
Task
Computer

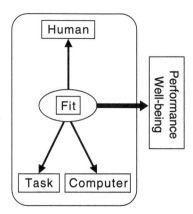

**Figure 1.4** The fit of HCI elements leads to performance and well-being.

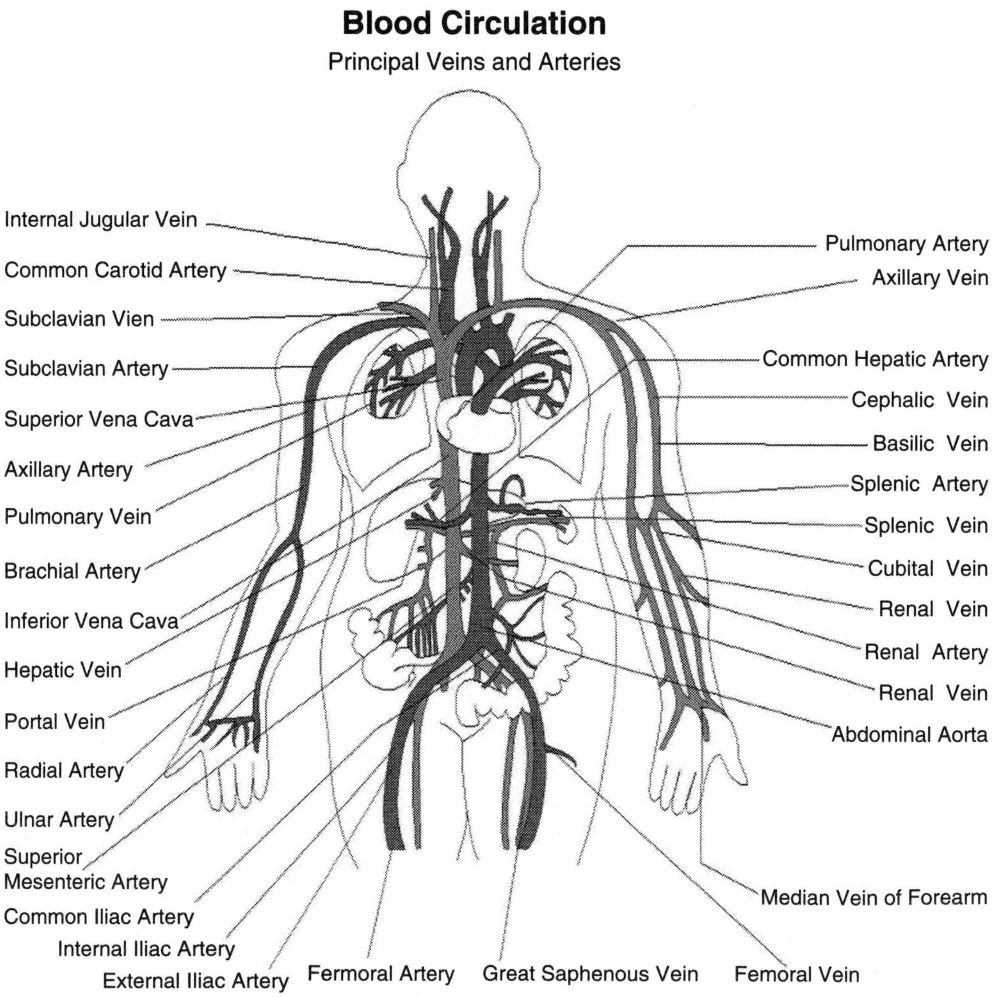

Blood Circulation
Principal Veins and Arteries
Internal Jugular Vein
Common Carotid Artery
Subclavian Vien
Subclavian Artery
Superior Vena Cava
Axillary Artery
Pulmonary Vein
Brachial Artery
Inferior Vena Cava
Hepatic Vein
Portal Vein
Radial Artery
Ulnar Artery
Superior Mesenteric Artery
Common Iliac Artery
Internal Iliac Artery
External Iliac Artery
Fermoral Artery
Great Saphenous Vein
Femoral Vein
Pulmonary Artery
Axillary Vein
Common Hepatic Artery
Cephalic Vein
Basilic Vein
Splenic Artery
Splenic Vein
Cubital Vein
Renal Vein
Renal Artery
Renal Vein
Abdominal Aorta
Median Vein of Forearm

**Figure 1.5** Blood circulation (see also color plate I).

and blue color symbols may lead to errors in identification of real blood vessels, which in reality are not painted blue and red. The design of the HCI must fit the task. Furthermore, tasks in the organizational context differ from tasks in other contexts such as command-and-control tasks in the cockpit. Hence, our design philosophy requires a thorough understanding of the nature of the task. Accordingly, we devote an entire chapter to some typical tasks found in organizations.

Fit can be achieved not only by design but also by user training. Users can also be trained to achieve a better fit. Training is part of creating effective HCI. Moreover, the task can be redesigned. Task analysis is also part of building effective HCI.

## 2.2 Levels of Interaction

The notion of fit leads to two of the three themes that organize the presentation in this book: a multilayer model of HCI and the analysis of user activity as a function of human resources (e.g., memory and attention). User activity encompasses the user's interaction with the computer to accomplish a task. A multilayer model of user activity (Figure 1.6) can explain how the task context affects the physical design by showing the transition from psychological intentions to physical implementation. The example of using red and blue for learning about blood vessels can be examined at different levels. On one level, we examine the user's goal of learning the concept of arteries and veins. On another level, we examine the use of colors to enhance pattern recognition in memory. These are different levels of understanding behavior that range from the user's goals to the physical aspects of the human resources used to achieve these goals. The goals provide the context for the use of resources. In other words, the higher level provides the context for the lower level. Designers must be able to discriminate between these levels but also integrate across them consistently. For example, say the user is moving the cursor (the low level of interaction) to advance from the leftmost character in a text string to the rightmost character (the high level). Imagine how difficult it is for the user to press the *left* arrow in order to advance one character to the *right*. It is probably even hard to imagine, let alone to implement. Well, unfortunatelythis inconsistency often happens when American word processors originally designed for left-to-right English are used for writing texts in languages that progress from right to left. And, indeed, it is very frustrating.

> **User activity:** The physical and psychological aspects of the user's interaction with the computer to accomplish a task.

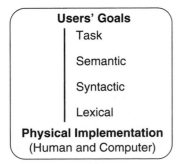

**Figure 1.6** The multilayer TSSL model of HCI.

Put more formally, we will examine HCI as a *multilayer activity* (i.e., user activity that is conceptually viewed at multiple and distinct levels of interaction). Of the several multilayer models that exist, we adopt a model with four levels of interaction: task, semantic, syntactic, and lexical (Moran, 1981). We call it the TSSL model. The *task level* pertains to the information requirements that have to be met (e.g., create a word processing document). It relates to the user's goals most closely. The *semantic level* pertains to the set of objects and operations through which the computer becomes meaningful to the user (e.g., the object "document" can be opened as "New"). It relates to the user's world of meaning but also to the computer's logical structure. The *syntactic level* dictates the rules of combining the semantic objects and operations into correct instructions. For example, first designate an object and only after that choose an operation (e.g., select a file and then choose "Open"). The syntactic level directs the user how to manipulate the computer system. The *lexical level* describes the way specific computer devices are used to implement the syntactic level (e.g., move a mouse pointer to the document label and click twice to open it).

Figure 1.6 shows the four levels of interaction, each layer providing the context for the layer below it. The uppermost layer (the task) is closest to the user's goals. The lowermost layer (lexical level) is closest to the resources that are needed to physically implement these goals. Thus, Figure 1.6 depicts the translation of goals to physical implementation as an activity at different levels of interaction. The levels of task and semantics can be viewed independently of their physical implementation. The levels of syntax and lexicon are tied to their implementation. As demonstrated in the example of a cursor moving in the wrong direction, it is important to let the user move smoothly from one level to another. For example, the colors chosen for the interface (lexical level) should not interfere with the interpretation of their meaning (semantics), as in using the color red for a command button "OK." While the discussion above is about operating the computer, we use the same ideas to talk about more abstract tasks such as computer-supported decision making (Chapter 9). Interestingly, the same hierarchical structure can be used to characterize conversation in natural languages by looking at the characters, words, and sentences as the different levels needed for communication. As we learn to converse, these levels collapse, in practice, into one seamless channel. Good HCI aims to achieve this seamless transition between our goal and the way we implement it. Our job as HCI designers is to make this interface almost transparent so that the user can get on with his or her work.

## 2.3  Human Resources in HCI and Their Impact

The second theme for organizing the material in this book examines the impact of user characteristics on HCI. Users rely on physical and psychological resources in their interaction with computers. We assume that the need to enhance limited human resources determines the potential roles of HCI. For example, using windows can enhance cognitive control, reduce demands on memory, and support shared attention to concurrent information sources. Using graphics can support memory, facilitate comprehension, and enhance cognitive processing for certain tasks such as trend comparison. Furthermore, many users consider graphics or color use to be more pleasing

---

**Multilayer activity (TSSL model):** A model of user activity that includes four levels: task, semantics, syntax, and lexicon.

---

**Task level:** Pertains to the information requirements that have to be met.

**Semantic level:** Pertains to the set of objects and operations through which the computer becomes meaningful to the user.

**Syntactic level:** Dictates the rules of combining the semantic objects and operations into correct instructions.

**Lexical level:** Describes the way specific computer devices are used to implement the syntactic level.

---

**Human resources in HCI:** the physical and psychological resources needed for user activity.

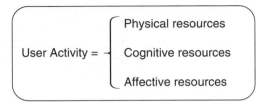

**Figure 1.7**   User activity is a function of human resources

than numbers or black text. Pleasing is an affective, rather than cognitive, function that has been shown to have an important role in users' acceptance and use of technology. Affect, together with motivation and other functions, will be discussed in the book as well. People tend to regard the computer as if it were a medium for interaction with other human beings rather than merely an innate tool (Brave & Nass, 2003; Picard, 1997). Hence the importance of emotions and attitudes in understanding how people react to computers and how we should design HCI more effectively should not be overlooked.

Figure 1.7 can be seen as the rationale underlying a strategy for defining the possible roles of any interface-oriented technique—that is, optimizing the physical, cognitive, and affective resources to produce the best possible HCI. Detailed lists of cognitive and affective resources will be developed and will then be used as templates for identifying potential roles of HCI. In general, these resources tend to inhibit performance when pushed to their limits. As a general principle of design, we strive to reduce the need for physical, cognitive, and affective resources and extend human capabilities in order to enhance HCI.

## 2.4 Context

The TSSL model and the human resources that determine the roles of HCI must be analyzed in *context*. This book uses the term *context* at different levels of abstraction. This is because context can be relative to content, which itself is context to more specific content. Thus, context consists of multiple layers, like the coats of an onion. The outer coat provides the context of the inner coats. Looking at the term *context* in relation to a word in a sentence, the word's immediate context is the sentence. The more distant context is the paragraph, and that of the paragraph is the whole story. Examining HCI requires an analysis of the immediate context (what the user was doing just before she moved the mouse to click on the option "Save"). It also requires an analysis of the distant context, say of the particular decision-making activity for which the interaction is taking place (e.g., planning a budget). The decision-making activity itself may need to be understood in the context of a great time pressure to get the budget out on time. Time pressure may affect the way we act and therefore the optimal design of the human–computer interface.

The general context of HCI in this book is organizational work. When we get down to building an application, the context must be refined even further. Some of the tasks performed with computers are highly structured and others are less structured. The HCI developer will usually find it simpler to analyze the highly structured tasks, such as filling a predefined form of personal data. The less structured tasks will require a deeper understanding of the task and its context. Most of the examples of HCI for less structured tasks will be developed for tasks in a managerial or an office environment. We will look at a broad class of tasks—managerial and decision-making tasks. This type of task has become central to organizations in the information age and is highly representative of the less structured activities in modern organizations. The next chapter provides several examples of this type of task.

Not only different situational contexts but also different users affect HCI design. Different people have different styles and preferences (e.g., learning styles, decision styles, graphic versus verbal orientation). Individual differences can sometimes be accommodated by flexible systems or individually tailored support. Individual styles will be studied whenever possible to supplement the more general approach taken in Figure 1.7.

**Context of HCI:** The situation and the physical and social factors in the environment that affect HCI.

Using the organizing themes in context will prove necessary when we begin to cover the vast amount of knowledge needed for effective design. We need several sources of knowledge. One is basic knowledge drawn from the fields of ergonomics, cognitive and affective psychology, computer engineering, information systems, and the relevant domain of the applications (i.e., organizational work). The second source is design and implementation paradigms, which build on the basic knowledge. The TSSL view of HCI refers to user goals and their physical implementation. The resources for physical implementation are human and computer, hence the need for basic knowledge about human capabilities for information processing and about design possibilities for the computer system. Additionally, the context for understanding users' goals requires basic knowledge of managerial work, decision making, and other various tasks. However, these three fields (user, IT, organizational context/task) are inadequate when treated in isolation. Designers need methodologies to apply this knowledge in an integrated fashion. They also need heuristics for thinking about the fit between task, user, and components of the human–computer interface because it is too complex to evaluate all possible design alternatives.

To sum up, our design philosophy is to develop the technology so as to achieve a good fit between the user, the task, and the technology, within a given context. Designers should strive to reduce the user's expenditure of physical, cognitive, and affective resources and to enhance the user's capabilities. In parallel, designers should think of the four interaction levels and an easy, almost transparent, movement from task to implementation. The upcoming chapters develop this design strategy as a sequence of steps that include defining information processing needs (e.g., memory), using predefined functions that computerized systems can provide (e.g., graphical displays of quantitative data), and matching the appropriate functions to the task (e.g., according to the type of decision-making task).

## ▶ 3. APPLICATION—A METHODOLOGY FOR HCI DEVELOPMENT

**Human concerns of HCI:** Physical, cognitive, affective, and usefulness.

The foundational knowledge of the user, the computer, the task, and the organizational context is applied by pursuing a development methodology that is built around human concerns. The methodology revolves around a systems development life cycle that includes four phases: planning, analysis, design, and implementation. Each phase includes several techniques that help meet four human concerns: physical, cognitive, affective, and usefulness. In particular, each phase includes evaluation techniques that encompass these four concerns. Together, the four concerns explain the user's behavior and motivation and therefore serve as the basis for design and evaluation. While the physical, cognitive, and affective concerns reflect aspects intrinsic to the user, the fourth is determined by extrinsic motivation. In the organizational context, the extrinsic motivation is usually tied to performance and well-being. In the last chapters of the book, we expand the discussion to consider sociological, ethical, cultural, and global issues that broaden the scope of extrinsic motivation. The methodology shown in Figure 1.8 is explained in detail in Chapter 11 and briefly overviewed below.

The project selection and planning phase determines the organizational information needs. This first phase is usually general to the entire system being developed without special attention to HCI, unless the HCI needs determine the project's feasibility. The second phase, analysis, involves several unique HCI techniques. Unlike many popular texts that first address HCI in the design phase, we believe that HCI considerations should start in the analysis stage to uncover user needs and opportunities. HCI analysis therefore begins by determining user requests and then validating them through user feedback. In addition, three major analyses are conducted: context, user, and task analyses. *Context analysis* determines the technical, environmental, and social settings of the human–computer interactions. *User analysis* identifies and characterizes the target users, referring to their demographic characteristics, job- or task-related factors, and anticipated use patterns of the target system. *Task analysis* determines how users meet their organizational goals and how they perform the tasks in terms of information processing, information needs, and representations.

Task analysis involves two typs of tasks: organizational-level and tool-level. Using the concept of levels of interaction described above, organizational-level tasks are decomposed into tool-level tasks. Organizational-level tasks are defined in terms of what needs to be done to accomplish organizational goals (e.g., make a purchase order or find a new location for the organization). Tool-level tasks are accomplished by using a tool (the computer) (e.g., select a product from an online list). Task analysis progresses from the organizational-level tasks to the tool-level tasks. As part of the analyses, human constraints and special considerations are identified and serve as a basis for design. The results of the analysis form the HCI expectations of the target system, which are called evaluation metrics. Alternative design strategies can then be constructed and the most likely alternative selected for the next stage.

The design phase specifies the user interface on the basis of the analysis according to HCI principles and guidelines and tested against the evaluation metrics. The main techniques of this phase are interface specification and formative evaluations. *Interface specification* translates the tool-level tasks into their lower interaction levels: semantic, syntactic, and lexical designs (this follows the TSSL model discussed previously). It includes metaphor, media, dialogue, and presentation designs. Metaphor and visualization design determines appropriate metaphors to understand the system (e.g., using a shopping cart in e-stores). Media design selects the medium that best fits the information requirements, such as text, static images, dynamic images, and sound. Dialogue design determines the specific HCI components used (e.g., the use of menus, form fill-ins, natural languages, dialog boxes, and direct manipulation). Presentation design determines

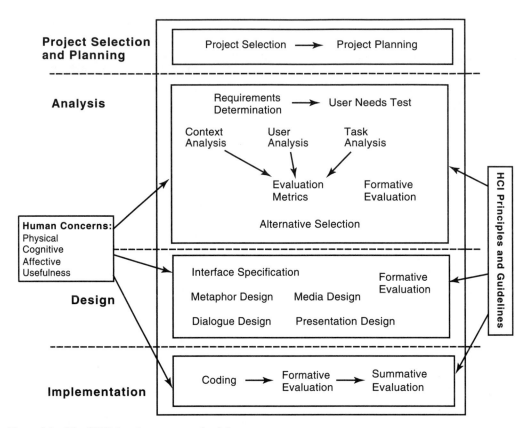

**Figure 1.8** The HCI development methodology.

the overall display layout. *Formative evaluations* identify the need for further design iterations and refinements.

Finally, the implementation stage makes the target system a reality. This includes coding, testing, and evaluating it to determine whether the completed system meets the user's expectations. In this book, we do not cover the technical aspects of implementation. We assume that readers have the technical skills necessary to use prototyping tools in order to demonstrate their HCI development ideas and considerations.

## ▷ 4. THE STRUCTURE OF THE BOOK

The structure of the book follows the general discussions developed previously and, in particular, exemplifies the principle of informed design. In other words, design principles are based on theories of how people behave and interact with computers. The book has four parts: Context, Foundations, Application, and Additional Context. The overall structure is depicted in Figure 1.9. The first part (especially Chapter 2) explains the organizational context. Organizational and business systems, such as office systems and e-stores, rely on effective HCI in order to function and compete.

The second part lays the foundations of effective HCI development. Chapter 3 provides a concise description of basic interactive technologies currently employed

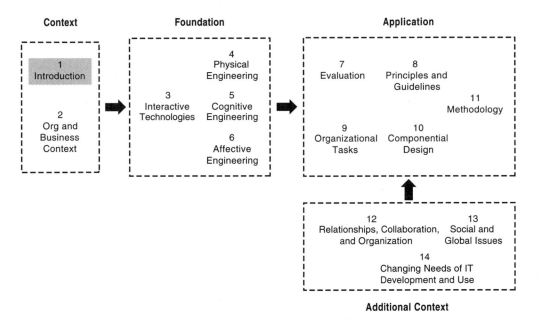

**Figure 1.9** The book's roadmap.

in the development of effective systems. Next, we turn to understanding the human concerns from the physical, cognitive, and affective perspectives (Chapters 4, 5, and 6, respectively). These discussions correspond to the first three human concerns of HCI we overviewed earlier. For example, we discuss ergonomic designs of input/output devices, such as an ergonomic mouse, safe screens, and appropriate noise levels. In cognitive engineering, the designer may want to know the performance implications of the user's limited capability to recall information (e.g., the maximum number of menu items that can be displayed simultaneously or the implications of the user's imperfect memory on the provision of feedback to the user).

The third part of the book deals with the application of basic knowledge to the developmental process. The intent is not to provide a comprehensive list of design guidelines but to demonstrate how the foundations are applied to the design and use of representative technologies of interaction. The HCI development methodology described above integrates several elements that are detailed in separate chapters. Central to the development methodology is the evaluation of each phase, which is examined in Chapter 7. This chapter describes in detail the different HCI concerns and the specific methods for conducting evaluations. Chapter 8 deals with HCI design principles and guidelines on issues such as control, consistency, and the use of metaphors. These are applied during the analysis and design phases. Chapter 9 examines the central role of task analysis in HCI development, concentrating on organizational tasks. It complements the discussions of the organizational context (Chapter 2) by examining organizational tasks and their implications on user requirements. Furthermore, it shows how tasks are decomposed into the tool-level tasks that are then modeled by the TSSL levels of interaction. Chapter 10 continues the discussions in Chapter 9 on task analysis to show how specific designs enable the tool-level tasks. It describes several design components of the interfaces such as graphics, color, windows, screen layout, and forms. Finally, Chapter 11 describes in detail the development methodology (Figure 1.8) that integrates the various components, principles and guidelines, and techniques to produce comprehensive HCI designs.

The fourth and last part of the book is designed to provoke thought beyond the organizational context as we described it into what we see as a rapidly changing world for HCI. Chapter 12 introduces relevant knowledge of relationships and collaboration in the organizational context. In organizations today, many tasks are performed as collaborative activities. Information systems must therefore support not only individual work with computers but also group and organization-wide work. For example, designs of computer systems that support collaboration and organization-wide work should rely on knowledge about how people interact, become aware of each other, share knowledge, make joint decisions, trust each other, and work as a team. Chapter 13 looks at the social and global aspects of HCI, which are becoming an important part of organizational life in the age of globalization and humane societies. Social aspects of HCI include the impacts of computerization and ethics as dimensions of designing HCI, and global aspects include international and intercultural considerations in HCI. Finally, Chapter 14 examines emerging changes and trends in both IT development and IT use and their implications for HCI design.

A few words about what this book does not do. This book does not provide a list of exhaustive guidelines on how to design HCI. Several books provide such lists, and they are listed in the bibliography. The book does describe in detail several HCI techniques, but this is to demonstrate how to apply the conceptual foundations to practical applications rather than to provide a recipe. Furthermore, the book concentrates on analysis and design issues and mentions only briefly issues of physical construction or implementation of interactive systems. Programming issues and User Interface Management Systems (UIMS) are raised only in the context of design issues. Usability issues constitute an important part of the book, but the management aspects of development, such as usability centers, are not discussed. Each chapter provides popular references and advanced readings on topics covered and those relevant but omitted for lack of space.

## ▶5. SUMMARY

This introductory chapter presents a view of HCI that will help organize the material in later chapters. Figure 1.9 shows the structure of the book, which has four parts: Context, Foundation, Application, and Additional Context. The main ideas to be developed further in the foundations are depicted concisely in Figures 1.4, 1.6, and 1.7. The notion of fit underlies many of the discussions, and the notion of levels of interaction—the task, semantic, syntactic, and lexical levels (TSSL)—provides a powerful concept that will appear in most chapters of this book. Furthermore, Figure 1.8 depicts the methodology that integrates the application chapters. Thus, the book can move logically through these various sections and provide the student with an understanding of HCI concepts that is grounded in theory and reinforced by concrete examples.

Below is a list of concepts covered in this chapter. These concepts will be used and developed further in later chapters. The bibliography includes a list of other texts on HCI. It also includes advanced readings on specific topics so as to provide researchers with some leads into advanced research topics. This practice will be repeated in each chapter. Additionally, we list several resources that may become useful as we progress. These include journals that provide not only new technologies and techniques but also new evidence on the impact of HCI designs. Similarly, academic and professional firms publish activities that will be of interest to students thinking of research or practice in the area of HCI.

## ▶ 6. SUMMARY OF CONCEPTS AND TERMS

| | |
|---|---|
| Multilayer activity model (the TSSL model) | User activity |
| HCI development methodology | Context of HCI |
| Performance | Human resources in HCI |
| Usability | Human concerns of HCI |
| Fit | Well-being |

## ▶ 7. BIBLIOGRAPHY AND ADDITIONAL READINGS

Booth, P. A. (1989). *An introduction to human-computer interaction.* Hove & London, UK: Lawrence Erlbaum Assoc.

Brave, S., & Nass, C. (2003). Emotion in human-computer interaction. In J. Jacko & A. Sears (Eds.), *The human-computer interaction handbook.* Mahwah, NJ: Lawrence Erlbaum Associates, Inc.

DeSanctis, G. (2006). Who is the user? Individuals, groups, communities. In P. Zhang & D. Galletta (Eds.), *Human-computer interaction and management information systems: Foundations.* Armonk, NY: M.E. Sharpe.

Gibbs, W. W. (1997). Taking computers to task. *Scientific American,* 82–89.

Kehoe, C., Pitkow, J., Sutton, K., Aggarwal, G., & Rogers, J. D. (1999). Results of GVU's Tenth World Wide Web User Survey: Graphics Visualization and Usability Center, Georgia Institute of Technology. Retrieved from http://www.gvu.gatech.edu/user_surveys

Moran, T. P. (1981). The command language grammar: A representation for the user interface of interactive computer systems. *International Journal of Man-Machine Studies, 15*(1), 3–50.

Nielsen, J. (1993). *Usability engineering.* New York: AP Professional.

Picard, R. W. (1997). *Affective computing.* Cambridge, MA: MIT Press.

Preece, J., Rogers, Y., & Sharp, H. (2002). *Interaction design: Beyond human-computer interaction.* New York: John Wiley & Sons.

Preece, J., Rogers, Y., Sharp, H., Benyon, D., Holland, S., & Carey, T. (1994). *Human-computer interaction.* Boston: Addison-Wesley.

Shneiderman, B., & Plaisant, C. (2005). *Designing the user interface: Strategies for effective human-computer interaction.* New York: Addison-Wesley.

Te'eni, D. (2006). Designs that fit: An overview of fit conceptualizations in HCI. In P. Zhang & D. Galletta (Eds.), *Human-computer interaction and management information systems: Foundations.* Armonk, NY: M.E. Sharpe.

Zhang, P., & Li, N. (2004). An assessment of human-computer interaction research in management information systems: Topics and methods. *Computers in Human Behavior, 20*(2), 125–147.

## 7.1 Academic Journals That Frequently Publish HCI Studies (Broadly Defined):

| | |
|---|---|
| ACM Interactions | http://www.acm.org/interactions/ |
| ACM Transactions on Computer-Human Interaction (ACM TOCHI) | http://www.acm.org/tochi/ |
| Behaviour and Information Technology (BIT) | http://www.tandf.co.uk/journals/tf/ 0144929X.html |
| Communications of the ACM (CACM) | http://www.acm.org/cacm/ |
| Communication of the Association for Information Systems (CAIS) | http://cais.isworld.org/ |
| Computers in Human Behavior (CHB) | http://www.elsevier.com/locate/issn/ 07475632 |
| Computer Supported Cooperative Work (CSCW) | http://www.springerlink.com/(search CSSW) |
| Human-Computer Interaction | http://hci-journal.com/ |
| Information Systems Research (ISR) | http://isr.katz.pitt.edu/ |
| International Journal of Human-Computer Interaction (IJHCI) | http://www.leaonlin.com/loi/ijhc |
| International Journal of Human-Computer Studies (IJHCS) | http://www.academicpress.com/www/ journal/hc/h.htm |
| Interacting with Computers (IwC) | http://www.elsevier.com/locate/intcom |
| Information & Management (I&M) | http://www.elsevier.com/homepage/ sae/orms/infman/menu.htm |
| Journal of AIS | http://jais.isworld.org/ |
| Journal of Management Information Systems (JMIS) | http://jmis.bentley.edu/ |
| Management Information Systems Quarterly (MISQ) | http://www.misq.org |

## 7.2 Academic Associations with HCI Focus or Special Interest Group:

| | |
|---|---|
| ACM SIG/CHI | http://www.acm.org/sig (Association of Computing Machinery) |
| AIS SIGHCI | http://sigs.aisnet.org/SIGHCI/ (Association of Information Systems) |
| ASIST SIG/HCI | http://www.asis.org/SIG/SIGHCI/sighci.html (Association of Information Science) |
| HFES | http://www.hfes.org (Human Factors and Ergonomics Society) |
| BCS | http://www.bcs.org.uk (British Computer Society) |

## 7.3 Professional HCI-Related Associations and Companies:

| | |
|---|---|
| Usability Professional Association | http://www.upassoc.org |
| IBM's User Interfaces Research | http://www.research.microsoft.com/research/ui/ |
| User Experience Network | http://www.uxnet.org/ |
| User Interface Engineering | http://www.uie.com/ |

## ▶ 8. CASE STUDY

The following section introduces a case study that runs through the entire book. This example uses an e-Shop development project to illustrate the incorporation of HCI guidelines, principles, and development into a commercial Web site.

### World Gourmet Setting

Majorca Fleming has a small imported-food shop in a small town in Illinois. Her shop is called "World Gourmet." Recently she has been thinking about finding someone to create a Web site to sell her products. She imports products from all over the world in small lots. This approach makes her freight costs quite high and requires her to add a hefty markup to the items she sells. She would like to order larger quantities and save on delivery costs.

### Requirements

There is a local company that builds, hosts, and maintains Web sites. She has seen their work and feels that they can produce an adequate Web site for her. She has met with the designer several times and decided on the following requirements for her Web site:

*   Clear navigation through product category is a must-have feature.
*   Consistent formats from page to page are important.
*   Third-party payment transactions will be contracted with a secure and trusted e-payment vendor.
*   The product information will be stored in a database from which the records will be read to populate the product Web pages.
*   The customers will fill out forms with their essential information. The forms will write customer records and sales transactions to a database.
*   The system should be able to identify a repeat customer and tailor some suggested products based on past purchases.
*   Customers should be able to get a response from the Web master or the owner within 24 hours of submitting an inquiry.

Each of the remaining chapters in the book will use this running case study to illustrate the concepts introduced in the chapter. Chapter 2, for example, will use the running case study to illustrate HCI issues in the small-business context.

## ▶ 9. EXERCISES

Ex. 1.  Where can you find HCI?

Ex. 2.  Why is it important to study HCI?

Ex. 3.  Design a simple online bio for the class, and write a report about your design.

The objectives of this assignment are (1) for you to experience some design issues and intuitive justifications (uninformed) and (2) for the professor, the TA, and your fellow classmates to get to know you so that groups can be formed later.
In your written report, write down any criteria or considerations you may have when designing your bio page. This includes even tiny decisions you made such as use of colors, icons, font sizes, positions of different parts, requiring or not requiring scrolling, using or not using frames, and so on.

Ex. 4.  Explain what the TSSL model is. Use examples to illustrate the different levels of concerns and how they connect to each other.

# 2

# ORGANIZATIONAL AND BUSINESS CONTEXT

## CONTEXT AND PREVIEW

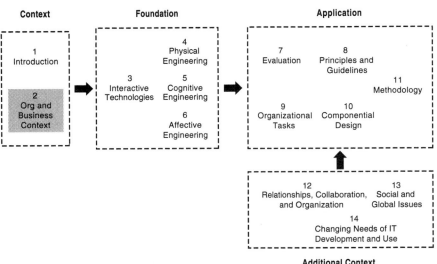

This chapter gives the student an overview of HCI issues within an organizational context. This chapter is unique to this book. We believe that the context in which the interfaces and interactions between humans and computers exist is critically important. The four levels of users, namely the individual, the work group, the organization, and the interorganizational level, create a structure that students should be familiar with and serve to anchor new knowledge about HCI. At each level, example systems and their HCI issues are articulated. Additionally, the chapter follows the task, semantic, syntactic, and lexical format that was introduced in Chapter 1 and is used throughout the book.

This chapter sets the stage for the study of HCI in the organizational and management context. The various systems that support people at work and the functions of the organizations are laid out at four different levels. For each level, example systems are described and HCI issues are highlighted for each of these sample systems. The first level is the individual level. Three examples of systems at the individual level are office automation systems, decision support systems, and executive support systems. The next level is the work group level, which includes project management systems, work flow management systems, and group support systems as examples. The next level of interest is the organizational level, which includes communications systems and enterprise resource planning systems as examples. The last level is the interorganizational level, and it includes supply chain management (SCM) systems.

## LEARNING OBJECTIVES

Upon completing this chapter, the student should be able to understand the organizational context of HCI and should be able to do the following:

- Understand the difference between the levels of individual, work group, and organization and the HCI issues related to these systems.
- Define and discuss the individual-level systems including office automation systems, knowledge work systems, decision-support systems, and executive information systems, and the HCI issues related to these systems.
- Define and discuss the work group–level systems including project management systems, work flow management systems, and group support systems, and the HCI issues related to these systems.
- Define and discuss the organizational-level systems including communication systems and enterprise resource planning systems, and the HCI issues related to these systems.

## ▶ 1. INTRODUCTION

This chapter sets the stage for the study of human–computer interaction (HCI) in organizations. It also incorporates and makes more concrete several of the organizing structures introduced in Chapter 1. The levels of interaction (task, syntax, semantics, and lexical) help to organize the different sections of this chapter. We also introduce some general ideas about tasks that are expanded upon later. Tasks are categorized as structured, semi-structured, or unstructured. Additionally, we introduce the various types and levels of information systems found in organizations. The levels of interaction also help to structure the rest of the book. Finally, HCI as a means for overcoming human limitations is another organizing theme that is introduced in this chapter and continues throughout the book.

Every chapter includes a running case to reinforce the concepts. The running case is an e-Shop development project that illustrates the incorporation of HCI guidelines, principles, and development for a commercial Web site. A fictitious small food import business demonstrates the concepts presented in the book. For this chapter on organizational context, the running case sets up the small business organizational context within which this project is embedded.

The context of the organization and a business orientation are critical to the understanding of HCI. This chapter explores the importance of human–computer interaction to the overall success of IS and, ultimately, to businesses themselves. The HCI focus of interest is not confined merely to the interface between the computer and the user. Our goal is to help students understand the relationships and variables that impact human–

computer interaction within an organizational setting. This understanding can then be used in the following ways:

- To help make IS users (both employees and customers) more productive and satisfied with IS
- To help IS professionals develop more usable and enjoyable, and therefore more successful, systems
- To enhance organizational effectiveness as an outcome of productive users and IS professionals
- To provide researchers with cohesive and cumulative knowledge in order to extend the boundaries of scholarly theory
- To apply this theoretical knowledge to enhance real information systems

Human–computer interaction focuses on increasing user effectiveness and improving user computer experiences with organizational systems. It does so by enhancing the user interface through an understanding of the tasks and organizational contexts in which HCI occurs (Carey et al., 2004). Workers who use computers on the job do not function in an isolated environment. They work within organizations and utilize computers for various purposes. Human–computer interaction does not occur in a vacuum. Variables such as user satisfaction, worker productivity, IS departmental structure, technical support for communication, balance of power, and many other factors impact the use of information systems. The organizational context shapes the expectations, prior experiences, priorities, preferences, and specific tasks of both users and developers. For example, the so-called structured revolution of the 1970s grew out of an effort to make the software development and maintenance process more manageable and less costly for organizations (Grudin, 1996). It is important for HCI designers to understand the particular organizational context within which software is being developed and systems are being utilized.

## ▶ 2. INDIVIDUAL LEVEL

It is helpful to categorize users according to the work they perform. In general, workers can be categorized as office support staff, knowledge workers (such as engineers, designers, and programmers/analysts), middle managers, and executives. Figure 2.1 depicts individual-level systems internal and external to the organization.

For each industry, there are alternative but similar worker classifications. Consider the environment of a hospital. There are office support staff persons, but the knowledge workers would be the doctors, nurses, and technicians, the middle managers would be logistics managers, and the executives would be directors of the hospitals. Also, the role of the insurance providers (external to the organization) in the hospital decision-making process adds additional complexity when thinking about creating information systems and interfaces. All of these workers perform their work tasks with computer support and often with systems that are single-user oriented, but the tasks are varied and range from routine, repetitive, and highly structured to intermittent, complex, and ill structured. The organizational concerns about these systems are varied and include individual productivity, technology acceptance, motivation to use any voluntary systems, and trust of these systems by both internal and external users.

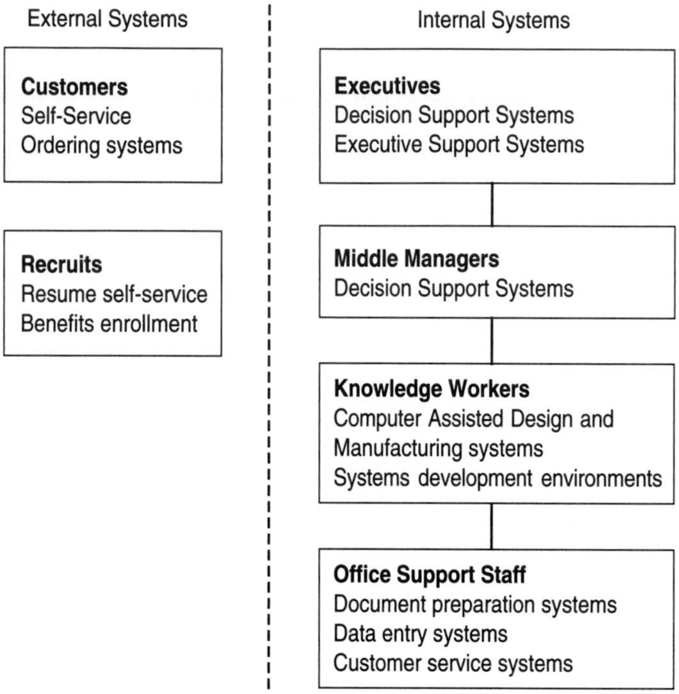

External Systems | Internal Systems

**Customers**
Self-Service
Ordering systems

**Executives**
Decision Support Systems
Executive Support Systems

**Recruits**
Resume self-service
Benefits enrollment

**Middle Managers**
Decision Support Systems

**Knowledge Workers**
Computer Assisted Design and
Manufacturing systems
Systems development environments

**Office Support Staff**
Document preparation systems
Data entry systems
Customer service systems

**Figure 2.1**   Individual-level systems.

An office support staff typically performs routine, repetitive, and highly structured tasks. Examples of these types of tasks include word processing and other types of document preparation, data entry, spreadsheet creation, and so on. The systems that support this type of work are frequently purchased as "off-the-shelf" software. These systems rely on a predefined set of parameters and therefore have limited flexibility and limited tailoring options. Although organizational efficiency is greatly impacted by these systems, users are not given much latitude in the choice of software. Consistency is critical in upgrading from one version to the next. Changes in the user interface can be very frustrating to users. The interface in this type of repetitive task should be very unobtrusive and almost disappear when the user has mastered the task. When changes occur, the natural rhythm of the work is disrupted and organizational efficiency plummets while the users are adapting to the new interface.

In the following section, we explore three types of single-user systems that belong to office support systems that support routine, repetitive, and highly structured tasks. These systems are electronic document preparation systems, data entry systems, and customer service systems.

## 2.1  Office Automation Systems

### 2.1.1  Electronic Document Preparation Systems

Many office support staff personnel spend a great deal of time creating, editing, storing, duplicating, and disseminating work documents. In this context, the documents may be disseminated to multiple people both in and out of the organization, but the creation of these documents is the responsibility of a single person rather than the work of a group.

**Office automation systems:** Systems designed to automate and support the work of white-collar support staff members. Interface consistency is critical to the success of these systems.

Shared workspace and documents created by multiple workers will be covered in a later section.

Examples of such systems are word processors, spreadsheet software, presentation software (such as PowerPoint), and desktop publishing software. The interfaces for such single-user systems are very familiar to many users of graphical user interface (GUI) environments. In word processing and desktop publishing software, the basic tasks are not very different from the days when typewriters were the main tools. The goal is to support easy and accurate input, management, and output of free-form data with some structured data such as tables. The basic workspace is like a piece of paper (white screen) upon which the office worker inserts and formats text and images. The final product may be a letter, memo, newsletter, brochure, report, and so on. The audience may be internal to the organization, such as members of a department, or external, such as customers.

Many office machines that were previously stand-alone have been connected via local area networks. Even remote copy machines and mail processing machines that fold documents, stuff them into envelopes, add postage, and sort them into zip-code bundles are now accessible from an office worker's workstation. The semantics of document preparation systems are concerned with the functionalities that directly support end users' various tasks as they use this type of software. The semantics include the documents themselves, which are usually referred to as files, with all the standard operations that are associated with files, such as open, save, save as, convert, and print. Blocks of text or entire documents can be edited by operations such as cut, paste, copy, move, duplicate, find, and replace. Various objects can be inserted such as pictures, charts, and symbols. The format of all the objects in a document can be altered. There are tools that can be used to check the spelling and usage of text. The language of the text can be enhanced through the Thesaurus tool. Tables and charts are often used in organizations to convey meaning about financial and tabular information. There are a number of operations associated with tables including column and row specifications. The window in which the document is displayed can also be split or otherwise arranged to support the document preparation task. The syntactic level of document preparation systems is closely aligned with the semantic level. In the early days of word processors, operation codes were inserted directly into the text and the document had to be compiled or "executed" to render the final version. An example of this type of system was the IBM Mainframe system called "Script." Today, HTML (Hypertext Markup Language) continues this tradition.

The lexical level of today's systems is concerned with building blocks that support syntactic-level considerations. Today's GUI-based systems are quite standard at the lexical level thanks to the object-oriented approach. Menus and navigation by mouse clicks as well as keystrokes are common. Blocks of text may be highlighted and then the menu choices can be selected through the pull-down menu options. Additionally, various icon-based menus provide desktop support for the most often used operations. Other toolbars such as formatting and drawing are available to be placed on the desktop as needed. Document systems also support OLE (Object-Linking and Embedding) so that graphs from spreadsheets and diagrams from a draw tool can be inserted directly into the text from other applications. Figures 2.2 and 2.3 are screen shots of the File menu and Edit menu document preparation operations.

> **Document preparation systems:** Office automation systems that are designed to support document preparation such as word processors, presentation software, publication software, and others.

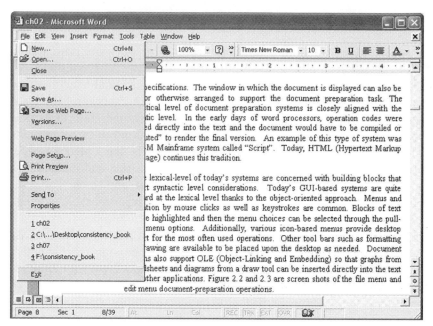

**Figure 2.2** Screen shot of File menu and text in Microsoft® Word®.

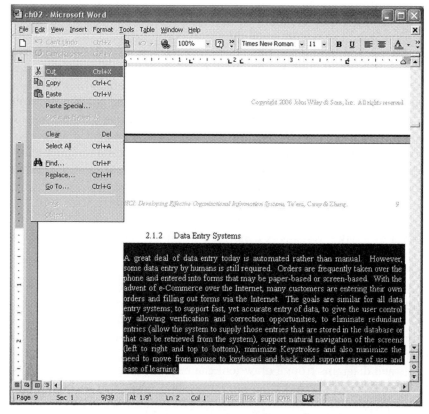

**Figure 2.3** Screen shot of Edit menu in Microsoft® Word®.

### 2.1.2 Data Entry Systems

A great deal of data entry today is automated rather than manual. However, some data entry by humans is still required. Orders are frequently taken over the phone and entered into forms that may be paper-based or screen-based. With the advent of e-commerce over the Internet, many customers are entering their own orders and filling out forms via the Internet. The goals are similar for all data entry systems: to support fast yet accurate entry of data, to give the user control by allowing verification and correction opportunities, to eliminate redundant entries (allow the system to supply those entries that are stored in the database or that can be retrieved from the system), to support natural navigation of the screens (left to right and top to bottom), to minimize keystrokes and minimize the need to move from mouse to keyboard and back, and to support ease of use and ease of learning.

> **Data entry systems:** Systems used to support the manual processes of data entry. These systems are generally proprietary and developed in-house specifically to accomplish data entry tasks.

The semantic level of data entry systems includes the various operations that are file- and record-oriented such as save, open, update, delete, create, and append. The fields in the form can be labels, text boxes, check boxes, list boxes, combo boxes (a combination of text and list), option buttons, command buttons, and so on.

The lexical level of data entry systems is similar to that of document preparation systems. The operations typically have shortcut keys to allow the experienced user to use keystrokes and thus minimize the amount of finger and hand travel that occurs when moving from keyboard to mouse. The focus of the cursor moves from control to control via the tab key. The mouse may be used to click on command buttons, but if the focus moves from control to control in the proper manner, minimal mouse clicks or insertions are needed. The data entry systems are designed to provide fast yet accurate data entry with interfaces that are easy to read and easy to learn.

Numeric keypads were introduced to the keyboard for the very purpose of streamlining the repetitive data entry of numbers and minimizing finger travel. It is critical that data entry systems provide user control and verification of destructive write operations such as submitting a file. Whenever possible, automatic field verification should be programmed in so that accuracy is supported. Errors messages that not only explain the error but also tell the user how to correct the error are also critical. If the data entry task requires multiple screens, navigation through the screens should be clearly marked and "bread crumbs" or a navigation path backward should be provided. These ideas are expanded in Chapters 8 and 10, but to make this discussion more concrete, consider Figures 2.4 and 2.5, which illustrate data entry screens. Figure 2.4 is an internal customer support screen used by a company employee. Figure 2.5 is an Internet-based e-commerce order form that is filled out by the customer.

### 2.1.3 Customer Account Management Systems

Reception and management of customer queries, appointment scheduling, order filling, complaints, and so on, are often supported or executed by computer-based systems. Automated telephone systems that route calls to appropriate customer representatives or account access are ubiquitous today. The cost of providing and training human operators to route calls greatly exceeds the cost of installing an automated voice system. These automated systems are also able to record transactions, provide a standard level of quality, and reduce costs. The Internet allows customers to self-serve without human interaction of the company employees. These systems have reduced service costs even more than the automated phone systems while at the same time empowering the customers to answer their own questions and manage their own accounts without having to wait in the phone queues or in a line at the customer service counter.

> **Customer account management systems:** These systems support the management of customer accounts. They may be purchased as part of an "off-the-shelf" system.

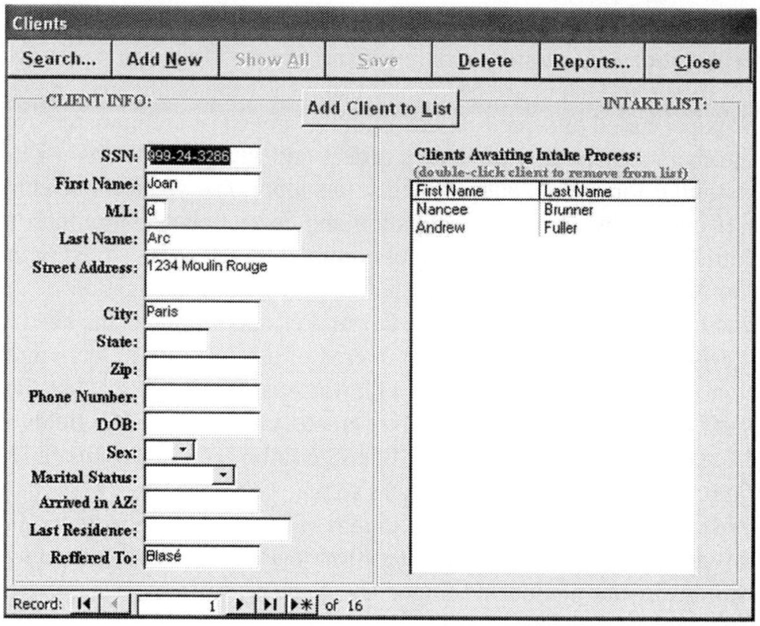

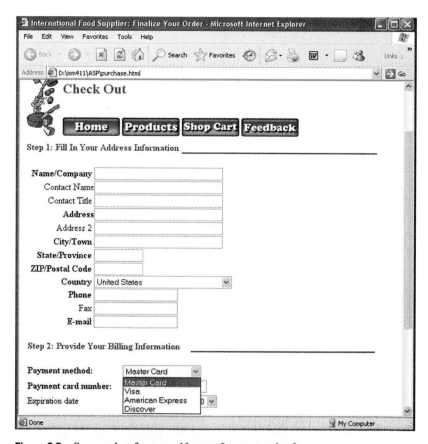

**Figure 2.4**  Screen shot from an internal system data entry order form.

**Figure 2.5**  Screen shot from a self-serve Internet order form.

Trust is another organizational issue. Trust is extremely important in customer self-service systems that are conducted over the Internet. Customers must believe that the financial and personal information that is being transmitted is secure and will not be compromised. In the early days of Internet e-commerce, many shoppers would browse retail products online, and once they found the item they wished to purchase, they would either order it over the phone or go to the "mortar" location of "click-and-mortar" stores to get the desired product. Today, when most banks, utilities, credit card companies, and other organizations that support customer accounts provide secure Internet access to accounts, customers are more trusting of the safety of their transactions and enter into them more willingly.

The semantic-level operations for these account management systems include logging in via login screens with login account IDs and passwords, retrieval of various snapshots of the account activity (usually organized by months from the present backward), payments, transfers between accounts, stop payments, and so on. Some financial institutions also support online loan applications.

The syntactic level is fairly simple and is limited to a few operations that usually involve submitting a parameter (like an account number) and retrieving information. The lexical level is typically supported by mouse clicks with a few keystrokes or list selection. Figures 2.6 and 2.7 illustrate customer account screens. Figure 2.6 is a login screen. Figure 2.7 is an account summary screen.

## 2.2 Knowledge Work Systems (KWS)

Knowledge work systems (KWS) support individuals who create intellectual property such as software programs and physical designs such as buildings and products. Architects, engineers, and information technology professionals are examples of individual KWS users. KWS include CAD/CAM (computer-aided design/computer-aided manufacturing), expert systems shells, computer-assisted software engineering (CASE), virtual reality environments, and others. KWS supports tasks such as architectural design, engineering new products, and creating computer-based software, among others.

**Knowledge work systems:** Single-user systems designed to support knowledge creation activities. KWS components include diagram support, stress and capacity testing, simulations, and prototyping tools.

The semantic-level operations of KWS include diagram and schematic support, simulations, stress and capacity testing, and prototyping tools, among others. The syntactic level is very task- and domain-specific. For example, for the architect who is using a CAD (computer-aided design) system, the syntactic level includes a collection of diagram symbols and draw tools that fit to a specific scale (e.g., 1 inch equals 5 feet). The architect uses the CAD system to create plans or blueprints for buildings and other spaces. The software programmer may use an expert system shell that allows the programmer to set up a rule base and a search algorithm to allow end users to find solutions to problems. The search algorithms may be breadth-first or depth-first or may use deductive reasoning or inductive reasoning.

The lexical level of KWS varies from domain to domain and from task to task. In the example of an architect using a CAD system, the lexical level is very mouse-oriented and includes a lot of drag-and-drop actions on specific symbols, shapes, and text. The resultant output in this example is a scale drawing or blueprint for a building or a manufacturing plant or some other

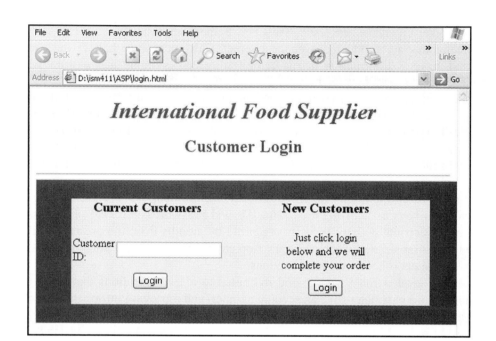

**Figure 2.6** Login screen for account management.

| 08-02-2005 | 2691 | Checking Withdrawal<br>Withdrawal (Item #2691) (eff. date 08/02/2005) | | 206.86 | 2,917.55 |
|---|---|---|---|---|---|
| 08-02-2005 | 2687 | ARCWF AUTO FINANCE (CHECKPAYMT)<br>Withdrawal (Item #2687)-ACH-A-WF AUTO FINANCE ARCWF AUTO FINANCE (CHECKPAYMT) (eff. date 08/02/2005) | | 195.61 | 3,124.41 |
| 08-01-2005 | | Checking Withdrawal<br>Withdrawal TRAVELERS CHECK PURCHASE (eff. date 08/01/2005) | | 500.00 | 3,320.02 |
| 08-01-2005 | | Checking Withdrawal<br>Withdrawal (eff. date 08/01/2005) | | 300.00 | 3,820.02 |
| 08-01-2005 | | Checking Purchase<br>Deposit (eff. date 08/01/2005) | 250.00 | | 4,120.02 |
| 08-01-2005 | 2688 | ARCAMERICAN EXPRESS<br>Withdrawal (Item #2688)- (CHECKPAYMT) (eff. date 08/01/2005) | | 442.99 | 3,870.02 |
| 08-01-2005 | | OPPENHEIMER (FUND PUR.)<br>Withdrawal-ACH-A-OPPENHEIMER OPPENHEIMER (FUND PUR.) (eff. date 08/01/2005) | | 100.00 | 4,313.01 |

Export August 01, 2005 to August 15, 2005

| Export |
|---|
| All transactions in the selected date range will be downloaded |

08 01 2005 to 08 15 2005

**Figure 2.7** Account summary screen.

physical space. In the example of the programmer creating an expert system, the lexical level may be couched in if/then rules with the true and false branches specified. The search algorithms are set up as inductive (forward chaining from the beginning states to the goal) or deductive (backward chaining from the goal to the beginning states).

In the following section, we explore two systems that support intermittent, semi-structured, or unstructured tasks. Individual users of these systems are typically middle- or upper-level managers. The two systems are decision support systems (DSS) and executive support systems (ESS).

## 2.3 Decision Support Systems (DSS)

There are numerous single-user systems that allow mid-level and top managers to make decisions. These systems often use corporate databases and models (such as statistical models) to make decisions. Sales forecasting, resource allocation, scheduling, routing, cost minimization, profit maximization, and so on, are all decision-making tasks. Chapter 9 examines such tasks in detail. They often require some intelligent interface to support model selection and interpretation of the output from these systems.

The semantic-level operations for decision support systems are often organized into four phases: problem definition, data selection, model selection, and execution. The syntactic level is frequently couched in table-related language using rows, columns, and cells (as in spreadsheets). It also includes mathematical functions and algorithms that can be applied to the data in the tables. Because of the ill-structured nature of the tasks, the semantics must be flexible to allow the user to be creative and perform operations that could not be anticipated by the designer.

The lexical level varies depending on the sophistication of the user and the intelligence that is built into the system. A less sophisticated user may interact with the system by answering a series of questions about the decision-making task at hand. The answers to the questions provide the system with the information needed to frame the problem, select the data, choose the model, and apply the model to the data and present the output to the user in a manner that is clear and well-explained. The output is often in graphical format. One very frequent decision task that upper-level managers often need to

> **Decision support systems:** Single-user systems designed to support decision making. DSS components include database, model-base, and user interface. The user interface is critical to the success of a DSS.

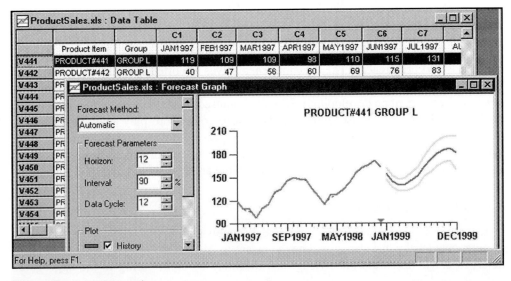

**Figure 2.8**  Sales forecasting.

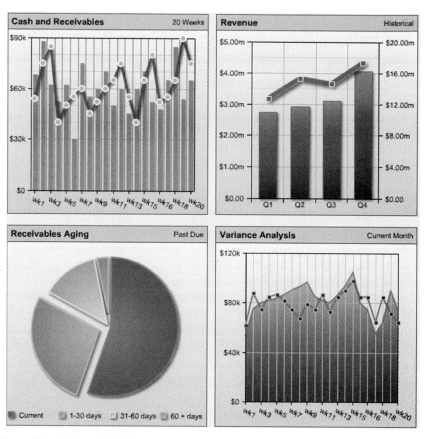

**Figure 2.9** Various ESS displays.

accomplish is that of sales forecasting. A critical feature of sales forecasting is sensitivity analysis. Managers are not certain about the future. To determine forecasted sales, they may run various scenarios that are optimistic, pessimistic, or in between. Figure 2.8 illustrates a sales forecasting system. The screen shot displays the sales forecast figures based on the selected data range and the input parameters.

In this type of single-user system, technology acceptance takes on a more critical role because use is typically at the discretion of the user. Typically, we design DSS of this type for a single user or a small set of users and can therefore tailor the system to particular needs and preferences. The decisions themselves are often critical to the success of the organization. All of these factors make acceptance even more important. Many dollars have been spent on developing DSS that sit unused because proper attention was not paid to the design of the user interface. Trust also comes into play again. In this case, trust or lack of trust may exist between the developers of the system and the users of the system. Good communication, end user involvement and ownership of the system, and a strong belief that the system is accurate and reliable are extremely important.

## 2.4 Executive Support Systems

Executive support systems (ESS) provide managers with the capacity to explore data at an aggregate level while also providing the means to "drill down" to data at lower levels of detail to chase down the underlying data that may be contributing to the aggregated

**Executive support systems:** Strategic systems designed to support executives. These systems give executives the capability of viewing data from an aggregate level and allow "drill down" to the more detailed level of data to help executives understand the nature of the aggregate level of data.

picture. Visualization is an area of HCI that has yielded various techniques for presenting information in formats designed to assist the user in understanding the trends and patterns of data.

Typically, we design ESS around a set of critical success factors (CSF) that the executive is interested in assessing on a daily or even more frequent basis. ESS are often designed to alert executives when prespecified levels of these CSF are not achieved or are out of normal range. The executive can then start to explore the data (drill down) to determine the cause of the problem and what corrective actions to take.

The interfaces of an ESS must be highly graphical in nature and allow the executive to scan both internal and external conditions at a glance. They must also be easy to use. Today's executives are often technically savvy but do not have the time or the inclination to be burdened with an interface that requires highly technical skills to use.

As with DSS, technology acceptance by the user and trust are two factors that impact the use of ESS. First, the use of an ESS is often voluntary rather than required. Technology acceptance is even more critical in voluntary-use systems than in nonvoluntary systems. Secondly, an ESS usually supports unstructured and high-impact decisions in which executives receive a variety of information from internal as well as external sources and anecdotal cases. In such situations, trust plays a more crucial role than in situations in which the information is structured, straightforward, and repetitive.

The semantic-level operations of ESS focus on information retrieval files, tables, and records that require finding, opening, extracting, summarizing, and so forth. The underlying syntactic level is based on Structured Query Language (SQL) operations, for example, "SELECT field1, field2, from TABLE1 WHERE condition exists." However, many of today's ESS do not require busy managers to create SQL queries as they are

**Table 2.1** Summary Table for Individual User Level in the Organizational Context

| Task Nature | User Type | System | Organizational Considerations | Interface Focus |
|---|---|---|---|---|
| Routine, repetitive, highly structured | Office support staff | Document preparation | Technology acceptance User productivity User satisfaction | Document |
| | Data entry staff or customer self-entry via Internet forms | Data entry | User productivity User satisfaction Trust Technology acceptance | Data entry form |
| | Customer service representatives or customer self-service via Internet | Customer account management | Technology acceptance Trust Motivation to use | Account |
| Intermittent, semi-structured, or unstructured | Upper- or middle-level managers | KWS Decision support systems | Technology acceptance Trust Motivation to use | Graphs and charts |
| | | Executive support systems | Technology acceptance Trust Motivation to use | Graphs and charts Visualization |

needed. Instead, we build a series of reports and the executive merely selects the desired report from a menu of all available reports. A natural language interface may also be provided to support the generation of new queries. In some cases, the lexical level is supported by voice activation. Figure 2.9 illustrates the frequent use of graphics in ESS to help display large quantities of data in meaningful ways.

Table 2.1 summarizes the tasks, users, systems, interface foci, and relevant organizational considerations at the individual-user level that are presented in this section.

## ▶ 3. WORK GROUP LEVEL

> **Work group level:** Groups of people who work together, such as departments and project teams.

Much of the work done in organizations is done by groups of workers. They may be organized in project teams, departments, management teams, quality circles, sales groups, or any one of a number of configurations. In this section, we look at work performed by groups, the systems that support these tasks, and relevant organizational issues. We divide the work into two sections. The first is project-oriented, where the work group forms specifically to accomplish an assignment; after the assignment is completed, although the project may require ongoing maintenance, the entire work group is dismantled. Most of the workers go on to tackle other projects. Project management systems and work flow management systems are used to discuss this concept. The second type of work group is a management team. This type of group is fairly stable and consists of various upper-level managers who are charged with strategic decision making for the organization. We use group support systems to discuss this concept, although such systems can also be used for ad hoc teams.

### 3.1 Project Management Systems (PMS)

> **Project management systems:** Systems designed to support the management of projects. These systems include mechanisms for decomposing large tasks into smaller, more manageable subtasks. They also include modules that help to manage resources including time, labor, and money.

A project is a temporary endeavor undertaken to accomplish a unique purpose. Projects are temporary in nature, require resources (often from various areas), often have a primary sponsor and/or customer, and usually involve uncertainty. Project groups are often referred to as teams. Project teams vary from purpose to purpose. In this discussion, the goal of the project team is to create a software system. The team consists of a project sponsor, a project leader or manager, technical staff members including analysts, programmers, a database specialist, an HCI specialist, and other technology specialists, and at least one user representative who understand the target environment in which this project will function.

Project managers must be able to manage project scope, time, cost, and quality by effective use and coordination of human resources, communication mechanisms, risk, and procurement management and, through it all, achieve project integration. Unfortunately, the track record for many IT projects is not very positive. Projects often come in over budget, behind schedule, and lacking in quality and functionality. Project managers need all the support they can get. Chapter 1 talked about technology's role in overcoming human limitations by identifying the specific cognitive and affective resources needed and by designing the interactive technology that can best support these needs. One of the specific problems project managers encounter is the need to organize multiple activities in a meaningful order. They need this organization to identify problems in the progress of the project. One of the graphical techniques that present the relevant information in a meaningful way is the Gantt chart, explained below.

Project management systems generally provide a centralized project repository that can provide the information necessary for showing the "big picture." All team members are able to access the repository. The general outline of the project management system is to first divide the complex task into smaller, more manageable tasks generally referred to as work breakdown structures. Usually each of these tasks is small enough and cohesive enough to be accomplished by a single team member. Once the tasks have been decomposed and assigned to personnel, they are entered into the project management system. Some tasks may be overview tasks, which can be expanded. The tasks are given an estimated duration and sequenced in the proper order. Some tasks may be dependent on the completion of a previous task and some can be accomplished in parallel while other tasks are being accomplished. Once all the tasks are entered and the relationships and durations set up, it is possible to calculate an estimated project completion date and a total cost for the project. As tasks are completed, the actual time taken to complete a task is entered. If tasks take longer than estimated, the entire schedule can ripple forward as needed.

Most project management systems can depict projects and milestones in a Gantt chart. A Gantt chart is expressed in time intervals. Figure 2.10 is a Gantt chart built in Microsoft® Project.® Its main purpose is to present the multiple activities in a form that highlights relationships between these activities on a time scale. This helps the project manager overcome the cognitive limitation on our natural (unaided) ability to mentally visualize such a complex structure. When this structure is presented to the project manager, it is easier for her to identify what, if anything, is wrong and how to cope with it. We note that this tool helps to coordinate group work but that most users view the screen

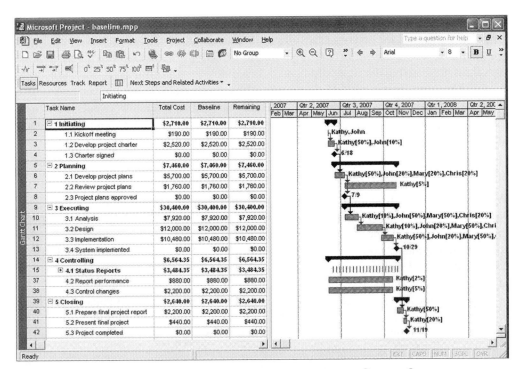

**Figure 2.10**  Gantt chart and work breakdown structure in Microsoft® Project®.

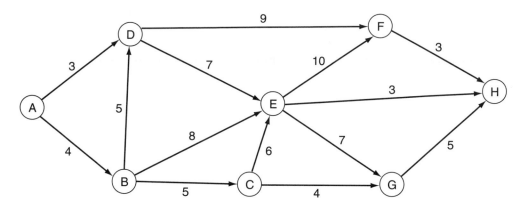

**Figure 2.11**   Network diagram.

on an individual basis. The fifth column shows the resources (people) responsible for the activities in column 1.

Another visual aid frequently available in PMS is the network diagram or PERT (Program Evaluation and Review Technique) chart. The PERT chart is useful for critical path analysis that determines the longest path through the network diagram and thus the time frame for the project. Figure 2.11 is a network diagram.

The semantic level of the PMS includes objects such as activities durations, costs, labor units, charts, and work breakdown structures, as well as the operations allowed on these objects. For example, two activities are related to each other either in sequence (one comes before the other) or in parallel. At the syntactic level, the rules by which we link activities, for example, are to draw an arrow between two activities so that the arrowhead points at the activity that follows its precedent. At the lexical level, the boxes are similar to a spreadsheet. There are columns of activities associated with each other. Activities are listed in the first column and then duration, start time, end time, predecessors, and resource names are listed for tasks when appropriate.

More generally, PMS include at the semantic level objects such as events, activities' durations, costs, labor units, charts, and work breakdown structures, along with the operations allowed on these objects.

**Work flow management systems:**
Systems that are designed to manage the flow of work. These systems include routing information (the path that work follows from person to person or from department to department. Other components of work flow systems include version control and work specification.

## 3.2  Work Flow Management Systems

Work flow management deals with the specification and execution of business processes. Work flow management systems execute business processes as well as support their specification. General work flow specifications include the actions to be performed, statements on control and data flow among these actions, agents allowed to execute actions, and policies that describe the organizational environment. Frequently, graphical user interfaces may be used to support the specification work.

Typical work flows are executed in distributed computing environments within large enterprises. Due to frequent modifications in the enterprise (e.g., new business processes, new departments), work flow management systems have to be scalable in order to satisfy

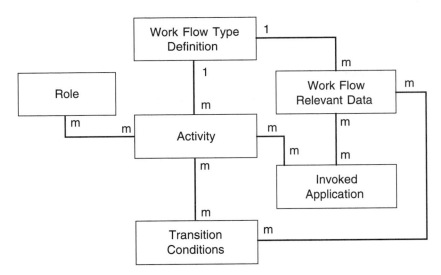

**Figure 2.12** Process definition meta-model.

the new requirements. Ownership and control is very important to allow for modifications to work flows by the properly authorized persons.

A process definition normally comprises a number of discrete activity steps, with associated computer operations and human rules governing the progression of the process. The process definition may be expressed in textual or graphical form or in a formal language notation. At definition time, the process-related roles for all activities of the process are defined. At execution time, each activity instance must be assigned to potential work flow participants. The following are semantic-level definitions associated with work flow management:

- Work flow type definition such as process name, version number, process start and termination conditions, and security, audit, or other control data
- Activities such as activity name, activity type, pre- and post-activity conditions, and other scheduling constraints
- Transition conditions such as flow or execution conditions
- Work flow–relevant data such as data name, data path, and data types
- Invoked application such as generic type or name, execution parameters, and location or access path

Figure 2.12 depicts a process definition meta-model for a work flow management system (Lawrence, 1997, p. 271). Figure 2.13 depicts a work flow diagram chart used in work flow management systems. Notice that the work flow diagram in Figure 2.13 looks like a flowchart for programming logic.

General systems theory and organizational theory both address the boundaries of an organization along with boundary-spanning activities and agents. Work flow management systems (WFMS) typically manage work processes that are internal to organizations. However, researchers have designed and developed a WFMS that is able to manage work that exists in dynamic virtual enterprises where one or more organizations combine in a contractual relationship such as outsourced software development (Grefen, Aberer, Hoffner, & Ludwig, 2000). One of the downsides of outsourcing is the loss of

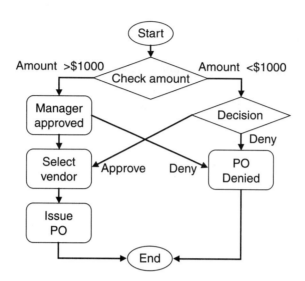

**Figure 2.13**   Work flow diagram chart.

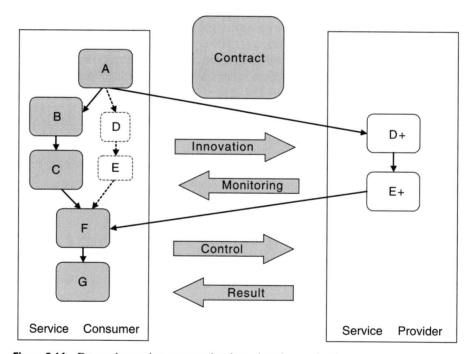

**Figure 2.14**   Dynamic service outsourcing in a virtual organization.

control, which may be overcome by effective representations of the work flows—an important component of work flow management systems. There are four main aspects that characterize this approach:

- Dynamic service outsourcing—Finding an outsource partner with compatible WFMS

- Contract-based service specification—Articulating the cross-flow WFMS technology and details

- Fine-grained, advanced interaction—Operating with the cross-flow WFMS advanced cooperation support services
- Contract-dependent generation of enactment infrastructure—Implementation of the contracted cross-flow WFMS

Figure 2.14 depicts dynamic service outsourcing in a virtual organization.

## 3.3 Group Support Systems

Group support systems (GSS) can be defined as technologies that support group processes such as decision making, communication, meetings, document control, and calendaring. The technology can be as simple as regular electronic mail systems or as complex as structured meeting support software. Teleconferencing is a computer-based technique for groups of people to access an electronic conference or dialogue. One of the advantages of teleconferencing is that group members can participate from different locations at various times. This is referred to as asynchronous communication. Additionally, simultaneous entries allow for multiple messages and reduction of "production blocking" or waiting to speak while others have the floor, which often occurs in face-to-face meetings (Diehl & Stroebe, 1987). Also, low-status or shy members of the group may feel freer to contribute when using teleconferencing (Siegal et al., 1986). The disadvantages of teleconferencing are that (1) this text-based communication does not offer the richness that audio, visual, graphical, and nonverbal cues provide, (2) those group members who lack keyboarding skills may be frustrated or restricted from full participation in the group, (3) the simultaneous entries that are facilitated by teleconferencing require additional cognitive processing, and (4) outcomes from virtual team interactions may be less positive than outcomes from face-to-face interactions (Potter & Balthazard, 2002).

> **Group support systems:** Systems designed to support group processes including decision making, communication, meetings, document control, calendaring, and others.

### 3.3.1 GSS User Interface

The user interface is critical to the efficiency of GSS. There are some important issues that need to be considered in GSS design:

- Design of the shared screen(s)
- Interaction between the shared and individual screens
- Ergonomic design of the individual's workstation in the group environment
- Interface support for communication among the participants
- Adapting to cognitive style differences among participants
- Adapting to cultural differences among participants
- Nature of the task to be supported
- Individual and group information needs (Gray, et al., 1993)

These issues frame the design choices in physical facilities, hardware, and software.

One of the key overarching design issues is that of access control (Shen & Dewan, 1992). Allowing individual users to access any and all shared information on demand can serve to detract from task accomplishment. However, restricting individual user access can lead to frustration. Agenda setting and chauffeur-driven systems can help alleviate control problems but require training and facilitation skills that many group leaders don't have. In addition, leaderless teams will not adapt well to such restrictions. Imposed structure disrupts the group's familiar meeting protocols, and therefore flexibility in social protocols and support for the existing social structures of the meetings are important dimensions of the interface (Elwart Keys et al. 1990). The major issues associated with the design of multimedia GSS interfaces are cross-media links, searchability and granularity, and interface consistency.

### 3.3.2 Shared Workspace

Shared workspace in distributed computer environments include such activities as sharing information, pointing, marking, annotating, and editing (Ishii, Kobayashi, & Grudin, 1992). This shared workspace has been referred to as "What you see is what I see" or WYSIWIS. In face-to-face meetings, nonverbal behaviors such as eye contact, facial expression, posture, and gesture are significant in developing a climate of confidence among the group members. In text-based GSS, these nonverbal cues tend to disappear unless they are purposely built back into the system. Some systems have mood indicators (often faces with expressions that reflect the mood of the individual). Users of instant messaging, teleconferencing, and bulletin boards have developed a large set of emoticons. The smiley face (☺) is used to indicate a good mood or a joking comment.

In current GSS environments, there are three major seams or interfaces:

- Seam between individual work modes and cooperative work modes
- Seam between the computer-supported work and other work
- Seam between asynchronous and real-time communication (Ishii, 1990)

Jessup and Valacich (1993) suggest that GSS need to focus on the following issues:

- "Anytime/anyplace" requires focus on technologies for distributed groups.
- "Orchestrated work flow" requires focus on groups of groups.
- "Virtual team rooms" requires focus on creation of its own collaboration workspace by the group.
- "Culture bridging" requires focus on enhancing the performance of the groups with members from diverse culture.

**Table 2.2**   Summary Table of Work Group Level in the Organizational Context

| Tasks | Duration | User Type | System | Organizational Considerations | Interface Focus (Semantics) |
|---|---|---|---|---|---|
| Project management | Ad hoc | Technical staff<br><br>User reps | Work flow systems<br><br>Project management systems | Shared workspace Group satisfaction<br><br>Coordination Leadership Motivation | Tasks Flow diagrams<br><br>Work breakdown Structures Gantt charts PERT charts |
| Managerial strategic decision making | Ongoing | Managers | Group support systems | Coordination Anonymity Leadership | Graphs Charts Organization Charts |

- "Just-in-time learning" requires focus on more online information repositories and memories.
- "Window to anywhere" requires focus on video wall or video window to simulate tele-presence of dispersed group members at the same location.

Table 2.2 summarizes the tasks, users, systems, interface foci, and relevant organizational considerations at the group level that are presented in this section.

## ▶ 4. ORGANIZATIONAL-LEVEL SYSTEMS

Organizational-level systems are designed to support the entire organizational entity. These systems may also reach beyond the organization to serve to connect the company with external constituencies such as customers, suppliers, stockholders, and so on. Although there are many possibilities for discussion, we focus on organizational communication systems, CRM, and enterprise resource planning (ERP) systems. These systems have dramatically altered the structure and core processes of organizations. Table 2.3 summarizes the various organizational-level systems within the organizational context and includes tasks, users, organizational considerations, and interface foci.

> **Organizational level:** These systems are designed to support the entire organizational entity and include communications, personnel management, and organizational learning.

### 4.1 Communication Systems

Organizational communication systems are designed to support enterprise-level communications and encompass various media and software. The most ubiquitous system is the e-mail system. Other media and systems such as voice mail, teleconferencing, computer conferencing, and Listservs also exist. Millions of dollars are spent on these types of systems. Additionally, many viruses have been transmitted through e-mail systems. Successful attacks by hackers can result in hundreds of hours of time spent to recover, clean, and defend these systems.

> **Enterprise communication systems:** Systems designed to support enterprise-level communications including e-mail systems and conferencing systems.

**Table 2.3**  Summary of Organizational Levels in the Organizational Context

| System Type | User Type | System | Organizational Considerations | Interface Focus |
|---|---|---|---|---|
| Communication | All levels and types of users | E-mail systems and document management systems | Communication effectiveness Anthony's pyramid | E-mails Documents Calendars |
| Personnel management | | Intranet human resource portal | Locus of control | Forms Announcements Policies |
| Organizational learning | | E-training | Organizational learning | Training modules |
| Functional systems | | ERP | Organizational effectiveness and efficiency | Reports and data retrieval |
| Extra-organizational | | CRM | Revenue generation and customer service | Customer service |

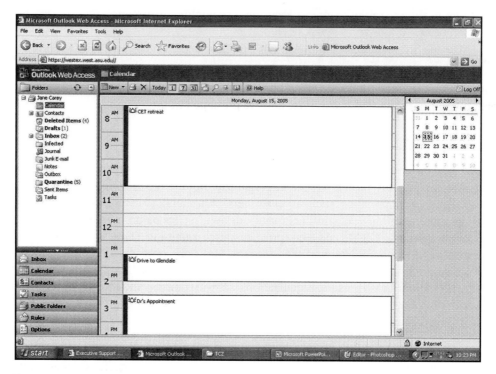

**Figure 2.15** Screen for Outlook Calendar.

Many empirical studies have examined the relationship of communication systems (specifically e-mail) with various organizational variables such as power, span of control, structure (flat versus tall), centrality, boundary spanning, employee motivation, feedback, and leadership, to name a few. In general, e-mail communications have supplanted face-to-face communications and telephone communications within organizations. E-mail is considered a "lean" rather than "rich" media due to the lack of interpersonal cues such as body language and tone of voice that are present in face-to-face and telephone communications. E-mail communications are more efficient but less personal than other modes of communication. E-mail systems also support one-to-many communications that are less time-consuming, more accurate (less likely to vary the message each time it is conveyed), and more efficient than multiple face-to-face communications.

In addition to e-mail messages, most organizational systems also support calendaring functions such as setting up meetings, reminders of activities, determining available dates for functions, and so on. This capability cuts down on the amount of phone calls and coordination that can occur when trying to bring several busy employees together for an ad hoc meeting.

The general tasks of communication systems include messaging, threaded discussions, chatting, asynchronous communication, and calendar-related functions. Some systems (like Lotus Notes) also support group document preparation.

The semantic level of e-mail focuses on lists of messages and associated operations such as send, open, reply, organize, delete, and so forth. The syntactic level of the Outlook Calendar function is shown in Figure 2.15. Notice that most of the syntactic-level concepts are time- and/or date-related. The main window shows the current day in an hour-by-hour format. Another window shows the current and next month. There is also a "to do" list of actions that can be checked off (indicated by crossing out the task). The lexical level includes mouse-clicks to activate operations and keystrokes to type in text.

## 4.2 Enterprise Resource Planning (ERP) Systems

Enterprise resource planning (ERP) systems are designed to support the functions and activities of an organization and integrate the various company information systems including human resources, inventories, and financials while simultaneously linking the company to customers and vendors. ERP systems are most frequently purchased from a third party such as SAP, Oracle, or PeopleSoft rather than created in-house. ERP can provide significant improvements in efficiency across a company, but only when implemented correctly. Planning for ERP systems and their implementations requires an integrated approach to meet the requirements of various functional areas.

> **Enterprise resource planning (ERP) systems:** Systems designed to support all the major functions and activities of an organization including marketing, production management, order fulfillment, accounting, personnel management, and financial management.

IT managers responsible for managing their organization's ERP implementation view their ERP systems as their organization's most strategic computing platform. However, despite such strategic importance, ERP projects report an unusually high failure rate, sometimes jeopardizing the core operations of the implementing organization. The results from a field study of 34 organizations show that ERP implementation success significantly depends on the organizational fit of ERP (Hong & Kim, 2002). In order to take advantage of this finding, organizations must understand their own culture and structure first.

ERP systems promise to increase productivity by standardizing processes, enhance decision making by sharing information throughout the organization, and create more cooperation among organizational entities by linking them together seamlessly. However, ERP systems typically reinforce the organizational status quo, rather than contributing to significant organizational change (Legare, 2002). Long-term creativity and solution development may be limited by the presence of an ERP.

A successful ERP can provide critical business intelligence for an organization and give management a unified view of its processes and systems. Unfortunately, ERPs have a reputation for costing a lot of money and providing suboptimal results. Training usually covers only how to do specific job-related tasks, without exploring the role those actions have within the rest of the business cycle. New ERP systems usually require employees to do more or different administrative tasks that do not add obvious value to their jobs. If they do not understand why that information is important to other members of the company, they will find ways to work around it (Gale, 2002). Even if they do understand why that information is important to other members of the company, they need additional motivation and need to be held accountable for the successful implementation of the ERP. Five post-implementation best practices that can help organizations reap all of the benefits of ERP-enabled include (1) focusing on capabilities and benefits, not just on going live, (2) aligning the organization on the true destination, (3) achieving balanced people, process, and technology changes across all areas, (4) applying program management practices throughout the program cycle, and (5) extending capabilities beyond the ERP platform ("ERP's Second Wave," 2002).

Most ERP systems do not allow much in the way of tailoring or accommodations to various organizational processes or cultures. Recently, many organizations have been migrating their ERP systems to the Web, causing even more interface complications.

Some researchers are exploring the relationship of ERP and organizational power. Although an ERP tightens management control by monitoring almost all core organizational activities, another outcome of an ERP is to empower employees through new process design. Management often resists empowerment by adding new process constraints on top of the ERP processes (Sia et al., 2002).

Organizations have discovered that when an ERP system is introduced, the new interface and navigation methods are very different from the old system. The change is disruptive and often causes a fall in worker productivity for a period of time, until the users get adjusted to the new interfaces. On the positive side, an ERP introduces a lot of interface standardization from subsystem to subsystem, which may help in the learning process. Consistency is a cardinal rule in interface design, and certainly ERP systems provide consistency across applications.

### 4.3  Customer Relationship Management (CRM)

> **Customer relationship management (CRM) systems** : Systems that enable organizations to better serve their customers via software. The term *CRM* can be used to describe either the software itself or the whole business

Customer relationship management (CRM) systems enable organizations to better serve their customers via software in contrast to customer service systems (mentioned above). The term *CRM* can be used to describe either the software itself or the whole business strategy.

Major areas of CRM focus on automated service processes, personal information gathering and processing, and self-service.

There are three parts of application architecture of CRM:

- Operational—Automation of the basic customer processes (marketing, sales, service)
- Analytical—Analysis of customer behavior
- Cooperational—Ensures the contact with customers (phone, e-mail, fax, Web, etc.)

Many call centers use CRM software to store all of their customers' details. When a customer calls, the system can be used to retrieve and store information relevant to the customer. By serving the customer quickly and efficiently, and also keeping all information on a customer in one place, a company aims to make cost savings and encourage new customers.

CRM solutions can also be used to allow customers to perform their own service via a variety of communication channels including the Internet and mobile phones (Nelson, 2000).

Many Web-based companies such as Amazon.com tailor the user interface to each individual customer based on past purchasing patterns. Product recommendations and individual buttons such as "My Stuff" give the customer a personalized experience. Figure 2.16 shows a sample customer recommendation screen for e'Gourmet.

**Figure 2.16**  Customer recommendations from e'Gourmet.

## ▶ 5. INTERORGANIZATIONAL SYSTEMS

Interorganizational systems are those systems that link companies with external organizations (not individual customers). Usually this link is a B2B (business-to-business) link between suppliers and business customers. With the advent of e-commerce, this link is primarily Internet-enabled and has taken the place of EDI (Electronic Data Interchange). These systems support computer-to-computer transactions that focus on order fulfillment and raw material requisitioning for manufacturing. These systems often eliminate the need for human intervention in the management of the supply chain.

It is difficult to determine the total revenues from interorganizational systems. It has been estimated that worldwide B2B e-commerce revenues surpassed $1.4 trillion in 2003 (e-Marketer, 2001). That is less than 10% of total U.S. revenues of $10.8 trillion. However, it is expected that B2B revenues will double each year for the foreseeable future.

Figure 2.17 shows the architecture of Enigma 3C software, which is one of the top-selling interorganizational systems for supply chain management.

> **Interorganizational systems:** Those systems that link companies with external organizations (not individual customers). Usually this link is a B2B (business-to-business) link between suppliers and business

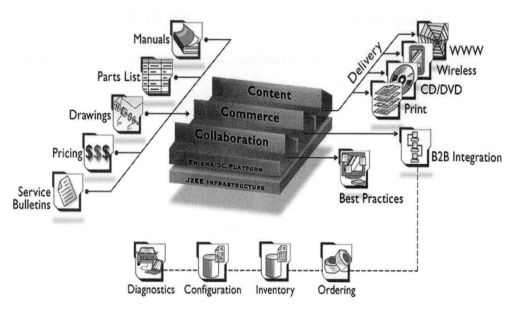

**Figure 2.17**   Enigma® 3C® architecture.

## ▶ 6. SUMMARY

In this chapter, we explore the organizational context within which human–computer interaction takes place. We present and discuss the impact of organizations on the tasks of HCI and the impact of HCI on organizations.

This chapter is structured around four levels of information systems: the individual, the work group, the entire organization, and the interorganizational level. At each level, various systems that support the level are presented along with the four levels of HCI (task, semantic, syntactic, and lexical) and the organizational theories that relate to the specific system.

The systems presented at the single-user level are divided between routine, repetitive, highly structured tasks performed by office support staff and intermittent, complex, unstructured tasks performed by middle and upper managers. The first group includes document preparation systems, data entry systems, and customer support systems. The second group includes KWS decision support systems and executive support systems. A discussion of Web-based self-service interactions is included in this section. Table 2.1 summarizes the single-user-level systems. The systems presented at the work group level include work flow systems, project management systems, and group support systems. Table 2.2 summarizes the work group–level systems. The systems presented at the organizational level include organizational communication systems, enterprise resource planning systems, and customer relationship management systems. Table 2.3 summarizes the organizational-level systems. We also introduce and discuss interorganizational systems including supply chain management systems.

In conclusion, understanding the organizational context of HCI is critical to the design and implementation of successful information systems. Conversely, understanding the impact of HCI on organizations is critical to understanding the theoretical underpinnings of organizational performance.

## ▶ 7. SUMMARY OF CONCEPTS AND TERMS

Work group level

Office automation systems

Customer account management systems

Work flow systems

Data entry systems

Executive support systems

Project management systems

Organizational level

Document preparation systems

Decision support systems

Group support systems

Enterprise communication systems

Enterprise resource planning (ERP) systems

## ▶ 8. BIBLIOGRAPHY AND ADDITIONAL READINGS

Carey, J., Galletta, D., Kim, J., Te'eni, D., Wildermuth, B., & Zhang, P. (2004). The role of HCI in IS curricula: A call to action. *Communication of the AIS, 13*(23):357–379.

Daft, R. L., & Macintoshm N. B. (1981). A tentative exploration into the amount and equivocality of information processing in organizational work units. *Administrative Science Quarterly, 25*:207–224.

Diehl, M., & Stroebe, W. (1987). Productivity loss in brainstorming groups: Toward the solution of a riddle. *Journal of Personality and Social Psychology, 53*(3):497–509.

Elwart Keys, M., Halonen, D., Horton, M., Kass, R., & Scott, P. (1990). *User interface requirements for face-to-face groupware.* Paper read at Human Factors in Computing Systems, CHI'90.

ERP's second wave: Post-implementation best practices. (2002). *Government Finance Review, 18*(1):48–49.

Gale, S. F. (2002). For ERP success, create a culture change. *Workforce, 81*(9):88–94.

Gray, P., Mandviwalla, M., Olfman, L., & Satzinger, J. (1993). The user interface in group support systems. In L. M. Jessup & J. S. Valacich (Eds.), *Group support systems—New perspectives.* New York: Macmillan Publishing Company.

Grefen, P., Aberer, K., Hoffner, Y., & Ludwig, H. (2000). Cross-flow: Cross-organizational workflow management in dynamic virtual organizations. *International Journal of Computer Systems Science and Engineering, 15*(5):277–290.

Grudin, J. (1996). The organizational contexts of development and use. *ACM Computing Surveys, 28*(1):169–171.

Hong, K. K., & Kim, Y. G. (2002). The critical success factors for ERP implementation: An organizational fit perspective. *Information and Management, 40*(1):25–40.

Ishii, H. (1990). *Teamworkstation: Towards a seamless shared workspace.* Paper read at Computer Supported Cooperative Work.

Ishii, H., Kobayashi, M., & Grudin, J. (1992). *Integration of interpersonal space and shared workspaces.* Paper read at Computer Supported Cooperative Work.

Jessup, L. M., & Valacich, J. S. (1993). Future directions and challenges in the evolution of group systems. In L. M. Jessup & J. S. Valacich (Eds.), *Group support systems—New perspectives.* New York: Macmillan Publishing Company.

Lawrence, P. (Ed.). (1997). *Workflow handbook.* New York: John Wiley & Sons.

Legare, T. E. (2002). The role of organizational factors in realizing ERP benefits. *Information Systems Management, 19*(4):21–42.

Nelson, S. (2000). *From e-commerce to CRM: The database as core system.* Research report from the Gartner Group. Retrieved from http://www.ncr.com/repositor/research_reports/pdf/gartner_dbcore.pdf

Potter, R., & Balthazard, P. (2002). Understanding human interactions and performance in the virtual team. *Journal of Information Technology Theory and Application, 4*(1):1–31.

Shen, H., & Dewan, P. (1992). *Access for collaborative environments.* Paper read at Computer Supported Cooperative Work, New York.

Sia, S. K., Tang, M., Soh, C., & Boh, W. F. (2002). Enterprise resource planning (ERP) systems as a technology of power: Empowerment or panoptic control? *Database for Advances in Information Systems, 33*(1):23–37.

Siegal, J., Dubrovsky, V., Kiesler, S., & Mcguire, T. W. (1986). Group processes in computer-mediated communication. *Organizational Behavior and Human Decision Processes, 37*:177–187.

Spears, R., & Lee, M. (1992). Social influence and the influence of the "social" in computer-mediated communication. In M. Lea (Ed.), *Contexts of computer-mediated communication.* Hemel Hempstead: Harvester Wheatsheaf.

Sprague, R. H., Jr., & McNurlin, B. C. (1993). *Information systems management in practice* (3rd ed.). Englewood Cliffs, NJ: Prentice-Hall.

Te'eni, D. (2001). A cognitive-affective model of organizational communication for designing IT. *MIS Quarterly, 25*(2):251–312.

## ▶ 9. CASE STUDY

Although small businesses differ in size and scope from large business organizations, they have many aspects in common. Here we use the e'Gourmet case to discuss the business context and HCI.

All businesses must be profitable. Majorca's main goal for establishing an e-commerce Web site is to improve sales. She also wants to reduce costs and the time she spends filling orders manually. A third goal is to enhance her own understanding of her customer base. Eventually, she would like to be able to use the data in her new database to better understand her customer base in order to enhance her sales and inventory management process.

Lance Redux is the owner and main designer from "Web Solutions," a small Web site development firm. He has met with Majorca several times and has explained to her about the various e-business models and Web site architectures available.

E-business models include the following:

- Storefront model
- Brokerage/auction model
- Advertising/portal model
- Manufacturer—Manufacturers to buyers directly
- Subscription—Pay for access
- Utility—Pay as you go

### Storefront Model

The storefront model combines transaction processing, security, online payment, and information storage to allow merchants to sell via the Web. Most e-commerce storefronts use the shopping cart to allow users to accumulate products they wish to purchase.

Shopping carts utilize *cookies* stored on the client machine to record information on the products selected. Online product catalogs allow users to browse the products and services the merchant has to offer. Product catalogs are often contained in a database on the merchant server and then put into dynamic Web pages based on user requests.

Storefront business models include the following:

- Virtual merchants—A business that operates only over the Web
- Catalog merchants—The migration of mail-order to a Web-based order business
- Surf-and-turf or click-and-mortar—Traditional brick-and-mortar establishment with Web storefront (e'Gourmet)
- Bit vendor—A merchant that deals strictly in digital products and services and conducts both sales and distribution over the Web (online entertainment, online learning, or software)

After much discussion and exploration of existing sites, Lance and Majorca have selected a basic storefront model for a "click-and-mortar" establishment with a catalog-type structure for the architecture. They feel that this model and structure will fit the goals of their site best.

## ▶ 10. EXERCISES

### Short-Answer and Discussion Questions

Ex. 1. Why is the organizational context of HCI important?

Ex. 2. What are some of the ways in which HCI can impact organizational performance?

Ex. 3. Discuss the ways in which organizational communication systems can impact an organization.

Ex. 4. Many customer support systems are moving to the Internet from phone centers. Discuss the cost savings and the importance of the user interface in such systems.

# 3

# INTERACTIVE TECHNOLOGIES

## CONTEXT AND PREVIEW

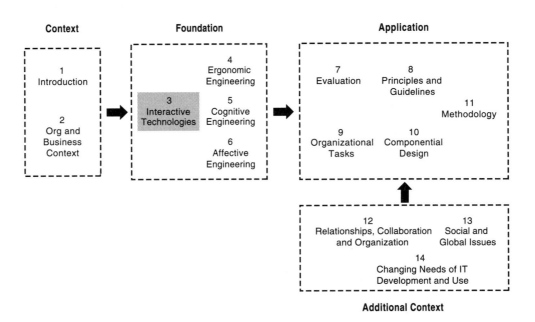

The "Foundations" part of the book includes three types of human engineering: physical, cognitive, and affective. This chapter explores the technologies that support physically related interactions with the computer. These technologies are then used in the ergonomic engineering process. The interactive technologies are organized by input, output, and other devices, and within each category we look at the various devices that support sensory preceptors including vision, audition, and touch. In this chapter, we emphasize the HCI implications of these interactive devices. This understanding serves to inform HCI design in the "Applications" section. We also look at the support of diverse users.

## LEARNING OBJECTIVES

Upon completion of this chapter, students should be able to do the following:

- Understand and discuss human perception and interactive technologies that support the various sensory perceptors including:
  - Vision
  - Audition
  - Touch
- Understand and discuss interactive input technologies including:
  - Keyboards
  - Pointing devices
- Understand voice recognition interactive input devices
- Understand touch-related haptic interactive input devices
- Understand and discuss visual display interactive output technologies
- Understand and discuss voice synthesis.
- Understand the human–computer interaction (HCI) implications of all these technologies
- Understand the HCI implications of wireless, wearable, and other emerging technologies

## ▶ 1. INTRODUCTION

This chapter explores interactive technologies. We have confined this chapter to the exploration of only those technologies that interact with the user and thus support human–computer interaction. In Chapters 5 and 6, we introduce cognitive and affective engineering. These two chapters focus on the cognitive and affective aspects of human–computer interaction. It is important to point out that the whole book emphasizes the cognitive and affective aspects of HCI more than the physical aspects. However, we must remember that the human being is also a physical entity. We can't forget that the physical aspects of the human must be addressed in order for any of the engineering done for the cognitive side of the human to be effective. So this chapter explores the actual technologies that support interaction with the computer, and Chapter 4 presents physical engineering with a focus on accommodating physical human requirements and constraints. This chapter is organized around input devices and output devices. These devices are discussed from the perspective of utilizing our human senses. We then introduce newer technologies such as the wireless PDA (personal digital assistant) and discuss the physical constraints imposed by these new technologies to *fit* the design.

## ▶ 2. SENSORY PERCEPTION AND INTERACTIVE INPUT DEVICES

**Input device:** Any machine that feeds data into a computer.

This section introduces input devices and is organized around the senses including vision, audition, and touch. An input device is any machine that feeds data into a computer. Input devices that support or rely on each of these perceptors are defined, and illustrations are presented to clarify the HCI issues for each technology.

## 2.1 Devices That Rely on Vision

### 2.1.1 Keyboards

Keyboards are the sets of typewriter-like keys that enable the user to enter data into the computer. The existing computer keyboard layout hinders human productivity more than any other factor. Most of the key positions in the keyboard layout on computers today are the result of the design of the keys for the typewriter. The early typewriter characters were positioned at the end of a long piece of metal and struck the paper through a ribbon when the user pressed the key on the keyboard. When the typist typed too fast, the keys would get caught on each other. Therefore the keyboard design strategy was to position the most frequently used keys as far apart as possible to minimize the possibility that the keys would stick together. That design makes no sense for the computer keyboard since there are no mechanical arms striking anything, only electronic signals. However, the early designers of computers determined that adhering to current keyboard layouts would make typists more comfortable with the computer. The result is a keyboard layout that maximizes finger movement instead of minimizing it.

> **Keyboard:** The set of typewriter-like keys that enable the user to enter data into the computer.

Other keyboard layouts such as the Dvorak (Shneiderman, 1987, 1998; Shneiderman & Plaisant, 2005) have been designed and tested and proven to yield faster typing speeds, but vendors are not willing to make the transition to the new layouts. If you use several keyboards on different computers, you are aware of the difficulty of switching from one layout to another. Even the placement of one key in a different position can cause you to commit errors and/or spend time searching for the correct position.

Over time, new keys have been added to the original typewriter layout to increase functionality. Most keyboards contain 12 function keys that can be programmed in various ways for individual software packages. The escape, print screen, scroll lock, break, control, alternate, pipe, backslash, backspace, and other keys are all commonly included in computer keyboard layouts. Most keyboards include a numeric keypad that also doubles as arrow keys, home, end, page up, page down, insert, and delete keys when the number lock key is not depressed. Many keyboards offer an additional set of arrow keys and insert, home, page up, page down, delete, and end keys that function separately in order to allow the user to use the numeric keypad and these other keys simultaneously. Figures 3.1 and 3.2 illustrate two very popular layouts for the computer keyboard. The two keyboards contain most of the same keys in the same placement; however, the shape of the second keyboard relieves some of the stress placed on the wrists and fingers of the user. This keyboard is not only curved to bring the wrists out and the finger position in but also curved upward in the center. The upward position allows the wrists to be much more relaxed and natural.

**Figure 3.1** Traditional Keyboard.

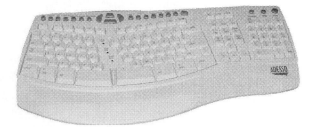

**Figure 3.2** Split Keyboard.

### 2.1.2 Pointing Devices

**Pointing device:**
Controls the movement of the cursor on a display screen.

Aside from using the keyboard, computers can be manipulated by various pointing devices such as mice (Figure 3.3), graphic tablets, touch pads, trackballs, joysticks, pen-based input, touch screens (Figure 3.4), light pens, and voice. A pointing device controls the movement of the cursor on a display screen. There are six different interaction tasks that can be performed by pointing or manipulation devices:

1. Select (point and click)
2. Position (drag and click)
3. Orient (rotate)
4. Path (combination of orientation and position movements)
5. Quantify (point and click)
6. Text (the pointing device merely initiates the position where the text is to begin and then gives control to the keyboard)

The touch screen and the light pen operate directly on the surface of the screen. The light pen can point to a spot on the screen, and then by pressing a button on the pen, the user can initiate action. There are several problems associated with the touch screen and the light pen. The first is fatigue caused by the direct control on the screen that is both upright and some distance away. Also, the user's hand and the device obscure part of the screen, and constant movement is required to go from manipulation to visual verification and back.

**Figure 3.3**   Mouse.

**Figure 3.4**   Touch screen flat panel monitor by Novitatech®.

A graphics tablet is a flat surface that is drawn on by a stylus. The surface of the graphic tablet has a one-to-one correspondence with the pixels on the computer screen. As the user moves the pen, he or she can watch the screen to observe the effect of this movement. Graphic tablets are frequently used by commercial art packages and in some children's art software. Figure 3.5 depicts a graphics tablet.

Touch pads are relatively new on the market as stand-alone devices (versus embedded in laptops). These devices do not require any force to operate; they have reduced the finger and hand stresses related to grasping and moving the mouse and button clicking.

Trackballs are sort of upside-down mice. The user moves the cursor on the screen by rotating the trackball with fingers, thumb, or the flat of the hand. Once the cursor has been positioned, a button on the trackball is pressed to initiate action. It has a distinct advantage over the mouse in that no operating surface is needed. Some laptops include small, thumb-operated trackballs with two buttons that are handy for operating in small spaces such as airplane seats. Figure 3.6 depicts a trackball.

Joysticks are devices that originated with automobile and aircraft controls. There are various designs for joysticks, but most of them are grasped by the fingers and flat of the hand with the thumb at the top. There is usually a button or trigger at the top position that can be pressed by the thumb. Joysticks are popular interfaces for interactive computer games. They allow the user to track movements on the screen easily because direction changes are easy and small changes in the joystick correspond to large changes on the screen.

Pen-based input is a combination of a light pen and a graphics tablet used with a software package that can interpret the text-based input or handwriting (either printing or cursive) of the user. The user must first train the software to interpret his or her handwriting. Pen-based input is more natural than keyboarding. Executives who have resisted computer usage are good candidates for this type of input. Figure 3.7 depicts pen-based input for a personal digital assistant (PDA).

Studies have been conducted to evaluate the performance of these various input devices. Murata (1991) investigated the mouse, joystick, light pen, trackball, and touch screen for pointing speed, accuracy, and usability and found that the joystick was fastest

**Figure 3.5** Graphics Tablet.

**Figure 3.6** Trackball.

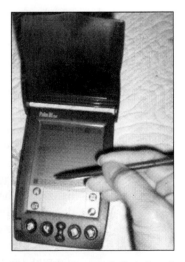

**Figure 3.7** Personal digital assistant.

while the light pen was the most accurate and that subjects preferred the joystick for overall usability. Kelley and Charness (1995) found that mouse input is difficult for older persons to use. They recommend pen-based input to replace the mouse.

Some of these devices are commonly found in business organizations and some are not. Joysticks are not very common. The mouse is probably the most common business-related input device. Touch pads are also common due to laptop usage.

## 2.2 Devices That Rely on Audition—Speech Recognition

Speech recognition is the ability of the computer to recognize human speech. The goal of speech recognition systems is to narrow the gap between human–computer interactions (HCI) and human–human interactions (HHI). In order to create successful speech recognition interfaces, HCI developers should know and understand user characteristics, the tasks that users are attempting to accomplish, and the context within which these interfaces will be used (Karat, Vergo, & Nahamoo, 2003).

Understanding user characteristics is important when designing any type of user interface; however, some aspects are unique to speech recognition systems. It is particularly important to know whether users are native or nonnative speakers of the language that is the target language of the system. Age is also a concern. If users are too young, they may not have mature language usage patterns. The recommended lower age limit is 14. This is partly due to the fact that voices change as users mature. However, older persons may also have difficulty because of possible medical conditions, which may affect their speech patterns. Education levels are another important aspect. Studies have shown that performance is best if users have at least a fifth-grade level of reading comprehension.

Understanding the target task is also very important. The four major types of tasks supported by speech recognition technologies include composition, transcription, transaction, and collaboration. The goal of a composition task is to create a document. The generation of e-mail, word processing documents, and instant messaging all fall into the composition task. Transcription tasks generally convert human speech (like a news broadcast, interview, or speech) into a document. This is closely aligned with composition, except that speakers in this setting are concerned with human-to-human communication and may not pay close attention to grammar and organization in the same way they would if they were writing a letter or an article. Transaction tasks are not focused on documents at all but rather on completion of a transaction. Transactions are varied. Some examples include purchases, stock trades, bank transactions, Internet searches, and so on. Collaboration tasks may be synchronous (performed at the same time by two or more collaborators) or asynchronous (performed at different times by two or more collaborators). Examples of collaboration tasks include group generation of documents, setting meetings through e-calendars, e-mail, and others.

The physical and social context of use for speech recognition systems is critical. Military use environments are often noisy and environmentally harsh. The presence of water, dirt, and chemicals may put stress on the conversational devices. Knowing the nature of the audio channel and the actual device characteristics is important when designing conversational interfaces. For example, inputting via a handheld microphone may require a different design than inputting via a telephone. Additionally, the social context of use may be critical. The task of transcribing a public speech at a dinner meeting may require different interface designs than composing a word processing document in a quiet office.

> **Speech Recognition:** The ability of the computer to recognize and understand human speech.

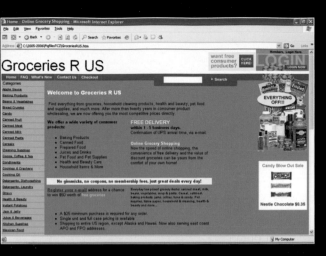

▶Figure 1.2a    An e-store Web page

▶Figure 1.2b    An e-store Web page

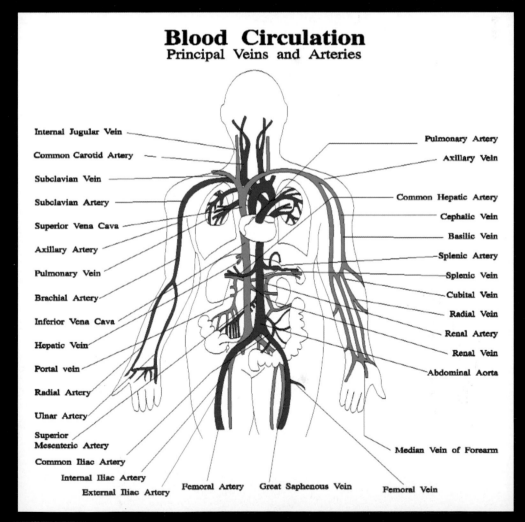

▶Figure 1.5    Blood circulation

**A** Classical

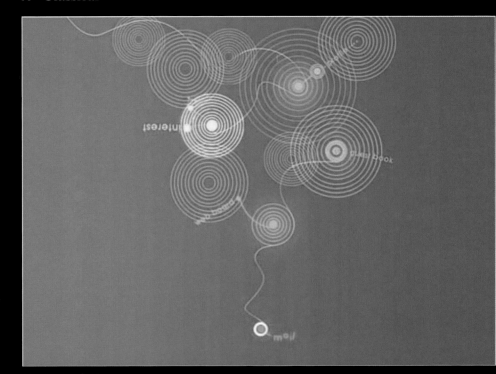

**B** Futuristic

▷ **Figure 6.3** Affective impressions in home pages

▶ Figure 7.7

▶ Figure 7.8

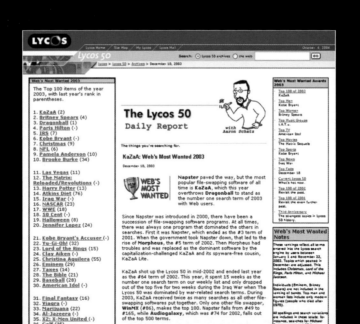

▶ Figure 7.9

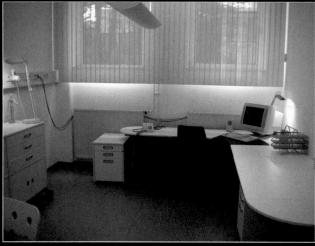

▶ Figure 7.28

▶ Figure 9.1

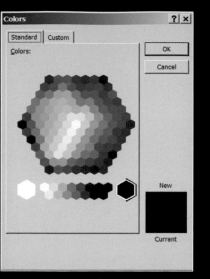
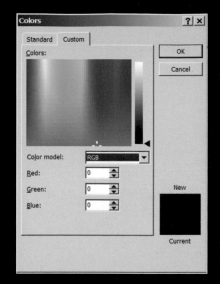
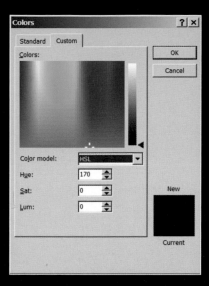

▶ **Figure 10.2** Dialog box to define color

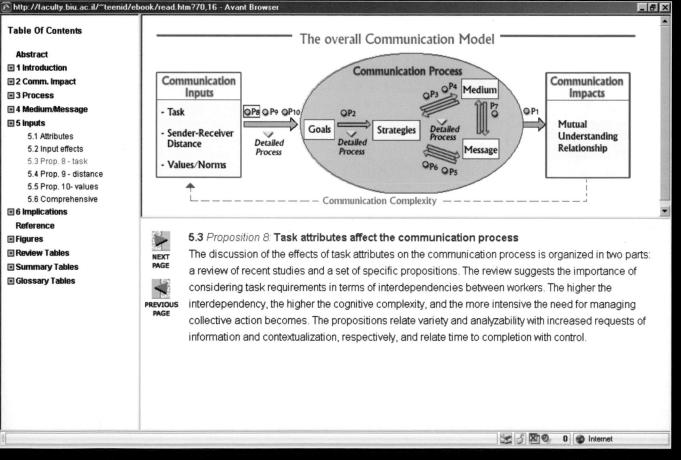

▶ **Figure 10.5** Navigation in an e-book uses a clickable image-based menu and a corresponding vertical menu.

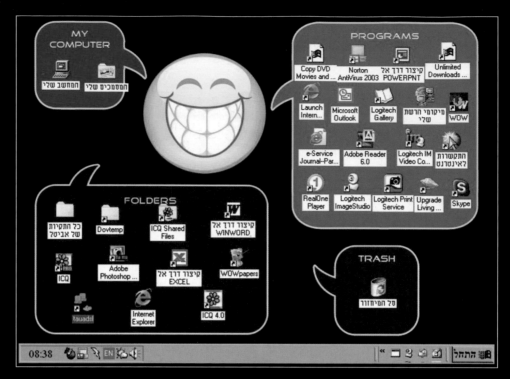

▶ **Figure 10.7**

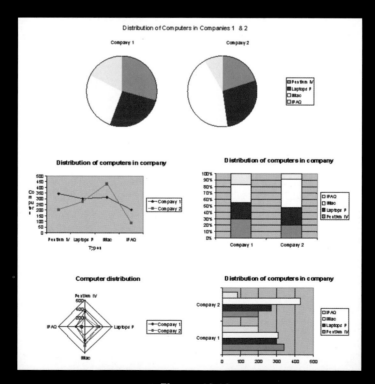

▶ **Figure 10.10**

**Figure 10.16** Not enough white space and too much color

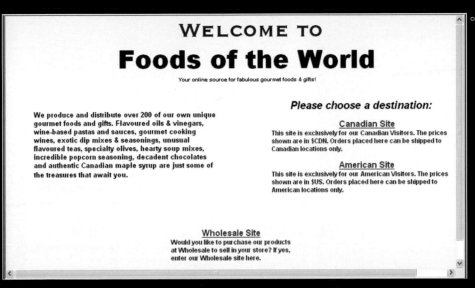

**Figure 10.17** Too much white space and too few colors

**Figure 10.18** E'Gourmet design using sufficient white space and two main colors

▶ **Figure 11.6**

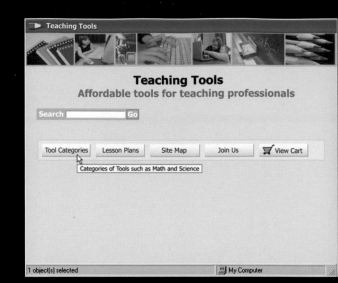

▶ **Figure 11.10**

▶ **Figure 11.11a**

▶ **Figure 11.11b**

▶ **VIII**

▶ **Figure 14.2 abc**

Voice input has evolved to a level where it is feasible for many situations. Devices that process human voice usually recognize a limited subset of words. However, the set of recognizable words is expanding all the time. Speech recognition devices usually have to be trained by the user. They are not totally reliable. However, they are reliable enough to allow "hands-free" dictation that may be stored as text-based documents. These systems also assist physically challenged individuals who are unable to move their hands and fingers. They can be used to control wheelchairs, operate equipment, and act as interfaces to computers. They are useful for situations where the speaker's hands and/or eyes are occupied, mobility is required, and harsh or cramped conditions exist.

Global Positioning Systems (GPS) are being included in various interaction devices, such as onboard computers with voice interaction and pilot interaction environments in planes. Other forms of technology are entering the environment at a fast pace; the general trend is to make interaction easier, faster, and more in tune with the task that the user is trying to accomplish.

## 2.3 Devices That Rely on Touch

The sense of touch is vital to understanding the world at large. Haptic interface devices generate sensation to the skin and muscles through touch, weight, and relative rigidity. It is often difficult to synthesize these sensations. Haptic devices are commonly used as interfaces in virtual reality applications. Haptic feedback is generally divided into four categories: somatic (skin) sensation, force display, full-body interaction, and tactile (touch) display (Iwata, 2003).

> **Haptic devices:** Devices that generate sensation to the skin and muscles through touch, weight, and rigidity.

Somatic devices generate changes that are perceived by the skin, such as temperature changes. Some somatic devices allow the user to detect the edge of a stationary object and the speed of a moving object. Force displays are mechanical devices that generate a reaction force from virtual objects. These take the form of exoskeleton force displays that are attached to the hand or body and have actuators at various points, such as virtual reality gloves. There are also tool-handling force displays, such as joysticks. Full-body haptic devices are often used to support virtual locomotion. Tactile displays are often applied to communication aids for blind persons. These devices can convey a sense of roughness or smoothness.

## ▶ 3. OUTPUT DEVICES

Output options are not as varied as the input options for human–computer interaction. An output device is a machine capable of representing data from a computer. General output categories include (1) printers, (2) visual display, (3) auditory output, (4) synthesized speech, and (5) haptic devices.

> **Output device:** A machine capable of representing data from a computer.

## 3.1 Visual Display

A visual display is an output device that is capable of rendering data from a computer and presenting it in a visual format such as graphic, tabular, text, or other. One of the most important aspects of visual-display output is response time. Human performance can be degraded if the computer response time is too long. However, optimal or maximum acceptable response time varies from task to task. Response time is usually defined as the time that the user must wait for a computer response following a command. Too long or erratic response times will probably result in a negative attitude toward the computer on the part of the user. In an interactive dialogue between the user and the computer, a key determinant of success is continuity—a feeling of uninterrupted conversational flow. Waiting too long for a response can interfere with continuity. A two-second response time was found to be acceptable in several task situations by Williams (1973). Nielsen (1994) suggests that a response time of 2 to 10 seconds is appropriate depending on the task.

**Visual display:** An output device that is capable of rendering data from a computer. Data may take the form of graphic, tabular, text, or other.

One of the most frustrating aspects of human–computer interaction using a visual display unit (VDU) occurs when a command is initiated and a wait period ensues with no indication of progress. A status bar or message indicating that processing is occurring and that the user should wait for a signal of completion is mandated for this situation. For example, Macintosh software generally displays an hourglass or watch face to indicate such activity. The user understands this and waits until the hourglass disappears before trying any other action. Mainframe computer interfaces are particularly annoying in this regard. Mainframe response time is highly variable and dependent on computer load; therefore, sometimes a long wait period is necessitated. Usually no feedback is given to the user about the status of the command, and often users give up and begin to press keys (usually the Enter key), which can throw them out of the environment that they intended to work in. Once they are out, there is seldom a corrective message to get them back to where they wish to be.

## 3.2 Printers

Printers are devices that output computer information on paper. There are a myriad of printer types.

Ink-jet printers spray ionized ink at a sheet of paper. Magnetized plates in the ink's path direct the ink onto the paper in the desired shapes. Ink-jet printers are capable of producing high-quality print approaching that produced by laser printers. A typical ink-jet printer provides a resolution of 300 dots per inch, although some newer models offer higher resolutions.

In general, the price of ink-jet printers is lower than that of laser printers. However, they are also considerably slower. Another drawback of ink-jet printers is that they require a special type of ink that is apt to smudge on inexpensive copier paper.

Laser printers utilize a laser beam to produce an image on a drum. The light of the laser alters the electrical charge on the drum wherever it hits. The drum is then rolled through a reservoir of toner, which is picked up by the charged portions of the drum. Finally, the toner is transferred to the paper through a combination of heat and pressure. This is also the way copy machines work.

One of the chief characteristics of laser printers is their resolution—how many dots per inch (dpi) they lay down. The available resolutions range from 300 dpi at the low end to 1,200 dpi at the high end.

In addition to text, laser printers are very adept at printing graphics. However, you need significant amounts of memory in the printer to print high-resolution graphics.

Because laser printers are nonimpact printers, they are much quieter than dot-matrix or daisy-wheel printers. They are also relatively fast, although not as fast as some dot-matrix printers. The speed of laser printers ranges from about 10 to 20 pages of text per minute (ppm).

Color printers are capable of printing more than one color. Most color printers are based on the CMYK color model, which prints in four basic colors: cyan, magenta, yellow, and black. By printing combinations of different colors close to each other, the CMYK model can simulate most other colors (Webopedia, http://www.webopedia.com). In general, the higher the resolution, the more expensive the printer. Business organizations use many different printer types depending on need. Most companies have at least a few high-resolution, full-color laser printers for printing color brochures, newsletters, color transparencies, and so on. They will probably have more high-speed black-and-white laser printers. Many individual desktop computers will be connected to a fairly inexpensive ink-jet printer that can print color or black and white.

## 3.3 Auditory Output—Nonspeech

In some environments and for some tasks, nonspeech auditory outputs such as beeps are very useful. An auditory nonspeech output is any sound that is generated by the computer or other device that can be detected by the human ear but is not speech-related. The main reasons for using nonspeech auditory outputs include the interdependence of vision and hearing (reinforcement), faster reaction times, reduction of the user's visual load, to simplify the screen, to grab attention, and to support visually impaired users more effectively (Brewster, 2003). There are some drawbacks to using nonspeech auditory output, such as inability to differentiate between similar sounds, transience (once the sound is generated, it is usually not repeated), and annoyance (some environments are already noisy and the sound output becomes part of a noisy and difficult environment).

> **Auditory nonspeech output:** Any sound that is output by a computer device that is not speech-related.

There are few guidelines for the use of auditory nonspeech output. Shneiderman (2002) and others suggest sparse use of sounds. They should be reserved for critical signals. Auditory icons (Gaver, 1997) and earcons (Blattner, Sumikawa, & Greenberg, 1989) are information presentation techniques for sounds. The auditory icon is defined as "everyday sounds mapped to computer events by analogy . . . sound effects for computers" (Gaver, 1997, p. 69). An example of an auditory icon from SonicFinder is illustrated in Figure 3.9 (adapted from Gaver, 1997). Sounds are applied to the action of selecting a folder (paper shuffle sound), dragging the folder (scraping sound), dropping the folder into the "recycle bin" (clinking sound), and emptying the recycle bin (smashing sound). An earcon (Blattner et al., 1989) is defined as "non-verbal audio messages that are used in the computer/user interface to provide information to the user about some computer object, operation, or interaction" (p. 13). Unlike auditory icons, there is no intuitive link between the earcon and what it represents. Studies suggest that in representational situations auditory icons perform better, while in abstract situations earcons perform more effectively. Nonspeech auditory output is often used to assist blind and partially sighted individuals in their use of computers.

## 3.4 Auditory Output—Speech

It is much easier for a computer to synthesize the human voice than to recognize and interpret human speech. Voice output is useful for phone systems, for blind and partially sighted individuals, for situations where the user's visual attention is needed elsewhere (e.g., driving a car, monitoring plant processes), and other situations. Voice output can be recorded and then selected by a computer program. Most voice messaging systems use this technique. Alternatively, the computer can synthesize speech by digitizing it.

Synthesized speech is a reasonable choice if the following conditions are met:

1. The required message is short and simple.
2. The message needs an immediate response.
3. The user/receiver is visually occupied.
4. The environment is too brightly or poorly lit for ordinary visual displays to be used.
5. The user is moving around too much to visually attend to a single screen.
6. No screen exists, but an audio receiver does (e.g., telephone).

## ▶ 4. WEARABLE DEVICES

There is a great deal of interest in the design and implementation of wearable computer devices that are small, durable, and useful particularly in a military setting. Vision enhancement, translation (text-to-speech, speech-to-text, and language-to-language), pen-based input, navigation, environmental scanning, and detection are among the many tasks performed by wearable devices. Small GPS (global positioning systems) are often a critical component of these devices. Once these devices are tested and found useful in a military setting, many of them become available as commercial products. Watches with GPS and maps designed to help travelers navigate in foreign locales are already available. Onboard navigators with connections to a dispatching system with human operators are helping car owners find destinations, call for roadside assistance, unlock car doors, and perform many other useful and perhaps lifesaving activities.

Another device that is not wearable by itself but is often placed on wearable products is radio frequency identification (RFID). RFID is a method of remotely identifying, storing, and retrieving data using devices called RFID tags. An RFID tag is a small object, such as an adhesive sticker, that can be attached to or incorporated into a product. RFID tags contain antennas to enable them to receive and respond to radio-frequency queries from an RFID transceiver. This technology is revolutionizing the retail inventory management and will soon change the way customers check out of retail establishments. Instead of standing in line at a cashier station, whole shopping carts will be scanned at one time. The bill will be paid by automatically debiting an account or credit card. Customers will receive a receipt and be on their way with almost no time spent on the checkout process.

The RFID technology will make shopping very convenient, but it has potential problems associated with it. One such concern is privacy. Since the RFID is capable of sending signals, if the consumer does not remove the tag, tracking devices may pick up the signals after the sale allowing tracking of shopping and other behavior patterns.

## ▶ 5. WIRELESS DEVICES

We have many improved tools to support our everyday life. Mobile or wireless devices are allowing people to compute on the run. A wireless device is any device that is connected to networks and other devices through nonwire media such as infrared signals.

Personal digital assistants (PDA), text-based cell phones, palm tops, and other small, portable devices are abundant.

These mobile devices offer some interesting challenges for HCI. Keyboarding in such a small space is difficult, although many of these small devices can be fitted with a collapsible keyboard that normal-size fingers can readily use. Pen-based input is still rather crude and can only capture images rather than interpret the pen strokes in a meaningful manner. Voice input holds promise, but it is still rather limited. Certainly, "hands-free" and "eyes-free" interaction is important when attempting to operate a car or other machine while interacting with a mobile device. Another solution to the keyboarding problem is offered by Compaq's iPAQ. An infrared lens is fitted on the handheld device. This lens projects a red light that displays in the familiar QWERTY pattern on a solid object. The user then types on the hard surface using the red pattern like a keyboard. A motion sensor detects the pattern and inputs the keystrokes into the handheld device. The name of this device is the Canesta keyboard. There are plans to install this device into cell phones, PDAs, and other small computing devices (Bretz, 2002).

> **Wireless devices:** Devices connected to networks and other devices through nonwire media such as infrared signals.

## ▶ 6. VIRTUAL DEVICES

Virtual devices are those that support virtual reality interaction. Virtual reality is an artificial environment that simulates reality. There are a myriad of technologies available for physical HCI today. However, we are still a long way from achieving the seamless interaction that has been depicted in sci-fi films, such as the humanoid robot C-3P0 in *Star Wars* and HAL of *2001: A Space Odyssey*. These two computer-enabled personas seemed to understand natural speech and human behavior to a fault. They responded with humanlike speech and, in the case of C-3P0, humanlike movements. HAL seemed to have sufficient levels of artificial intelligence to anticipate human behavior and plan a response to preserve its own existence. The C-3P0 character was depicted as a very "human" machine capable of filling in for human companionship and performing complex tasks to support human needs. The sophistication of current levels of artificial intelligence, speech recognition, and robotic programs cannot begin to achieve the level of performance of C-3P0 or HAL.

> **Virtual devices:** Devices that support virtual reality interaction. Virtual reality is an artificial environment that is computer-generated and simulates a real but limited environment.

There are many interaction devices for the world of virtual reality. A combination of exotic headgear, gloves, and body suits orient the user to the virtual world. Even simple interaction devices such as a mouse and keyboard can be used to manipulate the virtual environment. Figure 3.8 illustrates an interaction device for virtual gaming environments—a glove that allows finger movements and pressure to interact within the gaming environment.

There are also many interaction devices for the gaming world. Joysticks, footpads, rumble sticks, and other devices allow gamers to interact with the characters and environment in the game.

There are wearable devices that allow users to interact with computers in an unobtrusive manner. A wristband records forearm and wrist movements that in turn operate a nearby computer. A small pad can be inserted into a pocket and used to operate a nearby computer by touching the pad.

What relevance does virtual reality have in the business world? A variety of business applications are augmented by virtual reality techniques. Real estate and design sales often use virtual reality to take the prospective buyers through a "virtual tour" of a home or design choices. The research and development departments in many businesses use

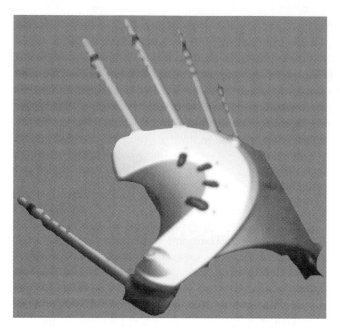

**Figure 3.8** Virtual reality glove.

virtual reality techniques to test out new designs. Medical applications of virtual reality abound. Virtual offices, office space, and virtual assistants are cutting costs for business activities. There is a new markup language called VRML (virtual reality markup language). This language can be used in CAD (computer-aided design), CASE (computer-assisted software engineering), and data warehousing applications. Virtual tours are also available for museums, parks, historic sites, and other places that travelers would like to visit but don't have the time or perhaps the money to visit.

Every day brings new technologies to the market, and many of these technologies present new challenges to ergonomic engineers. If a new computing device is not usable from a physical perspective, it will not sell in the marketplace.

## ▶ 7. SUMMARY

This chapter presents various computing technologies that interact with users. The users may bring with them physical challenges that must be overcome by ergonomic engineering. The interactive technologies in this chapter are organized by input devices, output devices, and advanced technologies. For each of these technologies, various sensory perceptors are discussed. For example, under input devices, we discuss technologies that are perceived by vision, audition, and touch. The various technologies are discussed with particular focus on the way in which they interact with the user.

Input devices are the most obvious interactive technologies. The human user manipulates the target technology (e.g., keyboard) to accomplish a task such as word processing. Keyboards, joysticks, mice, trackball mice, voice input, and haptic devices (to support the sense of touch) are all discussed as various input mechanisms.

Output devices are also critical for human–computer interaction. Many times, the output devices are intended to confirm the input of the user. Monitors, printers, auditory output, and voice synthesis are all discussed in the chapter.

This chapter also explores some of the more recent interactive technological developments including wearable, wireless, and virtual devices. The chapter concludes by exploring some technologies for the support of diverse user interactions.

## ▶ 8. SUMMARY OF CONCEPTS AND TERMS

| | | |
|---|---|---|
| Input device | Keyboard | Pointing device |
| Voice recognition | Haptic device | Visual display |
| Virtual devices | Wireless devices | Output devices |
| Voice synthesis | Auditory nonspeech output | |

## ▶ 9. BIBLIOGRAPHY AND ADDITIONAL READINGS

Blattner, M. M., Sumikawa, D. A., & Greenberg, R. M. (1989). Earcons and icons: Their structure and common design principles. *Human Computer Interaction, 4*(1):11–44.

Bretz, E. A. (2002). When work is fun and games. IEEE Online. Retrieved from http://www.spectrum.ieee.org/WEBONLY/resource/dec02/tool.html

Brewster, S. (2003). Non-speech auditory output. In J. A. Jacko & A. Sears (Eds.), *The human-computer interaction handbook: Fundamentals, evolving technologies, and emerging applications.* Mahwah, NJ: Lawrence Erlbaum Associates, Inc.

Gaver, W. W. (1997). Auditory interfaces. In M. Helander, T. K. Landauer, & P. Prabhu (Eds.), *Handbook of human-computer interaction.* Amsterdam: Elsevier Science.

Iwata, H. (2003). Haptic interfaces. In J. A. Jacko & A. Sears (Eds.), *The human-computer interaction handbook: Fundamentals, evolving technologies, and emerging applications.* Mahwah, NJ: Lawrence Erlbaum Associates, Inc.

Karat, C. M., Vergo, J., & Nahamoo, D. (2003). Conversational interface technologies. In J. A. Jacko & A. Sears (Eds.), *The human-computer interaction handbook: Fundamentals, evolving technologies, and emerging applications.* Mahwah, NJ: Lawrence Erlbaum Associates, Inc.

Kelley, C. L., & Charness, N. (1995). Issues in training older adults to use computers. *Behaviour and Information Technology, 14*(2):107–120.

Murata, A. (1991). An experimental evaluation of mouse, joystick, joycard, lightpen, trackball, and touchscreen for pointing. In H.-J. Bullinger (Ed.), *Human aspects in computing: Design and use of interactive systems and work with computers.* Amsterdam: Elsevier.

Nielsen, J. (1994). *Usability engineering.* San Francisco: Morgan Kaufman.

Shneiderman, B. (1987). *Designing the user interface: Strategies for effective human-computer interaction.* Reading, MA: Addison-Wesley.

Shneiderman, B. (1998). *Designing the user interface—Strategies for effective human-computer interaction* (3rd ed.). Reading, MA: Addison-Wesley.

Shneiderman, B. (2002). *Leonardo's laptop: Human needs and the new computing technologies.* Cambridge, MA: MIT Press.

Siemens. (2002). Webzine. Retrieved from http://w4.siemens.de/Ful/en/archiv/pof/heft2_02/artikle13/

Williams, C. M. (1973). System response time: A study of users' tolerance. *IBM Technical Report.*

▷ 10. CASE STUDY

Lance Redux is interested in creating a Web site for e'Gourmet that will accommodate differing interactive style preferences. The most common Web interaction style is to use the mouse for direct manipulation. Lance has already built an interface that supports this type of interaction. He has incorporated two horizontal navigational menus on every screen. One is located at the top of every screen and has buttons. The other is located at the bottom of every screen and has text-based links; both are activated by pointing at a button (or text) and clicking the left mouse button.

Lance also wants to support those users who prefer keystrokes to mouse clicks. To do this, he creates shortcuts for each of the menu choices in the button-based navigation menu. To indicate that a shortcut is available, the text on each button has one character underlined to indicate which alphabetic character is to be used with the alt key to create the shortcut key. Lance will also create a floating text bubble for each button that says, "To activate, either click with mouse or press alt key and the letter S simultaneously" (see Figure 3.9).

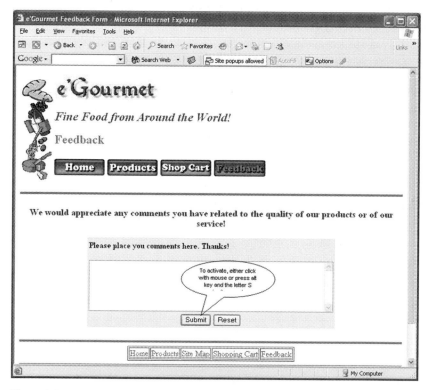

**Figure 3.9**  Illustration of optional interaction choices (mouse click or keystroke).

Questions regarding the case study:
1.    As a user, do you prefer keystrokes or mouse actions?
2.    Can you think of a situation where keystrokes might be preferable?
How important is it to provide options to your users and why?

## ▶ 11. EXERCISES

Ex. 1.    There are many ways to manipulate cursors. There are mice, trackballs, graphics pads, joysticks, and so on. List three different technologies that you have used to interact with the computer. Which did you like and why?

Ex. 2.    If you or someone you know owns a laptop computer, what type of input device comes loaded on the machine? Have you used it? Do you like it? Why or why not?

Ex. 3.    Use the Web to discover and explore three emerging HCI technologies. Assess usefulness and the likelihood that you would be willing to use or purchase the emerging technology.

# 4

# PHYSICAL ENGINEERING

## CONTEXT AND PREVIEW

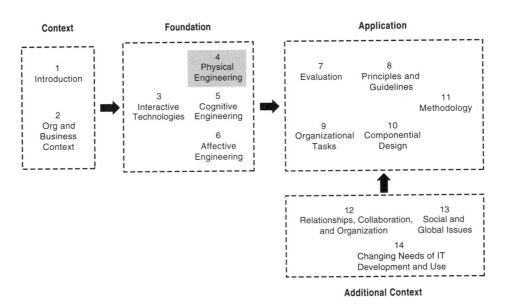

The "Foundations" part of the book includes three types of human engineering: physical, cognitive, and affective. Physical engineering, which refers to design aspects related to physical attributes of users, is explored in this chapter. Chapters 5 and 6 look at design aspects related to psychological attributes. This chapter on physical human engineering examines how users' physical capabilities affect the way users perform tasks. This understanding serves to inform HCI design in the "Applications" section. This chapter also looks at designing technologies that support disabled users; this, in turn, relates to Chapter 13, which focuses on the social and global context of HCI.

## LEARNING OBJECTIVES

Upon completion of this chapter, students should be able to do the following:

- Define physical engineering
- Understand and discuss human performance
- Understand and discuss human limitations
- Understand and discuss human perception through the various sensors including:
  - Vision
  - Audition
  - Touch
- Explain Fitts' law and how it pertains to HCI understanding and physical engineering
- Understand and discuss possible health problems associated with computer use including:
  - Emissions
  - Repetitive motion problems
  - Vision problems
  - Muscular problems
- Understand, explain, and design technologies to support disabled users including those who are:
  - Visually impaired
  - Hearing-impaired
  - Physically disabled

## ▷ 1. INTRODUCTION

**Ergonomics:** The physical fit between human and machine.

Ergonomics is synonymous with human factors. The word was coined in 1949 from two Greek words, *ergos*, which means work, and *nomos*, which means *natural laws*. It has come to mean "the fit between man and machine." The group that coined the word *ergonomics* was interdisciplinary and included psychologists, design engineers, work study engineers, industrial medical officers, and others with an interest in human performance. This group first met in Oxford, England, in 1949 and formed the Ergonomics Research Society. During this postwar era, much of the research in ergonomics was centered on human performance in relation to military technology. Although the study of ergonomics has expanded to include psychological ergonomics, most of the early work concentrated on engineering geared toward human physiology. In this chapter, we will use the word *ergonomics* to refer primarily to physical ergonomics.

Ergonomics has also been defined as "the science of human engineering which combines the study of human body mechanics and physical limitations with industrial psychology" (Hussain & Hussain, 1984, p. 624). The ergonomics of information systems deals with topics such as the physical workstation and furniture design, lighting, noise, and keyboard height and arrangement. These are all physical aspects of human engineering within an information systems context.

Still another definition can be found in the introduction to Woodson's *Human Factors Design Handbook* (1981). Here the definition of human factors is:

the practice of designing products so that the user can perform
required use, operation, service, and supportive tasks with a minimum
of stress and a maximum of efficiency. To accomplish this, the
designer must understand and acknowledge the needs, characteristics,
capabilities, and limitations of the intended user and design from the
human out, making the design *fit* the user instead of forcing the user to
*fit* the design. (p. vii, our emphasis)

The more traditional definition of human factors has been "the scientific study of the
relationship between humans and their work environment" (Chapanis, 1965). The goal
of most ergonomic research has been to improve system performance by improving the
fit between the human and the machine. This book devotes three chapters to the research
on issues of fit between human and computer: the present chapter looks at the physical
aspects of fit, and Chapters 5 and 6 concentrate on the cognitive and affective aspects,
respectively. The cognitive and affective attributes of computer usage concentrate on the
actual conscious (and subconscious) mental activities that occur during the use of the
computer. Most of this book is centered on these mental aspects of human–computer
interaction because they are particularly applicable to the organizational context.
Although a complete understanding of both the physical and the mental attributes of
human–computer interaction does not yet exist, we will attempt to provide as comprehensive a view as we currently can.

The physical aspects of human–computer interaction come into play primarily in the
operation of input and output devices. Currently, the main use of input devices is to control the system's operations and input or manipulate data. As explored in the previous
chapter, manual input is usually performed with pointing input devices, such as a mouse
or a joystick, or text, numeric, and graphic data input devices for keying in data and
drawing and manipulating objects, such as keyboards and numeric pads. In addition to
manual input, we also rely on other human faculties for input such as audition, voice,
and touch. Similarly, for output we rely primarily on visual devices such as the VDT
and, to a lesser extent, on other senses. Our discussion below is organized around these
physical resources (motor, vocal, and sensory) used in HCI. We begin with a discussion
of performance and limitations on performance due to our physical resources and continue with an analysis of the implications on the design of input and output devices. We
then follow with a general discussion of health problems that result from a mismatch
between the human body and the technology and a discussion of the need to design for
people with special physical needs.

## ▶ 2. HUMAN PERFORMANCE AND LIMITATIONS

### 2.1 Performance and Other Criteria for Physical Engineering

Physical engineering is concerned with the physical interfaces between the human user
and the computer and has three main categories: analysis, design, and assessment (Bullinger, 1988). The analysis category focuses on human attributes and capabilities, the
tasks to be performed, and the technology that is being used to aid in task performance.
The performance-related goals of ergonomics are to improve (1) the human ability to
handle physical load or demands of the work situation, (2) performance (reduce errors,

**Physical engineering:**
The science of human
engineering, which
combines the study
of human body
mechanics and
physical limitations
with industrial
psychology.

improve quality, reduce time required to complete task), and (3) end user acceptance of the system.

This section discusses three important points: the criteria for good physical engineering including performance, the effect of context on performance, and the notion of fit (contingency).

In physical engineering, well-being goes beyond satisfaction to include health aspects such as those discussed later in this chapter. Furthermore, performance is usually characterized as speed and accuracy of a task and the computer-supported actions leading up to it. For example, if the task is to key in a 100-word document from a printed paper, activities leading up to the task can be reading a few words and then typing them, continuing to do so (reading and typing) until the document is complete, and then proofreading the new soft copy (from the computer). The overall time from start to end is one measure of performance, and another is the average speed of uninterrupted typing. While the former measure directly affects work efficiency, the latter is also of importance to the ergonomic engineer because the two measures in combination may indicate, for example, that reading (rather than typing) is the bottleneck to more efficient work. Devising an adjustable device for holding the page in an upright position and close to the screen may be an effective solution.

> **Performance measures:**
> Performance is usually measured by reducing errors, improving quality, and reducing time required to complete a task.

Performance is affected by the context of work. The measures of physical engineering discussed above are influenced by several factors in addition to the specifics of the computer. These measures are determined by the *combined* effect of the person, the task, and the computer input/output devices but also by the physical work environment and procedures. Table 4.1 lists the physical engineering concerns of the devices, the immediate physical workspace, the general physical environment within which the user is operating, and the nature of work being performed. For example, the visual display unit (monitor) is generally located on a desktop. The environmental aspect of lighting is critical to the users' ability to see the monitor clearly. Since the monitor (VDU) is the main purveyor of all visual information, content is the aspect of work most closely associated with the monitor.

As noted in the introduction to this chapter, physical engineering seeks to improve system performance by improving the fit between the human and the computer. From our discussion above, the fit between the human and the computer must be examined in combination with the task and the work environment. Indeed, as we examine the design implications on various input and output devices, we see that different devices are better for one task but yield poorer performance for other tasks. For example, a joystick may

**Table 4.1**  Ergonomic Design Issues (Adapted from Bullinger, 1988, p. 13)

| Device | Physical Workspace | Environment | Nature of the Work |
|---|---|---|---|
| Visual display unit (VDU) | Desk | Lighting | Content |
| Keyboard | Chair | Ventilation | Workflow |
| Documents | Footrest | Noise | Structure |
| Peripheral devices | Document holder | General layout | Time |
| Other | Arrangement | Distractions | Ergonomics |

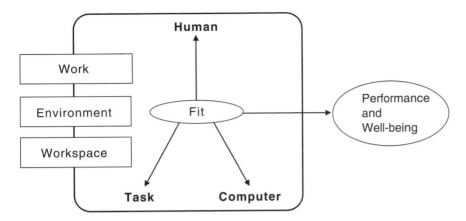

**Figure 4.1** The expanded fit between human, task, and computer in the work context.

be good for continuous tracking of objects on a screen but poor for rapid pointing, while a touch screen may be good for rapid pointing but poor for continuous tracking. Figure 4.1 models the fit between human, computer, and task in the workplace context.

Performance can be defined as "the result of a pattern of actions carried out to satisfy an objective, according to some standard" (Bailey, 1982, p. 4). To measure human performance, the standards must first be known and measurable. It is easy to see how human performance pertains to such tasks as flying an airplane, operating a forklift, shooting a rifle, or riding a bike. However, many of the tasks that humans wish to accomplish in the organizational context have performance-related problems. First of all, what is the specific objective of computer usage? Second, is there a known and measurable standard associated with the objective?

## 2.2 Limitations

Humans are limited creatures. If we weren't limited, there would be no need to work or design computers to support us in our work. Of course, humans have psychological and other types of limitations, but this chapter is primarily focused on physical limitation. Physical human limitations include sensory limits (what and how much our senses can perceive), motor (responder) limits (reach and strength), and cognitive processing limits (reaction time, accuracy). Other chapters in this book deal with cognitive processing, so this chapter will focus on the physical limitations of sense and response.

> **Physical human limitations:** These include such aspects as levels of hearing, arm reach, muscular strength, visual distance, and others.

To make matters more complex, there are no two people who have the exact same limitations. Part of performance enhancement is the assessment of individual limitations within a work context. Designers should begin with an understanding of physical human limitations of the general population regarding the specific task that the designer is targeting for computer support.

For example, some people can type 200 words or more per minute, but the average speed is closer to 60 words per minute. Therefore, designers of computer-based systems with keyboard interfaces should design with the average typing speed in mind.

### 2.2.1 Sensory Limits

The human senses of sight, hearing, smell, touch, and taste have thresholds and deficiencies associated with them. Examples of thresholds include the smallest amount of light that can be detected, the slightest sound that can be heard and understood, and so on. Deficiencies such as color blindness, blindness (or even the need for vision correction), deafness, and the inability to smell all have to be considered in some interfaces.

The opposite end of the spectrum relates more to tolerance than perception. For example, how much noise can humans tolerate before experiencing degradation of health or performance? Which types of attention-getting devices (such as blinking cursors, use of color, beeps, etc.) are effective and which are distracting? There are guidelines for answering such design questions, but once a design is executed, sensory tests should be conducted to verify the correctness of the design choices. These tests should measure not only users' performance but also their preferences.

### 2.2.2 Responder (Motor) Limits

Humans have limited reach and strength. You may think that reach and strength have little to do with computer usage, but that is not true. Many desktop computers do not even allow you to turn the system on and off from a normal working position. Keyboard layout designs and required mouse actions often cause users to change body positions in order to execute them. Computers do not require actions that exceed our normal range of strength, but some keyboards require more pressure than necessary that over time results in muscle fatigue. Even the position of keys relates to reach. Our fingers can only reach so far, so placing frequently used keys in positions that require either a change in hand position or a stretch can negatively affect performance and also result in health problems.

### 2.2.3 Fitts' Law

> **Fitts' law:** Measures the time it takes for a human to move a certain distance.

Fitts' law is important to this discussion and provides much of the theory underpinning our understanding of human performance and limitations. Fitts' law is a robust model of human psychomotor behavior developed in 1954. The model is based on time and distance. It enables the prediction of human movement and human motion based on *rapid, aimed* movement, not drawing or writing.

It seems intuitive that the distance moved would affect movement time and the precision demanded by the size of the target to which one is moving. Fitts discovered that movement time was a logarithmic function of distance when target size was held constant and that movement time was also a logarithmic function of target size when distance was held constant. Mathematically, Fitts' law is stated as follows:

$$MT = a + b \log2(2A/W)$$

where

- $MT$ = movement time

- $a, b$ = regression coefficients

- $A$ = distance of movement from start to target center

- $W$ = width of the target

Fitts' law is often used to predict the performance of humans when using various input and/or output devices. A study by Card, English, and Burr (1978) compared use of a touch screen (finger pointing), mouse, joystick, and keystrokes and used positioning time as the performance measure. This study determined that finger pointing with a touch screen is optimal, with the mouse a close second (5 percent slower). The joystick was 83 percent slower. Using text keys was even slower at 107 percent slower. Using function keys was slowest of all at 239 percent below touch screen with finger pointing. Fitts' law has been used for hundreds of experiments where response speed by the user is the performance measure of interest.

## ▶ 3. SENSORY PERCEPTIONS AND IMPLICATIONS FOR DESIGN

### 3.1 Vision

Scientists, engineers, and health researchers have studied vision more than any of the other senses, probably due to its importance. Visual stimuli that can be perceived by humans are only a small part of the total spectrum of light waves. There is a certain amount of variability of perception within each individual that complicates the design process. For example, if a person is trying to focus on an object in a dark room, it will be more difficult if he or she has just entered the room from outside where there is bright sunlight. Background, angle, size of object, length of time of exposure, and other situational variables impact the ability of an individual to see an object clearly.

Vision plays an important role in computer usage. The color of the foreground and background on the screen, the size of the characters, the angle of the tilt of the screen, brightness, contrast level, resolution, and others are all important considerations when designing a computer system. The most frequent computer response to user actions is in the form of textual screen output. Understandability and learnability of this output is more of a cognitive issue, but before something can be understood, it must be perceived and perception is truly a physical aspect of computer usage.

**Vision:** The human process of seeing and comprehending objects.

The following are the Guidelines for Physical Characteristics of Visual Displays (Bailey, 1982; Shneiderman, 2005):

- Characters in displays must be readable from a distance and angle that is representative of the normal range. The typical height of a single screen character for a word processor is approximately 5 mm. The width of a character should be 3/5 of the height.
- Fonts should be as simple as possible. Fancy fonts may lead to difficulty in understanding.
- Character definition should be as sharp as possible without leading to eyestrain.
- Characters should sufficiently contrast with the background.
- There should be adequate space surrounding each character.
- Highlighting should facilitate the task and not be distracting.
- Levels of intensity should not lead to fatigue.
- Underscoring should be used appropriately.
- Attention devices such as blinking and reserve video should be used sparingly.

- Displays should be relatively inert. Excessive movement and change in placement is distracting.
- Displays should read from left to right and from top to bottom in order to conform to natural tendencies (assuming cultural).
- Navigation within the screen and from screen to screen should be consistent and easy to understand.
- The display rate should be fast enough to combat frustration but not too fast.

The design criteria mentioned above include standardization, and the ISO 9241 is an excellent source for ergonomic standards. Part 3 of the standard refers to visual display requirements. Consider the following excerpt, and its accompanying table (correct for March 2004).

> The purpose of this standard is to specify the ergonomic requirements for display screens that ensure that they can be read comfortably, safely, and efficiently to perform office tasks. Although it deals specifically with displays used in offices, it is appropriate to specify it for most applications that require general-purpose displays. The Display Screen Regulations require displays to be clear, legible, and stable under normal working conditions.

**Table 4.2** Visual Display Requirements (Summary of Main Points)

| Design Requirements and Recommendations | Measurement |
| --- | --- |
| Design viewing distance | Minimum 400 mm for office tasks |
| Maximum line-of-sight angle | Less than 60° below horizontal |
| Angle of view within which display is legible | At least 40° from normal to display surface |
| Character height | 16' minimum, 20' to 22' preferred |
| Character format | Minimum 5x7 for numeric and uppercase Minimum 7x9 where legibility is important |
| Character size uniformity | Not vary by more than 5 percent anywhere |
| Display luminance | Minimum of 35 cd/m$^2$, higher preferred |
| Luminance contrast | Minimum 0.5 contrast modulation (CM) |
| Luminance balance | Average luminance ratio less than 10:1 for frequently viewed areas |
| Glare | Should be avoided without jeopardizing luminance or contrast requirements |
| Blink coding | For attention, 1 to 5 Hz, 50% duty cycle For reading, 1/3 to 1 Hz, 70% duty cycle |
| Spatial instability (jitter) | Location within 0.0002 mm per mm of design viewing distance in range 0.5 Hz to 30 Hz |

## 3.2 Audition

The sense of hearing is also important to human performance. Perceived sound is the result of pressure fluctuations on the eardrums that come from vibrations from some sound source. The eardrum transmits the waves to receptors in the inner ear and the nerve impulses are transmitted to the brain. Sound is characterized by frequency and intensity. Frequency is the number of cycles per unit of time. We refer to frequency as pitch. The human ear can hear frequencies from 20 to 20,000 hertz (Hz). However, most often we respond to frequencies in the 1000 to 10,000 Hz range. Intensity, or loudness, is the amount of pressure that is striking the eardrum. Decibels (Db) are used to measure intensity. The normal hearing range is from 20 Db (whisper) to 120 Db (thunder). Figure 4.2 illustrates various sounds that humans can hear at various decibels. Prolonged exposure to sound over 110 Db can result in damage to hearing and inability to hear particularly higher frequencies.

> **Audition:** The human process of hearing and comprehending sound.

Auditory messages are often used in computer-based systems to supplement visual displays. There are systems that use synthesized speech to convey information; however, more frequently auditory messages are in the form of beeps or sounds with no syntax. Beeps are often used to warn users that an inappropriate action has been attempted.

The following are the Guidelines for Physical Characteristics of Auditory Messages:

- The message should be short.
- Auditory messages are useful when a response is time-critical.
- Auditory messages are useful when the user's visual field is overburdened.
- Auditory messages are useful when the user is already focusing visual attention elsewhere.
- Auditory messages should be of high enough frequency and intensity to be heard by the user but not so high and intense that they annoy the user.
- The auditory message duration is important. If the message is designed to alert the user to perform some action, the message should continue until the user adequately performs the task or turns off the sound manually.
- Modulated sound will attract more attention than a continuous sound.

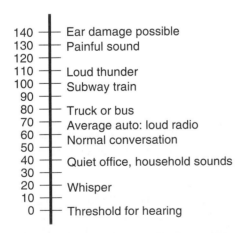

**Figure 4.2** Decibel levels for typical sounds.

- Use all auditory messages sparingly because they can cause annoyance, as they are almost impossible to ignore (unlike visual messages).
- The user should be allowed to turn on or off keystroke clicks that signal that a key has been pressed.

## 3.3 Touch

> **Touch:** The human process of sensing environment objects and conditions such as temperature through skin as a sensory organ.

The surface of the body acts as a sense organ through the nerve endings. Skin stimuli can take the form of pressure, pain, cold, and warmth. In the computer environment, the only skin stimulus that we are directly concerned with is touch or pressure. Sensitivity to touch in the fingertips is dependent on the concentration of nerve fibers and skin thickness. The keyboard and other direct manipulation devices such as the mouse have some relation to touch. Notice that the keys on the keyboard have a curved face. The curved face keeps the fingers from sliding off easily. Many keyboards have small bumps on the *f* and *j* keys. These give users a kinetic signal that their fingers are on these "home" keys. They can then recognize without looking whether or not their hands are positioned correctly on the keyboard. The amount of pressure that the fingers must exert on the keys to get the key to register is also important. If the necessary pressure is too much, the result will be muscle fatigue. If the necessary pressure is too light, the result can be key bounce or an unintentional repetition of characters and a constant need on the user's part to verify that the intended action has occurred. The keys themselves can be separated or they can be covered with a membrane that uses a nonmoving, touch-sensitive surface. The membrane keys are not suitable for touch-typing; however, they are durable and effective for restaurant cash registers and other environments where dirt is likely to be a problem.

The ISO 9241 includes a section (BS 7179, Part 4) on keyboard requirements. Below is an excerpt from these requirements and part of its accompanying summary table (March 2004):

> The purpose of this standard is to specify the ergonomics design characteristics of an alphanumeric keyboard that may be used comfortably, safely and efficiently to perform office tasks. Although it deals specifically with keyboards used for office tasks, it is appropriate to specify it for most applications that require general-purpose alphanumeric keyboards. It contains both design specifications and an alternative performance test method of compliance. The Display Screen Regulations require that the keyboard should afford tilting, be separable from the display and be easy to use without causing fatigue in the arms or hands.

The notion of fit between the computer, the user, and the task can further be demonstrated by comparing several of the pointing devices discussed in the previous chapter. Table 4.4, adapted from Greenstein (1997), compares the pointing devices on aspects related to the human–computer fit and on aspects related to the human–computer–task fit.

Similar tables can be constructed for other input devices such as a keyboard and numeric pad for inputting text and numeric data. The overall conclusion from research in this area is that different devices appear to be better for certain tasks and for certain working environments (e.g., noisy or quiet). One exception has been the QWERTY keyboard; despite its technical, rather than ergonomic, design rationale (see Chapter 3), it has been found to be relatively efficient for most tasks. Indeed it has been adopted by

**Table 4.3** Specification for Keyboards (Summary of Main Points)

| Design Requirements and Recommendations | Measurement |
| --- | --- |
| Alphanumeric keyboard layout | QWERTY layout |
| Numeric keypad | Either 123 or 789 layouts |
| Cursor control for text processing | "Cross" or "inverted T" required |
| Keyboard slope | Between 0° and 25°, preferably adjustable |
| Keyboard height (home row) | Less than 50 mm preferred |
| Keyboard placement | Independent of display and stable |
| Key-top legends | Robust, durable, minimum height 2.6 mm and minimum contrast ratio 3:1 |
| Key spacing | Between 18 mm and 20 mm horizontally and vertically between center lines of adjacent keys |
| Key-top size | Minimum 12 mm × 12 mm if square (maximum 15 mm) or 113 mm² if not square |
| Key-top shape | Molded concave |
| Key travel | Between 1.5 mm and 6 mm<br>Between 2 mm and 4 mm preferred |
| Keying feedback | Tactile feedback preferred<br>Audible shall be able to be switched off and should be adjustable in volume |
| Keyboard mode (e.g., caps, shift lock) | Clear indicators should be provided |
| Fitting numeric keypads to task | Data entry and numeric-based input |

several international standards (see Table 4.3). This may very well be a catch-22 in which the ubiquity of this standard makes it impossible for more efficient keyboards to replace it because we cannot demonstrate their efficiency, as most people perform better with the familiar devices. In contrast are most other devices, which have been found to differ according to task and environment. For example, numeric keypads can be designed with a layout of a phone (1, 2, 3 on the top row) or a calculator (7, 8, 9 on the top row). The calculator layout appears to be optimal for massive (numeric) data entry and calculations but the phone layout appears to be better for locating digits (Lewis, Potosnak, & Magyar, 1997). Finally, some devices appear to score higher on some criteria but lower on others. Consider, for example, the split keyboards. They have been found to be slower than standard keyboards but appear to result in lower muscle load in the wrist/forearm area (Lewis et al., 1997). The ergonomic engineer should be aware of these contingencies and, whenever possible, strive for optimal fit. However, as the phone and other technologies merge, there will be some contention, and further study will be needed to determine the optimal layout for numeric keypads.

**Table 4.4**  Relative Performance of Several Pointing Devices (Adapted from Greenstein, 1997)

| | Touch Screen | Light Pen | Tablet & Stylus | Mouse | Trackball | Joystick |
|---|---|---|---|---|---|---|
| **Human–computer fit** | | | | | | |
| Eye-hand coordination | Strong | Strong | Neutral | Neutral | Neutral | Neutral |
| Unobstructed view of display | Weak | Weak | Strong | Strong | Strong | Strong |
| Minimal skills | Strong | Neutral | Neutral | Neutral | Neutral | Neutral |
| Comfort in extended use | Weak | Weak | Neutral | Neutral | Neutral | Neutral |
| **Human–computer–task fit** | | | | | | |
| Rapid pointing | Strong | Strong | Neutral | Strong | Neutral | Weak |
| Accurate pointing | Weak | Weak | Neutral | Strong | Strong | Neutral |
| Point & confirm | Weak | Neutral | Neutral | Strong | Neutral | Neutral |
| Drawing | Weak | Neutral | Weak | Neutral | Weak | Weak |
| Tracing | Weak | Weak | Weak | Weak | Weak | Weak |

## ▶ 4. HEALTH PROBLEMS ASSOCIATED WITH HCI

### 4.1 Emissions

**Emissions:** Electronic radiation waves emitted by visual display terminals.

Visual display terminals (VDT) emit electromagnetic radiation waves. Studies conducted by various researchers and accepted by the U.S. National Academy of Sciences have shown that VDT emissions are well below accepted occupational and environmental health and safety standard limits. These limits are set at 2.5 mill roentgens per hour (Mr/h) at a distance of 40 centimeters from the screen. The studies also show that the normal ambient background level of ionizing sources to which the general population is exposed is higher than the levels emitted from VDTs (Grandjean, 1987).

Studies show that emissions from VDTs do not pose a health threat. However, there is some anecdotal evidence suggesting that pregnant women using VDTs experience a higher rate of miscarriage than the general population. No empirical evidence has been found to support this notion, however. Some pregnant women who use VDTs daily have elected to guard against exposure to emissions by using a lead shield or limiting their contact with VDTs during their pregnancy.

### 4.2 Repetitive-Motion Problems

**Repetitive-motion problems:** Physical discomfort and inflammation of tendons and tendon sheaths caused by frequent use of keyboards and other input devices.

While emissions from VDTs seem to pose no threat to the health of users, the heavy use of keyboards does. The traditional keyboard requires an unnatural position of the wrists and forearms in an inward position. This stress has contributed to physical discomfort and inflammation of the tendons and tendon sheaths (carpal tunnel syndrome). In some cases, heavy use of the computer keyboard has resulted in permanent nerve damage and physical incapacity.

To combat this problem, split keyboards have been developed that reduce the discomfort associated with lateral abduction and relax the neck, shoulder, arm, and hand regions. The keyboards are split in the middle, turned out at an angle, and raised at the middle to approximate natural hand and arm positions (see Figure 4.3). Although these split keyboards have been available for some time, very few of them have been purchased

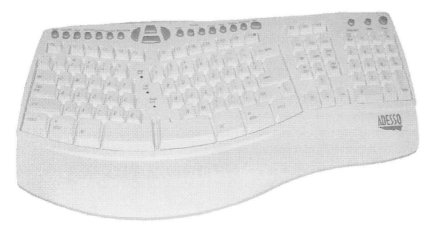

**Figure 4.3**  Split keyboard.

by U.S. businesses for office automation workers. A less expensive measure that seems to provide some aid is to provide a depth of at least 15 centimeters of support for the forearms and wrists of users.

## 4.3 Vision Problems

As more and more of the white-collar work population uses VDTs in their daily jobs, eye complaints have increased. Visual strain and physical discomfort such as visual fatigue, pain, burning, itching, blurred vision, and double vision have all been studied. Many studies have been conducted, but frequently without the benefit of a control group. The results are therefore inconclusive, but they do seem to suggest that heavy use of VDTs will result in eyestrain. In fact, eyestrain strikes 88 percent of the 66 million Americans who work on computers for at least 3 hours per day. The American Optometric Association projects that 10 million Americans will develop eyestrain every year (Shay, 1998).

Good design of the VDT can ameliorate eyestrain significantly. Such characteristics as (1) readability, (2) luminance and contrast, (3) resolution, (4) lighting conditions, (5) sharpness, (6) drift (slow change in position), and (7) jitter (abrupt change in position) can all contribute to eyestrain. Most of these characteristics are visible to the untrained eye and should be evaluated before purchasing VDTs from a vendor.

> **Vision problems:**
> Blurred visions and degraded ability to see brought on by frequent use of computers.

## 4.4 Muscular Problems

In addition to hand and arm strain, computer-based work can also contribute to other muscular problems such as neck, back, and shoulder strain and other posture-related problems. There are two kinds of muscular effort: dynamic and static (Grandjean, 1987). Almost all computer work requires static effort for all muscles except those in the fingers. Static muscular effort represses blood supply and does not result in removal of waste products that contributes to muscle fatigue. Constrained postures such as those required in prolonged computer-based work result in static muscular work and such symptoms as

> **Muscular problems:**
> Sore and damaged muscles brought on by frequent use of computers.

- inflammation of the joints (arthritis),
- inflammation of the tendon sheaths (tendinitis or peritendinitis),

- inflammation of the attachment points of the tendons,
- chronic degeneration of the joints (arthroses),
- painful hardening of the muscles, and
- intervertebral disc problems.

These symptoms vary from worker to worker and from environment to environment. In general, prolonged static positions will lead to the aforementioned problems. To combat these problems, furniture should be as flexible as possible to allow the worker to adjust the furniture to his or her own specifications. Chairs should provide lumbar support and also be adjustable. It is important to remember that support that is not at the proper level can do as much damage as no support at all. VDTs and keyboards should also be adjustable in order to minimize static posture effects.

One-third of all lost-workday injuries are repetitive stress injuries or musculoskeletal disorders and can be traced to computer use. These injuries cost employers as much as $20 billion a year in direct costs (Lindsey, 1999).

For years, the desktop PC has been the subject of much discussion among ergonomic engineers. Consequently, there is an array of products to compensate for its ergonomic failings—screens to control glare, special keyboards and wrist pads, footrests, and even mice sized to fit the user's hand. The laptop has not received the same amount of attention. However, as more employees are using laptops, related problems will become a pressing issue for employers. The intrinsic benefit of laptops—that they are portable—also generates specific ergonomic problems. Most people carry the laptop slung over their shoulder, which creates discomfort in the neck, shoulder, and back (Labar, 1997; Summerhoff, 1999).

Most workers use computers and view visual displays from a seated position. The seated position is recommended for work of long duration. The following rules for workplace layout are adapted from (Tichauer, 1978):

- The best height for a worktable or desk is dependent on the physical needs of the worker. The chair should be adjustable and adjusted to a height that allows the worker to place his or her feet flat on the floor when knees are bent at a 45-degree angle. The surface of the worktable upon which the computer monitor is resting should be low enough to allow the worker to view the screen at a downward angle (10 degrees down from the horizontal line of sight). The screen itself should be adjustable to achieve proper angle, to allow for movement to avoid glare, and so on.
- The angle and position of the keyboard should be adjustable. The keyboard angle is crucial to combat muscular fatigue and potential physical damage from repetitive-motion problems (covered earlier in this chapter).
- In addition to being adjustable, the chair should provide adequate support for the lower back.
- Illumination levels should be adequate to avoid eyestrain (200 to 500 lux).
- Glare should be minimized.
- The amount of work surface around the computer should be adequate to accommodate documents and other needs. If the worker does a lot of transcription from document to computer, a stand that holds books or documents upright should be provided.

## ▶ 5. TECHNICAL SUPPORT FOR THE DISABLED

### 5.1 Support for the Visually Impaired

Blind and partially sighted individuals can be taught to use the computer keyboard for input. Often, Braille characters are etched into the regular keys for training purposes. Output for the blind must be audible or tactile, because of the users' inability to see the visual display. Braille printers are fairly common and require special paper so that the raised dots can be felt. Braille output is limited to 64 characters. The special characters that can be represented in addition to the standard alphabetic characters are limited.

The generation of Braille output and the use of keyboard input allow blind and partially sighted individuals a wide spectrum of work possibilities in today's office automation environment that was not possible before computers.

There are several screen-reading systems that turn text and icons into language (Brown, 1992). One of these systems is called Outspoken for the Macintosh (Bosman, 1990). There are also devices that are external to the monitor that can magnify all or part of the screen for partially sighted individuals. These systems replace the eyes of a blind person and allow them to enter into the world of computing for work and personal communication.

> **Technical support for the visually impaired:** Software and hardware design that accommodates visually impaired users.

### 5.2 Support for the Hearing-Impaired

Computers can also expand the communication and work opportunities of the hearing-impaired. Hearing-impaired individuals can use standard off-the-shelf computers with no problems. The only possible limitations would be related to beeps and warning sounds that can usually be tailored with substitute attention-getting activities such as blinking lights or colors such as red. Electronic mail is ideal for hearing-impaired communication since no audible signals are necessary.

Johns Hopkins University (Wagner, 1992) funded a series of research grants directed at developing computer applications to assist persons with disabilities. The Americans with Disabilities Act (ADA) of 1989 has also spawned quite a few technological advances to support hearing-impaired individuals. One of the requirements of the ADA is the establishment of a nationwide telephone relay service for the speech- and hearing-impaired. A key component of such a system would be a keyboard-type interface for input. Gallaudet University has established an Electronic Networks for Interaction (ENFI) on which students interact with each other and for teaching (Didio, 1988). In addition to interpersonal communication, the ENFI facilitates instructional delivery and includes an option for printing out the lesson that eliminates the need for note taking.

Citibank and other corporations have set up toll-free numbers for the hearing-impaired to call both for assistance (Waldrop, 1990) and to help determine how the computer systems can better meet their specialized needs.

> **Technical support for the hearing-impaired:** Software and hardware design that accommodates hearing-impaired users.

### 5.3 Support for the Physically Impaired

One of the most exciting aspects of computer-supported assistance for individuals with disabilities is in the area of support for people who have lost the use of their limbs. Computers can help people control their wheelchairs, move their arms and legs, and even walk again. The area of biomedical engineering has made great strides in the development

> **Support for the physically impaired:** Software and hardware design that accommodates physically disabled users.

of neuromuscular stimulation and feedback control (Abbas & Chizek, 1991). Most paraplegic and quadriplegic individuals have severed spinal cords, and therefore the brain cannot signal and control the large muscle groups that are needed in walking, grasping, and other activities. Computer-driven devices stimulate appropriate muscles in the appropriate sequence to achieve the ability to walk. The software that controls the computers is very complex and can be categorized as artificial intelligence software. As the individual walks, millions of decisions have to be made and signaled to the muscles to achieve the appropriate balance and motion. Not only do these systems allow individuals more mobility, but they also provide the additional benefit of exercising muscles that would otherwise atrophy. This miracle of walking could not be achieved without the support of the computer.

## ▶ 6. SUMMARY

Physical engineering combines the study of human body mechanics and physical limitations with industrial psychology to achieve a fit between human and machine and thereby improve performance and the user's well-being.

The ergonomics of information systems deals with topics such as the physical workstation and furniture design, lighting, noise, and keyboard height and arrangement. These are all physical aspects of human engineering within an information systems context.

The performance-related goals of physical engineering are to improve (1) the human ability to handle load or demands of the work situation, (2) performance (reduce errors, improve quality, reduce time required to complete task), and (3) end user acceptance of the system.

Physical human limitations include sensory limits (what and how much our senses can perceive), responder limits (reach and strength), and cognitive processing limits (reaction time, accuracy). Computer interfaces and other interaction devices should ameliorate human limitations and improve human performance.

Well-designed computer interfaces must take into consideration human limitations and characteristics of vision, audition, touch, and motor-related activities. Computer interfaces such as screens, monitors, keyboards, mice, hard copy output, and synthesized voice must all be designed to support improved user performance and overcome human limitations.

Many individuals in today's white-collar, information-based workforce spend hours at their computer workstations; thus insurance companies and organizations are concerned about potential health-related problems associated with computers. Studies have shown that emissions from computers pose no significant health risks; however, eyestrain and muscular problems can have a negative impact on the health of users.

Computers are being used more and more to aid disabled individuals. Hearing-, vision-, and physically impaired individuals can all benefit from computer-based support. In many cases, computers are equated with independence and an improved quality of life for disabled individuals.

Although today's computers have nowhere near the sophistication of HAL from *2001: A Space Odyssey*, great progress has been made in the physical interaction of humans with computers. Voice input and synthesis is becoming more and more sophisticated, allowing pilots and vision-impaired users the option of interacting without the use of keyboards and other vision-based techniques. Simple robots exist that can do simple tasks. Biomechanical engineering is making strides in the use of computers to support human ambulation.

## ▶ 7. SUMMARY OF CONCEPTS AND TERMS

| | | |
|---|---|---|
| Ergonomics | Ergonomic engineering | Performance measures |
| Physical human limitations | Fitts' law | Vision |
| Audition | Touch | Emissions |
| Repetitive-motion problems | Vision problems | Muscular problems |
| Technical support for visually impaired | Technical support for hearing-impaired | Technical support for physically disabled |

## ▶ 8. BIBLIOGRAPHY AND ADDITIONAL READINGS

Abbas, J. J., & Chizek, H. J. (1991). Feedback control of cornal plane hip angle in paraplegic subjects using functional neuromuscular stimulation. *IEEE Transactions on Biomedical Engineering, 38*, 687–698.

Bailey, R. W. (1982). *Human performance engineering: A guide for system designers.* Englewood Cliffs, NJ: Prentice-Hall.

Bosman, J. S. (1990). Macs talk to visually impaired. *Computerworld, 17.*

Brown, C. (1992). Assistive technology: Computers and persons with disabilities. *Communications of the ACM, 35*(5), 36–45.

Bullinger, H. J. (1988). Principles and illustrations of dialogue design. In H. J. Bullinger and R. Gunzenhauser (Eds.), *Software ergonomics: Advances and applications.* Chichester, UK: Ellis Horwood.

Card, S. K., English, W. K., & Burr, B. J. (1978). Evaluation of mouse, rate-controlled isometric joystick, step keys, and text keys for text selection on a CRT. *Ergonomics, 21,* 601–613.

Chapanis, A. (1965). *Man machine engineering.* Belmont, CA: Wadsworth.

Didio, L. (1988). Deaf students talk over 10NET LANs. *Network World, 5*(14), 79–81.

Grandjean, E. (1987). *Ergonomics in computerized offices.* London: Taylor and Francis.

Greenstein, J. S. (1997). Pointing devices. In H. M., L. T. K., & P. P. (Eds.), *Handbook of human-computer interaction.* Amsterdam: Elsevier Science.

Hussain, D., & Hussain, K. M. (1984). *Information resource management.* Homewood, IL: Irwin.

Labar, G. (1997). Ergonomics for the virtual office. *Managing-Office-Technology, 42*(10), 22–24.

Lewis, J. R., Potosnak, K. M., & Magyar, R. L. (1997). Keys and keyboards. In H. M., L. T. K., & P. P. (Eds.), *Handbook of human-computer interaction.* Amsterdam: Elsevier Science.

Lindsey, E. (1999). Keying in on computer problems. *Business-Insurance, 33*(37), 3–10.

Shay, S. (1998). The eyes have it. *CIO, 11*(9), 18.

Shneiderman, B. (1998). *Designing the user interface—Strategies for effective human-computer interaction* (3rd ed.). Reading, MA: Addison-Wesley.

Summerhoff, E. W. (1999). Positioning laptops for future use. *Facilities-Design-and-Management, 18*(6), 34.

Tichauer, E. R. (1978). *The mechanical basis of ergonomics.* New York: John Wiley.

Wagner, C. G. (1992). Enabling the "disabled." *Futurist, 26*(3), 29–32.

Waldrop, J. (1990). From handicap to advantage. *American Demographics, 12*(4), 32–35.

Woodson, W. E. (1981). *Human factors design handbook: Information and guidelines for the design of systems, facilities, equipment, and products for human use.* New York: McGraw Hill.

## ▶ 9. CASE STUDY

Lance Redux is working on an e-commerce Web site for World Gourmet. He recently took a short workshop on ADA (Americans with Disabilities Act) compliance for Web sites. Although commercial sites such as the one he is designing for World Gourmet are not required to be compliant, Lance is interested in putting his new knowledge to work. At some future time, he may wish to bid on a project that requires such compliance, and he will be able to demonstrate that he is competent in this area.

Browsing most Web sites is challenging for blind and partially sighted individuals. There are many applications that convert screen text to synthesized voice output, such as "Jaws." However, the abundance of graphics on most Web sites causes a problem. Graphic images cannot be interpreted by software. In order to avoid this problem, Lance will create an alternative version of the site that is text-based only. When a customer who has the voice synthesis software enters the site for the first time, he or she has the option to switch to the text-based version. A cookie is set on the user's machine that will be read upon future visits and will automatically set the version to the text-based one. To see a demo of "Jaws" and the rules for ADA Web compliance, visit the following URLs:

- http://www.freedomscientific.com/
- http://www.adata.org/
- http://www.access-board.gov/about/ADA.htm

## ▶ 10. EXERCISES

Ex. 1.  What are the HCI issues that arise from PDA (personal digital assistant) and cell phone application development (both input and output)?

Ex. 2.  Place your fingers on the keyboard. Place both thumbs on the space bar. How does it feel? What are the long-term effects of continued keyboard usage? Now lift your wrists up from the keyboard and away from each other. How does that feel?

# 5

# COGNITIVE ENGINEERING

## CONTEXT AND PREVIEW

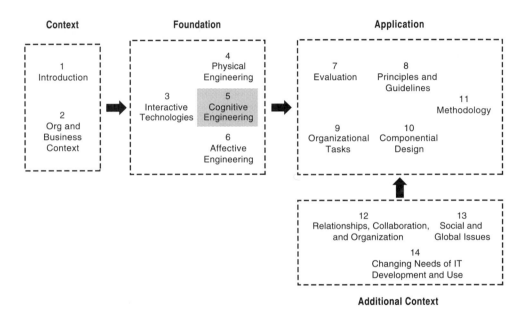

In contrast to Chapter 4, which explores the physical aspects of human engineering, Chapters 5 and 6 examine the psychological aspects: the cognitive and affective, respectively. Together, the three chapters of human engineering examine how users' physical and psychological attributes affect the way users perform tasks. For now, we deal with simple tasks, and later in Chapter 9 we expand the discussion to include more complex tasks such as decision making. But even with simple tasks such as adding two numbers, developers need to know about cognitive psychology to understand how human capabilities affect performance. Cognitive engineering applies knowledge of cognitive psychology in the development of interactive systems. A simplified cognitive model of human information processing serves as the basis for understanding how cognitive resources such as memory and attention are utilized in HCI. Norman's model of user activity and the GOMS model further demonstrate how users interact with computers. The notion of HCI complexity is introduced to represent the utilization of scarce cognitive resources. Reducing complexity is one of the goals of cognitive engineering.

## LEARNING OBJECTIVES

Upon completion of this chapter, students should be able to do the following:

- Describe the main elements of human information processing (HIP) and their interrelationships
- Understand the causes and importance of HCI complexity
- Explain Norman's seven-stage model and the design implications of the execution and evaluation gaps
- Use the Goals, Operators, Methods, and Selection (GOMS) model to describe a simple task
- Demonstrate how this material can be used to compare two different HCI designs

## SCENARIO

What makes the interaction with one system an easy and pleasurable engagement and turns the interaction with another system into a difficult and sometimes annoying experience even though both systems support the same task? Consider two systems that can help you add three numbers. One is a calculator (either a pocket calculator or one available on your computer) and the other system is a spreadsheet. Examples of such systems are shown in Figures 5.1 and 5.2. Say the user's task is to add the numbers 22, 33, and 44. Interacting with the computer calculator, the user inputs 22 by clicking twice (left mouse button) on the number 2 icon and then clicks once on the plus icon, twice on the number 3 icon, once on the plus icon, twice on the number 4 icon, and finally once on the equals sign icon. Alternatively, the user can also use the numeric pad to directly key in the numbers and the "+" operator and then click on the equals sign icon. Interacting with the spreadsheet to accomplish the same task is easier. The user uses the numeric keypad to key in 22, moves down one cell by depressing the downward arrow key, keys in 33, moves down, and keys in 44. Once the three numbers are in the cells, the user moves down one cell and clicks on the Σ icon ("auto sum" is a function in Excel that invokes the summation function, setting the range of summation automatically to the set of numbers immediately preceding the location of your pointer on the spreadsheet). The "auto sum" function highlights the range of summation (in our example, the range includes the three cells that contain the three numbers), and the user confirms by pressing the Enter key or clicking on "√".

Most users, perhaps not all, would prefer the spreadsheet to the calculator for this task, assuming both systems are readily available. The spreadsheet seems easier and has a more "natural" interface. People sense that this kind of interface accomplishes the task in a very direct fashion. The present chapter explains this sensation in detail.

Intuitively, some of the attributes of the spreadsheet that do not exist in the calculator seem to make the spreadsheet more usable. Past experience and recent developments have established improved standards of human–computer interaction that are now expected of new systems. A popular example is Jakob Nielsen's toolkit for usability engineering, which includes a set of rules for heuristic evaluation. One of these rules states that designs should minimize the user's memory load, and another rule states that designs should provide feedback. Using this rule, we compare the calculator with the spreadsheet. The calculator has one input area so that the second number keyed in overrides the previous input. The user therefore has to recall what has already been keyed into

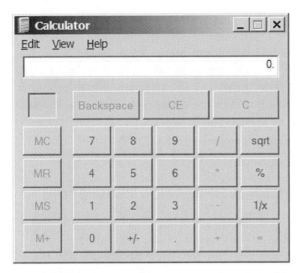

**Figure 5.1** A calculator screen that can be operated by mouse clicks as well as by numeric keys on the keyboard. The screen shot is from the Microsoft Windows program in Accessories.

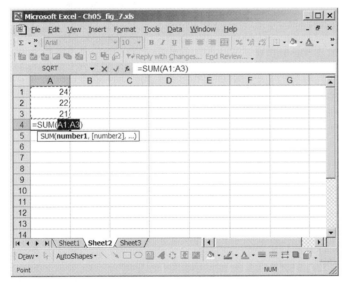

**Figure 5.2** A spreadsheet screen that supports direct insertion of numbers and functions such as SUM. The screen shot is from Microsoft Excel®.

the calculator. The spreadsheet, on the other hand, relieves the user from the need to memorize this information, as it is constantly visible to the user. The spreadsheet provides feedback about all user actions so that there is a smaller chance of error and a greater sense of user confidence. In contrast, when you key in a number into the calculator and then click on the plus sign, nothing happens. This is a poor form of feedback, namely none at all. The user may mistakenly click twice to make sure the input was received and then perhaps on the equals sign, producing an incorrect result. In any event, the user is left with an unpleasant sense of uncertainty about the impact of her action. Note, however, that in this example we artificially divorce the task of adding three numbers from its context by assuming that the calculator and the spreadsheet are equally accessible. A user who has some experience with calculators but none with spreadsheets may well prefer the calculator.

Our aim as developers is to make human–computer interaction easy and error-free. The present chapter examines HCI from a cognitive perspective, explaining how human information processing enables and limits performance. Thus it is possible to determine what creates complexity and how technology should be designed to reduce it. The next sections deal with the issues of complexity systematically and explain the intuitive judgments about the calculator versus the spreadsheet, but first we present an overview of the cognitive foundations.

## ▷ 1. A SIMPLIFIED VIEW OF HUMAN INFORMATION PROCESSING

Figure 5.3 presents a simplified model of human information processing (HIP). It attempts to capture part of the vast field of cognitive psychology that is especially relevant to our discussions of cognitive engineering. The simplified cognitive model includes processors and memories that interact in order to process information. There are three types of processors, namely, perceptual, cognitive, and motor processors, and two types of memory, namely, working memory and long-term memory. Attention is needed to facilitate and control this cognitive system. The figure is a simplified version of a model developed by Stuart Card, Tom Moran, and Allen Newell (1983).

Each processor has specific functions. The perceptual processor senses, detects, and accepts inputs from the external world and stores parts of the input in the working memory. The most prevalent data in HCI today are either visual or auditory. The cognitive processor interprets, manipulates, and makes decisions about the inputs. Finally, the motor processor is responsible for interpreting cognitive decisions into physical actions, such as using the keyboard. As noted, the processors work with memory. For example, the cognitive processor may access information stored in the long-term memory when interpreting incoming data.

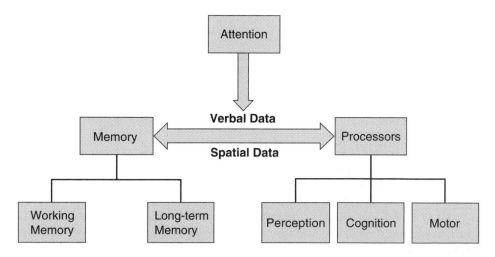

**Figure 5.3**  A simplified model of human information processing (HIP), including memories and processor. The processors and memories operate differently for verbal and spatial information.

The processors and memories are limited in the speed at which they can process data and their capacity to store data. Consider the following three limitations. The processors can process data within approximately 100 milliseconds (the motor processor is the slowest). The capacity of the working memory is roughly five to seven chunks of data that can be retained for 10 to 20 seconds (a chunk is a unit of information such as a name). And the capacity and retention of long-term memory is practically unlimited, although retrieval may be difficult. People face many more limitations on their ability to process information, and these limitations affect performance.

Cognitive engineering takes a narrow view of performance. Generally, performance reflects the efficiency and effectiveness of performing a task. Cognitive performance is the speed and accuracy of the information-processing task. As developers of HCI, we need to predict the speed and accuracy of the intended outcome of the interaction. Speed and accuracy will depend, in part, on the constraints posed by the human information processing system. Speed depends on the rate of processing and transfer of data within the system and between the human system and the external world. Accuracy depends on the capacity to store and retain information and then the ability to retrieve it correctly. Thus speed and accuracy depend on how well the processors and memory function as a whole given the constraints of the shared resources.

> **Cognitive performance:** The speed and accuracy of the information-processing task.

How do the limitations on processors and memories mentioned above impact performance? First, the user will not notice screen changes that fall within an interval of 100 milliseconds. Second, the user cannot be expected to work with more than seven chunks of information simultaneously. Displaying more chunks means the user will concentrate on some parts of the screen, ignoring others parts. Third, retrieval of information that is not expected to be in working memory will probably degrade both speed and accuracy. The human–computer interaction should be designed to avoid such performance loss by appropriate support.

Several principles of operation that govern HIP aim at overcoming the limitations on processors and memories. We demonstrate only a few principles that have special bearing on HCI development. Cognitive processes are characterized as *automatic behavior* (fast and relatively undemanding of cognitive resources) or *controlled behavior* (slower and highly demanding of attention and memory). For example, entering 50 numbers into a spreadsheet would quickly become an automatic activity that requires little attention and practically no long-term memory. However, deciding to use the summation function and defining its parameters requires access to long-term memory, selection of appropriate functions and parameters, and control to ensure correct operation. Developers need to be sensitive to this distinction and build the system to fit the expected type of behavior.

> **Automatic behavior:** Behavior characterized by cognitive processes that are fast and cognitively undemanding.
>
> **Controlled behavior:** Behavior characterized by cognitive processes that are relatively slow and cognitively demanding.

Another distinction is between image and verbal processes. The cognitive processor can process both information presented as *images* (processing is more spatial, graphic, and holistic) and *verbal* information (processing is more sequential, linguistic, verbal, and procedural). Verbal descriptions are characterized by functional and logical relationships that are processed in sequence, while images exist as units in which relations and can often be detected in parallel. Given that neither mode universally leads to better performance, developers must know when to use each mode. Indeed, later in the book we look at the importance of both text and graphics in HCI.

> **Processing of images:** Processing characterized as spatial, graphic, and holistic.
>
> **Processing of verbal information:** Processing characterized as sequential, linguistic, and procedural.

Cognitive strategies (our plans of mental action) are not rational in the sense that they follow strictly the rules of logic, as we know them. People tend to select cognitive strategies that minimize cognitive effort. In particular, cognitive processing involves *heuristics*, which are rules of thumb to perform a task that depend heavily

**Heuristics:** Rules of thumb to perform a task that depend heavily on the content and context of the task.

on the content and context of the task. Heuristics, like shortcuts, tend to use fewer cognitive resources and provide us with a natural way to overcome our limited cognitive resources. Often, these heuristics lead to correct answers, but not always. Moreover, whatever cognitive strategies the user may have, they are not applied perfectly and they are usually sensitive to the context in which they are applied. Hence cognitive processing may be subject to error. For example, the same information presented in negative terms will lead, under certain conditions, to different decisions than when presented in positive terms, even though the rules of logic would assess both presentations as identical. Heuristics are therefore vulnerable to changes in context.

**Metaphor:** A cognitive process in which an experience is related to an already familiar concept.

Metaphors and mental models are also forms of highly organized knowledge that help us overcome cognitive limitations in complex tasks. A *metaphor* is a cognitive process in which an experience is related to an already familiar concept. The "desktop" metaphor has been used extensively in HCI design. The developer creates screens (e.g., for office applications) that build on the familiar notion of a desk, enabling the user to anchor understanding to familiar objects. This general metaphor may trigger more specific metaphors such as the "cut-and-paste" metaphor. Metaphors are useful, for instance, in training (e.g., the typewriter metaphor can be used to learn about a computer keyboard). A *mental model* is a person's representation of the conceptual structure of a device or a system. In a sense, metaphors are components of models. For example, a user may build a mental model of the computer system in which files are stored in rows, like books on a shelf. When you delete a file, you throw it away. This design uses the trash bin metaphor. The user points at a file and drags it to the trash bin. Note that in this mental model, it is perfectly natural (consistent with the model) to pick a file out of the trash bin and put it back on the shelf.

**Mental model:** A representation of the conceptual structure of a device or a system.

To sum up, Figure 5.3 depicts a simplified model of HIP that is used here as the basis for cognitive engineering. The three processors interact with working and long-term memory to produce speedy and accurate information needed to perform tasks. The simplified model highlights the differences in the way image and verbal materials are processed, the role of heuristics in processing information, and the need to rely on metaphors and mental models in memory functions. The limited cognitive resources in face of task demands induce complexity in HCI, and reducing complexity is one of the objectives of HCI developers. Complexity is discussed in the next section.

## ▶ 2. THE COMPLEXITY OF HCI

### 2.1 HCI as a Bridge between Human and Computer

Cognitive engineering is a discipline that applies the combined knowledge of cognitive psychology and information technology to the design of artifacts. Its pioneers are Don Norman from the United States and Jens Rasmussen from Denmark. To date, cognitive engineering has produced most of the rigorous work on designing human–computer interaction. Its basic assumption is that users are faced with limited cognitive resources and, therefore, human–computer interaction should be designed to complement and fit these limitations.

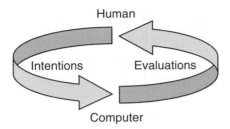

**Figure 5.4**  HCI as a bridge between human and computer.

The previous section focused on cognitive resources without reference to the computer. The remainder of the book looks at the interaction between user and technology in the context of performing a given *task*. The task, as the user sees it, can be represented as a set of intentions and evaluations. The user engages in human–computer interaction to achieve these intentions and evaluations. Figure 5.4 depicts this view graphically and serves as a framework for applying the simplified model of HIP to human–computer interaction.

When a user is faced with a task and a computer system, she perceives some level of complexity with this situation. Each factor in the human–computer–task triad is, separately and in combination, a source of complexity. The perceived complexity of HCI is the user's perceptions of difficulty, which can be viewed in three ways:

- Accomplishing a task with no computer in mind
- Operating a computer with no ulterior task in mind
- Combining both (i.e., using the computer to accomplish the task)

We concentrate on the latter because it is the main concern of organizations. Complexity is therefore a function of the amount of cognitive resources needed by the user to accomplish a given task with a given computerized system. The more resources needed, the higher the complexity. Note that the same task may be of different complexity when supported by different systems. Moreover, the same task on the same system may be of different complexity to different users. Generally, developers aim to minimize the complexity of all but the most trivial systems. More formally stated, developers strive to optimize the level of HCI complexity and thus maximize task performance.

**Complexity of HCI:** The amount of human resources needed for interacting with the computer to accomplish the task.

## 2.2  The Gulfs of Execution and Evaluation

Don Norman, author of several important books on HCI (see reading list), uses an amusing example to demonstrate the complexity of HCI. Think of John Smith trying to fill up a bathtub so that it is just the right temperature and does not overflow. John has in his mind two variables: temperature and rate of flow. (Temperature and rate of flow are psychologically constructed variables.) To manipulate the temperature and rate, John can adjust two physical valves—the hot and cold taps. Notice, though, that any adjustment of a valve affects both temperature and rate. This makes it difficult for John to relate the physical valves directly to the psychological variables. The modern one-handle tap can move horizontally to adjust temperature and vertically to adjust rate of flow. This new design enables a more direct mapping between the physical control device and the psychological

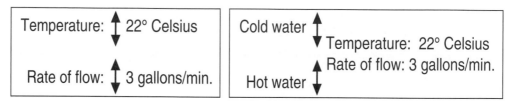

**Figure 5.5** Two interfaces. In left panel, user increases temperature and rate and observes directly the impact of each. In right panel, user increases cold and hot water and observes the integrated impact.

variables because there is a one-to-one mapping between the physical control and its psychological counterpart. Similarly, consider a high-tech bathtub that has an electronic control panel (see Figure 5.5). In the right panel, the user adjusts cold and hot water flows by increasing or decreasing the respective arrow and observing the impact on the water temperature. In the left panel, like the modern handle, each psychological variable has its own control and feedback showing its direct impact. Which panel is better? The left panel makes it easier to relate the action to the consequence, thereby reducing complexity and better serving the user. The virtual controls, however, introduce new complexity compared with the physical valves because users may be unfamiliar with the controls (e.g., the measures of flow and temperature may be abstract and ambiguous in comparison to watching the water flow and feeling the heat by putting your hand in the water). A moving picture of the water flowing as a result of changing the rate may give the user a better sense of the impact of the true rate of flow.

Our goal as developers is to understand the principles of human behavior in order to improve performance through effective design. In other words, we wish to reduce the complexity of the human–computer interaction to accomplish a given task. We also want to design a pleasurable engagement. To discuss these goals, Norman expanded Figure 5.4 by looking at how the gap between the human and the computer can be bridged by a sequence of user activities (Norman, 1986). He introduced the terms *gulf of execution* and *gulf of evaluation* to denote, respectively, the gap from human to computer and the gap from computer to human. These gulfs refer to the distance between (1) our internal goals and expectations and (2) the external representation of prior states, control devices, and states resulting from our action. The former is the psychological world and the latter is the physical world. A task is accomplished by a set of activities that bridge the two gulfs. These gulfs are the basic idea behind Norman's seven-stage *model of user activity* (Figure 5.6). Earlier we defined *user activity* as the physical and psychological aspects of the user's interaction with the computer to accomplish a task. Here we concentrate on the cognitive aspects of user activity.

> **Gulf of execution:**
> The gap between the user's goal and its computerized implementation.
>
> **Gulf of evaluation:**
> The gap between the computerized implementation of the user's goal and its evaluation by the user.

### 2.3 Norman's Seven-Stage Model of User Activity

Figure 5.6 shows how to approximate the accomplishment of a task by decomposing user activity into seven more-specific activities:

- Establish a goal that needs to be accomplished.
- Form the intention (or hierarchy of intentions) that will accomplish the goal.
- Specify the action sequence to implement the intentions.
- Execute the action.

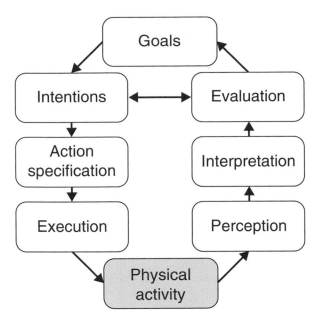

**Figure 5.6**  Norman's seven-stage model of user activity.

- Perceive the state of system resulting from the action.
- Interpret the system state.
- Evaluate your interpretation against the expectation based on your intentions.

These seven stages jointly describe the user activity for a particular goal. The intermediary stage labeled "physical system" is performed by the computer and is therefore not part of the user activity. The user (through the execution of actions) provides inputs to the system and perceives its outputs.

Norman's model of user activity can explain the differences between the use of the calculator and the use of the spreadsheet for completing the task of summing up three numbers (Figures 5.1 and 5.2). For both systems, the intention, given the goal of summing up three numbers, is to enter the three numbers and receive their total. The sequence of actions as well as its execution, for both the calculator and the spreadsheet, follows exactly the sequences described in the scenario. The calculator supports these first three stages of Norman's model by displaying a structure with one input area, one output area, and several icons, including the plus and equals signs. These elements of the calculator may remind the user of the notions of inputting, adding, and displaying that are relevant to intention formation and action specification. The plus sign needs to be understood as the arithmetic operator that adds one number to another, which is a semantic issue (recall the four levels of interaction). Similarly, the meaning of the equals sign is not always clear: Does it mean add last number and display total or display whatever has been added so far? The two interpretations will lead to two different executions with two different results! Furthermore, the single area for entering data and the set of single digits constrain the user options, which actually help execution. Nevertheless, without previous knowledge of calculators, the user may be left wondering if the first step should be pressing the plus sign and only then entering the number or vice versa (note that this is a syntactical issue). Additionally, the user is free to decide whether the digit 2 should be keyed in using the numeric key "2" or by clicking with a mouse button, which is a lexical issue.

The spreadsheet's similarity to a table of figures on paper helps form intentions and implies that one possible sequence is to fill the table and then add up the numbers. The $\Sigma$ icon reminds the user of summation of a given list (as opposed to adding one number at a time). Indeed, the summation operation, which is part of the action sequence, is very close to the notion of summing up the numbers stated as the goal of the task. In other words, the gap between the goal and its execution when using the spreadsheet is smaller than the parallel gap when using the calculator. The user of the spreadsheet is faced with lexical, syntactic, and semantic difficulties similar to those experienced by the user of the calculator. For instance, knowledgeable users will usually type a number and use the down arrow to simultaneously input the number and advance one cell. As there are many options open to the user, the novice may type a number, hit the Enter key, and then use the mouse to point at the cell below. This sequence is not only long but also likely to incur errors.

The more dramatic differences between the two systems are in the evaluation gap of Norman's model. The calculator receives a number and immediately displays it (which is perceived and interpreted as feedback that the number has been correctly, or incorrectly, received by the calculator). The calculator then receives the add operation but shows no feedback until a new number is keyed in. The user goes on working with uncertainty about the impact of his previous actions. In contrast, the user of the spreadsheet receives immediate feedback throughout the task, leaving visible the user's entries continuously. When issuing the summation, the user sees (perceives) the range to be summed (see Figure 5.2), making it very easy to interpret the operation and evaluate it in relation to the original task. Thus, closing the evaluation gap when using the spreadsheet seems easier compared with the calculator. The smaller evaluation gap for the spreadsheet-based summation task is one of the main reasons for users' perceptions that it is less complex than the calculator-based summation task.

At a more general level, minimal effort at each of Norman's seven stages and small execution and evaluation gaps represent low complexity. Note also the relationship between Norman's model and the four levels of interaction. The three stages between goals and physical activity relate to all four levels of interaction. Intentions that formulate which operators and objects are needed to accomplish the goal (and the corresponding evaluation) involve both the task level and the semantic level. Action sequence specification (like interpretation that must be done in the context of the specified sequence) combines both semantics and syntax (i.e., order and relationships between operations and objects) in order to produce a feasible plan of action. Execution translates the higher levels into action using the lexical level. You can perform a similar analysis for the evaluation gap. It appears that all four levels of interaction contribute to the complexity of HCI.

### 2.4  Fit and Complexity

In Chapter 1, we claimed that HCI should be designed to achieve a fit between the user, computer, and task. How is fit related to complexity? Consider the SUM function in Figure 5.2, which adds the numbers in cells A1 to A3. The dotted box around these cells on the spreadsheet helps the user ascertain that the summation will be performed in line with his intentions. The user's mental model of the numbers is in tabular format, corresponding to the spreadsheet. One fits the other. Now imagine that in the user's dialogue with the spreadsheet, SUM(A1:A3) would appear only in the Edit area (as it does just above columns C and D). The user would have to translate this symbolic notation to the physical locations in the spreadsheet before he could evaluate whether these are the numbers he intended to add. This would represent a misfit between the user's mental model and the computer's presentation, and this misfit requires the user to utilize additional cognitive resources. In other words, misfit increases HCI complexity.

The idea of fit applies to all stages of the user activity. The greater the fit, the easier it is to determine how to translate goals into action. The greater the misfit, the more difficult and more erroneous is the process of bridging the execution and evaluation gulfs. Compare the calculator with the spreadsheet. Most people have no idea how the calculator is built and how it operates. In contrast, the user's model of the spreadsheet resembles the system model. This may be because most users are accustomed to two-dimensional tables from school. The idea of tying together two numbers on a table is natural. The idea of updating results with every change in the spreadsheet is easily incorporated into the user's model.

Errors do occur, however, when the user's model deviates from the system's model. For example, some users find it difficult to manipulate relative addresses (e.g., copy a formula that changes automatically according to the new position of the destination). In the user's model, the copy operation carries what is seen to a new location. In the system's model, the formula stated with a relative address is copied and updated. The negative consequences of such deviations between models can be minimized by appropriate training or by changes in the interface (e.g., an animation of what happens during the copy). However, the model of the spreadsheet the user uses to perform a simple operation such as summation usually leads to a smooth and error-free performance.

## ▶ 3. USER ACTIVITY WITH MULTIPLE INTENTIONS

Users in organizational settings usually interact with computers to achieve complex goals. For example, summing numbers is usually part of a more complex task such as examining a stream of revenue in light of a new sales forecast. Norman's model of user activity can be used to describe the user activity involved in more complex tasks by modeling multiple intentions to accomplish a single goal—for example, checking a new sales forecast (which is the first intention) and summing the corresponding revenues (a second intention for the same goal). Each of these two intentions should be described by a separate user activity (i.e., Norman's stage model is constructed twice with one common goal). For each intention, Norman's model advances from abstract to concrete and back to abstract. Intentions, actions, specification, and execution progress from the abstract to the concrete. Perception, interpretation, and evaluation progress from the concrete to the abstract. The following example demonstrates these ideas in the context of decision making supported by a spreadsheet.

Say the user examines profit as a function of three variables: volume, price, and discount rate. Costs are fixed and given, so they are not displayed. The user's immediate goal is to examine the sensitivity of profit to changes in the discount subject only to the restriction that profits do not fall below zero. Figure 5.7 depicts a very simple screen for analyzing input-output relationships. This is a typical decision support system in which the user converges on an answer by asking repeatedly, "What if the discount changes?" When the user changes the discount rate from 11 percent to 10 percent, two things happen. First, the new price is calculated and rounded to cents. Second, volume of buyers rises through some exponential function. Both changes affect the profit. The formula for calculating the profit is shown in the computation line in the spreadsheet (Figure 5.7).

Imagine working with the screen in Figure 5.7. The user's activity for examining the discount's sensitivity is based on small changes around the current discount rate. In particular, the user increases the discount rate up to the point at which the net profit turns negative. Intention 1 is the starting point in Figure 5.8: "Increase discount until profit is negative." The goal and the intention are part of the user's psychological world. Figure 5.8 shows both the psychological world and its corresponding physical implementation. The actions under Intention 2 ("Increase discount rate by 1 percent") are part of the physical world. Even though the example is intended primarily to demonstrate how to

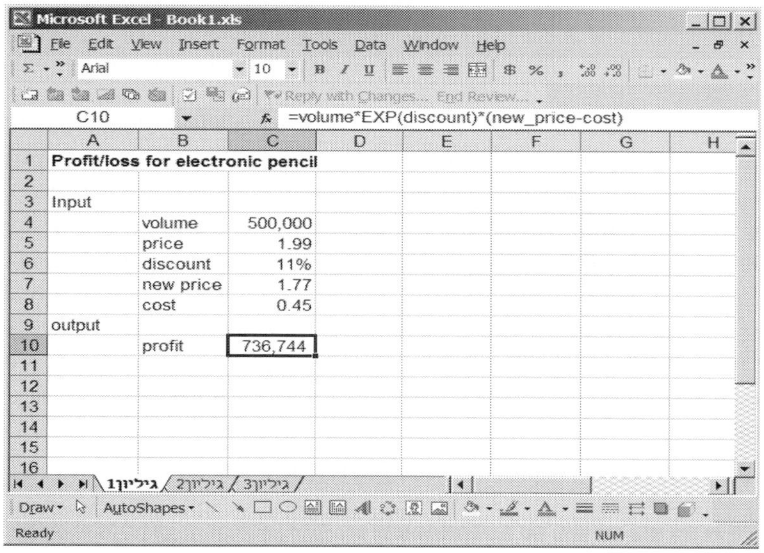

**Figure 5.7** Spreadsheet to compute profits (see Figure 5.8 for its activity specification).

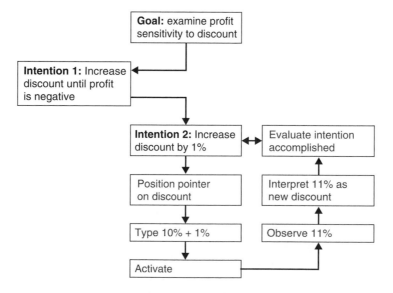

**Figure 5.8** Norman's model of user activity for spreadsheet in Figure 5.7.

articulate the higher levels (the psychological world), it is important to note the entire cycle that involves both the psychological and the physical world.

To translate a goal into intention requires a decision to act so as to achieve the goal. The first intention is to increase the interest rate until profit is no longer positive. Intention 1 is translated, through a process of problem solving, into two intentions that are more operational: Intention 2 is to increase the discount by 1 percent and Intention 3 (which is not shown in Figure 5.8) is to repeat Intention 2 if the profit is still positive.

Intention 2 needs to be translated into a sequence of actions. Going from an intention to a sequence of actions requires a transition from considering a psychological state to considering a physical state. In other words, the combination of a specific human–computer interface and the task determines the appropriate action. Assume we are using Excel with a regular keyboard. Intention 2 may be translated into the following sequence: position cursor on the discount rate cell, calculate (in your head) the current discount + 1 percent, type the result, and activate the spreadsheet by pressing Return. This would constitute the action specification stage for Intention 2. Intention 3 would be decomposed in a similar fashion.

Consider the complexity of going from the psychological intentions to the (physical) system-oriented sequence of actions. Positioning a cursor can be done in several ways. One way is to move the cursor with the arrow keys horizontally and vertically up to the desired cell. Another way is to press a function key and type the cell identifier. The user must know the control mechanisms used to position a cursor (moving the cursor cell after cell up to the required one or jumping directly to a given cell address) and know how these control mechanisms are activated physically (using arrow keys or using a function key and a cell label). A lack of this knowledge, imperfect knowledge, or faulty application of the knowledge increases complexity, slows down performance, and increases the likelihood of errors. Therefore, training can reduce complexity.

Once the sequence of actions has been specified, the next step is to execute it. The new discount value is entered in place of the old. Once the new discount becomes visible, the user perceives this change and interprets the new value as the new discount rate, which should be 1 percent higher than the old. If it is, the user evaluates Intention 2 to be accomplished. Figure 5.8 summarizes this breakdown of user activities. The accomplishment of Intention 2 activates Intention 3, which repeats Intention 2 until the profits become negative and the higher-level Intention 1 is accomplished. By modeling the task as a hierarchy of intentions and modeling each intention with Norman's stages of user activity, we can analyze how users accomplish complex tasks that involve multiple intentions, which are all translated into physical action.

The scenario above may give the wrong impression that user activity always proceeds sequentially from the first to the seventh stage. This is not so. Often, the user begins with perception and interpretation of events, followed by appropriate action, gradually forming a goal. Thus the order advances from the right-hand side of Figure 5.6. Moreover, like any simplification of real-life phenomena, the seven activities are not necessarily exact descriptions of the psychological processes going on in our heads. They are, however, useful in making more concrete the notion of complexity in human–computer interaction and the causes of complexity.

Good designs should reduce complexity by supporting each of the seven stages in the user activity cycle. The most obvious example concerns the use of visual displays. Because of cognitive limitations on working memory, relevant information should be displayed throughout the "what-if" session. This would include not only the information in Figure 5.7 but also information produced during the interaction (e.g., the best, in terms of profits, discount rate so far). But good designs should go beyond this to consider opportunities for supporting the entire cycle of activities in Norman's model of user activity. For example, menus remind users of the possible options, thus supporting the formation of intentions and the specification of actions. Pointing at icons supports easy and correct execution. Structured feedback displayed together with a reminder of the intention supports interpretation and evaluation. The list of opportunities for supporting user activity is practically endless.

This section demonstrated the model of user activity with a slightly more complicated task than the summation of three numbers described in the previous section. This task involved a hierarchy of intentions, which were translated into physical implementation using Norman's model. The breakdown of tasks into the stages bridging the gulf of execution and the gulf of evaluation directs the developer's attention to support all stages of the user activity model, and minimize the transition between stages, in order to improve the quality of the interaction. The next section discusses a more detailed method for describing user activity.

## ▷ 4. USING GOMS TO DESCRIBE USER ACTIVITY

### 4.1 Goals, Operators, Methods, and Selection Rules

Complexity is the result of task requirements that draw on limited cognitive resources as outlined in the simplified HIP model (Figure 5.3). Relating Norman's model to these cognitive resources is therefore the basis for assessing complexity of the user activity. For example, resources are needed to generate intentions, maintain them in working memory, and later retrieve them from long-term memory for evaluation. An analysis of the user activity involved in the use of a spreadsheet reveals that it requires a high degree of decision making about the order of task execution and about choice of methods (Olson & Nilsen, 1988). It also requires a relatively high degree of perceptual processing and high amounts of both working memory and long-term memory. In order to define more precisely the processor and memory operations needed for the user activity, we use a model called GOMS.

GOMS (Goals, Operators, Methods, and Selection rules) is a technique that maps the user activity to the operations of the simplified model. The GOMS model was devised by three cognitive scientists: Stuart Card, Tom Moran, and Allen Newell (Card, Moran, & Newell, 1983). The model is a way of representing knowledge of purposeful human–computer interaction. It has been used extensively in human–computer interaction research on rather routine and very structured tasks, such as text editing. Although the GOMS is applied only in very specific and structured incidents of HCI (e.g., the design of "cut and paste" in Office applications), it has had a very significant impact on the field of HCI. Moreover, the general approach represented by GOMS can also be applied to poorly structured and less specific human–computer interactions, which are relevant to the organizational context.

Much like the user activity model, the GOMS model too is based on levels of interaction that bridge the gap between the abstract (psychological) task and the concrete (physical) system. The terminology is slightly different, however. Furthermore, the GOMS does not make a distinction between execution and evaluation (Figure 5.6). In the GOMS model, methods (similar to action specifications in the user activity model)

**GOMS:** Goals, Operators, Methods, and Selection rules are the elements of a model that describes purposeful HCI.

are the means to implement goals (or intentions). The methods are described as a series of steps consisting of operators. Finally, if different methods can be used to implement a goal, selection rules describe which method to choose. A GOMS description includes a specification of each of the four components:

*Goals* specify what the user wants and intends to achieve. Goals are therefore the basis for control and evaluation and are needed to determine satisfactory achievement and what to do next.

*Operators* are the building blocks for describing human–computer interaction at the concrete level. For example, the operator "move the mouse pointer to the HCI folder icon" refers to human resources (e.g., long-term memory) and computer resources (e.g., folder icon).

*Methods* are programs built with operators that are designed to accomplish goals. One method to open a file may include "point to an item on screen." Another method to accomplish the same goal may include "choose OPEN option in file menu." These are two different methods to accomplish the same goal.

*Selection rules* predict which method will be used—for example, "If mouse working, select 'point to an item on screen'; if not, select 'choose OPEN option in file menu.'"

## 4.2 Using GOMS

The remainder of this section concentrates on a methodology for creating a GOMS description developed by David Kieras. The original and more detailed guide appears in the list of advanced readings (Kieras, 1988). The guide is often referred to as NGOMSL, which stands for the Natural GOMS Language (we use the terms interchangeably in this book). It supplies good rules of thumb on how to go about implementing this approach.

Figure 5.9 is a flowchart for building a GOMS description of human–computer interaction. The first step is to articulate the user's primary goals, which can then be broken down into more detailed subgoals. For each goal or subgoal it is then necessary to draft a method to accomplish it. This step requires you to determine how a user would go about doing what he has to do but without too many details and without any special considerations such as shortcuts.

The original studies of GOMS used the model to evaluate designs of text editing in which the operators are specified in the most specific level possible. The operators in Figure 5.10 (used in the original studies of text editing) illustrate well the link between the GOMS and the simplified HIP model. Note how the different operators use the cognitive resources differently. Mental primitives for control of flow are associated with controlled processing performed by the cognitive processor. "Accomplish goal" and "report accomplish" are operators that control the activity at the highest level. "Decide" and "Go to" are control operators necessary for nonserial logic, particularly for selection rules. The second group of operators is associated with memory. Interesting is the unintuitive operator "forget from working memory," which has proven useful in describing the user's intentional activity. The final group of external operators is associated with the motor and perceptual processors. The GOMS model can therefore show quite accurately how the user activity utilizes cognitive resources.

We demonstrate this methodology with an example from (Kieras, 1988). The example concentrates on defining a method to accomplish the goal of selecting an arbitrary text from some online document. An intermediary result (which needs to be refined)

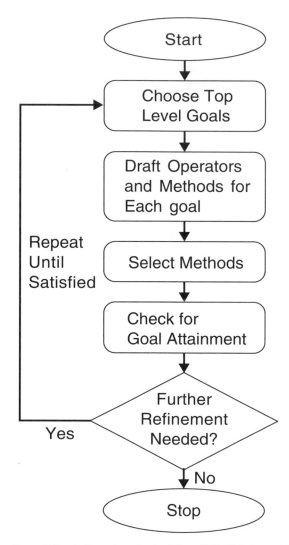

**Figure 5.9**  A flowchart for building GOMS (adapted from Kieras, 1988).

appears in Figure 5.11. The method has eight steps, which is usually considered too long. A good rule of thumb is to construct methods of up to five or six steps. One way to ensure shorter methods is to construct a higher-level operator such as "indicate beginning" and "indicate end" and then, if necessary, decompose them into more detailed submethods. Recall the idea of a gulf between intentions and physical implementation. The higher-level operation "indicate beginning" is an intention. Steps 2 and 3 in Figure 5.11 would become part of a submethod that describes the activation of the physical device.

Once the GOMS description of a task has been completed, it may be necessary to highlight the use of cognitive resources, particularly the use of working memory. For example, the operator "Retain" should be used whenever information is acquired. Too many "Retain" operators represent an overload of information in the working memory. Thus, these requirements on cognitive resources are important for assessing the exact

**Operators**
Mental primitives for flow of control:
Accomplish the goal of <goal description>
Report goal accomplished
Decision: if<operator> then<operator> else<operator>
Goto step <number>
Verify Selection

**Memory stage and retrieval**
Recall that <working memory object>
Retain that <working memory object>
Forget that <working memory object>
Retrieve LTM that <long-term-memory object>

**Primitive external operators**
Move mouse
Press key <key name>/mouse button
Type in <string of characters>

Move-cursor to <target coordinates>

**Figure 5.10**   A list of general operators used in a GOMS of text editing.

Method to accomplish goal of selecting arbitrary text:
1.   Determine position of beginning of text.
2.   Move cursor to beginning of text.
3.   Press mouse button down.
4.   Determine position of end of text.
5.   Move cursor to end of text.
6.   Verify that correct text is selected.
7.   Release mouse button.
8.   Report goal accomplished.

**Figure 5.11**   An example of a method with eight steps (taken from Kieras, 1988).

reaction times and the complexity of interaction by showing what parts of the interaction strain cognitive resources.

How is GOMS used in practice? As noted above, its use for evaluating HCI designs is limited to very simple and structured tasks in which performance in terms of time and accuracy is crucial, such as tasks that are done over and over again. This is because even simple interactions, such as text editing, can mushroom into scores of methods, each method decomposed into several operators. One of the most important lessons from the cognitive engineering approach is the need to minimize the human–computer gap, the distance from the psychological intentions to the physical materialization. Assuming that the length of a method is a good measure of the complexity of HCI, the GOMS model can provide a measure of the quality of alternative interfaces. Interfaces can then be chosen so as to minimize complexity. Moreover, the GOMS model makes it possible to predict accurately the time for completing a task with alternative designs. Performing such tests, for example, on alternative designs of a new palm interface may be worthwhile. Other practical applications of the GOMS model that have been suggested include checking for consistency between methods that serve similar goals and assessing mental workload of particular methods (e.g., number of information items in working memory). More on this subject can be found in Kieras and Polson (1985).

## ▶ 5. ERRORS

When user activity is described as GOMS (e.g., Figure 5.11), behavior may deceptively appear to be flawless. But to err is only human to the extent that users have been "accused" of being error-prone. Errors can occur at every stage in Norman's model and are usually attributed to our limited cognitive resources. In fact, as the complexity of HCI grows, so does the likelihood of error. This section examines the different classes of errors and their causes as a basis for future guidelines on designing for error.

### 5.1 A Classification of Errors according to Behavior Type

Cognitive engineering studies errors in the context of different types of human behavior in which errors occur. For example, errors during typing are treated differently than errors during work on a business problem supported by a decision support system. Jens Rasmussen (1986) described the automatic-controlled processing described in the simplified HIP model as a three-level model of information processing: skill-based, rule-based, and knowledge-based. Skill-based behavior is governed by readily available programs of action. This type of behavior is completely automatic. Rule-based behavior is governed by available programs that need to be selected according to the particular conditions given at the particular time of action. Rule-based behavior is not completely automatic because it requires the decision maker to be conscious of the problem and the particular conditions in place. Knowledge-based behavior requires the decision maker to create new patterns of behavior because old programs are not appropriate for the new conditions.

Knowledge-based behavior is the most thoughtful type of behavior. Skill-based behavior is found in routine actions. Rule-based and knowledge-based behaviors are characteristic of problem-solving activities. James Reason (1990) uses the skill/rule/knowledge model of behavior to describe human error. In skill-based behavior, slips and lapses are deviations from intended behavior and are due to failures in processing or memory. In rule-based behavior, mistakes occur when inappropriate programs of behavior are applied. In knowledge-based behavior, mistakes occur when inappropriate or insufficient programs are devised. Thus, the terms slip and lapse are associated with deviations from automatic behavior, while the term mistake is associated with deviations from controlled behavior.

This classification of errors is important for understanding errors and knowing when to expect them. Skill-based and rule-based errors (which Reason calls "strong-but-wrong") are more predictable. Strong-but-wrong errors are behaviors that jump to mind forcefully but are applied incorrectly because of a slip of attention or a lapse of memory. We know these strong behaviors and can predict how they may go wrong. In skill-based behavior, the focus of attention is usually on some other activity and therefore slips occur because control is lacking. In rule-based behavior, strong rules are misapplied. Moreover, skill-based errors are most easily detected. Once a skill-based error is committed, the user will usually notice the error. Rule-based and especially knowledge-based errors are harder to detect and often need a critical perspective to uncover such errors.

> **Errors:** Deviations from intentional behavior that is either skill-, rule-, or knowledge-based.

> **Skill-based behavior:** Automatic behavior that is predefined and requires minimal cognitive resources.
>
> **Rule-based behavior:** Controlled behavior that relies on predefined rules of behavior that are contingent on particular situation encountered.
>
> **Knowledge-based behavior:** Highly controlled behavior that requires assessment and generation of new rules of behavior and is demanding of cognitive resources.

## 5.2 The Causes of Error

We now associate classes of errors with the three types of behavior. Figure 5.12 is an abridged adaptation from Reason (1990, p. 69). Skill-based errors are due to either inattention or overattention. *Inattention* refers to failure to monitor performance at the critical nodes. *Overattention* involves inappropriately and unnecessarily checking routine behavior. Here are some examples of inattention errors. Habitual slips occur when one gets used to a certain behavior and fails to see that a change is needed (e.g., I just now started to use a new version of a word processor and repeatedly use the old function key that is no longer valid). An omission may occur due to an interruption (e.g., a phone call that occurs in the middle of typing can lead me to continue typing at a wrong place). Competing actions reduce the level of intentionality so that a user finds herself going on to do something other than what she had intended (e.g., she gets to a place in the document and begins to edit the paragraph but forgets to break a new paragraph as intended). Perceptual and inferential confusions are incorrect readings of the situation (e.g., aiming to press one key and hitting another).

Overattention can have similar effects, although it is due to too much monitoring rather than too little. For example, mistimed checks on automatic activity such as typing can cause the user to repeat characters due to the interference with the automatic sequence. Better timing would be to check the typing upon its completion.

In rule-based behavior, the reading of the situation is used to identify a program of behavior that is most suitable. In any given situation, several programs may compete to be selected. Selection will go to the closest on the salient features, the most successful, the most specific, or the most compatible with the active program at the time. Rule-based errors are due either to the misapplication of good rules or to the application of bad rules. *Misapplication of good rules* may occur on first exceptions to well-versed cases (e.g., the first time the system hangs up when you press the Ctrl /C key sequence and you discover that this sequence does not work under certain conditions). Countersigns are indications that the program is inappropriate, yet they are ignored and the program is activated (e.g., you try to paste immediately after a cut, even though the cut did not succeed and the "paste" icon is not active). Information overload is a common

**Skill-based behavior**

| *Inattention:* | Habitual slips; Omissions following interruptions; Reduced intentionality; Perceptual confusions |
| *Overattention:* | Repetitions |

**Rule-based behavior**

| *Misapplication of good rules:* | First exceptions; Countersigns; Information overload; Rule stength |
| *Application of bad rules:* | Encoding deficiencies; Action deficiencies |

**Knowledge-based behavior**

Selectivity; Availability; Biased reviewing; Confirmiation bias; Overconfidence; Problems with causality; Problems with complexity

**Figure 5.12** Error classification (adapted from Reason, 1990).

reason for ignoring countersigns. Frequently used rules are usually stronger in the user's mind than infrequent rules, and the stronger rules may overpower the weaker yet appropriate rules. For example, when logging off at the end of the day, I usually follow the shutdown procedure even when I decide to reboot.

The *application of bad rules* is the result of either encoding the situation incorrectly or performing unsuitable actions. When creating a formula in a spreadsheet, the user may fail to identify the need for absolute addressing rather than relative addressing (this has to do with the way the spreadsheet is organized). Alternatively, the situation is correctly encoded, but the sequence of actions leads to a formula that does not do the job because the spreadsheet cells in the formula were combined incorrectly.

Knowledge-based mistakes occur because of two main reasons: limited cognitive resources and inaccurate representations of the problem situation. Errors at this level are particularly dependent on the context of the problem-solving activities. In contrast to performance in skill-based and rule-based behavior, here extrinsic factors, rather than intrinsic factors such as frequency of prior use, are likely to dominate. Hence, a detailed discussion of knowledge-based errors relevant to decision making is presented in Chapter 9.

## ▶ 6. FIT AND COMPLEXITY EXTENDED

Cognitive engineering introduces the task into the interaction between the user and the computer, thereby forming a triad of the human, computer, and task (recall Figure 1.3 in the introductory chapter). This triad suggests to developers several directions. First, it is meaningful to talk about the complexity of HCI because complexity is associated with the cognitive resources needed to accomplish a given task with specific interactive technologies. Developers provide computer functionality to reduce complexity by relieving the user from utilizing cognitive resources. The models we have discussed show the way. First, Norman's seven-stage model of user activity depicts the cognitive functions for performing computer-supported tasks. These cognitive functions can be supported by appropriate designs, hence the importance for developers to understand this model. The discussion around this model (Figure 5.6) suggested that the developer actively seek opportunities for supporting each of the cognitive functions. Second, the focus on task makes it meaningful to examine user activity by bridging the psychological world of goals and intentions to the physical implementation. Indeed, Norman's model of user activity and the GOMS model begin with an explicit consideration of the task.

These two aspects of the task have been discussed at length. Both directions are, in effect, strategies for designing HCI. Minimizing complexity, which is to say minimizing effort, without compromising on performance, is a fundamental design principle. For example, reducing the need for memory reduces complexity and is therefore an objective that developers should pursue. Supporting every phase of user activity is another principle. For example, many systems fail to support the phase of evaluation, concentrating primarily on execution. An explicit consideration of all phases of user activity encourages the developer to think of new opportunities to support the user.

Supporting every phase of user activity and minimizing complexity often have the same design implications. Nevertheless, looking at both strategies provides the developer with additional guidance, increasing the chances of a better and more complete design. The GOMS model, for example, can be used to compute complexity of alternative designs by measuring the number and sophistication of the methods needed to characterize the HCI (see Kieras & Polson, 1985, for a theory of complexity as a basis for HCI design). The GOMS model can also be used to determine the consistency within an application (or between applications) by comparing the methods used for similar goals. Increasing consistency reduces the requirements of memory, thereby reducing the complexity of the HCI. These and other design principles are elaborated in Chapter 8.

In particular, one design principle to be developed later concerns the fit between the user's mental model of the task and the computer's representation of the information needed to complete the task. The idea of fit between the user's mental model and the system's representation is central to cognitive engineering (see our previous discussion of fit and complexity). It has been called "naturalness" by Donald Norman (1986) and "cognitive fit" by Iris Vessey and Dennis Galletta (1991), who argue that "for most effective and efficient problem solving to occur, the problem representation and any tools or aids employed should all support the strategies required to perform that task." So, basically, cognitive fit is the result of a match between the characteristics of the problem-solving strategy included in the user's mental model and the problem representation as it appears on the system display. For example, a cognitive fit exists between a spatial representation (such as a map) and a spatial problem (such as navigation). In contrast, a tabular representation for the same problem would produce a poor cognitive fit. Cognitive fit can be seen as a determinant of low HCI complexity.

A word of caution, however, about the triad of user, computer, and task. Cognitive engineering should not be applied to this triad as if it were independent of its context because tasks are always performed by the user in a particular context. The user's model obviously affects the user's actions, and thereby it determines actual work but it is not necessarily identical to actual work. Any representation simplifies the real world and may omit details that in reality force a behavior that is different from that planned according to the user's model. Say that the user assumes he will have all the necessary information on time but then discovers that he has to make a decision with incomplete data (an example of organizational context) or finds it difficult to implement a decision because of group pressure (an example of social context). The models and output of the computerized system may no longer be valid. These discrepancies reduce fit, confuse the user, and result in poor support. Chapter 9 discusses tasks in the organizational context and shows how to consider this context in HCI.

## ▶ 7. SUMMARY

Cognitive engineering focuses on developing systems that support the cognitive processes of users. The simplified model of HIP demonstrates how cognitive resources such as memory and attention are utilized. Norman's seven-stage model of user activity is a framework for applying the simplified model to HCI. Complexity is seen to represent the utilization of scarce cognitive resources. A good fit between the user's mental model of the system and the actual mental model is one way of reducing complexity. Another is to support the stages of user activity and the transition between them, thereby reducing the execution and evaluation gaps. The GOMS model is also introduced (GOMS stands for Goals, Operators, Methods, and Selection rules) to explain in more detail how cognitive resources are used in specific interactions. Much like Norman's user activity model, the GOMS model is based on levels of interaction that bridge the gap between the abstract (psychological) task and the concrete (physical) system. Thus, the notions of fit, complexity, and levels of interaction are central to understanding cognitive engineering in HCI.

## ▶ 8. SUMMARY OF CONCEPTS AND TERMS

| | | |
|---|---|---|
| Model of user activity | GOMS | Performance |
| Gulf of evaluation | Errors | Controlled behavior |
| Gulf of execution | Complexity of HCI | Automatic behavior |
| Images | Metaphor | Heuristic |
| Verbal materials | Mental model | Skill-based behavior |
| Rule-based behavior | Knowledge-based behavior | Cognitive fit |

## ▶ 9. BIBLIOGRAPHY AND ADDITIONAL READINGS

Card, S., Moran, T. P., & Newell, A. (1983). *The psychology of human-computer interaction.* Hillsdale, NJ: Lawrence Erlbaum Associates.

Kieras, D. E. (1988). Towards a practical GOMS model methodology for user interface design. In M. Helander (Ed.), *Handbook of human-computer interaction.* Amsterdam: North-Holland Elsevier.

Kieras, D. E., & Polson, P. G. (1985). An approach to the formal analysis of user complexity. *International Journal of Man-Machine Studies, 22,* 365–394.

Norman, D. (1986). Cognitive engineering. In D. Norman & S. Draper (Eds.), *User centered design: New perspectives on human-computer interaction.* Hillsdale, NJ: Lawrence Erlbaum.

Norman, D. (1988) The psychology of everyday things. New York: Basic Books.

Olson, J., & Nilsen, E. (1988). Analysis of the cognition involved in spreadsheet software interaction. *Human-Computer Interaction, 3,* 309–349.

Rasmussen, J. (1986). Information processing and human-machine interaction. Amsterdam: North Holland.

Reason, J. (1990). *Human error.* Cambridge: Cambridge University Press.

Vessey, I., & Galletta, D. F. (1991). Cognitive fit: An empirical study of information acquisition. *Information Systems Research, 2*(1), 63–84.

## ▶ 10. CASE STUDY

Lance Redux is interested in maximizing the usability of the World Gourmet site. He has decided to conduct a GOMS assessment to determine the exact nature of the user interactions for this site. GOMS stands for Goals, Operators, Methods, and Selection rules.

He visits existing Web sites and searches and makes hypothetical purchases to help him understand the nature of these B2C (business-to-consumer) interactions. He determines the following:

Goals specify what the user wants to achieve. In the case of the World Gourmet customer, there are two goals. The first is to search for and find a particular product. In some cases, the user knows exactly what he or she is searching for. In other cases, the user may browse the site and become attracted to various products that can be purchased. Once the user has chosen a product or set of products, the goal is to purchase the product(s).

Operators are the basic operations used for describing human–computer interaction at the physical level or close to it. In the case of World Gourmet, the physical interaction level is primarily a set of mouse clicks to effect operators such as move to the next field within a form, select an item from a list of options, and confirm an instruction. Some parts of the interaction also require the user to enter text (keystrokes) in blanks on a form.

Methods are programs built with operators that are designed to accomplish goals. One of the methods that will be used in the World Gourmet site is filling a form with data that builds on the operators, entering text in a blank field, and moving to the next field.

Selection rules predict which method will be used. In the World Gourmet site, the rules are oriented toward filling in the order form. Some of the rules are listed below:

If the current field contains appropriate information and the user presses the Enter key, the cursor moves to the next blank.

If the system can "look up" information (such as the date), it should supply the date (relieving the user from doing so).

If the user has already supplied the information during this session or a previous one, the system should supply the information whenever needed (don't require the user to reenter it). In the case of previous sessions, "cookies" may be used to store the user's information on the user's machine or the information may be pulled from a database that has stored the user's information.

If empty blanks exist, prompt the user to supply information.

## ▶ 11. EXERCISES

Ex. 1. Extend the scenario at the beginning of the chapter about adding three numbers to the following problem:

Instead of finding the sum of three numbers, calculate the sum of the absolute deviations from their mean—for example, for the numbers 22, 33, and 44, the expression should be $|22 - 33| + |33 - 33| + |44 - 33| = 22$. As in the previous scenario, compare the calculator to the spreadsheet for this task. When considering the calculator, use its memory functions.

Ex. 2. Assume the following GOMS description for cutting text when working with a word processor on a document:

Method to accomplish the goal of cutting text

If text is a word, then Accomplish goal of selecting a word,

else,

Accomplish goal of selecting an arbitrary text.

Accomplish goal of issuing a CUT command.

Report goal accomplished.

This method includes a selection rule that determines which type of selecting text is appropriate (a word or arbitrary text) and a submethod for issuing the CUT command. According to the result of the selection rule, the appropriate submethod is invoked. The method for selecting an arbitrary text is given in Figure 5.11.

Your task is to write a method for selecting a word.

Compare your method with that in Figure 5.11, and identify any consistencies and inconsistencies between the two methods. Clearly they are not identical, but you are asked to examine similarities and differences that may affect the way the user performs.

Ex. 3.   * Identifying errors in HCI

Observe a fellow student searching for a book in the online catalog in your campus library and report. Ask the student to perform several such searches according to the details you supply. In one case, all the details should be correct and should reflect a book currently in the library. In another, the book is in the library, but the details are incorrect in one of the fields (e.g., author name). In the third case, the details are correct, but the book is not in the catalog. Your report should consist of all the errors the student made, which include hesitations, not knowing what to do or guessing what to do, performing an action and correcting it or repeating it, or simply expressing frustration about some failed action. When you observe some unexpected action or repeat trial and are not sure that it is indeed an error, don't hesitate to intrude and ask the student if a particular action was an error or not.

Classify the errors in your report according to Figure 5.12.


* This is a more difficult exercise.

# 6

# AFFECTIVE ENGINEERING

## CONTEXT AND PREVIEW

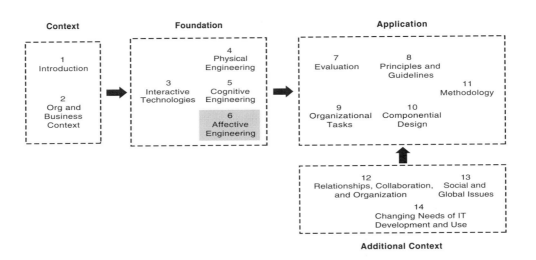

This chapter complements the previous two chapters on physical engineering and cognitive engineering by providing the foundations for affective aspects of HCI design. It covers several concepts that are important in HCI such as affect, attitude, flow, and satisfaction. The chapter describes models of affect that help explain how and why users interact with computers and how this knowledge is relevant to design. Some of these ideas are expanded in Chapter 12, which puts the individual model in the organizational contexts, and in Chapter 7, which discusses HCI evaluation. The foundational knowledge in this chapter is later translated to concrete guidelines to achieve positive affect by appropriate designs (e.g., by designing aesthetic interfaces).

## LEARNING OBJECTIVES

Upon completion of this chapter, students should be able to do the following:

- Explain the importance of affect and how it can be engineered
- Describe the main elements and mechanisms of affect

- Explain the Technology Acceptance Model and the perceptions of usefulness, ease of use, and enjoyment
- Explain attitudes and their place in HCI, including satisfaction and computer anxiety
- Explain the concept of flow
- Demonstrate how this material could be applied

## SCENARIO

Denver, October 16, 1998. A large audience of Windows developers, filling an entire auditorium hall, witnessed the execution of the Microsoft® Office Assistant (see Figure 6.1). This was not a sad occasion to almost everyone in the room. The well-known paper clip Office Assistant (nicknamed "Clippy the Paper Clip") has become a popular demonstration of how to evoke negative feelings. The Office Assistant appears as a paper clip with expressive eyes and hyperactive eyebrows, offering tips and help. What can possibly go wrong with such a friendly and helpful character? Apparently, a lot! Most developers disliked the paper clip's "cuteness" and complained gravely about its intrusiveness. At that same meeting, when shown how to invoke the option "Kill the Assistant," and as the paper clip cried back, "I'm melting, I'm melting," one of the developers commented, "Good riddance."

In a thesis entitled "Why People Hate the Paperclip," Luke Swartz notes on the basis of interviews with frustrated users that the Assistant's appearance is one of the main reasons for users' negative reactions to it. While it is known that baby-like features such as large heads, short arms and legs, round skulls, and big eyes are perceived to be likable, the paper clip has virtually none of these features. It has longish "limbs" and a minute face. Can appearance alone trigger such strong negative feelings? Apparently, feelings are formed on the basis of many different cues. You might think of other reasons for not liking the paper clip. For instance, people don't like intruders, even if they have the best intentions. People expect and certainly want other people to be sincere. In this vein, computerized assistants or software agents that look like

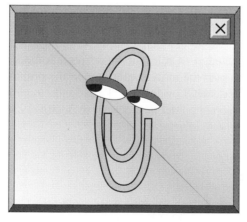

**Figure 6.1**  Microsoft Assistant® paper clip.

humans (this is called anthropomorphism) are expected to display humanlike characteristics so that fake expressions are disconcerting and annoying.

How should we therefore design the interface so that it evokes positive rather than negative feeling? The paper clip is the default appearance for the Assistant and can be changed, but few people bothered to change it. In fact, Microsoft Office offers a gallery of alternative characters for the Assistant—for example, a dog, a genius, a cat, and others (right-click on the Assistant to scroll through the characters). Do you like any of these? Do you think you would still like it the ninth time it appears? What other feelings do these characters evoke? Or more generally, in the terminology of this chapter, how can these designs generate positive affect? This chapter begins to answer such questions.

## ▶ 1. INTRODUCTION: FEELING AND ATTITUDE

Affect is a general term that refers to psychological processes and states such as feelings, emotions, moods, attitudes, affective impressions, and satisfaction. In this chapter, we have organized several aspects of affect that are particularly important to HCI as three subtopics: (1) feelings (emotions, moods, and affective impressions), (2) attitudes and related factors, and (3) the possibility of designing to please.

> **Affect:** A general term for a set of psychological processes and states including emotions, moods, affective impressions, and attitudes.

The new psychological basis of HCI that balances and integrates affective and cognitive aspects is rapidly gaining popularity. The dramatic move from pure cognitive aspects of HCI to a more balanced view is demonstrated in Donald Norman's new emphasis on emotions in computing (Norman, 2004). He begins with the realization that cognition and affect play distinct but equally important roles. Both subsystems of human information processing act as interfaces with the world around us. Both subsystems prepare us for action and help evaluate the action. Cognition interprets and makes sense of the world. Affect evaluates and judges, modulating the operating parameters of cognition and providing warning of possible dangers. Thus it is clear that knowledge of how the two systems work independently and in conjunction is essential for HCI developers.

Consider the following examples: a robot smiling at you when it welcomes you to a new day, or your desktop computer adjusting its screen background color from a light to a deeper color when it recognizes that your tone of voice is grave. These are two examples of *affective computing*, a term introduced in the late 1990s by Picard (1997). (In this book we use the term *affective engineering* to connote a broader application of affect to the development of HCI.) Both examples are technically feasible ideas that rely on our knowledge of affect. Much like the cognitive models we explored in the previous chapter, we need models of affect that explain how feelings affect function, what the limitations on feelings are, and how feelings impact behavior and performance. On the basis of such models, it will be possible to design HCI that considers the affective, as well as the cognitive, aspects of human behavior.

The second type of affect we discuss is attitudes toward computers. In today's competitive market of computer systems and the Internet, attitudes toward systems determine whether customers will use and revisit systems, because many instances of use are discretionary. Understanding discretionary use, especially when the user is a client rather than an employee of the organization, is rapidly becoming one of the most important issues in HCI. Take, for example, the behavior of online shoppers. Recent studies reveal that 53 percent of total online revenues are generated from repeat visits of customers who are satisfied with their experience (quoted in Moon & Kim, 2003). Online stores that managed to improve the customer's experience by incorporating more pleasing designs reaped an increase in repeat visits (the ratio of buyers to unique visitors) from 40 percent to 140 percent. This kind of "stickiness" toward the online store depends on experiential motivations that rely on a balance of emotions and cognition.

Affect and cognition can hardly be treated separately. When analyzing the user's feelings during the process of human–computer interaction, it appears that only the combination of affect and cognition can holistically characterize the state that the user experiences (this state is called *flow*, a concept that will be expanded on later). Furthermore, our discussion of attitudes in this chapter demonstrates how intentions to behave combine both cognitive and affective considerations. In this respect, this chapter not only examines the affective aspects of behavior but also extends the discussion of cognitive aspects outlined in the previous chapter.

The next section provides an overview of affect and its relation to design. Sections 3 and 4 explain attitudes, choosing to highlight only a few of the many attitudes relevant to HCI. Section 5 describes the important concept of flow in HCI. Finally, Section 6 discusses some applications of affect in HCI development.

## ▷ 2. A SIMPLIFIED VIEW OF AFFECT IN HCI

### 2.1 Some Core Concepts of Affect

What is affect? The field of psychology has not yet settled on a common definition. James Russell (2003) offers a comprehensive framework, from which we extract the parts that are particularly relevant to HCI. The human (user) has a potential set of core affects such as feeling elated, upset, tense, or comfortable. People direct these core affects at objects, which can generally be other people, conditions, things, or events, but in our discussions the object will be related to the computer system (e.g., the computer, a particular screen, a manual or computer help desk). Thus, the computer system has affective qualities that are able to trigger or change the user's core affects. Each of these terms (core affect, object, and affective quality) is expanded and related to HCI.

*Core affect* (or feeling) is a neurophysiological state that integrates two dimensions: pleasure-displeasure and activated-nonactivated. Pleasure-displeasure is the hedonic dimension. Activated-nonactivated is the arousal dimension, which measures the extent to which one feels energized and engaged. These two dimensions are orthogonal. In Figure 6.2, the vertical dimension is activation and the horizontal dimension is pleasure. An example of a particular core affect is "tense/jittery" and exactly opposite it is "placid/calm." "Placid/calm" is very low on activation and quite high on pleasure, while "tense/jittery" is very high on activation but at the same time very low on pleasure. Similarly, the feeling of "elated/happy" is high on activation and very high on pleasure, whereas "sad/gloomy" is low on both dimensions.

On the core affect circle, we can draw another dimension called positive-negative affect, which is tilted 45 degrees from the pleasure and activation dimensions. It integrates activation and pleasure into one, suggesting the common connotation of feeling good or feeling bad. This dimension clearly shows "elated/happy" as a very positive affect and "sad/gloomy" as a very negative one. The core affect circle helps to identify scores of feelings and characterize them. This is a first step in modeling affect in general and in HCI in particular.

---

**Core affect (or feeling):** A neurophysiological state that integrates two dimensions: pleasure-displeasure and activated-nonactivated.

**Affective quality:** The object's ability to cause a change in the user's core affect.

**Emotion:** A core affect that is intentional and directed toward a certain object.

**Moods:** Unintentional core affects that exist within a person independently of external objects.

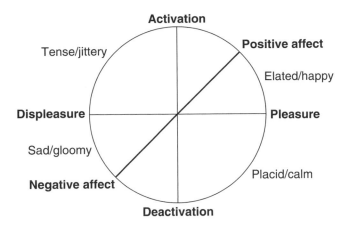

**Figure 6.2** Core affect circle (adapted from Russell, 2003).

At this point we can distinguish between (specific) emotions and (general) moods. An *emotion* (also called "attributed affect") is a core affect that is intentional and directed toward a certain object. *Moods*, in contrast, are unintentional core affects that exist within a person and are therefore not dependent on affective qualities of an object, as are emotions. In some instances, moods may seem to relate to a number of external causes, but in other instances, moods may also relate to some inner feeling regardless of external circumstances. Emotions tend to be more acute and exist for a short time in comparison with moods, which are usually less severe and can exist for longer time intervals (hours and sometimes days).

How do feelings interact with objects? Affective quality is the object's ability to cause a change in the user's core affect. For example, the rhythm of the music is an affective quality of music that makes me feel calm. The affective quality of the computer system is to be found in the human–computer interface or, to a lesser extent, in documentation and other descriptions of the system. The next section concentrates on the affective qualities relevant to HCI and the impressions they leave on the user.

## 2.2 Affective Qualities and Affective Impressions in HCI

This section relates the general discussion of affect to HCI. We seek to explain how objects of the human–computer interface influence core affect. For this we identify the affective qualities in the interface and determine the process in which these qualities are perceived by the user and thereby affect the user's feelings. In Russell's framework, the object's affective qualities are input to a perception process by which the qualities are appraised in terms of their capacity to impact feelings. These reactions to the object's affective qualities, which we call "affective impressions," form the basis for change in core affect.

In the design of HCI, we therefore concentrate on affective qualities of HCI components (e.g., color and animation) and on affective impressions that are linked to core affect but are specific to the HCI domain. Recent studies have identified a large assortment of affective qualities in HCI. Affective qualities of Web sites and screens include beauty, overview, title, shape, structure, texture, menu, main images, and color (Zhang &

Li, 2005). We look into the impact of some of these affective qualities exhibited in three research projects.

Two characteristics have drawn special attention in the context of online stores: interactivity and vividness (Moon & Kim, 2003). *Interactivity* is the extent to which the user can manipulate and communicate with the computer in real time. Interactivity is influenced by speed of users' actions and effects, range of user actions, and mapping of actions to effects. *Vividness* is the richness of representation in the human–computer interface. Vividness is influenced by sensory breadth (e.g., auditory and visual) and sensory depth (e.g., the screen resolution).[1] Interactivity and vividness are examples of affective qualities: they influence core affects and, thereby, influence attitudes and behavior. In subsequent chapters we discuss how the design attributes of the interface generate interactivity and vividness. For instance, in the case of Web pages, three common design attributes are graphics, background color, and response time.

Other characterizations of affective qualities in the context of Web pages include beauty, whether the page is mostly graphics versus mostly text, the availability of overview, and the page structure (Schenkman & Jonsson, 2000). Recall the two Web pages for online stores in the introductory chapter, which differed primarily in the relative amount of graphics versus text. It appears that the affective quality of "mostly graphics" generates a more positive attitude for Figure 1.2b, which is predominantly graphical, than for Figure 1.2a, which is predominantly text.

An interesting study on affective qualities of home pages demonstrates well the link between design and affect. Kim, Lee, and Choi (2003) performed an elaborate study of the affective impressions evoked by a set of diverse home page designs. In the first stage, affective impressions were determined from a survey of users. As the users were asked to judge static screens with no opportunity to experience the interactive qualities of the system, this study is necessarily limited in the scope of affective impressions.[2] Thirteen affective impressions of home pages were identified: bright, tense, strong, static, deluxe, popular, adorable, colorful, simple, classical, futuristic, mystic, and hopeful.

In a second stage, the key design factors of home pages were identified. This was done in order to be able to generate the set of diverse home pages. The primary design factors identified included texture, shape, and color. For example, the shape of an object on a screen is determined by its orientation relative to the screen's base dimension, by its size, by its form, and by its boundary line. Texture refers to whether the shape and color are mixed or not (i.e., rich texture is when there are multiple colors and types of shapes).

Two very different home pages are presented in Figure 6.3. The colors used are very different. Large portions of the left screen (a) are in dark brown, and large portions of the right screen (b) are in light blue. The textures of both are mixed. The shapes of screen B are generally rounded, in contrast to the straight lines in screen A. Thus, different designs are established and tested in the next stage.

In the third stage, the authors wished to determine how the design factors of the home pages evoked the affective impression. To do so, they presented to potential users several designs of Web pages. The two screens shown in Figure 6.3 are examples. The label "classical" for Figure 6.3a represents an affective impression evoked by the particular

---

[1]  See advanced reading by Steuer (1992) for detailed characterizations of these qualities.
[2]  In this limited static context, the authors preferred to use the term *aesthetic impression* rather than *affective impression*, which is the term used in this book.

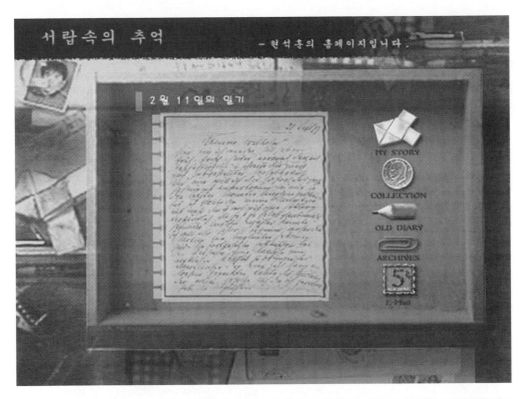

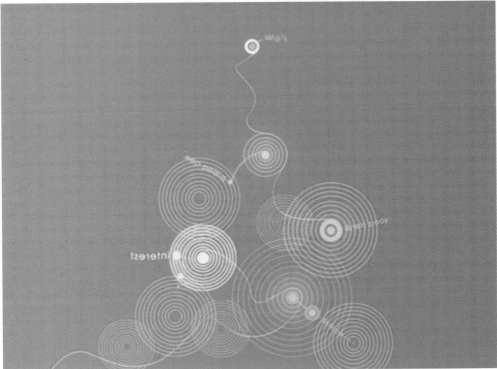

**Figure 6.3** Affective impressions in home pages (adapted from Kim, Lee, & Choi, 2003) (see also color plate II). (a) Classical. (b) Futuristic.

combination of design factors present in the home page. Similarly, the label "futuristic" is evoked by the very different design factors in Figure 6.3b. Other designs of home pages elicit other affective impressions from the list of thirteen impressions mentioned previously. Although the results are tentative, they suggest that these design factors (shape, color, and texture, and especially color) indeed have affective qualities that impact emotions.

In another attempt to capture aesthetic impressions of Web sites, Lavie and Tractinsky (2004) identified two dimensions in users' perceptions: "classical aesthetics" and "expressive aesthetics." The classical aesthetics dimension pertains to aesthetic notions that emphasize orderly and clear design. The expressive aesthetics dimension is manifested by the developers' creativity and originality and by the ability to break design conventions. Thus, their study offers a reliable tool that can be used to capture the affective impressions of Web sites on these dimensions. Interestingly, the classical dimension is closely related to elements of perceived ease of use and usability (discussed in Chapter 7), while the expressive dimension is not.

Clearly, these are only demonstrations of affective qualities in HCI and are developed in a limited context. Other studies will surely produce different sets of affective impressions. The general implication, however, is that developers should know how the design factors impact emotions in order to fit the overall image to the emotions they consider to be most appropriate for the person or situation characteristic of system usage.

We have looked at the relationship between HCI design factors, affective qualities, and emotions: certain elements of HCI have affective qualities that evoke certain affective impressions, which impact emotions. Figure 6.4 shows an example of how design can influence emotions based on the studies cited above. Note, though, that at this early stage of research into the role of affect in computing, this example is tentative and many other design factors may be found to elicit affective impressions. In Chapter 10, we return to some of the specific design factors shown in Figure 6.4 when we study in more detail the HCI design components.

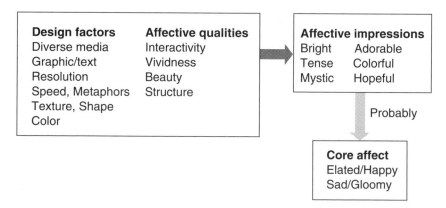

**Figure 6.4** Design impacts emotions—examples of design factors, affective qualities, impressions, and affect in Web-based design. These lists are tentative and partial.

## 2.3 Applications of Affect to Computing

Affective engineering in HCI is a new and exciting area (see advanced reading by Hudlicka, 2003). Affect concerns four major activities in the design of HCI:

1. Modeling affect in the user and the computer

2. Sensing and recognizing the user's affective state

3. Adapting the computer's state to fit the user's affective state

4. Generating on the computer (artificial) affective expressions

Modeling affect is the basis for sensing the user's affect, for adapting to it, and for generating affective expressions. Developing systems that can recognize automatically the user's affective state relies on models of affect. Indeed, even if the user is asked to report manually his affective state, it is important to anticipate the relevant types of emotions in order to produce designs that fit those emotions. Of the many possible types of affect, it is important to identify those relevant to particular contexts and to determine how they should impact our design. For example, consider the grief and anxiety patients normally experience in hospitals. A system open to the public for registering the patient's details should be designed with special care and sensitivity to the user's affect. A worried user is more likely to commit errors in recognizing and understanding instructions and in completing details on a form because of lower levels of attention. Designs should be relatively simple and supportive and should include more checks on data input.

New HCI developments in sensing affect include the detection of speech tone, pitch intensity, pupil size, skin conductance, blood pressure, body movement, and body temperature. New research and developments in affect recognition aim at determining anger, fear, grief, joy, sadness, frustration, and the neutral state.

Generating affective expressions relies on modeling affective states and implementing them with HCI technologies. Developments in simulating expressions of affect include head position, facial expressions, posture, gaze, gestures, speech tone, and body movement. The story of the paper clip assistant demonstrates well how careful developers should be when generating expressions. The expression generated (simulated) to show a merry assistant when called for or a sad one when called away proved quite irritating to many users. It seems most people don't like the obviously insincere affective expression that appears continuously on the assistant's "face."

At the MIT media lab (http://www.media.mit.edu), researchers investigate possibilities of generating affective expressions. "Kismet" is the name of an expressive robot that imitates human expressions in interpersonal communication. The robot displays human-like expressions of emotions. Designs of affective expressions rely mainly on the ears, eyebrows, eyelids, and lips. Kismet can perk its ears in an interested fashion or fold them back in "anger." Eyebrows can furrow in frustration, elevate upward for surprise, or "sadly" slant upward. Kismet can also wink an eye or blink both. Kismet can also shape its lips upward to produce a smile or downward to express disappointment. Figure 6.5 shows the mechanisms in Kismet for generating facial expressions.

A more general question is whether to design computer interfaces that appear and behave like human beings. Shneiderman and Plaisant (2005), for example, are against designing systems that appear as though they were human. Such designs are called anthropomorphic designs. It seems that children readily accept anthropomorphic designs for most objects, while adults usually prefer a clear distinction between computers and humans. One reason may be that computer systems dressed with humanlike features are

**An anthropomorphic** design resembles human beings.

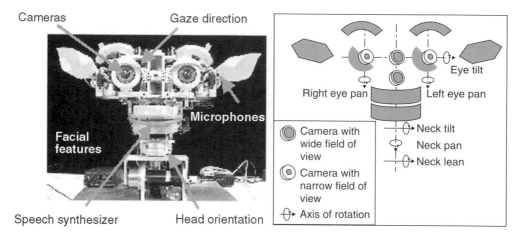

**Figure 6.5**   Generating affective expressions in a robot—Kismet from MIT Media Lab.

perceived to be deceiving and generate computer anxiety in many users. Others, in particular Reeves and Nass (1996), have advocated that users tend naturally to regard interacting with computers as communicating with people. This dilemma is ongoing. While some experiences, such as the Office paper clip, have failed, others, such as the broadcaster of interactive video reports by an information supplier named Ananova (www.ananova.com), appear to have succeeded.

## 2.4  Affect and Performance

Following the fit framework introduced in Chapter 1, the three human aspects—namely physiology, cognition, and affect—interact with the task and the computer to impact performance and well-being (Figure 6.6). While the discussion of physical engineering addressed both performance and well-being, the discussion of cognitive engineering concentrated on performance. This reflects the emphasis of current research and knowledge. With regard to the impact of affect, people usually think of well-being rather than performance. But this is not necessarily true. For certain tasks, particularly those involving

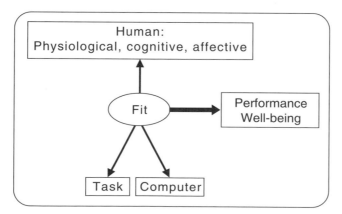

**Figure 6.6**   Affect, as well as physiology and cognition, impacts both performance and well-being.

judgment, cognition and affect work hand in hand to accomplish the task. Cognition is necessary to process and make sense of information, and affect is necessary for evaluating and judging people, objects, behaviors, and consequences (Norman, 2004, discusses this aspect at length). We therefore consider the impact of affect on performance too.

Affect and cognition interact in many ways. For instance, affect changes the way cognition works. When people feel good, they tend to think more creatively. This finding may explain how an aesthetic design affects performance. In a study of the effect of beauty on performance, Tractinsky, Katz, and Ikar (2000) found that attractive ATM layouts led to better performance than functionally equivalent but less attractive layouts. Interestingly, this study of Israeli subjects replicated the results of an earlier study of Japanese subjects. If this case can be generalized, then affective computing may play an important role in promoting not only well-being but also performance.

Not all systems need to incorporate affective computing. Filling out standard weekly forms and reporting mundane activities such as the number and time of services rendered this week are examples of tasks that need not reference affect. In general, frequent, structured, and factual transactions are less likely to be influenced by our emotions in comparison with the novel, unstructured, and knowledge-based processing. Nevertheless, even in such conditions in which human information processing is relatively automatic, certain moods, such as boredom, increase the plausibility of errors due to lack of attention. For example, centers for manual data input involve typing repeatedly standard and invariant data into online forms. This activity can easily become boring to the extent that people begin to pay little attention to the activity and consequently do not detect errors of inattention such as typing the same data twice (see Figure 5.12).

Knowledge of the impact of affect on cognition is the first step in adapting HCI to ensure positive performance. Sensing the user's state and acting accordingly is a goal of affective engineering. Knowing that repeated data input may generate a state of boredom and being able to detect characteristic behavior of bored users, such as poor attention, could trigger a process of adaptation in the human–computer interface or in the work conditions. For instance, the system could highlight feedback that demonstrates recent errors and attributes them to the user's inattention. The system would then suggest taking a break or would notify the user that the stricter input validation checks will be enforced.

Affect impacts cognition and behavior in more ways. A pleasant core affect directs attention to positive material, while unpleasant affect facilitates attention to negative material. In practice, this means that people seek information that is congruent with their

**Table 6.1**  Effects of Emotions on Cognition (Adapted from Hudlicka, 2003)

| | |
|---|---|
| **Anxiety and attention:** | Anxiety limits attention, predisposing attention to sources of danger. |
| **Affect and memory:** | Mood biases memory recall (positive mood induces recall of positive information). |
| **Obsessiveness and performance:** | Obsessiveness delays decision making, reduces recall of recent events, and reduces confidence in ability to distinguish between real and imagined events. |
| **Affect and judgment:** | Negative mood decreases and positive increases perception of self-control; anxiety predisposes toward interpretation of ambiguous stimuli as threatening. |

mood (this tendency is referred to as "mood congruence"). Table 6.1 demonstrates some of the impacts of affect on cognition and behavior. The reader is invited to stipulate what can be done to enhance positive impacts and minimize negative impacts. To learn more about these developments, see advanced reading by Hudlicka (2003).

## ▷ 3. ATTITUDES

From the early days of IS research and practice, users' attitudes toward computers have been a major concern. Studies of attitudes have often involved questionnaires that measure general attitudes toward using a computer, satisfaction with a particular system, and anxiety about the implications of using a computer. Knowledge of attitudes has served developers in determining advantageous and disadvantageous features of systems and in detecting resistance to the introduction of systems.

Attitudes are commonly measured before or after interacting with the system. This is in contrast to our earlier discussions of affect experienced during the process of interacting with computers. In the field of IS, the word *use* is commonly employed in association with attitude to denote the user's interaction with a computer. Although the connotations of use and interaction may differ, we generally interchange the terms in this book, unless specified otherwise. Furthermore, attitude integrates affect and cognition.

### 3.1 Attitudes—Concept and Measurement

**Attitude:** A summary evaluation of an object.

An *attitude* toward an object, such as a computer system, "represents a summary evaluation of a psychological object captured in such attribute dimensions as good-bad, harmful-beneficial, pleasant-unpleasant and likable-dislikable" (Ajzen, 2001, p. 27). Attitudes are influenced by cognition (beliefs about the object) as well as affect (emotions toward the object) and result in a tendency to behave in a certain way toward the object (i.e., an intention to act). Attitudes, therefore, come close to predicting how people will interact with computers, although actual behavior, as opposed to intentions to act, depends also on a person's perceptions of control over behavior (Ajzen, 1991). For example, a person who believes using a computer is beneficial and feels positively about the computer will most probably intend to use it. However, the same person may not use the computer in reality if there is doubt in his mind about being able to operate the computer easily. Indeed, predicting users' behavior is one important role of attitudes in information systems.

Attitude can be measured directly or implied from its antecedents and consequences without measuring attitude directly. When attitudes are measured directly, they are usually gauged by questionnaires or interviews. For example, in a questionnaire developed by Igbaria, Parasuraman, and Baroudi (1996), respondents are asked to rate on a 1–7 scale statements such as "I'd like to use a computer because it is oriented to user needs" and "I wouldn't use a computer because it is too time-consuming." However, recent research and practice has tended not to measure attitude directly but rather to concentrate on its antecedents and consequences. TAM is the most popular of these models in IS.

### 3.2 TAM—Technology Acceptance Model

The Technology Acceptance Model (TAM) (Davis, 1989) is one of the leading models in IS to explain attitudes toward using a system. TAM has been widely used to predict the acceptance and use of information technology. In Figure 6.7, attitude is shown in the middle of the figure. On the one hand, a user's attitude toward using a system is determined by two main beliefs: the system's usefulness to the user and the ease of using it. Perceived usefulness and perceived ease of use generate commensurate attitudes. High perceived usefulness and high perceived ease of use result in positive attitudes. Both beliefs have consistently been shown to be important in innovation diffusion, in general, and in computer diffusion, in particular.

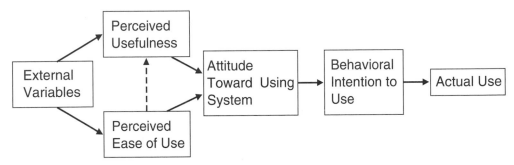

**Figure 6.7**   The Technology Acceptance Model (TAM) (adapted from Davis, 1989).

> **Perceived usefulness:** The users' belief that using the system will enhance their performance.
>
> **Perceived ease of use:** The users' belief that using a particular system will be free of effort.

On the other hand, the resulting attitude shapes the user's intention to use the system, which in turn predicts actual use. Although attitudes play a central role in the model, in practice most TAM studies attempt to predict intentions directly from measures of perceived usefulness and ease of use. Venkatesh, Morris, Davis, and Davis (2003) provide a comprehensive review of TAM studies.

The model can be improved by including individual and organizational variables (we elaborate on individual variables in the next section and on organizational variables in Chapter 12). The external variables impact perceived usefulness and ease of use. For example, experienced users may find the system easy to use, while novices experience the same system as difficult. Similarly, in certain organizations the use of technology per se is valued, increasing the perceived usefulness regardless of the system's direct impact on work.

The causal linkages between two key beliefs (perceived usefulness and perceived ease of use) and users' intentions and between intentions and actual usage are founded on the "theory of planned behavior" (Ajzen, 1991), which is one of the most influential theories of human behavior. In TAM, a behavioral intention to use the system is directly determined by a person's belief that using a specific application will increase his or her job performance (perceived usefulness) and by the belief that using the system will be relatively free of effort (perceived ease of use). Thus these two beliefs—perceived usefulness and perceived ease of use—predict the user's intention to use the system, which in turn predicts actual use of the system.

Knowledge of users' attitudes can be employed in the management of system development. Organizational investments in information technology to support planning, decision-making, and communication processes are inherently risky. To make effective use of this technology, managers, professionals, and operating employees must accept the applications, learn how to interact directly with aspects of the hardware and software, and adapt the technology to their tasks' requirements. Understanding why people

**Attitude**                                                                    **Use**

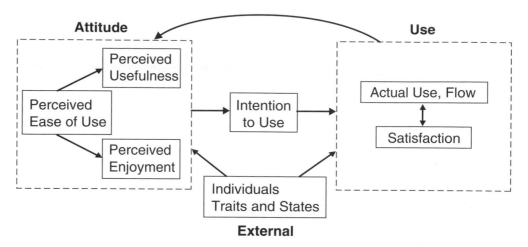

**Figure 6.8** Expanded view of affect and its impact on use.

accept or reject computers has proven to be one of the most challenging issues in information systems research. Davis (1989) introduced the TAM to explain and predict computer usage behavior. TAM can be used to evaluate systems very early in their development or to assess user reactions to systems on a trial basis in advance of purchase decisions (Davis, Bagozzi, & Warshaw, 1989). Using TAM for evaluation is developed further in Chapter 7.

## ▷ 4. EXPANDED VIEW OF AFFECT IN HCI

This section integrates our discussions of affect and attitude and furthermore puts them in context. Figure 6.8 presents the expanded view. It includes attitude (the factors that constitute attitude), intention to use the system, use (actual use and satisfaction), and external variables (individual traits that affect attitude and use). Users with positive attitude are likely to form intentions to use the system and, as a result, actually use it. Use results in high or poor satisfaction, depending on how well the users' expectations are met. Furthermore, the users' personal traits and self-perceptions may affect the way they form intentions and behave. The curved arrow going from "use" to "attitude" reflects a flow from satisfaction back to perceptions of usefulness, enjoyment, and ease of use, affecting attitudes in future interactions. We now examine separately each of the elements in Figure 6.8.

### 4.1 Attitudes Revisited

The upper-left box labeled "attitude" in Figure 6.8 contains the antecedents of attitude in TAM (although there is no specific measure of attitude, following the common practice of TAM, the integrative effect of the antecedents reflects attitude). The two antecedents in the original model (Figure 6.7), namely perceived usefulness and perceived ease of use, may not capture the user's impression of affective qualities discussed earlier in the chapter. As attitudes combine both cognitive and affective processes, we add affective impressions (perceived affective quality) as a third antecedent of attitude. Note, however, that affect is a very new topic of research in HCI and there has been very little empirical research supporting the impact of affective impressions on attitudes toward computers. We choose here one example of affective impressions, namely perceived enjoyment.

Perceived enjoyment focuses on the intrinsic motivation to seek pleasure or fun from the process of interacting with the computer. It "specifies the extent to which fun can be derived from using the system as such" (van der Heijden, 2004). Perceived enjoyment, like perceived usefulness, has to do with the impact of using the computer, but it differs from perceived usefulness with respect to motivation. Perceived usefulness has to do with the extrinsic motivation of some benefit that is effected by using the computer but not dependent on the process of interacting with the computer. In this respect, perceived enjoyment is similar to perceived ease of use, which has to do with the process of interacting with the computer. However, while ease of use is not associated with the goal of using the computer but rather with the means of achieving the goal, perceived enjoyment can be regarded as a goal. In most studies of user perceptions using organizational systems, usefulness has been found to dominate enjoyment and to influence intentions to use more forcefully (Cheung, Chang, & Lai, 2000). However, it may be that the relative importance depends on the context. Van den Heijden (2004) suggests that in systems that are predominantly productivity-oriented, perceived usefulness is indeed most important, but in systems that are predominantly pleasure-oriented, perceived enjoyment will take precedence.

There are many possible external variables posited in TAM; here we look only at the individual variables that demonstrate affective states. An affect factor that has received considerable attention in IS is *computer anxiety*. You may be surprised to learn that many people, particularly from the older generation, are still anxious about computers, especially computer systems in high-impact and sensitive services such as health and financial. Computer anxiety taps the users' fears of the consequences of using computers (Thatcher & Perrewe, 2002). For example, a user may be afraid of losing important information as a consequence of storing and maintaining the data on the computer instead of keeping printed records. Another fear may be the loss of face in revealing how little you know about working with a computer. Some people are afraid of making mistakes that will cause them to lose money, order the wrong product, or send a message to the wrong person. Finally, some people fear they may lose control over private information, unfortunately with very good reason. Like perceived enjoyment, computer anxiety affects intention to use and actual use.

In sum, the model of acceptance shown in Figure 6.7 is expanded to include affective impressions in addition to perceived usefulness and perceived ease of use. Figure 6.8 shows how these factors interact to form the user's intentions to use, which in turn lead to actual use.

## 4.2 Satisfaction

Satisfaction is perhaps the most commonly used factor in behavioral IS research. Satisfaction is a positive affect resulting from the evaluation of the use of the computer system. A model called the expectation-confirmation theory explains how satisfaction is formed (Bhattacherjee, 2001): users have certain expectations, and they then confirm (or disconfirm) these expectations and, as a result, form a feeling of satisfaction. Thus, satisfaction necessarily involves some comparison of expectation versus experience. For example, one may have very high expectations of fun before interacting with the system, then interact and enjoy the interaction but not as much as expected, and therefore end up

**Perceived enjoyment:** The extent to which fun can be derived from using the system as such.

**Computer anxiety:** Emotions about the implications of using a computer such as the loss of important data.

**Satisfaction:** A positive affect resulting from the evaluation of the use of the computer system based on a comparison of expectations versus experience.

unsatisfied. Here we present two popular examples of satisfaction questionnaires to demonstrate satisfaction measured at two levels: general system satisfaction and satisfaction with the human–computer interface.

Many different measures of satisfaction are available to IS developers, so it is important to first determine the purpose of measuring satisfaction and accordingly select the appropriate measure. One important purpose of measuring satisfaction is to evaluate a system (this is done in place of or in addition to measuring system use). One of the most popular measures of satisfaction is called End-User Computer Satisfaction (Doll & Torkzadeh, 1988). This measure is composed of five subfactors, each measured with two to four questions: (1) content (e.g., Does the information content meet your needs?), (2) accuracy (e.g., Is the system accurate?), (3) format (e.g., Is the information clear?), (4) timeliness (e.g., Do you get the information you need in time?), and (5) ease of use (e.g., Is the system easy to use?).

Increasing user satisfaction is an important goal in developing and managing information systems. Satisfaction is the basis for users' attitudes in continued (repeated) use so that low satisfaction may inhibit use and drive the system to failure. For many years, measures of user satisfaction have served as early indicators of a system's failure or success (Ginzberg, 1981). Moreover, developers can impact satisfaction by taking action before and during implementation. Developers should therefore attempt to manage expectations. Exaggerated expectations, which invariably are not met, lead to low satisfaction. Appropriate expectations, if confirmed, raise satisfaction. Training, in addition to instructing and coaching users, can serve to set the right expectations.

Other measures of satisfaction that are more specific to certain aspects of the system can serve developers as feedback for improving their initial designs. A reliable measure of user satisfaction is the Questionnaire for User Interaction Satisfaction (QUIS) (Shneiderman & Plaisant, 2005). Like the End-User Computer Satisfaction questionnaire, QUIS is composed of subfactors, but the subfactors are more specific to HCI: screen factors, terminology and system feedback, learning factors, system capabilities, technical manuals, online tutorials, multimedia, voice recognition, virtual environments, Internet access, and software installation. The questionnaire can be configured according to the needs of each interface analysis by including only the relevant sections. Specific questionnaires such as QUIS are used to improve the HCI design according to users' feedback. The specific feedback helps to pinpoint the reasons for dissatisfaction (e.g., dissatisfaction with unfamiliar terminology), fix the problems, and increase the user's satisfaction.

In conclusion, satisfaction can be defined at the level of the entire system and at the more specific level of the human–computer interface. Both types of satisfaction measure users' attitudes toward a system after having used it or having been exposed to its design. The two questionnaires introduced here (many others exist), representing the general and the specific, overlap in the components of the system that pertain to the human–computer interface (i.e., format and ease of use). Each type is used for different purposes: the general for overall assessment, management of implementation, and indication of success and the specific for interface evaluation and feedback to improve the design.

## 4.3  Individual Differences and Training

Attitudes toward computers are influenced by individual characteristics such as personality and background. Individual differences in these characteristics affect the user's beliefs about use (perceived usefulness, ease of use, and enjoyment) and hence affect user attitudes. These individual traits can be classified as general traits, such as trait anxiety (a general feeling of anxiety when faced with some problem), or as specific traits that are defined for particular computer-related objects, such as computer anxiety. In this section we look at specific traits and mention the general traits only as a reference for comparison. This classification is analogous to the distinction between core affect and affective impressions described previously.

Acknowledging user diversity is an important guideline that we discuss in Chapter 8. We noted in our discussions of cognitive engineering that individuals differ in their cognitive capabilities, and these differences may imply different interactions by different people with the same system. Affect is personal, perhaps more so than cognition. Different people will react differently to a new laptop. One person may be amazed at the beauty of curves while another may be disappointed because he is used to straight lines (see Figure 6.3). A high proportion of respondents agreed with the labels "classical" and "futuristic." However, some people prefer classical and others futuristic. Some would be very pleased and aroused by the color and shapes in the futuristic design, while others would experience displeasure with it under certain conditions and would feel indifferent under other conditions. This section discusses differences in attitudes.

Individual differences in people's general attitudes toward computers take many forms. We have already examined computer anxiety. Another prime example is computer self-efficacy (Compeau & Higgins, 1995). Computer self-efficacy (CSE) refers to a person's evaluation of his or her capabilities to use computers in diverse situations. People with high CSE tend to form more positive perceptions of the benefits of using computers and therefore, according to the TAM discussed above, tend to use computers more frequently than those lower in CSE. This is similar to the influence of computer anxiety on attitudes and behavior (see Figure 6.8). Indeed, the two are usually correlated yet distinct. CSE is associated with a person's feelings about capabilities regardless of a particular act of using the computer. Computer anxiety is associated with feelings about the possible impact of using a particular system or class of systems.

Computer self-efficacy can be an obstacle to successful acceptance and effective use of a system. Individuals who are confident in their computer-related capabilities use computers more readily and achieve better performance. It is therefore imperative that we learn about our users and attempt to influence their CSE by appropriate training. In particular, Compeau and Higgins (1995) found that having model users demonstrate computer skills to trainees can significantly increase CSE. For example, users observed a videotaped model user solving problems with a spreadsheet. This experience of learning by observation appeared to boost their CSE and improve their performance.

Knowledge of individual differences is also important for designing computer training (Thatcher & Perrewe, 2002). For example, knowing the sources of self-efficacy or anxiety helps to shape the content and student composition in training classes. The right placement of users in training programs will allow the instructor to tailor the training to the particular predispositions. Coping with the specific trait of computer anxiety may be possible by focused instruction on the impact of the computer; however, this instruction may hardly be effective if the problem is general trait anxiety.

### 4.4 Summary of Attitudes

The measures we have discussed are not independent of one another. Using the measures reviewed here, Figure 6.8 presents a schematic view of how different factors of affect interact. It is based on the studies described above and meant to clarify the topic with a tentative picture rather than provide a definitive model. Perceptions of ease of use, usefulness, and enjoyment form the user's attitude toward using the system, thus determining the intention to use the computer. Once intentions materialize into actual use, we can also tap into the user's satisfaction from the system or its human–computer interface. In fact, use is a prerequisite for satisfaction; conversely, satisfaction will affect future use. The view in Figure 6.8 is of course a simplified view, but it does raise some interesting points. First, computer anxiety affects our perceptions of the effort and benefits in using computers. Reducing anxiety may well increase the positive perceptions. Second, following van der Heijden (2004), perceptions of usefulness and enjoyment determine our attitudes and intention to use, but their relative influence probably depends on whether the system is viewed as fun (pleasure-oriented) or as work (productivity-oriented).

In summary, we used several factors to demonstrate attitudes associated with using a computer. Others exist, and it may be important to find the factor that is most closely related to the issues that warrant measurement (see advanced reading by Sun & Zhang, 2006). In Chapter 7, which discusses evaluation and usability, we return to these factors and their measures and discuss their application in more detail.

## ▶ 5. FLOW AND PLAYFULNESS

We now turn to affect and cognition associated with the process of interacting with computers. How can we characterize the user's feeling during interaction with a computer? One of the most popular characterizations is the affective-cognitive concept of *flow*.

The theory of flow (Csikzentmihalyi, 1975) is a general psychological theory that has important implications for HCI design. Flow represents the user's perception of the medium as playful and engaging. The theory of flow suggests that involvement in a playful, exploratory experience is self-motivating because it is pleasurable and encourages repeated experiences (Webster, Trevino, & Ryan, 1993).

Flow is a complicated and multidimensional factor. Csikzentmihalyi (1975, p. 72) describes the flow state: "Players shift into a common mode of experience when they become absorbed in their activity. This mode is characterized by a narrowing of the focus of awareness, so that the irrelevant perceptions and thoughts are filtered out; by loss of self-consciousness, by a responsiveness to clear goals and unambiguous feedback; and by a sense of control over the environment . . . it is this common flow experience that people adduce as the main reason for performing an activity."

Flow is regarded as an optimal experience. However, the connotations of being absorbed in the interaction, lack of awareness of the surroundings, loss of control, or self-consciousness may seem troubling to some. Obsessive use of computers is often associated with loss of one's control of whether and when to use the computer. Clinical centers now address people characterized as computer addicts because they exhibit extreme dependence on computers and loss of control over daily decisions due to their need to access the Internet. Clearly, such attraction and absorption in the interaction is well beyond the notion of flow.

Flow can be measured. It can be defined as a continuous variable, ranging from lack of flow to intense flow. Trevino and Webster (1992) defined four dimensions of flow experience: (1) the extent to which the individual perceives a sense of control over the interaction with technology (control), (2) the individual perceives that his or her attention is focused on the interaction (attention focus), (3) the individual's curiosity is aroused during the interaction (curiosity), and (4) the individual finds the interaction intrinsically interesting (intrinsic interest).

HCI design should be undertaken with the above dimensions of flow in mind. Interfaces should afford users a perceived sense of control. Direct manipulation devices, navigation support, the ability to tailor the interface to meet individual preferences, validation of destructive actions, and so on all serve to enhance the user's perceived sense of control. The interface must also disappear into the background in order to give the user the perceived sense of interaction focus. The task is foremost, and the interface (like a pencil during the writing process) should require little or no attention from the user. Ease of use and learning and above all consistency in the interface design will support the perception of attention focus. Arousing the user's curiosity and creating intrinsic interest are related more strongly to content than to interface. However, the interface design can be used to draw the user into the content. Such design features as use of color, animation, sounds, and so on can draw the user's attention toward aspects of the content. The design of the content itself is all-important. The intrinsic aspect of "intrinsic interest" suggests that a user brings this interest to the interaction a priori. Therefore, attention to design aspects may have only limited impact on a preexisting interest or lack of interest in the content. For example, the organization of the Web site content, ease of navigation, speed, and general ease of transactions all affect the perception of control and playfulness and enhance the user's flow experience when interacting with a Web site (Raymond, Niekerk, & Berthon, 1999). If the Web site content is lacking, the other design factors will have little positive impact.

> **Flow:** The user's optimal experience of control, focus of attention, curiosity, and intrinsic interest.

## ▶ 6. SUMMARY

Affective engineering is an emerging element of HCI development that promises to become a common activity alongside physical and cognitive engineering. We look at affect in the process of interacting with the computer as well as attitudes before and after use. Attitudes and emotions feed into each other. Affective, as well as cognitive, processes generate attitudes, but at the same time, attitudes can be seen to affect the formation of emotions. Both aspects have practical implications.

We identify four major roles of affect in the process of interacting with computers: (1) modeling affect, (2) sensing and recognizing the user's affective state, (3) adapting the computer's state to fit the user's affective state, and (4) generating on the computer affective expressions. As HCI technologies advance, developers will increasingly engage in these activities. Unfortunately, evidence of affect and its impact on behavior is still scarce, so there are few clear-cut design guidelines. Developers are encouraged to be aware of the foundations explored in this chapter, be sensitive to the dilemmas (e.g., for or against anthropomorphic [humanlike] designs), and keep up-to-date with new developments.

The idea of recognizing the user's affective state and adapting the computer design accordingly parallels our discussion about cognitive aspects of fit in the previous chapter. Cognitive engineering strives to accomplish a fit between the design of the information

**Table 6.2** Attitudes and Related Factors in HCI

**Person and situation before interaction**

| | |
|---|---|
| Computer self-efficacy (CSE) | People's belief about their capabilities to use computers in diverse situations (Compeau & Higgins, 1995) |

**Interaction process**

| | |
|---|---|
| Flow | Holistic sensation that people feel when they act with total involvement (Trevino & Webster, 1992) |

**Impact of interaction**

| | |
|---|---|
| Perceived usefulness | People's belief that using the system will enhance their performance (Davis, 1989) |
| Perceived ease of use | People's belief that using a particular system would be free of effort (Davis, 1989) |
| Computer anxiety | Anxiety about the implications of using a computer such as the loss of important data or other important mistakes (Thatcher & Perrewe, 2002) |
| Perceived enjoyment | The extent to which fun can be derived from using the system as such |
| Satisfaction | The fulfillment of positive expectations of using a computer (Doll & Torkzadeh, 1988; QUIS) |

presented to the user and the user's intentions of using the information to complete the task at hand. Similarly, developers may consider accomplishing a fit between the affective impressions, the user's mood, and the task. The idea is to avoid a state of emotional conflict, which is an unpleasant state of dissonance. Computer-generated messages or affective expressions that trigger a user's reaction such as "I'm not in the mood for that" obviously do not represent a good fit. In contrast, tailoring the design factors to produce affective impressions that promote task accomplishment and the user's well-being represents a good fit. For example, using pastel colors for an e-commerce site that leaves the user feeling calm may generate a more compliant attitude and readiness to purchase (Zviran, Te'eni, & Gross, 2006). This view is depicted in Figure 6.6.

We also look at the important role of attitude and its related factors. Attitudes combine cognitive and affective processes to form evaluations of computers in general or of specific systems. Attitudes are of practical importance. First, attitudes represent evaluations of computer systems in terms of success or problems. Systems developers can react to users' perceptions of systems prior to or during systems development. Second, attitudes can be shaped and managed to some extent. Training users to appreciate the qualities of the system and their own skills is instrumental in reducing computer anxiety and enhancing positive attitudes. Furthermore, managing expectations and involving users in development have shown to be effective in easing acceptance and boosting satisfaction.

The application of attitudes to training begins with measurement. Table 6.2 summarizes several attitudes relevant to HCI and provides references that describe the corresponding measurement tools. These are tools developers can adapt to their own local needs. Strictly speaking, these measures are a mix of attitudes and their components (beliefs and emotions) as shown in Figure 6.8, but they can all be utilized in the development and management of IS. The measures are classified into three categories: measures associated with the situation or person before interaction with the computer, measures associated with the process of interaction, and measures associated with the expected impact of using the computer.

The concepts and tools of affective engineering covered in this chapter, along with those of physical and cognitive engineering, will be revisited and applied in the evaluation, analysis, and design of HCI. They provide the physical and psychological foundations for understanding the user.

## ▷ 7. SUMMARY OF CONCEPTS AND TERMS

| | |
|---|---|
| Affect | Affective quality |
| Core affect | Affective impression |
| Affective computing | Interactivity |
| TAM | Vividness |
| Emotion | Flow |
| Mood | Perceived ease of use |
| Attitude | Perceived usefulness |
| Perceived enjoyment | Computer anxiety |
| Satisfaction | Computer self-efficacy |

## ▷ 8. BIBLIOGRAPHY AND ADDITIONAL READINGS

Ajzen, I. (1991). The theory of planned behavior. *Organizational Behavior & Human Decision Processes, 50*(2), 179–211.

Ajzen, I. (2001). Nature and operation of attitudes. *Annual Review of Psychology, 52*, 27–58.

Bhattacherjee, A. (2001). Understanding information systems continuance: An expectation-confirmation model. *MIS Quarterly, 25*(3), 351–370.

Cheung, W., Chang, M. K., & Lai, V. S. (2000). Prediction of Internet and World Wide Web usage at work: A test of an extended Triandis model. *Decision Support Systems, 30*(1), 83–100.

Compeau, D. R., & Higgins, C. A. (1995). Computer self efficacy: Development of a measure and initial test. *MIS Quarterly, 19*(2), 189–211.

Csikzentmihalyi, M. (1975). Play and intrinsic rewards. *Humanistic Psychology, 15*(41–63).

Davis, F. (1989). Perceived usefulness, perceived ease of use, and user acceptance of information technology. *MIS Quarterly, 13*(3), 319–340.

Davis, F. D., Bagozzi, R. P., & Warshaw, P. R. (1989). User acceptance of computer technology: A comparison of two theoretical models. *Management Science, 35*(8), 982–1003.

Doll, W. J., & Torkzadeh, G. (1988). The measurement of end-user computing satisfaction. *MIS Quarterly, 12*(2), 259–274.

Ginzberg, M. J. (1981). Early diagnosis of MIS implementation failure: Promising results and unanswered questions. *Management Science, 27*(4), 459–479.

Hudlicka, E. (2003). To feel or not to feel: The role of affect in human-computer interaction. *International Journal of Human-Computer Studies, 59*(1–2), 1–32.

Igbaria, M., Parasuraman, S., & Baroudi, J. J. (1996). A motivational model of microcomputer usage. *Journal of Management Information Systems, 13*(1), 127.

Kim, J., Lee, J., & Choi, D. (2003). Designing emotionally evocative homepages: An empirical study of the quantitative relations between design factors and emotional dimensions. *International Journal of Human-Computer Studies, 59*(6), 899–940.

Lavie, T., & Tractinsky, N. (2004). Assessing dimensions of perceived visual aesthetics of web sites. *International Journal of Human-Computer Studies, 60*(3), 269–298.

Moon, J. Y., & Kim, J. (2003). Can interfaces affect users' feeling? A model of the impact of the customer interface on the shopping experience. Working paper.

Norman, D. A. (2004). *Emotional design: Why we love (or hate) everyday things.* Cambridge, MA: Basic Books.

Picard, R. W. (1997). *Affective computing.* Cambridge, MA: MIT Press.

QUIS. Retrieved from http://www.lap.umd.edu/QUIS/index.html

Raymond, D. N., Niekerk, V., & Berthon, J. P. (1999). Going with the flow: Web sites and customer involvement. *Internet Research, 9*(2), 109–116.

Reeves, B., & Nass, C. I. (1996). *The media equation: How people treat computers, televisions, and new media as real people and places.* New York: Cambridge University Press.

Russell, J. A. (2003). Core affect and the psychological construction of emotion. *Psychological Review, 110*(1), 145–172.

Schenkman, B. N., & Jonsson, F. U. (2000). Aesthetics and preferences of web pages. *Behaviour & Information Technology, 19*(5), 367–377.

Shneiderman, B., & Plaisant, C. (2005). *Designing the user interface: Strategies for effective human-computer interaction.* New York: Addison-Wesley.

Steuer, J. (1992). Defining virtual reality: Dimensions determining telepresence. *Journal of Communication, 42*(4), 73–93.

Sun, H., & Zhang, P. (2006). The role of affect in IS research: A critical survey and a research model. In P. Zhang & D. Galletta (Eds.), *Human-computer interaction and management information systems: Foundations.* Armonk, NY: M.E. Sharpe.

Thatcher, J. B., & Perrewe, P. L. (2002). An empirical examination of individual traits as antecedents to computer anxiety and computer self-efficacy. *MIS Quarterly, 26*(4), 381–396.

Tractinsky, N., Katz, A. S., & Ikar, D. (2000). What is beautiful is usable. *Interacting with Computers, 13*, 127–145.

Trevino, L. K., & Webster, J. (1992). Flow in computer-mediated communication. *Communication Research, 19*(5), 539–573.

van der Heijden, H. (2004). User acceptance of hedonic information systems. *MIS Quarterly, 28*(4).

Venkatesh, V., Morris, M. G., Davis, G. B., & Davis, F. D. (2003). User acceptance of information technology: Toward a unified view. *MIS Quarterly, 27*(3), 425–478.

Webster, J., Trevino, L. K., & Ryan, L. (1993). The dimensionality and correlates of flow in human-computer interactions. *Computers in Human Behavior, 9*(4), 411–426.

Zhang, P., & Li, N. (2005). The importance of affective quality. *Communications of the ACM.*

Zviran, M., Te'eni, D., & Gross, Y. (2006). Colored e-mail is cheap, but does it make a difference? *Communication of the ACM.* Forthcoming.

## ► 9. EXERCISES

Ex. 1.   Computer addiction

Perform a short Internet search on computer addiction in order to learn about the problem and compare it with the notion of flow. Summarize in brief (no more than one page) your findings and, in particular, refer to the dangers of computer addiction to individuals. Your summary should consist of your definition of computer addiction, an assessment of how prevalent the problem is, and a list of symptoms by which to identify computer addiction. Given your one-page summary, compare the symptoms of computer addiction with the notion of flow.

Ex. 2.   * Affective expressions

Work in pairs so that you can compare your individual impressions. Choose, together, a humanlike character on the Internet. One example is the broadcaster in Ananova (www.ananova.com).

A. Individually, make a list of at least five features of the character that you like. Similarly, make a list of features that you do not like. Answer the following questions: Do these features affect your attitude toward the system (and if so, how)? Do you feel more relaxed and less anxious with the system in comparison to similar systems without humanlike characters? Does the humanlike character add to the system's credibility, and are some features more important than others?

B. Compare your answers and summarize where you agree and disagree.

* This is a more difficult exercise

# 7

# EVALUATION

## CONTEXT AND PREVIEW

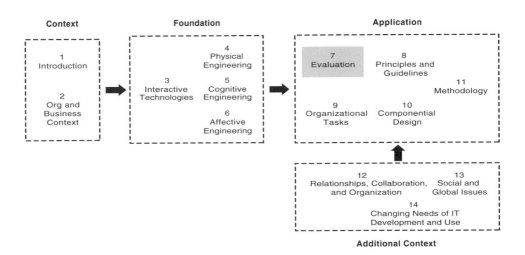

This chapter answers the questions of What to evaluate, Why to evaluate, When to evaluate, and How to evaluate. It outlines the ultimate concerns of human–computer interaction that are classified into multiple types. These ultimate concerns of HCI build on our discussions in early chapters of the book. Evaluations should be structured around supporting and verifying these concerns. Owing to the importance of usability and usability engineering in the HCI discipline and their broad coverage in many HCI-related books, we will briefly introduce the origin and historical development of usability concerns, and the issues in usability, usability engineering, and universal usability. Although many evaluation methods were presented as usability evaluation methods in other books, we point out that these methods can be used for evaluations that address other concerns besides usability, which is one of the several types of HCI concerns in this chapter. Specific evaluation methods and techniques are introduced along with examples of applying them. Finally, we introduce some standards that play an important role in the practice of HCI, usability, and evaluation. One particular standard is the Common Industry Format, whose detailed format is given in Appendix A. In Appendices B and C, we briefly describe some research tools and laboratories related to HCI studies.

This is also the first chapter in the Application section of the book. The purpose of the Application section is to demonstrate how various aspects we have studied so far can be put together to guide the development of human-centered information systems. In order to keep this goal in context, we will add one more figure, the HCI development methodology figure, at the beginning of all five chapters of the Application section. Each chapter's emphasis is highlighted in the methodology figure. For example, from the figure below, we can see that the materials of this chapter relate to three stages of the HCI development methodology, as shown by the shaded activities.

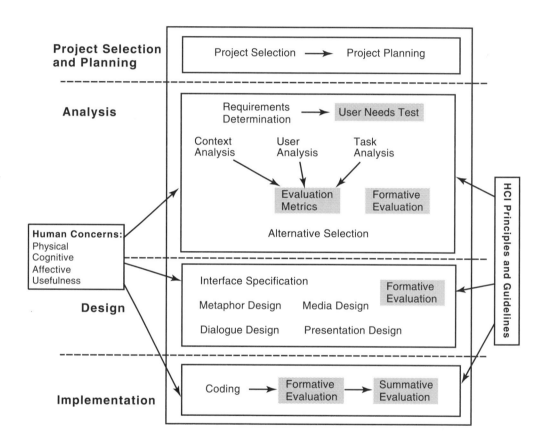

## LEARNING OBJECTIVES

Upon completion of this chapter, students should be able to do the following:

- Explain what evaluation is and why it is important
- Understand the different types of HCI concerns and their rationales
- Understand the relationships of HCI concerns with various evaluations
- Understand usability, usability engineering, and universal usability
- Understand different evaluation methods and techniques
- Select appropriate evaluation methods for a particular evaluation need
- Carry out effective and efficient evaluations
- Critique HCI designs or evaluations done by others
- Understand the reasons for setting up industry standards

## ▷ 1. INTRODUCTION

Evaluation is a general term for the determination of the significance, worth, condition, or value of something of interest by careful appraisal and study. Evaluation of an information system for organizational and individual use occurs constantly throughout the entire life cycle of the system. These evaluations can be grouped into two clusters. The first cluster of evaluation occurs when the system is being developed and prior to release and actual use, that is, during the development stage. The primary purpose of these evaluations is to test the system for functionality, usability, user experience, and any other aspects. All bugs, annoyances, and problems must be detected and fixed before the official release. User-needs testing, module testing, system testing, usability testing, and user experience testing all occur during this prerelease stage. We call this cluster Development Evaluations. The other cluster of evaluations happens when the system is released and is used by targeted users in a real context, that is, during the use and impact stage. The purpose of these evaluations is to better understand how the system impacts organizational, group, and individual tasks and activities. Such evaluations can further guide and change the design of future systems. We will call this cluster of evaluations Use and Impact Evaluations. The two clusters of evaluations differ in terms of at what stage of the system life cycle they occur. Many issues and concerns, such as what to evaluate and how to evaluate, are the same or similar to both clusters.

| **Evaluation:** The determination of the significance, worth, condition, or value by careful appraisal and study. |
| --- |

### 1.1 What to Evaluate: Multiple Concerns of HCI

The recent development and work on HCI from several related disciplines call for a reexamination of the fundamental concerns of human interaction with technologies. For example, Zhang and colleagues suggest revisiting Maslow's basic need hierarchy to ask what humans want or what they need in their lives, then to use technologies to support humans' higher needs in the need hierarchy (Zhang et al., 2002). From a slightly different angle, Maxwell suggests using Maslow's need hierarchy as an analogue for a HCI maturity model to represent a progression in the types of human needs and goals that the HCI discipline supports (Maxwell, 2002). Specifically, from the perspective that HCI is primarily a discipline focused on people, Maxwell identified three levels of HCI maturity: level 1 is basic usability; level 2 is collaborative, organizational, and role-based interaction; and level 3 is individualized and holistic interaction (Maxwell, 2002). The message is that human interaction with technologies should be driven by human's different levels of needs and goals; thus HCI can be viewed as using technologies to support a progression from basic to higher-level needs and goals of users (Zhang et al., 2002; Maxwell, 2002).

In order to take a systematic approach to identifying the true concerns of HCI, we can step back and think about humans interacting with technologies as a goal-driven behavior that has two main questions: what causes users to use technology, and why the use of technology is different among users or among situations (Zhang, Carey, Te'eni, & Tremaine, 2005). These questions fall in the general area of modern motivation studies, which attempt to answer two questions: what causes behavior, and why does behavior vary in its intensity (Reeve, 2005). Reeve suggests four sources of motivation: external events, needs, cognitions, and emotions. The latter three form internal motives that are internal processes that energize and direct behavior. External events are environmental incentives that have the capacity to energize and direct behavior. Needs (biological and psychological) are conditions within the individual that are essential and necessary for the maintenance of life and for the nurturance of growth and well-being. Cognitions refer to mental events, such as beliefs, expectations, and self-concept. Cognitive sources of motivation revolve around the person's ways of thinking. Emotions are short-lived attributed core effects (see Chapter 6). They orchestrate how we react adaptively to the important events in our lives (Reeve, 2005).

Building on the human-centered view where HCI support is driven by humans' needs and goals, we consider the following four types of HCI concerns along with the four aspects derived from the motivational theories discussed above: physical, cognitive, affective, and extrinsic motivational. The early chapters of the book provided the foundations to discuss these concerns. Next, we present the detailed discussions.

The first concern is at the user's physical level. The efforts and results in related disciplines (such as ergonomics, HCI, and MIS disciplines in studying human interaction with technologies) can be examined within the motivation framework using the human-centered view. For example, physical engineering (see Chapter 4) considers the physical aspect of humans interacting with devices including computers. The key issue is to design systems to achieve physical fit between humans and machines. This is based on the understanding of human physical limitations and potentials. Most concerns are studied around human sensors that interact with computers. For example, eyes should not become uncomfortable due to color uses or brightness of the computer screen displays; audio signals should be within the comfortable range of our normal hearing; muscles should not be hurt due to the operation demand the system imposes on its users; and people with certain disabilities should be considered properly in system designs. In general, the system should be safe for our health concerns.

The second concern has to do with the cognitive side support. Cognitive psychology and engineering (see Chapter 5) plays an important role in HCI. Perception, memory, mental models and metaphors, knowledge representations, problem solving, errors, and learning are all topics under cognitive psychology that have direct implications to HCI design. Usability engineering has largely built on cognitive psychology studies and applications in practice. Usability, or basic usability, includes aspects such as ease of use, ease of learning, error prevention, error recovery, and efficiency of performance. Usability has a strong cognitive component in that users need to comprehend the system to some extent in order to utilize it. Basic usability considerations are continuously needed for any systems to be used by humans. Among the four HCI concerns, the cognitive and physical concerns are relatively mature owing to more than two decades of work, especially in usability engineering. We will provide more details on usability and usability engineering in section 2 of this chapter.

The third type of HCI concern has to do with supporting the affective needs of the users (see Chapter 6). A significant movement in the psychology discipline in recent decades is that the affective aspect is moving to the mainstream of psychology (Russell, 2003; Forgas, 1995) with the realization that in a realistic situation, a human being has more than just the physical and cognitive aspects to be concerned with. This has also been reflected in studies in HCI (Brave & Nass, 2003) and in MIS (Sun & Zhang, 2006). This coincides with a shifting emphasis away from worker productivity and performance and toward enrichment of human lives. While productivity and performance concern the outcome of user tasks, affective experiences focus on the process of the task and overall well-being of the users. Being effective and efficient on tasks is now only one of the goals. Users want to be able to enjoy and be engaged in what they are doing. Recent studies indicate that beautiful things are easy to use (Tractinsky, Katz, & Ikar, 2000), pleasant things work better (Norman, 2004), and fun things make time fly (Agarwal & Karahanna, 2000). This is because these things have certain affective qualities (Zhang & Li, 2005) that meet our emotional needs. Studies on perceptions of affective quality (Zhang & Li, 2004, 2005) and aesthetics of IT (Kim, Lee, & Choi, 2003; Lavie & Tractinsky, 2004), the optimal flow experience (Chen, Wigand, & Nilan, 1999; Csikszentmihalyi, 1990; Ghani, 1995; Finneran & Zhang, 2003, 2005; Webster & Martocchio, 1992), cognitive absorption (Agarwal & Karahanna, 2000), emotion and affect (Norman, 2002; Sun & Zhang, 2005; Brave & Nass, 2003), engineering joy (Hassenzahl, Beu, & Burmester, 2001), and satisfaction (Bhattacherjee, 2001) are all related to this type of HCI concern. Chapter 6 covers some of the foundations of the affective dimension of HCI, as well as some of the concepts mentioned here such as optimal flow (or simply flow) and affective quality. Interested readers can find more from the references provided above on related concepts.

---

Personal story

Ping had a chance to visit Japan with a group of colleagues in the summer of 2002. One colleague brought her 17-year-old daughter along, who brought all her savings with her. During our shopping trip to the biggest electronic store in Tokyo, the girl went up to the digital camera section and bought one cute blue camera without any hesitation. When we asked her why she was buying this relatively expensive camera, she said, "Because it was in blue color, my favorite. I have been looking for such a camera in the U.S. for a long time. And this one was the only type that has blue color. I am so happy I finally found it."

The camera is more than just a tool for taking pictures. This girl regards it as a personal favorite and as a way of distinguishing and representing herself. We have seen this phenomenon in cell phone skins, desktop skins, and even cars.

Cars are even more typical examples of people's desire to achieve a holistic experience while interacting with them. A car is more than a tool to get someone or something from point A to point B. We desire a lot more from a car: its aesthetic design, chosen color, convenient features, and other aspects that make us feel powerful and in control. The competition of similar products eventually gets down to the point when we must decide which product and all its properties and features would make us feel better overall. There is a reason for such markets: People have higher desires or needs. These desires and needs are beyond what the basic functionality and usability can support.

---

Finally, the fourth concern is about the extrinsic motivation of using the technology. Within the organizational context, it is about technology being useful to one's job or work. In the MIS discipline, it is well understood that some extrinsic motivation, such as the usefulness of IT, plays an important role in users' IT behavior (Davis, 1989; Venkatesh, Morris, Davis, & Davis, 2003). Usefulness, or *utility* in Grudin and Nielsen's terminology (Grudin, 1992; Nielsen, 1993), is an HCI concern. It links closely to system functionality and requirements specification. From an HCI perspective, if a system is useful or even perceived to be useful, users will be more likely to start the initial interaction and continue to interact with the system. That is, users interact with, adopt, and use technologies largely because they perceive that the technology can be used to achieve desired goals. Technology should extend humans' capabilities, be they physical, cognitive, affective, or behavioral, and allow them to do things in certain ways that they could not do otherwise. In other words, no matter how easy or how attractive an IT may appear to the potential users, few people will use it if its functions are not perceived to be useful to help fulfill some needs or goals.

While the above discussions all have to do with the direct layer between human and IT, there is another external event that can play an important role in the ways humans behave around IT. This is the sociological, organizational, and cultural impact of computing (Maxwell, 2002). In other words, this is between the IT and the context while humans interacts with IT, namely the organizational, social, and cultural context. This is largely due to the broad adoption of IT by organizations and society to support organizational functions and goals and to enhance society's development. For example, organizational efficiency may be expected due to redesign of work flows among critical business units that are affected by the implemented IT; satisfaction and retention of customers/clients are anticipated due to accurate and fast information gathering and presentations, to name a few. It is noteworthy that some of the organizational or societal impacts may not be tangible or directly attributed to HCI considerations. This is in line with the issues of determining IT values in organizations and societies. To make HCI concerns clear to the students and designers to guide their practice, we consider the direct layer concerns between humans and IT.

Personal story

Ping once owned a classic Macintosh in the early 1990s, one that had a nine-inch mono-colored monitor as part of the body of the machine. The machine came with several preinstalled software applications and games. Many of these applications did not have a good online manual indicating what they could do or what games they were and how to play. As a result, most of these applications were never used during the five-year life of the machine.

There are still many software applications out there these days that are in a similar situation. Their purposes or functions are not well documented and revealed. If these are popular applications such as MS Word, then there is little problem. But given that there are so many applications or freeware programs available, not every one of them will be popular. For example, a technical staff member installed the following software on Ping's new machine: Ad-Aware. She might have explained to Ping what it was. But later on, Ping forgot what it was about. Ping might be able to find out by surfing the Internet. But why would the user take the effort to do so? Why cannot such important information be included in its online manual or on the first page once it is displayed?

Not knowing the usefulness of a software application, no matter how easy it might be, how attractive it may look, or how cheap it is, users would not accept or adopt it. The result is a total waste.

Table 7.1 summarizes the human concerns of HCI with some measurable items for each type of concerns (Zhang et al., 2005). These items can represent different aspects of the type. Generally speaking, these four types of HCI concerns have influence on each other. For example, physical and cognitive concerns are less relevant if the usefulness concern is not resolved. Simply speaking, few people would use any technology that is easy to use but useless. Emotional support depends on high usefulness, usability, and beyond.

**Table 7.1**  Multiple Concerns of HCI (Adapted from Zhang et al., 2005)

| HCI Concern | Description | Sample Measure Items |
|---|---|---|
| Physical | System fits our physical strengths and limitations and does not cause harm to our health | Legible<br>Audible<br>Safe to use |
| Cognitive | System fits our cognitive strengths and limitations and functions as the cognitive extension of our brain | Fewer errors and easy recovery<br>Easy to use<br>Easy to remember how to use<br>Easy to learn |
| Affective | System satisfies our aesthetic and affective needs and is attractive for its own sake | Aesthetically pleasing<br>Engaging<br>Trustworthy<br>Satisfying<br>Enjoyable<br>Entertaining<br>Fun |
| Usefulness | Using the system would provide rewarding consequences | Support individual's tasks<br>Can do some tasks that would not be possible without the system<br>Extend one's capability<br>Rewarding |

The multiple concerns of HCI can also be closely linked to the fit idea (fit between human, computer, and task) and to the outcomes such as performance and well-being, as demonstrated in Figure 1.4 in Chapter 1. Performance can be considered at both the micro level and the macro level. At the micro or action level, users' error rates, action speed, learning speed, and so on are important to consider. This is exactly what the cognitive concern is about. At a macro level, we are concerned with whether users can achieve their organizational task goals. This is linked to the usefulness concerns in Table 7.1. Finally, a user's well-being may not be directly measured by performance alone but has its own worth. In our discussion, well-being can be considered from all three aspects: physical, cognitive, and affective. These are linked directly to the first three types of concerns in Table 7.1.

The human concerns of HCI guide the development of an HCI project, as depicted in the Human-Centered Systems Development Life Cycle (HCSDLC) methodology, to be introduced in Chapter 11. The multi-type concerns are particularly relevant to the development of HCI evaluation metrics, to be discussed later in this chapter.

## 1.2  Why to Evaluate

At the beginning of this chapter, we discussed that *evaluation* is a general term for the determination of the significance, worth, condition, or value of something we are interested in. The goal of the evaluation is to provide feedback in system development, thus supporting an iterative development process (Gould & Lewis, 1985). System development is a complex process. A different kind of evaluation feedback is needed to provide insight on whether the development is moving toward the desired values and significance. It is also important to understand whether the development and the final product achieved the intended values and significance.

Personal story

Ping received a Palm PDA as a Christmas gift in 1999. It was a thrill at the time. In five minutes, she figured out all the functions and tricks and loved it. It was certainly easy to use. Everything was clearly self-explanatory and she had no trouble understanding any part. She immediately put it in use and started to rely on it for all scheduling-based activities. She also used the hot sync to share data with her desktop PC.

Then there was an accident. The desktop Palm program crashed, so she had to reinstall a new one. After the installation, she put the PDA on the hot sync seat and pushed the button, intending to back up the data from the PDA to the desktop. Then on the desktop, everything showed blank! Checking on the PDA, all data entries were gone! After a few minutes of troubleshooting, she realized that the Palm hot sync program automatically detects the most recent version of data, either on the PDA or on the desktop, and then overrides the less recent version without any warning or confirmation from the user. Since she just installed the desktop one, the date of the data files was newer than that of the PDA. So the PDA was "updated" to be consistent with the desktop! This accident erased six months' worth of data. Unfortunately, no backup was made prior to that.

The supposed "smart" feature of automatically detecting the most recent version of data can backfire at some unexpected occasions. This example illustrates that if such occasions were either considered in the design stage of the system or identified during the evaluation stage and then fixed before release, they would not cause damage to the users.

Preece and colleagues list four main reasons for conducting evaluation (Preece et al., 1994):

1. Understanding the real world. How do users employ the technology in the workplace? Can designs be improved to fit the work environment better?

2. Comparing designs. Which is the best? There are various occasions when designers want to compare two or more designs or design ideas. For example, early in the design process, there may be debate about exactly which functions are essential and how best to represent them on the screen. On such occasions designers may run tests to compare two or more designs.

3. Engineering toward a target. Is it good enough? Here the design process can be viewed as a form of engineering. The designers have a target, which is often expressed as some form of metric, and their goal is to make sure that their design produces a product that reaches this goal. Two possibilities are that a product is at least as good as that of a competitor's for a particular set of features and that the newer versions are at least as good as the older ones.

4. Checking conformation to a standard. Does this product conform to the standard? For example, is the screen legibility acceptable? Standards bodies or institutes have rigorous testing procedures to ensure that products conform to the standards that they have set.

In the previous section of this chapter, we presented four types of human–computer interaction concerns. Evaluations are to ensure that each of these concerns are targeted and achieved.

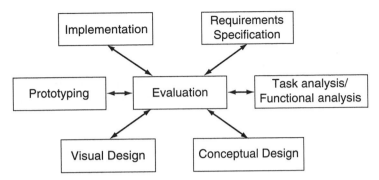

**Figure 7.1**  Evaluation as the center of systems development (adapted from Hix & Hartson, 1993).

## 1.3  When to Evaluate

A product is evaluated during its entire life cycle. Therefore, evaluation is basically an ongoing process. Figure 7.1 depicts the central role of evaluation during a system's development. In this "Star Life Cycle" model (Hix & Hartson, 1993), evaluation occurs at each stage of the development process and is regarded as the center of the development. Different evaluation methods can be used to address specific evaluation issues at each development stage

According to the purpose and timing, evaluations can be classified as formative evaluations and summative evaluations. *Formative evaluations* take place during the development of a product in order to form or influence design decisions. They answer the question "What and how to redesign?" (Rosson & Carroll, 2002) *Summative evaluations* are conducted after the product is finished to ensure that it meets a certain level of quality, meets certain standards, or satisfies certain requirements set by the sponsors or other agencies. They answer the question "How well did we do?" (Rosson & Carroll, 2002).

Besides evaluations that occur during development (formative evaluations) and after the product is finished but prerelease (summative evaluations), evaluations should continue after release and during the actual use by real users in real contexts. This type of evaluation is called *use and impact evaluation*. There are several reasons for use and impact evaluations. First, resistance to IT is a widespread problem in organizations. IT cannot improve individual and organizational performance if it is not used. The use evaluation can provide a realistic picture of how users actually react, adopt, accept, and use the product in the real context. The Technology Acceptance Model (TAM) and related studies that we introduced in earlier chapters explain and predict user acceptance, intentions, and behavior (Davis, 1989; Venkatesh et al., 2003). Second, just using IT does not mean that expected performance and productivity can be achieved. A fit between user tasks and technology features is a key to achieving desired task and organizational performance and productivity. There are several IS models on fit, such as cognitive fit (Vessey & Galletta, 1991; Vessey, 1991) and task-technology fit (TTF) (Goodhue & Thompson, 1995). These models address the issues related to use evaluation. The understanding of actual use can provide feedback for the next version or future development of similar products. Third, it is of great concern to the research and design community to know the impact of a software product on users, organizations, society, and culture. This impact evaluation has value beyond interface design and system design. It has high-level contributions to our overall understanding of human interaction with IT and the impact of such interaction within a large context, thus to our decision on future IT development.

**Formative evaluation:** Conducted during the development of a product in order to form or influence design decisions.

**Summative evaluation:** Conducted after the product is finished to ensure that it possesses certain quality, meets certain standards, or satisfies certain requirements set by the sponsors or other agencies.

**Use and impact evaluation:** Conducted during the actual use of the product by real users in real context.

**Longitudinal Evaluation:** involving the repeated observation or examination of a set of subjects over time with respect to one or more evaluation variables.

An evaluation can consist of a one-time data collection of evaluation measures. The collected data reflects the current state of the system, whether in development or in actual use. Software systems progress through many states, and the users' interaction with them can evolve as well. Thus one-time data collection is more of a snapshot-based approach that cannot reveal other dynamic natures of the system or its use by users. An alternative approach is longitudinal evaluation, which involves the repeated observation or examination of a set of subjects over time with respect to one or more evaluation variables. A series of data collections and associated analyses are conducted over a period of time. Longitudinal evaluations provide much rich understanding on the dynamics of users interacting with the product. On the other hand, this type of evaluations is more expensive and time-consuming.

## 1.4 Issues in Evaluation

There are several issues related to evaluations. One issue concerns the objectivity and subjectivity of an evaluation. Evaluations should be based on real phenomenon and should be repeatable. Thus evaluations should be objective. On the other hand, evaluations are dependent on the subjective interpretation of the evaluators. Thus evaluations may be biased.

Another important issue in evaluations is to follow established human rights protection procedures if human subjects are involved. This normally includes a consent from the subjects (either signed or clearly stated in a coversheet) so that subjects are aware of what is involved in the evaluation. The privacy and personal data of individual subjects should be protected. Many universities, organizations, and professional societies require evaluators to file a petition for using human subjects in their studies. Such petitions are reviewed by a board pertinent to using human subjects in studies. No evaluations should be conducted before such petitions are approved. Tables 7.2 and 7.3 show two sample consent forms that can be used in different situations.

The third issue is to identify several determinants of an evaluation plan. For example, Shneiderman and Plaisant (2005) listed the following:

- Stage of design (early, middle, late)
- Novelty of product (well-defined versus exploratory)
- Number of expected users
- Criticality of the interface (e.g., life-critical medical system versus museum exhibit support)
- Costs of product and finances allocated for test
- Time available
- Experience of the design and evaluation team

Once the above factors are identified and determined, one or more evaluation methods can be used. Normally evaluation methods determine the data collection method and the nature of data (such as quantitative or qualitative, one-time or longitudinal). Yet, there are some general issues on conducting evaluation, analyzing data, and interpreting and presenting results.

**Table 7.2** Sample Consent Form That Can Appear at the Beginning of a Survey Instrument

This is a survey of students' opinions on WebCT. It is conducted by School of Information Studies at Syracuse University under the supervision of Dr. Ping Zhang. The result of this survey will help us better understand how students react to WebCT, thus provide potential suggestions for necessary improvement. Your candid participation is greatly appreciated. This survey will take you about 10 minutes. There are no right or wrong answers. Please answer all the questions in the order presented. All answers are confidential and for research purposes only. Completing the survey signifies consent to participate in the research.

**Table 7.3** Sample Consent Form That Needs Signature

My name is Dr. Ping Zhang, Professor at Syracuse University. I am inviting you to participate in a research study. Involvement in the study is voluntary, so you may choose to participate or not. Please feel free to ask questions about the research if you have any. I will be happy to explain anything in greater detail if you wish.

I am interested in learning more about the impact of Web page designs on an individual's information-seeking performance. You are to look for information on specifically designed Web pages and answer questions. You are also expected to compete with other members in the group on task performance. To appreciate your effort, I will give away some prizes based on task performance. The Instruction sheet will provide more details. Information related to this study will be kept anonymous and confidential. This means that your identity will not appear anywhere and no one will know about your specific answers except myself.

The benefit of this research is that you will be helping me as a researcher to understand the impact of Web page designs on individual performance. The risk to you of participating in this study is possible eye fatigue, which is very minor and no more than that caused by your daily computer use. The risk is minimized since the experiment lasts a very short period. If you no longer wish to continue, you have the right to withdraw from the study, without penalty, at any time.

**** **** **** ****

All of my questions have been answered and I wish to participate in this research study.

_____   _____   _____
(Print participant name)   (Signature)   (Date)

Reliability of a method is how well it produces the same results in a different study but under the same circumstances. Different methods have different degrees of reliability. For example, lab experiments, when conducted correctly, have high reliabilities. In contrast, an unstructured interview may lead to a very low reliability.

Validity is concerned with whether the evaluation technique measures what it is meant to measure. This has two aspects: the method itself including its instrument, if any, and the process of conducting this evaluation.

## ▶ 2. USABILITY AND USABILITY ENGINEERING

Owing to the importance of usability in the history and the fact that it is covered extensively in many HCI-related textbooks and other reference books, we will use this section to give a brief introduction to its development and major achievements. Although work on usability has historically emphasized cognitive aspects, many of the evaluation methods labeled as usability methods can also be applied to evaluate the other concerns of HCI.

### 2.1 The Origin of Usability Concerns

Early computers were designed for professionals to use and were constrained mainly by the hardware (e.g., processing power and memory). Software was not a major concern as software was relatively simple compared to today's software and was used for specific needs. The use of the software required special training and was not intended for people other than professionals. Thus there were no "end users."

In the 1960s, the challenges of software development became enormous due to advancements on the hardware side and various information processing needs in science and business domains. Software systems grew with greater scale and complexity. The resulting failures, cost overruns, late deliveries, and ineffective and unreliable systems were labeled the software crisis. This crisis led to the emergence of software engineering as a professional discipline (Rosson & Carroll, 2002).

Through the 1970s, it became clear that an important component of software engineering would be the user interface design. As more and more software was developed for interactive use, attention to the needs and preferences of end users intensified (Rosson & Carroll, 2002).

With the wide adoption of the PCs in the early 1980s, many nonprofessionals became the primary users of the interactive systems, making the demand on easy-to-use interfaces much higher than ever.

As end users became more diverse and less technically savvy, interactive systems came to be compared and evaluated with respect to usability—the quality of a system with respect to ease of learning, ease of use, and user satisfaction (Rosson & Carroll, 2002).

### 2.2 Usability Definitions

> **Usability:**
> The extent to which a system with given functionality can be used by specified users to achieve specified goals with effectiveness, efficiency, and satisfaction in a specified context of use.

ISO (International Standards Organization) defines *usability* as "the extent to which a product can be used by specified users to achieve specified goals with effectiveness, efficiency, and satisfaction in a specified context of use" (ISO, in Bevan, 2001). This is the definition we adopt in this book, where *product* is taken to mean a computerized system with given functionality.

Jakob Nielsen uses slightly different definitions for the same terms. He considers usability part of system acceptability and defines it as how well users can use the functionality or utility of a system (Nielsen, 1993). Figure 7.2 demonstrates this idea. According to Nielsen, system acceptability is determined by social acceptability and practical acceptability. The latter has five aspects; one of them is usefulness, which is determined by utility and usability. Usability is not a one-dimensional property of a system but has multiple components and is associated with five attributes: learnability, efficiency, memorability, errors, and satisfaction (Nielsen, 1993). Table 7.4 lists the detailed definitions for the usefulness-related concepts in Figure 7.2.

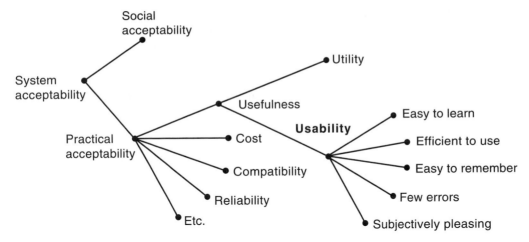

**Figure 7.2**  System acceptability and usability (adapted from Nielsen, 1993).

**Table 7.4**  Nielsen's Definitions

**Usefulness:** The issue of whether the system can be used to achieve some desired goal.

**Utility:** The question of whether the functionality of the system in principle can do what is needed.

**Usability:** The question of how well users can use that functionality.

**Learnability:** The system should be easy to learn so that the user can rapidly start getting some work done with the system.

**Efficiency:** The system should be efficient to use, so that once the user has learned the system, a high level of productivity is possible.

**Memorability:** The system should be easy to remember, so that the casual user is able to return to the system after some period of not having used it, without having to learn everything all over again

**Errors:** The system should have a low error rate, so that users make few errors during the use of the system; if they do make errors, they should be able to easily recover from them. Further, catastrophic errors must not occur.

**Satisfaction:** The system should be pleasant to use, so that users are subjectively satisfied when using it; they like it.

## 2.3  Usability Engineering

*Usability engineering* is a process through which usability characteristics are specified, quantitatively and early in the development process, and measured throughout the process (Hix & Hartson, 1993). The term *usability engineering* was coined by usability profession-als from Digital Equipment Corporation in the 1980s (Rosson & Carroll, 2002). They used the term to refer to concepts and techniques for planning, achieving, and verifying objectives for systems usability. Usability engineering is a set of activities that ideally take place

> **Usability engineering:** A process through which usability characteristics are specified, quantitatively and early in the development process, and measured throughout the process.

throughout the life cycle of the product, with significant activities happening at the early stages before the user interface has ever been designed (Nielsen, 1993). Usability engineering became a major movement in industry. There are "discount usability engineering" and usability engineering life cycle models to guide interactive systems development practice (Nielsen, 1993; Mayhew, 1999). Discount usability engineering emphasizes simple methods, fast process, and cheap cost for conducting usability studies.

### 2.4 Universal Usability

With the globalization of computer technology and software applications, especially with the development and utilization of the Internet, the diversity of human users and their potential interaction with the available IT became a major concern (Shneiderman, 2000). Understanding the physical, intellectual, personality, cultural, demographic, and hardware/software differences between users is vital for expanding market share, supporting required government services, and enabling creative participation by the broadest possible set of users (Shneiderman & Plaisant, 2005). Shneiderman thus envisioned and defined that "Universal Usability will be met when affordable, useful, and usable technology accommodates the vast majority of the global population: this entails addressing challenges of technology variety, user diversity, and gaps in user knowledge in ways only beginning to be acknowledged by educational, corporate, and government agencies." (Shneiderman, 2000)

## ▶ 3. EVALUATION METHODS

There are many evaluation methods and techniques, and there are different ways of clustering them. For example, Baecker and colleagues summarized research and evaluation methods into four types, as depicted in Table 7.5. This table gives readers a summary of the types of evaluation methods that are used in research and practice.

In this chapter, we do not intend to cover all evaluation methods that appeared in Table 7.5. Instead, we focus on several ones that are either commonly used or are beneficial to use in our opinion. We group these evaluation methods into the following categories: analytical evaluations and empirical evaluations. The former includes methods such as heuristic evaluation, guideline review, cognitive walk-through, and TSSL-guided evaluation. The latter includes lab experiment, survey, interview and focus group, field study, and field experiment. The main difference is that analytical evaluations normally do not need collected evidence from users but rely on evaluators using structured approaches for inspections and evaluations, while empirical evaluations draw conclusions based on empirical data, which can be qualitative or quantitative in nature. For each method, we try to describe it from the following six aspects:

- Method and key ideas
- Special framework or model to be used
- Context or environment
- Whether to involve users
- Whether to consider user task, work, or activity
- The status of the artifact being evaluated (early, late or finished, or in use)

**Table 7.5**  HCI Research and Evaluation Strategies (Adapted from Baecker, Grudin, Buxton, & Greenberg, 1995)

| Field Strategies | Respondent Strategies |
|---|---|
| (Settings under conditions as natural as possible) | (Settings are muted or made moot) |
| **Field studies**<br>Ethnography and interaction analysis<br>Contextual inquiry | **Judgment studies**<br>Usability inspection methods (e.g., heuristic evaluation) |
| **Field experiments**<br>Beta testing of products<br>Studies of technological change | **Sample surveys**<br>Questionnaires<br>Interviews |

| Experimental Strategies | Theoretical Strategies |
|---|---|
| (Settings concocted for research purposes) | (No observation of behavior required) |
| **Experimental simulations**<br>Usability testing<br>Usability engineering | **Formal theory**<br>Design theory (e.g., Norman's seven stages)<br>Behavioral theory (e.g., color vision) |
| **Laboratory experiments**<br>Controlled experiments | **Computer simulations**<br>Human information processing theory |

## 3.1 Analytical Methods

Analytical methods are normally conducted by experts or designers to inspect potential design problems. Most of them do not need to involve users. Most of them use rather structured approaches to conduct evaluations. The commonly used methods include (1) heuristic evaluation, (2) guideline review, (3) cognitive walk-through, (4) pluralistic walk-through, (5) framework-based inspection such as using the Task-Semantic-Syntactic-Lexical (TSSL) model, and (6) user model-based analysis, such as using the GOMS model (Card, Moran, & Newell, 1983) to predict user's behavior and performance during interaction with a computer system. In this section, we introduce the first five types of analytical methods. For the GOMS model and evaluation method, see Chapter 5 for more discussions.

### 3.1.1 Heuristic Evaluation

Heuristic evaluation is an informal usability inspection method developed by Nielsen and colleagues (Nielsen & Mack, 1994). In a recent study, it was identified as the most widely adopted usability evaluation approach in practice due to its ease of application, low cost, shallow learning curve, applicability early in the development process, and ability to generate effective evaluation without the need for professional evaluators (Vredenburg, Mao, Smith, & Carey, 2002). A group of evaluators (experts, developers, or even novices who can be trained to conduct the evaluation), guided by a set of higher-level usability principles known as usability heuristics, evaluate whether user-interface elements conform to the principles. User interface elements can include dialog boxes,

> **Heuristic evaluation:** A group of experts, guided by a set of higher level design principles or heuristics, evaluate whether interface elements conform to the principles.

menus, navigation structure, online help, and so on. These heuristics closely resemble the design principles in Chapter 8, although there are more principles in practice than what we cover in Chapter 8.

The conduction of a heuristic evaluation requires first an adoption of a limited set of heuristics that are easy to understand and relevant to the product and on which evaluators can be trained if necessary. Then the process of heuristic evaluation takes place, which consists of the following:

- A briefing session, in which the evaluators are told what to do. A prepared script is useful as a guide and to ensure that each person receives the same briefing.
- The evaluation period, in which each evaluator typically spends one to two hours independently inspecting the product, using the heuristics for guidance. Several passes may be necessary to develop a better understanding of the product and thus detect its problems. Depending on the nature of the product and its status in the development process, sometimes evaluators have to put user tasks in mind when going through the product.
- A debriefing session, in which the experts come together to discuss their findings, remove duplicates, prioritize the problems found, and suggest solutions.

There are generic heuristics, such as the 10 usability heuristics by Nielsen (see Table 7.6) and eight golden rules by Shneiderman (Table 7.7). The design guidelines introduced in Chapter 8 have a function similar to that of heuristics. If these heuristics are too general for a particular system or product, they can be tailored to specific products. For example, the HOMERUN heuristics (Table 7.8) by Nielsen (2000) are more appropriate for evaluating commercial Web sites. For designing documentations of software and hardware, either hard copies or online manuals, there is a set of design principles or heuristics by Mehlenbacher (2003).

Empirical evidence shows that five evaluators can normally detect around 75 percent of the total usability problems (Nielsen & Mack, 1994). The expertise of evaluators does matter, and more-experienced evaluators can detect more problems.

**Table 7.6**   Ten Usability Heuristics (From Nielsen & Mack, 1994, p. 30)

| Rules | Description |
| --- | --- |
| Visibility of system status | The system should always keep users informed about what is going on, through appropriate feedback within reasonable time. |
| Match between system and the real world | The system should speak the users' language, with words, phrases, and concepts familiar to the user, rather than system-oriented terms. Follow real-world conventions, making information appear in a natural and logical order. |
| User control and freedom | Users often choose system functions by mistake and will need a clearly marked "emergency exit" to leave the unwanted state without having to go through an extended dialogue. Support undo and redo. |
| Consistency and standards | Users should not have to wonder whether different words, situations, or actions mean the same thing. Follow platform conventions. |
| Error prevention | Even better than good error messages is a careful design that prevents a problem from occurring in the first place. |

| | |
|---|---|
| Recognition rather than recall | Make objects, actions, and options visible. The user should not have to remember information from one part of the dialogue to another. Instructions for use of the system should be visible or easily retrievable whenever appropriate. |
| Flexibility and efficiency of use | Accelerators—unseen by the novice user—may often speed up the interaction for the expert user such that the system can cater to both inexperienced and experienced users. Allow users to tailor frequent actions. |
| Aesthetic and minimalist design | Dialogues should not contain information that is irrelevant or rarely needed. Every extra unit of information in a dialogue competes with the relevant units of information and diminishes their relative visibility. |
| Help users recognize, diagnose, and recover from errors | Error messages should be expressed in plain language (no codes), precisely indicate the problem, and constructively suggest a solution. |
| Help and documentation | Even though it is better if the system can be used without documentation, it may be necessary to provide help and documentation. Any such information should be easy to search, be focused on the user's task, list concrete steps to be carried out, and not be too large. |

**Table 7.7**  Eight Golden Rules for User Interface Design (Shneiderman & Plaisant, 2005)

| Rules | Description |
|---|---|
| Strive for consistency | This rule is the most frequently violated one, but following it can be tricky because there are many forms of consistency. Consistent sequences of actions should be required in similar situations; identical terminology should be used in prompts, menus, and help screens; consistent color, layout, capitalization, fonts, and so on should be employed throughout. Exceptions, such as required confirmation of the delete command or no echoing of passwords, should be comprehensible and limited in number. |
| Cater to universal usability | Recognize the needs of diverse users and design for plasticity, facilitating transformation of content. Novice–expert differences, age ranges, disabilities, and technology diversity each enrich the spectrum of requirements that guides design. Adding features for novices, such as explanations, and adding features for experts, such as shortcuts and faster pacing, can enrich the interface design and improve perceived system quality. |
| Offer informative feedback | For every user action, there should be some system feedback. For frequent and minor actions, the response can be modest, whereas for infrequent and major actions, the response should be more substantial. Visual presentation of the objects of interest provides a convenient environment for showing changes explicitly. |
| Design dialogs to yield closure | Sequence of actions should be organized into groups with a beginning, middle, and end. Informative feedback at the completion of a group of actions gives operators the satisfaction of accomplishment, a sense of relief, the signal to drop contingency plans from their minds, and a signal to prepare for the next group of actions. |

**Table 7.7**  Eight Golden Rules for User Interface Design (Shneiderman & Plaisant, 2005)

| | |
|---|---|
| Prevent errors | As much as possible, design the system so that users cannot make serious errors. If a user makes an error, the interface should detect the error and offer simple, constructive, and specific instructions for recovery. Erroneous actions should leave the system state unchanged, or the interface should give instructions about restoring the state. |
| Permit easy reversal of actions | As much as possible, actions should be reversible. This feature relieves anxiety, since the user knows that errors can be undone, thus encouraging exploration of unfamiliar options. The units of reversibility may be a single action, a data-entry task, or a complete group of actions, such as entry of a name and the address book. |
| Support internal locus of control | Experienced operators strongly desire the sense that they are in charge of the interface and that the interface responds their actions. Surprising interface actions, tedious sequences of data entries, inability to obtain or difficulty in obtaining necessary information, and inability to produce the action desired all build anxiety and dissatisfaction. |
| Reduce short-term memory load | The limitation of human information processing in short-term memory requires that displays be kept simple, multiple-page displays be consolidated, window-motion frequency be reduced, and sufficient training time be allotted for codes, mnemonics, and sequences of actions. Where appropriate, online access to command-syntax forms, abbreviations, codes, and other information should be provided. |

**Table 7.8**  HOMERUN Heuristics for Commercial Web sites (Nielsen, 2000)

**Description**

- **H**igh-quality content
- **O**ften updated
- **M**inimal download time
- **E**ase of use
- **R**elevant to users' needs
- **U**nique to the online medium
- **N**et-centric corporate culture

### 3.1.2 Guideline Review

The interface is checked for conformance with the organizational or other guidelines document (Shneiderman & Plaisant, 2005). Example guidelines include those early Apple and Microsoft guidelines that were influential for desktop-interface design and were followed by many designers. A guidelines document helps by developing a shared language and then promoting consistency among multiple designers in terminology, appearance, and action sequences. It records best practices derived from practical experience or empirical studies with appropriate examples and counterexamples. Since many guidelines documents are very detailed and specific, guideline review can be very lengthy and time-consuming.

Guideline reviews occur in the design context or environment. They normally do not require using real users. They are conducted by designers or experts outside the design team. Some guideline reviews do consider user tasks or activities. For example, there are specific guidelines for navigation, data entry, and getting the user's attention. These types of evaluations can happen at both early and late stages of the development. They can also be used for summative evaluation on finished products.

### 3.1.3 Cognitive Walk-Through

Imagine that someone asks you how many windows there are in your parents' house, which is far away from where you live now. It is impossible for you to physically examine the house. Very likely, however, you would mentally walk through every room of the house and count the windows while "walking." This is a simple example of a cognitive walk-through. Experts can examine and discover potential usability problems by cognitively walking through the system pretending they are the users, especially novice users.

Cognitive walk-throughs "involve simulating a user's problem-solving process at each step in the human-computer dialog, checking to see if the user's goals and memory for actions can be assumed to lead to the next correct action" (Nielsen & Mack, 1994). Cognitive walk-throughs are conducted by evaluation experts and do not need to involve users. A typical example would be to walk through the activities (cognitive and operational) that are required to get from one screen to another in order to get certain tasks done (Preece et al., 1994). Before doing the walk-through, experts determine the exact task that will be done, the context in which it will be done, and their assumptions about the user population. They then walk through the task, reviewing the actions that are necessary to achieve the task, and attempt to predict how the user population would most likely behave and the problems that they would encounter. Ideally, all user tasks are evaluated, rather than just high-frequency tasks.

The following steps are involved in cognitive walk-throughs (Preece, Rogers, & Sharp, 2002):

1. The characteristics of typical users are identified and documented and sample tasks are developed that focus on the aspects of the design to be evaluated. A description or prototype of the interface to be developed is also produced, along with a clear sequence of the actions needed for the users to complete the task.

2. A designer and one or more expert evaluators then come together to do the analysis.

3. The evaluators walk through the action sequences for each task, placing it within the context of a typical scenario, and as they do this they try to answer the following questions:

   - Will the correct action be sufficiently evident to the user? (Will the user know what to do to achieve the task?)
   - Will the user notice that the correct action is available? (Can users see the button or menu item that they should use for the next action? Is it apparent when it is needed?)
   - Will the user associate and interpret the response from the action correctly? (Will users know from the feedback that they have made a correct or incorrect choice of action?)

   In other words, will users know what to do, see how to do it, and understand from the feedback whether the action was correct or not?

4. As the walk-through is being done, a record of critical information is compiled in which:

- The assumptions about what would cause problems and why are recorded. This involves explaining why users would face difficulties.
- Notes about side issues and design changes are made.
- A summary of the results is compiled.

5. The design is then revised to fix the problems presented.

Cognitive walk-throughs are effective in detecting design problems very early on so that they may be removed or fixed. This method focuses on users' problems in detail, but users do not need to be present, nor is a working prototype necessary. However, it can be very time-consuming and laborious to do. It is task-specific and thus has a relatively narrow focus.

### 3.1.4 Pluralistic Walk-Through

Like cognitive walk-throughs, pluralistic walk-throughs were originally developed for desktop systems but can be applied to Web-based systems, handheld devices, and other products such as VCRs.

Pluralistic walk-throughs are "another type of walkthrough in which users, developers, and usability experts work together to step through a task scenario, discussing usability issues associated with dialog elements involved in the scenario steps" (Nielsen & Mack, 1994). Each group of experts is asked to assume the role of typical users. The walk-throughs are then done by following a sequence of steps (Preece, Rogers, & Sharp, 2002):

1. Scenarios are developed in the form of a series of hard-copy screens representing a single path through the interface. Often just two or a few screens are developed.

2. The scenarios are presented to the panel of evaluators and the panelists are asked to write down the sequence of actions they would take to move from one screen to another. They do this individually without conferring with one another.

3. When everyone has written down their actions, the panelists discuss the actions that they suggested for that round of the review. Usually, the representative users go first so that they are not influenced by the other panel members and are not deterred from speaking. Then the usability experts present their findings, and finally the developers offer their comments.

4. Then the panel moves on to the next round of screens. This process continues until all the scenarios have been evaluated.

Pluralistic walk-throughs include a strong focus on users' tasks and how they would proceed with doing tasks. The approach extends itself well to another important approach: participatory design. Participatory design is a design approach that attempts to actively involve the end users in the design process to ensure that the final system meets their needs and is usable. Pluralistic walk-throughs use such key ideas in participatory design to involve multidisciplinary teams in which users play a key role. The pluralistic walk-through method is limited to only a number of scenarios that can be evaluated, and the evaluation process can be slow.

### 3.1.5 Inspection with Conceptual Frameworks Such As the TSSL Model

Another structured analytical evaluation method is to use conceptual frameworks as bases for evaluation and inspection. One such framework is the TSSL model we introduced earlier in the book. Recall that TSSL was used as a framework for design. User tasks should be identified first. Then semantic designs should be provided to support achieving the tasks and goals. Semantic designs can have different syntactical designs; some are better than others in terms of considering human cognitive, affective, and behavioral constraints. Finally lexical design uses the building blocks to fulfill syntactical requirements.

This framework can be used to evaluate whether a design is an effective one. From the procedure perspective, this method is similar to the heuristic evaluation. However, this method emphasizes starting from identifying user tasks and then evaluates the system from the angle of supporting the tasks. No real users are needed. But user tasks need to be identified first within the use context. The evaluation can be conducted at any stage of a design including early or late stages, as well as after the product is finished. The process of conducting the evaluation is the same as applying the T-S-S-L steps. Next, we use two examples to illustrate how to conduct such analytical evaluations. The first example is about evaluating option/configuration specification interfaces of two software applications. The second example is about top search results of 2003 of three top Web portals.

### Example 1. Evaluating option/configuration specification interfaces

Software applications have grown richer in features and functions and have thus become more complex on user-configurable options. This complexity, measured by the sheer number of user settings, poses a challenge to the designers of the user interface. Designers must determine the most appropriate means of categorizing and presenting a myriad of application options, each of which should not only be easy to manipulate and access by the user but also be intuitive in both their use and semantic meaning within the context of the application.

When an application is in its infancy, and the number of settings is minimal, the designer can use a simple dialog box as an appropriate metaphor for presenting the user-configurable options. Analogous to the instrument control panel on a motor vehicle, the dialog box with its buttons, sliders, and check boxes seems the perfect fit for this particular scenario (Figure 7.3). As the application matures and the number of features and user-configurable options increases, the dialog box is typically replaced by a tabbed dialog box (Figure 7.4). The tabbed dialog box uses a page metaphor, allowing the user interface designer to group a similar set of configuration options onto separate named pages of the same dialog box. However, most of today's applications are so rich in user-configurable options that they have even outgrown the tabbed dialog box metaphor and are now resorting to other user interface elements to present all the settings to the end user.

This example will explore two applications, each with a different approach for presenting a large number of user-configurable options. For both applications, the user interface will be examined in terms of its task, semantic, syntactic, and lexical levels. Based on the human factors of the design of the user interface, each example will be critiqued accordingly.

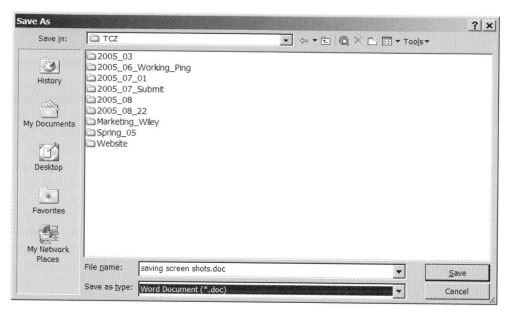

**Figure 7.3**  A sample dialog box.

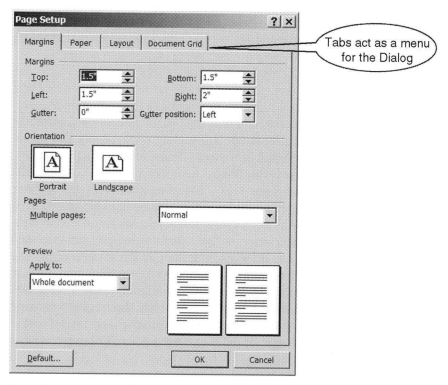

**Figure 7.4**  A sample tabbed dialog box.

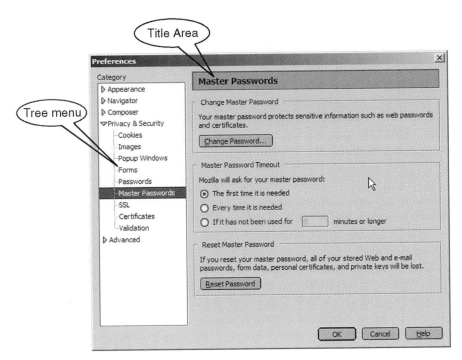

**Figure 7.5** The preferences dialog box with tree menu (taken from Mozilla).

Figure 7.5 is the window for configurable options in Mozilla, the open-source Web browser. Rewritten from the ground up from what was originally Netscape Communicator 4.7x source code, Mozilla has a robust set of configurable options in the application. These options, which can be accessed by selecting "preferences" from the "edit" menu, are organized using a tree menu on the left-hand side of the dialog box to navigate the vast set of options. The options are divided into nine categories, each containing a set of subcategories. Selecting a category from the tree menu with the mouse causes the right-hand side of the dialog box to display the appropriate information based on the selected option.

As an example, let us examine the task of setting the master password, in terms of its semantic, syntactical, and lexical components. The master password is a convenience feature of Mozilla, which allows the user to create one password to manage all of his or her logins and passwords for Web forms on the Internet. The semantics of this task are fairly straightforward, since many users who are familiar with most user interfaces know that application settings are found in the menus. Users must then use semantics to navigate the tree menu on the left-hand side of the preferences dialog box. Good organization of the tree menu structure makes this easy, since "master passwords" intuitively falls under the "privacy and security" menu section.

The preferences dialog box is syntactically well organized, too. It reads top-left to bottom-right and uses consistent fonts, capitalization, buttons, and justifications. Most importantly, because the look of the right-hand side of the dialog box changes in context to the menu selection on the left-hand side, a title area exists at the top of the dialog box always keeping the user informed of the current tree menu selection.

The lexical components of the dialog box are the tree menu (along with various labels), option box, text boxes, command buttons, check boxes, and drop-down lists. The tree menu is by far the most elegant lexical component of the interface, providing a simplistic means of navigating the categories of options. The tree menu is designed with a shallow menu depth (two levels) and nine items in the menu breadth, keeping it within the range for efficient traversal time.

The Mozilla preferences dialog box elegantly handles the challenge of dealing with a large number of user-configurable options by using a tree menu. This syntax fits easily within the overall user's mental model and does not distract the user from the actual task. After the user selects "preferences" from the "edit" menu, the tree view displays a menu of preferences that the user can edit, navigable in a left to right fashion.

While the user interface Mozilla presents a large number of configurable options in an easy, convenient, and intuitive manner, the same cannot be said about a similar type of dialog box, part of Novell's Console One network administration application. Novell's Console One is an application for manipulating network objects. It is used for just about any network administration task such as creating user accounts, giving a user rights to print to a printer, or increasing a user's file storage quota. While network administrators are typically the primary users of Console One, other nonadministrators can be set up to access key features of the application. For example, large organizations might set up nonadministrator accounts with rights to assist with typical information technology help desk requests, such as resetting passwords or unlocking accounts. Console One is very feature-rich, and the quantity of settings an administrator can change for an arbitrary network object can be overwhelming. The argument could (and will) be made that it is not the complexity or quantity of the features but rather how Console One presents them with little thought to the semantic, syntactic, and lexical levels of design that makes the software so difficult and frustrating to use.

To illustrate some of the problems in Console One, let us analyze the task of resetting an account password. The user's mental model is fairly straightforward because, at one level, the Console One user interface uses good metaphors: icons representing users, printers, and servers as well as context-sensitive menu commands, thus making it easy to change a password for a user account by just double-clicking on the user icon. Semantically, the concept is also fairly simple. To change a user's password, the administrator needs two things: the account name of the user and the new password. It is at the syntactic level that the design begins to break down. Once the administrator double-clicks on the user icon and the properties dialog box appears (Figure 7.6), confusion begins to set in.

Next, let us follow through with what must be done syntactically to complete the task of resetting that password. First, search through tabs for the proper tab, which in this case is "Restrictions." Next, from the drop-down menu off the tab, select "Password Restrictions." Then, click the "Change Password" button that appears in the dialog box. Last, the administrator must enter the new password twice and click the "OK" button.

Of the lexical components of the user interface, the most interesting is the tabbed drop-downs. Using the tabbed drop-down dialog box is awkward and poses several problems. First, there are over 20 tabs displayed in the menu, so the menu breadth is out of balance. The administrator sees only a handful of menu items at a time, because of the tab navigators in the top-right corner of the dialog box. While at first glance this might prove beneficial to a user's short-term memory stores, that notion is debunked

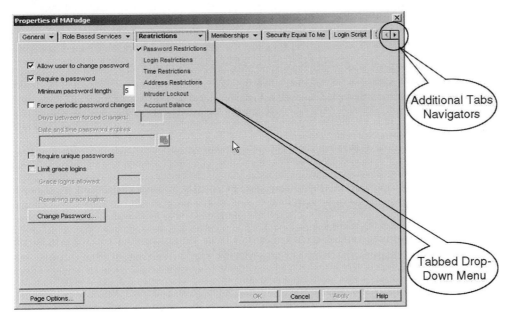

**Figure 7.6** The object properties dialog box with tabbed drop-down menus (taken from Novell Console One).

when the administrator attempts to find the correct tab using these tab navigators. To find the correct tab, the administrator must click the arrows several times until the corresponding tab heading appears and then must click on the tab heading to view the drop-down menu.

There are other lexical problems with the tab navigators in the tabbed drop-downs. To search for the correct tab, the control forces the user to navigate the dialog box from right to left instead of from left to right. Another annoyance is that although they must be accessed frequently, they are the smallest-sized controls in the entire dialog box, thereby requiring precision to operate. While the administrator's eyes try to read the moving tabs searching for the desired menu item, she also must try to focus attention on clicking the correct navigator controls with the mouse. The exercise is both confusing and exhausting at the same time.

Lexically, there are two ideas for improving Console One's interface. First, replacing the tabbed drop-down menu with a tree menu, such as the one we explored in the preferences dialog box of Mozilla, would have been an improvement. Another improvement might be to arrange the large breadth of top-level menu items alphabetically. Because it is difficult to determine the functional arrangement of the menus, it might prove beneficial in terms of faster retrieval times to organize them alphabetically.

Another key problem with the design is that the syntactic level is too complicated for the mental model. There are far too many steps required to get to the desired result, which is mainly due to the poor menu structure of the tabbed drop-down menus. There are far too many top-level items in the menu structure, resulting in a menu with too much breadth and not enough depth. In addition, not much care was taken to logically group the tasks in the organization of the tabbed drop-down menus. To consider our original example, not many individuals would think the "change password" function would be in the category of "restriction" or even "password restriction."

One way to improve this would be to alter the set of visible options based on user roles and permissions. For example, a helpdesk operator, with specific administrative permissions such as reset password or unlock account, would only see those menu items in the tabbed drop-down menus. Currently, Console One displays the exact same dialog box regardless of the user's access permissions and just disables the actual fields for each option the user is not allowed to access. So while someone cannot change the options they don't have access to, they can still select them from the tabbed drop-down menu.

### Example 2. Evaluating the most popular search results of 2003 displayed by three top Web portals and search engines

At the beginning of 2004, three topic Web portals and search engines—Yahoo, Google, and Lycos—reported the results of top searches over the entire year of 2003. Figures 7.7, 7.8, and 7.9 display the first screens of the three Web pages that report the results.

All three can target the same type of user tasks: to find out the most popular searches. The three Web sites show different semantics. Yahoo's and Google's pages focus mainly on the search results, thus providing primarily search results–related information. On Lycos's page, the search results seem secondary and the page has something more than just the search results in the central panel and the right column. Google does not provide a navigation tool to go to other places within the Google Web site. Both Yahoo and Lycos do provide a navigation bar at the top of the screen. Thus Yahoo and Lycos can support navigation tasks of the users within the Web site while Google cannot. Finally, Google lists the contact information (name, phone, and e-mail address) right on top of the page. Such information allows interested readers to contact the person with questions or additional comments. It also gives readers a sense of reliability of the content of the page. Yet such information is not shown on the first screens of Yahoo's and Lycos's Web pages.

At the syntactical level, Yahoo and Google are similar in organizing the overall display to center the search categories within the focal area of the screen and then use well-formatted tables to indicate categories and the results within the categories. Lycos uses hyperlinks on the left panel and uses the center panel for other types of information. Readers cannot know the results of a search category without clicking a link. The well-balanced layout and use of coordinating colors make the Yahoo and Google pages more pleasant and exciting than the Lycos one.

At the lexical level, both Yahoo and Google utilized short text messages, coordinated colors, well-formatted tables with headers and hyperlinks, and charts (not shown on the first screens). Yahoo also uses a rather large image on the left side to highlight the overall top search results. Lycos, on the other hand, uses long text descriptions, overall text-based presentations, some images (although not all related to search results), and minimum use of color.

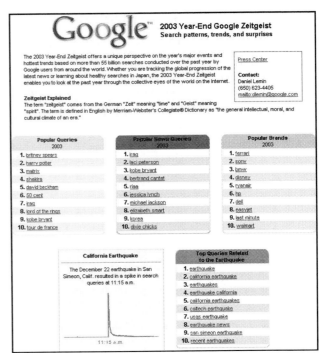

**Figure 7.7**  Yahoo 2003 top search results (first screen). See also color plate III.

**Figure 7.8**  Google 2003 top search results (first screen). See also color plate III.

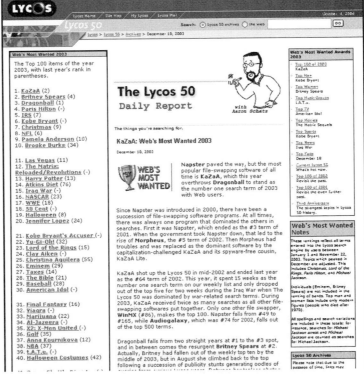

**Figure 7.9**  Lycos 2003 top search results (first screen). See also color plate III.

## 3.2 Empirical Methods

Empirical methods are normally conducted by involving users and collecting facts about users interacting with the system. Data being collected can be either quantitative or qualitative in nature. The commonly used methods include (1) survey or questionnaire, (2) interview including focus groups, (3) lab-controlled experiment, and (4) field studies on observing and monitoring usage. We introduce each of these methods.

### 3.2.1 Survey/Questionnaire

Surveys are commonly used to collect quantitative data from a large poll of respondents. A survey may focus on opinions or factual data depending on its purpose. But all surveys involve administering questions to individual respondents. Surveys can be conduced in ways such as telephone, e-mail, or mail; they can be paper-based or online. Very often, the questions are administered by the respondent in the form of a questionnaire. If the questions are administered by the researcher or evaluator, then it is called an interview or a focus group, depending on the respondent numbers at the time of the study (see section on interview and focus group methods later in chapter).

The advantages of the survey methods include being inexpensive and flexible to conduct; involving a large number of respondents, thus offering validity, reliability, and statistical significance; allowing anonymity of respondents, thus encouraging more candid and honest responses; and providing unbiased understanding if using validated or standard instruments.

There are several disadvantages of the survey methods. The reliability of survey results depends on how truthful respondents' self-reports are. Respondents may sometimes be unmotivated or unable to answer questions well. The latter may occur if the question calls for the respondent to remember past actions or asks them to provide reasons for those past actions. Since studies have shown that users typically overrationalize their actions, the findings may be misleading. Surveys cannot reveal the complex or dynamic nature of certain phenomena. Sometimes the respondents are selected based on convenience or economical concerns; thus they do not truly represent the intended population, making the results less valid or generalizable.

Most questionnaires use a Likert scale (5 or 7 points) to collect answers on questions about a specific concern, such as opinions, perceptions or beliefs, attitudes, satisfaction, behavior, or specific assessment. For example, a statement can be presented, followed by a scale similar to the ones following:

Likert 5-point scale

| Strongly agree | Agree | Neutral | Disagree | Strongly disagree |
|---|---|---|---|---|

Likert 7-point scale

Strongly agree                                              Strongly disagree

    3       2       1       0       −1     −2     −3

Bipolar anchored scales can also be used to collect answers. For example, the following can appear in a questionnaire:

Bipolar scale:

| Vague | 1 | 2 | 3 | 4 | 5 | 6 | 7 | Specific |
|---|---|---|---|---|---|---|---|---|
| Discourage | 1 | 2 | 3 | 4 | 5 | 6 | 7 | Encouraging |
| Pleasant | 1 | 2 | 3 | 4 | 5 | 6 | 7 | Unpleasant |

There are other questions where the answers can fall into a range of possible values. For example, for gender, there are two possible answers: female or male. If a classification of ethnicity is predefined, then the answer is one of the categories. Sometimes, a question requires a specific value, such as age or number of hours using an IT per day. Sometimes, a range instead of a specific value is more appropriate. For example, for some user groups, it might be better to ask age in ranges of "< 20," "20–29," "30–39," and so on instead of a specific age. The same may be true for asking about household income. This will make subjects feel more comfortable to answer than in the case where they are asked to report a specific number.

Surveys can be on paper or online. It is popular nowadays to have a survey on the Web for participants to answer.

---

Examples

The questions below are not well designed:

1. Do you currently have access to a computer with connection to the Internet via broadband?

2. Regarding the calendar feature of the software, how useful is it for you?

Very Useful     Useful     Not Useful

*----------------------*----------------------*

3. Rate your choices by circling your answers: 1 (lowest) – 5 (highest)

| Familiarity with computers | 1 | 2 | 3 | 4 | 5 |
|---|---|---|---|---|---|
| Design Features: Screen layout | 1 | 2 | 3 | 4 | 5 |
| Design Features: Color choices | 1 | 2 | 3 | 4 | 5 |
| Design Features: Ease of use | 1 | 2 | 3 | 4 | 5 |

Comments: For (1), if the answer is "no," then it cannot rule out whether the subject has no computer at all, or has a computer but no Internet connection, or has Internet connection but no broadband. The problem with (2) is that it is unclear whether subjects should select one of the three asterisks (*) or whether they can mark anywhere on the line. If they did mark on places other than the asterisks, the researchers have to decide how to interpret such answers so that they can do analysis. For (3), the scales do not make sense for some questions. For example, what does it mean if 1 or 5 is circled for screen layout or for color choices? These two questions should be separated from the others, and meaningful scales should be developed for measuring them.

---

In this section, we present a few sample instruments for collecting data on some aspects or measuring some commonly interested variables. Some of these instruments are validated by various studies.

### Demographic Data Collection

A section on demographics and other related data can be very useful and thus should be included in a questionnaire as well. Table 7.9 is a sample instrument for collecting demographic data of the participants who might be college students. Certain items can be customized to reflect the nature of the participants and purpose of the evaluation study.

### Technology Acceptance Model (TAM) Measures

The Technology Acceptance Model (TAM) was introduced in Chapter 6. The main variables for this model are perceived ease of use, perceived usefulness, and behavioral intention to use the IT. TAM measures can be used in a variety of places, such as the user-needs test in the project initiation and analysis stages of the HCI development life cycle (see Chapter 11 for more details) and use and impact evaluation after the system is released and being used in real contexts. As the name suggests, "perceived usefulness" measures the user's perception of the usefulness of a computer system, and is therefore one possible reflection of one of the four HCI concerns. Perceived ease of use reflects the cognitive concern regarding how easy the system is to use. TAM measures have been validated by a large number of empirical studies and have been proven to be robust across a variety of IT types and use contexts. For an example of TAM measures, see Table 7.10.

**Table 7.9**  A Sample Instrument for Collecting Demographic Data

1.  My age is ____ <20      ____ 20–29      ____ 30–39      ____ >40

2.  My gender is:  ____ Male  ____ Female

3.  My ethnicity is:  a. ____ African-American
    b. ____ Native American
    c. ____ Asian/Pacific Rim
    d. ____ Caucasian/White
    e. ____ Hispanic
    f. ____ Multiracial
    g. ____ Other (please specify): _____

4.  I am currently a
    ___ Freshmen   ___ Sophomore   ___ Junior   ___ Senior
    ___ Graduate (Master)   ___ Doctoral   ___ Other

5.  I have been using computers for ____ years.

6.  I have been using the Web for ____ years.

7.  On average, I use the Web ____ hours/week.

8.  On average, I use this ZYX system ____ hours/week.

9.  I have been using system ZYX for about ____ months.

**Table 7.10**  Technology Acceptance Model (TAM) Measures

| Perceived case of use | Strongly disagree | | | | | | Strongly agree |
|---|---|---|---|---|---|---|---|
| It was easy for me to become skillful at using the system. | −3 | −2 | −1 | 0 | 1 | 2 | 3 |
| Learning to operate the system was easy for me. | −3 | −2 | −1 | 0 | 1 | 2 | 3 |
| I find it easy to get the system to do what I wanted it to do. | −3 | −2 | −1 | 0 | 1 | 2 | 3 |
| I find the system easy to use. | −3 | −2 | −1 | 0 | 1 | 2 | 3 |
| Perceived Usefulness | | | | | | | |
| Using the system would enhance my effectiveness at work. | −3 | −2 | −1 | 0 | 1 | 2 | 3 |
| Using the system would enhance my productivity at work. | −3 | −2 | −1 | 0 | 1 | 2 | 3 |
| I find that the system would be useful in my work. | −3 | −2 | −1 | 0 | 1 | 2 | 3 |
| Using the system would improve my performance at work. | −3 | −2 | −1 | 0 | 1 | 2 | 3 |
| Intention to Use | | | | | | | |
| I plan to use the system, assuming I had access to it. | −3 | −2 | −1 | 0 | 1 | 2 | 3 |
| Given that I had access to the system, I predict that I would use it. | −3 | −2 | −1 | 0 | 1 | 2 | 3 |

### 3.2.2 Interviews

An interview is "a conversation with a purpose" between one or more interviewers and one or more interviewees. A focus group is a form of group interview where the interviewees are a group of people that are selected to represent typical users. Interviews can be productive if specific issues are addressed and discussed directly with the users. Interviews can also be costly and time-consuming, and they require skilled interviewers. Therefore, usually only a small number of users are involved.

Interviews can be open-ended (unstructured), semi-structured, or structured. They indicate the level of control the interviewers impose on the conversation by following a predetermined set of questions. Open-ended interviews focus on a topic and can go to a deep level. The interviewees are not restricted by format or content and thus can go as deep or as broad as they want. They may also reveal rich information that goes beyond what interviewers have considered or anticipated, which can be interesting, surprising, or explored further. Because the interviewees can go deep and broad, the interview can also go in several possible directions. This thus requires the interviewers to have the skills to prevent the interview process from drifting off course. Transcribing and analyzing interview results can also be a challenge and require certain training and skills.

Structured interviews use a predetermined set of questions, similar to those in a questionnaire format. This is more appropriate when the evaluation goal is very clear and the specific issues are well identified and put into questions. These questions are normally considered "closed" since they require a precise or specific answer from a set of pre-identified potential answers. This type of interview is thus relatively easier to conduct and analyze than the open-ended interview and can be easily replicated.

Semi-structured interviews fall between the above two types. They combine both closed and open-ended questions.

Regardless of the structure of the interviews, all questions should be carefully thought out and presented. There are many guidelines or tactics on how to develop questions. A few quick guidelines are listed below (Robson, 2002):

- Avoid long questions, as they are hard to remember.
- Avoid compound sentences/questions by splitting them into two questions. That is, one sentence is for one idea or question.
- Avoid using jargon or language that interviewees may not know but may feel embarrassed to admit.
- Avoid imposing or implying any bias when presenting the question to the interviewees.

### 3.2.3 Lab Experiment

Lab experiments are appropriate if evaluators have a clear focus on some specific aspects such as certain design features, particular tasks, or specific consequences of design features on user performance or reactions. A lab experiment allows evaluators to address specific aspects of design by manipulating a number of factors associated with the design and assessing the related user performance. That is, some other factors can be controlled or excluded so that a better understanding of the issues at hand can be achieved. Lab experiments can be small in scope and scale and do not require installation of the real system in the real setting, and thus they are relatively easy and inexpensive to conduct. A lab experiment can be conducted on a system in different development stages, such as a mock-up, an advanced prototype, or a finished system. Thus, lab experiments can be used for both formative and summative evaluations.

A lab experiment study can involve the following steps:

- Develop a research question that outlines the relationships between several concepts or constructs.
- Develop theory-driven hypotheses to be tested that outline the specific relationships between dependent variables and independent variables.
- Design the experiment including operationalizing constructs into measurable variables, constructing manipulations and treatments, designing tasks, designing data collection methods, identifying data analysis methods, and designing incentives and procedures.
- Pilot test the experiment.
- Recruit subjects and take care of the requirements for using humans as participants.
- Conduct the experiment, collect and analyze data, and draw conclusions.

### 3.2.4  Observing and Monitoring Usage through Field Studies

One way to evaluate a system is to observe and monitor the real users actually using the system in a real setting. Field study means that the study is conducted in a normal working environment, or the real field. Field studies can be valuable in formative evaluations and in use and impact evaluations. Longitudinal data collection is possible by observing users over an extended period of time.

Ethnographic observation attends to actual user experience in real-world situations with minimum interruption or intervention from the evaluators. Data may be collected by evaluators taking notes, recording with video or audio devices, or using computer logs. Several actual use episodes can be observed if necessary. Data analysis can be tedious and time-consuming. Depending on the data collected and evaluation goals, both qualitative (notes, video or audio data) and quantitative (logs) data analyses may take place.

## 3.3  Comparison of Methods

Earlier we discussed that there are certain factors to consider when planning an evaluation. These factors are stage of design, novelty of product, number of expected users, criticality of the interface, costs of product and finances allocated for test, time available, and experience of the evaluation team. We have discussed the four types of HCI concerns: physical, cognitive, affective, and usefulness. We also mentioned the four reasons for evaluation: understanding the real world, engineering toward a target, comparing designs, and conforming to a standard. All of these come into play when one is planning an evaluation and selecting appropriate methods.

Each method has pros and cons and there is no one-size-fits-all method. Selecting which method to use is important when planning an evaluation. As we have already learned, some of the methods are good for certain HCI concerns (e.g., cognitive), while some might be appropriate for all of them. Some are good for early stages of development, while others are good for late stages. Some require the use of real users, while others do not.

Table 7.11 lists the evaluation methods and their characteristics along several dimensions. These dimensions include the stage of the development life cycle at which the evaluation will occur, the system's status (paper prototype or final product), the environment or setting of the evaluation, whether real users will participate in the evaluation, and whether real user tasks will be used in the evaluation. Finally, we also list the main advantages and disadvantages of each method. Some of the comparisons are from existing works by Nielsen (Nielsen, 1993) and Preece and colleagues (Preece et al., 1994; Preece, Rogers, & Sharp, 2002), among others. In Table 7.11, "life cycle stage" means at what time of the development or use process the system should be evaluated. We will discuss the life cycle model in Chapter 11, "HCI Development Methodology." For now, just think about any artifact that can be viewed from a life span perspective: from the time it is initiated and crafted to the time it is completed, to the time it is put in use in the real context, and finally to the time it is retired or replaced.

## ▶ 4.  STANDARDS

Standards are concerned with prescribed ways of discussing, presenting, or doing things to achieve consistency across the same types of products. Standards exist for many things we interact with in our lives—for example, video standards for recording and playing in VCRs, DVDs, or camcorders; standards for the peripherals to be plugged into

> **Standards:** Standards are concerned with prescribed ways of discussing, presenting, or doing things to achieve consistency across the same types of products.

**Table 7.11** Comparison of Evaluation Methods

| | Life Cycle Stage | System Status | Environ. of Evaluation | Real Users Participation | User Tasks Used | Main Advantage | Main Disadvantage |
|---|---|---|---|---|---|---|---|
| Heuristic evaluation | Any stage; early ones benefit most | Any status (mock-up, prototype, final product) | Any | None | None | Finds individual problems; can address expert user issues | Does not involve real users and thus may not find problems related to real users in real context; does not link to user's tasks |
| Guideline preview | Any stage; early ones benefit most | Any status | Any | None | None | Finds individual problems | Does not involve real users; does not link to user's tasks |
| Cognitive walk-through | Any stage; early ones benefit most | Any status | Any | None | Yes, need to identify tasks first | Less expensive | Does not involve real users; limited to expert's view |
| Pluralistic walk-through | Any stage; early ones benefit most | Any status | Any | Yes, real users work together with designers | Yes, need to identify tasks first | Input from both users & designers | Limited to only a number of scenarios; evaluation can be slow |
| TSSL-based inspection | Any stage | Any status | Any | None | Yes, need to identify tasks first | Direct link to user tasks; structured with fewer steps to go through | Does not involve real users; limited to the tasks identified |
| Survey | Any stage | Any status | Any | Yes, a lot | Yes or no | Finds subjective reactions; easy to conduct and compare | Questions need to be well designed; need large sample |
| Interview | Task analysis | Mock-up, prototype | Any | Yes | None | Flexible, in-depth probing | Time-consuming; hard to analyze and compare |
| Lab experiment | Design, implement, or use | Prototype, final product | Lab | Yes | Yes, most time artificially designed to mimic real tasks | Provides fact-based measurements; results easy to compare | Requires expensive facility, setup, and expertise |
| Field study with observation and monitoring | Design, implement, or use | Prototype, final product | Real work setting | Yes | None | Easily applicable; reveal user's real tasks; can highlight difficulties in real use | Observation may affect user behavior |

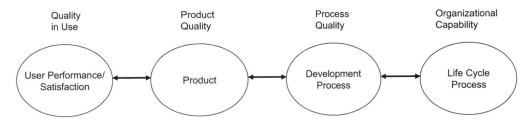

**Figure 7.10**  Categories of HCI-related standards (adapted from Bevan, 2001).

computers; standard bed sizes and beddings; standard paper sizes; and standards for constructions, to name a few. Standards can indicate quality, safety, or merits we know. Standardization makes people's lives easier and safer.

Standards for software are being developed to prevent the development of poor-quality software that may bring disasters to businesses and people's lives. Agencies such as the National Institute of Standards and Technology (NIST) in the United States, the International Standards Organization (ISO), the International Electrotechnical Commission (IEC), and the British Standards Institute (BSI) set standards that are used for software products. As we have discussed earlier in this chapter, standards are important for summative evaluations of the finished products.

## 4.1  Types of Standards for HCI and Usability

Standards related to HCI and usability can be categorized based on their purposes. Figure 7.10 depicts this categorization (Bevan, 2001). These categories are logically related: the objective is for the product to be effective, efficient, and satisfying when used in the intended contexts. A prerequisite for this is an appropriate interface and interaction. This requires a user-centered design process, which to be achieved consistently requires an organizational capability to support user-centered design.

HCI and usability standards have been developed over the last 15 to 20 years. One function of the standards is to impose consistency, and some attempt has been made to do this by ISO and IEC standards for interface components such as icons, PDA scripts, and cursor control. However, in these areas de facto industry standards have been more influential than ISO, and the ISO standards have not been widely adopted. Table 7.12 lists the sources of some standards. Since many user interface standards can quickly become out of date, all international standards are reviewed at least once every five years.

## 4.2  Common Industry Format (CIF)

### 4.2.1  Background and Current Status

In October 1997, the U.S. National Institute of Standards and Technology (NIST) initiated an effort to increase the visibility of software usability, the Industry USability Reporting (IUSR) Project. Cooperating in the IUSR project are over 300 prominent suppliers of software and representatives from large consumer organizations. A common usability reporting format for sharing usability data with consumer organizations was developed and pilot tested. On November 30, 2001, ANSI approved ANSI/INCITS 354-2001 Common Industry Format for Usability Test Reports. In May 2005,

**Common Industry Format (CIF):** A standard method for reporting summative usability test findings.

**Table 7.12** Sources for HCI and Usability-Related Standards

| Information | URL |
|---|---|
| Published ISO standards | www.iso.ch/projects/programme.html |
| ISO national member bodies | www.iso.ch/addresse/membodies.html |
| BSI: British Standards Institute | www.bsi.org.uk |
| ANSI: American National Standards Institute | www.ansi.org |
| NSSN: A National Resource for Global Standards | www.nssn.org |
| TRUMP list of HCI and usability standards | www.usability.serco.com/trump/resources/standards.htm |

CIF was approved as the worldwide standard by the International Standards Organization in Geneva (Thibodeau, 2005). The document is called "ISO 25062 Software Engineering—Software Quality and Requirements Evaluation—Common Industry Format for Usability Test Reports."

The Common Industry Format (CIF) for Usability Test Reports is a standard method for reporting usability test findings. The purpose of the CIF is to encourage incorporation of usability as an element in decision making for software procurement. The CIF targets two audiences: usability professionals and stakeholders in an organization. The CIF is designed for usability professionals who generate reports to be used by stakeholders. Stakeholders can use the usability data to help them make informed decisions concerning the release of software products or the procurement of such products. Current adopters of CIF include Apple, IBM, HP, Sun, Oracle, Compaq, and Microsoft, among others, as suppliers and Boeing, US West, Northwest Mutual Life, State Farm Insurance, Fidelity, and Kodak, among others, as purchasers. The type of information and level of detail that is required in a CIF report is intended to ensure the following:

- Good practice in usability evaluation has been adhered to.
- There is sufficient information for a usability specialist to judge the validity of the results (for example, whether the evaluation context adequately reproduces the intended context of use).
- If the test was replicated on the basis of the information given in the CIF, it should produce essentially the same results.
- Specific effectiveness and efficiency metrics must be used, including the unassisted completion rate and the mean time on task.
- Satisfaction must also be measured.

It is important to note that the CIF assumes that best practice is used in designing and conducting a usability test. The CIF does not tell you what to do; it tells you how to report on what you did. The CIF is based on the usability definitions of ISO 9241-11: the extent to which a product can be used by specified users to achieve specified goals with effectiveness, efficiency, and satisfaction in a specified context of use.

### 4.2.2 The CIF Format

The CIF is designed for summative testing rather than formative testing. The CIF format is primarily for reporting results of formal usability tests in which quantitative measurements were collected and is particularly appropriate for summative/comparative testing. The format includes the following main sections: Executive Summary, Introduction, Method, and Results. The Method and Results sections are particularly important and provide usability professionals with a good framework for the report. The Method section prescribes the inclusion of details concerning the participants and their profiles, the details of the context of use employed in the test, technical aspects of the testing facility and apparatus, and finally all the study design aspects (such as variables and measurements). The Results section includes subsections for the presentation of performance data (e.g., times or error rates) and a subsection for the presentation of satisfaction results. Appendix A at the end of this chapter shows the details of the CIF report format.

### 4.2.3 How to Use the CIF

According to NIST, the CIF can be used in the following fashion. For purchased software:

- Require that suppliers provide usability test reports in CIF format.
- Analyze for reliability and applicability.
- Replicate within agency if required.
- Use data to select products.

For developed software (in house or subcontract):

- Define measurable usability goals.
- Conduct formative usability testing as part of user interface design activities.
- Conduct summative usability test using the CIF to ensure that goals have been met.

Although the CIF was designed for usability tests only, not for other HCI concerns we have discussed in this chapter, one can borrow its spirit to include any test that is of interest.

In the "HCI Development Methodology" chapter later in the book, we will present a template for documenting HCI development processes and deliverables. At the time, we will mention that our template can be streamlined with the CIF format. That is, our template focuses on both the process and the outcomes, whereas the CIF emphasizes primarily the outcomes. But the outcomes part can be streamlined, especially for the evaluation metrics and results of the HCI development methodology.

## ▶ 5. SUMMARY

Evaluations are driven by the ultimate concerns of human–computer interaction. In this chapter, we present four types of such concerns along the following four dimensions of human needs: physical, cognitive, affective, and usefulness. Evaluations should occur during the entire system development process, after the system is finished, and during the period the system is actually used. This chapter introduces several commonly used evaluation methods. Their pros and cons are compared and discussed. The chapter also provides several useful instruments and heuristics. Standards play an important role in practice. This is discussed in the chapter. A particular standard, Common Industry Format, is described and the detailed format is given in Appendix A. Some tools and laboratories for HCI studies are briefly described in Appendices B and C.

## ▶ 6. APPENDIX A. THE DETAILED CIF TEMPLATE (WWW.NIST.GOV/IUSR)

### 1 Title Page

    a) Identify report as Common Industry Format for Usability Test Report v2.0 and contact information
    b) Name of the product and version that was tested
    c) Who led the test
    d) When the test was conducted
    e) Date the report was prepared
    f) Who prepared the report
    g) Customer company name
    h) Customer company contact person
    i) Contact name(s) for questions and/or clarifications
    j) Supplier phone number
    k) Supplier e-mail address
    l) Supplier mailing or postal address

### 2 Executive Summary

This section provides a high-level overview of the test. The intent of this section is to provide information for procurement decision makers in customer organizations. These people may not read the technical body of this document. This section shall begin on a new page and end with a page break to facilitate its use as a stand-alone summary.

A high-level overview of the test shall be provided that includes the following:
    a) Name and description of the product
    b) Summary of method(s) including number(s) and type(s) of participants and tasks
    c) Results expressed as mean scores or other suitable measure of central tendency

The following information should be provided:
    a) Reason for and nature of the test
    b) Tabular summary of performance results
    c) If differences between values or products are claimed, the probability that the difference did not occur by chance

### 3 Introduction

#### 3.1 Full Product Description
The following information shall be provided:
    a) Formal product name and release or version
    b) The parts of the product that were evaluated
    c) The user population for which the product is intended

The following information should be provided:
    a) Any groups with special needs that are supported by the product
    b) Brief description of the environment in which it should be used
    c) The type of user work that is supported by the product

### 3.2 Test Objectives
The following information shall be provided:
  a) The objectives for the test and any areas of specific interest (note: possible objectives include testing user performance of work tasks and subjective satisfaction in using the product)
  b) Functions and components with which the user directly and indirectly interacted

The following information should be provided:
  a) Reason for focusing on a product subset, if the whole product was not tested

## 4 Method

Sufficient information shall be provided to allow an independent tester to replicate the procedure used in testing.

### 4.1 Participants
The following information shall be provided:
  a) The total number of participants tested (note: in order to generate valid summative statistical analyses, it is necessary to test sufficient numbers of subjects; eight or more subjects/cells [segments] are recommended for this purpose)
  b) Segmentation of user groups tested, if more than one
  c) Key characteristics and capabilities of user group
  d) How participants were selected; whether they had the essential characteristics
  e) Differences between the participant sample and the user population
  f) Table of participants (row) by characteristics (columns), including demographics, professional experience, computing experience, and special needs

The characteristics shall be complete enough so that an essentially similar group of participants can be recruited. Characteristics should be chosen to be relevant to the product's usability; they should allow a customer to determine how similar the participants were to the customers' user population.

The following information should be provided:
  a) Description of any groups with special needs

Participants should not be from the same organization as the testing or supplier organization.

### 4.2 Context of Product Use in the Test
The following information shall be provided:
  a) Any known differences between the evaluated context and the expected context of use

### 4.2.1 Tasks
The following information shall be provided:
  a) The task scenarios for testing
  b) Why these tasks were selected
  c) The source of these tasks
  d) Any task data given to the participants
  e) Completion or performance criteria established for each task

### 4.2.2 Test Facility

The following information should be provided:

    a) The setting and type of space in which the evaluation was conducted

    b) Any relevant features or circumstances that could affect the results

### 4.2.3 Participant's Computing Environment

The following information shall provide enough information to replicate and validate the test:

    a) Computer configuration, including model, OS version, required libraries, or settings

    b) If used, browser name and version; relevant plug-in names and versions

### 4.2.3.1 Display Devices

The following information shall be provided:

    a) If screen-based, screen size, resolution, and color setting

    b) If print-based, the media size and print resolution

    c) If visual interface elements (such as fonts) can vary in size, specify the size(s) used in the test

### 4.2.3.2 Audio Devices

The following information should be provided:

    a) If used, the relevant settings or values for the audio bits, volume, etc.

### 4.2.3.3 Manual Input Devices

The following information should be provided:

    a) If used, the make and model of devices used in the test

### 4.2.4 Test Administrator Tools

The following information shall be provided:

    a) If a standard questionnaire was used, describe or specify it here (note: customized questionnaires are included in an appendix)

The following information should be provided:

    a) Any hardware or software used to control the test or to record data

### 4.3 Experimental Design

The following information shall be provided:

    a) The logical design of the test

    b) The independent variables and control variables

    c) The measures for which data were recorded for each set of conditions

### 4.3.1 Procedure

The following information shall be provided:

    a) Operational definitions of measures

    b) Descriptions of independent variables or control variables

    c) Time limits on tasks

    d) Policies and procedures for interaction between tester(s) and subjects

The following information should be provided:
- a) Sequence of events from greeting the participants to dismissing them
- b) Details of nondisclosure agreements, form completion, warm-ups, pre-task training, and debriefing
- c) Verification that the participants knew and understood their rights as human subjects
- d) Steps followed to execute the test sessions and record data
- e) Number and roles of people who interacted with the participants during the test session
- f) Whether other individuals were present in the test environment
- g) Whether participants were paid or otherwise compensated

### 4.3.2 Participant General Instructions
The following information shall be provided:
- a) Instructions given to the participants (here or in an appendix)
- b) Instructions on how participants were to interact with any other persons present, including how they were to ask for assistance and interact with other participants, if applicable

### 4.3.3 Participant Task Instructions
The following information shall be provided:
- a) Task instruction summary

### 4.4 Usability Metrics
Usability is measured by three types of metrics: effectiveness, efficiency, and satisfaction.

The following information shall be provided:
- a) Metrics for effectiveness
- b) Metrics for efficiency
- c) Metrics for satisfaction

Effectiveness and efficiency results shall be reported, even when they are difficult to interpret within the specified context of use. In this case, the report shall specify why the supplier does not consider the metrics meaningful. If it is necessary to provide participants with assists, efficiency and effectiveness metrics shall be provided for both unassisted and assisted conditions, and the number and type of assists shall be included as part of the test results.

### 4.4.1 Effectiveness
Effectiveness relates the goals of using the product to the accuracy and completeness with which these goals can be achieved. Common measures of effectiveness include percent task completion, frequency of errors, frequency of assists to the participant from the testers, and frequency of accesses to help or documentation by the participants during the tasks. It does not take account of how the goals were achieved, only the extent to which they were achieved. Efficiency relates the level of effectiveness achieved to the quantity of resources expended.

### 4.4.1.1 Completion Rate
The completion rate is the percentage of participants who completely and correctly achieve each task goal. If goals can be partially achieved (e.g., by incomplete or suboptimum

results), then it may also be useful to report the average goal achievement, scored on a scale of 0 to 100 percent based on specified criteria related to the value of a partial result. For example, a spell-checking task might involve identifying and correcting 10 spelling errors and the completion rate might be calculated based on the percent of errors corrected. Another method for calculating completion rate is weighting; for example, spelling errors in the title page of the document are judged to be twice as important as errors in the main body of text. The rationale for choosing a particular method of partial goal analysis should be stated, if such results are included in the report.

The following information shall be provided:

a) The percentage of participants who completely and correctly achieve each task goal

### 4.4.1.2 Errors

Errors are instances where test participants did not complete the task successfully or had to attempt portions of the task more than once. Scoring of data should include classifying errors according to some taxonomy.

### 4.4.1.3 Assists

When participants cannot proceed on a task, the test administrator sometimes gives direct procedural help in order to allow the test to proceed. This type of tester intervention is called an *assist* for the purposes of this report.

The following information shall be provided:

a) The unassisted completion rate (i.e., the rate achieved without intervention from the testers) as well as the assisted rate (i.e., the rate achieved with tester intervention) where these two metrics differ

For example, if a participant received an assist on Task A, that participant should not be included among those successfully completing the task when calculating the unassisted completion rate for that task. However, if the participant went on to successfully complete the task following the assist, he could be included in the assisted Task A completion rate. When assists are allowed or provided, the number and type of assists shall be included as part of the test results. In some usability tests, participants are instructed to use support tools such as online help or documentation, which are part of the product, when they cannot complete tasks on their own. Accesses to product features that provide information and help are *not* considered assists for the purposes of this report. It may, however, be desirable to report the frequency of accesses to different product support features, especially if they factor into participants' ability to use products independently.

### 4.4.2 Efficiency

Efficiency relates the level of effectiveness achieved to the quantity of resources expended. Efficiency is generally assessed by the mean time taken to achieve the task. Efficiency may also relate to other resources (e.g., total cost of usage). A common measure of efficiency is time on task.

The following information shall be provided:

a) The mean time taken to complete each task, together with the range and standard deviation of times across participants.

#### 4.4.2.1 Completion Rate/Mean Time-On-Task

Completion Rate/Mean Time-On-Task is another measure of efficiency. The relationship of success rate to time allows customers to compare fast error-prone interfaces (e.g., command lines with wildcards to delete files) to slow easy interfaces (e.g., using a mouse and keyboard to drag each file to the trash).

### 4.4.3 Satisfaction

The following information shall be provided:

    a) One or more measures of user satisfaction

Satisfaction describes a user's subjective response when using the product. User satisfaction may be an important correlate of motivation to use a product and may affect performance in some cases. Questionnaires to measure satisfaction and associated attitudes are commonly built using Likert and semantic differential scales. A variety of instruments are available for measuring user satisfaction of software interactive products, and many companies create their own. Whether an external, standardized instrument is used or a customized instrument is created, subjective rating dimensions such as Satisfaction, Usefulness, and Ease of Use should be considered for inclusion, as these will be of general interest to customer organizations. Suppliers may choose to use validated published satisfaction measures or may submit satisfaction metrics they have developed themselves.

## 5 Results

### 5.1 Data Analysis

The following information shall be provided in sufficient detail to allow replication of the data scoring methods by another organization if the test is repeated:

    a) Data collection and scoring
        EXAMPLE: How data was treated with respect to exclusion of outliers, categorization of error data, and criteria for scoring assisted or unassisted completion.
    b) Data reduction
        EXAMPLE: How data were collapsed across tasks or task categories.
    c) Statistical analysis
        EXAMPLE: Statistical procedures (e.g., transformation of the data) and tests (e.g., t-tests, F tests, and statistical significance of differences between groups). Scores that are reported as means shall include the standard deviation and optionally the standard error of the mean.

### 5.2 Presentation of the Results

The following information shall be provided:

    a) Tabular performance results per task or task group

Various graphical formats are effective in describing usability data at a glance. Bar graphs are useful for describing subjective data such as that gleaned from Likert scales. A variety of plots can be used effectively to show comparisons of expert benchmark times for a product vs. the mean participant performance time. The data may be accompanied by a brief explanation of the results but detailed interpretation is discouraged.

### 5.2.1 Performance Results

A table of results may be presented for groups of related tasks (e.g., all program creation tasks in one group, all debugging tasks in another group) where this is more efficient and makes sense. If a unit task has subtasks, then the subtasks may be reported in summary form for the unit task. For example, if a unit task is to identify all the misspelled words on a page, then the results may be summarized as a percent of misspellings found.

The following information should be provided:
  a) Summary Table(s) of Performance Results across all tasks
  b) Graphical Presentation of Performance Results

Additional tables of metrics should be included if they are relevant to the product's design and a particular application area.

### 5.2.2 Satisfaction Results

The following information shall be provided:
  a) Tabular Satisfaction Results
  b) Summary table(s) of Satisfaction Results
  c) Graphical presentation of Satisfaction Results

## 6 Appendices

The following information shall be provided:
  a) Custom questionnaires, if used
  b) Participant general Instructions (if not in the body of the report)
  c) Participant task Instructions

The following information may be provided:
  a) Release Notes explaining or updating the test results

## ▷ 7. APPENDIX B. RESEARCH TOOLS

With the advancement of technologies for research, there are quite a number of companies building research tools for conducting behavioral or usability studies. Many of these tools are quite advanced so that researchers can concentrate on the studies and get the results relatively quickly and easily. In this section, we briefly describe tools from two different companies and some of the tools' functions and features in order to give readers some ideas about how such tools would help research.

### 7.1 Mangold

Mangold (http://www.behavioral-research.com) is a company that offers a broad range of equipment and software packages for behavioral analysis, from ready-to-go lightweight mobile solutions to fully equipped stationary labs.

INTERACT is a software solution for studies on behavior that runs on any up-to-date Windows PC, helping a researcher to save hundreds of hours of time during analysis of video recordings and live observations. It is designed with the following philosophy: (1) completely method independent; no predefined behavioral codes or categories—researchers can use their own observation methods and category systems; (2)work as with "paper and pencil" (e.g., record any free text, behavioral code, or annotation whichever way you want at any time); (3) multiple users can work with one observation result list at any time to change any prerecorded data, to add new events, or just to fill new behavioral codes into existing events.

INTERACT can be used in the following ways: with multimedia, with conventional videotapes, and with real-life observation. (1) Multimedia. Using INTERACT with multimedia files offers easy control possibilities and frame-to-frame accurate analysis. It allows behavioral observation in any place where the movie on CD-ROM or DVD can be played, without the need of additional hardware (VCRs, video monitor, control equipment, etc.). This makes a researcher independent of a stationary video observation lab. Researchers can do the analysis in their lab, at home at their private PC, or while traveling, using a notebook computer. Figure 7.11 depicts this way.

(2) Conventional videotapes. For those users not willing or able to use multimedia, INTERACT is able to control a wide range of analog and digital VCRs. This allows a researcher to migrate smoothly if multimedia should be wanted in the future. See Figure 7.12.

(3) Real-life observation. One can use INTERACT in real-life observation, for example, in places where video recording is prohibited or not possible. A researcher may also easily integrate and synchronize live recordings with results of video analysis. This allows the researcher to use both methods at the same time: while recording a video, the researcher may already make some live annotations and codings. He or she can use those results later on as basis for the detailed video analysis. This can speed up the process incredibly, thus saving time (and money).

INTERACT is an open structured system and thus can be used in any environment where observation of behavior takes place. It uses standard Windows multimedia files for scoring processes (text, videos, audios, pictures) and allows assignments of any multimedia file to any event for annotation, thus providing further description of

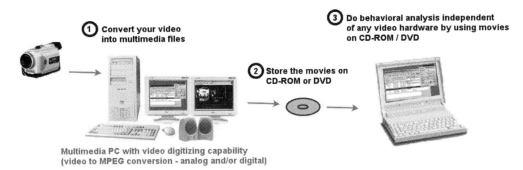

**Figure 7.11** INTERACT with multimedia (from Mangold Web site).

**Figure 7.12** INTERACT with conventional videotapes (from Mangold Web site).

that event. It can let the software remotely control the video player and can use digital camcorders directly. Also, INTERACT can open a practically unlimited number of video sources at the same time and control them synchronously. This is necessary if several video sources are being recorded during a test (e.g., screen contents, environment video, user's face) and researchers don't have the option of mixing them all into one video or don't want to mix them to preserve the original size and quality of the different videos.

**INTERACT** provides a graphical representation of the coded behavior, showing "what happened when." This makes it easy to immediately see interesting patterns of behavior without the need to do statistical analysis first. With a mouse click into the graph, the video will jump to the corresponding picture or play the selected sequence. Figure 7.13 shows the main screen and the visualization function called "Interaction Graph."

INTERACT offers a variety of statistics including calculation of frequencies, sequential analysis, calculation of relative duration, and so on. One useful function is the calculation of interrater reliability, using Cohen's Kappa. A researcher can select any observation to be compared with any other observation (e.g., from a different coder) and let INTERACT calculate the congruence between the analysis sessions.

INTERACT's Data View can visualize third-party data (or any kind of external acquired data) synchronous to a researcher's video recording. This allows the researcher not only to see what's going on in the video but also to evaluate the recorded data in parallel. Figure 7.14 shows the idea.

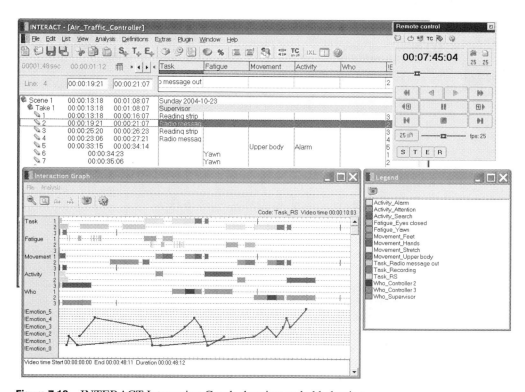

**Figure 7.13**  INTERACT Interaction Graph showing coded behavior.

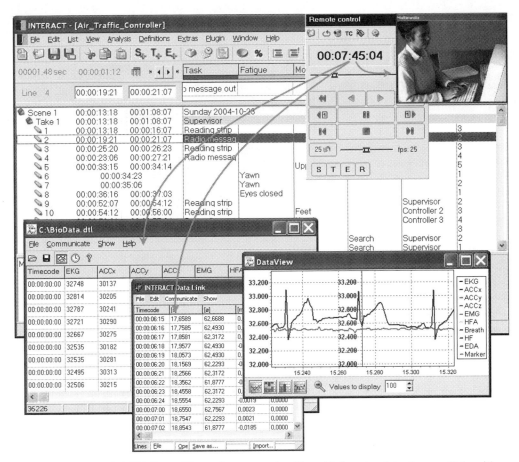

**Figure 7.14** INTERACT Data View that can visualize third-party data in parallel with a researcher's video recordings.

INTERACT includes a variety of export possibilities. The represented data can be exported in spreadsheet programs, work processors, or statistical software (e.g., to SPSS, SAS, Excel).

Finally, INTERACT offers a so-called plug-in technology allowing the user to add any functionality that is not yet integrated (special data import, export, or manipulation routines).

Other interesting INTERACT add-on tools are the Screenalyzer and the Soundalyzer. The Screenalyzer allows the automated collection of user data and screen contents during PC-based (usability) tests. The collected data integrates seamlessly into INTERACT, thus allowing the researcher to jump to a specific user event in the videos and other data files with a simple mouse click from within INTERACT. Figure 7.15 shows an example screen recording snapshot and the final mouse activity chart

The Soundalyzer helps in the analysis of video files by identifying parts of interest automatically, where special audio events happen (e.g., all parts where a person in the video is saying something). This saves a tremendous amount of time, because only the detected fragments have to be analyzed in detail later on (e.g., What was the person saying? What was he doing at the same time?).

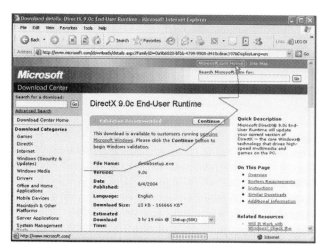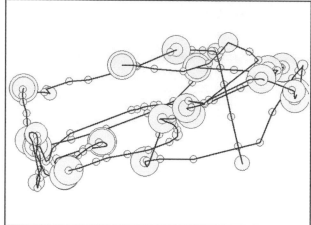

**Figure 7.15** The Screenalyzer can record user activities as INTERACT-compatible events as well as the user's screen contents and mouse movements.

## 7.2 Noldus Information Technology

Noldus Information Technology (http://www.noldus.com/usability) provides professional software and instrumentation for the collection and analysis of behavioral data. Their products cover the following categories: event logging for data collection (The Observer), video highlighting for summarizing and presenting results (The Observer Video-Pro), instant reports for immediate availability of standard reports, analysis to reveal relationships and structure in data, and mobile solutions for collecting data informally or on the site with portable devices. The latest version of The Observer (The Observer XT) also offers the integration of various data modalities such as multiple video sources, physiological data, and events recorded in other systems. Possible events to use include Web page views, mouse clicks, button presses, and eye movements. All ofthese data are synchronized, so that the user can find the relationships between video, physiology, and recorded events. The pattern detection software Theme is capable of finding complex time relationships in behavioral data that standard methods miss. It can be used to gain insight into how people structure their work or how they navigate through Web sites. Noldus staff also help clients set up customized usability labs (see Appendix C).

## ▶ 8. APPENDIX C. SAMPLE LABORATORIES FOR HCI STUDIES

Depending on a number of factors, a lab can have different scopes and functions; it can be fully portable, medium-sized, or stationary (usually large). Here we assemble several real-world labs to give readers some ideas on types and considerations of suchlabs. They may have different names: usability labs, human factors labs, HCI labs, or user experience labs. Some organizations have multiple labs, including portable/mobile labs and stationary ones. All sample labs described here are supported by Noldus Information Technology; the following information has been taken from its Web site (http://www.noldus.com/site/doc200406061) with the permission of each lab.

## 8.1 Thales Naval Netherlands

Thales is a European high-technology group renowned worldwide for its expertise in electronics-based defense systems and services, particularly for naval forces. Thales Netherlands creates high-tech defense solutions for naval and ground-based environments. They combine their extensive and long experience with an ongoing search for new techniques and possibilities. This has resulted in a vast expertise in the fields of radar, infrared, weapon control, display technology, and communications equipment. The product range comprises systems suitable for all classes and types of naval vessels, any weapon system, and any mission. Modern and highly capable sensor suites, together with their combat management system TACTICOS, equip new generations of frigates, corvettes, and fast attack craft throughout the world. Naval capabilities include sophisticated Anti-Air Warfare systems, featuring APAR, SMART-L, and SIRIUS. Thales Ground Based provides solutions for integrated air defense surveillance, track and fire control purposes, and border and battlefield surveillance.

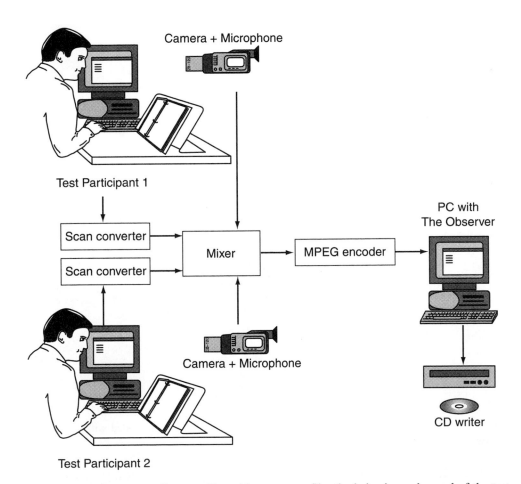

**Figure 7.16** Thales system diagram. Two video cameras film the behavior and sound of the test subjects. Two scan converters convert the signal from the computer screen into a normal video signal. The mixer (quad unit) combines these four video signals into one video signal. This combined video image is then recorded on the computer's hard disk (MPEG-format).

**Figure 7.17** The test room where two participants work as a team to operate the "Hybrid Fire Control" station.

**Figure 7.18** The observation room where a team of observers evaluate the participants' actions.

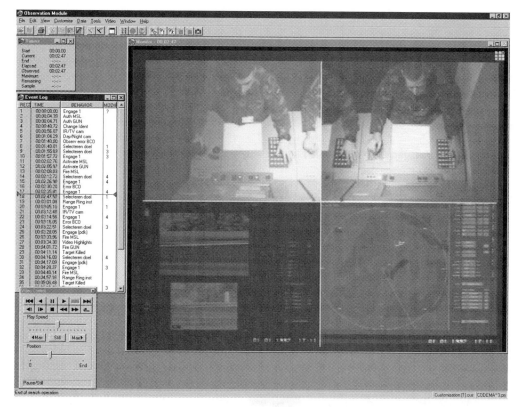

**Figure 7.19** The coding station where the combined video streams are coded with The Observer software.

In 2002, Thales Naval Netherlands, the Royal Netherlands Army, and the Dutch Department of Defense joined forces in the project "Hybrid Fire Control." The purpose of the project is to test a new concept for a ground-based air-defense system. In the human factors lab, The Observer Video-Pro facilitates the usability testing of this particular system. During the usability test, teams of two users are operating the system, while a team of observers is marking important and/or special events using The Observer.

After the test, the observations are evaluated with both the users of the system and the system developers.

Researchers use The Observer to:

- repeatedly analyze video recordings at specific points;
- observe used procedures and communication between the users;
- analyze the use of different input (and some output) devices and compute response time, rate, frequency, and so on.

Readers can contact Theo Hendriksen at Theo.Hendriksen@nl.thalesgroup.com for more information.

## 8.2 CURE's User Experience Laboratories

CURE's mission is to develop innovative and usage-oriented systems utilizing methodological and qualitative usability and usability engineering knowledge. Leading-edge research activities as well as intensive industrial experience enable us to provide added value for users, producers, and principals.

CURE's User Experience Laboratories are fully equipped with the most advanced research and demonstration facilities. All rooms can modularly be connected with each other. This allows numerous settings for studies and observations.

Most of CURE's studies conducted in the labs include qualitative observations as well as quantitative measurements. The main focus is on the collection of qualitative data. For usability tests whose main goal is the detection of usability problems, CURE uses a tailored Excel sheet that enables the observer to log the data in real time duringthe observation. If CURE proves clearly defined scientific hypotheses or if it compares the efficiency or error rate of two or more systems, CURE uses The Observer Video-Pro for logging. The quantitative analysis of the data is then made with Excel and SPSS. Highlight videos are produced with Apple's iMovie.

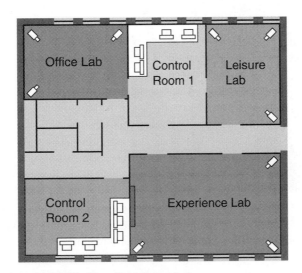

**Figure 7.20**  Floor plan of CURE's User Experience Labs.

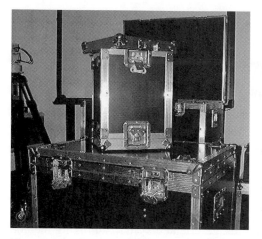

**Figure 7.21** The functionalities of CURE's mobile lab facilities do not differ from the ones of our stationary labs. The most important difference is that it is transportable. Three cameras monitor the test setting. Signals are transmitted to a video mixer and to a digital video recorder. Also the audio signals are recorded digitally.

**Figure 7.22** A small high-resolution camera mounted on mobile devices facilitates tests of applications used with different device classes. CURE's leisure labs, where most of the tests of mobile applications take place, simulate a comfortable living room atmosphere.

**Figure 7.23** Two control rooms support the usability engineer's tasks. From his/her console the usability engineer is able to operate numerous cameras (which are located in three different labs) remotely and simultaneously. He/she can make close-ups, swivel the cameras, and zoom in/out. The recorded videos/pictures can be sampled in various settings: numerous picture-in-picture combinations as well as different sizes and formats can be produced.

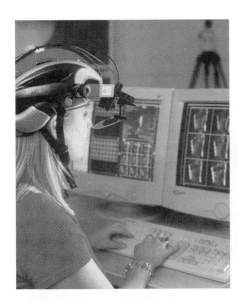

**Figure 7.24** The eye-tracking equipment is used if the research question requires the analysis of users' eye movements. The visual output of the eye-tracking recordings (points/circles on the screen visualizing the user's eye focus as well as the duration of fixations, eye-movement paths, etc.) can be added to the video material.

**Figure 7.25** The Experience Lab can be monitored from either of the two control rooms. It is used for, for example, focus groups and participatory design sessions. Apart from that, the Experience Lab can also be used to monitor any room of the User Experience Laboratories (via video and audio transmission from the respective room/s). Such settings are used when designers want to discuss the results of a test or a trial while watching a test session.

### 8.3 TNO Human Factors Lab

The Intelligent Interfaces group at TNO Human Factors develops and applies guidelines, methods, and user interface concepts that guide the software development process to improve the task support, accessibility, and ease of interaction.

Usability testing is an important instrument for systematically addressing the user and usage perspective during system (re)development. The UE group applies generic and customized methods, tools, and facilities to apply cost-effective tests of software and services (Web sites, mobile services, desktop applications) in different development stages. The usability tests are performed on location or in the Usability Lab.

The Usability Lab offers a flexible number of rooms, which can be arranged as needed (for individual or parallel software testing purposes). The rooms are connected via a computer network and a routing system for all audio and video signals. From the observation room, user behavior is monitored, recorded, and scored using The Observer (by Noldus Information Technology). In addition, the lab is equipped with an eye-tracking device, tools for measuring mental load, and a tool (TIATO) for task and question provision. In specific research projects, customized solutions are developed for the simulation of interaction. The data gathered in the test is analyzed using dedicated statistical software packages to assess efficiency, effectiveness, satisfaction, trust, mental load, and emotional state.

Currently, three of the rooms are converted to intelligent environments (a home, an office, and a museum) in which physical (lighting, heating, appliances, etc.) and information (route planning, weather, news, movies, etc.) services can be triggered by the user and/or the control room for usability tests in the ubiquitous computing domain.

**Figure 7.26** The observation room during a parallel test session.

**Figure 7.27** Usability test with eye-tracking equipment for point of view, mental load, and scan-path assessment.

(a)

(c)

(b)

**Figure 7.28**  The intelligent rooms. See also color plate IV. (a) The intelligent home. (b) The intelligent office. (c) The intelligent museum.

## ▶ 9. SUMMARY OF CONCEPTS AND TERMS

| | | |
|---|---|---|
| Evaluation | HCI concerns | Usability |
| Usability engineering | Usefulness | Universal usability |
| Field experiment | Formative evaluation | Summative evaluation |
| Longitudinal evaluation | Use and impact evaluation | Guideline review |
| Cognitive walk-through | Heuristics evaluation | Focus group |
| Lab experiment | Survey | Field study |
| Common Industry Format | Standard | |

## ▶ 10.  BIBLIOGRAPHY AND ADDITIONAL READINGS

Agarwal, R., & Karahanna, E. (2000). Time flies when you're having fun: Cognitive absorption and beliefs about information technology usage. *MIS Quarterly, 24*(4), 665–694.

Baecker, R., Grudin, J., Buxton, W., & Greenberg, S. (1995). *Readings in human-computer interaction: Toward the year 2000* (2nd ed.). San Francisco, CA: Morgan Kaufmann Publishers, Inc.

Bevan, N. (2001). International standards for HCI and usability. *International Journal of Human-Computer Studies, 55*(4), 533–552.

Bhattacherjee, A. (2001). Understanding information systems continuance: An expectation-confirmation model. *MIS Quarterly, 25*(3), 351–370.

Brave, S., & Nass, C. (2003). Emotion in human-computer interaction. In J. Jacko & A. Sears (Eds.), *The human-computer interaction handbook*. Mahwah, NJ: Lawrence Erlbaum Associates, Inc.

Card, S., Moran, T. P., & Newell, A. (1983). *The psychology of human-computer interaction*. Hillsdale, NJ: Lawrence Erlbaum Associates.

Chen, H., Wigand, R. T., & Nilan, M. S. (1999). Exploring web users' optimal flow experiences. *Information Technology and People*.

Csikszentmihalyi, M. (1990). *Flow: The psychology of optimal experience*. New York: Harpers Perennial.

Davis, F. (1989). Perceived usefulness, perceived ease of use, and user acceptance of information technology. *MIS Quarterly, 13*(3), 319–340.

Finneran, C. M., & Zhang, P. (2003). A person-artefact-task (PAT) model of flow antecedents in computer-mediated environments. *International Journal of Human-Computer Studies, 59*(4), 475–496.

Forgas, J. P. (1995). Mood and judgment: The affect infusion model (AIM). *Psychological Bulletin, 117*(1), 39–66.

Ghani, J. (1995). Flow in human computer interactions: Test of a model. In J. Carey (Ed.), *Human factors in information systems: Emerging theoretical bases*. New Jersey: Ablex Publishing Corp.

Goodhue, D. L., & Thompson, R. L. (1995). Task-technology fit and individual performance. *MIS Quarterly, 19*(2), 213–236.

Gould, J. D., & Lewis, C. (1985). Designing for usability: Key principles and what designers think. *Communications of the ACM, 28*(3), 300–311.

Grudin, J. (1992). Utility and usability: Research issues and development contexts. *Interacting with Computers, 4*(2), 209–217.

Hassenzahl, M., Beu, A., & Burmester, M. (2001). Engineering joy. *IEEE Software* (January/February), 70–76.

Hix, D., & Hartson, H. R. (1993). *Developing user interfaces: Ensuring usability through product and process*. New York: John Wiley.

Kim, J., Lee, J., & Choi, D. (2003). Designing emotionally evocative homepages: An empirical study of the quantitative relations between design factors and emotional dimensions. *International Journal of Human-Computer Studies, 59*(6), 899–940.

Lavie, T., & Tractinsky, N. (2004). Assessing dimensions of perceived visual aesthetics of web sites. *International Journal of Human-Computer Studies, 60*(3), 269–298.

Maxwell, K. (2002). The maturation of HCI: Moving beyond usability toward holistic interaction. In J. M. Carroll (Ed.), *Human-computer interaction in the new millennium*. New York: Addison-Wesley.

Mayhew, D. J. (1999). *The usability engineering lifecycle—A practitioner's handbook for user interface design*. San Francisco, CA: Morgan Kaufmann Publishers, Inc.

Mehlenbacher, B. (2003). Documentation: not yet implemented, but coming soon! In J. A. Jacko & A. Sears (Eds.), *The human-computer interaction handbook: Fundamentals, evolving technologies and emerging applications*. Mahwah, NJ: Lawrence Erlbaum Associates, Publishers.

Nielsen, J. (1993). *Usability engineering*. New York: AP Professional.

Nielsen, J. (2000). *Designing web usability*. Indianapolis, IN: New Riders.

Nielsen, J., & Mack, R. L. (1994). *Usability inspection methods*. New York: John Wiley & Sons.

Norman, D. A. (2002). Emotion and design: Attractive things work better. *Interactions: New Visions of Human-Computer Interaction, IX*(4), 36–42.

Norman, D. A. (2004). *Emotional design: Why we love (or hate) everyday things*. Cambridge, MA: Basic Books.

Preece, J., Rogers, Y., & Sharp, H. (2002). *Interaction design: Beyond human-computer interaction*. New York: John Wiley & Sons.

Preece, J., Rogers, Y., Sharp, H., Benyon, D., Holland, S., & Carey, T. (1994). *Human-computer interaction*. Wokingham, UK: Addison-Wesley.

Reeve, J. (2005). *Understanding motivation and emotion* (4th ed.). New York: John Wiley & Sons, Inc.

Robson, C. (2002). *Real world research: A resource for social scientists and practitioner-researchers*. Oxford, UK: Blackwell.

Rosson, M. B., & Carroll, J. M. (2002). *Usability engineering: Scenario-based development of human-computer interaction*. New York: Morgan Kaufmann Publishers.

Russell, J. A. (2003). Core affect and the psychological construction of emotion. *Psychological Review,* 110(1), 145–172.

Shneiderman, B. (2000). Universal usability. *Communication of the ACM, 43*(5), 84–91.

Shneiderman, B., & Plaisant, C. (2005). *Designing the user interface: Strategies for effective human-computer interaction*. New York: Addison-Wesley.

Sun, H., & Zhang, P. (2006). The role of affect in IS research: A critical survey and a research model. In P. Zhang & D. Galletta (Eds.), *Human-computer interaction and management information systems: Foundations*. Armonk, NY: M.E. Sharpe.

Thibodeau, P. (2005, June 20). Large users hope for broader adoption of usability standard. *Computerworld*.

Tractinsky, N., Katz, A. S., & Ikar, D. (2000). What is beautiful is usable. *Interacting with Computers, 13*, 127–145.

Venkatesh, V., Morris, M. G., Davis, G. B., & Davis, F. D. (2003). User acceptance of information technology: Toward a unified view. *MIS Quarterly, 27*(3), 425–478.

Vessey, I. (1991). Cognitive fit: A theory-based analysis of the graphs versus tables literature. *Decision Sciences, 22*, 219–240.

Vessey, I., & Galletta, D. F. (1991). Cognitive fit: An empirical study of information acquisition. *Information Systems Research, 2*(1), 63–84.

Vredenburg, K., Mao, J., Smith, P. W., & Carey, T. (2002). *A survey of user-centered design practice*. Paper read at Computer Human Interaction (CHI).

Webster, J., & Martocchio, J. J. (1992). Microcomputer playfulness: Development of a measure with workplace implications. *MIS Quarterly, 16*(1).

Zhang, P., Benbasat, I., Carey, J., Davis, F., Galletta, D., & Strong, D. (2002). Human-computer interaction research in the MIS discipline. *Communications of the AIS, 9*(20), 334–355.

Zhang, P., Carey, J., Te'eni, D., & Tremaine, M. (2005). Integrating human-computer interaction development into the systems development life cycle: A methodology. *Communication of the AIS, 15*, 512–543.

Zhang, P., & Li, N. (2004). *Love at first sight or sustained effect? The role of perceived affective quality on users' cognitive reactions to IT.* Paper read at International Conference on Information Systems (ICIS'04), Washington, DC.

Zhang, P., & Li, N. (2005, September). The importance of affective quality. *Communications of the ACM, 48*(9), 105–108.

## ▶ 11. CASE STUDY

Lance Redux is designing and implementing a Web site for Majorca Fleming's e-Gourmet international food import store. He is aware of the importance of usability for any e-commerce Web site. In addition, he wants his customers to enjoy using the Web site. Customers are expected to place their own orders through the Web site. Since use of the site is voluntary, any difficulties encountered by customers may cause the customers to leave the site and never return, which translates into lost sales.

In order to ensure usability, Lance has enlisted several of his friends (both technical and nontechnical) to test out the Web site. He has created a short questionnaire and set of tasks for each of his usability testers. He also has several open-ended questions that will allow the testers to make suggestions for improving the site.

## ▶ 12. EXERCISES

Ex. 1.    Web Accessibility Guide

There are several standards on Web content accessibility. There are also tools on testing the accessibility of a Web site. Go to the Watchfire® Bobby™ Web site (http://www.watchfire.com/products/desktop/bobby/default.aspx) to find out what it is about. What standards is it based on?

1.a. Evaluate a number of Web pages such as your university's Web site and your personal home page in light of these two standards and provide examples of how (if at all) they are supported by the example Web pages.

1.b. Write your own impression of the Watchfire® Bobby™ Web site. This can include any aspect of it, such as whether it is a useful tool, whether its own design is a good one based on what criteria, whether it is easy to work with, and so on.

Ex. 2.    Use the TSSL model to evaluate existing interface design.

Select a good computer user interface that interests you in terms of interface design and human characteristics that should be considered. Distinguish the lexical, syntactic, and semantic levels of factors of the interface. Discuss how a task is supported based on the three levels. Analyze how human characteristics are addressed on the interface at each level. Describe how the interface can be redesigned or revised at any of the three levels to achieve either the same or better results. Select a bad interface and do the same exercise described above. Example interfaces include but are not limited to the following:

Web pages for

- Information presentations
- Information searching
- Online registrations
- E-commerce transactions
- Downloading applications

Computer desktop

- With multiple windows
- A dialog window of an application
- A screen of an electronic game

Other interfaces such as

- ATM
- Palm PDA

Ex. 3.   Use CIF to report an evaluation of an existing system.

The objective of this assignment is to apply learned evaluation methods to examine an existing system and report the evaluation results in CIF. Identify a small computer system or a subsystem of a computer system. Select one evaluation method with justification of its appropriateness for this evaluation task. Then conduct the evaluation using this method and produce the report in CIF format.

# CHAPTER 8

# DESIGN PRINCIPLES AND GUIDELINES

## CONTEXT AND PREVIEW

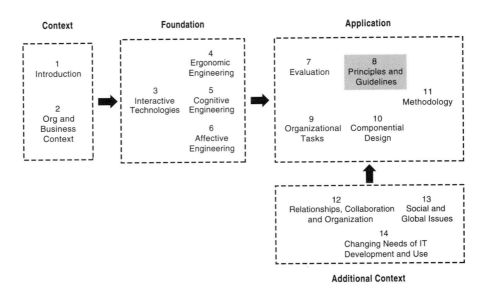

The current chapter presents a set of design principles and guidelines that form a transition between the Foundation chapters and their application to HCI development. On the one hand, the design principles summarize the theoretical foundations (Chapters 3 to 6). On the other hand, the principles and the more operational guidelines are formulated with an eye to HCI development (Chapters 9 to 11). They are applied throughout the analysis, design, and implementation stages of the development life cycle, as indicated below in the methodology map.

The principles and guidelines are stated in Table 8.1. In this book, principles shall be defined as high-level design goals that hold true regardless of task or context. The principles are extracted from the discussions of physical, cognitive, and affective engineering with a view to achieving a seamless fit between the user, computer, and task. Guidelines shall be defined as specific rules that are dependent on task and context and are means for accomplishing the design principles. We present the pros and cons of these guidelines, challenging the reader to critically evaluate their application.

## LEARNING OBJECTIVES

Upon completion of this chapter, students should be able to do the following:

- Explain the difference between theory, principles, and guidelines and how they relate to each other
- List and discuss the seven HCI principles introduced in this chapter
- List and discuss the five HCI guidelines introduced in this chapter
- Utilize the principles and guidelines to design and develop sound HCI
- Assess existing HCI for adherence to the principles and guidelines
- Recognize good and bad examples of HCI and understand their underlying causes

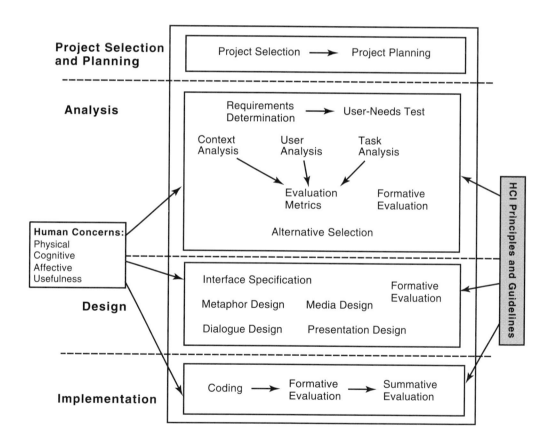

## 1. INTRODUCTION

The underlying theory presented in the Foundations section must now be translated into principles of HCI development, as well as the more specific design guidelines. The principles build on the previous chapters to formalize high-level and widely applicable design goals. The guidelines are more specific rules for designers to follow in order to achieve the principles. They tend to be more dependent on the task and the context and

**Table 8.1** Design Principles and Guidelines

---

**Design Principles**

---

- Improve users' task performance and reduce their effort
- Strive for fit between the information representation needed and presented
- Direct and constrain user affordances to capture real-world knowledge
- Design for error
- Enable an enjoyable and satisfying interaction
- Promote trust
- Support diversity of users

---

**Design Guidelines**

---

- Maintain consistent interaction
- Provide the user with control over the interaction, supported by feedback
- Use metaphors
- Use direct manipulation
- Design aesthetic interfaces

---

are tied more closely to the interactive technologies. In the transition from theory to practice, you may want to think of the principles as representing the theory with an eye to what we should practice and the guidelines taking the principles one step further toward their application. For example, promoting an enjoyable interaction (a principle) can be accomplished by providing an aesthetic screen (a design guideline).

The overarching goal of the principles and guidelines is to achieve fit between the user, technology, and task. Although we espouse the adoption of these guidelines by HCI practitioners, we understand that each guideline has advantages as well as limitations and stress the need to apply such rules with caution. We have included tables, figures, examples, and discussions to articulate development strategies and choices for each of the guidelines and principles included in the chapter. We therefore limit the coverage to several guidelines in contrast to more comprehensive lists such as those devised by Smith and Mosier (1984). Furthermore, we claimed in the Introduction that effective design should be user, task, and context dependent. The same user can undertake different tasks in different contexts, having different expectations of the technology. Designs must therefore be flexible.

Consider a particular user, a college student, who interacts with a computer to accomplish three different tasks. The student uses a word processor to write a term paper for a class, plays an online bridge game with unknown partners from all over the world using a PC in her dormitory, and uses an ATM machine to withdraw some cash. The developer's first step is to understand the user, the tasks from the user's point of view, and the context in which the user accomplishes the tasks. The college student would usually have some experience in using PC. She may be young and relatively impatient and accustomed to performing multiple tasks simultaneously. Providing this user with lengthy instructions on how to use the word processor would not fit her temperament. Similarly, not being able to leave the word processor to do something else and return exactly to the location she left it would also reflect poor fit between the design and the user's way of performing the task. In longer tasks, the user expects to be distracted from time to time to attend to other tasks. When playing bridge, she would expect that the computer game should indicate the status of the current game, provide her with an area

**Design principles:** High-level and largely context-free design goals based on theories of human–computer interaction.

**Design guidelines:** Specific and usually context-dependent rules for designers to follow in order to achieve the principles.

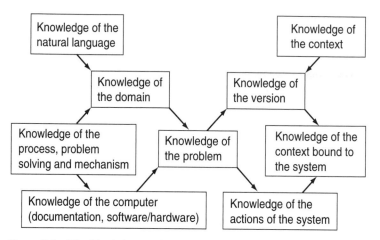

**Figure 8.1**  The block interaction diagram (adapted from Hammond & Barnard, 1984).

for communicating with her partner, and not distract her by flashing images or ads. When using the ATM, she wants to get the task done as quickly as possible. The user expects no interruptions and expects no fun associated with this short and structured task. She would appreciate a shortcut for getting commonly needed amounts (such as $50, $100) so that she spends minimum time on getting the task accomplished. Thus, the three different tasks dictate different user expectations and priorities and therefore a different emphasis on aspects of design to achieve the right fit.

One framework for characterizing the user is to specify the user's knowledge needed for the interaction. The sources of knowledge pertain to the user, the computer, the task, and the interactions between the three. The user has several categories of previous knowledge: computers in general, the use of natural language, problem solving, the task domain, and general work procedures in the organization. Furthermore, the user has knowledge of how these characteristics interact (e.g., how problem solving can be enhanced with computers). Figure 8.1 (adapted from Hammond & Barnard, 1984) is a map of the knowledge necessary to perform the task with the computer. This diagram (called the Block Interaction Model) is a useful design tool. At the minimum it serves as a checklist for considering what kind of background knowledge the user needs and what the user knows coming into the dialogue. But the knowledge map is also the basis for determining the user's habit or mental model associated with the task. Other characterizations of users, such as gender and age, may also be relevant in some situations (e.g., bigger fonts for the elderly or more colorful interfaces for children). Finally, we go beyond the task to consider affective aspects of HCI to include aspects such as trust, flow, and satisfaction. Equipped with an understanding of user and task characteristics, we turn to the principles and guidelines.

## ▶ 2. DESIGN PRINCIPLES

It should be noted that it is impractical to list an exhaustive set of principles that may lead to good HCI designs. The goal of this chapter is to demonstrate some of the principles and explain in detail their pros and cons. Readers are encouraged to select appropriate principles and guidelines when designing HCI to support a particular user group for particular tasks in a particular context of use.

## 2.1 Improve Users' Task Performance and Reduce Their Effort

Figure 1.7 suggests that user activity depends on the utilization of the user's resources, such as memory and attention. In nontrivial situations, we assume that any reduction in the resources that the user needs to expend to complete the task will improve performance. Our first design principle is therefore to automate or partially automate the user activity (this is the functionality aspect, which has to do with the system's services and operations available to the user) and to do so with minimal user effort (this is the usability aspect). As we discuss in task analysis (elaborated in Chapter 9), the first step focuses on functionality, that is, what functions should the system provide in order to support the task? Usability (Chapter 7) addresses issues of efficiency, ease of use, and comfort in using the system, given that the functionality has been established. There is sometimes a trade-off between functionality and usability, and often compromises in functionality produce higher usability. For example, added options on the menu facilitate additional functionality but may render the menu difficult to use. This design principle dictates a combined effort to achieve high functionality along with high usability.

## 2.2 Strive for Fit between the Information Representation Needed and Presented

Figure 1.4 in the Introduction calls for a fit between user, computer, and task. In Chapter 5 (Cognitive Engineering) we discuss the user's and computer's representations of the task and the fit between them. Given some real-world task, the user constructs a mental representation of the task in order to act (this is the user's mental model). The user's representation is simply the way the user depicts and usually simplifies the real world. The designer also constructs a representation of the real-world task in order to design a way of supporting the user in performing the task (this is the designer's conceptual model). Finally, the computer system is designed to display elements of the task externally in order to communicate with the user about the task and internally in order to process the information. Our second design principle concentrates on the "cognitive fit" between representations.

> **Representation:** A simplified depiction of a real-world phenomenon constructed to support some activity.

Figure 8.2 shows the interaction between three types of representations (models): the user's mental model, the designer's conceptual model, and the system's representation of the designed model as it is displayed and seen by the user. The idea of cognitive fit

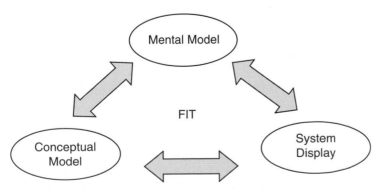

**Figure 8.2** Three models—the designer's conceptual model, the user's mental model, and the display of the system.

between the user's mental model and the system's representation is central to cognitive engineering as explained in Chapter 5. The same principle applies to the expanded partnership among the designer, user, and system. Deviations between any pair bring about inefficiency and room for error.

A natural representation for a particular problem requires minimal transformations and, indeed, can be measured as the inverse of the number of steps needed to complete the task in comparison with other representations. Fewer steps means less cognitive effort on behalf of the user and a smaller chance of errors (assuming, simplistically, that each step requires the same effort). We have already discussed this approach and demonstrated it with GOMS, claiming that a shorter GOMS description is superior to a longer program, assuming both programs can accomplish the common goal. A good fit between the mental models of user, system, and designer is the second design principle.

> **Cognitive fit:** The state in which the system's representation of the problem supports the user's strategies for performing the task.

### 2.3  Provide and Constrain Affordances to Capture Real-World Knowledge

The third design principle dictates a search for both affordances and constraints that are appropriate for the particular users and tasks at hand.

Affordances are "the perceived and actual properties of the thing, primarily those fundamental properties that determine how the thing could possibly be used" (Norman, 1988). For example, a keyhole in a door is designed to make it obvious and easy to correctly insert the key by signaling only one possible position (e.g., a vertical position of the key). The general idea here is that the knowledge required to act effectively resides both in the person's head and in the real world around him. There is always a trade-off between the amount of knowledge the user has to memorize and the amount of knowledge evident in the design of the artifact. A vertical slot that allows only one possibility for placing the key relieves the person from remembering the correct position. However, it is often inefficient to use real-world knowledge in the interface design because it may overload the user with information displayed on the screen. The designer's dilemma is how to provide affordances that relieve cognitive effort (reduce the need to retrieve information or plan a procedure) and at the same time constrain the user's inappropriate actions. In a sense, this design principle is an expansion of the previous principle of fit. The designer, in striving for a good fit, must also consider the balance between information assumed to reside in the mental model and that displayed on screen.

> **Affordance:** The aspects of an object that the user perceives as indicating how to use the object (e.g., the handle of a teapot).

Consider some examples. Anyone who has connected the various cords from a desktop computer to the screen, mouse, keyboard, power, phone, network, speakers, and so on, knows how rewarding it is to have only one possible slot for each plug. By a careful design, the shape (and often color) can indicate how to set up the connections with minimal effort. This is the power of designing constraints into the interface. As opposed to the boundless command-based interfaces such as those offered by UNIX, consider a pull-down menu that allows you to select from a limited set of options. Moreover, in certain situations when some of the options are irrelevant, those options are dimmed (grayed out) and inactive, thus further constraining unwarranted action.

A set of good examples of affordances can be found in Gaver (1991). In Figure 8.3, the raised "OK" button invites the user to click on it (which is equivalent to pushing a key on the keyboard to type a character). This is an affordance that draws the user's attention to a possible action, while deemphasizing other actions. The user needs to resort to previous (nonafforded) knowledge about how to depress the button (e.g., using the mouse to move the pointer to the button and clicking the right mouse button).

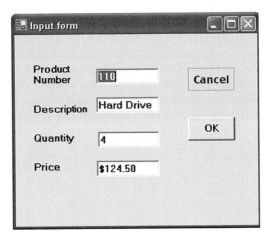

**Figure 8.3** Affordance in the design of buttons—the "OK" button invites you to push it.

Another action, such as pressing the Tabs, may intentionally or unintentionally bring about the same affordance for the "Cancel" button. Balancing the affordances and constraints is the third principle.

## 2.4 Design for Error

The famous saying "To err is human" suggests that users are *error-prone*. Not that we, as designers, should cast the blame on users, but we must assume that errors are part of any human activity. Designers must therefore (1) attempt to minimize the occurrence of errors, (2) indicate that an error has occurred, (3) help correct or undo the error, and (4) indicate the impact of the error and possibly minimize the cost of error.

Chapter 5 explains the sources of error as they related to the three types of information processing: skill-based, rule-based, and knowledge-based. Figure 5.12 classifies the many types of error accordingly. Only after performing an analysis of possible errors by using Figure 5.12 as a checklist can we design to minimize error occurrence. Norman (1983) provides a classification of errors and some rules on how to avoid them, which are summarized in Table 8.2.

The format of error messages is discussed below under the design guidelines for feedback, but generally speaking, such messages should be specific and constructive. Helping the user correct or undo errors has become commonplace. The command *Undo* (e.g., Microsoft applications usually have the *Undo* under menu option *Edit* or a shortcut though Ctrl + Z), which is today a standard, allows the user to undo the most recent operation or choose from a list of recent operations. Finally, the fourth aspect of designing for error is to indicate the possible or actual damage generated by the error and to minimize it. This aspect is difficult and often impossible to do comprehensively. For example, the system can provide an indication of all files that could be affected by a recent change in the current file (e.g., change of files linked by hyperlinks). This warning can be supplemented by an option of recovering some of them from backups.

Moreover, some errors can be corrected, or at least suggestions for corrections given, automatically. In skill-based behavior, some errors, such as spelling mistakes, can be

**Table 8.2**   Classification of Errors

| Source | Design Rule |
|---|---|
| Mode errors: erroneous classification of the situation (e.g., insert mode versus strikeover mode). | Do not have modes. Distinguish clearly between modes. Distinguish between commands associated with different modes so that inappropriate commands do no damage. |
| Description errors: ambiguous or incomplete specification of the intention (e.g., specifying the destination for moving files by imprecisely pointing at a location in a directory). | Arrange controls (menus, fields) in functional patterns, procedures. Distinguish between controls (dialogs, displays) with a different look and feel. Make it especially difficult to perform actions with serious cost of error. |
| Capture errors: when performing a sequence that is similar to a more frequent one, the frequent one will capture control (e.g., shutting down a system instead of an intended but less frequent "restart"). | Minimize overlapping sequences. Try to catch it when it occurs by identifying the critical point of deviation from the correct sequence (requires knowledge of the intention). |
| Activation errors: inappropriate actions get performed and appropriate actions do not. | Maintain a display of incomplete sequences to prompt the user to act appropriately. |

detected and often corrected automatically when the error is defined unambiguously. In word processing, the automatic correction of spelling proves to be very popular. The guidelines on control and feedback discussed below are forms of reducing the propensity and cost of errors.

## 2.5  Designing for an Enjoyable and Satisfying Interaction

High levels of functionality and usability are expected to produce high user satisfaction. As noted earlier, although usefulness and ease of use have traditionally been considered the main contributors to user attitudes toward using computers, emotions are beginning to play an equally important role. For example, an aesthetic interface may trigger positive feelings toward the system and in fact is found to correlate with measures of usability (Tractinsky, Katz, & Ikar, 2000). Flow, defined as a feeling of optimal experience, has to do with a state of being completely absorbed by the interaction. A sense of flow in the interaction and closure toward the end of the interaction may produce a satisfying and fulfilling experience. In particular, the vividness (richness of the representation), interactivity, and adaptability of the human–computer interface affect the flow of HCI. For example, a higher quality of the image and range of colors (vividness) or a better response time and control over the navigation (interactivity) positively affect the user's attitude toward the system.

These aspects of design have more to do with a general positive feeling that goes beyond the accomplishment of the task at hand. As designers of HCI, we strive to create more satisfying systems for people. It appears that pleasing interfaces are also perceived to be more usable and create a more productive workplace. However, the main business incentive for providing pleasing Web sites is to win the competition for user attention and loyalty. When the organization's customers, rather than its workers, are the users, a pleasurable interaction attracts visitors that are free to choose from scores of competing Web sites. Indeed, research has shown that a fundamental objective of an online consumer is to enjoy the shopping experience (Keeney, 1999).

The fifth principle of design encourages designers to consider enjoyment, pleasure, and satisfaction as an important element of interacting with computers. The terms "engineering joy" and "emotional usability" (Hassenzahl, Beu, & Burmester, 2001), symbolize the move from task-related usability to a broader concern for emotions and attitudes.

## 2.6  Promote Trust

Trust is another aspect of HCI that requires analysis beyond task analysis. In e-commerce systems where the interactions translate directly into revenue, trust is a critical component. As developers, we ask the question, "How can we design HCI that positively affects the user's trust in the system and in the services it provides?"

Trust is based on both cognitive and emotional components (Lewis & Weigert, 1985). Cognitive trust is based on knowing enough about the trusted agent to have good reasons for trust, such as acknowledged expertise of the trusted party. Interestingly, trust actually involves some kind of leap beyond the expectations based on the information available. Emotional trust consists of feelings that are part of an emotional bond. It is therefore usually associated with established or close relationships. On the basis of cognitive and emotional trust, people undertake risky action on the expectation that the trusted partner will act appropriately. Behavioral trust feeds back to emotional and cognitive trust, so, for example, unexpected behavior (e.g., betrayal) or faulty behavior will quickly erode trust. We expand on trust in Chapter 12, but we now concentrate on the design implications.

What has trust to do with computers? Well, if we assume that people fundamentally interact with computers in a social and natural manner that resembles their interaction with other people in real life, then we can examine how the human–computer interface affects cognitive and emotional trust. Reeves and Nass (1996), among others, make a persuasive argument to adopt this assumption, labeling it "The Media Equation."

One interesting stream of work based on this assumption resulted in research on computer credibility (see Fogg & Tseng, 1999). Although the empirical research that supports these deductions is quite tentative, it is worth noting them as they have intuitive appeal. Table 8.3 summarizes several determinants of computer credibility. Some of the design implications apply to all users, while other implications are dependent on the type of user, particularly whether the user is a novice or an expert on the subject matter. Experts are generally more critical, judging the system as less credible, especially when the views presented in the system conflict with their own.

Hoffman, Novak, and Peralta (1999) make one last point about building trust online. Users of Web sites expect them to honor a social contract between the Web site operators (owners) and the users. The contract should be accessible and explicit. Whatever is not announced and not agreed on must not allow any invasion of privacy and consumer rights. Most notable is an understanding that any personal data belongs to the user and nobody else has any right to use it. Any breach of this contract erodes trust completely and any guarantee, stated and acted, enhances trust.

**Table 8.3**  Sources and Barriers of Computer Credibility

- Computer errors damage credibility. In fact, even small errors reduce credibility and do so disproportionately.
- In situations where people feel they need help, computers seem more credible.
- Users who consider themselves experts judge computers as less credible.
- Users who consider themselves to be similar in some sense to the system will judge it as more credible.
- Signs of affiliation to expert or known other sources enhance credibility (e.g., association with known groups, credentials).
- Certain characteristics of the interface that project an attractive but professional aura enhance credibility.

## 2.7  Support Diversity of Users

As designers we have the responsibility to open our design to the effective use of diverse populations of users. First, in many cases we do not know in advance who will attempt to use the system if it is open to all users (e.g., users of a particular Web site). We should assume that users from different nationalities with different backgrounds may use the system. Second, some of the users may be handicapped in one way or another and find it difficult or impossible to use certain features. For example, color-blind users may not be able to understand information displayed on a graph that relies on the use of color to differentiate categories. We should not put some users at a disadvantage when using the system. Indeed, Section 508 of the Rehabilitation Act reendorsed by the U.S. Congress in 1998 sets Accessibility Standards that are regulated in all federal procurements. See specific guidelines at http://www.access-board.gov.

## ▶ 3. DESIGN GUIDELINES

As noted above, we take a deeper look at five illustrative guidelines. The alternative approach would be to make a shallow attempt to cover all guidelines, which would be less effective in our opinion. Two elements run through most of the discussions in this section: (1) design is often about trade-offs and therefore designers need to prioritize and compromise, and (2) guidelines often apply to the four levels of interaction—task, semantic, syntactic, and lexical (see Figure 1.6). The guidelines apply to these levels of interaction in different ways with differences in importance. For example, the design and effect of consistency at the task level (the same options on a menu in all situations) may be different from those at the lexical level (the consistent use of pop-up menus).

The overall approach is to critically examine the tasks and users of the target system and from this examination and an understanding of common practice decide how to apply the appropriate guidelines in order to achieve a well-designed information system. The guidelines are based on theory covered in the Foundations section of the book. Additionally, general rules for implementation are offered for each guideline. More specific applications of these and other guidelines will be explored in the coming chapter on design components and within the integrated examples.

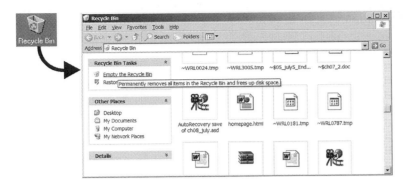

**Figure 8.4** Recycle bin in the Windows environment illustrating analogical consistency.

## 3.1 Issue I: Consistency Guidelines

"Maintain consistency in interface design" has been considered the heart of design philosophy. Scholars from Shneiderman to Bailey suggest that consistency is the "golden rule" of good design. In practice, this guideline has acquired universal acceptance. Some of this acceptance is driven by the "look and feel" that has been standardized first by Sun and Apple (Macintosh) and then by Microsoft (Windows). It has been said that humans are adaptable. If we provide users with a consistent interface (no matter how usable it is) users will adapt to fit the interface. Is consistency always preferable? We look into this guideline and leave you at the end pondering whether indeed consistency is universally good.

In general, consistency is believed to lead to faster task performance, with fewer errors and less effort, and to facilitate learning and easier transfer from one application to another. There are at least three types of consistency: internal, external, and analogical (Grudin, 1989). *Internal consistency* is the degree to which the same appearance, meaning, and operation of interface attributes hold within the same application. Similarly, *external consistency* is the degree to which the same appearance, meaning, and operation hold across various applications. *Analogical consistency* is the correspondence between the appearance, meaning, and operation of objects represented in the human–computer interface and the real-world (external to the system) objects being represented. Figure 8.4 illustrates the metaphor of the recycle bin in the Windows environment. The recycle bin, like a garbage can, is a storage space that holds deleted files until it is actually emptied by the user. Files that are accidentally deleted may be retrieved until the recycle bin is emptied.

A prime example of achieving consistency is the use of standard controls (e.g., those supported by Visual Studio.Net) to produce in the interface the same (consistent) "look and feel" throughout the human–computer interaction in a single application and across other applications. For example, standard dialog boxes are consistent in look and feel (properties and methods) and can be added to an application with little effort. Figure 8.5 illustrates the standard "Save As" and "Open" dialog boxes that are used by the Microsoft Word application. The same dialog boxes are available across all Microsoft Office applications and the Visual Studio.Net development environment for Visual Basic.Net, C#, or J++. The standard dialog boxes are both internally consistent (across a single application) and externally consistent (across multiple applications).

Figure 8.6 illustrates external consistency across two different applications. The user encounters the same filters, titles, and formats from dialog to dialog and uses them in a consistent manner to perform similar actions. There is no need to learn new tools

**Internal consistency:** The same appearance, meaning, and operation hold true for all the user's interactions within the same application.

**External consistency:** The same appearance, meaning, and operation hold true for the user's interactions across applications.

**Analogical consistency:** The correspondence between the system's representation and the real-world phenomenon in terms of appearance, meaning, and operation.

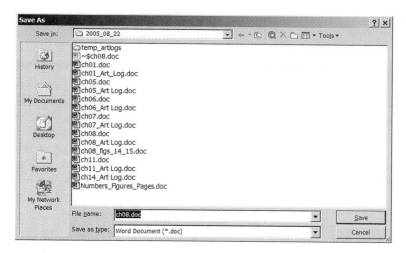

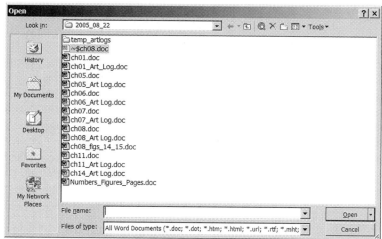

**Figure 8.5** "Save as" and "Open" dialog boxes in Microsoft Word illustrating internal consistency.

because the same toolkit is available for a very wide range of actions. The same behavior leads to more efficient and more accurate action. These are two fundamental measures of performance. Consistency is also related to the distinction between controlled and automatic behavior. Consistency is critical to automatic behavior because without it the user must stop the flow of work to choose an appropriate tool for the task, which clearly stymies the automatic behavior and introduces an element of decision and control into user behavior. A consistent "look and feel," therefore, enhances learning and efficient operation.

Table 8.4 includes several designs rules that enhance consistency, as summarized by Tognazzini (1990). The first four rules are straightforward conclusions derived from the realization that people prefer and expect consistency. The first rule is "Follow accepted (usually published) guidelines whenever possible" and is a simple method of ensuring consistency. The second rule has to do with stability and is "Do not change something unless it really needs changing." Figure 8.7 illustrates a violation of this rule. The two screen shots are the main database windows from Access 97 and Access 2000. The look and feel between these two versions is very different. The functionality is much the

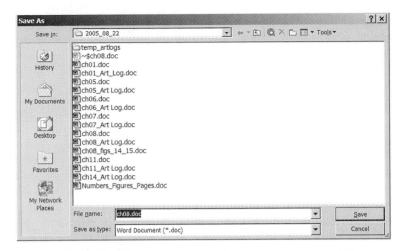

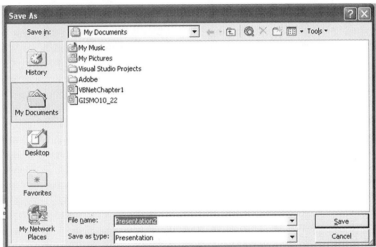

**Figure 8.6** "Save as" dialog boxes in Microsoft Word and Microsoft PowerPoint illustrating external consistency.

same. It seems that the user would have been better served by keeping the interface as stable as possible unless there is a need to change and improve the system. Or consider stability within a session. You have on your desktop 20 icons, of which you would typically use only 10 a day. Your computer system is configured to rearrange your desktop according to what it predicts (on the basis of your previous behavior) which icons you will probably use. Such "efficient" design would violate the rule of stability.

The third rule has to do with training and is "Add new skills to the user's skill set rather than expecting the user to modify existing skills." The fourth rule states, "If you must make a change, make sure it is a large and obvious one." Rule 4 recognizes that any break away from the expected can be made easier if it is more noticeable. An effective change of behavior should result from an obvious change in the interface. If the change is small and subtle, users will likely become more confused and try to hold on to their learned behaviors either subconsciously or consciously. The fifth rule may be less obvious. People expect consistency (perhaps most of all from artifacts) and therefore assume that in the absence of any obvious reason or contradictory evidence the object of interaction

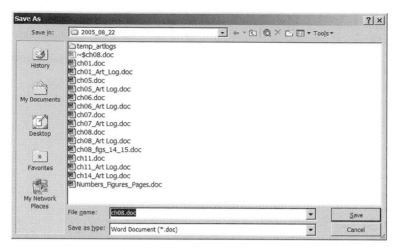

**Figure 8.7**  Access 97 interface versus Access 2000 interface. Violation of the second rule of Consistency Guideline I ("Do not change anything unless it needs changing").

will behave consistently from use to use. In particular, the users' intentions should be interpreted consistently. Any violation of this expectation that is not a consequence of their own intention shatters their perception of that object, reduces their confidence, and leaves them undecided about their future actions. The implicit part of the system's behavior must, therefore, be consistent, that is, the interpretation of the users' identical intentions as represented by the same actions. While a change in the color of a screen background from one day to another may be tolerated, different reactions to the same keystroke or mouse click from use to use or from version to version is extremely frustrating. Apparently inconsistent system behavior can be due to changing circumstances of which the user is unaware. Under Windows, for example, a request to copy a directory may be interpreted as duplicating the directory when the destination is on another device and as moving the directory (without duplication) when it is on the same device. This inconsistency problem could have been avoided by sufficient differentiation between moving and copying a directory. The two actions should not be confused. They are different tasks in the user's mind.

**Table 8.4**  Design Rules for Consistency

1. Standardization of interface designs: Follow accepted (usually published) guidelines whenever possible.
2. Stability: Do not change something unless it really needs changing.
3. Training: Add new skills to the user's skill set rather than expecting the user to modify existing skills.
4. If you must change, make it a large and obvious one.
5. Consistent interpretation of user behavior by the system is more important than consistent system objects or behaviors.

These observations can be redefined in terms of the models of cognitive engineering. Referring back to the "gulf of execution" and the "gulf of evaluations" (see Figure 5.6), consistency in "gulf of evaluation" is the more important. This is because from the user's perspective there is more uncertainty in how the machine reacts than how the user himself reacts. Consistency in how the machine reacts is essential for mastering the user's interaction with it. For example, high external consistency occurs when the same icon (designed like a printer with a page in it) appears to designate a print command in two different applications. It is also high analogical consistency because the printer resembles a physical machine and the association with the printing operation is strong. However, if the reaction to a click on the printer icon produces a print menu (with options to specify the print scope, number of copies, etc.) in one situation and begins to print directly (without a menu) in a second situation, there is no consistency in the evaluation gulf. Such inconsistency raises the uncertainty about the user's mental model of the system, inhibits learning, and slows down performance in the next encounter with the print command.

Furthermore, consistency should be considered at each of the four levels of interaction. Consistency at the lexical level, that is, using the same physical characteristics of the objects (e.g., shape and color of icons), improves performance by promoting faster recognition, although the user may be able to overcome inconsistency (e.g., change of colors of the same shape) with some effort. The same icon, appearing in different locations on the screen, also hampers performance (an example of inconsistency in syntax) because the user can no longer expect to find the icon above or below some point in the screen and has to engage in a search for the desired icon. Consistency at the higher levels of semantics may be detrimental because there is no certainty about what the communication means. Finally, inconsistency at the task level is probably most damaging to the user's ability to form a correct mental model of the system. Say the user learns that clicking on the printer icon results in a setup of the printer attributes (it happened to be the first time the user printed with a newly connected printer) but then finds out that, on another occasion, he accidentally printed out a private document on the departmental printer (the default printer). The second encounter reflects the designer's conceptual model of the system, that is, a click on the printer icon activates the print command with a default scope of the currently active document. Thus, an inconsistent system's reaction to the same user operation results in an unwarranted result. The way to design this option to give the user maximum control and support all three types of consistency is to always have the printer dialog box pop up when the printer icon is clicked.

Can consistency be measured? We have already learned about GOMS and how a comparison of different GOMS descriptions of similar operations can indicate the degree of consistency between two actions such as "cut" and "copy." Similarly, other methods such as the activity list can be compared to gauge consistency. In fact, we see how such measures are used to study the effect of consistency on transfer of learning (e.g., Kieras & Polson, 1985, explained in Chapter 5).

Is consistency universally good? Grudin (1989) makes an interesting case against consistency. One reason is that consistency may actually hinder performance by over-looking certain situational knowledge. For example, a pull-down menu presents the options of the "Edit" command (namely Undo, Cut, Copy, Paste, Special Paste, and Find). Internal consistency requires that the same options be presented whenever Edit is invoked. However, note that options "cut" and "copy" are grayed out when there is no selected text because they are irrelevant. This inconsistency is beneficial because it constrains the user and helps avoid errors.

Figure 8.8 shows three Edit menus. The first two are from Microsoft Word showing the difference between the menu option Edit in the two conditions of an active selection and no selection, respectively. The third Edit menu is the result of clicking the right mouse button in the identical situation of the second menu (i.e., no active selection). Note that although the special paste option is relevant, it does not appear. We leave it to the reader to ponder whether consistency and inconsistency in the design is good or bad.

As in other issues of design, the designer may be faced with a trade-off between consistency and efficiency. In the "Edit" example, changing the default option according to the previous operation may be inconsistent but efficient. For example, the default option of Edit may be "cut" when a text has been selected, but it changes to "paste" after "cut" has been used. Moreover, the notion of consistency at different levels of interaction begs the question of the relative importance of consistency at the different levels of interaction. Ideally, the analogical consistency between the user's expectations of the system's response (based on the user's experience in the real world) should be compatible with the internal consistency; when such compatibility is impossible, the higher-level consistency (at the task level) takes precedence over the consistency at lower levels (Tero & Briggs, 1994).

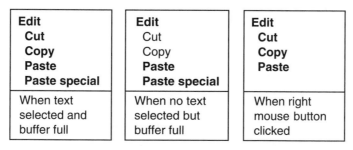

**Figure 8.8** Inconsistency in Edit menu—good or bad?

## 3.2 Issue II: User Control and Feedback Guidelines

Control and feedback go hand in hand. Providing feedback is probably the most accepted guideline in the design of any interaction. However, it is important to understand the rationale for each specific feedback instance. Feedback can support three important factors of user activity: motivation, control, and learning. The designer should consider which of these three is the objective or goal of the feedback. The content of the feedback and the manner in which it is presented depend on the goal of the feedback (Te'eni, 1992). Our main focus in this section is on providing feedback designed to promote control.

Control feedback is designed to enhance the user's control over the interaction and the completion of the task at hand. Two aspects of control should be considered. One is that control is needed to cope with reactions different from those expected or reactions that cannot be predicted due to changing (and uncontrollable) conditions. The need for control grows with the plausibility of errors (it follows closely from the principle of "design for error"). Without such control, the chances of successful completion of the task are diminished. Secondly, users want to *feel* in control. Users do not want to feel that the machine has taken over. In other words, the locus of control should be with the user and shifted to the machine only when the user decides to do so, like a pilot moving to automatic control when conditions are appropriate. The first guideline of control is therefore to ensure that the user perceives that he or she is in control. For example, the user should always be able to abort one activity and initiate another (the system should not "take over" control). Furthermore, the user should be able to control the pace and format of presentation (e.g., controlling the speed of scrolling and the size of the font).

Our basic assumption is that optimal control depends on both the *type of user activity* that needs to be controlled and the *level of interaction*. Some activities require highly controlled processing while others are skill-based and practically automatic (recall the discussion in Chapter 5). For example, in skilled typing there is hardly any control during the process, only a check of the final product. In contrast, purchasing a book online requires the user to exercise control and judgment in the process. Moreover, activities such as purchasing a book, designing an artifact, or navigating an e-book require different classes of feedback to ensure control, depending on which aspects of the activity are more prone to error. In navigation, for example, the phrase "lost in hyperspace" suggests that feedback on the current location within a hypertext system is crucial to control navigation. In a multistage process of purchasing a book, feedback on the current state of the user vis-à-vis the entire process can help to control the activity.

Control can be applied to all levels of interaction but is not always needed and is not needed with the same urgency. Under normal conditions, control is needed at the task level of interaction rather than at the lower implementation levels. Furthermore, by "levels of interaction" we refer not only to the task, semantic, syntactic, and lexical levels but also to the expansion of the task level, which may be decomposed into subtasks. For example, if the task is "purchase a book," one of the subtasks could be "choose among all possible retailers of the selected book." The higher-level processes in the task decomposition require more control and attention. This is true for normal conditions, but when breakdowns occur, control shifts to the lower levels. For example, in using a spreadsheet to determine the price of a product, the user may check various interest rates. A mistake with the decimal point may produce a large jump in the price, which shifts the user's focus to the level of inputting the correct interest rate, dropping even further down to the level of the physical interface, that is, pressing slowly the decimal point to avoid another mistake. Thus, the control that the user exercises depends on both the type of activity and the level of interaction.

This relates to the second guideline of control: What is the appropriate control for the type of activity and level of interaction expected in normal conditions and also when breakdowns occur?

We now turn to what feedback should be provided (feedback content) and how it should be provided (its format and timing) to promote control effectively. First, feedback must correspond to the control it is to support, that is, the focal level of interaction and the type of behavior controlled. Feedback on an input action that violates a syntax operation such as inserting an incomplete formula (e.g., a missing parenthesis) should help the user proceed by identifying the input (or better yet, part of it) as incorrect, direct the user to possible solutions, and signal that activity can proceed upon successful action. For example, if the rule is that opening and closing parentheses should be matched, mismatched parentheses can be highlighted by color and optional locations for a parenthesis can be marked. Feedback on the action of specifying the information necessary for purchasing a book can be in the form of a confirmation that the input is adequate and no further action is now required of the user. Feedback on the subtask of specifying supplier X (say number 9 on a list of 20) for a given book may state, "You have selected X—the second cheapest on the list." This last example confirms the supplier by name to avoid errors of misspecification but goes beyond that to alert the user on a possible violation of a possible decision rule, that is, choosing the cheapest supplier. Such speculations on behalf of the system designer are not always welcome. Ensuring that the user feels in control would suggest that such feedback would be provided only by user request.

Depending on the type of type of activity (e.g., navigation vs. purchasing), different contents of feedback will be more or less beneficial. Specific examples of feedback are developed in coming chapters. Nevertheless, the content of feedback should generally consist of at least one or all of the elements listed below. Once the designer has specified the action at a certain level of interaction, feedback on that action should inform users regarding the following:

- The effect their action has on the system
- Possible consequences of that action
- The new system state
- The new location of the user in the system or state

If we accept as a given that the content of feedback, its format and timing, should be specified, like any other system output, the format and timing of feedback should demand minimal use of cognitive resources while ensuring accurate processing. Feedback serves to control action and navigation. If the user does not understand where he or she will end up or what effect a user action will have on the state of the target application, the feedback is not effective. In the manipulation of interface tools, feedback should be introduced when it can be recognized (i.e., when the tool or icon can be seen) and used (active). In skill-based (automatic) behavior, feedback should not be provided at a time when it disrupts behavior but rather at the end of the activity. The only exception is to halt an incorrect process or correct high-cost errors (e.g., erasing a file). In contrast, in knowledge-based behavior (highly controlled), feedback during the process is effective when it is introduced at the time it can be used by the user rather than the time it is created by the system. Prematurely presented feedback is overlooked by the user or requires that the user remember to use it at a later-stage. Conversely, late feedback is either useless or costly to apply. Thus timing should be determined according to possible effect on action (Te'eni, 1991).

Feedback should be presented in the manner that most directly supports the action to be taken. In other words, apply the principle "Strive for fit between the information representation needed and presented." The feedback should be sufficiently specific to guide action but at the same time should not require unnecessary translations or reformation. For example, when a consumer specifies a withdrawal amount beyond available credit,

**Table 8.5**  Design Rules for Feedback to Promote Control

- Feedback should correspond to goals and intentions.
- Feedback should help evaluate goal accomplishment.
- Feedback should be sufficiently specific to control user activity.
- Feedback should help develop accurate mental models.
- Feedback should fit the task representation (verbal and visual).
- Feedback should fit the type of behavior (controlled, automatic).

the feedback should not force her to perform mental calculations to determine the maximum amount of available funds. Instead, the feedback should state the available balance in straightforward terms. In sum, well-designed feedback should reduce cognitive effort within the context of a specified activity. Here are some examples:

- Alert users to legal actions and dependencies between objects as they become relevant.
- Give feedback in the most usable way.
- Minimize attention needed to process feedback if it is in the context of automatic behavior.
- Provide feedback when it can be used if it is in the context of knowledge-based behavior.

More generally, Table 8.5 summarizes the design rules discussed above on what feedback to provide and how to provide it. Figure 8.9 illustrates user feedback that states the error, gives the corrective action, and gives the user control. Additionally, when the user presses the OK button to go back to the application, the focus is reset to the position where the error was committed.

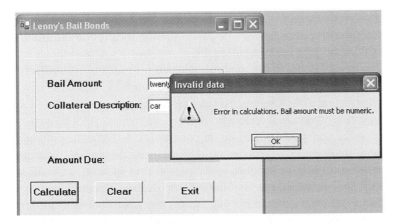

**Figure 8.9**  User feedback.

### 3.3  Issue III: Metaphor Guidelines

Metaphors relate user actions to an already familiar concept (see Chapter 5). Metaphors may evolve into an invisible web of terms and associations that undergirds the way we speak and think about the concept. How can we make use of metaphors in HCI?

The metaphor of the "desktop" (originated by Apple and now used by Windows) is one of the most commonly used metaphors in HCI. It makes the abstract concept of a file-based system with directories and subdirectories seem more concrete by relating it to the well-understood metaphor of a desk with drawers. Consider the many similarities between the desktop metaphor as displayed by the system and the real-life parallel of a physical desk, including the flat work surface. You need supplies such as paper and pencil to write on the work surface of your desk. You also need a place to store the papers you write and those you have received from others. The storage drawers in the desk need to be organized for storing items, retrieving them, and moving them from one folder or drawer to another. The most basic configuration of the desktop metaphor supplies the user with a screen that represents a desktop and on it a writing pad and several storage options (folders). Because most users are familiar with the real-life desktop and know how to use it and manipulate the objects on it, they quickly learn how to use the computer desktop as it is displayed to them. For instance, they expect to be able to move a document from one folder to another just as they do on their real-life desks. Moreover, they form expectations of the computer system that may not be apparent immediately. For example, a user that has a calendar on her desk, which she often uses while working, may search for it among the desktop options, even without reading a tutorial.

We also note that a designer can also benefit from using a metaphor to form the conceptual model of the system by using it to formulate user scenarios of actual work. The general idea then is to transfer knowledge from the familiar, usually more concrete world to the unfamiliar and more abstract world. The similarity between the familiar source and the unfamiliar target need not be perfect, but it must be sufficient to enable the user to function effectively in the new environment even without perfect understanding.

Most users perceive a move of a document icon from one folder to another to be a real move of the document itself from one place to another. Of course, what "really" occurs is a change in the value of a pointer from one file address to another. The pointer, by the way, is another metaphor that is also used within the desktop metaphor. A user moves the pointer (shown as a little hand with an extended index finger) to an object in order to manipulate it. This is easily understood by the user. Consider the difficulty of explaining the concept of a physical address pointer, which points to the file location in the address registers of the read-only memory of the computer CPU.

The similarity between the real desk and the computer desktop is limited by the difference in physical sizes. Standard-size screens can include only a limited number of legible icons and writing space. Larger screens (e.g., 19-inch screens) can include slightly more information and indeed will typically display more desktop functions such as a calendar, clock, or calculator, which are all objects that you would often find on your real desk. Once the difference between the familiar source and designed target is acknowledged by the designer and accepted by the user, additional controls (tools) are supplied to the user to deal with the "anomalies." For example, the scroll bar lets you expose parts of the desktop outside the current view.

Erickson (1980) presents a metaphor example that causes a misperception. Consider a scenario in which a visitor arrives at a hotel to meet her awaiting boyfriend. The visitor phones from the lobby to tell her friend that she has arrived. Unfortunately, the friend is in the shower, so the voice mail system answers: "The guest at this number is currently unavailable, so please leave a message after the beep." The visitor leaves a message, but the friend does not recognize that the message is there. The visitor is quite annoyed when the friend shows up in the lobby a half hour later and asks what kept him. What neither person knew is that there was a half-hour delay between the time at which she left the message and the time it became available to the friend. This is because the voice mail system resides on a machine, which under certain conditions takes time in transferring messages. The metaphor

**Table 8.6**  Use of Metaphors

| Metaphor | Application | Examples |
|---|---|---|
| Typewriting (typing, using keyboard) | Word processor | Word |
| Document (elements of a document and their attributes and operations) | Desktop publishing | PageMaker, Etude |
| Ledger sheet (matrix structure for numbers) | Spreadsheet | Lotus 1-2-3, Excel |
| Drawing (with paper, pencil, and palettes) | Drawing and painting | MacPaint, MacDraw, Paintbrush |
| Table of data (managing data organized in rows and columns) | Database | QBE, Access |

created in the mind of the user is one of an answering machine that stores the message until the user returns to his expected place. A different, more appropriate metaphor is the messaging service in which a third agent takes a message from the "sender," stores the message, and at a later stage transfers the stored message to the "receiver." Mistakes and delays in transmission are comprehensible, understandable, and in some cases even acceptable.

Table 8.6 is adapted from work by Carroll, Mack, and Kellogg (1988). It lists several metaphors, applications that use the metaphors, and examples of software. Carroll and colleagues (1988) identified three stages in the use of metaphors of computer systems: instantiation, elaboration, and consolidation. In instantiation, the user recognizes something from a familiar source that can potentially be applied to the new target. In elaboration, the user considers how to go about applying the knowledge from the old source to the new target. Finally, in the third stage, the user consolidates the knowledge of the old and new into a new mental model. Ideally, this consolidated mental model acknowledges both the similarities and the differences between the source and the target. Carroll and colleagues suggest four steps in designing interface metaphors to capitalize on this understanding of metaphor use: identify candidate metaphors, identify user scenarios and their computerized parallels, identify matches and mismatches, and identify designs to cope with the mismatches.

Figure 8.10 depicts a metaphor. It is a globe with a chain link over it. This metaphor is supposed to represent a hyperlink. If we follow the steps suggested by Carroll and colleagues (1988), first we identify the globe and chain link as a candidate metaphor. We then identify the user scenario as inserting a link to travel from one point in the text to another location, using the globe icon. Does the globe with the chain match the concept of hyperlink as a way of getting from one place to another? That is debatable. However, with the introduction and use of this metaphor over time, users now recognize and "match" the metaphor with the desired action. Nevertheless, to cope with the initial mismatch, the design includes floating or "hovering" text to verbalize the action that the metaphor icon is intended to represent and thus aids the user in determining the target task of the metaphor. Table 8.7 provides a list of metaphor design guidelines.

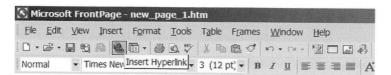

**Figure 8.10**   Use of metaphors—icon of globe with chain link used to represent "insert hyperlink."

**Table 8.7**   Guidelines on Metaphor Design

---

Make use of common metaphors that have readily anticipated characteristics

Determine which of the metaphor characteristics are essential

Make explicit any mismatch between system functions and features of the metaphor

Provide analogies that explain to the user the implications of the metaphors

Do not mix major metaphors

Use terms that refer to the source object of the metaphor

Ensure that the tone of the metaphor matches the attitude that the user should have towards the system

Preserve in the metaphor the order of the actions that are common in the source object

---

### 3.4  Issue IV: Direct Manipulation

According to Shneiderman (Shneiderman & Plaisant, 2005), three ingredients characterize *direct manipulation*:

1. Continuous representation of the objects and actions of interest

2. Physical actions or labeled buttons instead of complex syntax

3. Rapid incremental reversible operations whose impact on the object of interest is immediately visible

> **Direct manipulation:** An interaction style in which objects are represented and manipulated in a manner analogous to the real world (e.g., by directly pointing at an object and dragging it to a location rather than issuing logical instructions to bring about the same effect).

The general guideline is to use direct manipulation whenever possible. Recall the gulf of execution and evaluation in Chapter 5. In direct manipulation these gulfs tend toward one harmonious action, thus minimizing the effort required to perform the action and embedding in the action effective and direct feedback to ensure its accuracy. Consider the simple example of moving a file to a trash bin by clicking on its icon and dragging it to the trash bin icon. Contrast this with the same action carried out by a sequence of menu options and commands, for example, locating the appropriate directory of files, finding the exact name of the file, specifying a "delete" command, and receiving (at least in some operating systems) confirmation that "the file had been deleted." In direct manipulation the sequence of Norman's seven stages (see Figure 5.6) is reduced to manipulation of a specific object (the file icon) in relation to another (the bin icon), all processed in graphical form with the feedback presented continuously through the very same objects. In the nondirect manipulation, each of these elements is distinct. Each of the seven stages requires effort to articulate and evaluate. In fact, some of the subactions (find the file and then delete it) require an execution and evaluation cycle before continuing to the next stage. Some may be presented spatially (e.g., a tree of directories), but most are represented verbally. The specification of execution stages is separate from the feedback in the evaluation stages. The feedback is produced at the end of the process confirming the result but not accompanying the process. Direct manipulation in such activities is certainly more effective.

Indeed, Hutchins, Hollan, and Norman (1986) generalize these concepts as a "feeling of involvement directly with a world of objects rather than of communicating with an intermediary." A question is whether such direct interaction with objects is always feasible and effective. Can activities that assume a task representation that involves abstract relationships and manipulations always be transformed into a dialogue involving objects and manipulations on the objects? The designer is faced with a trade-off. On the one hand, the designer strives for a fit between the natural task representation and the display. On the other hand, the designer wishes to give the user direct and involved communication with objects on the screen.

To illustrate the trade-off concept, we use an example of finding data in a database. Suppose an instructor desires to determine those students who are failing in a class in order to call the students and communicate with them. The instructor verbalizes the task as, "Find students with grades below 50 and show their names and phone numbers." Such a query can be implemented in several ways. The most common way is to construct an SQL statement (Structured Query Language) according to predefined syntax rules. This requires a translation of the user's thoughts, presumably in natural language, into a different language. A second method would be to construct a predefined query and substitute the old values with the new ones; this is often referred to as "query by example." This method requires a matching of the user's thought into a familiar format. A third method may be to let the user specify the query in natural language and present to the user as feedback the translation in an understandable form before execution. This method requires only the user's verification, which is usually an easier cognitive act than specification, and in the event of a machine misinterpretation, it requires the user to reformulate the query. Finally, a fourth (semi-) direct manipulation method can be devised by translating the database attributes to visual objects (e.g., icons for each field) and constructing with these objects the query and required output format (e.g., Access Query Builder).

## 3.5 Issue V: Aesthetics in Screen Design

There are really two important aesthetic issues of concern. One is "how important are aesthetics," including the possible trade-offs between aesthetics and functionality or usability. The second issue is "how to create an aesthetically pleasing design."

Designs should be aesthetically pleasing, ideally without compromising on the usefulness and usability of the system. HCI educators have frequently paid minor attention to aesthetics because of their focus on usefulness and usability. We often say, "Get it right before you worry about making it look pretty." Today, perhaps because of the growing use of e-commerce interfaces for direct purchase on the part of consumers, aesthetics are becoming a necessary ingredient of design. E-purchases are almost always voluntary in nature. If the look and feel of the Web site is unattractive, the user may go elsewhere to find the desired product or service. The nature of the aesthetic aspect of the site may serve to attract or repel customers. Market researchers are beginning to explore the particular aspects of Web sites that draw consumers in and ultimately lead them to commit to a purchase. Recent research has determined, as noted above, that beautiful is also usable (Tractinsky, Katz, & Ikar, 2000). In other words, there is no trade-off between aesthetics and usability because one leads to the other. Norman (2002) offers a more balanced view

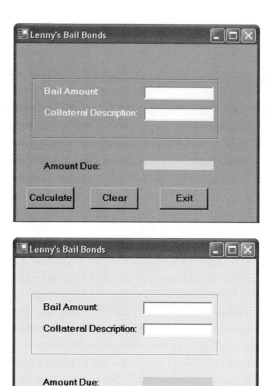

**Figure 8.11**   Aesthetics in screen design.

acknowledging the possible trade-offs by claiming that the designer's choice should be contingent on the user's state of mind and type of activity. Aesthetics are especially important to induce positive affect when the user is relatively relaxed and engaged in creative activities. Stressful situations and focused activities require highly usable interfaces at the possible cost of aesthetics. Thus, the concept of fit between user, activity, and computer (see Figure 1.4) should also be applied to aesthetical considerations. Figure 8.11 compares two VB.Net® interfaces. The first is not aesthetically pleasing due to lack of contrast between the background and text and lack of consistency in the color of the text. The second interface has a sufficient level of contrast and is consistent in appearance. Thus not only is the second interface more aesthetically pleasing, but it also supports the usability of the application by making it easier to read the labels.

There are very few attempts to provide cookbooks for aesthetics in the design of the human–computer interface, although several very general working assumptions are commonly noted. Aesthetically designed Web sites do not necessarily correspond to beautiful works of art in a museum. A good Web site design includes "instant aesthetics." Visitors form immediate impressions and accept or reject the site with only a few seconds. They have no intention of dwelling on a home page to appreciate its beauty (although a visitor to a Web site of an art gallery may expect to do so). A common working assumption is that an aesthetic design should be simple and in fact minimalistic (e.g., a small number of graphics and few colors). Another assumption is that good design incorporates a sense of

**Table 8.8**  Aesthetic Criteria of Screen Design

| Criterion | Aesthetic Rule | Example |
|---|---|---|
| Balance | Balance the optical weight of screen elements. | Do not place heavy (large) elements on one side of the screen and light elements on the other side. |
| Equilibrium | Maintain a midway center of suspension. | Place the center of the layout on the center of the screen. |
| Symmetry | Arrange elements so that elements on one side of the center line are replicated on the other side. | Background colors gradually fade off similarly in upper and lower parts of the screen. |
| Order | Order elements to correspond with hierarchy of perceptual prominence. | Arrange the objects on the screen according to their size from left to right in descending order. |
| Consistent ratios | Maintain a consistent ratio between height and width. | If the width of the overall frame is greater than its height, arrange the elements to follow this ratio. |
| Unity | Attempt coherence of the layout by keeping elements in relative proximity. | Arrange elements in closer proximity one to another than distance to frame. |
| Alignment | Align elements horizontally and vertically. | Three text boxes roughly of the same size but misaligned are usually disturbing to the eye. |
| Density | Optimize the occupied areas of the screen. | Leaving about half of the screen area as white space is pleasing to the eye. |
| Rhythm | Introduce regular patterns of changes in the elements. | Two moving elements on the screen should move at the same pace. |

being well-organized. Organization includes well-ordered placement rather than random placement, a regular pattern rather than irregularity, consistent rather than inconsistent forms and dimensions, and balanced rather than imbalanced distribution of elements and white space on the screen. Overall, this suggests that an acceptable level of lexical and syntactic complexity on the screen is key to aesthetic designs. These aspects of aesthetics are not easy to apply uniformly. For one, aesthetics are sensitive to the context of viewing the design and, in particular, the culture of theusers. A diversity of users makes it difficult to please everyone. Second, it is easy to "overkill." Applying these aspects automatically may lead to boring interfaces that may conform to all aesthetic criteria but leave the user untouched.

Some very recent studies look at some commonly accepted elements of aesthetic screen design and the types of emotions that are evoked in HCI. Table 8.8 is constructed from Ngo and Byrne (2001), who use these criteria to evaluate data entry screens. Consider the unattractive screen notifying us that a page we are looking for

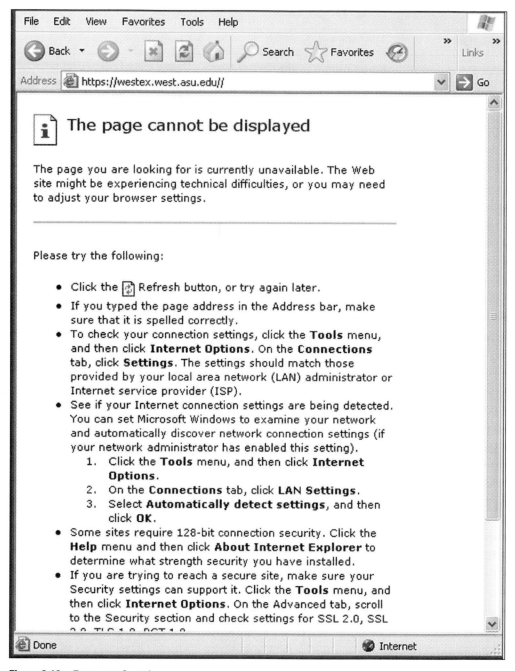

**Figure 8.12** Page not found.

on the Web was not found (Figure 8.12). The "news" is bad enough, so why make it ugly? Notice how skewed it is to the left, leaving most of the white space to the right. There seems to be no balance between the bullets and between the upper and lower sections. The perceptual prominence of the colored sentences, the underscored words, and the graphics are associated with several elements that are completely out of the expected sequence of reading. The two colored (in red) elements seem out of place and out of balance.

Clearly there are potential trade-offs between criteria that may arise and need to be resolved by the designer. For example, introducing rhythm may increase complexity and break alignment and balance. Nevertheless, to some there is no pleasure without rhythm. Indeed, beauty is in the eye of the beholder. Moreover, aesthetics may conflict with usability or functionality. For example, perfect regularity and symmetry come in the way of emphasizing and controlling attention. Aesthetic order of elements may not be the most efficient order of, say, input fields. The relative importance of the various aspects of design will surely depend on the type of task, system, user, and general context.

## ► 4. SUMMARY

It is important to note again that the five issues on design guidelines are not intended to be a comprehensive list of guidelines. They are only a demonstration of design guidelines that are based on the theories and principles in this book. Nevertheless, they explain the line of thought on which guidelines can be developed and the contingent nature of such guidelines on the type of user activity and the conditions in which it takes place. Moreover, the notion of fit and levels of interaction have been used to critically examine the applicability of these guidelines.

Other guidelines that should be considered include, but are not limited to, individual differences among users, flexibility of user interfaces, user confidence and trust, and navigation. Each of these issues is worthy of examination not only in itself but also in relation to the issues discussed above. For instance, novices and experienced users behave differently and require different types of support. Guidelines about how to provide differentially for different levels of experience are common (e.g., provide shortcuts for experienced users). Moreover, novices and experts reveal different levels of control for the same interaction and therefore should ideally receive different feedback. One way would be to design an adjustable interface that adjusts the level of help and specificity of the feedback to the level of user experience.

Even within the guidelines covered there is still much to consider. For example, the content of feedback designed to promote motivation will likely follow different rules. Similarly, feedback for learning environments will stress long-term effects above and beyond the immediate action. Some of these issues are covered in the context of specific applications later in the book. Others should be evaluated ad hoc in the particular context in which they are to be applied.

Recently there has been a tendency to balance the task orientation traditionally dominant in HCI design with a broader view that encompasses the user's emotional reactions to the technology. While it may be very reasonable to strive toward enjoyable and satisfying interactions, the designs based on affective engineering may conflict with simpler designs derived from the task analysis. For example, aesthetic designs may dictate a symmetric layout that requires more hand movement than a less pleasing yet more efficient design. In the final analysis, it is the designer's job to resolve the trade-offs between design solutions emerging from the different principles. Similarly, the notion of user empowerment goes beyond the given task to provide the user with capabilities of producing new and creative outcomes not yet specified by the designer. Shneiderman (2000), for example, talks about providing the user with a toolset to support searching digital libraries, consulting peers, visualizing information, associating, exploring solutions, composing artifacts, and reviewing interactions. Clearly the right toolset empowers the user with the capabilities to solve creatively new situations and problems unforeseen by the designer. A simpler, predefined procedure to solve a specific known problem may be more efficient but is limited. Decomposing the user activity into smaller tasks and enabling the user to work creatively may be the more effective solution for unstructured activities such as problem solving.

## ▶ 5. SUMMARY OF CONCEPTS AND TERMS

| | | | |
|---|---|---|---|
| Functionality | Usability | Consistency | Direct manipulation |
| Performance | Effort | Feedback | Trust |
| Fit | Representation | Feedback format | Empowerment |
| Affordances | Diversity of users | Creativity | Metaphor |
| Error | Pleasing interaction | Aesthetics | Flow |
| Feedback content | Control | | |

## ▶ 6. BIBLIOGRAPHY AND ADDITIONAL READINGS

Carroll, J. M., Mack, R. L., & Kellogg, W. A. (1988). Interface metaphors and user interface design. In M. Helander (Ed.), *Handbook of human-computer interaction*. Amsterdam: Elsevier.

Erickson, T. D. (1980). Working with interface metaphors. In G. Lakoff & M. Johnson (Eds.), *Metaphors we live by*. Chicago: University of Chicago Press.

Fogg, B. J., & Tseng, H. (1999). *The elements of computer credibility*. Paper read at Human Factors in Computing Systems (CHI).

Gaver, W. W. (1991). *Technology affordances*. Paper read at Human Factors in Computing Systems (CHI).

Grudin, J. (1989). The case against user interface consistency. *Communications of the ACM, 32*(10), 1164–1173.

Hammond, N., & Barnard, P. (1984). Dialogue design: Characteristics of user knowledge. In A. Monk (Ed.), *Fundamentals of human-computer interaction*. London: Academic Press.

Hassenzahl, M., Beu, A., & Burmester, M. (2001). Engineering joy. *IEEE Software* (January/ February), 70–76.

Hoffman, D. L., Novak, T. P., & Peralta, M. (1999). Building consumer trust online. *Communications of the ACM, 42*(4), 80–85.

Hutchins, E. L., Hollan, J. D., & Norman, D. A. (1986). Direct manipulation interfaces. In D. A. Norman & S. W. Draper (Eds.), *User centered systems design: New perspectives on human-computer interaction*. New Jersey: Lawrence Erlbaum Associates.

Keeney, R. L. (1999). The value of Internet commerce to the customer. *Management Science, 44*(4), 533–542.

Kieras & Polson (1985). An approach to the formal analysis of user complexity. *International Journal of Man-Machine Studies, 22*(4), 365–394.

Lewis, J. D., & Weigert, A. (1985). Trust as a social reality. *Social Forces, 63*(4), 967–985.

Ngo, D. C. L., & Byrne, J. G. (2001). Application of an aesthetic evaluation model to data entry screens. *Computers in Human Behavior, 17*(2), 149–185.

Norman, D. A. (1983). Design rules based on analyses of human error. *Communications of the ACM, 26*(4), 254–258.

Norman, D. A. (1988). *The design of everyday things*. New York: Doubleday.

Norman, D. A. (2002). Emotion and design: Attractive things work better. *Interactions: New Visions of Human-Computer Interaction, IX*(4), 36–42.

Reeves, B., & Nass, C. I. (1996). *The media equation: How people treat computers, televisions, and new media as real people and places.* New York: Cambridge University Press.

Shneiderman, B. (2000). Creating creativity: User interfaces for supporting innovation. *ACM Transactions on Computer-Human Interaction, 7*(1), 114–138.

Shneiderman, B., & Plaisant, C. (2005). *Designing the user interface: Strategies for effective human-computer interaction.* New York: Addison-Wesley.

Smith, S. L., & Mosier, J. N. (1984). *Design guidelines for user-system interface software.* Hanscom Air Force Base, USAF Electronic Systems Division.

Te'eni, D. (1991). Feedback in DSS: Experiments with the timing of feedback. *Decision Sciences, 22,* 597–609.

Te'eni, D. (1992). Process feedback in DSS. *Accounting, Management and Information Technology, 2*(1), 1–18.

Tero, A., & Briggs, P. (1994). Consistency versus compatibility: A question of levels? *International Journal of Man-Machine Studies, 40*(5), 879–894.

Tognazzini, B. (1990). Consistency. In B. Laurel (Ed.), *The art of human-computer interface design.* Reading, MA: Addison-Wesley.

Tractinsky, N., Katz, A. S., & Ikar, D. (2000). What is beautiful is usable. *Interacting with Computers, 13,* 127–145.

## ▶ 7. CASE STUDY

Lance Redux, a small-business Web applications developer, is very much aware of the importance of usability in the e-commerce environment. Most B2C (business-to-consumer) applications are dependent on consumers to place orders through an interactive Web site. Usability is critical for these applications. If the site is too difficult to use, the consumer abandons the order process. Another aspect that is important to e-commerce Web applications is security, which in turn generates "trust." If consumers do not "trust" that their personal information and financial data are safe from identity theft and misuse, they will not place an order over the Internet.

Lance is exploring various sources to determine the most important guidelines for usability. He compiles a list of the guidelines that he considers most crucial for the World Gourmet site. They include the following:

- Design for the Web-based environment. Remember, the destination is a computer, not the printed page. Research indicates that users read hypertext very differently than printed information.

    Craft the look and feel.

    Make your site consistent and easy to use.

    Better sites support the way *users* want to approach the problems. (Users will leave sites that have unique designs or terminology.)

- **Content design** requires that the Web designer determine the best approach to describing each unit of information.

- Use a standardized **information architecture**. An example that has already happened is the *"About the company"* area of most corporate Web sites.

- Design for the whole site, not just individual pages. Your choices of colors, fonts, graphics, and page layout should communicate a visual theme that orients users to your site's content.

- Design for the target user audience and only include content on your site that is of direct benefit for your intended audience.
- Give away something valuable: information, software, advice, or humor.
- Create an interface that will be familiar and easy to use.
- Plan the overall site by using a specification document.
- Use consistent text-based navigation bars to link users to other pages on your site.
- Use other text-based links to help users move through a long page of information or through a table of contents. If you use graphical navigation links:

    Reuse the same images to reduce download time.

    Use the ALT attribute to provide alternative navigation options for users.

    Have a consistent text-only link/navigation bar at the bottom of every page.

- Keep a flat hierarchy. Do not make users navigate through too many layers to find the information they want.
- Consider providing a site map that graphically shows users the layout of your entire site.
- Make your design portable. To be successful, your Web design must be portable and accessible across different browsers, operating systems, and computing platforms.
- Design for low bandwidth:

    Plan your pages so that they are accessible at a variety of connection speeds.

    Break large pages into smaller units.

    Use fewer graphics.

    Use the ALT attribute with your images so that the user has information to look at while the graphics are downloading.

- Plan for clear presentation and easy access to information:

    Highlight keywords (hypertext links serve as one form of highlighting; typeface variations and color are others).

    Use meaningful subheadings (not "clever" ones).

    Use bulleted lists.

    Only one idea per paragraph (users will usually skip over any additional ideas).

    Start with the conclusion and then add details.

    Have half the word count (or less) than print writing.

    Limit the number of fonts and colors used on the site.

- Use the power of hypertext linking
- Provide targeted links that will allow users to jump through a long document quickly.
- Plan the page structure and content.
- Place the important information "above the fold." This is a newspaper term. The fold is what appears on a standard screen when the Web page first loads. This is very important for the home page. Users will resist using the scroll bar to go "below the fold."
- Use cascading style sheets (CSS) to attain a uniform look and feel throughout the site. CSS allow designers to standardize the following:

    Choices of colors, fonts, and graphics

Page layout

Backgrounds

Hyperlinks (it is often desirable to change the color of a hyperlink once the user has clicked it; it is also possible to change the hyperlink when the user is "hovering" above a link)

- Create smooth transitions.
- Plan to create a unified look among the sections and pages of your site. Web sites should have the following:

  Consistent background graphics

  Consistent placement of navigation information

  Consistent font usage

  Logo that brands the site

- Use a grid to provide visual structure and stability.
- Do not crowd too much information on each Web page.

Lance is so concerned about usability that he has designed a short questionnaire to measure usability (see Chapter 7). He is planning to have several friends and fellow developers test out the site once a first version is up. He will give his testers a copy of the usability instrument to fill out as they attempt to use the site.

## ▶ 8. EXERCISES

Ex. 1.  Accessibility Guide

Please go to the online site that describes Section 508 on design for people with disabilities (see URL in the text). In the site, visit the guide to the standards and concentrate on software applications. The first two standards are about executing functions from the keyboard and about accessibility features.

1.a. Summarize these two standards.

1.b. Evaluate your university's Web site in light of these two standards and provide examples of how (if at all) they are supported.

Ex. 2*  Combining the use of metaphors with learning

The following box printed on paper could be the result of one of the three manipulations in Microsoft Word: (1) drawing "borders" around a block of text, (2) creating a "text box," and (3) creating a "frame."

| This is in a box. This is in a box. This is in a box. |
| --- |

**Figure 8.13**  Small text box.

The assignment consists of several stages; the first two are background stages and the stages that follow are meant to design a better interface.

**Background**

First, distinguish between the three manipulations (borders, text box, and frame) by stating generally what each is intended for (use the Help feature or manual). Next, create a

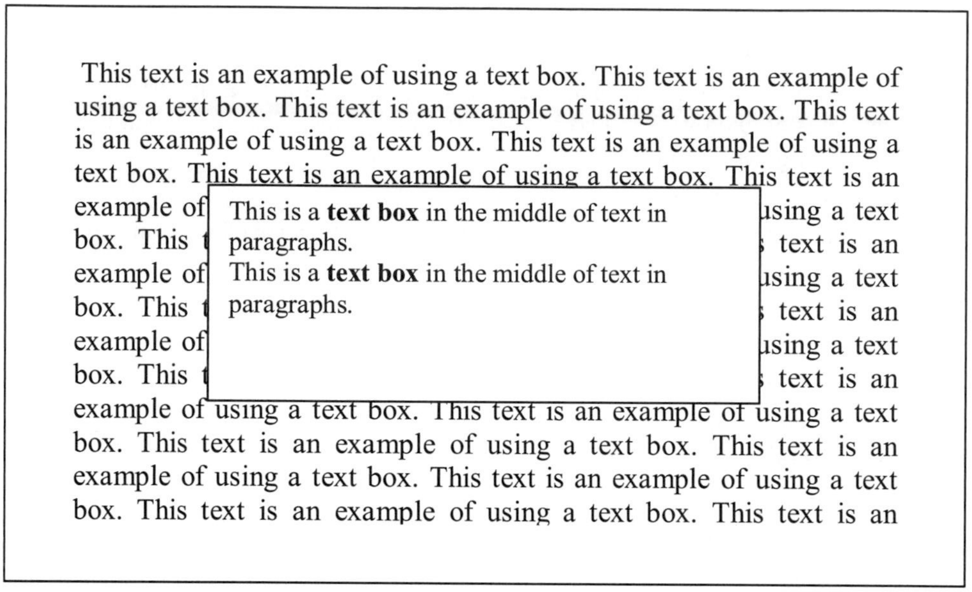

This text is an example of using a text box. This text is an example of using a text box. This text is an example of using a text box. This text is an example of using a text box. This text is an example of using a text box. This text is an example of using a text box. This text is an example of using a text box. This text is an example of using a text box. This text is an example of using a text box. This text is an example of using a text box. This text is an example of using a text box. This text is an example of using a text box. This text is an example of using a text box. This text is an example of using a text box. This text is an example of using a text box. This text is an example of using a text box. This text is an example of using a text box. This text is an example of using a text box. This text is an example of using a text box. This text is an example of using a text box. This text is an example of using a text box. This text is an example of using a text box. This text is an

This is a **text box** in the middle of text in paragraphs.
This is a **text box** in the middle of text in paragraphs.

**Figure 8.14**  Big text box.

text box as shown in Figure 8.14. Describe, as an activity list or flowchart, how you accomplished this.

## Design

1. State two goals that can be accomplished with a text box (e.g., enabling the structure above).

2. For each of these goals, review how the current design of using a text box in Word supports the goal and how you would improve the current design (e.g., what kind of feedback that is not given today you would provide). Demonstrate with figures how this would appear to the user.

3. Write a section in a manual on how to use a text box. Provide a short (around 1–2 pages) section to guide the user (refer to the two goals you staged in #1). Hints: Use a metaphor. Use graphics.

# TASKS IN THE ORGANIZATIONAL CONTEXT

## CONTEXT AND PREVIEW

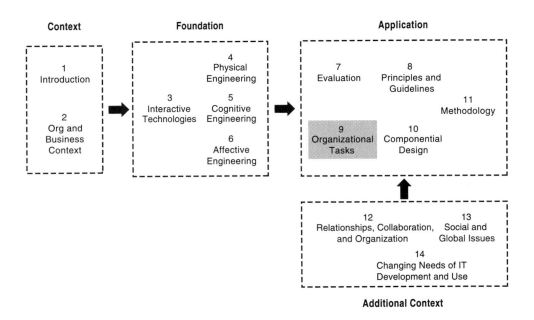

In the TSSL (Task, Semantic, Syntactic, Lexical) model, task refers to the level of operating the computer (e.g., copy a text). But these "tool-level tasks" are meant to support organizational tasks (e.g., write a letter). This chapter discusses the organizational tasks that contextualize and shape the tool-level tasks.

The chapter does three things. First, it shows how organizational tasks are decomposed into subtasks that eventually translate into tool-level tasks represented by the TSSL model. This activity is called task analysis. Second, it puts tasks in the context of work to examine how characteristics of organizational tasks and work affect user requirements. Finally, it goes back to a specific type of task, namely decision making, to show in detail how a decision task should be analyzed. This is demonstrated with a method for analyzing decision tasks that has three steps: analyze the user and the task as the user sees it, determine human limitations and strengths in accomplishing the task, and provide the appropriate support. As shown in the methodology map, this chapter is applied in the analysis stage.

## LEARNING OBJECTIVES

Upon completion of this chapter, students should know and understand as follows:

- Know the attributes of organizational tasks pertinent to HCI and how they provide the context of tool-level tasks
- Understand the need for task analysis in HCI
- Understand how the work context affects HCI design and differentiates between structured and nonstructured tasks
- Understand how organizational-level tasks are decomposed hierarchically and mapped to tool-level tasks, which are described by the TSSL model
- Understand and apply a method for analyzing HCI requirements for decision support

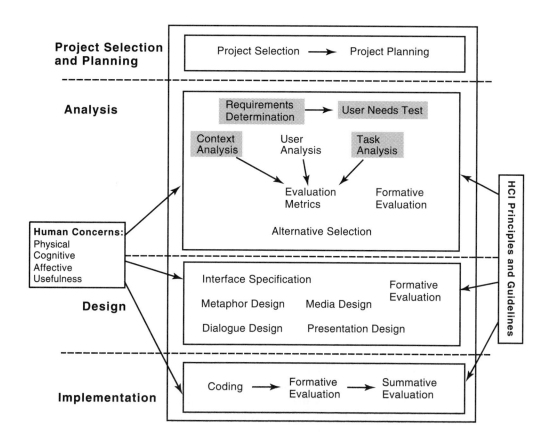

# SCENARIO

This scenario demonstrates the relationship between organizational tasks and HCI.

A young company called e-Opus is a network of e-book and e-music providers that combines both virtual and physical shops. In addition to books and music, it supplies services for photocopying, drawing, desktop publishing, editing, and so on. The e-Opus chain is growing rapidly and opening new sites nearly every week. Once a month, the general manager decides on new sites for the physical shops. She strives to choose the best location from a given set of possible sites. She chooses the location according to

1. The size, cost, and condition of the physical space available for conducting business, and

2. Its accessibility to its potential clientele

The manager wants a decision support system (DSS) that helps her select office space by interactively showing alternative locations and comparing them on preselected criteria such as size and cost. The task is complex. It includes several subtasks such as comparing alternative locations, forecasting the number of clients in alternative locations, and analyzing the probable impact of local regulations such as property taxes. You, as a designer, need to build the system that supports the process of choosing the best option. Where would you start?

User-centered development means that we start the design process with an understanding of the user and the user's task. The cognitive engineering approach included three main steps:

1. Analyze the user and the task demands.

2. Articulate users' strengths and limitations in performing the task (such as short-term memory limitations).

3. Design HCI to enhance strengths and overcome limitations (e.g., use multiple windows to reduce the need for memorizing information).

We employ the same three-step strategy here too by asking what tasks and subtasks are involved in the decision to locate a new office, what are the user's strengths and limitations in accomplishing these tasks, and what are the types of support that we can provide.

Consider part of the office selection process: generating alternative locations and comparing them visually. People are usually very effective in visually examining pictures. The computer is therefore charged only with presenting the relevant pictures in an accessible and legible fashion. A hypothetical DSS may include an interactive session that elicits the user's preferences for two attributes of the office location and shows alternative locations that meet these preferences. For example, the user specifies the preferred type of building (e.g., open-space houses versus apartment buildings) and geographical regions (Northeast, Midwest, etc.). The DSS presents a map and highlights preferred buildings (Figure 9.1). The user can click on an apartment building to zoom in and open another window depicting the building's exterior (the smaller picture in the upper part of Figure 9.1). The user can then zoom in on the layout of a particular level, opening yet another window on the screen. In order to compare two possible levels in the same building, the user would like to view both levels at once and see a typical room from each level (this is shown in Figure 9.2). Thus, the system provides the user with appropriate visualizations, capitalizing on the user's visual strengths.

**Figure 9.1** Map of buildings from which to select ideal location (taken from http://www.tau.ac.il Tel-Aviv University). See also color plate IV.

**Figure 9.2** Two levels within the building as possible locations for the site.

In most cases, computer support is aimed at overcoming user limitations. Consider two difficult elements of the decision to find the best location for the office: projection and probabilistic analysis. The optimal location of an office depends on the number of clients projected to frequent the location. The user needs therefore to forecast the expected clients in each of the alternative locations. As we note below, most users are not very good at forecasting due to several recurring biases (such as concentrating on recent events and discounting earlier events). The DSS could be designed to help the user overcome such biases.

The DSS could also help with calculating probabilities. In determining the expected cost of the office space, the user may need to incorporate probabilities in the cost estimation. For instance, there may be a 0.60 likelihood of a 10 percent tax increase that would be fully reflected in the price of the office space. Most people find it difficult to take into account probabilities. Again, the DSS could be designed to help users deal with probabilities and thereby reduce effort, errors, and uneasiness.

Both examples, prediction and processing probabilities, show how one can identify the user's tasks, find the likely limitations or biases, and build appropriate support. The visual comparison of locations stresses the parallel need to extend the user's strengths. Note, though, that unlike the cognitive engineering chapter, we need to work here at the level of decision making (the "organization-level task") rather than the level of operating the computer (the "tool-level task"). The current chapter shows how this can be done.

## ▶ 1. INTRODUCTION

The information systems discussed in Chapter 2 are designed to support work in organizations. In an attempt to link HCI to the workplace, Dowell and Long (1989) regard the workers and the information systems as "work systems" that affect some domain (e.g., customer services) through work aimed at achieving organizational goals by means of a set of tasks. Task analysis determines how tasks achieve the work. In this book, the work systems consist of one or more human and computer components situated in the workplace. Thus task analysis must dictate not only which tasks achieve work but also how they are allocated to the computer and the user. In this chapter we cover the topics of task, work, and their relation to HCI.

The chapter does three things. It begins by examining the task, at both the organizational level and the tool level, and then concentrates on characteristics of organizational tasks. It then goes on to examine the impact of work on user requirements. The HCI developer needs to understand how the work is structured and performed in order to understand how workers divide and coordinate their work into specific tasks. It is also important to understand the dynamics of work patterns to recognize opportunities to support work over time. Finally, the workplace, with its computers and other artifacts, does not always behave as expected. People behave in unpredicted and unplanned ways. HCI developers must be aware of actual patterns of behavior at the workplace. Having discussed tasks and work, we go back to one specific type of task, namely the decision task, and provide a detailed method for analyzing decision tasks and the implications for HCI.

We know that task is central to HCI. The task-semantics-syntax-lexicon (TSSL) model describes HCI by representing the user's view of the task and its human–computer implementation. However, up to now we have referred to tasks in the context of operating the computer (e.g., an operation such as "cut and paste") as "tool-level tasks." In contrast, tasks in the organizational context, like the task of selecting an office location, are defined at a higher level of abstraction. They have to do with satisfying some organizational demands. A task in the organizational context is often regarded as a piece of work allocated to a worker. Conversely, work can be seen as an ensemble of organizational tasks performed or managed by the organization's workers.

The organizational context affects HCI in two ways: (1) in general, characteristics of the organizational tasks and the workplace affect user behavior and user requirements, and (2) specific organizational tasks map onto specific tool-level tasks.

How do the characteristics of organizational tasks affect user behavior and user requirements? Consider two very different activities in the e-Opus example. One activity is the seller's tasks related to selling a book (e.g., checking the book, registering its product number, receiving payment, and issuing a receipt). The other activity is the executive's selection of a new site (described above). Selling a book dictates a different emphasis in user requirements (e.g., the efficiency of performing transactions quickly and accurately, the possibility of inexperienced and rotating personnel, multiple concurrent activities, and a noisy shop). Selecting a new site, in contrast, is composed of many interrelated subtasks, many of which are relatively complex, such as forecasting. In site selection, the main user requirements involve guidance and feedback in solving problems and overcoming difficulties by providing computerized support. Therefore, knowing about characteristics of the organizational tasks helps the developer decide on the general directions in determining user requirements before specifying the details of the tasks. Moreover, developers should also understand the broader context of work at the particular workplace being analyzed. Are people expected to be involved in multiple activities at the same time or can they concentrate on one task to its completion? Answers to such questions determine what type of computer support they will need.

How are tasks at the organizational level related to tasks at the tool level? A particular task can usually be placed into a hierarchy of tasks. In the scenario above, the task of viewing two alternative office locations is part of the higher-level task of selecting an office space. Furthermore, the task of viewing two alternatives can itself be decomposed into several subtasks (e.g., determining which two locations to view, defining the information to be displayed for each location, and then examining visually the two displays). By the same token, each of these subtasks can be related to the tool-level tasks that facilitate it. Finally, each of the tool-level tasks can be described using the TSSL interaction levels.

Figure 9.3 depicts the partial hierarchy of tasks (the broken lines indicate incomplete descriptions). The upper part represents the tasks at the level of the organizational context and the lower part of the figure describes the tools level, which follows the TSSL model. Thus, the HCI developer can picture a hierarchy of tasks beginning with a high-level and abstract task that is decomposed into subtasks, which are decomposed further until eventually the lowest-level task is then translated into the four-level description of HCI (TSSL).

When the task is relatively well defined (e.g., selling a book in e-Opus), the analyst can directly apply the hierarchical task decomposition to represent a tree of the task and its subtasks. Each task is broken down into several subtasks (usually not more than seven) that are hierarchically related. The task decomposition should be continually refined down to the level that the analyst can match the lowest-level subtask to a pattern of human–computer interaction.[1]

As already evident from the scenario above, for well-defined tasks, the application of a hierarchical task decomposition is straightforward. However, for less structured tasks such as decision making, it is necessary to first characterize the task systematically in

---

[1] For a detailed exposition of task analysis, see Diaper & Stanton, 2004.

order to identify user requirements and define the specific tasks involved. For this reason, we revisit task analysis at the end of the chapter when analyzing decision tasks.

## ▶ 2. CHARACTERISTICS OF ORGANIZATIONAL TASKS

The two main aspects of organizational tasks relevant to the development of HCI are the nature of the task and the interrelations between tasks. The first aspect relates to the nature of the individual task, particularly its structure (e.g., whether the task is well-defined or ill-defined, routine or nonroutine). Knowing about the nature of the task can help predict what type of behavior is expected (e.g., automatic or controlled) and determine the appropriate computer support.

For example, guidance and feedback are welcomed by the user in unstructured tasks but may be rejected as redundant in routine tasks. Knowledge of the task's structure, its requirements, and its impact are the subject of task analysis, and this chapter concentrates on task analysis for decision tasks. A *structured task* is well defined and, has clear and explicit goals, which can be accomplished by following predefined procedures.

The second aspect of interest is the interrelations among tasks performed by the same or different users. Knowledge of these interrelations influences the users' requirements and determines the appropriate computer support. Consider, for example, a receptionist at an office. The receptionist may be asked to perform two tasks in parallel. One task is to identify and keep track of incoming visitors using a registration system. The other task is to prepare a document using a word processor. In addition to supporting each task separately, the receptionist could be supported in coordinating the two tasks. For instance, the system would identify the transition from word processing to registering a visitor and ensure that it is easy for the receptionist to resume working on the word processor after the interruption. The system can highlight the most recently completed or uncompleted actions and suggest the next actions. Thus, knowledge of the interrelations between tasks influences design. This knowledge is gained by analyzing work characteristics and, moreover, by analyzing users' work habits (e.g., how they choose to organize their tasks). In this chapter, we look at the characteristics of work at the office (as opposed to other workplaces such as a production floor) because of its wide diversity of users and tasks.

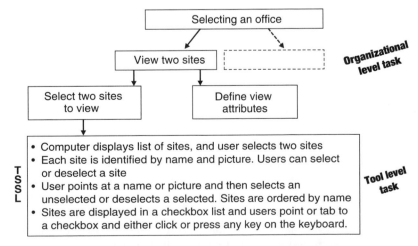

**Figure 9.3** Hierarchical task decomposition, with both the organizational-level tasks and the tool-level task described by the TSSL levels of how to operate the computer.

**Organizational-level task:** A worker's designed effort to accomplish an organizational demand.

We have differentiated between tasks at the organizational level and tasks at the tool level. We can regard the organizational-level task as the context of the related tool-level tasks. Furthermore, the organizational-level task itself should be examined in the context of the work environment, which consists of many other tasks. These layers of context have been ignored in the previous chapters on cognitive and affective engineering. In particular, Chapters 4, 5, and 6 examined, respectively, the physical, cognitive, and affective aspects of HCI without considering the context of the task. For example, the activities of choosing among several options in a pull-down menu or dictating a requirement to a voice-based system are found in many different systems. From the user's perspective, searching a menu is a task, but it is different from the more abstract task such as finding a hotel room. Using the menu is a means of operating and controlling the computer in order to facilitate the higher-level tasks of finding a room. We claim that the design of the tool-level task should depend on the higher-level organizational task. For example, (current) voice-based menus with a predefined terminology may be appropriate for choosing a hotel room but not for formulating an unstructured decision such as devising a new marketing strategy. In other words, the design of HCI should fit the task and its context.

We define an organizational-level task as the worker's designed (intended and planned) effort to accomplish an organizational demand. Workers are assumed to understand the organization's goals and the demands the organization places on them. The workers work to satisfy these demands. In some cases the workers simply follow set procedures, in other cases they interpret or redefine the demands to their own way of accomplishing the demands, and in yet other cases workers initiate tasks that are believed to serve personal and organizational goals. We regard all these intended efforts as tasks.

**Structured task:** Is well-defined, has clear and explicit goals, and can be accomplished by following predefined procedures.

**Nonstructured task:** Task that is ill-defined, has ambiguous goals (if it has any at all), and has no explicit procedures that can ensure successful completion of the task.

The main question we ask about the nature of the tasks is whether they are structured or nonstructured. Structured tasks involve specific and predefined procedures and have clear and explicit goals. For example, filling a customer order usually follows very clear and well-defined procedures. Nonstructured tasks, in contrast, are ill-defined, creative, ambiguous, and without predefined rules or procedures. Some nonstructured tasks are partially structured (e.g., preparing a quarterly budget), whereas others are completely unstructured (e.g., research and development). We will see that different types of systems and different modes of HCI fit different degrees of structure. Furthermore, we should expect different types of behavior for different degrees of task structure. Skill-based (automatic) behavior is found in highly structured and usually routine tasks. Rule-based behavior and knowledge-based (controlled) behavior are needed for nonstructured tasks. (These types of behavior are covered in Chapter 5.)

In addition to the degree of task structure, tasks are characterized as routine or non-routine (novel), repetitive or occasional, and uniform or diverse. Routine tasks are well-known to the user and can be performed according to known rules or on the basis of past experience (e.g., reading your daily e-mail at the beginning of the day). Repetitive tasks are performed repeatedly in the same session or close by (e.g., a teller at the bank enters the details of 20 checks, repeating the same sequence of operations 20 times). Repetitive and routine tasks can be repeated almost uniformly (e.g., depositing a check varies only minimally from one check to another). Alternatively, the task can be performed many times but incidents differentiate one instance from the other (e.g., reading your mail may require substantial effort one day and hardly any on another day, or entering information about new patients at a clinic can follow very different procedures depending on the type of illness, insurance, residency, or manner of admittance).

These task characteristics affect the focus of HCI design. Chapter 2 describes the type of computer systems used in organizations, including Office Information Systems, Management Information Systems, and Decision Support Systems. Office Information Systems (OIS) include end-user computer systems such as word processing, hypertext, database management systems, spreadsheets, graphics, desktop publishing, electronic mail, and so on. Management Information Systems (MIS) are designed to integrate and analyze information for management control, coordination, and planning. Decision Support Systems (DSS) are designed specifically to support managerial decision making. In addition, the professional staff uses various systems that support its particular profession such as legal or financial systems. Most importantly, these different systems support tasks that vary significantly in their degree of structure, repetitiveness, and routineness (Tables 2.1 and 2.2 in Chapter 2 summarize these differences). Consequently, the focus of designing HCI will change accordingly. Each type of task requires the designer to concentrate on different strengths and limitations of users.

In highly structured tasks, the pattern of work is well-known and can be determined in advance. The main concern is to enhance productivity by easing the work flow and speeding the completion of each task but at the same time ensuring accurate work. Errors of inattention in skill-based and rule-based behavior due to boredom are one source of inaccuracies. Experienced users may be frustrated from a lack of shortcuts. Creating the perception of seemingly inefficient work and providing unnecessary feedback are other issues to avoid. Repetitive work is usually the source of physiological problems too (e.g., carpal tunnel syndrome). In general, systems that support routine, repetitive, and highly structured tasks require less flexibility than systems designed to support nonroutine and less structured activities. Moreover, in highly structured tasks, it is easier to automate the task and relieve the user from the effort. In comparison, the more unstructured the task, the more effort one has to invest in its analysis.

Nonstructured tasks dictate a different set of user requirements. First, as they cannot be completely specified in advance, users are expected to vary in their use of the system to support the task. The system must therefore be designed for flexibility. Furthermore, users are expected to engage in knowledge-based behavior, demanding mental resources to engage in complex problem solving, simulating solutions, building mental models, calculating, and planning. Memory, cognitive processing, comprehension, and attention are often stressed to their limit and require computerized support. Additionally, individual styles of thinking and feeling will play a greater role in unstructured compared with structured tasks. Being able to adapt to personal tastes should therefore be another design concern. Because of the complexity of analyzing and supporting such tasks, we devote a special section on the topic of decision analysis.

Systems that support multiple tasks performed concurrently or tasks that are highly interdependent must satisfy a unique set of requirements. When working on several tasks concurrently, users find it difficult to coordinate their activities, to manage the different tasks, to recall what they have done and what they should be doing on each individual task, and generally to shift from one task to another. High information stress (overload) is a common source of errors in such situations. Cumbersome transitions from one system to another (e.g., inconsistent interfaces) add additional complexity, cause errors, and invariably leave users frustrated. Similarly, managing interrelated tasks, even if not performed concurrently, requires the user to maintain a global view of the tasks, understand thoroughly their interrelations and how changes in one task affect the other, and recall and manage large amounts of information. In demanding tasks, memory, comprehension, and attention often limit performance and are a source of error.

Table 9.1 summarizes the impact of task characteristics on the focus of HCI design. It emphasizes the differences in the impact of different types of tasks on the users and their performance because different types of tasks require different resources. The different impacts, in turn, determine the corresponding type of support.

## ▶ 3. WORK AT THE OFFICE AS CONTEXT—TASKS AND THEIR INTERRELATIONS

Work in organizations is composed of many different tasks located in a network of task hierarchies (see Figure 9.3). Some tasks are completely automated (e.g., payroll processing) and others are performed with the support of computers (e.g., the selection of office space in the scenario). Some tasks are performed entirely by one agent (worker), whereas others are divided among several agents (e.g., one person selects the office space and another contracts it). Other tasks are performed by groups rather than by individuals. Finally, one person may be responsible in his job for several tasks, which may or may not be interrelated. Although we do not examine how work is allocated among agents, we do look at the implications of a given task allocation on the design of HCI and of work habits. These are expanded below.

**Table 9.1**  The Importance of Task Structure to HCI

| Type and Context of Task | Example | Main Implications |
|---|---|---|
| Structured, routine, uniform, repetitive tasks | Intensive data entry | Minimal user effort and maximum speed; minimal learning time; errors due to inattention and boredom; frustration with ill-fitted interfaces (e.g., no shortcuts); physiological stress |
| Structured to semistructured, routine but diverse tasks | Word processing | Minimal user effort and maximum speed for certain operations; piecemeal but efficient learning; recall and skill necessary to operate; errors due to misapplication of rules; fit to specific tasks and to specific work habits; limited problem solving and calculations |
| Unstructured tasks | Supported decision making | Comprehension; creativity and flexibility; complex problem solving and planning; simulations, calculations, and mental models; errors and biases in judgments; fit to individual style |
| Multiple tasks concurrent | Operating several office systems | Managing attention to several tasks; controlling states and operations in several systems; confusion and overload leading to errors and frustration |
| Interrelated tasks | Project management | Comprehension; complex problem solving; memory; simulation and planning; flexibility |

This section examines the impact of the work context on the way users think, feel, and behave. As noted above, the more we as designers know about the user, the easier it will be to fit the technology to the user. The first part of the section looks at the special characteristics of the work environment, the second part identifies the users' information processing needs that HCI can support, and the third part briefly discusses the analysis of the workplace as context to HCI.

## 3.1 Characteristics of Different Types of Work

The variety of tasks found in most organizations is very large. This variety is perhaps best reflected in the various types of computer systems found in the organization, including TPS (Transactions Processing Systems), OIS (Organizational Information Systems), MIS (Management Information Systems), and DSS (Decision Support Systems). Furthermore, the different users of these systems represent the variety of types of users. We develop this idea of a variety of tasks and of users as a basis for examining the implications on the type of required computer support.

Workers at the office engage in several categories of work: clerical, professional, and managerial work. We further differentiate between clerical workers who specialize in a particular task usually found in transaction processing systems, such as order entry, and clerical workers who function as support staff dealing with a wide variety of office services, such as reception, document management, communication, and coordination. Using Table 9.1 as a rough classification, we can anticipate users of TPS to perform largely structured routine and relatively uniform tasks. Clerical support work usually involves multiple tasks that tend to be routine and structured or semi-structured but are often performed in parallel.

Professional work is very often unstructured, usually involving many interrelated tasks. Managerial work is probably the most complex, as described in detail below, and appears to combine most types of tasks.

Typically workers from all categories interact and are interdependent in the sense that they rely on information received and produced by other workers' tasks. For instance, it is difficult to talk about managerial work without considering the office as a whole because of the strong interrelationship of managers with their clerical and professional staff. This interrelationship dictates intense flows of information between the parties, collaborative work, and the use of common information systems.

In contrast to users of TPS, the users of OIS and MIS are more diverse in their skills and styles. Time, particularly the time of managers and professionals, is expensive. Office work is usually less structured and more difficult to assess. Overall, the complexity of work is expected to be higher than in performing TPS-related tasks. In order to design the HCI for OIS, MIS, and DSS, we need to know more about the user's behavior at the workplace. We should also consider users who are the organization's customers, rather than workers (e.g., users of e-commerce systems). Customers are not accustomed to the particular organizational culture and are not obliged to interact with the particular organization.

Striking is the flexibility managers need in shifting between modes of breadth and depth of work. Office work is typically pictured as a set of multiple activities performed concurrently. Occasionally it involves in-depth and all-consuming activities such as decision making. Thus there is a mix of modes: breadth is characterized by multiple but shallow activities and depth is characterized by one in-depth activity. HCI for the former should support concurrency (e.g., remembering to attend to interrupted activities). HCI

**Table 9.2** Propositions about Managerial Work (Adapted from Kurke & Aldrich, 1983)

- Managers perform a great quantity of work with little free time (34 different activities per day, 44 hours per week).
- Managerial jobs are characterized by brevity, variety, and fragmentation (63 percent of activities lasted less than nine minutes; only 5 percent lasted more than an hour).
- Managers favor verbal over written contacts (desk work and tours take up only 29 percent of their time and the rest is for phone calls and meetings).
- Scheduled meetings consume more time than any other activity (four meetings a day with half involving three people or less).
- Managers link their organization with outsiders in a variety of ways (external contacts took 52 percent of verbal contacts; internal contacts, over a third).

for the latter requires detailed and comprehensive support for an individual task (e.g., ensuring that alternatives in a selection task be considered as comprehensibly and extensively as possible).

Henry Mintzberg in the *Nature of Managerial Work* (1973) proposes that all managers play three types of roles: interpersonal, informational, and decisional. He suggests managers across all levels of management engage in the same roles but with different emphasis. Interpersonal roles include being a figurehead, a leader that directs and motivates, and a liaison between the organization and its environment. Informational roles include being a monitor of information and events within and outside the organization, a disseminator of information from outside the organization to people in the organization, and a spokesperson about the organization to the outside world. Decisional roles include being an entrepreneur, a resource allocation expert, a disturbance handler, a negotiator between subordinates, and a technical expert.

Several surveys on how managers really work in practice support Mintzberg's early proposals (e.g., Pavett & Lau, 1983). Table 9.2 summarizes some of the results from a study by Lance Kurke and Howard Aldrich. It lists some of Mintzberg's propositions about managerial work and includes additional evidence. In parentheses are results on average behavioral indicators. Although these data were gathered quite some time ago, the long hours and diversity of activities are still high and have probably even grown in past years.

We note then the various types of managerial roles and the evidence on observed behavior—frequencies of activities, preferences, and so on. In the remainder of this chapter, we look more closely at these roles and observed behavior to identify potential needs that can be supported with interactive technologies. We start with a picture of the user, concentrating for now on the manager. Later, other types of users (e.g., the clerical staff, which interact with the manager and support the managerial work) will also be considered.

The typical managers seem to be jumping all over the place, both mentally, between issues, and physically, between places and people. They work long and hard hours. They need to take care of urgent issues as well as plan. They use several alternative means of communication. More and more, they are expected to work all the time and everywhere.

HCI must be designed to fit this work style, but it needs to be flexible to provide different types of support. First, the system should not slow down the work when the user wishes to work on several tasks. On the contrary, HCI can be designed to support shifts between tasks by enabling the user to move from one task to another rapidly and seamlessly, reducing confusion or oversight. Similarly, the system should not slow down moving between people and places, so mobile computing and continuous accessibility may be important. Second, the system should allow the user to concentrate on one task when the user decides to do so. This means that the user can choose not to receive indications of incoming calls, alerts about new messages, or requests to acknowledge completion of other tasks, akin to closing your office door and asking for no calls when you want to concentrate. Long working hours with a computer may require ergonomic solutions too. Clearly, the way people work has significant impact on the design of HCI. We develop this notion in the next section.

## 3.2 Information Processing Functions Supported by HCI

Based on the characteristics of work environment, particularly the work habits of workers and the interrelations between the tasks and the people, we reexamine the implications of Table 9.1. The description of the work environment highlights the aspects of human information processing that are more likely to suffer from the limitations and biases mentioned previously. We choose to compare two types of work: managerial and clerical. We begin with the managers' needs for support and then compare them with those of the clerks.

The typical manager is likely to suffer from information overload unless she takes preventive action. To function effectively as monitor, disseminator, and spokesperson, information must flow to and from the manager quickly. The cognitive limitations on memory and processing become a critical threshold. Support is needed in both reducing the amount and complexity of information processing and increasing the capability of memory, processing, attention, and comprehension. Managers need to shift attention from one issue to another and back again (Vandenbosch & Huff, 1997). Drawing and holding attention needs support, as well as reducing errors in comprehension due to a multiplicity of issues. They also need to be able to store issues and access them in future periods or circumstances. These requirements make it necessary to support memory and cognitive management.

Managers also appear to need flexibility in the way they communicate. Different modes of communication need to be available to users so that they select the one that best fits their preferred way of processing and communicating information. Logistically, too, information technology needs to be flexible and adaptable. The time pressure and the relative high opportunity cost of time for managers and professionals make it nearly impossible to devote time to training beyond the bare minimum necessary to get started. Piecemeal and continuous learning must be supported.

These needs arise predominantly from the informational roles of managers. The decisional roles play a major part too and are discussed after a brief overview of managerial decision making. In both informational and decisional roles, managers interact heavily with clerical and professional workers. The clerical staff supports management and performs many of the structured and labor-intensive tasks of receiving, filtering, organizing, accessing and retrieving, transmitting, and processing information. Although we concentrated on the manager's perspective, many of the characteristics of office work apply also to the clerical staff, such as pace and time pressure, dealing with multiple issues simultaneously, and working with many diverse parties and styles.

**Table 9.3**  Managerial and Clerical Work with Corresponding User Limitations

| Characteristics of Managerial Work | Characteristics of Clerical Support Work | User Limitations |
|---|---|---|
| Information overload | Information overload | Memory, attention, cognitive processing |
| Concurrent tasks overload | Concurrent tasks overload | Cognitive management |
| Complex problem solving | | Memory, cognitive processing |
| Use of multiple media for communication | | Perceptual processing |

Furthermore, the brevity and fragmentation of managerial work often hides long hours of preparation on tasks that involve clerical and professional work. For example, word processing and communication through electronic mail (e-mail) may require hours of continuous interaction with the computer. A piece of information from a data bank may take hours to find but minutes to consider in the context of some decision.

On the whole, operations in clerical work are structured. They require technical and, often, interpersonal skills. When faced with irregular tasks, the clerical staff commonly seeks guidance from superiors or defers them to another agent in the organization. There is little restructuring of tasks or redesign of procedures that is typical of managerial and professional work. The complexity of information processing lies usually in the quantity of information processed and less in the depth of analysis and judgment that are characteristic of decisional roles in managerial work. The quantity and pace of incoming information is frequently very high relative to the resources available. It becomes a bottleneck and a source of errors when information is communicated incorrectly, ignored, stored incorrectly, or forgotten.

The primary cognitive functions that need support are memory, processing, and cognitive management. Long-term memory is commonly supported by elaborate filing systems, which in turn require long-term memory to enable efficient accesses to the stored material (e.g., the efficient use of keywords requires knowledge about the way the thesaurus is used). Short-term memory and cognitive management are stretched when working with multiple tasks. For example, working on a document and answering incoming calls requires memorizing information about the interrupted task and ensuring that you get back to it when the new task is dealt with. These functions are summarized in Table 9.3. In addition, clerical work requires a high degree of motor functions, primarily in typing information and using the mouse. More generally, many aspects of physical engineering discussed in Chapter 4 are particularly relevant to continuous and lengthy interaction with the computer that is typical of clerical work.

### 3.3 Work Modeling

The previous sections describe the organizational context in general terms, stressing the types of tasks, the interrelations among tasks, and the work habits of the workers who perform the tasks. The application of these ideas in a particular work setting for a particular computer system (or systems) may require a special analysis. One approach that begins the development of IS by looking at the work context is contextual design (Beyer & Holtzblatt, 1998).

Contextual design is based on an understanding of how users (workers or customers) work. It relies heavily on interviews, of all kinds, and observations of work as it is done in reality. This approach assumes that a careful understanding of work will provide insight into what is really important to the users and what are their most important needs and wants.

Contextual design has seven parts: contextual inquiry, work modeling, consolidation, work redesign, user environment design, test with customers, and putting into practice. Chapter 11 of this book deals with a systems development methodology that includes some of these parts. Here we are interested only in the first three parts, which overlap our general characterization of work:

1. *Contextual inquiry:* Determines the stakeholders and attempts to model how they work in practice. Using a variety of interview techniques, contextual inquiry represents the users' work habits, motivation, needs, and desires.

2. *Work modeling:* Represents the tasks performed by individual workers and interacting workers. Modeling techniques resemble object orientation tools and diagrams. One diagram represents the allocation of tasks to workers and another represents the interrelations between tasks. Additionally, each task is described individually (like a flowchart). Moreover, modeling also includes the interactions between workers, both the formal interactions around tasks and the informal interactions.

   Work modeling goes further, however, by looking closely at the physical environment too. It seeks to identify how workers use physical artifacts such as notes and desks to manage their work. For example, how one worker arranges his desk may indicate certain needs that would have to be satisfied in a paperless office.

3. *Consolidation:* This is needed when (and this is assumed in contextual design) the design is done in teams. It combines the information gained from individual interviews to form a holistic view of work.

Put together, these three parts, each consisting of several steps, produce a characterization of the particular work environment relevant to the intended system. This section completes the discussion of organizational tasks and work as the context for understanding HCI. As described in the development methodology in Chapter 11, the process of understanding the work context and analyzing tasks constitute a major part of the HCI analysis.

## ▶ 4. DECISION MAKING AS ORGANIZATIONAL TASK

Having looked at the work context and organizational tasks, we now focus on the task analysis for nonstructured decision tasks. This section discusses the idea of a decision life cycle and its implications for design and the idea of levels of interaction as it applies to decision support. The next section provides a specific method for analyzing decisions.

### 4.1 A Decision Life Cycle as a Basis for Determining Requirements

The idea of a decision life cycle helps to identify the opportunities for supporting the user (Te'eni, 1992). This life cycle should not be confused with the HCI development life cycle, which describes how to develop a computerized system. The decision life cycle defines the main activities involved in a decision-making process and how they

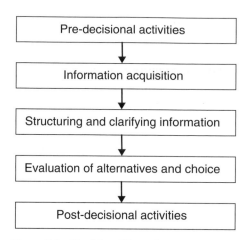

**Figure 9.4** Decision life cycle.

progress from one activity to another. We can then use the life cycle to determine what resources are needed for each activity, what the user's limitations and strengths are in performing the activity, and, accordingly, what functionalities are needed to overcome the limitations and extend the strengths. Five main stages of the decision life cycle are shown in Figure 9.4. In practice, people do not always engage in all these stages, nor do they always pursue this particular sequence. This schematic view of decisions should therefore be taken as a simplified view of decision making that drives the designer to consider the potential role of HCI.

Pre-decisional activities include complex processes such as problem detection, strategy formulation, and strategy selection. For example, in the selection decision at e-Opus, pre-decisional activities may include identifying the need for more frequent decisions on where to open new sites, formulating a strategy in which every month a different part of North America is considered for potential new sites, and selecting this strategy so that information about any other parts of North America is ignored for the coming month's decision.

Information acquisition includes all forms of obtaining information from external sources as well as retrieving information from one's own memory. Searching in national databases for information about the socioeconomic status of inhabitants in selected areas provides information for projecting the clientele in that area. The decision maker's memories complement and often dominate information acquired from external resources. For instance, remembering from a previous visit the scene of crowded coffee shops around the site may adjust favorably the computed forecast of potential clients.

Structuring and clarifying information involves complex processes aimed at making sense of the decision situation and the available information so as to be able to make a decision. It involves interpreting information, assigning values to variables, generating and updating beliefs, and constructing a structure for evaluating alternatives. For example, information about an expected wave of immigrants to a southern state needs to be interpreted as an impact on the clientele forecast. Establishing weights to combine the cost and size of the potential shop is a necessary step before evaluation of alternatives can take place. Similarly, constructing a formula that projects the clientele on the basis of socioeconomic status will be an ingredient in the evaluation of alternatives.

Evaluation of alternatives and choice is the most obvious part of decision making. It involves comparisons of alternatives with some structure defined in the previous stage.

For example, a matrix in a spreadsheet could represent three alternative sites, with information about clientele, cost and size, and calculations of expected profit stated for each site. The user is expected to compare the three alternatives and select the most profitable site. As there is uncertainty about the information and also some ambiguity about the manager's preferences (reflected in the weights), the user finds it necessary to examine the projected profits using slightly different weights to see whether such differences affect the choice of alternatives (this is called a sensitivity analysis). Finally, a choice is made.

Post-decisional activities are the last stage. It is often valuable to examine the activities after the choice is made in order to identify further opportunities of supporting the user. First, it is important to consider the affective aspects that follow from a decision and, in particular, the user's confidence in and conformance with the decision made. Both underconfidence and overconfidence are detrimental. A second aspect of post-decisional activities is learning from feedback about the decision and revising accordingly all or part of the earlier stages in the decision life cycle.

In each of the decision stages, human limitations and biases make certain activities especially difficult and prone to error. These limitations, as well as human strengths in making decisions, represent to the designer opportunities for supporting the user. We review some of the findings about human limitations in the stages of decision making.

Information acquisition, both from external and internal (memory) sources, is subject to several biases. Consider the following three biases:

1. *Availability* (Tversky & Kahneman, 1974). People tend to use information that is readily available to them and ignore information that is less available, even if it is from reliable sources. Information that is easy to recall is considered more probable.

2. *Confirming information* (Hogarth, 1987). People tend to seek and accept information that confirms rather than disconfirms their expectations. Note that more information will usually strengthen this impact rather than cure it.

3. *Selective perceptions* (Hogarth, 1987). The bias toward confirming information is a form of selective perception. Attending to first and last impressions is another.

Additionally, people find it difficult to organize information and manage it. In consequence, information gets lost or becomes inaccessible; it is ignored when needed and misused when irrelevant.

Biases and limitations are prevalent in the stage of structuring and clarifying information too. Consider the following biases:

1. *Anchoring* (Tversky & Kahneman, 1974). People tend to adjust their initial impressions more slowly than optimal rules derived from decision theory.

2. *Base rate.* People tend to judge probabilities of events according to the number of times the event occurred but ignore the rate of their occurrence. For example, seeing two black men and two black women in a class may suggest to an observer that the chances of higher education among black men and women must be close to equal, despite previous reports on lower rates among women. The correct likelihood of black women in higher education may be much lower.

3. *Regression effects* (Tversky & Kahneman, 1974). People tend to consider extreme values without considering the effect of randomness, which would dictate a regression toward the mean.

4. *Gamblers fallacy.* People mistakenly assign high probabilities to events that have not occurred recently. For example, a run of odd numbers may seem to suggest an even number in the next round.

5. *Illusion of correlation.* People tend to see relationships between variables even if there is no covariance. This is a symptom of a wider tendency to put structure where there is none.

All in all, people find it difficult to deal with probabilistic information and their projections are often erroneous. Furthermore, people usually find it difficult to structure problems that involve ill-defined or conflicting objectives. Although people seek structure, they often find it difficult to create comprehensive and correct structures and, paradoxically, create relationships when in fact they do not exist. Finally, given a structure, they often find it difficult to visualize changes and their impacts.

The main limitations in evaluation of alternatives and choice are due to processing and memory limitations. People find it difficult to compute, particularly calculations involving probabilities, and analyze results. These difficulties and inaccuracies occur even with specified procedures. Difficulties also abound in post-decisional activities. For one, people find it difficult to incorporate feedback into their decisions, particularly in dynamic decision making (Sterman, 1989). A second common bias is the decision makers' overconfidence with their decisions. In comparison with normative theories of decision making, people are usually overconfident, leading them to seek less information than desirable, reach incorrect decisions, and, most importantly, interfere with learning.

The limitations and biases discussed in relation to each of the five stages in the decision life cycle imply several types of support for users engaged in decision making. One attempt to organize the needs for supporting decision making is provided in Table 9.4, which takes after Silver (1991). The common needs include fuller exploration of alternatives than usually practiced, an earlier detection of problems and opportunities than most current practices, support for coping with multiple objectives, support in dealing with risk and probabilities, reduction of biases such as those elaborated above, triggers and support for creativity, support for structuring problems, and learning from feedback and experience. In addition to these provisions to overcome essentially cognitive biases and limitations demonstrated above, support is also needed for social phenomena such as communication (this topic is developed in Chapter 12).

The functionality the system provides the user reduces the need for cognitive resources and overcomes biases and errors. But it goes beyond that to change the way people make decisions by influencing their choice of decision strategies. Consider two decision strategies: additive and elimination by aspects (EBA). In the additive strategy, the decision maker evaluates one alternative at a time along all relevant attributes. Referring back to the example of e-Opus at the beginning of the chapter, the general manager would examine each location comprehensively, considering its cost, condition, size, and so on. In contrast, in the EBA strategy, for each attribute, its value for each alternative is compared with some threshold, and if it falls short, the alternative is eliminated from further consideration. The e-Opus manager would, in this case, decide on a threshold for cost (e.g., not more than $1,000 a month) and would eliminate all locations with higher costs. She would then decide on a threshold for every other attribute and follow the same procedure to identify the candidates that satisfy all thresholds.

**Table 9.4** Common Needs of Decision Making (Silver, 1991)

- Fuller exploration of alternatives
- Earlier detection of problems
- Coping with multiple objectives
- Treat risk
- Reduce cognitive biases
- Creativity
- Communication
- Structure decision-making process
- Learning

Now we can ask how the system's functionality affects user behavior. First, working with the system, appropriate functionality can reduce the user's effort in each step of the decision life cycle (Figure 9.4). Second, it can reduce errors (e.g., in computation). Third, it can affect the user's selection of decision strategy by making one strategy more attractive to the user than other strategies (Te'eni, 1989; Todd & Benbasat, 1992). Todd and Benbasat (2000) showed how different designs of DSS could induce users to select either the additive or EBA strategies. This observation has important implications on design because if one decision strategy is superior to the other (e.g., the additive is often more effective than EBA), the designer should provide the functionality that makes it less cognitively demanding. In the next chapter, we see a very similar conclusion with the use of graphics in decision making.

## 4.2 Levels of Interaction in Decision Making

We now apply the hierarchical decomposition of tasks to decision tasks in particular. As noted above, in the four-layer model of HCI (TSSL), the task constitutes one level. However, it can be decomposed into a hierarchy of task descriptions as shown in Figure 9.3. Concentrating on the selection decision in the e-Opus scenario, we demonstrate how similarly the decision task is decomposed. The user's goal is to locate a new shop. This goal is the primary decision task, which consists of subtasks such as predicting the number of customers at each potential location. Some of these subtasks are performed by the computer and some by the user. Those performed by the computer can be described in more detail using the four-layer model of HCI. As in Figure 9.3, we distinguish between the task level of decision making (e.g., locate a new shop) and the tool level of operating the computer (e.g., display a new potential location). The decision-making level is independent of which resource is used, that is, whether computer or human. Any task that includes an input or output operation, and all its subtasks, should be categorized at the level of operating the computer. Note that the decision-making level is closer to the primary decision task (the user's goal) and the operating level is closer to the resources that facilitate the task. This follows the general notion of layers of interaction that bridge the gap between goals and resources.

In Figure 9.5 the decision to locate a new shop is shown as the topmost level. It consists of four subtasks shown at the second level. These are task descriptions at the level of decision making. (Of course, there can be more than two levels of decision-making tasks, the lower levels describing even finer operations.) The subtask "view the site" involves the use of the computer, which is to display a picture of the site. Level 3

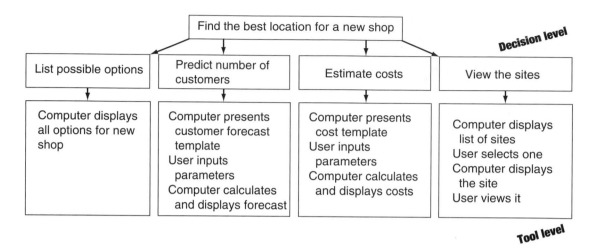

**Figure 9.5** Hierarchical task decomposition, where upper levels represent the decision task and the lower (tool) level represents how to operate the computer.

describes how subtasks are allocated between the user and the computer to implement "view the site." In this section we concentrate only on the distinction between the decision-making level and the tool level without expanding the latter with the TSSL model as we did in Figure 9.3.

The following example demonstrates the importance of addressing both levels: the level of decision making as well as the tool level. The decision context is the choice of the best location for the new shop, and the particular aspect of HCI design in question is feedback. In general, HCI should be rich with feedback (Chapter 8). Feedback, however, can be designed for different levels of human–computer interaction. Say the user is now looking at a computerized display of a map of buildings (Figure 9.1). Imagine the following scenario: The screen shows part of the map and the user wants to move around the map to see other parts of the zone. He can use the mouse or the four arrow keys (up, down, right, and left) to move north, south, east, and west on the map. When pointing at any building, the user can then double-click (or press function keys) to zoom in on a building (Figure 9.2) and then point at a specific level (a floor) to enter it.

In this scenario there may be several types of feedback to the decision maker. One potential type of feedback could be an arrow at the bottom of the map (added to Figure 9.1). The arrow would show the direction in which the user is moving—for example, up or down the floors (levels) of the building. An arrow pointing upward would appear in response to the user's action of pressing a function key to move up one floor.

The counterpressure of the keyboard key confirming that indeed the user has pressed it is feedback at yet a lower level (lower in the sense that it is closer to the machine operations and further from the user's goal of finding the best office location). At a higher level than the up/down feedback is feedback that the user reaches the floor he intends to inspect. He starts at floor number 1 and presses twice to get to floor number 3, each time receiving feedback that he is moving up. Showing the floor number is a higher-level feedback in response to an accumulation of subtasks (advancing one floor at a time). This feedback corresponds to the higher-level task of reaching floor number 3. Finally, if the user's intention is to examine locations on several floors, a check on whether all the intended floors are examined should be fed back to the user (e.g., the number of floors that have or have not been examined so

|          | Task                             | Feedback                  |
|----------|----------------------------------|---------------------------|
| Level III | Compare all floors on attributes. | "Covered 2 out of 3 floors" |
| Level II  | Reach floor 3.                   | "On floor #3"             |
| Level I   | Up/Down a floor.                 | "Going up"                |

**Figure 9.6**  Different feedback messages are designed for distinct levels of task. The specificity of the feedback should match the task level.

far). Figure 9.6 shows some of these feedback messages at the different levels of interaction.

Is this relationship between levels important for design? In Chapter 1 we made a general statement about the need to design computer support so that it considers the multiple levels of user activities (Figure 1.6). But how exactly are these levels related? Concentrate on the feedback messages at levels II and III (Figure 9.6). From the user's viewpoint, the two messages are information items that are shown on the screen and need to be processed. In other words, the user needs to expend limited cognitive resources on both information items, perhaps to the extent that one piece of information may be ignored on account of the other. If so, is one piece of information more important than the other? Should the timing of one necessarily coincide with that of the other? Should the format of one differ from the other? These are crucial questions for the designer that can be answered only if the designer considers both levels. Detailed solutions about the design of feedback are discussed in Chapter 8. In general, these questions require an understanding of the psychological aspects of decision making.

For example, during the process of making a decision, attention shifts from one level of interaction to another. The circumstances under which such shifts occur should determine when to provide feedback. Under normal conditions, the higher-level feedback should override lower levels of feedback messages. However, if the normal procedures fail, attention transfers to lower levels of interaction and, therefore, should receive lower levels of feedback. Say the user is comparing all floors from the ground floor upward. Floor number 3 is unexpectedly closed and disrupts the normal procedure, so the user's attention focuses on the problem of floor number 3, shifting away from the higher-level focus on comparing floors. This calls for a corresponding shift in the level of feedback provided by the computer. For example, "On floor #3—cannot enter" is more appropriate than the more general message "Covered 2 of 3 floors." Further, say the arrow key is depressed but the elevator does not move. This calls for a message explaining why the elevator is not moving (e.g., "No more floors").

Our main conclusion is that the designer should consider multiple levels of interaction and, in particular, combine the views of the decision level with the tool level.

## ▶ 5.  A METHOD FOR TASK ANALYSIS AND DECISION SUPPORT

### 5.1  An Overview of the Method

This section offers a template for applying the discussions above of context and task. Wane Zachary (1988) was one of the first to integrate design tools for DSS that are based on cognitive engineering. Zachary's methodology rests on the assumption that human decision making depends on the following:

1. Use of internal representations

2. Pursuit of goals

3. Chunking of information

Furthermore, human decision making is limited by five factors:

1. Working memory

2. Cognitive processing

3. Retrieval from long-term memory

4. Numerical operations

5. Projection in time and space

Chapter 5 discusses in detail the first three limitations on human information processing. The fourth and fifth limitations, numerical operations and projections, are higher-level cognitive operations that are especially relevant to decision making. The difficulty with these operations goes back to the limitations on memory and processing. Zachary's methodology assumes that these characteristics of decision making lead to several recurring problems, which can be minimized by a systematic process of analysis and design.

Figure 9.7 describes a process of designing a DSS that is adapted from Zachary's methodology. It begins with an analysis of the task and its constraints, continues with a specification of the functionality required, and then proceeds to a design of the technology. Concentrating on decision making as the central task allows us to define tailored tools and products for each stage. These tools are discussed below. Note also the lists of factors at each stage of Figure 9.7, which are pertinent to decision-making settings. These are the unique characteristics of the decision task as opposed to other types of tasks.

In stage 1, the work context is determined and a detailed task analysis is performed that includes a definition of objectives and measures of performance, dynamics, the underlying process, and elements of the behavioral decision making. The next section shows this process at length. In stage 2, we compile a list of relevant human limitations, such as cognitive constraints, decision biases, communication failures, and so forth. These are identified on the basis of Tables 9.4 and 9.5 in relation to the product of the task analysis. Again, this stage is described below in section 5.3. Stage 3 is the most creative part. It matches the limitations to the task analysis in order to define new functionality. Taking an open view of the decision process often results in a new procedure, new methods, and a new allocation of tasks between the user and the computer. Usually, this stage is not a simple automation of the current process but an improvement (e.g., introducing a new forecasting method that is feasible thanks to new neural network technologies or enabling real-time decisions thanks to mobile technology). Once the new functionality is defined, we enter the stage of design. In particular, we concentrate here on the design of HCI. This stage is deferred to the next chapter, but essentially it will be accomplished using the TSSL model. Referring back to the methodology map at the beginning of the chapter, this is shown as the design stage.

We add a fifth stage to Zachary's original methodology to ensure an iterative process. Once the designer has a good idea of the design, it is imperative to reexamine the work with the system. Say the system lets the user access information on the World Wide Web (WWW). Working with the system opens new information sources that were not previously available. The designer must ask how this will change the user's work, which in turn may call for further changes in the design. Work with the Web is often slow due to

---

1. **Situational and Functional Analysis**
   (organizational context, work style, task attributes, objective and perceived effectiveness, task dynamics, decision process, data and knowledge resources, problem representation, required judgments, errors)

2. **Constraint Analysis**
   (human limitations & biases, data constraints, communication failures, stress)

3. **Propose New Functionality**
   (redefine elements of the decision process and the allocation of tasks to human and computer)

4. **Design HCI, Models, Data, and Control**
   (design detailed human–computer interfaces, computerized decision techniques, data management, and control over the system operation throughout the human–computer interaction; develop prototype)

5. **Reanalyze Work with New DSS and Modify**
   (for objective and perceived effectiveness and for new constraints)

---

**Figure 9.7** Analysis and design of decision support systems.

bandwidth limitations and needs to be carried out in parallel to other operations with the DSS. This would most probably affect the design of the interface.

## 5.2 Situational and Functional Analysis

In the first stage, the designer analyzes the decision situation and functional aspects of the decision task. The essence of this stage is to define the decision problem and decompose its goal into subgoals. Its main tool is a protocol for collecting and analyzing information. Its product is a *Summary Tabulation of Aiding Requirements* (STAR Table; see Figure 9.8).

Goal decomposition should (1) concentrate on concrete goals and (2) work top-down from the more general to the more specific goals. Decision makers (DM for short) can usually articulate what it is they are trying to achieve in terms of events or states. The new states they attempt to achieve are frequently an observable effect on the environment, such as a certain profit level, but can also be an accumulation of knowledge (e.g., a better understanding of the competition). For each high-level goal, at least one level of subgoals should be completed. This follows closely the strategy of building a GOMS model. At this stage, it is sufficient to state the goal and the primary methods for achieving it. For example, a student needs to decide about his college education. Two high-level goals are choosing the best college and choosing the most rewarding subject.

The activity around each high-level goal is called a decision situation. The analysis includes several categories of information about the decision situation. The first two categories are situational objectives and task dynamics. These are the task context for the more specific needs and corresponding techniques shown in Figure 9.8. Categories 3–8 expose the decision-making needs. A complete protocol for collecting information on decision decomposition is given in Zachary (1988). A sample of interview questions in eight categories is given in the appendix.

The short entries of the STAR form are only summaries of the extensive knowledge gathered through the protocol. Consider some example questions and answers about choosing the best college. What is the DM trying to achieve? Where to study next year? The choices are confined to the top 10 universities in the Northeastern United States.

---

**Decision situation: (Name of decision situation)**

**Task dynamics:**
(state types—closed loop, iterative, unfolding, or single instance)

**Situational objective:**
(highest level goal that the DM is trying to achieve)

**Value criteria:**
(list of individual criteria by which alternative decisions are evaluated)

**Underlying process:**
(a brief description of the observable process in which the decision situation is embedded)

**Information environment:**
Inputs (list of available information items)
Outputs (list of information items that are created)
Parameters (list of information items that do not change value)

**Intermediate reasoning/analysis steps:**
(list of intermediate reasoning steps or types of analysis that the DM typically applies in the baseline process)

**Representation:**
(a simple description including both the external world and the internal world)

**Judgment:**
(required judgments, which are unstructured and intuitive activities)

---

**Figure 9.8**  STAR table for decision support (adapted from Zachary, 1988).

When would the decision be repeated? Only if the first choices did not work out would the decision maker make this decision again.

Choice criteria for the school decision include school reputation, tuition, average starting pay on graduation, and distance from home. One way to combine these criteria is to assess each criterion on a 1–5 scale and then calculate a weighted average.

The information environment consists of three categories: inputs, outputs, and parameters. The inputs are information items that the DM considers relevant and may change throughout the decision process. Parameters are inputs that do not change during the decision process. The outputs are information items created during the decision process. One may start with subjective impressions of school rankings and then obtain survey results. The updated rankings are outputs. Locations of the schools and the DM's home are parameters.

Intermediate analyses are the analytic and reasoning processes employed. It is usually easier to uncover the analytical portion of the DM's decision strategy. It is harder to reveal the implicit commonsense reasoning, heuristics, and shortcuts that experienced decision makers use. The prospective student may insist on talking to a graduate of each college who comes from the same high school. If some of the recommendations are not warm, those colleges are put into a second class that is evaluated only after the class of recommended colleges is exhausted.

Decision representations are the forms of knowledge that the DM works with. These may be abstract or concrete mental models and metaphors such as tables, sentences, business graphs, still pictures, moving pictures, and so forth. If such representation can be captured effectively, they will serve as excellent decision aids. The prospective student trying to imagine the distance between home and each of the colleges may benefit from a map showing the travel distances.

Required judgments are those parts of the decision process that do not lend themselves to analytical or objective descriptions of how they are performed. Intuition, "gut feelings," and overall judgment that cannot be explained are all descriptions of judgments. Although one cannot explain these judgments, it is important to note their existence. The student's final choice may rest on the feel he gets for the place.

## 5.3 Constraint Analysis

This second stage identifies the decision-making needs that arise from the constraints on unaided or the baseline decision-making process. The general direction is to refer to common limitations or biases in decision making and examine what is relevant to the particular decision situation as characterized in the prior stage of situational and functional analysis. Section 4.1 above outlined several examples of such limitations and biases, associated with the various stages of the decision life cycle, and general compilation of possible functions to help overcome the limitations (Table 9.4). Zachary (1988) too offers a similar list in Table 9.5 and relates them to the categories of the decision situation (Figure 9.8). For example, the difficulty in predicting scenarios is particularly relevant to the underlying process; the difficulty in combining attributes is relevant to the choice criteria, and so on.

**Table 9.5** Common Limitations on Decision Making (Zachary, 1988)

---

*Inability to predict processes*—It is difficult to project processes, particularly uncertain processes, due to limitations on working memory, attention to detail, and numeric processing. Possible outcomes are projecting with errors, relying on suboptimal techniques, and ignoring information.

*Difficulty in combining attributes and objectives that are competing*—It is difficult to combine ill-defined objectives or conflicting objectives, due to limitations on working memory and numeric processing. Possible outcomes are incorrect integrated criteria and omission of important attributes or objectives.

*Inability to manage information*—due to limitations on working memory and long-term memory and also limited attention. Possible outcomes are errors in using the information and ignoring information intentionally and unintentionally.

*Difficulty in analyzing and reasoning*—Limitations on knowledge, time, and effort make it difficult to formulate an effective decision strategy or to carry it out correctly.

*Difficulties in visualizing*—It is difficult to visualize abstract manipulations and semantic data. It is easier to visualize concrete situations but difficult to manipulate them, due to limitations on working memory and cognitive processing. A major outcome is limiting the ability to manipulate information and therefore producing less effective solutions.

---

Tables 9.4 and 9.5 are no more than checklists that need to be matched with the analysis documented in the STAR table. The product of this stage is a list of specific decision-making difficulties. For example, in choosing a college (without decision aids) there may be difficulties in nearly every category mentioned in the tables. The student choosing a college may limit himself to only 20 alternatives and, of those, look closely only at three. This is because of the difficulty comparing and combing multiple attributes. For example, the student may find it hard to compare alternatives on the basis of college prestige with home distance because they both seem necessary and no alternative has both. Moreover, some information is not available online, so the student may not learn that several colleges have deteriorating conditions until his site visit, at which stage he gave up on other alternatives. The risk of postponing one to get into the other may prove to be too difficult to undertake. With unlimited cognitive resources, the student may not need to restrict his search. Computer support that enables the student to examine hundreds of options according to specified attributes would help the student overcome his difficulties in combining attributes. In sum, most unaided decision processes suffer from most of the problems mentioned in the checklists above. The designer should painstakingly examine each one for potential difficulties.

## ▶ 6. A DEMONSTRATION OF THE METHOD FOR TASK ANALYSIS

This section demonstrates part of the methodology above on the e-Gourmet running case study, concentrating on the selection of a supplier. e-Gourmet has been selling international foods through its store and Web site. Recently, customers have been asking about American ethnic cuisine, particularly Cajun. e-Gourmet has decided to explore various suppliers of Cajun food and to select a new supplier for this line of product. Because this business is so dynamic and subject to new trends, the managers expect to reevaluate their selections every three to four months.

The managers first select from a database all the Cajun food suppliers authorized by the health department and narrow them down to three suppliers who are located in Louisiana (USA). They now wish to evaluate them more closely. Quotes for representative products are invited from each supplier. The three alternatives are as follows:

Supplier 1 is Bon Temps Rouler. It is located in New Orleans, Louisiana, and has a good reputation for quality products. However, it has difficulty keeping up with demand and doesn't often deliver in the time promised. Its prices seem to be very expensive.

Supplier 2 is Cajun Cabin. It is located in Baton Rouge, Louisiana. The products it carries are unique and difficult to duplicate. They are based on "secret Cajun recipes." It also has difficulty with delivery fulfillment, which is due to both the small size of its operation and the distance from Baton Rouge to a major U.S. airport.

Supplier 3 is Red Hot Cuisine. It is located in Monroe, Louisiana. It carries common Cajun items such as red beans and rice and crawfish etouffee. Its prices are low to medium. It has a large operation and can guarantee shipping within five days.

On the basis of the STAR in Table 9.6, we can build a hierarchy of tasks (similar to Figure 9.5). In order to help structure this task representation, it is helpful to use the decision life cycle (Figure 9.4) as a framework. The main activities for choosing a supplier are organized as five subtasks for the user: (1) deciding to expand the list of suppliers; (2) deciding on required criteria for a new supplier; (3) finding acceptable candidates from a general database; (4) gathering detailed information about at most five candidates and structuring the information in a useful manner; and (5) evaluating the finalists and choosing the best among them. For each of these subtasks (and their coordination), we determine the user's limitations or strengths. Of these activities, we concentrate on three subtasks that exhibit very different design implications: gather information, structure and interpret information, and evaluate alternatives.

**Gather information.** The main problem the user faces is to ensure a complete and unbiased set of relevant information items. Access to a database to retrieve all feasible alternatives ensures an unbiased selection and helps manage the information. Once the

**Table 9.6** STAR for e-Gourmet Supplier Selection

**Decision situation:** Select food supplier—Cajun food.

**Task dynamics:**

These are simple. Once the information is gathered, the choice of supplier can be made in a single session. A new decision of Cajun food suppliers is expected every three to four months. It is likely that the same system will be generalized in future to other types of food.

**Situational objective:**

The manager's highest-level goals are to choose the best-known supplier according to the information available and to reevaluate the decision according to actual performance (best in terms of criteria below).

**Value criteria:**

Prices are the most important criterion, the lower the better. Type of food: unique products are preferred to regular ones. Delivery time—over 25 days is unacceptable, and in general below 14 days is sufficient.

**Underlying process:**

A list of all Cajun food is queried to select only the authorized suppliers that are located in Louisiana. From these, information is sought by going to the Internet and calling directly for a quote on five representative products. These prices are then translated into a high, medium, and low price scale. From consumer reports, a delivery time is specified. Once the information is gathered, the managers organize the information and evaluate the alternatives.

**Information environment**

| Inputs and Parameters | Outputs |
|---|---|
| For each supplier, five prices for selected products | A table of suppliers ordered according to given criteria |
| For each supplier, location, product type, and (unstructured) information about delivery practices | |
| Weights on criteria | |

**Intermediate reasoning/analysis steps:**

Translate the information about tardiness and delivery time into one estimated delivery time. Once the output table is ready, managers take the opportunity to review the options and sometimes choose immediately, without further calculations.

**Representation:**

The managers want to view a matrix of alternatives and attributes before any analysis is made. While they would like to employ analytical tools, they feel it is important to see the overall information so that they may choose immediately without resorting to any calculations.

feasible set of alternatives is generated, information about each alternative is gathered from the suppliers, from consumer reports, and from selected customers. At this stage it is important to promote consistency in gathering information from suppliers and customers, as this interaction involves human communication. Figure 9.9 depicts a task decomposition of this stage. Each lowest-level subtask is then translated into tool-level tasks. In the next chapters we talk about how to design the computer support for these tool-level tasks. For example, an information input screen (Figure 9.10) helps to structure the conversation with the customer and supplier and reduces inconsistencies.

**Structure and interpret.** Interpreting the data gathered is not easy because it is somewhat ambiguous. Using a structured procedure to form an average of the five prices available helps produce an objective measure that must then be combined with the

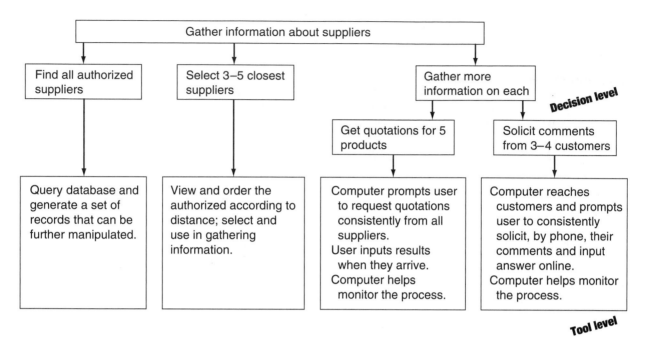

**Figure 9.9** Hierarchical task decomposition for one of the stages—gather information.

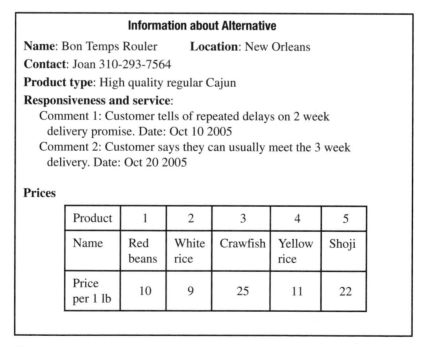

**Figure 9.10** Information input screen to promote consistent information gathering.

comments from customers. A dialog that guides the user to code these comments consistently would be helpful. Similarly, establishing weights for the attributes (preferences as input to the evaluation of alternatives is difficult (see Table 9.5). People usually are inconsistent in explicating preferences. Finally, interpreting the meaning of the location requires several transformations. Interpretation can be supported by automatically translating the locations into distances or by plotting the location on a map to show distances to customers and suppliers. Structuring the problem is complex because it involves several stages, including the interpretations discussed above. A trial-and-error approach, implemented in a spreadsheet, could be based on the matrix in Table 9.7. It would present the weights of the attributes and some integrative index (such as a weighted average) to be calculated for each alternative (supplier).

**Table 9.7**  Representation of Decision Problem

| Supplier | I | II | III |
|---|---|---|---|
| Attribute | Bon Temps Rouler | Cajun Cabin | Red Hot Cuisine |
| Product type | Regular; high-quality | Unique products | Common products |
| Responsiveness | 20 days | 20 days | 5 days |
| Relative prices | High | Medium | Low-medium |
| Location | New Orleans, LA | Baton Rouge, LA | Monroe, LA |

**Evaluate and choose.** One common way of supporting evaluation is to provide a sensitivity analysis. Typically users find it difficult to remember the results of different scenarios, so an important support is to collect results of simulated trials and then present them in a meaningful way. For example, knowing that indices of responsiveness are probabilistic and subject to errors of estimation, users may find it fruitful to show how the value of each supplier changes with small changes in their responsiveness.

## ▶ 7. SUMMARY

This chapter positions HCI within the organizational context by addressing task and work. We differentiate between task at the organizational level and task at the tool level and position both on one task hierarchy, where tool-level tasks are the means for accomplishing the higher organizational-level task. The chapter first looks at the characteristics of organizational tasks and work to help define user requirements by identifying needs or difficulties. It then looks at methods for analyzing and decomposing tasks.

Work is the ensemble of interrelated tasks and workers who perform the tasks. Understanding work is necessary for understanding how people actually, in everyday work conditions, perform the tasks. The general characteristics of a task, particularly the task's degree of structure, determine the types of computer support that are most appropriate in order to boost performance, ease work, and generally satisfy the user. The general characteristics of work, particularly the types of users and the interrelations between tasks performed by the same person or groups of workers, also dictate the limitations users face and the computer support they require. Thus the analysis of tasks in the work context they are performed is the basis for determining user requirements and designing HCI.

Having reviewed the general characteristics of organizational tasks and work, we examine methods applied to specific situations. We briefly discuss a method for analyzing work situations called contextual design. We then cover in detail a method for analyzing decision tasks. The demonstration of applying the method to the selection decision at e-Opus reveals how needs are compared to constraints in order to determine the necessary functionality of the system. The STAR table clarifies the activities, human resources, and information needed to accomplish the decision task. The constraint analysis detects the relevant difficulties the user may face in performing the task. Put together, the STAR and constraint analysis dictate ways the computer can support the user. The initial specifications of a system to support the e-Opus selection task produced at the end of this chapter are not the final product.

Given the general impact of the context on user requirements, the specific organizational tasks are decomposed into subtasks and mapped to tool-level tasks (e.g., Figure 9.10). The next chapters describe how to design the human–computer interaction to enable the tool-level tasks. For example, given that the user needs to collect information about customers, what is the best way to design the appropriate screen (e.g., designing a form-fill screen with suitable fields to ensure consistent and correct data entry)?

## ▷ 8. SUMMARY OF CONCEPTS AND TERMS

| | |
|---|---|
| Hierarchical task analysis | STAR table |
| Value criteria | Decision life cycle |
| Information environment | Roles of managers |
| Decision representation | Levels of interaction |
| Constraint analysis | Tool-level task |
| Organizational task | Structured task |

## ▷ 9. BIBLIOGRAPHY AND ADDITIONAL READINGS

Beyer, H., & Holtzblatt, K. (1998). *Contextual design: Defining customer-centered systems.* San Diego: Academic Press.

Diaper, D., & Stanton, N. A. (Eds.). (2004). *The handbook of task analysis for human-computer interaction.* Mahwah, NJ: Lawrence Erlbaum Associates.

Dowell, J., & Long, J. (1989). Towards a conception for an engineering discipline of human factors. *Ergonomics, 32*, 1513–1535.

Hogarth, R. M. (1987). *Judgment and choice* (2nd ed.). Chichester: John Wiley & Sons.

Kurke, L. B., & Aldrich, H. E. (1983). Mintzberg was right! A replication and extension of The Nature of Managerial Work. *Management Science, 29*, 975–984.

Mintzberg, H. (1973). *The nature of managerial work.* New York: Harper and Row.

Pavett, C. M., & Lau, A. W. (1983). Managerial work: The influence of hierarchical level and functional specialty. *Academy of Management Journal, 26*, 170–177.

Silver, M. S. (1991). *Systems that support decision makers: Description and analysis.* Chichester: John Wiley & Sons.

Sterman, J. D. (1989). Modeling managerial behavior: Misperceptions of feedback in a dynamic decision making experiment. *Management Science, 35*, 321–339.

Te'eni, D. (1989). Determinants and consequences of perceived complexity in human-computer interaction. *Decision Sciences, 20*, 166–181.

Te'eni, D. (1992). Process feedback in DSS. *Accounting, Management and Information Technology, 2*(1), 1–18.

Todd, P., & Benbasat, I. (1992). An experimental investigation of the impact of computer based decision aids on processing effort. *Management Information Systems Quarterly, 16*(2), 373–393.

Todd, P., & Benbasat, I. (2000). Decision aids and compensatory information processing. *Journal of Behavioral Decision Making, 13*(1), 91–106.

Tversky, A., & Kahneman, D. (1974). Judgment under uncertainty: Heuristics and biases. *Science, 185*, 1124–1130.

Vandenbosch, B., & Huff, S. L. (1997). Searching and scanning: How executives obtain information from executive information systems. *MIS Quarterly, 21*(1), 81–107.

Zachary, W. W. (1988). Decision Support Systems: Designing to extend the cognitive limits. In M. Helander (Ed.), *Handbook of human-computer interaction.* Amsterdam: Elsevier.

## ▷ 10. EXERCISES

Ex. 1.   You plan to take a friend out to dinner—it's his birthday. You now need to decide which restaurant to choose. Complete the STAR analysis for this decision. Assume at least three comparable alternatives.

Ex. 2.   Perform a constraint analysis for the STAR in Ex 8-1. Choose one constrain and propose the functionality that will support it. Provide a screen to demonstrate the proposed functionality.

## ▷ 11. APPENDIX: DECISION DECOMPOSITION PROTOCOL

### Sample questions (Zachary, 1988)

#### 1. Situational objectives
What is the DM's goal in this situation? If there are multiple goals, are they hierarchically related? What are the relationships? If not hierarchical, are they complementary or competing?
What event or relationship is the DM trying to achieve?
Which goals are imposed on the DM from a higher authority?
What are the relative priorities among the goals involved?

#### 2. Task dynamics
Is this decision likely to occur more than once in the current context?
Under what conditions would it be repeated? Is it made repeatedly as part of a larger task?
Is it one of a sequence of decisions that must be made to resolve the overall problem?

#### 3. Underlying process
Is there some real-world process underlying this decision situation?
Is this process being managed by other people or is it a natural process (e.g., weather)?
If others control the process, how do their goals relate to those of the DM?
How do the DM's options/resources affect this process and how are they affected by it?
How does the DM perceive the uncertainty and its sources?
How does the DM perceive the task structure or lack of it and its sources?
What metaphor/mental model does the DM use to think about the process?

#### 4. Choice criteria
What criteria does the DM use?
Can they be measured objectively? How?

If not, how can they be represented?

How are criteria traded off or combined?

Which are specified by a higher authority and which are defined by the DM?

How does the DM justify decisions?

### 5. Information environment

What data are available prior to or during the decision?

What parameters distinguish this instance of the decision from other instances?

Are the constructs used by the DM at the same level of abstraction as those in the external information environment? If not, how are they translated?

How much prior knowledge is needed to make the decision?

How does the DM access the information?

How is the DM updated and how current is the update?

### 6. Intermediate analyses

What are the DM's steps in formulating the decision problem?

What subproblems does the DM resolve separately from the others?

Are there intermediate states that the DM tries to create to facilitate the overall problem?

How does the DM integrate the subproblem solutions?

Are any of the subproblems optimization problems? Constraints? Criteria?

Does the DM lack time or expertise to perform effectively in any of the subproblems?

### 7. Decision representation

What common visual metaphors are used by the DM or others in this domain?

Is there a pictorial format commonly used to show the results/analyses of the subproblems?

How effective is the linguistic representation in describing the data and the problem?

Does the DM need simulations of data? What are they?

Is there a real-time control aspect to the decision?

### 8. Required judgments

What are the unstructured mental activities that qualify as judgments?

How precise must the judgment be?

What heuristics does the DM use?

How well is the DM able to verbalize the judgmental process?

Would the DM be willing to consider judgments of others (experts, expert systems)?

# 10

# COMPONENTIAL DESIGN

## CONTEXT AND PREVIEW

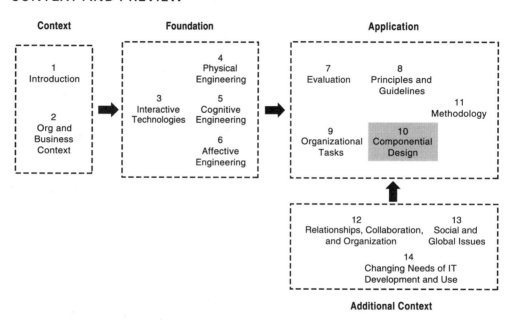

This chapter examines several important HCI design components. These are the building blocks of the human–computer interface, such as color, graphics, menus, and form fill-in. We look at the task, semantics, syntax, and lexicon (TSSL model) of each of these components. Using the material from previous chapters, we ask how we can design the component to best fit the user's task. Componential design is central to most of the design activities as indicated below in the methodology map.

## LEARNING OBJECTIVES

Upon completion of this chapter, students should be able to do the following:

- Know some of the popular HCI components
- Understand how to select and design components
- Learn how to apply HCI design guidelines to the design of HCI components.
- Learn how to apply the TSSL model to any HCI component.

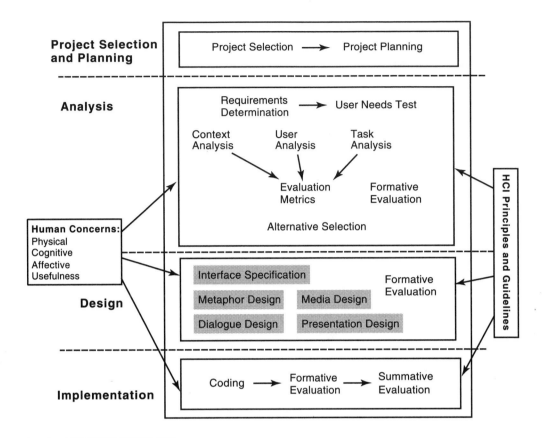

## ▷ 1. INTRODUCTION

Most designers build human–computer interfaces by assembling ready-made components. The previous chapters examined the tasks users perform, including organizational-level and tool-level tasks. The computer provides functions that enable the
tool-level tasks (e.g., given that the user's task is to key in data, the computer provides the user with data-input functionality). Functionality is usually built by assembling interface *components* into input-output designs that serves some *function* such
as presenting information to the user, enabling navigation, and accepting information
from the user. Take, for example, the simple screen shown in Figure 10.1, which
shows a graph and beneath it three controls. The graph depicts the profit history for
Company Y. Imagine that the user faces a task that involves inspecting and then
choosing the best-performing company among several companies, each company
with its corresponding graph of profit history. The screen in Figure 10.1 enables the
user to study each company and navigate from one company to another (by using the
forward and backward controls). The computer computes and displays the profit for a
given company and shifts between views of companies according to the user's
instructions. Overall then, the design in Figure 10.1 supports the task by enabling
presentation and navigation.

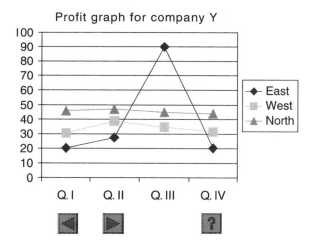

**Figure 10.1**   A screen with two types of components—graph and buttons.

Two types of components are used in this example: a graph and command buttons. In most window-based systems, both types of components are readily available and need only to be included (and, if necessary, adapted) into a specified application. Alternative components can also support the same task. For instance, a table (rather than the graph) can be used to display profits, and a list box of all companies (rather than the forward/backward buttons) can be used to navigate among companies. The designer thus faces a choice of which component to use. Moreover, in some cases, designers may decide that current components cannot effectively support the task and therefore design a new component. In any event, designers need to know which components exist, how to choose among them, how to fit them to the particular situation, and how to combine them into one screen. We call this process componential design.

This chapter reviews several components to demonstrate their application. We use the four-layer TSSL (task, semantics, syntax, and lexicon) model of interaction that translates the abstract function to the physical building blocks. However, to avoid confusion, the term *task* is reserved for describing the task as the user sees it, and the term *function* will be used to describe the designer's description of what the component does. The set of all functions constitutes the system's functionality. Of course, function should match task, and some functions support several types of tasks. So, for example, the user's task is to read information to answer a question such as, "Which organization shows the highest profit?" To support this task, the designer includes in the system a graph component. The graph's function is to present quantitative information in order to help answer the question, and the graph's lexicon includes labels and line graphs.

Any discussion of design must first determine the level of design specificity it addresses. For example, text can be examined at the level of a character (e.g., its font and size) or at the level of a paragraph (e.g., its direction and alignment). Similarly, graphic design can address the level of spatial elements (e.g., the line segment, angle, and circle) that are assembled into a specific image such as a face or the level of business charts (e.g., pie charts and bar charts). There are no absolute distinctions between levels. For instance, graphic objects considered to be high-level components by the graphic designer may be considered to be low-level components by the business analyst. Nevertheless, the notion of high versus low levels of design components is useful. First,

**Components:** The building blocks with which we construct the human–computer interface.

**Functions:** The component's services to the user.

**Componential design:** The process of selecting or adapting the appropriate component to fit the user and the user's task.

**Table 10.1a**  Low-Level Components—The Infrastructure

| Component | Functions |
|---|---|
| Color | Differentiate data items; group elements; signal order and meaning; impact mood |
| Voice | Convey meaning and emotion; signal importance; instruct tools |
| Text | Convey meaning and emotion |
| Video | Convey meaning and emotion; display dynamic behavior |

**Table 10.1b**  Higher-Level Components

| General Function | Description of Function | Components |
|---|---|---|
| Data input & feedback | Input data by selecting from predefined values or generating new values | Selection: radio button, check box, list box Generation: text box, message box for feedback, specific dialog boxes |
| Navigation controls & feedback | Control the intersystem and intrasystem flow of activities and user navigation of the system | Menu, command buttons, dialog box |
| Quantitative displays | Output quantitative information | Graphics (bar charts, etc.), tables |
| Input information about some entity | Input related data that describe some entity and therefore share some common context | Form fill-in |
| Output information about some entity | Output related data that describe some entity and therefore share some common context | Output screen |
| Search and browsing | Search for a specified piece of information located in some information environment or browse an information environment for targeted or nontargeted information | Query screen Browser |
| Exploratory decision making | Decide on a solution by investigating the impact of different values for given parameters | What-if screen |
| Navigation and control within some Web site; introduce a site | Navigate within a Web site so as to reach your destination and maintain control over your whereabouts and progress; in your first interactions, the same component introduces the site to improve (and invite) navigation | Home page (also menu); multiple windows for multiple views of the Web site |

the higher-level design components usually enable more general functions than the lower-level components. Second, the lower-level components are often subcomponents of higher-level components. For example, the business chart itself can be built from lower-level components such as a title, a bar chart, and a legend. These subcomponents constitute the building blocks of the higher-level component. Each subcomponent itself, however, has four levels of interaction (e.g., the title's task is to focus the user's attention on the main message and its lexicon includes text and artwork). Tables 10.1a and 10.1b list, respectively, low-level and high-level components (the classification is arbitrary but demonstrates the idea of levels). Not all the components listed in the tables are covered in the text, and hence the chapter is not exhaustive of HCI components but rather demonstrative of how to use components in the design of effective HCI.

Each component is examined through (1) the four-layer TSSL model, proceeding bottom up from the lower and concrete levels to the higher levels, and (2) the psychological parameters of user activity (memory, attention, comprehension, attitude, etc.), analyzing the impact of the component on cognitive and affective resources. Both perspectives rely on the materials covered in previous chapters. In particular, we build on the simplified model of human information processing that relies on scarce resources (see Figure 5.3 in Chapter 5). Components are generally designed so as to minimize the effort and maximize user performance. Similarly, the use of components should be evaluated for their affective impact. This examination of each component helps determine how to choose and fit the component to the user's task and needs.

## ▶ 2. COLOR

### 2.1 Color—Introduction

Color in human–computer interaction is used extensively. Color is particularly effective in calling attention to specific information on a display, differentiating information types, and grouping similar items. Color is also effective in helping comprehension by underscoring structures, by depicting multiple dimensions of data, and by more accurately representing known or natural phenomena associated with color. Color helps memory too by adding cues to data and building more associations. Moreover, color is appealing and convincing and is often pleasant to the eye. Hence, color facilitates recognition, attention, memory, comprehension, and positive affect. For all these reasons, especially as color in display and even in print becomes cheaper, color is an important component in design.

And yet color can be misused. For one, too much color is confusing and may be physically tiring. Extensive use of extreme colors may even have aftereffects. Therefore, one of the most important guidelines is not to overuse color. Another is the cultural sensitivity of color. The same color can be sacred in one culture and not in another, and therefore using it inappropriately may be offensive to some. This section examines these issues, providing the designer with important know-how.

**Color wheel:** A spatial representation of colors as a circle, where each color corresponds to a light wavelength.

### 2.2 Color—The Building Blocks

The eye receives incoming light and translates it into what our brain perceives as color. Certain cells in the eye's retina produce the sensation of shades of gray and other cells produce the sensation of color, using receptors of red, green, and blue. These receptors are located in different areas of the retina, so some colors, especially blue, are perceived to be deeper than other colors, such as red. Some color combinations, therefore, strain the eye because it must shift its focus to perceive the different colors. One such irritating combination is red and blue.

Figure 10.2 is a typical dialog box for determining the required color. It is organized as two tabs labeled "Standard" and "Custom." Think of the hexagon in the "Standard" tab as an approximation for a circle and its edges as a circumference. It is called a "color wheel" and it helps to explain the building blocks of color. Along the circumference of the color wheel are colors, including the base colors (red, blue, and green) as well as combinations such as blue-green and yellow-red. Each color corresponds to a light wavelength. Colors that are positioned opposite each other (e.g., blue-green and yellow-red) cancel each other out, leaving gray. At the center is the color white, which results from combinations of colors on the circumference. In fact, one can think of white as a generic name for a black–white continuum, which has gray in the middle. Imagine then a third and orthogonal dimension of the wheel that goes through the word "white."

Color is defined by three variables: hue, saturation, and brightness. As shown below, we can equivalently use the base colors red, green, and blue (RGB).

*Hue* corresponds to the normal meaning of color—changes in wavelength. Hue is located along the circumference of the color wheel. These are spectral colors.

*Saturation* (or chroma) is the relative amount of pure light that must be mixed with the white light to produce the perceived color. All colors on the circumference are highly saturated, and as you approach the center, the colors become less saturated. The point labeled "white" has zero saturation.

*Brightness* (or intensity or luminance) refers to the shades of gray going from white (very high brightness) through gray (medium brightness) to black (very low brightness). It is located on the (imaginary) third dimension, which is orthogonal to the two-dimensional circle. In the dialog box it appears as the horizontal line of small white, gray, and black hexagons beneath the color wheel.

---

Hue, saturation, and brightness define color:

**Hue** corresponds to the normal meaning of color—changes in wavelength.

**Saturation** is the relative amount of pure light that must be mixed with the white light to produce the perceived color.

**Brightness** refers to the shades of gray decreasing from white through gray to black.

---

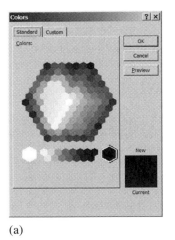

(a)

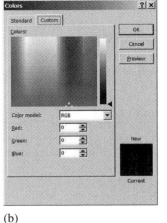

(b)

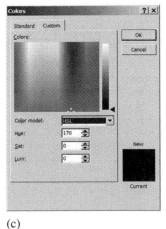

(c)

**Figure 10.2** Dialog box to define color. See also color plate V.

In Figure 10.2 the current color of the lower right-hand box is black (as the color has not yet been changed, the same color appears as "New" too). The user can change the color in three ways. In Figure 10.2a, the user points directly at the required location on the color circle. Alternatively, the user can directly determine the values for hue, saturation, and luminance (HSL). In Figure 10.2c, the value of hue is set to 170, while saturation and brightness are set to 0. Some find it easier to use the corresponding RGB scheme, as shown in Figure 10.2b. For example, bright green may have the respective values of 80 (hue), 255 (maximum saturation), and 128 (brightness). The same color would be defined in RGB by 30, 255, and 0, respectively.

## 2.3 Color—The Syntactic and Semantic Levels

Conservative use of color means not using too many colors. If users need to recognize the colors (i.e., be able to identify what information is colored in a particular color), then the maximum number of colors recommended varies between 5 and 11 (e.g., Post, 1997). If colors are used only to differentiate between data, more colors can be used. In general, it is best to use the colors located on the circumference of the color wheel (i.e., those differentiated by hue). For drawing attention, colors that are high on both saturation and brightness are most effective. When colors are used to signal an ordinal relation between data items, it is customary to use the spectral sequence: red, orange, yellow, green, blue, indigo, and violet. This presents a natural evolvement.

Care should also be taken concerning the combinations of colors used in a single display. As noted above, colors diagonally opposed on the circumference (high saturation) create strong contrasts and strain the eye. Here are some of these contrasts: red and green, blue and yellow, green and blue, and red and blue. Such combinations often create vibrations and confuse the user's perception of the relationships between the colored items.

Determining the semantics of color requires special care because of the diversity in the way people interpret color. The first step is to decide whether color will be used as a natural reference color, that is, whether the user is expected to identify the color as that of the real-world object or whether color will convey symbolic meaning with no physical (natural) association to the real-world object. Natural reference colors should obviously resemble as much as possible the common natural setting. Symbolic color needs to be selected with special care and sensitivity to the user, the task, and the organizational and social context. An immediate rule about choosing the color to represent an object or an abstraction is to use a familiar coding scheme (e.g., red is usually associated with danger or stop). One way to ensure familiarity is to ask users directly. It is equally important to use the coding scheme consistently. The task and the context of using the system impacts the meaning associated with a particular color. For example, green stands for "go" at the traffic lights, for "OK" on the ATM panel (same idea as "go"), vegetarian on the restaurant menu, and "sacred" in Islam. Similarly, the same idea is represented by different colors by different contexts or different cultures. For example, sacredness is green in Islam but blue or gold in Judaism.

Differences among individuals and cultures in the perception and interpretation of color have been detected on several dimensions. It is not always possible or feasible to fit the choice of color to the particular condition, but it is important to be aware of these differences and allow for adaptation. Two general design guidelines help in mitigating

**Table 10.2**  Fitting Colors to Function

| Functions of Color in Displays | Comments |
| --- | --- |
| Differentiate data itemsmale | Colors differentiated by hue (spectral); sparingly use as many colors as you wish, but not more than 11 |
| Group related elements | Colors differentiated by hue (spectral); use between one and five colors at most |
| Signal ordinal relation | Use the following sequence: red, orange, yellow, green, blue, indigo, and violet |
| Impact mood | Pastel colors are known to calm |
| Signal meaning by conventional connotations | Beware of intercultural differences and sensitivities |

the problem. First, allow for redundancy so that differentiation by color is also accompanied by differentiation by shape or size. For example, in Figure 10.1, the three data series can be differentiated by both color and shape. Between 8 percent and 10 percent of American males are color-blind! Without such redundancy, every one out of ten male users will not be able to understand your message. One way to ensure this guideline is to start your design in black and white and add color as a second stage. Secondly, whenever possible, empower the user to adapt colors to fit their preferences and their culture. Using the dialog box with the color wheel is a good example of how control over presentation is transferred to the user.

### 2.4 Color—The Task Level

As a low-level component, color supports many different tasks in different ways. Thus, the choice of color depends on the type of task it supports. In this section we demonstrate the need to fit color to the task with several, out of many, examples of tasks. We concentrate on tasks that are especially relevant to organizational work. These are summarized in Table 10.2 and expanded below.

Color is used frequently to attract attention. In reading long streams of texts, numeric and textual tables, business charts, and even detailed images, users need and often expect to focus their attention on part of the information. Colors high in brightness are most effective for drawing attention. However, too many information items highlighted in color confuses rather than helps. Furthermore, continued brightness eventually grows on you so that it is no longer effective.

Color is also used to help detect and recognize information. Data extraction from tables and graphs in decision tasks can benefit from color (Hoadley, 1990). As noted above, differentiating information by color should be in addition to some other technique such as using different shapes. Using color not only increases the speed and accuracy of data extraction but also enables higher density of information in comparison to black-and-white designs.

Color helps users understand and recall information in reading and decision tasks. Color adds cues to information items (e.g., colored photographs of coworkers in a collaborative application). These additional (redundant) cues boost recall and make it easier to recognize the coworkers in other situations or in future encounters. Additional cues also help users understand complex information such as diagrams showing relationships (e.g., scatter plots of the performance of different organizations). Color helps distinguish and then generalize patterns of behavior. In these cases, color is usually associated with some symbol (there is no natural reference), and therefore special care must be given to the semantics. Incongruent associations damage rather than help comprehension. Think of the chaos on the roads if for some reason traffic lights reversed the colors of the lights so that green (the uppermost light) would signal "stop." Now think of how many users would be confused to see in Figure 10.2 the command button "OK" in red and the "Cancel" in green. Finally, imagine a world atlas that has the oceans painted in brown and green and the continents painted in shades of blue. Color can certainly support comprehension and memory but only if the color fits the task and context.

Finally, color supports affective processes too. Some hotels paint their rooms in pastel colors because people seem to be more relaxed when surrounded by these colors (pastel colors are high in brightness). In contrast, colors high in saturation excite you. Applying this knowledge to marketing, advertisements are painted in pleasing colors in order to induce people to buy. Using the idea of the core affect diagram (Chapter 6), it is possible to examine how color relates to positive or negative affect. Placing two axes on the core affect diagram, boredom-excitement and relaxation-tension, a color of high brightness and high saturation generates a mood best characterized as being both excited and relaxed at the same time, and in this mood, the consumer is most likely to yield to the advertisement (Gorn, Chattopadhyay, Yi, & Dahl, 1997). Imagine now the implications for e-commerce!

We see, then, that color plays many different roles in different tasks. It supports detection and recognition in reading and decision making, aids in comprehension and memory, helps to attract attention, and impacts affect and thereby propensity to yield. Color is important in other respects that could not be covered here. For example, color is used for decoration to boost aesthetic appearance. Color should be used, but it should be used cautiously.

## ▶ 3. DATA INPUT

### 3.1 Data Input—Introduction

Data input is one of the most frequent input-output activities and yet one that is particularly prone to error. This section looks at the input of a single or a small number of related data items. Another section later in this chapter discusses how to organize the input of multiple data items when inputting relatively large batches of data (e.g., all relevant information about a new student in the university). In any event, the main design objectives of data input are to ensure correct input with minimal user effort.

There are two general methods of inputting data: in one method the user generates the data values, and in the other the user selects values from a display of predetermined data values. Typing your name in response to a system's prompt is an example of generating free-form text, and keying your password in a field labeled "Password" and formatted to allow four digits only is another example. The most common way users generate data for input is by typing on the alphanumeric keyboard or using the numeric keypad. More advanced techniques employ other media such as voice-based input. In contrast, inputting your country and state by selecting from a predefined list of states or checking the

> **Data input:** Enables the user to input data to the computer by generating values or selecting from predefined values.

range of your age from a set of age ranges are examples of input by selection. (Some books regard input by selection as a type of menu, while here we reserve the word *menu* for navigation and control, as demonstrated below.)

Inputting data, particularly selection from predetermined values, may also represent a choice among options for action. For example, in an e-commerce application, radio buttons can be used to determine which of four possible printers the customer wishes to purchase. The discussion in Chapter 9 revealed design concerns for the support of decision making; it is also applicable to consumer choice in e-commerce but is not expanded in this section.

### 3.2 Data Input—The Building Blocks

The common building blocks (controls) for selecting symbolic values include the radio button, check box, and list box. Other techniques for selecting analog values such as colors and volume have also become popular; for example, in Figure 10.2 (preceding), the dialog box for defining colors has a vertical slide bar for setting the brightness. Figure 10.3 shows a screen that includes a check box to designate whether you are entitled to a discount and radio buttons to choose the number of requested tickets. In addition, the user can select the required movie (currently Madagascar) from a pull-down list box by scrolling to locate the suitable option and then clicking on it to select it. Both radio buttons and list boxes are used to select one value from a predefined set. Multiple check boxes, unlike radio buttons, allow the user to select several values at once.

The common controls for enabling the user to generate values are the formatted input field (coded field), text box, and specific dialog boxes, which are often supported by guidance and feedback through a message box. In Figure 10.3, a text box is used to input the transaction summary. The "amount due" is presented in a formatted field. A similar formatted field (not shown) could be used to input the amount of money to donate to some voluntary cause. While the value for the transaction summary is not restricted in any way, the values of the amount of money to donate are restricted to numeric digits

**Figure 10.3** Screen with list box, check box, radio buttons, command buttons, and text boxes.

only. In cases where the input can be validated against certain restrictions, the user receives feedback when these restrictions are violated. The message box is used to notify an incorrect value for the phone number.

A combination of predetermined values and an option for user-generated values is possible too (sometimes called a combo box). This combination is used when the most frequent solutions can be identified but room must be left for the occasional unknown value or when the list of allowed values expands according to users' inputs.

### 3.3 Data Input—Syntactic and Semantic Levels

Some of the syntactic and semantic guidelines apply generally to all the input widgets and are derived here from the design guidelines in Chapter 8, stressing error and effort reduction. The guidelines that are tailored to particular controls (sometimes called widgets) are organized in Table 10.3. Labels for single and groups of data items must first be understandable and meaningful to the user (e.g., no medical jargon to a layman patient). Guidance and constraints afforded by the structure and appearance of the data entry fields reduce intentional and unintentional errors, for example, a data entry field that provides space for nine digits or a date format that indicates "JUL-10-2005." Such restrictions and examples clarify the semantic and syntactic rules. Third, immediate feedback that verifies input, detects errors, and helps correct errors is essential (e.g., detecting incorrect alphabetical data when a quantity is expected or indicating an empty field under name of spouse when another field indicates a spouse exists).

### 3.4 Data Input—The Task Level

From the user's point of view, providing information requires several cognitive resources: understanding what data to provide, recalling the data, and articulating and feeding the data. In general, selection from predetermined values is effective if the user can easily select the right value (i.e., the listed values are unambiguous and self-explanatory). This is usually possible only for structured input (e.g., a single or a few numeric quantities, labels of known objects, predefined scales). User-generated input is necessary when possible values of the input cannot be predetermined, when the data is

**Table 10.3** Fitting Control to Function

| Control | Function | Guidelines |
|---|---|---|
| Formatted (coded) fields | Enhance clarity of what is expected; prevent errors and guide specification of input; ease input | Use meaningful labels adjacent to the data entry field; the data entry field should be clearly visible and match the expected value in format and size; recognizable but restrictive formats when possible; provide explanations near the data entry field; provide constructive feedback upon incorrect input; use defaults when possible (e.g., common or personalized value) |
| List box | Display values and help select | Order values in obvious sequence (e.g., alphabetical); provide explanation of the list values or categories |
| Radio buttons | Display values to enable holistic view and easy choice | Organize values to enable parallel view of all options (e.g., order categories in increasing ascending value); provide explanation of the values or categories |

unstructured, or when it is important to maintain the user's style and personalized content (e.g., a person's explanation for some action documented for future analysis).

In structured input, information about expected values is used to guide and provide feedback. Field labels and instructions are used to reduce ambiguity on the meaning of the expected input, and the results of validity checks are fed back to the user. The higher the likelihood of misunderstanding, the more guidance and feedback are needed (here we follow feedback guidelines in Chapter 8). Table 10.4 summarizes the guidelines for fitting the data-input control according to the task.

## ▶ 4. NAVIGATION AND FLOW CONTROL

### 4.1 Navigation and Flow Control—Introduction

**Navigation:** Enables the user to control the inter-system and intra-system flow of activities and the user's navigation of the system.

In window- and Web-based systems, the main visual mechanisms for navigating and controlling systems and interactions are the menu, the command controls, and the dialog controls, all with appropriate feedback. Other mechanisms such as natural language and controls based on other media such as voice are becoming popular but are currently dominant only in specialized applications. This will undoubtedly change. For now, however, we concentrate on a sample of the most popular controls. Also, navigation on the Internet is not treated here.

**Table 10.4**  Fitting the Data Input Controls to Task

| Input Circumstances | Main Concerns | Controls Recommended |
|---|---|---|
| Possible values known; several values allowed | Recall and specification is difficult and accuracy of input is crucial (e.g., areas of interest for marketing purposes) | Check box for limited number of values |
| Possible values known; one value allowed | Free-form specification may be ambiguous and accuracy of input is crucial (e.g., spelling of country name) | Radio buttons for few possible values; list box for multiple values (ordered if possible) |
| Possible values known; one value allowed | Choice of value depends on comparison with other options (e.g., exact marital status on tax form) | Radio buttons to display simultaneously the possible values |
| Possible values unknown; free-form alphanumeric input expected | In some cases, specification of input is difficult | Text box with short labels when specification is straightforward and additional constant labels or pop-up message boxes to help with ambiguous or difficult specification |
| Possible values unknown; some predefined restrictions | Free-form specification may be ambiguous and accuracy of input is crucial (e.g., phone number with area code and country code) | Formatted input box with message box as feedback to validate input |

Menus let the user locate and activate the required system action by selecting from predefined options (each option is a menu item). Like a menu item, a command control activates a particular system action. Dialog boxes help the user control system actions by allowing the user to specify her intentions through questions and answers. Finally, feedback helps ensure that the user's intended controls are correctly implemented by confirming (or disconfirming) the user's specific inputs and by indicating the resulting system outcome (e.g., a command to shut down the system will begin a shutdown but also indicate on the screen that the system is in the process of shutting down).

## 4.2  Navigation and Flow Control—The Building Blocks

We describe the main types of menus, command controls and hotlinks, the dialog box, and feedback indicators.

Menus can be classified as text-based (verbal) menus, icon-based menus, and sensitive image-based menus. In text-based menus, each menu item is labeled with a meaningful term. The menu items are organized in some structure (e.g., a linear sequence or tree structure). Figure 10.4 shows a display of an article in Acrobat Reader. The upper part of the display shows a common tree-structure menu displayed as a horizontal menu that begins with the Acrobat icon as the first (leftmost) menu item, continues with "File," and ends with "Help." The "File" option has suboptions (not displayed), and some of the suboptions have their own suboptions. These levels of suboptions constitute the tree structure.

Text-based menus are often supplemented with command controls represented by icons. Beneath the horizontal menu in Figure 10.4 are two rows of icons (controls), each representing a command to help control the flow of interaction. While these commands are also accessible through the text-based menu, it is usually easier to simply-click on the appropriate icon. In some cases, the command controls function as an icon-based menu, replacing altogether the text-based menu. The typical desktop of a PC is an icon-based menu, providing direct access to your main software.

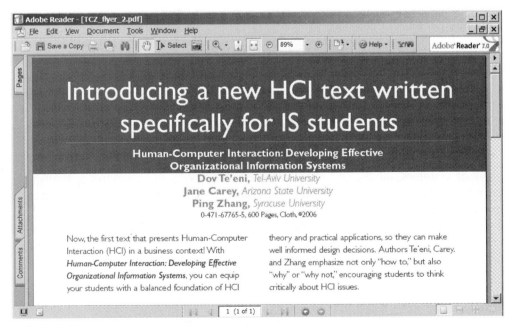

**Figure 10.4**  A control panel consisting of a horizontal menu and icon-based command controls.

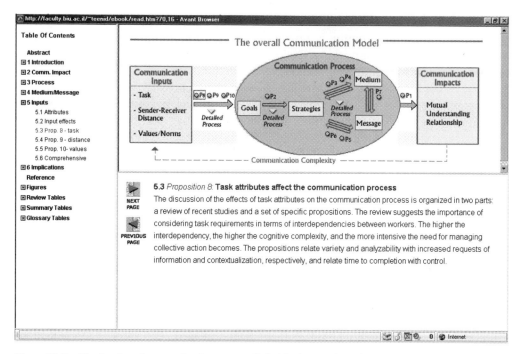

**Figure 10.5** Navigation in an e-book uses a clickable image-based menu and a corresponding vertical menu. See also color plate V.

Images sensitive to pointing devices, mouse clicks, or touch can function as menus too. A good example is a sensitive weather map that is used to indicate the relevant area, zoom in on it, and receive the corresponding weather data. Figure 10.5 shows, on the right, a clickable image that functions as a menu to an e-book application. The user can access directly different parts of the book that correspond to parts of the portrayed image. It works in concert with the vertical menu on the left-hand side, which is the more familiar table of contents.

Figure 10.6 shows two overlapping dialog boxes. The lower, partially hidden dialog box is a "Print" command, which is one of the options under menu item "File." The "Print" dialog box has a "Properties" button (not shown in Figure 10.6) that is expanded (by clicking on it) to the upper dialog box. The upper dialog box is organized in five tabs, the first of which is the "Advanced" tab shown in the figure. Dialog boxes usually combine several types of data input controls, as well as text and image displays.

Finally, feedback and status indicators using standard message boxes, simple displays of counters, labels, or images are used extensively in interactive systems. For example, in most text processors or readers, users see the current page number in relation to the total number of pages, and if they press the "Insert" key on the keyboard, an appropriate label appears at the bottom of the screen. Similarly, in using a dialog box, users expect and receive a confirmation on correct actions and alerts on incorrect actions.

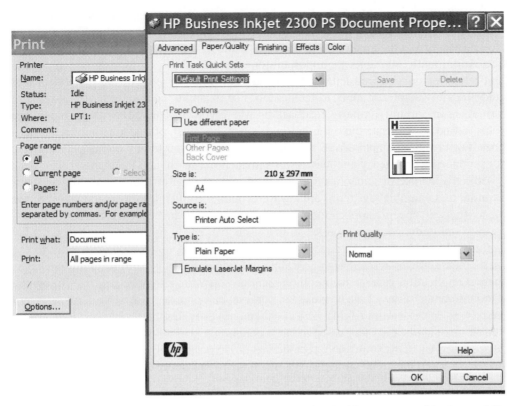

**Figure 10.6**   Two overlapping dialog boxes, the upper one invoked by a command in the partially hidden one. The upper dialog box is organized in five tabs, consisting of a variety of texts, images, and data input controls.

## 4.3 Navigation and Flow Control—Syntactic and Semantic Levels

In tree-structured menus the main design issues are the breadth-depth trade-off, the organization of menu items, the sequence of menu items, and the graphic layout. Breadth is the number of menu items displayed concurrently at the same level and depth is the number of levels. Clearly, breadth and depth are inversely related. There is substantial empirical research showing that depth slows down the search so that having more items on the highest levels of the menu (and consequently fewer levels) reduces search time. On the other hand, crowding (presenting too much information) confuses the user. Breadth is usually limited to eight items and depth to four levels. If more menu items need to be organized in the menu, the menu can be divided or additional support can be provided (e.g., feedback on your location within the tree structure).

Organizing the menu items into a tree structure can follow several alternatives. Menus can follow conventional wisdom (e.g., some temporal order) or some standard organizations (e.g., File, Edit, Format, and Help are common top-level options). More content-dependent organizations rely on alphabetical sequence or categories. In short lists, conventional order, if there is one, is preferred. In long lists, if there are distinctive and well-known categories, then they are preferred to alphabetical organization. Finally, if some menu items are used more frequently, in a significant way, they should lead the structure, particularly if the menu list is long. If categories are used, they should be visually distinct (e.g., a blank line between categories). In any event, the movement from one item to another is dictated by the tree structure. However, menus should let the user move backward in the menu as well as forward and also move directly to the root of the tree. Additionally, shortcuts are important for experienced users—for example, using the first letter (or underscored letter) of a menu item. Finally, most of the general design guidelines in Chapter 8 apply to menus too. For example, consistent terminology and format are important. Similarly, feedback on where you currently are within a menu tree helps to find and activate the right option. Beware, however, of tradeoffs between guidelines. For instance, adaptive Web site menus achieve a better fit and higher performance but produce inconsistency and may lower satisfaction (Te'eni and Feldman, 2001).

Effective choice of semantics is crucial for correctly and efficiently locating an item. Familiar and unambiguous terms are key to recognizing and interpreting the labels of the menu items. In specific applications, the subject matter is the best basis for building categories and items within categories so that users can easily relate the computer display to the real-world tasks (this is a good example of fitting the computer display to the user's mental model—see design guideline in Chapter 8). In general software packages such as application generators or communication software, it may be easier to follow the standard menu terms. Labels must be concise but precise. Users read menus very quickly, so the first word (if there is more than one) provides the strongest signal.

The main application text-based menu is commonly positioned at the top of the screen horizontally. By convention, more specific menus are positioned vertically on the left-hand side. Icon-based menus are arranged in a two-dimensional space to be read left to right and top to bottom by infrequent users. However, other patterns usually emerge when users rearrange the menu to their likings (e.g., positioning all frequent options at the bottom row). Such screens may quickly get crowded (this often happens when users simply add new software or shortcuts to their desktops). It seems that the younger users tend to feel comfortable with very large icon-based menus. Colors and shapes can be used to help sort out the clutter. Figure 10.7 is a typical youngster's self-constructed icon-based menu.

Image-based maps follow the rules of effective graphics—they should clearly represent the target object (e.g., an image-based menu of Europe should resemble maps of Europe closely enough so that it is immediately recognized and its resolution is sufficient for its intended functionality). For example, if the user is expected to point at the level of countries, the shape of the country should be recognized and the label legible. When necessary, it is possible to zoom in on an area to access a more detailed submenu. Additionally, users should be able to point and click on the target easily and accurately. It is useful to provide pop-up tips that indicate the link (e.g., name of the city) at which you are pointing. Often, image-based menus are combined with text-based menus to enable alternative access paths but also to provide feedback from one to the other—for example, pointing at a map and simultaneously seeing the menu item on the text-based menu (see Figure 10.5).

### 4.4 Navigation and Flow Control—The Task Level

Menus support several types of user tasks, all related to navigation and control. A well-designed menu helps the inexperienced user form intentions (e.g., it guides the user on which command to locate and activate or where to begin work). For example, "File," as a convention and for convenience, is usually located as the first option, and indeed it includes the first operations one usually performs when starting to work with documents or files. Once an intention has been formed, the user has a search target in mind. Forinstance, a user wishes to add a comment but does not know how to proceed, so she decides she needs help with comments. There are three types of searches in the menu:

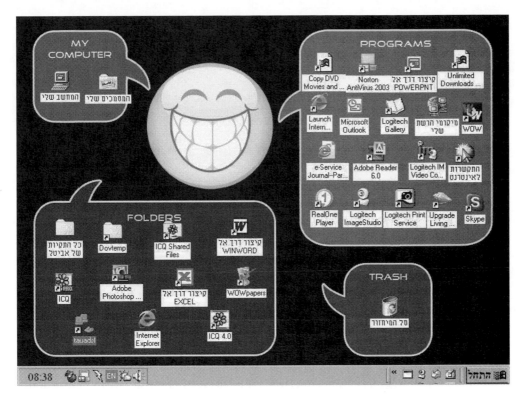

**Figure 10.7** A youngster's desktop arranged visually and rich with icons. See also color plate VI.

(1) matching the search target with an identical menu item label (e.g., matching "help" with a menu item labeled "Help"), (2) locating the category that includes the search target (e.g., "About" comments within "Help"), and (3) finding a label that is equivalent (but not identical) to the search target (e.g., "make remark" may be equivalent to "Insert Comment"). Moreover, when the search target is well-defined, the task is simpler than when the search target is fuzzy.

These distinct tasks impact the relative effectiveness of the menu designs discussed above. For example, when the search target is fuzzy, alphabetical order is not very helpful, while categories help the user get closer to the target and identify it when it shows up. Characterizing the users in terms of which tasks are more likely can help the designer determine what elements should be emphasized. For example, finding equivalent labels requires a good understanding of the displayed labels. This can be supported with short but informative descriptors of each menu item (e.g., as a tool tip that pops up when you point at a menu item).

The type of task should also affect the choice between text- and image-based maps. Looking for a hotel that is en route from Paris (France) to Berlin (Germany) involves spatial tasks. Both text-based menus and image-based menus could be used to categorize hotels by geographical area. However, the design principle of striving for fit between display and mental model suggests that image-based menus will be more effective (see Dennis & Carte, 1998).

Locating and activating an option in the menu or responding to a dialog box are part of higher-level tasks (e.g., deleting a file or configuring a printer). Users expect feedback at two levels. One level of feedback is a confirmation that the computer received the instruction. For the instruction "delete file," using the menu item "delete," the disappearance of all but the top-level menu items signals that the computer received the instruction. The second-level feedback indicates that the file has been deleted, usually with a message to that effect. Thus the feedback brings closure to the user's interaction to navigate and control the system.

## ▶ 5. QUANTITATIVE GRAPHICS

### 5.1 Graphics—Introduction

In recent years, graphics have played an increasingly important role in managerial work, primarily in decision making and communication. The increasing importance of graphics is, at least in part, due to the amazing graphical power that is found in today's graphical packages and the affordability of high-quality screens, printers, and plotters. Dedicated graphical packages include business software (Harvard Business Graphics) and desktop publishing packages (Ventura). In addition, other more general packages such as spreadsheets incorporate graphical tools, which generate an ever-growing demand for high-quality graphics in managerial work. Like many areas of computer applications, the technology has advanced much faster than the corresponding research into how it can be applied effectively.

Why use computer graphics?

1. Graphics are effective communicators for most types of quantitative information.

2. Computer-generated graphics are low-cost alternatives to manual charts (think how easy it is to construct a high-quality chart in most commercial spreadsheets).

3. Computer-generated graphics readily access corporate databases.

4. Computer-generated graphics help interactive decision making.

Many types of graphics are used in computerized applications of management and office work: simple pictures augment business presentations and make them more persuasive, graphics explain messages and add humor, business charts efficiently display quantitative data in 2-D (two dimensions) and 3-D, and graphics are used extensively for creating aesthetic interfaces in window-based systems (e.g., designing icons). Our discussion concentrates on graphics for displaying quantitative information, with a special focus on graphics for decision making.

Information displayed as graphs or text (e.g., tables) are processed differently (Chapter 5). This is because verbal material and imagery invoke different perceptual and cognitive processes and are stored in different forms in memory. Table 10.5

**Table 10.5** Graphics versus Text

|  | Text | Graphics |
|---|---|---|
| Lexicon | Text composed of words in clauses within paragraphs | Images composed of generic shapes |
| Syntax | Procedural—processes as sequence of elements | Holistic—process as a unit with parallel relations |
| Semantics | Functional, logical, and abstract relations | Spatial—built on proximity, ordering, and direction |

summarizes the differences between texts and graphics. Images are analog knowledge representations, and verbal information involves analytical encoding. Images are processed in parallel, i.e., the image is processed holistically rather than one part at a time, enabling faster scanning and decoding. Verbal presentations are processed in sequence, requiring more time, attention, and memory. Images are revived and restored in working memory faster and more accurately. Furthermore, simple images are retained in working memory for longer periods.

## 5.2 Graphics—The Building Blocks

Say we are given data about the computer purchases of two companies. The data are organized by type of computer and given as percentages of total purchases for each company. Figure 10.8 is a 3-D chart that represents the data in the table accompanying the chart.

The building blocks for representing quantitative data (the graphic's lexicon) include labels and numeric data represented by spatial elements such as lines, angles, circles, boxes, and so on. In Figure 10.8, the labels are types of computers and company names, and the numeric data are the quantities. Assume for simplicity that labels and numbers have very specific roles, particularly with respect to describing "raw data." (Raw data are measurements of the world we are trying to represent with numbers.)

Labels in graphs are used to describe (1) individual items, (2) groups of items, and (3) properties of items. For example, data about students in a class may include individual items such as names of students, groups of these items include men and women, and properties of students include age and height. Numeric data describe (1) quantities of items in groups or in time periods (e.g., a count of students in group "men") or (2) some property of an item or a group of items (e.g., the age of all men is 20). The numeric data are represented with spatial elements. The size of the spatial element is proportional to the numeric datum (e.g., the line that represents 20 is longer than that representing 10).

*Composite graphics* (such as business charts available in spreadsheets and presentation graphics packages) are assembled from labels and spatial elements to form a picture with a message. In the world of text, this is analogous to sentences that are composed of words. The words have no message individually, but the sentence does. Composite graphics are meaningful arrangements of labels and spatial elements that represent characteristics or relationships in the data. The chart in Figure 10.8 contains all the basic

> **Composite graphics** of quantitative information: Meaningful arrangements of labels and spatial elements that represent characteristics or relationships in the data.

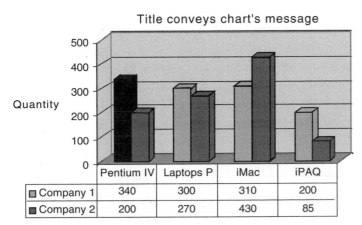

**Figure 10.8** A 3-D bar chart, representing quantitative data with a title, grid, legend, and labels.

elements that a graph should have: a title; the body of the chart, which is the graphical representation of the quantitative data; labels of items and groups of items; and a legend. Even though the graph is complete, it can be improved in ways discussed below. For example, the title should convey the main message in the graph (analogous to an opening or closing statement in a paragraph). Figure 10.8 could include a title such as "Company 1 is quick to adopt new mobiles."

### 5.3  Graphics—Syntactic and Semantic Levels

A good starting point for examining the syntactic level of graphics is the theory of data graphics developed by Edward R. Tufte in *The Visual Display of Quantitative Information*. One of his strong recommendations is to use graphics conservatively. In other words, control the popular urge to use fancy graphics wherever possible. Tufte uses the term *data ink ratio*. Data ink is the amount of ink devoted to the nonredundant display of information, which includes any necessary part of the labels, the quantitative data, title, and legend. Data ink is the complement of the amount of ink in the graph that can be erased without loss of information.

The data ink ratio = (data ink) / (total ink used to print the graphic).

According to Tufte, effective graphics (1) maximize the data ink ratio and (2) erase non–data ink, within reason. Data ink is a metaphor, of course, but it drives home the message of being conservative in the use of graphics other than the bare basics. For example, the chart in Figure 10.8 uses a 3-D bar chart to show unidimensional measures of items. There is no need for three dimensions in the graph when one would do. An extreme alternative is the dot chart in Figure 10.9 (each dot represents a quantity for one of the companies). In effect, each dot replaces a three-dimensional bar and "manages" to represent the single measure without loss of information. Although the information is all there (in fact, we added more meaningful titles), the dot chart does seem lacking. It is somehow difficult to comprehend and seems less pleasing to the eye. A two-dimensional bar chart would increase the data ink ratio (compared with Figure 10.8) but would appear more pleasing to the eye than the dot chart in Figure 10.9. Try it!

We must conclude that minimizing the data ink ratio cannot be applied automatically, hence the qualification "within reason." The schema that is invoked, the clarity and immediacy of the signals, and the overall aesthetics all play a role in the  way we use and

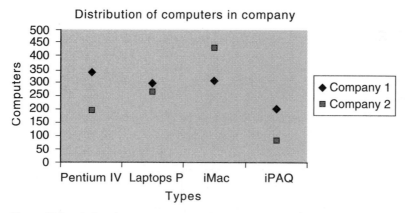

**Figure 10.9**   A dot chart, representing the same data as Figure 10.8.

appreciate a graph. For example, a circle in a pie chart invokes a strong sense of a whole. The data ink ratio of pie charts is certainly smaller than a comparable stacked bar chart, and therefore pie charts should not be used according to the data ink ratio rule. Yet the pie chart is the most popular graph for depicting percentage or fraction breakdowns (e.g., budgets).

## 5.4 Graphics—The Tasks of Deciding and Communicating

Graphs are effective in supporting many types of managerial tasks, particularly tasks that have to do with decision making and communication. This section first looks at the general impact of graphics in managerial tasks, based on earlier discussion of cognitive and affective engineering. We then concentrate on specific decision tasks and show how to choose from common business charts the one that best fits the specific task.

Graphics, in comparison with text and tables, support several activities common to managerial tasks. For certain types of tasks, graphics use memory more efficiently than verbal representation both in terms of time and accuracy. Graphics also support perception by providing immediately a structure for the data. As perception constantly seeks structure in order to interpret the environment, appropriate graphs speed interpretation and reduce errors. Comprehension, which involves recognition and interpretation, requires cognitive processing and memory, which generally work more efficiently with graphics than with text. Moreover, images are easily associated with analogies, improving our retrieval capability from long-term memory. Images can also help detect exceptions to common behavior and trends (e.g., outliers are quickly detected when located physically outside clusters of dots on a graph).

Chapter 9 examines the decision-making process in detail. Accordingly, Table 10.6 summarizes the main aspects of decision making that can be supported by graphics and the corresponding psychological variables that are pertinent to that aspect. These variables indicate to the designer opportunities for supporting user activity with graphics.

A great deal of research in IS has been devoted to the effectiveness of graphs in managerial tasks. Jarvenpaa and Dickson (1988) provide a good summary of earlier research on graphics in decision making. There is evidence that simpler graphics are more likely to be understood. However obvious this rule seems, it is hardly practiced. There is no conclusive evidence to suggest that graphics are always more effective than tables. It appears that the best display is a function of the task. A more detailed analysis of the task is therefore necessary to determine the most appropriate format. Moreover, people vary in their capability to process graphic information.

The survey of graphics in decision-making concludes that graphics are effective in several types of tasks:

1. Summarize data

2. Show trends

3. Compare points and patterns

4. Show deviations

5. Represent values for easy reading

**Table 10.6**  Resources Needed in Decision Making that Graphics Support

| Decision-Making Aspect | Psychological Resources Supported by Graphs |
| --- | --- |
| Problem finding | Detection, attention |
| Information analysis | Comprehension, memory |
| Performance review | Detection, attention, comprehension, affect |
| Forecasting | Detection, comprehension |
| Exception reporting | Detection, attention |
| Planning | Memory, comprehension, attention |
| Exploratory analysis | Detection, attention, comprehension |
| Simulation | Memory, comprehension, attention, affect |

Graphics lead to faster information processing when summarizing data. Graphics are faster and more accurate when detecting and understanding trends. The evidence on comparing points is inconclusive and may depend on the exact task or data. The same is true for reading points. Graphics are better in comparison of patterns. The survey includes findings about specific charts too. In showing trends over time, line graphs are best for dynamic comparisons, which are characteristic of interactive work. Bar charts are easier to read than line graphs, and multiple lines on a single graph are better than many single-line graphs. In comparing points and patterns, graphics are best for complex comparisons. Pie charts are read as accurately as divided vertical bars and are especially good for comparisons of less than five items. In general, judgments about points (positions on a space) are more accurate than length and angle judgments. Segmented bar charts are harder to process than grouped nondivided bars.

As explained in Chapter 8, good graphical design for decision making implies a good fit between the presentation of data and the way the data is processed in the decision-making process—this is the *cognitive fit theory*. Conversely, a mismatch between the graphical design and the decision strategy employed may increase complexity and thereby increase the likelihood of poor performance.

We now examine how to choose a composite graph to fit the decision task. Zelazny (1999) recommends five basic graphs for business presentations: the pie chart, the bar chart, the column chart (vertical bar charts), the line chart, and the dot chart. Figure 10.10 shows these charts and adds the radar chart (the 3-D bar chart and the dot chart are shown in Figures 10.8 and 10.9, respectively). Tasks that require graphs involve one of the following five types of comparison: component, item, time series, frequency distribution, and correlation. For each type of comparison, there is an optimal graph, sometimes contingent on other aspects such as number of data items.

Zelazny proposes a three-step strategy:

1. Determine your message—a single point to be made.
2. Identify the comparison (out the five types).
3. Select the type of chart.

Table 10.7 explains each of the five types of comparison and shows to its right the most suitable graph for the particular comparison.

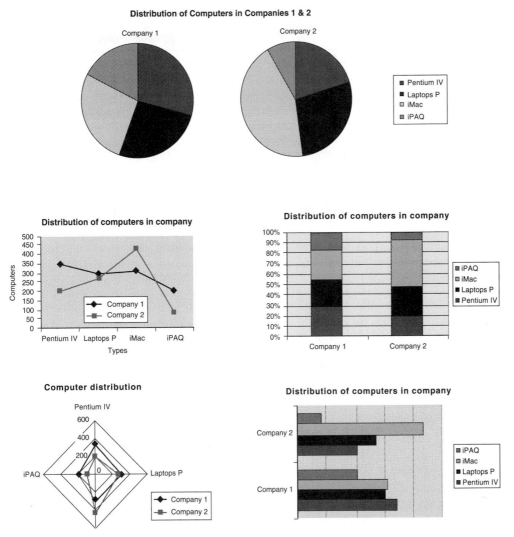

**Figure 10.10** Common business graphics—pie, line, vertical bar, horizontal bar, and radar charts. See also color plate VI.

Is it possible to demonstrate the impact of fitting the display to the task? Jim Treleaven attempted to answer this question in an interesting study on how people use graphs for decision making (Kennedy, Te'eni, & Treleaven, 1998). He asked people to trace their own actions by moving a pen on paper as they shifted their attention from one area to another. Treleaven managed to break down the process of reading the graph into a series of elementary information processes. (He used a GOMS-like analysis discussed in Chapter 5.) For example, consider the line graph shown in Figure 10.11. It plots the sales over time of two companies, A and B. It also shows a trace of the user's movements to answer the question "What were company A's sales in 1992?"

Most people used a common strategy that was highly efficient. People attempted to use the shortest possible strategies that provide correct answers most of the time (e.g., when asked to compare rates of growth, they compared the angles of the line graphs). This result is consistent with our discussions of cognitive engineering, which suggested

**Table 10.7**   Each Type of Comparison Matched with a Preferred Composite Graph

| Type of Comparison | Recommended Composite Graph |
|---|---|
| Component comparison—Show size of each part as a fraction of the whole | Pie chart—no more than six items; position the most important item against the 12 o'clock line |
| Item comparison—Show how items rank or compare between themselves | Bar chart—vertical dimension is not a scale, so arrange order logically; emphasize most important item |
| Time series comparison—Show how items change over time | Column chart if less than 7–8 time points, and line chart if more |
| Frequency distribution comparison—Show how many items fall into a series of progressive quantitative ranges | Column chart (histogram) if less than 7–8 time points, and line chart (histograph) if more; note ranges must be ordered |
| Correlation comparison—Show how the relationship between two items behaves | Dot chart that includes an expected trend |

that people seek to minimize cognitive effort. Clearly, different types of graphs will dictate different strategies for the same task. For example, when the same data was plotted as a pie chart rather than as a line chart, the strategy of comparing angles was no longer valid and was hardly used. It follows that for every combination of chart and task it is possible to define the best strategy, the one that is expected to produce the right answer with minimal cognitive effort. This finding is analogous to the result that the DSS functionality affects the user's selection of a decision strategy (section 4.1 in Chapter 9) and has similar design implications. From a designer's perspective, it is important to provide the user with the chart that best fits the task at hand (i.e., the chart that calls for the strategy of least cognitive effort). Treleaven's study showed that performance increases when the chart is selected in advance according to the expected strategy.

We have looked at relatively simple tasks, but graphs are used in organizations to support more complex decision tasks. In such cases, it may be useful to complement graphs with tables and color (Benbasat, Dexter, & Todd, 1986). Moreover, it appears that as

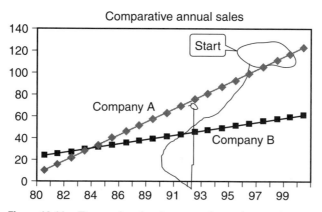

**Figure 10.11**   Traces showing how people read a graph to answer "What were company A's sales in 1992?"

complexity grows, the use of more complicated graphs results in improved decision making. For example, 3-D graphs outperform 2-D graphs when the task is more complex (Kumar & Benbasat, 2004). Using a single 3-D graph instead of two 2-D graphs to show a three-way relationship proved more effective. Interestingly, some of the difficulties encountered using complicated graphs, such as the ambiguity users face in the perception of depth in 3-D graphs, can be mitigated with straightforward designs such as dynamic labeling of data. Designers must therefore be sensitive to the context in which graphics are used.

## 5.5 More on Graphics: Training, Individual Differences, and Affective Impressions

One of the most important conclusions in the survey mentioned above (Jarvenpaa & Dickson, 1988) is that users need to be *trained*. This is not obvious to most designers. Users need to understand how to read the graph and, a fortiori, how to select and create one. Although most people read simple graphs efficiently, experts perform even better. More complex graphs, such as multiple-line graphs, divided graphs, 3-D graphs, and nonstandard graphs, require prior training and online help. The discussion below on integrity in the use of graphics reinforces the need for training.

Graphics, like color, are sensitive to individual differences. For both psychological and social reasons, users react differently and indeed have different capabilities to process graphs. Although there are few substantiated guidelines on how to tailor graphics to these differences, it is important to provide users with the ability to adjust graphic presentations, like color, to their own tastes.

In Chapter 6 we discuss anthropomorphic (humanlike) designs. In such designs, the affective impressions are usually in the facial expressions. An interesting application of facial expressions to capture quantitative data is the "Chernoff faces" (Chernoff, 1973). Figure 10.12 (generated by a mathematical software program called Mathematica) shows several faces, each representing a different set of data (e.g., financial data). Various mappings can be used (e.g., liquidity could be an eyebrow slant, revenue could be eye size, long-term deposits could be nose length). This is a multidimensional depiction of quantitative data that relies heavily on our familiarity with facial expressions.

> **Chernoff faces:**
> Graphics constructed as facial expressions to represent quantitative information.

**Figure 10.12** Chernoff faces convey quantitative data.

Interestingly, our very knowledge of facial expressions makes it important to use the dimensions (e.g., eyebrow angle, mouth shape) in a way that is congruent with our expectations. For example, a sad rather than a happy shape of mouth should display a fall in profits. As noted above, one should use the minimum necessary number of dimensions. In other words, one and only one facial characteristic should reflect a quantitative variable.

## ▶ 6. FORM DESIGN

### 6.1 Forms for Data Input—Introduction

As noted above, the input of data in transaction processing systems to create and update records in files or databases is a common activity and yet one that is prone to error. The relatively large quantity of data that the user keys in to the system magnifies the likelihood of error because in comparison with machine processing, humans are prone to error. In situations where keying in data is a routine and often boring activity, operators often make mistakes due to lack of attention. In situations that are new, users err because the instructions and terminology are complicated and confusing. Overcoming and reducing the propensity for error in data input is therefore an important objective in designing effective interactions. Additionally, the magnitude of the time and effort invested in this activity justifies a special concern with efficiency so that minimizing the user's effort in filling the required information is crucial. Finally, in some situations the user may also be reluctant to disclose information; thus promoting trust becomes important. For these reasons it is important to design the data input activity carefully, taking account of these and other objectives.

One common design technique is to build a form that includes all the relevant information about a particular entity (like an order or a person)—this is called a form fill-in. Its main advantages lie precisely in the full view of the relevant information to be

> **Form fill-in:** Enables the user to input information about some entity as a spatially organized set of data input controls.

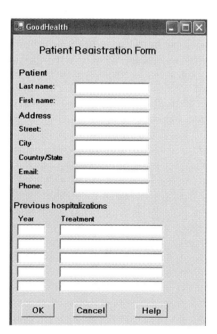

**Figure 10.13**  Initial design of patient form fill-in.

entered into the computer system. Figure 10.13 is an example of form fill-in for registering a new patient into the system. The typical form fill-in may not be appropriate for repeated situations characterized by little information. For example, a scrolling table in which each row describes an instance of the same entity is better than multiple forms.

The complete display of the entire patient's record serves several design objectives. It focuses the user's attention on the particular patient so that all the data keyed in is clearly associated with that patient and not with someone else. This is important, for example, in reducing the likelihood of error by detecting data that is clearly not related to the patient (e.g., date of admittance to the maternity ward for a male patient). Second, the full view helps the novice user understand the meaning of certain fields by their context (e.g., "spouse" would immediately be interpreted as the patient's spouse). It also helps the user remember certain data by triggering events and contexts, such as previous medical treatments. Third, the full view of the information helps maintain control over the input process by structuring and presenting what needs to be done and helping to ensure that the process is complete and correct. Furthermore, the user feels in control, knowing when the dialogue begins and where it ends and knowing how to terminate the process (usually) without penalty.

## 6.2 Form Fill-In—The Building Blocks

Form fill-ins are high-level components that are in fact assemblies of lower-level components. The main building blocks of the form fill-in include components for accepting and selecting data (e.g., text box, radio button, check box), feedback (message box, sound), and organizers such as order of the fields, groupings, and labels. The first two categories of components have already been described under low-level components. The new organizing components deserve some explanation.

Given that the required fields have been determined, the designer decides on the order of the data items (fields), considering primarily the design principles of reducing effort and reducing the likelihood of error. Second, the designer can use borders and physical spacing to form groups of data items and in conjunction use meaningful labels to eliminate confusion about the anticipated input. In the patient data entry screen, there are three groups: patient identification, address, and referring doctor.

The low-level components such as color and sound can be used in conjunction with form fill-ins too. For example, color and special fonts can be used to help form groups, highlight certain fields and feedback, or distinguish between optional and required fields.

## 6.3 Form Fill-In—The Syntactic and Semantic Levels

The sequence of entering data usually corresponds to the order in which the data items are presented. This minimizes the effort in locating and jumping to a remote field. If there are groups of data items, sequences within groups should be completed before advancing to the next group. Thus, the default is to automatically advance to the next field upon completing the input to a field and, therefore, from one group to the group immediately following it. The order and grouping of data items should fit the user's model of the information (e.g., a person thinks of his address and referring doctor as separate issues and usually introduces himself first by first name and only then by last name). This then dictates the grouping and order of the data items. Whenever possible, it is best to follow the standard order of fields, which is often also the logical sequence (e.g., street, city, and state). If the analysis of the interaction reveals the order of the input process, this information should dictate the order of fields on the screen, which may be different from the standard order. The designer's objective is to minimize the user's effort needed to move from one field to another. For example, if the operator is instructed to follow two stages—first to determine the customer's background and only then to ask an appropriate and different set of personal questions—the screens should fit this two-stage model of task.

Borders around data items and spatial proximity signal a group. In other words, the physical proximity also signals a logical proximity. Tullis (1997) builds on the physical–logical correspondence to suggest that the distance between fields in a group should be smaller than the distance between fields across groups. In English, people read from left to write in the same row and then, on completing one row, advance to the next row. Users will therefore associate fields on the same line as belonging to the same group. If there is reason to present two groups side by side (horizontally), they would need to be spaced out and surrounded with visible borders around each group (e.g., personal details of two parents could be displayed in two parallel groups).

Each field must be immediately understood. The most obvious guideline is a short informative label, using terminology well-known to the user. Short instructions are also useful, but longer instructions should be available on call (e.g., a sensitive help screen that pops up when requested or a tool tip that is displayed when the user points or jumps to a field). Like any other screen, the form fill-in must not be cluttered with information that can be retrieved when needed. Furthermore, the context of the group, the size and shape of the input field (e.g., date format), and feedback messages on the correctness of the input value all help in making the user's task clearly understood and efficient.

Finally, the form itself is a collection of data about some entity (e.g., an order for a product, a registration of a patient, or an evaluation of an event). A clear and meaningful title is necessary to focus attention on the task and on the object (instance) of interest. For example, "Patient registration" well defines the task, using known terms and doing so concisely. Once the name of the patient is in the system, adding the name to the title (on the same line or immediately under it) would help draw attention to the person and possibly avoid mistakes and confusion between patients.

Once the task-related organization is complete, the screen should be assessed for its aesthetic design. The discussion in Chapter 8 on aesthetics in screen design applies directly to the form fill-in too. Using density, balance, and equilibrium is particularly straightforward. Some of the other criteria may conflict with the design guidelines above—for example, aesthetic order (according to perceptual prominence) may conflict with the task-dictated order. As always, the designer is left to decide on design trade-offs. Figure 10.14 is a possible outcome of applying the aesthetic rules and, at same time, maintaining the task-related organization of the patient registration screen in Figure 10.13.

### 6.4 Form Fill-In—The Task Level

The task supported by a form fill-in is simply feeding data into the system. A person requesting a service or product can either fill in a form directly or indirectly through an operator. For example, a patient entering a clinic may interact directly with the computer and enter the required information, the patient may fill in by hand a printed form that is later inputted by a clerk, or the clerk can interact with the computer and read out to the patient the questions involved. The sources of error can be assumed to

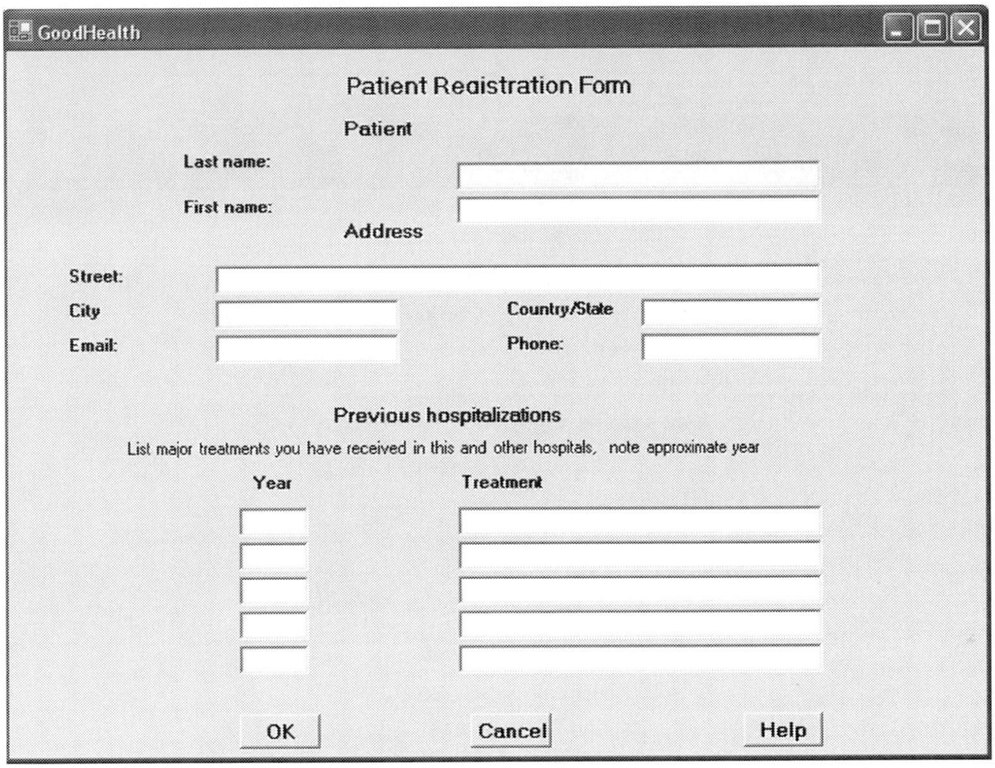

**Figure 10.14** Redesigned patient registration form for better balance.

be different in each of these scenarios. The clerk, after entering several patients into the system, can be assumed to know the meaning of each field and the appropriate way of feeding in the data but may be unfamiliar with the particular data (e.g., misspell a name) and may confuse data belonging to different patients. In contrast, the patient interacting directly with the system is very familiar with personal information but may misunderstand medical terms and may find it difficult to use the system. Moreover, in some cases, the user faces a blank screen for a new patient; in others, the information has been entered, and the user adds or updates information. Adding a completely new patient is different from updating an existing patient, creating two different modes of work. In updating, the user often neglects some fields and moves directly to selected fields to confirm, add, or change data. In the update mode, new data may introduce inconsistencies that are hard to notice (e.g., adding personal information for a new spouse but neglecting to correct the number of dependents in a remote field). Designers should therefore fit the design to the practices and potential difficulties in anticipated scenarios.

As noted in the introduction to form fill-ins, reducing the likelihood of error or misunderstanding is perhaps the most important design objective in addition to minimizing the effort required to complete the task. Looking back at Table 8.2 in Chapter 8, all four sources of error are relevant to data input: mode errors, description errors, capture errors, and activation errors. However, the frequency of these errors may depend on the experience of the user and the particular scenario. For example, an operator feeding and updating several users may be especially susceptible to activation errors in which the user starts updating one patient, is interrupted by another urgent admittance, and fails to

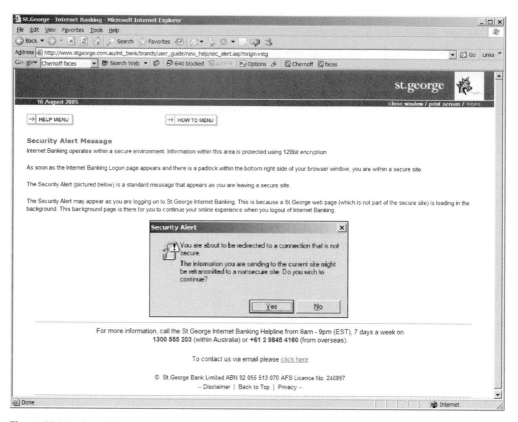

**Figure 10.15** Security alert dialog box promoting trust (http://www.stgeorge.com.au/int_bank/ brands/user_guide/new_help/sec_alert.asp?origin=stg).

complete the first patient correctly or feeds data belonging to one patient into the record of the other. On the other hand, users feeding their own data into the system do not confuse their data with others but rather fail to understand instructions or fail to specify correctly their intentions. In such cases, restricted input (e.g., using list boxes and check boxes) and guidance and feedback are the designer's topmost concerns.

The cost of erroneous data in the system is high for both the individual and the company. Detecting and correcting errors that have entered the system is extremely costly, hence the need to support the user and minimize the probability of error in data input. Feedback is also essential for promoting trust in the system by indicating the effort to ensure high data quality. Figure 10.15 shows a security alert dialog box that indicates that the user is about to leave a secure environment. This feedback mechanism helps to promote trust. The Web site is a bank (St. George), in which trust is essential. Good HCI designs of form fill-ins are those that, above all, reduce error and minimize effort.

## ▶ 7. SUMMARY

We enumerate several HCI components, but many others exist (see, for example, Tables 10.1a and 10.1b, from which we selected only a few components). We learn how to examine a component and decide when the component is useful and how it should be designed to fit the particular application. The same line of thought can be applied in the future to new components.

We look at low-level components such as color and higher-level components such as menus and form fill-ins. The idea is that the lower-level components help to build the higher-level components. Thus, color can be found in a form fill-in as well as in a menu. In all cases, we examine each component through the TSSL model (task, semantic, syntactic, and lexical levels). This model helps to relate the user's task to its implementation in human–computer interaction. It lays the basis for examining the impact of a component on the user's cognitive and affective processes and, thereby, on overt behavior. For example, we analyze how color is perceived, how it impacts our emotions, and how it influences our buying behavior.

We also apply some of the HCI guidelines elaborated in the previous chapter to the design of specific components. For instance, we created a form and then improved it by using one of the aesthetic guidelines. Similarly, we could analyze what types of menus best suit particular tasks.

The most important message throughout the chapter, however, is the effort to fit the component to the task at hand. Perhaps the most convincing case is the selection of graphics according to the task. The same strategy can be applied to nearly every component. It requires knowledge of the task characteristics, knowledge of the user's characteristics, and knowledge of the available components and their design options (e.g., color selection). This chapter, along with previous chapters, provides you with this knowledge.

## ▶ 8. SUMMARY OF CONCEPTS AND TERMS

| | |
|---|---|
| Componential design | Color wheel |
| Hue, saturation, brightness | Composite graphics |
| Data input | Chernoff faces |
| Navigation and control | Form fill-in |

## ▶ 9. BIBLIOGRAPHY AND ADDITIONAL READINGS

Benbasat, I., Dexter, S. S., & Todd, P. (1986). An experimental program investigating color-enhanced and graphical information presentation: An integration of the findings. *Communications of the ACM, 29*(11), 1094–1105.

Chernoff, H. (1973). Using faces to represent points in k-dimensional space graphically. *Journal of American Statistical Association, 68*, 361–368.

Dennis, A. R., & Carte, T. A. (1998). Using geographical information systems for decision making: Extending cognitive fit theory to map-based presentations. *Information Systems Research, 9*(2), 194–203.

Gorn, G. J., Chattopadhyay, A., Yi, T., & Dahl, D. W. (1997). Effects of color as an executional cue in advertising: They're in the shade. *Management Science, 43*(10), 1387–1400.

Hoadley, E. D. (1990). Investigating the effects of color. *Communications of the ACM, 33*(2), 120–125.

Jarvenpaa, S. L., & Dickson, G. W. (1988). Graphics and managerial decision making: Research-based guidelines. *Communications of the ACM, 31*(6), 764–774.

Kennedy, M., Te'eni, D., & Treleaven, J. (1998). Impacts of decision task, data and display on strategies for extracting information. *International Journal of Human Computer Studies, 48*, 159–180.

Kumar, N., & Benbasat, I. (2004). The effect of anchoring and encoding on information representation: A comparison of 2D and 3D graphs. *MIS Quarterly, 28*(2), 255–281.

Post, D. L. (1997). Color and human-computer interaction. In M. G. Helander, T. K. Landauer, & P. V. Prabhu (Eds.), *Handbook of human-computer interaction*. Amsterdam: Elsevier.

Te'eni D., & Feldman R. (2001). Performance and satisfaction in adaptive websites: a laboratory experiment on search tasks within a task-adapted website. *Journal of AIS*, 2(3), 1–28.

Tullis, T. S. (1997). Screen design. In M. Helander, T. Landauer, & P. Prabhu (Eds.), *Handbook of human-computer interaction*. Amsterdam: North-Holland.

Zelazny, G. (1999). *Say it with presentations: How to design and deliver successful business presentations* (3rd ed.). New York: McGraw-Hill.

## ▶ 10. CASE STUDY

Lance Redux is creating a Web site for World Gourmet, an international food retail outlet. Lance is interested in choosing colors for the Web site that will impart a global cultural feel and enhance the attractiveness of the pictures of the food. He has several color-oriented guidelines to help him make the decision. He first goes to several Web sites that sell food and other global products. He finds the following two Web sites (see Figures 10.16, 10.17, and 10.18) that he evaluates for their use of color according to the guidelines. He determines that site number 1 does not have enough white space and the colors are too intense and that site number 2 uses too much white space and too many different colors. He determines that two colors with appropriate use of white space willbe best. He finds that red and green (opposites on the color wheel) will serve his purpose and seem to enhance the look of the food. He designs a logo using these two colors. Then he incorporates the red and green in the other pages that make up his site. Figure 10.18 shows the final color choice for the e-Gourmet home page.

**Figure 10.16**  Not enough white space and too intense color. See also color plate VII.

**Figure 10.17**   Too much white space and too few colors. See also color plate VII.

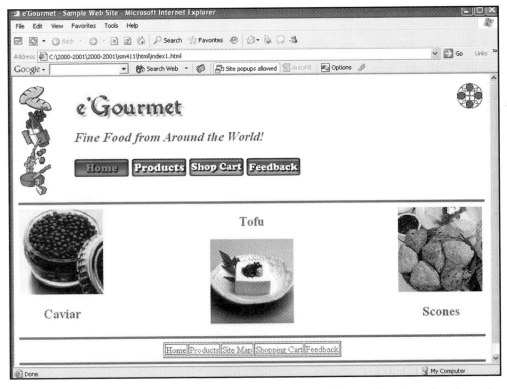

**Figure 10.18**   e-Gourmet design using sufficient white space and two main colors. See also color plate VII.

▶ **11. EXERCISES**

Ex. 1.  Figure 10.10 consists of five business charts showing the same data (based on the data in Figure 10.8). For each of the five charts, devise a chart title that expresses the most obvious message that emerges from that chart.

Ex. 2.  Specify a possible decision-making scenario that would fit the display of the two pie charts in Figure 10.10. Given this scenario, redesign (if necessary) the screens, add appropriate controls, and implement the interface. If you are using Visual Basic, use MDI (multiple-document interface). Take the two graphs as given data (so there is no need to enable any manipulation of the data). You can sketch them with a word processor or spreadsheet and incorporate them through the OLE control. As far as possible, explain the rationale for your design.

Ex. 3.  Form fill-in. Consider the case of a patient admitted to a clinic and asked to fill in her personal information. She fills in by hand a printed form that is later inputted by a clerk. What are the possible sources of error in the process of entering the data into the computer? What are the design implications on the form fill? First think of the main design principles and guidelines that are especially relevant, and then demonstrate their application with a specific example of the printed and online form.

# 11

# HCI DEVELOPMENT METHODOLOGY

## CONTEXT AND PREVIEW

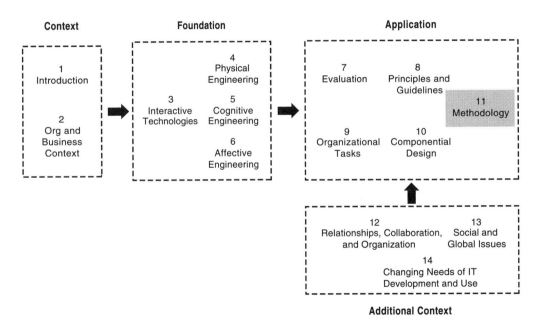

This chapter integrates many HCI concepts, models, and theories, as well as HCI principles and guidelines that were treated in previous chapters. The goal is to use them together to solve HCI development problems. This is thus the place where we present the HCI development methodology in its entirety. The following methodology figure will also appear in the chapter within certain contexts.

Because HCI development is normally part of the entire information systems development, this chapter contrasts modern SA&D development models to illustrate the different emphases of HCI development, as well as the relationship between HCI development and modern SA&D concerns. We accomplish this by presenting a human-centered systems development methodology (HCSDLC). Later, the chapter emphasizes the HCI part of the HCSDLC by depicting a self-containing HCI development methodology. This HCI development methodology runs throughout the entire systems development life cycle (SDLC). In a nutshell, this chapter shows what to consider when conducting an HCI development project and how to conduct it. The HCI methodology functions as a "cookbook" to provide high-level guidance to put the whole HCI project together. Detailed components and steps of the HCI methodology are discussed, and several techniques and methods are introduced. The application of the methodology is illustrated by examples. This chapter is primarily based on work by Zhang, Carey, Te'eni, and Tremaine (2005).

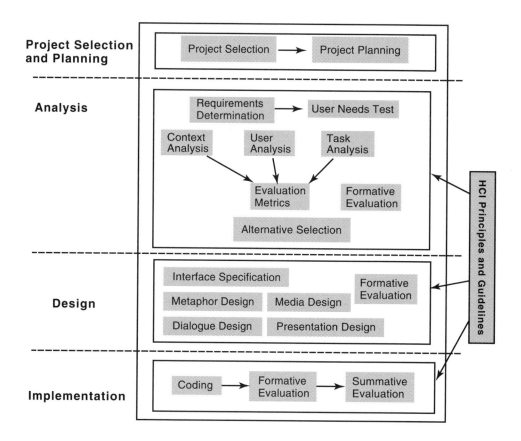

## LEARNING OBJECTIVES

Upon completion of this chapter, students should be able to do the following:

- Understand the role of HCI development in the system development life cycle (SDLC).
- Understand the relationship and differences between modern systems analysis and design (SA&D) and HCI development activities.
- List and discuss the activities and deliverables in different stages in the HCI development methodology.

- Connect important concepts, theories, principles, and guidelines learned in early chapters to the HCI development issues and concerns at the different stages of the methodology.
- Apply the entire methodology to an HCI development project.

## ▶ 1. INTRODUCTION

A systems development methodology is a standardized development process that defines a set of activities, methods and techniques, best practices, deliverables, and automated tools that systems developers and project managers are to use to develop and continuously improve information systems (Whitten, Bentley, & Dittman, 2004). Organizations use specific methodologies to develop and support their information systems (Valacich, George, & Hoffer, 2004). Methodologies provide a systematic approach that is based on science and engineering in practicing systems development to ensure correctness, rigor, effectiveness, and efficiency. This is in contrast to a piecemeal or complete craftsmanship fashion of developing systems. Methodologies thus are very important for successful practice in developing organizational information systems.

There are several successful and widely used systems development methodologies. Most of them mainly emphasize developing information systems to meet organizational needs. These methodologies are often referred to when discussing systems analysis and design (SA&D). Many of these methodologies can be found in popular textbooks for SA&D. The most popular one is the systems development life cycle model (SDLC). We will discuss this in great detail in section 2 of this chapter.

There have been several efforts to propose and promote methodologies that emphasize usability and human–computer interaction concerns, including the star life cycle model (Harson & Hix, 1989, also in Preece et al., 1994), the scenario-based development of HCI (Rosson & Carroll, 2002), and the usability engineering life cycle (Mayhew, 1999), to name a few.

Most of the existing usability or HCI methodologies are characterized by the dominant concerns for usability, which overshadow other concerns, such as organizational needs (the main concern in modern IS SA&D or software engineering), physical concerns, and affective concerns. Some of the methodologies focus heavily on the design stage and do not pay enough attention to the importance of analysis at an early stage of the systems development. Yet many usability and interaction problems are caused by inadequate understandings that should be addressed during an early stage, such as the analysis stage. Other HCI concerns, such as usefulness, physical concerns, and affective concerns, should be considered at the same time as usability concerns.

To develop information systems to meet a range of both organizational and user needs, modern SA&D concerns and HCI concerns should be integrated into a unified methodology for information systems development. The HCI methodology we introduce in this chapter is part of an overall human-centered systems development methodology that considers both organizational needs and human needs. Such a human-centered system development methodology can help us to develop truly human-centered organizational information systems that benefit the human users and ultimately contribute to successful businesses.

In this chapter, we first present an overall methodology for developing information systems, a methodology that considers both modern SA&D and HCI approaches (Zhang et al., 2005). It demonstrates that the term "human-centered systems development" can

> **System development methodology:** A standardized development process that defines a set of activities, methods and techniques, best practices, deliverables, and automated tools that systems developers and project managers are to use to develop and continuously improve information systems.

be broadened both for systems functionalities and for human–computer interaction development. Our goal is that the overall methodology should be instrumental for developing information systems that meet both organizational and human needs. We call this integrated approach the Human-Centered Systems Development Life Cycle (HCSDLC) Model.

Due to the maturity of modern SA&D approaches and the main focus of this book, in the later part of the chapter, we focus on the HCI development part (the HCI development methodology) of the HCSDLC model and refer to the modern SA&D counterparts only when necessary. The HCI development methodology is self-contained and can function as a stand-alone methodology without being dependent on SA&D knowledge. Thus, students who have not taken a course in SA&D can still understand the HCI development issues, concerns, and procedures. We emphasize the systematic and theory-based application of human-centeredness during all stages of the HCI project development life cycle. A philosophy and a set of high-level principles are laid out. We then discuss activities and methods for each of the main stages of the HCI methodology. Examples are used to illustrate the step-by-step procedure for applying the methodology.

## ▷ 2. THE ROLE OF HCI DEVELOPMENT IN SDLC

### 2.1 SDLC: The Systems Development Life Cycle Model

> **System development philosophy:** Follow formal scientific and engineering practice, yet make room for a strong creative element.

The development of computer-based information systems began in the 1950s and has gone through several revolutionary stages owing to the advancement of technological capabilities of computers and organizational IT needs. Key revolutions in systems development include the structured analysis and design approach in the 1970s, the object-oriented approaches in the 1980s, and more recently the Agile methodology (Fowler & Highsmith, 2001) or eXtreme Programming (Beck, 2000) approaches. Despite their differences, all of these approaches share a general philosophy of systems development, that is, to follow formal scientific and engineering practice yet make room for a strong creative element. Various systems development methodologies are developed to guide the systems development practice so that effectiveness and efficiency can be achieved. A methodology is a collection of a particular systems development philosophy, a set of strategies, principles, and guidelines, a multistep procedure dictating what and how to do things, and associated techniques and methods. Methodologies can be expected to differ from one organization to another.

User-centered systems development has come a long way to establish itself in the modern SA&D approaches. The thrust of user-centered systems development is that users of an information system should play an important role during the systems development process, especially at the early stages. The general principles of user-centered systems development include (1) involving users as much as possible so that they can influence design; (2) integrating knowledge and expertise from different disciplines that contribute to systems development and use; and (3) encouraging high interactivity so that testing can be done to ensure that the design meets users' requirements. User-centeredness has been reflected in several systems development approaches, including Joint Application Development (JAD), which started in the late 1970s at IBM. Fast prototyping and Rapid Application Development (RAD), as well as the Agile methodology, are user-centered. The concept of user-centered systems development is thus part of modern SA&D approaches.

Among the different ways of organizing and managing the complex and lengthy systems development processes, the life cycle idea has been appealing. An organizational information system, like many other artifacts, has a life cycle: it is created, tested, introduced to the market, and eventually retired from the market and replaced by new systems. Thus the process of developing information systems often follows this life cycle.

The systems development life cycle (SDLC) model is a commonly accepted modern approach for describing the complex processes and issues involved in information systems development. It captures the spirit of the systems development process (Hoffer, George, & Valacich, 2005) and is a general framework that can be found in many different systems development methodologies. Such a model can be found in many textbooks on modern systems analysis and design (SA&D). SDLC takes a structured approach and divides the development life cycle into different stages or phases. Some people consider two main stages: (1) systems development and (2) systems operations and maintenance. That is, first the system is built, and then the system is used and maintained (Whitten, Bentley, & Dittman, 2004). Others consider additional, more detailed stages. Figure 11.1 depicts a typical SDLC model with four phases: Planning, Analysis, Design, and Implementation.

> **SDLC:** A commonly used methodology for information systems development that breaks the whole systems development process into manageable phases.

The directional relationships among phases in Figure 11.1 are for high-level project management purposes. Iterations among stages are typical in real IS development projects. Figure 11.2 reflects the key ideas of the modern SA&D approach: iteration, fast feedback (such as developing prototypes and soliciting user feedback), accuracy, and user-centeredness. The key point is that the four phases in Figure 11.1 are at a higher level and are for project management purposes; within each phase, there could be multiple rounds of smaller scales of analysis, design, and implementation. For example, during Phase 1 (project selection and initiation/planning), analysts may need to do a quick mock-up or prototype to have some concrete ideas of system functionalities and to gain feedback from users and on market potential (such as acceptance tests on mock-ups/ prototypes). In Phase 2 (the analysis stage), system requirements can be more accurately specified with a prototype of the system for both analysts and users to gain an accurate understanding of the system functions. In Phase 3 (the design stage), certain design options or results from formative evaluations may prompt a re-analysis of certain aspects, and such re-work may be better demonstrated by another round of prototyping. All these possibilities indicate that each stage may have smaller-scale analysis, as well as design and implementation activities. Figure 11.2 is an attempt to illustrate this

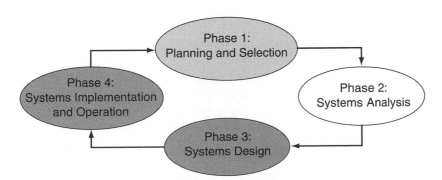

**Figure 11.1**   Modern SDLC model for systems development.

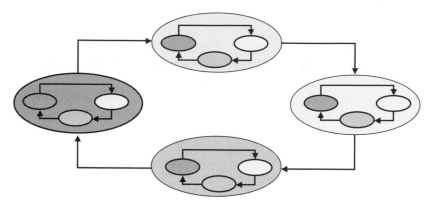

**Figure 11.2**  Modern SDLC: iteration, fast feedback, accuracy, user-centered.

iterative idea that is embedded in the modern SDLC model (note: labels for stages were removed for simplicity).

We can use another example to illustrate the life cycle idea and how it may help in project management. Assume that you are thinking about doing some home improvement to your parents' house. First, you identify that there are several things you can do, such as remodeling the kitchen, adding a patio, or building a Japanese garden. After some brainstorming and discussion with your parents, you select the patio first. You estimate that you would have sufficient funds and enough time to do it over the summer. You have some understanding of your own technical skills or are planning to hire professional help. This would be the first phase as depicted in Figure 11.1: project planning.

To add a patio to the house, you need to first figure out what kind of patio it would be, what specific parts or features it should have, who would most frequently use it for what purposes, and so on. For example, the patio could be large enough for a small party of eight people, it could have stairs going to the backyard, or it could eventually have screens during the summer to prevent mosquitoes and bugs from getting in. Different features would definitely have different possible designs, total costs, technical challenges to you, and length of time needed for completion. After several rounds of discussion with your parents, who will be the most frequent users of the patio, you eventually finalize the patio's main features and functions. This would be the analysis phase.

Next, ideas in the analysis stage are represented on paper with plans, or perhaps with a cardboard model. For the main features or functions, there are several possible design alternatives. For example, stairs to the backyard can have several designs, the fence can be in different styles, and so on. You draw the specific design ideas on paper so that your parents can fully understand what the patio will look like once it is really built. This is the design phase.

After the plans are approved by your parents, the real construction starts. This is when, if you are planning to build the patio yourself, you go out and buy the materials, tools, and so on. Once the patio is completed, it would be put into use. This is the last phase, the implementation and operation phase. However, there is a sense in which the patio is never truly finished. As long as the patio is in use, ongoing work is needed to help maintain it and keep it functioning and in good shape. At times the patio may need to be expanded or repaired. All these activities are part of the maintenance stage, which is implied by the looped arrows among the four phases in Figure 11.1. The patio's life cycle ends when it is no longer wanted, used, or maintained and is thus disassembled.

## 2.2 HCI in SDLC: What It Has Been

Some researchers understand that although usability engineering is making headway in industry, HCI has exerted only a minor influence on the current generations of object-oriented development methods. While HCI has created structured methods from both academic research and industrial authors, these have largely been ignored by software engineers (Sutcliffe, 2000). Argument for an engineering approach to HCI that complements and integrates with software engineering has proved elusive (Sutcliffe, 2000). This realization coincides with the fact that in the IS discipline, many popular SA&D textbooks contain only one or two chapters in the design stage of SDLC that cover some user interface issues. Undeniably, screen layout, menu design, buttons and colors, and so on, are HCI considerations in information systems development, but they are far from being the exclusive or the most important ones. Very often, users of an IS are most frustrated or annoyed by problems that are beyond the computer screen level. Illogical organization of data/information in the system, lack of task support, misfit between the nature of the task and the support provided, difficult navigation, and inconsistency between mental models and system operations are among the major difficulties users experience.

These incompatibilities affect user reactions, acceptance, and use of the information system. They may be rooted in the neglect of complex human cognitive, affective, and behavioral factors and the dynamics of human interactions with technologies. These issues affect users' interaction with the information system and can be addressed during the HCI development processes. A better understanding of various human cognitive, affective, and behavioral factors involved in user tasks, problem-solving processes, and interaction contexts is required in order to address these problems. Just as it is important to understand systems requirements as early as possible, it is critical that human technology interaction be addressed at the beginning of the SDLC.

There have been attempts in the past to tie usability and user factors into the systems development life cycle (Hefley et al., 1995; Mantei & Teorey 1989). Recently, the HCSDLC model was developed as a continued effort to develop better organizational information systems that support both human and organizational needs (Zhang et al., 2005).

Next, we introduce the overall human-centered systems development methodology. Then, we focus on the HCI part of such methodology, because the main focus of this book is developing HCI for organizational information systems.

## 2.3 The Human-Centered SDLC Model: HCSDLC

Figure 11.3 depicts the proposed HCSDLC methodology in contrast to the modern SA&D methodology: the left side (a) is a typical SDLC model, while the right side (b) is the HCSDLC model that covers both SA&D and HCI concerns and activities. Note that on the (a) side, user interface design is one task inside the design stage and is typically covered as one or two chapters in a modern SA&D textbook for a one-semester course. Modern SDLC and some systems development methods, such as RAD, JAD, and prototyping, attempt to capture systems requirements (that is, systems functionalities) as early and as accurately as possible. These methods, however, are not typically used to capture HCI factors that affect user interaction designs.

The vertical line in the middle of the (b) side of Figure 11.3 roughly divides the different emphases of the modern SA&D and the HCI development. The four boxes across the middle line of (b)—labeled Project Selection/Project Planning, Requirements Determination,

**HCSDLC:** A human-centered systems development methodology where organizational needs and human needs are considered together throughout the systems development life cycle.

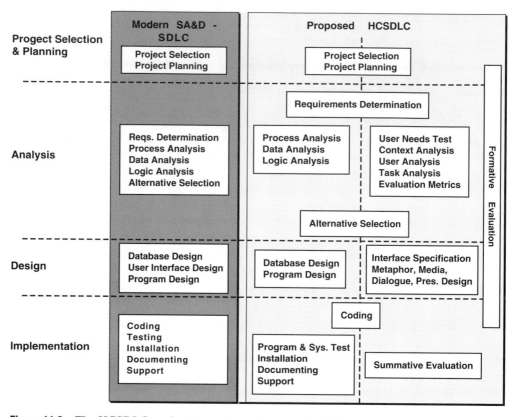

**Figure 11.3** The HCSDLC methodology (from Zhang et al., 2005).

Alternative Selection, and Coding—are about the same activities that occur in both SA&D and HCI development. Note that for the SA&D side of (b), user interface design activity is removed and should be replaced by the entire HCI side of (b). HCI development thus involves all phases of the SDLC. The HCSDLC methodology indicates that a successful development of an information system should consider all the activities as depicted in (b).

The HCSDLC methodology incorporates the parsimony of the SDLC model, which is helpful from the project management perspective. It lays out the connections and differences between SA&D and HCI activities and provides a step-by-step procedure for transformations among activities at different stages. Next, we briefly discuss the different emphases between modern SA&D and HCI concerns.

## 2.4 Modern SA&D and HCI: Different Emphases

In the development of organizational information systems, the modern SA&D approach focuses on system functionalities and data requirements to meet organizational needs. For example, Hoffer and colleagues consider information systems analysis and design as a complex, challenging, and stimulating organizational process that a team of business and systems professionals uses to develop and maintain computer-based information systems (Hoffer, George, & Valacich, 2005). Modern SA&D and HCI overlap with the concerns of system utility or functionality, although their perspectives are different.

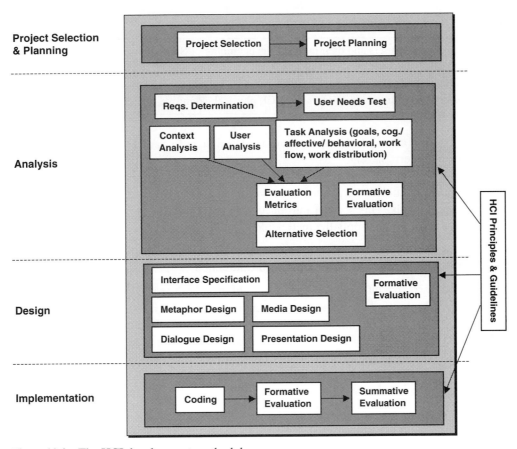

**Figure 11.4**   The HCI development methodology.

The HCI approach focuses on human–machine interactions and collaborations, and defines what a system should do from a user's perspective. HCI considers users' physical, cognitive, affective, and behavioral constraints and their impacts on system development and use. HCI development distinguishes between the user's responsibilities and the system's responsibilities during user interaction with the system and how users can interact with the system. Ultimately, HCI is concerned with how systems can fit users' needs, lifestyles, and well-being, as well as system utility or functionality. In order to develop information systems to meet both organizational and individual needs, modern SA&D concerns and HCI concerns should be integrated in a unified methodology.

## ▶ 3.  THE HCI DEVELOPMENT METHODOLOGY

In this section, we focus primarily on the HCI development methodology, the right side of Figure 11.3b. To make the methodology easier to understand, we outline it in Figure 11.4. It is worth noting that the HCSDLC is iterative in nature, just as that of the modern SA&D shown in Figure 11.2. Thus each of the four phases may involve multiple iterations of the smaller-scale interaction analysis, design, and implementation. We refer to certain activities in the SA&D part (the left side of Figure 11.3b) when necessary to

**Table 11.1** HCI Development Strategies

---

- Focus early on users and their tasks (at the beginning of SDLC).
- Evaluate throughout the entire system development process.
- Iterate when necessary.
- Consider all four human concerns of HCI: physical, cognitive, affective, and usefulness.

---

make discussion clear. Students who are not familiar with SA&D issues can read any textbook on modern SA&D.

As mentioned earlier in this chapter, a methodology is an ensemble of philosophy, strategies, principles, guidelines, activities, deliverables, techniques, methods, best practices, and automated tools. This section introduces most of these components in detail. Later sections illustrate how to apply the methodology in developing various HCI projects.

### 3.1 Philosophy, Strategies, Principles, and Guidelines

**HCSDLC philosophy:** Information systems should meet both organizational and individual needs; thus all relevant human factors should be incorporated into the SDLC as early as possible.

Our philosophy is that information systems should meet both organizational and individual needs; thus all relevant human factors should be incorporated into the SDLC as early as possible. Several strategies under this philosophy are listed in Table 11.1.

Chapter 8 discusses several important HCI principles and guidelines. They are summarized in Table 8.1. As mentioned in Chapter 8, these principles and guidelines are illustrative rather than exhaustive. Nevertheless, they play an important role in the HCI development process. In the discussion of the methodology, we refer to them to illustrate the role they play and how to apply them.

### 3.2 The Project Selection and Planning Phase

**Project selection and planning:** The first phase in SDLC where an organization's total information systems needs are analyzed and arranged, a potential information systems project is identified, and an argument for continuing or not continuing with the project is presented.

Project selection and planning is the first phase in the SDLC. In this phase, the HCI and SA&D issues and activities are the same. The organization's total information needs are analyzed and arranged, a potential information system project is identified, and an argument for continuing or not continuing the project is presented (Valacich, George, & Hoffer, 2004). A decision to continue with the project has to be made at this phase in order to go ahead with the rest of the methodology.

The process of identifying and selecting information systems development projects includes three primary activities:

1. Identifying potential development projects
2. Classifying and ranking projects
3. Selecting projects for development

The primary deliverable, or end product, is a schedule of specific IS development projects. Once a project is selected, it moves to the project planning stage.

The objective of the project planning process is to define clear and discrete tasks and the work needed to complete each task (Valacich, George, & Hoffer, 2004). One important activity during project planning is to assess project feasibility. This is also called a feasibility study. Most feasibility factors fall into the following six categories:

1. Economic or cost-benefit analysis

2. Operational

3. Technical

4. Schedule

5. Legal and contractual

6. Political

For the HCI issues and factors, a cost-benefit analysis can illustrate the importance of considering HCI issues up front and along the entire SDLC. This analysis also outlines the potential issues on the broad organizational, societal, and cultural impacts. For more details on this stage of the SDLC, interested readers can study the advanced readings at the end of the chapter and any textbook on systems analysis and design.

## 3.3 The Interaction Analysis Phase

In modern SA&D, the analysis phase studies the current system and proposes alternative systems. It involves determining the system requirements (functions to meet business needs), structuring requirements according to their interrelationships (normally conducted by process analysis, data analysis, and logic analysis), and generating and selecting design alternatives (Valacich, George, & Hoffer, 2004).

> **Analysis:** Studies the current system and proposes alternative systems.

From the HCI perspective, requirements determination is still one of the most important activities, and alternative generation and selection are also necessary before subsequent design is conducted. In addition, HCI analysis includes user-needs tests on the system requirements (which may be demonstrated by mock-ups or prototypes) and HCI evaluation metrics that are derived from context analysis, user analysis, and task analysis.

### 3.3.1 Requirements Determination and User-Needs Test

To determine the likelihood of target users accepting a system's functionalities, *user-needs tests* should be conducted as soon as the requirements are outlined or determined. Errors in requirements specifications are a major contributor to costly software project failures. Verifying requirements of a new system based on user evaluation of specifications measured during the earliest stages is beneficial (Davis & Venkatesh, 2004).

> **User-needs test:** A test during the analysis stage using simple mock-ups to assess the likelihood of the system's functionalities being accepted by its potential users.

In two longitudinal field experiments, Davis and Venkatesh found that pre-prototype usefulness measured by target users, who received information about a system's functionality without direct hands-on experience, can closely approximate hands-on usefulness measures and can predict usage intentions and behavior up to six months after implementation (Davis & Venkatesh, 2004). This distinction is key, because compared to ease of use, usefulness is generally much more strongly linked to future usage intentions and behaviors. A paper-based survey and paper-based prototypes or mock-ups can be administered to target users using Davis and Venkatesh's (2004) instrument, which is based on the original technology acceptance model (TAM) (Davis, 1989). Based on the testing results, designers and managers can decide whether to (1) go forward as planned, (2) modify or refine requirements to improve acceptability, or (3) abandon to avert major losses (Davis & Venkatesh, 2004).

User-needs tests can be conducted once or multiple times during this stage. The measurement instrument was discussed in Chapter 7 (see Table 7.10). A similar test can also be administered during the project selection and planning stage, even though the system requirements are at a higher level and less detailed.

### 3.3.2 Context Analysis

Once user-needs tests are passed, three major analyses are conducted and will determine the HCI evaluation metrics. *Context analysis* includes understanding the technical, environmental, and social settings where the information systems will be used. It examines whether and how the interaction between the physical and social environments and the physiological and psychological characteristics of the user would impact users interacting with the system. The concepts introduced in Chapters 2 (Organizational and Business Context), 3 (Interactive Technologies), 4 (Physical Engineering), and 5 (Cognitive Engineering) all help inform the process of context analysis.

There are four aspects in context analysis: physical context, technical context, organizational context, and social and cultural context. Overall, context analysis can provide ideas for design factors such as metaphor creation/selection and patterns of communications between users and the system.

1. *Physical context.* Where are the tasks carried out? What entities and resources are implicated in task operations? What physical structures and entities are necessary to understand observed task actions? For example, an ATM can be placed and used in a shopping mall, outside a bank branch, or in a nightclub. These environments provide different levels of lighting, crowdedness, and noisiness. Thus legibility of the screen, use of audible devices for input or output, or even the size of the working space to prevent people nearby from seeing the screen could be designed differently. Physical engineering principles gained in Chapter 4 help us to understand physical human limitations and how to design effective systems.

2. *Technical context.* What are the technology infrastructure, platforms, hardware and system software, network/wireless connections? For example, an e-commerce Web site may be designed to only allow people with certain browser versions to access it. The Web site may also be designed to allow access for small-screen devices such as PDAs or mobile phones. Chapter 3 (Interactive Technologies) gives us the knowledge to determine the appropriate technologies needed to address both physical (Chapter 4) and cognitive (Chapter 5) human limitations.

3. *Organizational context.* There are two different use situations where organizational context may play different roles. For an organizational information system to be used by the organization's own employees, organizational context analysis answers questions such as: What is the larger system into which this information system is embedded? What are the interactions with other entities in the organization? What are the organizational policies or practices that may affect the individual's attitude and behavior toward using the system? In an example of the e-commerce context, some businesses have both physical and online stores. Thus the online system is part of the entire organizational information system. Transactions occurring at the online store are eventually integrated into the entire information system. Design of the online information system has to consider the entire organizational information system.

The organization's policies, procedures, and other factors may affect the design and use of a system. For another example, assuming that Lotus Notes is used by an organization as a communication and collaboration tool, management may depend on using the tool to set up meetings by checking employees' calendars on mutually available time slots. The effectiveness of setting up meetings depends on whether employees use the tool and how they use it. The answers to the whether and how questions can be controlled by organizational policies.

For an organizational information system that is used by people outside the organization, this organizational context analysis emphasizes how the user's own organizational factors may come into play when the user uses the system. The significance of organizational context may be less than that in the previous Lotus Notes use situation, and the role of such an organizational context may be less controllable by the system developers. For example, in e-commerce where customers order products via the system, the customer's environment may put certain constraints on using the system. If the system is to be used by a broad range of customers, such contextual issues may be less controllable and less clearly identified. Nevertheless, realizing this uncertainty of customers' environments can help developers to put HCI development into perspective. Chapter 2 provides more details on organizational contextual considerations.

4. *Social and cultural context*. What are the social or cultural factor that may affect user attitudes and eventual use of the information system? Any information system is always part of a larger social system. Thus social norms and cultural issues must be reflected and considered in the information systems in supporting socially and culturally appropriate interaction with the system. In addition, globalization is more a reality than just a trend now, due to the interconnectivity of the Internet. The bigger context of the organization in which the information system is embedded should also be under consideration. For example, one sensitive design factor is the use of color. Different national cultures have different implied meanings for specific colors. Not being considerate will only hinder the potential success of the information system. In an e-commerce Web site example, the Web site can be accessed from all over the world. It thus is a design consideration whether the Web site allows access by people with any language and cultural background who can provide credit cards with USD exchange, or whether it should be accessible only to people who speak certain languages (such as English, Spanish, and French) and who are from certain cultures (such as the United States).

### 3.3.3 User Analysis

*User analysis* identifies the target users and their characteristics, including the following three aspects that have been demonstrated to affect user perceptions, attitudes, interactions, and eventual acceptance and use of information systems.

> **User analysis:** Identifies the target users of the system and their characteristics.

1. *Demographic data*, such as age, gender, education, occupation, cultural background, special needs, computer training and knowledge, experience with similar systems/products, and so on. Some of these demographic characteristics and the limitations they may bring with them are introduced in Chapter 4 (Physical Engineering).

2. *Traits and intelligence*, such as cognitive styles, affective traits, and skill sets or capability. Topics we discussed in Chapter 5 (Cognitive Engineering) and Chapter 6 (Affective Engineering) are relevant for this type of user analysis.

3. *Job- or task-related factors*, such as job characteristics, knowledge of application domain and job familiarity, frequency of computer use on the job, and usage constraints.

### 3.3.4 Task Analysis

> **Task analysis:** Studies what users do to reach their goals, how they do it, and what they think and feel during this process.

*Task analysis* is concerned with understanding what people do to achieve their goals. In Chapter 9, you learned that task analysis reveals patterns of information processing, information needs, and representations that users currently use to perform work. It includes scenarios and conditions under which humans perform the tasks. It also discovers patterns of exceptions. In developing organizational information systems, it is useful to analyze tasks at two levels: organizational level and tool level. Task analysis should start by identifying the tasks or goals that are meaningful to one's job or work within the organizational context. These are organizational-level tasks (OLTs). Then the task analysis should progress toward understanding OLTs by decomposing them into the tasks or actions that users have to do to interact with the information system or tools. We named these tasks tool-level tasks (TLTs). The user interface should be designed to directly support the TLTs with the OLTs and the organization as their high-level contexts. Chapter 9 demonstrated how to get to TLTs from OLTs.

The objective of task analysis is to identify opportunities to support user activities. For example, sound may be used to draw attention to a visually loaded screen, or the sequence of a presentation may be altered to help ameliorate biases caused by primacy and recency effects. In HCI, task analysis also distinguishes between what computers do and what humans do. It examines the task work flow and the distribution of work and work skills among users and computers. A key issue in building new systems is to realize that the new systems can change skill sets and can obstruct current work flows. Development of a new system must take into account the movement from one type of work environment to another.

There should be alignment and consistency between task analyses and the high-level process analyses (such as the most general level-0 data flow diagram) in SA&D. The highest-level OLTs are at the same abstract level with the processes in the level-0 data flow diagrams (level 0 shows all the major processes an information system has at a higher level without revealing the details of each process). Certain SA&D techniques such as use cases and scenarios can be used for both process and task analyses. It is worth noting that task analysis in HCI is a challenging and time-consuming activity and there is no one-size-fits-all method or technique to cover the entire spectrum of task analysis considerations. Task analysis may also depend on the nature of the system being developed and a number of other factors.

In order to illustrate some possible aspects of a task analysis from the HCI perspective, we use the example of developing a Web site for selling international foods over the Internet (the e-Gourmet example.) The task analysis may identify the following four aspects.

*User goals and use cases* identify five cases: (1) buy particular foods or ingredients that users already know about, (2) look for ingredients that make a known dish, (3) learn about a particular dish, its ingredients, and how to make it, (4) browse to decide what to cook for a particular occasion, and (5) recommend the site to others.

*Cognitive, affective, and behavioral analysis of user tasks* reveals that (1) in case 1, a user may forget the actual name but remember the characteristics of some food (thus may need to do a query on certain attributes of the food to find it first); (2) when examining an ingredient, users may need to refer to the dishes where this ingredient is used (the same is true when examining a dish where ingredients/recipe would be needed); (3) an aesthetically pleasing presentation would encourage browsing (cases 3 & 4) and eventually purchasing foods (cases 1 & 2) and recommending the Web site to others (case 5); and (4) users may use the forum for peer recommendations and exchange of recipes or cooking experiences (case 5).

*Work flow analysis* finds that case 1 would need a sequence of actions to be finished. Abortion of the task can occur at any stage of the sequence, and users may want to go back to any of the previous stages; case 4 may lead to any of cases 1 through 3.

*General work distribution between users and the Web site/machine* suggests that users make selections, and the Web site provides options and all related and relevant information for each selection.

### 3.3.5 Evaluation Metrics

*Evaluation metrics* specify the expected goals of human–system interaction for the designed system. Such metrics, often quantified into specific measures, guide the rest of the HCI development process and provide benchmarks for the formative and summative evaluations throughout the entire development process.

> **Evaluation metrics:** Specify the expected human–computer interaction goals of the system being designed. There are four types of HCI goals.

The evaluation metrics correspond to the multiple concerns of HCI that we discussed earlier in Table 7.1 in Chapter 7. The specific measures or quantitative aspects of the metrics come from the analysis results (context, user, and task analyses), formative evaluation tests on mock-ups or prototypes, industrial or international standards, if any, and the goals and constraints of the information system being developed. This last consideration may come from the "alternative selection" activity, which is the last activity in the interaction analysis phase (see the following section). Basically, the more stringent the HCI expectations (such as the expectation that users should not make any mistakes), the more costly it will be to develop the system. Thus trade-offs may be necessary to achieve reasonable HCI goals (e.g., less than 10 percent of users would make mistakes on certain tasks when using the system) within feasible development constraints.

In section 4 later, we will use a specific example to illustrate the quantified evaluation metrics based on Table 7.1. Each item in Table 7.1 may be quantified based on past studies or industry standards—for example, specifying the acceptable task completion time (e.g., a novice conducting a money transfer using an ATM should take less than 30 seconds), predictable error types and rates, and expected levels for satisfaction and enjoyment. It is noteworthy that not every measure is equally important for all types of information systems. This is based on the results from an empirical research study that investigated users' perceptions of important Web site features in six different domains: financial, e-commerce, entertainment, education, government, and medical. Results show that users have different ranks of the same features for different systems, that is, they regard certain features as more important than others depending on the types or purposes of the systems (Zhang, von Dran, Blake, & Pipithsuksunt, 2001).

### 3.3.6 Alternative Generation and Selection

Before transforming all gathered and structured information from the analysis phase into design ideas, there is a need to *select the final alternative design strategy* for the proposed information system because (1) there are competing ideas from different users on what the system should do, and (2) there are multiple alternatives for an implementation environment for any new system (Valacich, George, & Hoffer, 2004). Although SA&D emphasizes functionality in selecting design strategies, the approach of generating and selecting best alternatives can also be applied to HCI design strategies. The deliverables include (1) three substantially different design strategies (low, middle, and high range—see Table 11.4 in the Teaching Tools example below) that come from different requirements specifications and HCI evaluation metrics, and (2) a design strategy judged most likely to lead to the most desirable system, from functionality and HCI evaluation metrics, given all of the organizational, economic, and technical constraints that limit what can be done.

This alternative selection activity will help shape the final HCI evaluation metrics, as mentioned above. This is another example of iterations among activities within the same stage of SDLC. Other issues to consider when generating design strategies include examining different ways of constructing the system, such as outsourcing, off-the-shelf, or in-house development. If in-house development is chosen, the interaction design and implementation phases will continue.

The results of HCI analysis should provide feedback to and may even change the systems requirements. For example, user analysis may show that "trust" is important to user acceptance. In the case of an e-commerce site that relies on user trust, analysis may lead to an alternative functionality that signals that information is safe and will not be sold without the user's permission. This analysis may also lead to the use of "trusted" third-party software to handle the payment options.

## 3.4 The Interaction Design Phase

**Design:** To create or construct the system according to the analysis results.

In this phase the user interface is specified, sketched, developed, and tested. The goal is to support the identified issues during context, task, and user analyses and to meet the HCI evaluation metrics requirements. The main activities are interface specification and formative evaluations.

### 3.4.1 Interface Specification

*Interface specification* includes semantic understanding of the information needs to support HCI analysis results, as well as syntactic and lexical decisions including metaphor, media, dialogue, and presentation designs.

The TSSL (task, semantic, syntactic, and lexical) model introduced earlier in the book can be used to guide design decisions. Semantic understanding of the HCI analysis results should provide descriptions of the logical structures of information to support task-related information requirements for interface organizations. It should specify at what time what type of information should be displayed during a task. Its main emphasis is on the *what* and *when* questions of information requirements, not the *how*.

For example, task analysis of an ATM may indicate that a user would need to transfer a certain amount of money from one banking account (#1) to another account (#2) but is somehow uncertain of whether s/he has sufficient funds in account #1. Semantically, information regarding account numbers, current balances, transfer commands, transfer status, and transfer results should be displayed simultaneously on the interface to support this money transfer task.

Syntactic design provides specific ways of supporting and delivering semantic understandings and meanings. There can be different ways of supporting the same information requirements, and some are better than others in terms of effectiveness, efficiency, and aesthetic values. Specifically, the HCI principles and guidelines discussed earlier will play an important role in judging which syntactic design is best.

Recall that in Chapter 10 (Componential Design) we supply several examples to illustrate the decisions from one level to another in the TSSL model. Chapter 10 also demonstrates that the syntactic decisions will be further implemented or materialized by lexical decisions that utilize the primitive elements or building blocks of interface design. For example, ATM speech command input may have a limited number of clauses and word sequences that can be understood by the computer; command buttons may have a certain size, shape, and color; and a warning signal (e.g., insufficient balance) may be implemented by using flashing red text and a beeping sound (flashing or moving stimuli to attract a user's visual attention, a red color to reflect the normal implicit meaning of danger/warning in U.S. culture, and a beep sound to alert users in case their eyes are not or cannot be focused on the display).

Interface specification can have four aspects: metaphor, media design, dialogue design, and presentation design. Each of these four aspects contributes to the overall design of the final user interface.

### 3.4.2 Metaphor Design

*Metaphor design* helps the user develop a mental model of the system. It is concerned with finding or inventing metaphors or analogies that are appropriate for users to understand the entire system or part of it. There are well accepted metaphors for certain tasks, such as a shopping cart for holding items before checking out in the e-commerce context and lightbulbs for online help or daily tips in productivity software packages.

### 3.4.3 Media Design

*Media design* is concerned with selecting appropriate media types for meeting the specific information presentation needs and human experience needs. Popular media types include text, static images (e.g., paintings, drawings, or photos), dynamic images (e.g., video clips and animations), and sound. Different media types have different "bandwidths" for transmitting information. In addition, some media types can make presentations more interesting and stimulating, or annoying and distasteful.

For example, if an ATM is suboptimally lighted, (according to a context analysis) or used by visually challenged people (according to a user analysis), it is desirable to augment text output with speech and allow speech input for commands instead of buttons. If speech is considered as an alternative input method, then there is a series of design decisions for such media selection. For example, only limited clauses can be used to support the limited commands (semantic decision). For each clause, the word order should be specified for machine understanding (syntactic decision). Finally, in each clause, only limited words can be used (lexical decision).

### 3.4.4 Dialogue Design

*Dialogue design* focuses on how information is provided to and captured from users during a specific task. Dialogues are analogous to a conversation between two people. Many existing interaction styles, such as menus, form fill-ins, natural languages, dialogue boxes,

**Metaphor design:** Concerned with finding or inventing a metaphor or analog to help the users develop a mental model of the system.

**Media design:** Is concerned with the selecting of certain media types for meeting the specific needs.

**Dialogue design:** Focuses on how information is provided to and captured from users during a specific task.

**Presentation design:** Concerns the decisions on display layout and incorporation of metaphors, media, and dialogue designs with the rest of the displays.

and direct manipulation, can be used. Chapter 10 (Componential Design) also includes examples on dialogue design issues and methods.

### 3.4.5 Presentation Design

*Presentation design* concerns the decisions on information architecture and display layout incorporating metaphors, media, and dialogue designs with the rest of the displays. It is at a higher level of concern by considering all other components into one final outcome.

Commonly established user interface design principles and guidelines may be applied during the design stage. For example, the following are principles for presentation design that were suggested by Sutcliffe (Sutcliffe, 1997): (1) maximize visibility—all necessary information should be immediately available; (2) minimize search time with minimum keystrokes; (3) provide structure and sequence of display; (4) focus user attention on key data—important information should be salient and easily comprehended; (5) provide only relevant information; and (6) don't overload the user's working memory. In Chapter 8, there are several design guidelines (such as consistency, user control and feedback, and aesthetics in screen design) that can be applied here.

### 3.4.6 Formative Evaluations

*Formative evaluations* identify defects in designs, thus informing design iterations and refinements. A number of different formative evaluations can occur several times during the design stage to form final decisions. In fact, it is strongly recommended that formative evaluations occur during the entire HCI development life cycle, as depicted in Figure 11.4. A variety of different formative evaluations can occur several times during the design stage of an information system. Chapter 7 (Evaluation) introduces several commonly used methods for such evaluation purposes.

## 3.5 The Implementation Phase

HCI development in this phase includes (1) coding, (2) formative evaluations to fine-tune the system, (3) summative evaluation before system release, and (4) use evaluation after the system is installed and being used by targeted users for a period of time. *Summative evaluation* takes place after the system is developed to confirm whether the evaluation metrics or other industry standards are met. *Use and impact evaluation* collects feedback for understanding the actual behavior toward system use. This understanding helps in developing new versions or other similar systems. Both types of evaluations can use the techniques introduced in Chapter 7.

## 3.6 Prototyping

**Prototype:** A proof-of-concept representation of a design.

**Prototyping:** The process of quickly putting together a prototype.

In this section, we will only briefly mention prototyping due to the limited space and the emphasis of the chapter. Interested readers can find more details from other sources.

In the systems development context, prototyping is the process of quickly putting together a prototype in order to test various aspects of the design, illustrate ideas or features, and gather early user feedback. A prototype is a representation of a design concept; thus it is often called a proof-of-concept. Prototypes can be in many different forms. They can be drawings (hand- or machine-made), paper- or cardboard-based models, mock-ups of the screens of an application, or a running (but not fully functional) system.

Prototyping is an essential and integral part in the development process. It is a way of making an abstract conceptual model into a concrete physical form, even though this physical form could be very rough, incomplete, and not functional. Therefore, prototyping has the benefit of illustrating conceptual ideas, demonstrating a design's feasibilities and appropriateness, and overcoming potential users' misunderstandings of the final product or the designers' misunderstandings of user's needs.

Prototyping as an activity can occur many times at any stage of the HCI development process. For example, prototypes can be used in the project identification and planning stage. It can also be used for user-needs tests in the analysis stage. Of course, it is always a method that designers can use to explore different design alternatives and to fine-tune various aspects of the final product during the design stage.

Depending on the nature of the prototypes, different methods can be used to produce them. There are roughly two types of prototyping: low-fidelity and high-fidelity prototyping. Low-fidelity prototyping refers to the process where the developed prototype does not look very much like the final product. That is, the prototype is far from being close to the final product. These types of prototypes are useful because they tend to be simple, cheap, and quick to produce and modify. They are for exploration purposes. This can be especially beneficial during the early stages of development.

High-fidelity prototyping normally uses materials that would be expected to be in the final product, and the produced prototype looks (or even functions) very similar to the final product. Many such prototypes (often running and interactive systems) can be developed with computer-aided software engineering (CASE) tools, or end-user computing applications. For example, the prototype for the Teaching Tools example in this chapter was developed in Visual Basic.Net. The e-Gourmet example was created with tools such as HTML, cascading style sheets, and Java. Other software applications such as Microsoft Access can also be very powerful prototyping tools. Web development tools as simple as HTML, which we have used, can be handy when prototyping is needed.

### 3.7 Documenting HCI Development Activities and Deliverables

It is important to communicate HCI development activities and results to clients or teammates. Although there are many details that can be and should be documented, a rather standard format that gives an overview of the entire project will facilitate communication and understanding. Other detailed documents, such as task analysis results (which could involve many pages and levels), design alternative sketches, and so on, can be attached to the overview report. A template based on the HCI development life cycle methodology is presented in Table 11.2. Such a template gives a "one-glance" overview of the project, rather than the details. It is worth noting that this HCI-DLC report template can be easily streamlined with the Common Industry Format (CIF), which is designed for summative usability tests and is currently used in industry (Bevan, Claridge, Athousaki, & Maguire, 2002). See Chapter 7 for details on the CIF.

## ▶ 4. APPLYING THE HCI DEVELOPMENT METHODOLOGY

The case study at the end of the chapter shows how to apply the methodology for the e-Gourmet example that we have been studying in the previous chapters. Here we

**Table 11.2**   HCI Development Life Cycle (HCI-DLC) Report Template

| ID | HCI Development Activity | Deliverables |
|----|--------------------------|--------------|
| 1.1 | Project selection and planning | Schedule of IS projects development:<br>Cost-benefit analysis:<br>Other feasibility analyses: |
| 2.1 | Requirements determination | The specific system functionalities: |
| 2.2 | User-needs test | Sample profile:<br>Data collection time and setting:<br>Sketches or mock-ups used:<br>Test results:<br>Suggestions for revising system functionalities: |
| 2.3 | Context analysis | Physical context:<br>Technical context:<br>Organizational context:<br>Social/cultural context: |
| 2.4 | User analysis | Demographic:<br>Traits/skill sets:<br>Job- or task-related factors: |
| 2.5 | Task analysis | User goals and use cases:<br>Cognitive, affective, behavioral analysis of user tasks:<br>Work flow analysis:<br>General work distribution between users and the system: |
| 2.6 | Evaluation metrics | Physical:<br>Cognitive:<br>Affective:<br>Usefulness: |
| 2.7 | Alternative selection | Three alternatives:<br>The main constraints:<br>The chosen alternative: |
| 2.8 | Formative evaluation | Evaluation target, method, timing, and results: |
| 3.1 | Interface specification | Metaphor design:<br>Media design:<br>Dialogue design:<br>Presentation design: |
| 3.2 | Formative evaluation | Evaluation target, method, timing, and results: |
| 4.1 | Prototyping | Tools used: |
| 4.2 | Formative evaluation | Evaluation target, method, timing, and results: |
| 4.3 | Summative evaluation | Sample profile:<br>Data collection time and setting:<br>Test results:<br>Conclusions in light of evaluation metrics: |

present a slightly different fictional case, the Teaching Tools, to illustrate further how to apply the methodology to develop human-centered information systems.

"Teaching Tools" is a small company owned by two retired elementary school teachers, Janet and Chris. They have been creating teaching materials and tools for about 10 years. During this time, they have been selling their products at school bazaars, through flyers, and by direct mail to existing customers. The owners wish to develop an e-commerce Web site. They have contracted with HCD (Human-Centered Development Inc.) to build the site. The developers are recent graduates from an IS program that has implemented the HCSDLC curriculum.

Table 11.3 summarizes the HCI development activities and deliverables for the Teaching Tools case. Detailed explanations are embedded in the table.

**Table 11.3**  HCI-DLC Report for Teaching Tools

| ID | HCI Activity | Deliverables |
|----|-------------|--------------|
| 1.1 | Project selection and planning | Owners and consultants have completed an in-depth feasibility study and determined the cost/benefits of the site and created a tentative budget and schedule for the project. They have made a decision to go ahead and build the Web site. |
| 2.1 | Requirements determination | The potential systems requirements are (1) recommending a teaching tool that will meet customers' needs, (2) taking online orders by using credit cards, (3) providing sample lesson plans that go along with each tool, (4) providing learning objectives for each tool, and (5) providing a forum for teachers and learners to exchange ideas and experiences. The last one has a lower priority than the other four requirements. |
| 2.2 | User-needs test | A 10-person focus group was selected to help determine whether the proposed requirements will meet customer needs. The focus group consists of five long-term customers and five new customers. Through an iterative process, the user-needs test affirmed the four requirements and agreement that the discussion forum would be nice but not necessary to support sales. |
| 2.3 | Context analysis | 1. *Physical context*: Users may order or browse primarily from home or school. These two physical environments do not generally pose distracting physical aspects. The school environment can be a bit chaotic when students are present, but the teachers in the focus group said that they most likely order Teaching Tools products without students being present. However, one teacher said that she likes to get student input and often asks a small group of students to help her choose the tools at the beginning of the school year. The home environment can be a bit distracting also, but again the focus-group teachers said that they would wait for a quiet time at home to place orders. Overall, there were no special requirements due to the physical context and therefore they could choose a fairly standard e-commerce design. A decision has been made to make the Web site fully ADA (Americans with Disabilities Act) compliant. This decision ensures that the Web site will be adaptive to persons with both hearing and vision limitations. |

**Table 11.3**   HCI-DLC Report for Teaching Tools  (Continued)

| ID | HCI Activity | Deliverables |
|---|---|---|
| | | 2. *Technical context*: It is unlikely that users will browse the Web site using Palm PDAs or mobile phones. It is more likely that the users will be browsing from a desktop or laptop PC with a cabled Internet connection. The screen can be assumed therefore to be full-sized for a regular computer monitor. A later version of the site may be adapted to fit the small-screen requirements of the mobile devices. |
| | | 3. *Organizational context*: The Web site reflects the business strategies of the organization and thus is subject to business decision changes made at the strategic level. The site is primarily commercial and has the goal of making money and budget constraints that must be respected. However, the owners are emphatic that the site should reflect their student-centered philosophy. In addition, Teaching Tools does not have other computer-based information systems for the Web site to link to. |
| | | 4. *Social and cultural context*: The site is not really considered a global site; however, one of the owners is a teacher of English as a second language (ESL) and wants a Spanish version of the site and plans to add additional language versions as money allows. |
| 2.4 | User analysis | 1. *Demographic data*: Users are primarily female elementary school teachers in the U.S. who speak mainly English and some Spanish. |
| | | 2. *Traits and intelligence*: Users have a college degree and are fairly experienced computer users and often purchase items through the Internet |
| | | 3. *Job- or task-related factors*: Users may purchase items from the Teaching Tools Web site two times per year. |
| 2.5 | Task analysis | The overall goal is to select the appropriate teaching tool. Sample tasks: Task 1 is to specify the teaching requirements and selection criteria for the tool. The criteria include cost, author reputation, level of difficulty, level of study (grade level), and supplement. Task 2 is to evaluate the criteria and provide alternative options. Task 3 is to choose the tool. These tasks should be further decomposed into TLTs. |
| 2.6 | Evaluation metrics | After some research on existing Web sites and metrics published in trade journals, the following evaluation metrics are established (note: user-needs test has verified the usefulness of the Web site): |
| | | *Physical/ergonomic metrics*: <br> 1. 85 percent of the potential customers can read the text and image with ease. |
| | | 2. 85 percent of the potential customers feel that the sound produced by the system is audible and not hurting. |
| | | 3. 95 percent of the potential customers think that using the system does not impose health concerns. |
| | | *Usability metrics* <br> 1. New users are able to navigate and use the main functions within 10 minutes. |
| | | 2. Users are able to get to the main tasks with one or two clicks. |

**Table 11.3** HCI-DLC Report for Teaching Tools (Continued)

| ID | HCI Activity | Deliverables |
|----|--------------|--------------|
| | | 3. Ordering teaching tools should be done within one minute from the time the user clicks the submit button until a confirmation screen is returned. |
| | | 4. Error rate should be less than 1 in every 20 users for each purchase task. |
| | | 5. The number of complaints should be less than 1 in 100 uses. |
| | | 6. Secure connection should be alerted when the consumer is entering his or her credit card and personal information. |
| | | *Affective metrics*: <br> 1. 70 percent of the tested shoppers should have (a) aesthetic, (b) enjoyable, (c) engaging, and (d) satisfactory rating of at least 4 out of 5. |
| | | 2. No unnecessary anxiety imposed by the interface design such as "customers have to complete purchasing in 10 seconds." |
| | | 3. Relaxed atmosphere for ordering products. |
| | | 4. At least 70 percent of the potential target users would trust the Web site for credit card use. |
| | | *Usefulness metrics*: <br> 1. Customers can order the types of products that they normally cannot get from a local store. |
| | | 2. Customers can order the products with an affordable price and shipping. |
| 2.7 | Alternative selection | Three prototype designs were developed to reflect three alternative design strategies. They differed in systems requirements and HCI evaluation expectations. The low-range one has the very basic system functions and minimum evaluation expectations. The high-range one has the most powerful set of functions and the highest level of evaluation expectations. The middle-range one is a trade-off between the low- and high-range ones. The main constraints for choosing the final design strategy were financial and level of user sophistication. The chosen alternative is the one that meets the level of user sophistication and is the most affordable. Additional features may be added over time as money is available. |
| 2.8 | Formative evaluation | Ongoing testing to see if evaluation metrics are being met or should be adjusted. |
| 3.1 | Interface specification | 1. Storefront metaphor. <br> 2. Shopping cart metaphor. <br> 3. Navigational buttons and floating text. |
| 3.2 | Formative evaluation | Prototypes were reiterated and ongoing testing occurred via focus group and owner feedback to see if evaluation metrics are being met. |
| 4.1 | Coding | Visual Basic.Net is used as a coding tool. |

**Table 11.3** HCI-DLC Report for Teaching Tools (Continued)

| ID | HCI Activity | Deliverables |
|----|--------------|--------------|
| 4.2 | Formative evaluation | Prototypes and working systems reiterated and tested. |
| 4.3 | Summative evaluation | A Web site was created as a beta test site. Key customers were invited to visit the site and provide feedback. Then, a production version of the system was developed. The site has been modified and improved over time. The current site is stable but improvements are made according to customer and owner feedback. The current site has met the evaluation metrics set up in the early phases of the project. It took several months and countless revisions to meet these criteria. The site is beginning to pay for itself and has added 50 percent to overall revenues compared to the quarter prior to the installation of the Web site. |

Next, we discuss in detail the interaction design phase for Teaching Tools. The goal is to support the issues identified during context, task, and user analyses and to meet the HCI evaluation metrics requirements. Many discussions from Chapter 10 on componential design can be applied here. The design team for Teaching Tools created mock-up designs to demonstrate some design ideas and to gain feedback from the owners and potential users. One design incorporates stacked buttons and pop-up menus (see Figure 11.5). The second design uses navigational buttons and floating text (see Figure 11.6).

The search option was added at the focus group's suggestion. They wanted to be able to search from anywhere in the site for a specific tool for which they already knew the name. After trying out both options, the user focus group along with the store owners selected design option 2.

Once the user chooses the category of tool (from the pull-down list of Figure 11.6), the next task is to specify the values of the list of parameters of the tools that were identified during the analysis stage.

The selection criteria for the tool chooser screen includes (1) cost, (2) author reputation, (3) level of difficulty, (4) level of study, and (5) whether a supplement was included. Figure 11.7 depicts the design for the Tool Chooser screen.

In addition to the metaphor and dialog design, interaction design includes media design and presentation design. As noted above, presentation design follows established design principles. For example, the fields that are related logically are also placed physically at close proximity. For a particular choice of tool, the tool category, level of study, and level of difficulty are relatively inflexible. The user has more flexibility and room for compromise, if necessary, in determining the cost, author reputation, and whether a supplement is necessary. Hence, the first three fields are located within one physical group and the remaining three fields in another. Notice also that the level of difficulty of the tool is related to the level of study so that these two fields are positioned near each other. Finally, the order of the fields attempts to follow a logical or preferred order of input. These are all examples of design guidelines that we apply in presentation design.

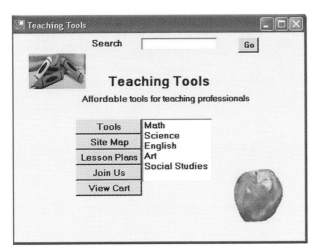

**Figure 11.5** Design option 1 for the Teaching Tools home page.

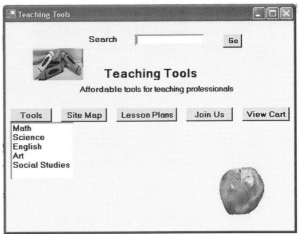

**Figure 11.6** Design option 2 for Teaching Tools home page. See also color plate VIII.

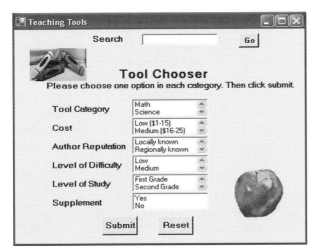

**Figure 11.7** Tool Chooser screen design.

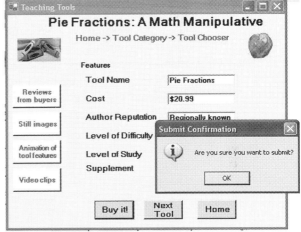

**Figure 11.8** Tool Features screen.

The Tool Chooser screen allows the user to select from various options by scrolling through the options so that the desired option appears in the text box. Once all the options are satisfactory, the user then clicks the Submit button. A confirmation message box for both the Submit button and the Reset button allows the user to confirm the choices made. Figure 11.8 shows the confirmation message box for the Submit button.

Once the user has confirmed the selection criteria in the Tool Chooser screen, the system searches the database of existing tools, finds all the tools that match the selection criteria, and presents them to the user one tool at a time. The user can explore the tool through many different avenues including Figure 11.9, which shows a tool that matches the selection criteria in Figure 11.8.

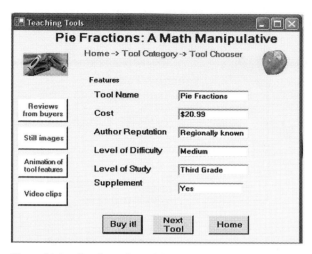

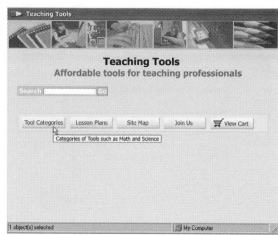

**Figure 11.9** Confirmation of Submit button click event.

**Figure 11.10** Final Teaching Tools home page. See also color plate VIII.

The screen in Figure 11.9 is meant to help the user evaluate a particular teaching tool. What is the best way of presenting the tool? Media design requires that we consider the alternative media and select those that are most helpful in evaluating the tools. In this case, it was important to provide not only textual descriptions but also pictures (still images) of the tool from revealing angles. Furthermore, to show how the tool's features are used dynamically, animations can be used to efficiently depict the sequential operation. Moreover, teachers are always concerned about how the tool is actually used in class. For this, a video clip of someone using the tool in a realistic session is also available. The result of the media design is reflected in the buttons at left side of the screen.

If the user wants this tool, he or she can click the "Buy it!" button, which leads to the shopping cart and subsequently to the purchase screen. If the user is not sure whether he or she wants to buy the tool, the user can place the tool in the shopping cart and view the cart at any time. From the cart page, the user can delete any of the tools not wanted. If the user knows that he or she does not want the tool, the user can click the Next Tool button, which brings up the next tool that matches the selection criteria. If there are no more tools, a message box pops up that indicates that there are no more tools and asks the user if he or she wants to try to find another tool (sends the user back to the tool chooser category page) or finish shopping by going to the shopping cart. The example ends here. The shopping cart screen and the payment screen would be similar to and consistent with existing e-commerce screens.

An iterative revision process was conducted with feedback from the user focus group and owners. Next, a Web site was created as a beta test site. Key customers were invited to visit the site and provide feedback. The site has been modified and improved over time. The current site is stable, but improvements are made according to customer and owner feedback. The current site has met the evaluation metrics set up in the early phases of the project. It took several months and countless revisions to meet these criteria. Figure 11.10 shows what the final home page looks like. This is based on the early design ideas in Figure 11.6, with users' feedback, an artist's touch, and fine-tuning.

## ▶ 5. SUMMARY

Methods and techniques in both the SA&D field (including software engineering) and the usability engineering field have matured over the years and are used for education, training, and guiding practice. However, little effort has been put toward providing integrated methodologies for developing human-centered information systems that consider both organizational and human needs. This lack of integration is problematic to our students, who often take different courses with different emphases. The same problem applies to information systems developers who are responsible for delivering both organizationally effective and human-centric systems but who often find reference books with one emphasis but not the other. Diverse approaches with different perspectives may help to isolate different issues, but they do not help with overall effectiveness and efficiency of systems development. The result of this situation is that developed information systems often either lack well-defined systems requirements to support organizational needs or lack human understanding, and thus they are frustrating to use.

This chapter positions HCI development in the overall system development life cycle by presenting the human-centered SDLC (HCSDLC) model first and then emphasizing the HCI development aspect. HCSDLC is an integrated methodology that emphasizes human-centeredness and considers HCI issues together with SA&D issues throughout the entire system development life cycle. The methodology has the parsimony of the SDLC model, which is helpful from the project management perspective. It lays out the connections and differences between SA&D and HCI tasks and provides a step-by-step procedure for transformations among tasks at different stages.

In this chapter, we provide very detailed materials on HCI development methodology that tie many earlier chapters together. An HCI-DLC Report template is used to summarize the activities and deliverables of the methodology. Examples are also used to illustrate how to apply the methodology.

## ▶ 6. SUMMARY OF CONCEPTS AND TERMS

| SDLC | SA&D | HCSDLC |
|---|---|---|
| Project selection | Project planning | Analysis |
| Requirement specification | User-needs test | Evaluation metrics |
| User analysis | Task analysis | Context analysis |
| Design | Implementation | Metaphor design |
| Dialogue design | Media design | Prototyping |
| Methodology | Method and/or technique | Maintenance |

▶ 7. BIBLIOGRAPHY AND ADDITIONAL READINGS

Beck, K. (2000). *eXtreme programming eXplained.* Upper Saddle River, NJ: Addison-Wesley.

Bevan, N., Claridge, N., Athousaki, M., & Maguire, M. (2002). *Guide to specifying and evaluating usability as part of a contract.* Retrieved from http://www.usability.serco.com/prue/

Davis, F. (1989). Perceived usefulness, perceived ease of use, and user acceptance of information technology. *MIS Quarterly, 13*(3), 319–340.

Davis, F., & Venkatesh, V. (2004). Toward preprototyping user acceptance testing of new information systems: Implications for software project management. *IEEE Transactions on Engineering Management, 51*(1), 31–46.

Fowler, M., & Highsmith, J. (2001). *The Agile Manifesto 2001.* Retrieved August 18, 2004, from http://www.sdmagazine.com

Hartson, H. R., & Hix, D. (1989). Toward empirically derived methodologies and tools for HCI development. *International Journal of Man-Machine Studies, 31*, 477–494.

Hefley, W. E., Buie, E. A., Lynch, G. F., Muller, M. J., Hoecker, D. G., Carter, J., & Roth, J. T. (1995). Integrating human factors with software engineering practices. In G. Perlman, G. K. Green, & M. S. Wogalter (Eds.), *Human factors perspectives on human-computer interaction: Selections from the Human Factors & Ergonomics Society Annual Meetings 1983–1994.* Santa Monica, CA: Human Factors and Ergonomics Society. (Original edition, *HFES Proceedings 1994*, pp. 315–319.)

Hoffer, J. A., George, J. F., & Valacich, J. S. (2005). *Modern systems analysis and design* (4th ed.). Upper Saddle River, NJ: Prentice Hall.

Mantei, M., & Teorey, T. (1989). Incorporating behavioral techniques into the system development life cycle. *MIS Quarterly, 13*(3), 257–274.

Mayhew, D. J. (1999). *The usability engineering lifecycle—A practitioner's handbook for user interface design.* San Francisco, CA: Morgan Kaufmann Publishers, Inc.

Preece, J., Rogers, Y., Sharp, H., Benyon, D., Holland, S., & Carey, T. (1994). *Human-computer interaction.* Reading, MA: Addison-Wesley.

Rosson, M. B., & Carroll, J. M. (2002). *Usability engineering: Scenario-based development of human-computer interaction* (p. 422). New York: Morgan Kaufmann Publishers.

Sutcliffe, A. (1997). Task-related information analysis. *International Journal of Human-Computer Studies, 47*, 223–257.

Sutcliffe, A. (2000). On the effective use and reuse of HCI knowledge. *ACM Transactions on Computer-Human Interaction, 7*(2).

Valacich, J. S., George, J. M., & Hoffer, J. A. (2004). *Essentials of systems analysis and design* (2nd ed.). Upper Saddle River, NJ: Prentice Hall.

Whitten, J., Bentley, L., & Dittman, K. (2004). *Systems analysis and design methods* (6th ed.). Boston: McGraw-Hill Irwin.

Zhang, P., Carey, J., Te'eni, D., & Tremaine, M. (2005). Integrating human-computer interaction development into the systems development life cycle: A methodology. *Communications of the AIS, 15*, 512–543.

Zhang, P., von Dran, G., Blake, P., & Pipithsuksunt, V. (2001). Important design features in different website domains: An empirical study of user perceptions. *e-Service Journal, 1*(1), 77–91.

▶ 8. CASE STUDY

We continue with the e-Gourmet example to illustrate how Lance Redux could apply the HCI development methodology. By now, you should be very familiar with the e-Gourmet case, which runs throughout the book. The description in this section is meant to be illustrative and does not represent the full scale of details involved in developing such a Web site. Using the HCI development report template, Table 11.4 summarizes the HCI activities during HCI development, the data captured, and issues and concerns for each activity.

Systems requirement specifications are very important to HCI development. Table 11.4 lists the four main functions of the e-Gourmet Web site. It is typical that this list is the result of several iterations, such as after a user-needs test and after some design considerations.

In order to do the user-needs test, sometimes using paper-based prototypes or mock-ups can better show potential users the system's functions or the potential usefulness of the system. In the e-Gourmet example, the functions are quite straightforward. Text-based descriptions can be sufficient for potential users to understand the functions. User-needs tests, especially if additional open-ended interviews are used, may provide opportunities to revise the systems requirements. In this case, potential users may want a discussion group; thus this function is added to the system requirements.

**Table 11.4**  HCI-DLC Report for e-Gourmet

| ID | HCI Activity | Deliverables |
|---|---|---|
| 1.1 | Project selection and planning | A decision is made to develop the e-Gourmet Web site. A cost-benefit analysis and other feasibility analyses are done. |
| 2.1 | Requirements determination | 1. Taking online orders of international gourmet foods using credit cards<br><br>2. Providing recipes of certain dishes<br><br>3. Providing explanations/history of certain ingredients and dishes<br><br>4. Providing a buddy forum for buyers to exchange recipes and cooking experiences (this function is added after initial user-needs test) |
| 2.2 | User-needs test | *Sample and data collection setting:* Shoppers from a supermarket answered a paper-based survey.<br><br>*Sketches or mock-ups used, if any:* Drawings on paper demonstrated systems functionalities and some design ideas.<br><br>*Results:* Shoppers suggested having a buddy forum for specialty food discussions among interested shoppers. |
| 2.3 | Context analysis | *Physical context:* Users may order from or browse the Web site from any location where they have access to the Internet.<br><br>*Technical context:* Users may use Web browsers from PC, Palm PDAs, or mobile phones.<br><br>*Org context:* None. Buyers' organizational context should not play any role in their using the system. |

**Table 11.4**  HCI-DLC Report for e-Gourmet  (Continued)

| ID | HCI Activity | Deliverables |
|---|---|---|
| | | *Social/cultural context:* The Web site can be accessed by anyone from any country with any culture who can provide a credit card with USD exchange. A cost-benefit analysis in the project planning phase determined that the e-Gourmet company will support only English at this moment. |
| 2.4 | User analysis | *Demographic:*<br>Upper-middle-income male and female shoppers with any occupation<br><br>Cosmopolitan and immigrant U.S. users and users outside U.S. (see context analysis above)<br><br>Users who speak English<br><br>*Traits/skill sets:*<br>Basic computer knowledge and experience<br><br>Basic understanding of buying things through the Internet<br><br>*Job- or task-related factors:* The frequency of users buying from the e-Gourmet Web site can range from once per month to daily with any dollar amount. |
| 2.5 | Task analysis | *User goals and use cases:*<br>Case 1: Buy particular foods or ingredients that users already know about.<br><br>Case 2: Look for ingredients that make a known dish.<br><br>Case 3: Learn about a particular dish, its ingredients, and how to make it.<br><br>Case 4: Browse to decide what to cook for a particular occasion.<br><br>Case 5: Recommend the site to others.<br><br>*Cognitive, affective, and behavioral analysis of user tasks:*<br>In case 1, a user may forget the official name but remember the characteristics of the foods (thus user may first need to do a query on certain attributes of foods to find it) (cognitive).<br><br>When examining an ingredient, users may need to refer to the dishes where this ingredient is used. The same is true when examining a dish where ingredients/recipe would be needed (cognitive, behavioral).<br><br>Aesthetically pleasing presentation would encourage browsing (cases 3 & 4) and eventually purchasing (cases 1 & 2) and recommending (case 5) (affective, behavioral).<br><br>A forum for peer recommendations and exchange of recipes or cooking experiences (case 5) (behavioral). |

**Table 11.4** HCI-DLC Report for e-Gourmet (Continued)

| ID | HCI Activity | Deliverables |
|----|-----------|------------|
| | | *Work flow analysis:*<br>Case 1 would need a sequence of actions to be finished; abortion of the task can occur at any stage of the sequence; and users may want to go back to previous stages.<br><br>Case 4 may lead to any of cases 1–3.<br><br>*General work distribution between users and the Web site/machine:*<br>Users make selections.<br><br>The Web site provides selections and all related and relevant info for each choice. |
| 2.6 | Evaluation metrics | *Physical/ergonomic metrics:*<br>1. 85 percent of the potential customers can read the text and image with ease.<br><br>2. 85 percent of the potential customers feel that the sound produced by the system is audible and not hurting.<br><br>3. 95 percent of the potential customers think that using the system does not impose health concerns.<br><br>*Usability goals:*<br>• New users (never used the Web site) should be able to navigate and use the main functions within one, three, or five minutes (for high-, middle-, low-range solution, respectively).<br><br>• Users should be able to get to the main tasks with maximum two clicks for middle-range solution.<br><br>• Ordering task should be done within one minute in normal situation (normal network traffic, user has no interruption) and with no more than two, four, or six clicks/actions (for high, middle, low range, respectively).<br><br>• The error rate should be less than 1 in every 10 users for each main task.<br><br>• The complaint rate of usability problems should be less than 1 in every 10 users.<br><br>• Credit cards are safe and secure to use.<br><br>*Affective metrics:*<br>• 80 percent of the tested shoppers should have (1) aesthetic, (2) enjoyable, (3) engaging, and (4) satisfactory rating of at least 4 out of 5.<br><br>• At least 50 percent of the shoppers would participate in the buddy forum at least once every three months (read or send postings).<br><br>• At least 80 percent of the potential target users would trust the Web site for their credit card use. |

**Table 11.4**   HCI-DLC Report for e-Gourmet  (Continued)

| ID | HCI Activity | Deliverables |
|---|---|---|
| | | *Usefulness goals:*<br>• Customers can order the type of foods that they normally cannot get from a local store.<br><br>• Customers can order small amount of foods with an affordable price and shipping.<br><br>• Customers can learn new ways of cooking international gourmet meals. |
| 2.7 | Alternative selection | Developed three (high, middle, and low ranges of potential solutions) alternatives using prototyping from the HCI evaluation metrics perspective and system functions perspective. Decided to go with the middle-range alternative after trade-off debate. |
| 2.8 | Formative evaluation | Conducted several tests on analysis results including evaluation metrics using paper drawings, mock-ups, and simple screen snapshots. Participants were friends and relatives of the developers who are interested in international gourmet meals. |
| 3.1 | Interface specification | *Metaphor design:*<br>"Product catalog" is used as a metaphor to help shoppers navigate the e-shop to find what they are looking for.<br><br>"Shopping cart" is used as a metaphor for holding items before checking out.<br><br>*Media design:*<br>Dishes are represented by images (photos of the master cooked dishes with great presentation) to make them look delicious. Certain ingredients will also be shown in realistic photos. Recipes will be brief and concise and will use common format. Forum will be similar to most successful online forums.<br><br>Other media types include text, buttons, hyperlinks, threaded discussion posts.<br><br>*Presentation design:*<br>The home page consists of virtual store map (with English), plus the section of language selection. It also indicates the main system functionalities. |
| 3.2 | Formative evaluation | Conducted several tests on various design decisions at semantic, syntactic, or even lexical levels using paper drawings, mock-ups, simple screen snapshots. |
| 4.1 | Coding | State-of-the-art Web development techniques were used to do this. |
| 4.2 | Formative evaluation | Conducted tests on various prototypes using laptop computers. Participants were friends and relatives, and some shoppers were recruited from a gourmet shop. |
| 4.3 | Summative evaluation | Real shoppers of the Web site are recruited to test the Web site on the Evaluation Metrics measures. |

Table 11.4 clearly lists the context analysis and user analysis results. For task analysis, each of the main system functions is analyzed in terms of user goals, use cases, cognitive/affective/behavioral analysis for each task, work flow analysis, and work distribution between users and the system.

Evaluation metrics are based on common practice, industry standards, if any, past experiences, and/or benchmarks. In Table 11.4, some quantitative numbers are used to illustrate that evaluation metrics or measures can be quite specific.

Finally, analysis may suggest at least three alternatives for the e-Gourmet Web site. In order to determine which alternative meets the clients' needs and results in the most usable interface, Lance uses prototyping to generate various screens to facilitate communication with the clients. For example, the high-range alternative may include an extensive list of system functions and high standards for evaluation measures. This also implies that it will be more costly and take longer to complete. A low-range alternative may have very limited system functions; it may fail to consider human needs or do so only to a minimum expectation level. This may affect the eventual user acceptance of the system and eventually the success of the business. There can be a middle-range alternative, as well. The final outcome of the analysis phase is the selection of a particular set of system functions and evaluation metrics. This alternative is passed to the design phase. For the simplicity of discussion, let us assume that the alternative selected is the middle-range one, as specified in Table 11.4 in terms of systems requirements/functions and evaluation metrics.

Figure 11.11 depicts two possible designs for the top-level layout, media selection, and presentation design considerations that should help users develop appropriate mental models of the Web site.

In the design stage, each of the identified tasks during task analysis should be carefully supported byppropriate design. The tasks should support the higher-level system functions as identified in the systems requirements specification. In the e-Gourmet example, let's focus on the fourth function, providing a forum to exchange ideas, recipes, and experiences. One task related to this function is to support users who wish to enter the forum. Figure 11.12 shows two possible designs for supporting this task. The (b) design allows a user to easily navigate the Web site, while the (a) design requires the user to go back to the previous page in order to go to other places on the Web site. Such a small difference in design can cause a big difference in a user's experience in using the Web site. Having a the navigation bar on the page is the result of a work flow analysis during task analysis.

In the implementation phase, modern techniques and methods of fast coding can be used to construct the systems. In addition, formative evaluations should be conducted to test various parts of the system. A summative evaluation should be conducted to conclude the evaluation of the system, typically in light of the evaluation metrics as specified in the analysis stage. For e-Gourmet, real shoppers should be used in real shopping contexts for this evaluation. Computer logs and surveys can be used as data collection methods.

We can move further with this case study. Assume that Lance Redux completed the development of the e-Gourmet Web site, as summarized in Table 11.4. During the beta testing stage (a summative evaluation), he received several suggestions from the owners to expand the system's functions, such as streamlining it with the company's physical store business and telephone ordering division and to target non-English speakers to use the Web site. This is because after seeing what the Wcb site does for the business, the

**Figure 11.11**   Two top-level design choices for e-Gourmet prototype. See also color plate VIII.

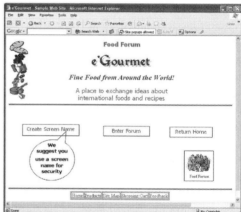

**Figure 11.12**   Two design choices for entering the Food Forum in the e-Gourmet Web site.

owners now have a better understanding of the role of this Web site. The owners want to attract people who may not speak English but who do speak one of the following languages: Spanish, French, Chinese, and Korean. In addition, Lance also received some complaints from online customers who wish that fewer clicks were required to go through the checkout process. All these prompted Lance to start thinking about the next version of the e-Gourmet Web site. Based on human-centered systems development philosophy, Lance decided to apply the HCI development methodology again for the new adventure. Can you use the HCI-DLC template to outline the next iteration of e-Gourmet for Lance?

▶ 9. EXERCISES

Ex. 1.  Review questions

Answer the following questions to test your understanding of the chapter materials.

1. What is a life cycle of an object or artifact? List some examples and the stages of the life cycle that you can identify.

2. What is the advantage of using the life cycle of a system to manage the systems development project, including HCI development?

3. Why should HCI development be part of the entire systems development process and take into account the entire life cycle, rather than just one activity in the design stage of the development life cycle?

4. Why do HCI concerns involve more than just usability?

5. Why do HCI issues exist beyond the user interface level?

6. How many main stages are there in the suggested HCI development methodology? List and discuss them.

Ex. 2.  Solving problems (1)

Assume that as the IT director of your organization, you are about to make a purchase decision on an organization-wide calendar system. How would you proceed with this task? Does the methodology help you to structure your choice? Why or why not? What factors do you need to consider?

If you think the methodology does help, try to use it to structure your task. List all factors or activities you need to consider. Which of them are more organizational-needs oriented, and which of them are more human-needs oriented? Write down as many details as you can.

Ex. 3.  Solving problems (2)

Assume that as the IT director of a university, you are to lead a team to develop a computer system to manage campus-wide book/meal/school-supply purchase needs. That is, anyone associated with the university can use a special card to purchase anything that is offered on campus. Users can add money to a card using any of the value-adding machines. They can also withdraw cash from the card by using the machine.

Use the HCI methodology to help you develop the value-adding machine, including its functionalities, and all other aspects so that eventually users can use it. Use drawings or sketches to illustrate your design ideas.

# CHAPTER 12

# INTERPERSONAL RELATIONSHIPS, COLLABORATION, AND ORGANIZATION

## CONTEXT AND PREVIEW

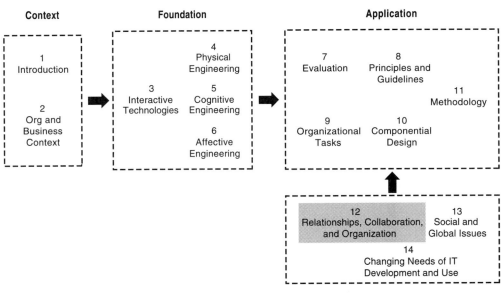

This chapter presents several models from referent disciplines such as psychology, management information systems, consumer behavior, organizational behavior, and others. These models explain various relationships between individuals, groups, and organizations and reveal the implications of the relationships on HCI practice and theory. The models are applied at the group level, at the enterprise level, and in the interorganizational context of e-commerce. In Chapter 2 and throughout the book, we focus on the individual's interaction with the system. This chapter expands our level of analysis to the work aspects of information systems that depend on interpersonal relationships and collaborative work.

## LEARNING OBJECTIVES

Upon completion of this chapter, students should be able to do the following:

- Understand and apply the organizational models at the group and organizational levels
- Understand and apply consumer models, models of trust, and TAM (the Technology Acceptance Model), and understand how they relate to e-commerce
- Understand how these various models form the theoretical underpinnings for HCI theory, guidelines, and principles in collaborative situations
- Be able to associate the various models with HCI practice

## ▶ 1. INTRODUCTION

Previous chapters have looked at the development of systems from the perspective of the single user. This chapter looks at the needs of two or more individuals working with a system, examining HCI beyond the single user. We study systems that support interpersonal relationships, as they exist within organizations and between organizations and their customers.

An organization relies on collaborations between its workers. Collaborations of all forms—within formal or informal groups, within small or large groups, co-located or dispersed—are the ideal manifestation of interpersonal relationships. We begin therefore with collaborations and then review some of the underpinnings of interpersonal relationships in organizations that affect collaboration, such as trust and communication.

Armed with some of the theoretical foundations, we explain user behavior with systems that support collaboration at different levels: (1) group work, including group decision making, intercultural teamwork, and the role of leadership; (2) enterprise-wide work, including communication support systems and issues of implementation; and (3) customer–enterprise relationships, which are especially prevalent in e-commerce. In reviewing the systems at these different levels, we rely on additional conceptual models, which are elaborated where needed.

## ▶ 2. COLLABORATION

Collaboration software allows people to work together and includes groupware, e-mail, instant messaging, data conferencing, and videoconferencing, among others. Collaboration was introduced in Chapter 2. The growth of the Internet has increased access to collaboration software and made it more affordable.

**Collaboration software:** Allows people to work together and includes groupware, e-mail, instant messaging, data conferencing, and videoconferencing, among others.

Lotus Notes debuted in 1989 and was one of the first products in the collaboration software genre to appear on the market. Today, more than 15 years later, there are several products in the genre. Today's products generally take the form of a suite of loosely integrated products. The user interfaces and back-end services have changed to meet the needs of users. Some of the important changes to collaboration environments are transparent to the vast majority of users. For example, databases that store documents and mail have traditionally been built around so-called flat databases but now are making a transition to object-oriented databases. There are also new development tools that allow tailoring of the user interfaces to fit each installation to the needs of its corporate users. Some vendors are approaching the trend toward lighter messaging systems as an opportunity to address the needs of the so-called deskless workers. The lighter messaging systems run on several of the more prevalent wireless platforms. The notion of "presence aware-ness," which involves determining whether a user is immediately reachable or is in a less-available status, is a new feature of recent collaboration software releases.

An early framework for understanding computer-supported collaborative work sys-tems (CSCW) classifies these systems on two dimensions: time and place (Ellis, Gibbs, & Rein, 1991). Same-time systems support interaction with synchronous communica-tion, such as instant messaging (IM), as opposed to different-time systems, in which communication is asynchronous and the users access the system at different times (e.g., e-mail). Such systems necessarily involve some form of memory to pass messages from one user to another; for instance, production rooms usually maintain a log that records events so that workers entering the next shift can quickly learn what happened during the previous shift. Same-place systems support interaction between colocated users, while different-place systems support interaction between distributed users. Four combina-tions of these two dimensions are possible; for example, systems can serve users who are interacting at the same time in the same place, which usually involves face-to-face inter-action, or at different places (Figure 12.1). Software companies strive to offer systems that can support more than one combination so that users will learn to interface with one system that will perform anywhere, anytime. For example, you will be able to use the same interface on a PDA in a conference room connected to a display projected on the wall or participate in the same virtual meeting from a hotel lobby.

CSCWs introduce a complex set of conflicting effects on user behavior. For example, teleconferencing is a computer-based technique that allows groups of people to access an electronic conference or dialogue. One of the advantages of teleconferencing is that group members can participate from different locations at various times. This is referred to as asynchronous communication. Additionally, simultaneous entries allow for multi-ple messages and reduction of "production blocking" or "waiting to speak" while others have the floor, which occurs in face-to-face meetings (Diehl & Stroebe, 1987). Also, low-status or shy members of the group may feel freer to contribute when using telecon-ferencing (Siegal et al., 1986). The disadvantages of teleconferencing are that (1) this text-based communication does not offer the richness that audio, visual, graphical, and nonverbal cues provide, (2) those group members who lack keyboarding skills may be frustrated or restricted from full participation in the group, (3) the simultaneous entries that are facilitated by teleconferencing require additional cognitive processing, and (4) outcomes from virtual team interactions may be less positive than from face-to-face

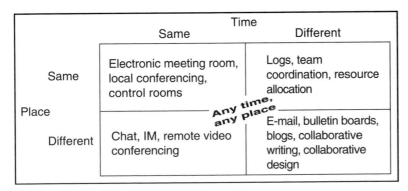

**Figure 12.1** Classification of CSCW

interactions (Potter & Balthazard, 2002). This section looks at some of the theories that explain these impacts.

## 2.1  Collaboration—The Building Blocks

All collaboration software designs have three commonalities. The first is a shared interface. The shared interface is also sometimes referred to as the workspace. All participants see the shared interface. The second commonality is that the shared user interface must be "WYSIWIS" or "What you see is what I see." When two or more people are collaborating in an online setting, the shared interface space must look and act the same to all participants. Imagine how confusing and potentially harmful to collaboration outputs a non-"WYSIWIS" interface would be. The third commonality is that each participant also has a "private" space. This space is used to prepare responses with available editing tools. These responses may then be sent to the "shared" space. Alternatively, the

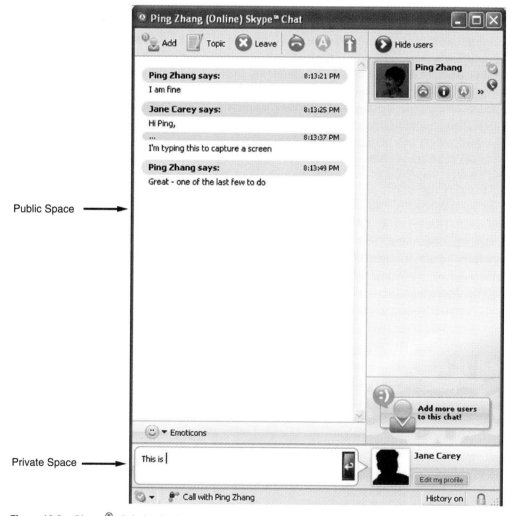

**Figure 12.2**  Skype® global telephony system illustrating public and private workspace.

private space may be used to take notes that may be saved or discarded but are not sent to the shared space. Figure 12.2 illustrates the concept of shared and private workspace. Figure 12.2 shows Skype®, a global telephony product that allows voice conversations and typed chats via the Internet.

Skype® runs on desktops but also on mobile devices such as a PDA. It aims at becoming a system that can serve the user at any time and any place that can link via wire or wireless connections to the Internet. E-mail applications (mailers) are also aiming at becoming more accessible by moving from the desktop to handheld devices such as the Blackberry (www.blackberry.com), which allows you to access your e-mail through cell phone providers that make your e-mail accessible from practically any place connected by mobile phones.

## 2.2 Collaboration—Semantic and Syntactical Level

The objects and operations available in the private workspace are similar to those we have already examined. Their primary purpose is to allow the user to compose in private and, when finished, upload the information to the public or shared space. The shared workspace enables the operations that directly support collaborative work. For example, in the system shown in Figure 12.2, users operate on objects such as "Contact," "Message," and "Call." Users can manage a contact by adding, editing, or deleting the contact from their contact list. They can initiate or terminate a call and add a contact to a call. Furthermore, users can control the way they are presented to others; for example, they can decide whether others will see their picture or just a general sketch of a person's head (see both options in Figure 12.2), and they can decide whether they are currently shown as being available or away from their desk. Moreover, in CSCW, users can generally decide to share messages or applications by opening them in the shared workspace or alternatively sending a message to some contacts but not others.

Some syntactical-level features can be seen in Figure 12.2. Since the shared workspace is the most important feature of collaboration, and design guidelines tell us that important information should be placed in the upper-left-hand space of the screen, the shared workspace is placed in the upper left. The private workspace is usually placed at the bottom of the screen. This is to facilitate keyboarding and editing. The user can see his or her typing and easily validate it before sending. There is a separate send button, but usually the return key also sends the work from the private space to the public space. In Figure 12.2, the standard text-based horizontal menu options appear at the top of the screen and the special-purpose vertical menu options appear in the right-hand portion of the screen. Of course, instant messaging (IM) is not the only software in the collaboration category. E-mail, videoconferencing, computer conferencing, groupware, and others in the collaboration category have some differences from IM. However, they all have the commonalities listed in section 2.1.

## 2.3 Collaboration—Task Level

Collaboration includes many different tasks such as sharing knowledge, coordinating action, informing colleagues or subordinates of events, and meeting. The task level for collaboration is based on communication. One such task is "chatting" or meeting to communicate ideas. This can happen in "real time" (as in IM), anytime (as in e-mail), or anytime and anyplace (as in Internet-based collaboration). A second task is to work on a

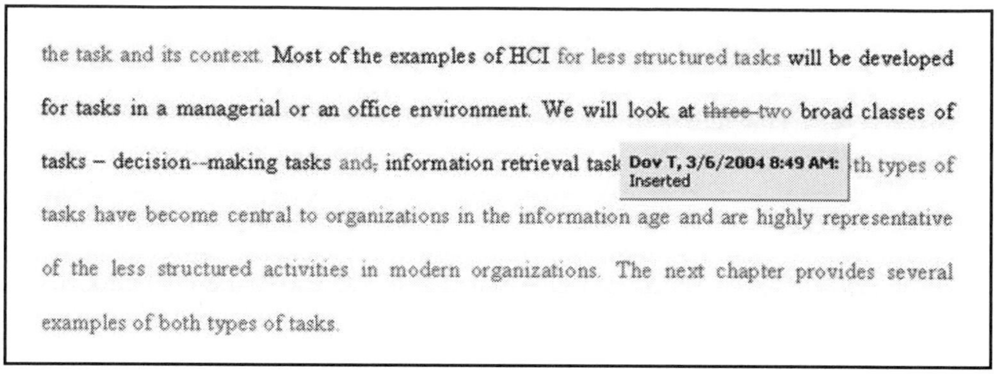

> the task and its context. Most of the examples of HCI for less structured tasks will be developed
>
> for tasks in a managerial or an office environment. We will look at ~~three~~ two broad classes of
>
> tasks – decision–making tasks and, information retrieval task **Dov T, 3/6/2004 8:49 AM:** th types of
> **Inserted**
>
> tasks have become central to organizations in the information age and are highly representative
>
> of the less structured activities in modern organizations. The next chapter provides several
>
> examples of both types of tasks.

**Figure 12.3**   Microsoft® Word® tracking feature for shared writing of a manuscript (this book).

document. The document could be a word processed document, a design, or a diagram. The collaboration software contains a repository that helps keep track of versions, updates, authors, edits, and changes. It allows for a designated person who has authority to accept or reject changes. Access privileges can be set so that some people are locked out, others are given read-only access, others have read/write access, and still others have accept/reject privileges. Figure 12.3 illustrates the tracking feature of Microsoft® Word®. It shows who inserted the highlighted text and the date it was inserted.

In the following sections we examine other collaborative tasks such as group decision making and knowledge sharing.

## ▶ 3. THE ISSUE OF TRUST

**Trust:** The willingness to rely on an exchange partner due to confidence that the partner will fulfill obligations.

Trust generally is viewed as an essential ingredient for successful interpersonal relationships. Moorman, Deshpande, and Zaltman (1993, p. 82) define trust as "a willingness to rely on an exchange partner in whom one has confidence." They propose that an expectation of trustworthiness results from the ability to perform (expertise), reliability, and intentionality. Morgan and Hunt (1994, p. 23) define trust as the perception of "confidence in the exchange partner's reliability and integrity."

We are concerned with three types of trust in HCI. First, users can trust the underlying technology and human-consumer interfaces, including Internet technologies and security safeguards such as digital signatures. We include here also expert systems or artificial agents that recommend to the user what products to purchase or what decisions to make. We have already looked at trustworthy interfaces (see design principle to promote trust in Chapter 8); here we expand and apply the issue of trust to specific types of systems. Second, users such as online customers can trust the institutions with which they interact via information technology. Sometimes, the users trust the Web site regardless of their trust of the institution (Kracher et al., 2005). But often, the computer (e.g., a Web site) comes to represent the institution (Jarvenpaa & Tractinsky, 1999). Third, certain systems include recommendations by particular people (e.g., other customers with similar backgrounds recommending a book on Amazon or even opinions from friends you select). Again, such recommendations can be seen as part of the Web site, but as some researchers strongly oppose the idea of projecting human–human trust to machines, we leave this third category of trust distinct from the first two.

Like other attitudes (Chapter 6), trust is based on both cognition and affect. While there has been considerable research on the cognitive antecedents of trust in computers, we know very little about the affective sources of trust. One distinction between cognitive and affective trust is tied to the impact of familiarity. Familiarity with e-commerce sites appears to affect cognitive trust significantly (Gefen et al., 2003), but familiarity with systems has little impact on affective trust (Komiak & Benbasat, 2004). Research shows that cognitive trust incorporates several types of processes: calculative (people evaluate costs and benefits), prediction (the user determines that the system's past actions reliably predict future actions), capability (the system's capabilities are assessed as sufficient to ensure that the user's expectations will be fulfilled), intentionality (the system's actions and semantics indicate trustworthy intentions), and transference (trust is projected from a known entity to the system). So, for example, familiarity will affect trust primarily through the prediction process, and recommendations from peers will affect trust through the transference process. Below we address trust in virtual groups and e-commerce.

## ▶ 4. COMMUNICATION AND TECHNOLOGY

The relationship between organizational theory and communication technology is very complex. For one, not all types of media are effective in supporting the various types of organizational tasks. We have already seen that tasks are more or less structured, that behavior is more or less controlled, and that these distinctions require different designs. Similarly, tasks can be characterized as being high or low on uncertainty (the amount of information required to complete the task) and high or low on ambiguity (the lack of knowing what information to seek and how to use it). It is not clear how technology can support the communication necessary for collaboration in these distinct types of tasks effectively. Another complication introduced by technology used for communication is that it affects human relationships in organizations, which, in turn, impact behavior in general and collaboration in particular.

We introduce two theories that address these two issues. These are, respectively, information richness theory and social identity theory. A third model that applies these ideas to the design of communication support systems is described later in the chapter.

### 4.1 Information Richness Theory

One of the key theories of study has been information richness theory (IRT) (Daft & Macintosh, 1981). The gist of IRT is that ambiguity can be reduced through rich media and uncertainty can be reduced through lean media. Designers should therefore strive to select the medium that best fits the type of task.

What is rich media? The richest communication mode is face-to-face. Media richness refers to social cues and meaning that can be conveyed by the message through the media: the diversity of channels, signals, and formats (e.g., ability to transfer both audio and visual signals, written versus graphic), the diversity of languages (e.g., natural language versus a predetermined subset of possible messages), and the ability to provide immediate explanations and feedback (usually associated with synchronous as opposed to asynchronous communication). Teleconferencing, for example, can provide a lot of social cues whereas e-mail would provide limited social cues. Figure 12.4 depicts a continuum of media ranging from rich to lean.

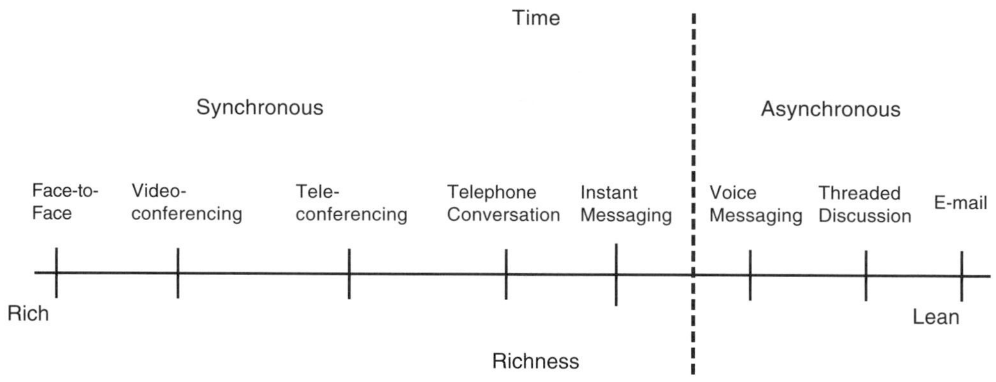

**Figure 12.4** Information Richness Theory.

## 4.2 Social Identity and De-individuation (SIDE) Processes

Another organizational theory that has been advanced and tested regarding communication systems is called social identity theory and de-individuation processes (SIDE) (Spears & Lee, 1992). This theory posits that information systems and in particular e-mail systems diminish social identity and de-individualize the user population. These psychological states reduce the normal impact of social norms and constraints and eventually result in "deregulated" behavior. An example of deregulated e-mail behavior is "flaming," which is a reactive and uncensored response. The person who engages in "flaming" in an e-mail setting is less likely to say the exact same things in a face-to-face conversation. In turn, some variables that are important to organizational success, such as belongingness, motivation, self-efficacy, and ownership, among others, are reduced, thus decreasing the likelihood of success for the organization.

Let us examine one of the leaner media and how it is used in an organization. One form of threaded discussions is the listserver (others are message boards, blogs, and newsgroups). In comparison to electronic message boards, where users know they need to access a board to read messages, the listserver delivers messages by e-mail. Members of an organization or a community are eligible for signing up to the listserver (often called a Listserv), supplying certain details including, of course, an e-mail address. Once a member of the listserver, the user can compose a message and send it out to the entire listserver mailing list, which can consist of hundreds or thousands of recipients. Listservers can be moderated or unmoderated. If moderated, an individual or team is appointed to oversee the smooth operation of the board and censor the messages in violation of a predefined agreed-upon code.

The ISWorld Listserv opened to the IS community in 1994 and now consists of over 5,000 members. Members can elect to receive messages as they are written or as a daily digest that includes all the messages of the day (you can also access the posted messages of the day at ISWorld and search in an archive of all messages to date). The Listserv has a manager, who controls the board and can go as far as banning users who violate the ISWorld policy. An interesting tradition that has developed on this Listserv is posting a compiled list of replies to members' queries. This enables efficient knowledge sharing within the community (see a description of this and other practices in "Conditions of Use of the ISWorld Listserv" (http://lyris.iswrold.org/isworldlist.htm).

**Social Identity and De-individuation Processes** such as email reduce the impact of social norms and constraints.

A recent study of the ISWorld Listserv revealed that members used the Listserv for five main tasks: information dissemination (e.g., notices on conferences), knowledge sharing (e.g., summaries of some topic), social binding (e.g., finding colleagues and building relationships), discussing an issue (e.g., the contents of an introductory course), and collaborating on a project (e.g., call for participation in a multicultural research project).

In general the Listserv has functioned smoothly to the high satisfaction of its members. There were very few instances of deregulated behavior in the last 10 years. One instance of flaming occurred on September 11, 2001, following the terror attack. Within three days the messages had escalated to such an offensive level that the Listserv had to be temporarily shut down and reopened under restricted conditions (see Te'eni & Schwarz, 2004, for an analysis of this incident of flaming).

## ▶ 5. WORK GROUP LEVEL

Group support systems (GSS) can be defined as any technologies that support group or collaborative work. The technology can be as simple as regular electronic mail systems or as complex as structured meeting support software.

### 5.1 Group Decision Support Systems (GDSS)

We have seen how systems can support decision making (Chapter 9). Group decision making builds on individual decision making but adds the collaboration that occurs at the different stages of the decision process. Decision makers in a group setting find themselves involved in both individual activities and group activities (e.g., work out some solution individually and then present to the group members to recruit their support).

**Table 12.1** McGrath's Classification of Group Tasks

| Type of Task | Group Losses |
| --- | --- |
| Planning tasks—generating plans | Coordinating, projecting, production blocking |
| Creativity tasks—generating ideas | Withdrawing, asymmetry, production blocking |
| Intellective tasks—solving problems with a correct answer | Groupthink, problem solving |
| Decision-making tasks—dealing with tasks for which an answer is judged to be correct | Groupthink, joint judgment |
| Cognitive conflict tasks—resolving conflicts due to different understandings of the issues | Resolving conflict |
| Mixed-motive tasks—resolving conflicts due to different values | Resolving value-laden conflict |
| Competitive tasks—resolving conflicts due to power | Power games |
| Psychomotor tasks—performing according to objective standards | Limited capacity |

Group decision support systems (GDSS) must therefore support both collaborative activities and enable an easy transition between individual and group activities.

The development of GDSS follows the methodology described in Chapter 9 for developing decision support: first analyze the decision task, then consider possible human constraints and strengths that might, respectively, inhibit and enhance task performance, and finally propose new functionality accordingly. A commonly accepted classification of group tasks, proposed by McGrath (1984), is shown in Table 12.1.

McGrath's typology of eight group tasks is classified into four activities (each with two types): generate, choose, negotiate, and execute. Each type of task involves difficulties leading to group process losses but also offers opportunities for process gains. For instance, in creativity tasks, one problem encountered in group processes is low participation because people tend to withdraw from the group when they feel unsafe. This is a process loss because high participation produces more and more diverse ideas that increase the likelihood of success. Indeed, groups offer an opportunity for diverse opinions that obviously are unlikely in individual decision making. This group capability leads to potential process gains.

Table 12.1 lists the eight types of tasks along with the main process losses associated with each task. They include difficulties in coordination between group members, problems of agreeing on forecasting and projections, production blocking in which people cannot contribute because they are waiting or interrupted by others, withdrawing from the group, asymmetry in status and knowledge of group members, groupthink in which members tend to think like the others instead of arguing their own views, difficulty in resolving conflicts, power games that lead to unproductive disputes, and limited physical, cognitive, and emotional resources to perform a task.

The GSS functions described below are designed to overcome these potential group losses. Let us demonstrate the general direction with an example of cognitive conflict tasks. One of the difficulties encountered in group decision making is the transition from individual thinking to one that takes into account the perspective and thoughts of other team members. The system can provide cognitive feedback such as graphic displays of the weights in multicriteria decision making to show the changes in the user's own thoughts after interacting with other members. Such feedback is instrumental in achieving effective group decision making. Similarly, systems can provide knowledge-based explanations of recommendations in group decision making and increase the likelihood of group effectiveness (these techniques are demonstrated in Sengupta & Te'eni, 1993, and Nah & Benbasat, 2004).

One of most documented GSS is the "same time, same place" Electronic Meeting System (EMS). An EMS is typically organized in a conference room that has a network of individual computer stations but also includes one or more large public displays. (Although the term EMS also applies to systems for dispersed teams, we treat such systems separately.)

EMSs include several components that support the various stages of group decision-making processes.

For logistics and control:

- Agenda and participants—Sets the agenda and rules of games; allows the moderator to monitor the progress.

- Control progress—Controls participation, ensures time limits and order, and enables anonymous contributions.

- Documentation tools—Supports collaborative writing (see Figure 12.3) and supports the process of developing consensus statements.
- Group memory—Supports the recording of information in an easily accessible fashion, including metadata such as common and individual definitions of important terms.

For idea generation:

- Electronic brainstorming—Allows members to generate ideas efficiently and share them with other members.
- Issue organizers—Enables moderated or unmoderated structuring of the ideas and issues presented. For example, all issues may be copied onto a public display and then, through discussion, issues are grouped, renamed, and deleted until a clear and categorized list of issues is reached.

For analysis:

- Support an agreed-upon set of criteria.
- Alternative evaluation to compare a set of alternatives according to stated criteria.

For choice:

- Voting systems that let members vote on ideas and priorities. For example, members may allocate a fixed number of points among several alternatives according to their own preference and the system computes the joint preference function.

Many of the studies of EMS have been conducted by a team of researchers led by Jay Nunamaker at the University of Arizona (Nunamaker et al., 1991). They report on several important lessons they have learned over the years of facilitating electronic meetings. Here are some of these lessons about designing EMS. First, the interface designs affect group dynamics. For example, screens that enable short comments usually result in more ideas being considered by the group. Second, users must be able to move easily from the individual tools they work with (e.g., a spreadsheet with sales data of a particular region) to the group tools (e.g., a graphic presentation of all regions). Third, the system must support flexible progress. Group processes cannot be planned to the last detail and carried out accordingly. Fourth, users must have continuous access to all information regardless of when it was generated. People go back and forth in their thought processes, one idea can trigger a new thought about a previous discussion, and a new opinion may change one's preference about an old issue. These nonsequential thought processes require effective group memory.

Noteworthy too are some more general lessons about the impact of EMS on group participation and decisions.

- Anonymity increases the amount of relevant contributions from the group members. The likelihood of a good idea is a function of the number of contributed ideas.
- The ability of members to work in parallel increases participation and a sense of group achievement.
- Anonymous criticism avoids premature convergence to suboptimal resolutions.
- Feedback to the group on each stage of the group process in relation to the overall agenda helps the group stay focused.

### 5.2 Virtual Teams

Virtual teams (i.e., distributed teams that rely to a large extent on information technology in order to collaborate) have become an important form of work. These teams can form for a one-time effort or continue to work together on a long-term project. Some teams meet face-to-face at the outset of their teamwork and continue to meet virtually; others never meet physically. Some are relatively homogeneous, coming from the same background; others come from different professional backgrounds and even different cultures. But all virtual teams pose difficult challenges to designers of the collaborative systems on which they rely. Among the serious communication problems in teamwork are failure to communicate and maintain contextual information, failure to transmit the information to all team members, difficulty in communicating the salience of information items in a message, difficulties of communication due to differences among team members in access to information, and difficulty in interpreting silence (Cramton, 2001; Majchrzak et al., 2000).

Let us examine these difficulties in reference to the screenshot of a typical virtual meeting system shown in Figure 12.5 (this system is of type "same time, different place"). Besides the general menu bar at the top of the screen, there are three areas: on the left is the public area currently showing the meeting agenda, on the top right is a list of participants and their status, and on the bottom right is access to potentially relevant materials. The relevant materials can be files, applications that can be displayed simultaneously on all client machines, or Web sites on the Internet. These relevant materials help maintain a shared context and transmit contextual information when necessary.

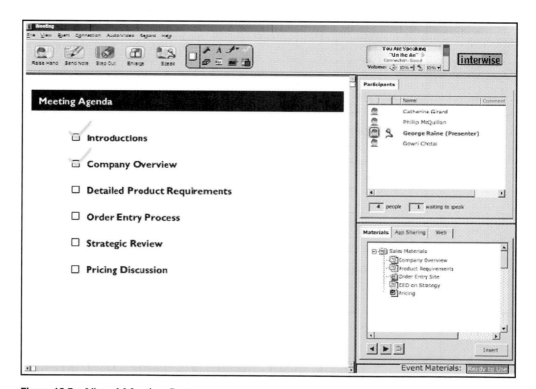

**Figure 12.5**   Virtual Meeting System.

Knowing (from the participants list) who is talking and who is listening is also a form of contextual information that helps clarify the messages. The microphone near the third member, George, indicates that he is now speaking. The list helps the users become aware of any changes in the status of a particular member (e.g., when a member signals that he or she has left the computer for a while). It also helps ensure that all members received the message. Often speakers ask for a quick raise of hands (near each participant, a hand-like icon is displayed) to acknowledge receipt of the message. Note also the use of an agenda (see discussion above on GDSS); it helps orient the participants as to the progress in the sequence of planned items.

Nevertheless, the communication remains problematic in comparison to, say, face-to-face. First, despite the fact that one can see who is listed as participating, one cannot be quite sure if they are really attentive to what is being said. In this particular virtual meeting, you can display one or two video pictures of members' faces. Members can detect whether the person is looking at the screen and can even detect certain facial expressions. Unfortunately, current quality limits the precision of these nonverbal signals (the media richness problem). Second, even though you can see when a person picks up the microphone to speak, it is still unclear whether silence reflects hesitation, confusion, anger, or just a technical problem. Third, it is impossible to detect the relationships between other members. Unlike a face-to-face meeting, people around a table send messages to each other; here you have no idea what is happening between other members. For instance, George can send a private message to Catherine with no indication to anyone else that such a message (not to mention its content) had ever been sent.

More generally, collaboration in virtual teams suffers from two potentially inhibiting effects on communication: technology mediation and distance between members. We have already seen the effect of technology on communication, as described in the information richness theory and the social identity theory. Distance refers to both physical (geographical) distance and psychological distance. Physical distance dictates technology mediation, when face-to-face is infeasible economically or logistically. Psychological distance is the lack of shared knowledge among team members. Examples of shared knowledge are shared professional knowledge from common backgrounds, shared knowledge about the project's processes and products, shared knowledge about who can do what in the team, and so forth. Without such shared knowledge, it is impossible or very difficult to collaborate effectively. The following discussion on communication support systems addresses these problems.

## 5.3 Culture and GSS

GSS are designed, developed, and tested in a particular cultural setting, which is typically Western and often English-speaking. Research studies demonstrate that the culture of the target environment is an important dimension in the successful use of GSS (Mejias et al., 1996; Watson, Ho, & Raman, 1994; Tan, Watson, & Wei, 1995). The driving theory of cultural investigation is Hofstede's (1991) Model of Cultural Differentiation.

Hofstede's model includes four dimensions of national culture including power distance, uncertainty avoidance, individualistic-collectivistic, and masculinity/femininity. The power-distance dimension describes the relative distance and relationship between a supervisor and a subordinate. Countries that score high on power distance can be characterized as autocratic or paternalistic, while countries that score low on power distance can be characterized as participative.

> **Hofstede's Model of Cultural Differentiation:** Includes four dimensions including power-distance, uncertainty avoidance, individualistic-collectivistic, and masculinity-femininity.

Uncertainty avoidance is the extent to which members of a particular culture feel uncomfortable or threatened by unknown outcomes. Countries that score high on the uncertainty-avoidance dimension tend to have little tolerance for uncertainty and a greater need for formal rules. Countries with high uncertainty-avoidance scores have less tolerance for people or groups with deviant ideas or behavior and are more likely to resist innovation. Countries with low uncertainty-avoidance scores were inclined to take more risks and were more tolerant of deviant behavior and innovative ideas.

The individualistic-collectivistic dimension refers to the relationship between the individual and his or her larger environment. In individualistic cultures, people are more self-reliant and are expected to look after mostly themselves and their immediate families; relationships or links to outside individuals are usually not very strong. Collectivistic cultures tend to have a preference for cohesive and tight-knit social networks. Collectivistic cultures strive to maintain harmony and avoid confrontation or disagreement among group members.

The masculinity-femininity dimension describes the relative trade-off between an assertive versus a supportive environment. High masculinity (low femininity) scores emphasize power, assertiveness, and individual achievement. Low masculinity (high femininity) scores indicate a greater emphasis on people, quality of life, nurturing, and collective cooperation.

The aspect of culture has important implications for the design of GSS interfaces. A lengthy discussion of global software development takes place in Chapter 13. For this chapter, we will summarize the design issues raised by the aspect of culture.

Design issues raised by culture:

- Language of the target culture requires significant translation and back-translation and often creates space problems. Almost all other languages take more space than does English.
- Icons and symbols must be meaningful and inoffensive in the target culture.
- Various colors may have different connotations in different cultures. For example, Chinese brides traditionally wear red dresses whereas white symbolizes death.
- Use of sound should be sparing.

User acceptance testing by users who are members of the target culture is critical to system success.

It is important to understand the target culture. There are several strategies that a software company can undertake to achieve this understanding. One is to hire an outside consultant who already understands the culture (it is reasonable to insist that the consultant be fluent in both the language of the country in which the original software was developed and the language of the target culture). Another strategy is to do a cultural study by sending human factors experts from the company to the target culture. The third strategy is to hire members of the target culture to become permanent members of the company or perhaps a subsidiary.

If a company decides to do a cultural study from within the company, to gain understanding of a target culture, the first step is to go to the target culture and establish a rapport. Once a rapport is established, some initial activities can be undertaken to customize the cultural study to the particular culture; then formal data collection occurs. This data collection is most effective if a cross-cultural observation team is put together with members from the original culture and members from the target culture. Once the data is collected, there should be a wrap-up or debriefing in which preliminary findings are discussed. Then the team either returns to the original culture and applies the knowledge from the study or continues to stay in the target culture, refining the product and testing it using subjects from the target culture in the actual target environments.

## 5.4 Leadership and GSS

One of the important areas for further research in GSS is the relationship between leadership and GSS outcomes (Briggs, Nunamaker, & Sprague, 1997/98). Extant research has shown that even with a simple GSS, a subtle difference in leadership method may lead to massive differences in group outcomes. The authors ask the following questions: What other leadership methods might lead to similar differences? Under what conditions do teams perform better under a leader who uses GSS to structure and focus group processes? Under what conditions do groups perform better when they use the GSS with no leader and no structure? How can leaders use GSS to uncover hidden agendas among group members? Is the uncovering of hidden agendas necessarily a good thing? Why or why not? What effect does it have on group processes for the group to surface hidden agendas?

We also ask the question, "How can GSS interface design be used to mitigate the role of dysfunctional leadership and augment the role of productive leadership?" This is not a simple question and assumes that we can determine when leadership is dysfunctional and/or productive.

Some answers are beginning to emerge in recent research. Parent and Gallupe (2001) found that leadership style might be a strong moderating factor in the success or failure of a GSS-supported meeting. They propose and validate a research model that depicts the moderating effect of leadership on meeting outcomes. Figure 12.6 illustrates this model.

Earlier research revealed how leadership can make a difference. An experiment that compared groups with and without a leader found that the use of a GSS resulted in a more equal distribution of influence with no leader than in the face-to-face setting (Lim, Raman, & Wei, 1994). However, the presence of an elected leader in the GSS setting resulted in a distribution of power that was just as uneven as that in a face-to-face setting.

What roles should leaders of group interactions undertake? Below is a list compiled by Beranek and colleagues (2005) for leaders of virtual project teams:

In the pre-project stages, establish and communicate project mission, priority, and success criteria; select team members and define their roles; and determine technology requirements.

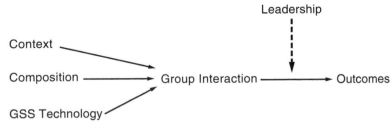

**Figure 12.6**   Group model of leadership.

In the project initiation stage, establish and manage team boundaries; develop shared mental models; create and maintain awareness; and manage communication processes.

In the wrap-up stage, review lessons learned and annotate successes.

Parts of these leadership functions can themselves be supported by GSS functionality. For example, creating and maintaining awareness involves awareness of others' activities, awareness of others' availability, awareness of how others fit into the processes, and social awareness of others (Weisband, 2002). In Skype® (Figure 12.2), an icon (which the user can control) indicates to others on an authorized list of contacts whether you are currently available. Holding an open calendar for all team members can show when people will be available. Characterizations of an individual's expertise are accessible to team members to suggest how he or she can effectively be mobilized to the project. For instance, nearly all the editorial work in *MIS Quarterly* is handled virtually. A repository of all associate editors describes their expertise, their current load, and their availability. The senior editor can effectively allocate new tasks on the basis of this information. Thus the leadership roles necessary for effective GSS are partially built into the functionality of the GSS.

### 5.5 Anonymity and GSS

Anonymity is an important aspect of group support systems (GSS). In GSS anonymity means that the electronic communication submitted by an individual does not contain any identifying attributes. In other words, other persons reading the communication cannot ascertain who submitted the communication. Anonymity is expected to improve communication and decision making, to enhance group performance, and to increase the number and quality of ideas generated in a brainstorming session.

Anonymity has been seen as an important variable in the encouragement of contributions from minorities and women, who are often less vocal in face-to-face situations. This lack of voice can be due to the nature of the individuals themselves (e.g., shy or retiring personalities). Sometimes this lack of voice is due to the leader in the face-to-face situation who consciously or subconsciously does not call on the minorities or women in the group to solicit their opinions.

Various social processes in decision-making groups (such as inhibition due to a low position in the management hierarchy) are considered detrimental to the quality of decisions. It is often assumed that removing the ability of groups to exert strong social influence on their members improves group decisions. Anonymity is seen as a tool to reduce the impact of the group over its members, and therefore as the key to improved group performance. However, some studies have shown that although anonymity does increase the number of ideas that are generated, these ideas are not necessarily of a high quality. Thus the gains of generating more ideas may be negated by the necessity of increased time for evaluation of these ideas (Connelly et al., 1990).

When designing GSS, it is important to consider the aspect of anonymity. A careful decision based on situational variables should be made as to whether to allow anonymous contributions. If the designer is not sure of the best option for the situation, a test run with anonymous and named contributions could be run to determine the best options.

## ▶ 6. ENTERPRISE-LEVEL SYSTEMS

An understanding of the enterprise level reveals new considerations for supporting communication and knowledge sharing. We review here two organizational models that explain the hierarchical structure of organizations and the distribution of power in organizations to examine their implications on support systems. These models are referred to as organizational macro models versus organizational behavior models, which relate to individual behavior within the organizational setting. We first introduce another collaborative technology, the "Wiki," which aims to promote knowledge sharing within and across organizations and communities.

### 6.1 Wiki

Think of a dynamic Web site that anyone can not only read but also edit and is used to create and share knowledge among members of an organization or community. This is a very crude description of Wiki as a collaborative system. Relying on relatively highly accessible technology, Wiki applications are rapidly spreading into corporations. They are inexpensive (usually built on open source), technologically simple (using standard HTML on the Internet), relatively quick to create knowledge, and well suited for decentralized organizations (Wagner, 2004).

The name Wiki means "quick" in Hawaiian. It's quick to learn and quick to create and share knowledge. One of the most popular Wiki-based systems is the Wikipedia, known as the free online encyclopedia (http://en.wikipedia.org). Figure 12.7 shows a typical entry of the encyclopedia, which has four tabs: "project page," "discussion," "edit this page," and "history." The first presents the current version of the article, the second enables an open discussion about the topic on a discussion board, the third lets

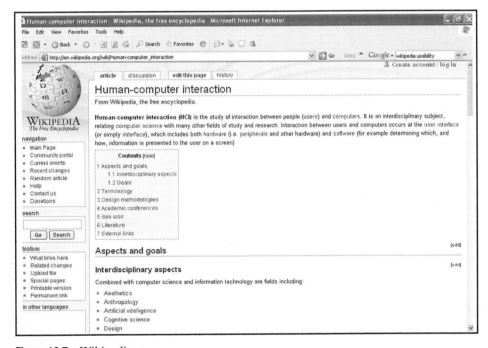

**Figure 12.7** Wikipedia.

the user edit the page, and the fourth keeps a record of all changes made to the page. The article in the figure is about the efforts of Wikipedia's usability group to redesign the main page.

Wiki-based systems are expected to adhere to several design principles. They are to be open to grant users complete freedom to do anything they wish to the Wiki pages. This sounds chaotic and it is, but generally users appear not to misuse this freedom. Another interesting design principle is that the Wiki design is organic, meaning that the system grows and evolves as the actual physical work and know-how develop over time. Ideally, there is no distinction between the actual and the representation (a perfect cognitive fit). Other principles such as incremental development and voluntary development characterize what has become known as "social computing." Perhaps the most striking feature of Wiki-based systems is the trust among their members. Members, who invest in creating knowledge and who are aware that other members are entitled to edit and delete their work, trust others not to act inappropriately. Unfortunately, Wiki can be abused or mistakenly misused. Wiki-based systems usually maintain some control mechanisms, such as rollback procedures.

New versions of Wiki are improving and adapting Wiki to business environments. A leading open-source supplier, JotSpot, is supplying versions of Wiki to serve as enterprise systems. They include more control mechanisms and more structured representations of knowledge and information. The idea is that the work processes use Wiki-based systems so that the actual work process becomes the knowledge managed. Figure 12.8 shows a screen that supports a work process for recruiting employees, but at the same time the application is also a Wiki page, part of the organizational system to help share knowledge. For example, members of the organization would be able to locate this screen when searching for information about recruiting practices. The recruiting screen, along with many other application screens, is taken from an Application Gallery of ready-made templates of common applications.

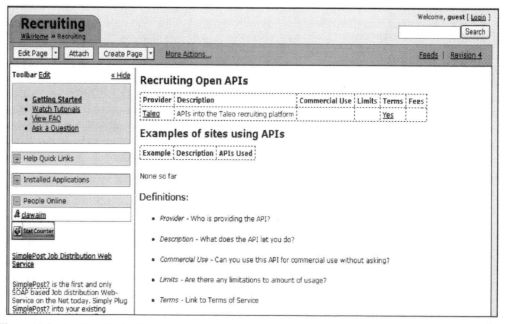

**Figure 12.8**  JotSpot Web site.

## 6.2 Anthony's Triangle (Also Known as Anthony's Pyramid)

A concept called Anthony's Triangle has been a guiding framework for (1) the classification of information systems, (2) the purposes of these systems, and (3) the corresponding levels of the managers who use the systems (Anthony, 1965). Figure 12.9 depicts Anthony's Triangle. The triangle or pyramid shape indicates that the systems at the bottom operational level are larger, serve more people, and require more organizational resources. The systems at the bottom level are referred to as operational information systems (OIS) or transaction processing systems (TPS). The users and managers who work with these systems are at the lower levels of the organization. The managers are generally supervisors and the workers are line workers. These systems support the basic business of the organization. Without these systems, most businesses would not be able to function. The level of information provided by these systems is quite detailed and usually accounting-oriented.

At the middle level of the pyramid are the management information systems (MIS). Middle managers are the primary users of these systems. These systems are often referred to as "reporting" systems and provide tactical information to organizations. Budgeting, forecasting, summarizing, and exception reporting are all tasks that these MIS perform. In the past 10 years, the number of middle managers in large organizations has declined. One reason for this is that computerized information systems have automated the duties of middle managers, and therefore fewer are needed. These systems have also allowed managers to expand the number of workers under their direction (span of control), which in turn reduces the number of managers needed for organizational effectiveness. The level of information provided by these systems is fairly summarized and is focused on current performance and tactical planning.

The top level of information systems are referred to as strategic information systems. Such systems as decision support systems (DSS), executive information systems (EIS), expert support systems (ESS), and strategic information systems (SIS) are all associated

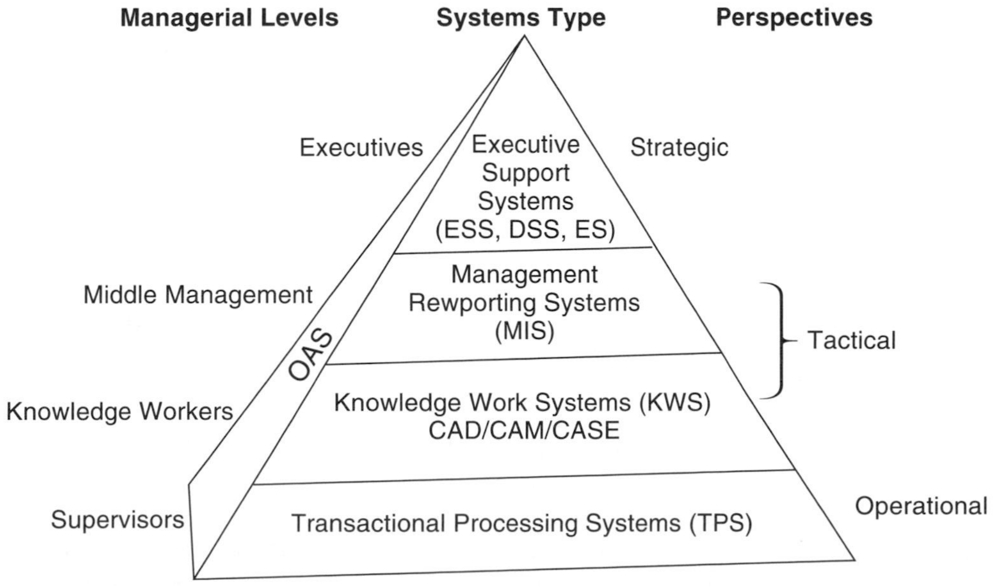

> **Anthony's Triangle:** Classifies the levels of information systems and the levels of managerial users of these systems.

**Figure 12.9**  Anthony's Triangle (Pyramid).

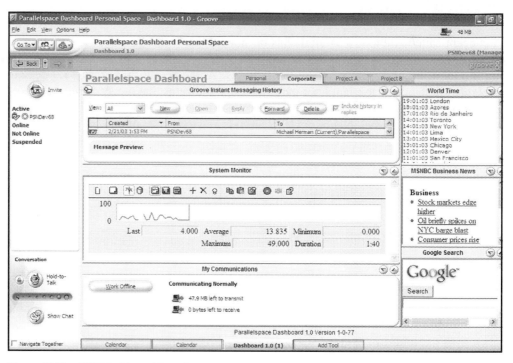

**Figure 12.10** ESS dashboard interface.

with this level. Top-level managers who are involved in strategic planning for organizations are supported by these systems (although both EIS and ESS are often found to support managers and workers lower on the pyramid as these systems mature). The information provided by these systems is often future-oriented and summarized. Information flows can also be illustrated through the triangle. In a formal organization, information typically flows from top to bottom. In a flatter, more informal organization, information flows from bottom to top and also across from peer to peer. The triangle is also useful for explaining the role of information within the various systems. For example, in executive support systems (ESS), drill-down capability (taking aggregate information down to the specific data that comprise the summary) can be easily understood by moving from the executive or top level (ESS) down through the MIS level (reporting systems) to the bottom level or OIS (operational information systems).

Anthony's pyramid is useful for understanding how information systems, their users, and their purposes fit into the organizational context.

Consider two ESS examples that involve HCI. Executives often want to drill down to a particular detail but find it very difficult to locate the textual detail out of context. With graphics, it is usually easier to capture the overall context and the detailed object within its physical context. One of the earliest reported ESS was a system at Lockheed that allowed the manager to zoom in on any area of the plant to see the status of a particular aircraft (Watson, Rainer, & Koh, 1991). Another example is the difficulty of keeping track of all the relevant information in the organization—the higher you are in the pyramid, the more information may be of interest to you. An interesting metaphor is the corporate dashboard. In one display, you organize an overview of the organizational activities and important links to people and information sources. The idea is first to select the relevant sources of information and then to display it in a manner that makes it easy to monitor changes and initiate action. Figure 12.10 is an example of a corporate dashboard.

## 6.3 Communication Support Systems

Whether positive or negative, it is certain that electronic communications systems impact organizations significantly and that the user interfaces of these systems can be designed to provide richer social cues and thus ameliorate the negative effects. One of the authors of this book, Dov Te'eni (2001), proposes a cognitive-affective model of organizational communication and suggests that "the issue for designers of communication support systems has become broader: how should technology be designed to make communication more effective by changing the medium and the attributes of the message itself?" (p. 251). His working assumption is that effective communicators adapt their behavior by changing the medium, the message, and the communication process itself to best fit their communication goal and the situation they face. He posits a model that incorporates three main ideas:

> **Cognitive-affective model of communication (Te'eni)** explains how effective communicators adapt their behavior to reduce complexity

- Communications have inputs including values and norms, task, and distance between the sender and receiver.
- Communication processes are both cognitive and affective.
- Communication processes impact actions and relationships.

A common thread that links these three ideas is a set of communication strategies aimed at reducing complexity by adapting to the situation and the communication goal. For instance, in culturally diverse teams, communicators include more contextual information in their messages, and in sensitive communications, communicators exercise more control over the communication. This model yields five area of focus for designers of communications systems:

- Mechanisms for structuring the context information
- Feedback that enhances sender control (e.g., receiver reactions, media manipulation, monitoring progress, and cataloging and storing of messages)
- Augmentation of attention and focus
- Conveying and monitoring affectivity
- Presenting receiver's perspective (via cognitive maps [see Figure 12.11] or physical objects)

Let us consider two examples of implications of the Te'eni model. An example of augmentation of attention and focus is creating *awareness* of the communication message and, more importantly, of the communication partner. Imagine, for example, a display of views of offices in which your colleagues work so that you can track their whereabouts throughout the day (putting privacy issues aside for the moment).

A second example has to do with structuring context information. *Spider* (Boland, Tenkasi, & Te'eni, 1994) is designed to present context in a variety of forms to support richer communication. The system displays the different rationales behind an issue in the form of cognitive maps that highlight the similarities and differences in the communicators' perspectives. But solving one problem may introduce another, namely information overload. Using dialog designs that hide information but make it available when needed through hypertext messages was implemented in kMail (Schwartz & Te'eni,

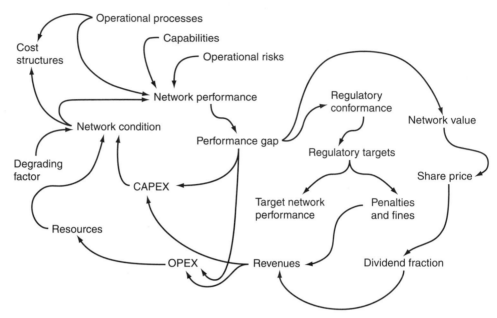

**Figure 12.11**  Sample cognitive map presents user's mental model.

2000). Regular e-mails are parsed to determine what context information is relevant to the message and then added as a set of hyperlinks. The receiver can then access this context information to understand the sender's perspective. Figure 12.12 shows a message that was augmented automatically in kMail.

## ▷ 7.  ENTERPRISE-LEVEL IMPLEMENTATION ISSUES

### 7.1  Innovation Diffusion Theory

> **Innovation Diffusion Theory:** Explains the way in which organizations implement innovations.

The relationship between organizational success and innovation is rather hazy and seems to be industry-specific. It is fairly widely accepted that high-tech companies must be innovative to be successful. What is the role between innovation and information systems? This section will explore this relationship and draw some conclusions.

An innovation is an idea, object, or process that is perceived as new and is transformed into action or implemented. An idea by itself does not become an innovation until it is implemented. A great deal of literature exists about the diffusion of innovation. Rogers (1983) lists five key characteristics about successful innovations:

- Relative advantage (compared to other products)
- Compatibility (with existing values)
- Complexity (or rather simplicity of implementation)
- Trialability (ability to produce and test with minimal effort)
- Observability (results are apparent to adopter and prospective adopters)

Information and communication channels play an important role in the innovation diffusion process. In consumer product diffusion, the communication channels are usually mass media and in particular television. In organizational innovation, the communication

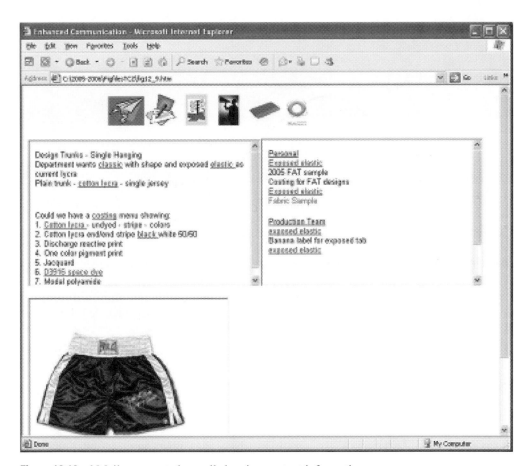

**Figure 12.12**   kMail-augmented e-mail showing context information.

channels vary from direct one-to-one communication or word of mouth, to observation, to formal reports, and so on. Much diffusion occurs by potential adopters modeling the behavior of their near-peers.

One successful technique for intentionally promoting information technology innovation is that of using an information technology (IT) champion to "sell" the technology to the organization (Beath & Ives, 1989). The IT champion should come from the early adopters and early majority categories in Rogers' (1983) innovation diffusion model (see Figure 12.13). Pioneers are seen by most members of an organization to exhibit "rash behavior" and therefore lack credibility. It is only when the early adopters adopt a new technology that the likelihood of organization-wide adoption occurs.

Rogers (1983) has determined that early adopters (and pioneers) are more highly educated, have more favorable attitudes toward science and education, are more able to cope with change, are more socially oriented, are more cosmopolitan, are more exposed to mass media, are more likely to engage in interpersonal communication, and are more upwardly mobile. All of these characteristics seem to ensure that others in the organization will respect their opinions.

Beath and Ives (1989) suggest that organizations that exhibit the following characteristics are most likely to foster successful IT champions:

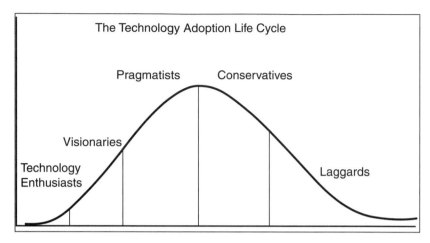

**Figure 12.13**  Innovation Diffusion Model.

- Norms and policies that encourage and reward innovation
- Interdependence or interconnectedness between members (to enhance information flows)
- Slack resources for scanning and experimentation (to explore innovations without penalty)
- Network-forming devices (such as matrix management and team formation)
- Specialization of individuals rather than generalization
- Placement of a high organizational value on accumulation of knowledge or learning

Once potential IT champions are identified, they need three tools to be successful (Kanter, 1985): (1) information for evaluation and persuasion, (2) resources (staff time and computers), and (3) support from the organization. It is not likely that a good IT champion will come from the internal ranks of the IT group.

The linkage between information systems and internal diffusion of innovation is fairly clear. Identification and support of IT champions can improve the likelihood that successful innovations will occur and then diffuse through the organization.

## 7.2  Technology Acceptance Model and the Organizational Level

We already introduced the Technology Acceptance Model (TAM) (Davis, 1989) at the individual level in Chapter 6. TAM has been widely used for predicting the acceptance and use of information technologies (IT). The factors determining attitude and intention posited by TAM are perceived ease of use and perceived usefulness. Perceived ease of use and complexity (opposite of ease of use) have been shown to be important in innovation diffusion in general and in IT diffusion in particular. Understanding TAM and applying it to organizational usage of technology has the potential to improve the payoff in IT investments.

Organizational investments in information technology to support planning, decision making, and communication processes are inherently risky. To make effective use of this technology, managers, professionals, and operating employees must accept the applications, learn how to interact directly with aspects of the hardware and software, and adapt the technology to their task requirements. Understanding why people accept or reject

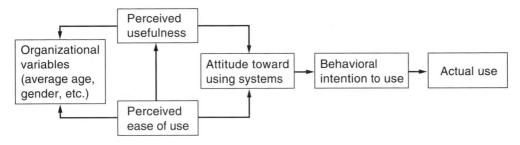

**Figure 12.14** Extended Technology Acceptance Model.

computers has proven to be one of the most challenging issues in information systems research.

Phillips, Calantone, and Lee (1994) used TAM to investigate the influence of culture and demand certainty on international technology adoption. They found that cultural affinity has a significant and positive influence on TAM through perceived ease of adoption. They found that when demand is certain, the influence of culture is stronger and more positive than when demand is uncertain.

Venkatesh, Morris, Davis, and Davis (2003) looked at eight different models and a multitude of data samples regarding technology acceptance and developed a "unified view." They determined that gender, age, experience, and voluntariness all had a significant effect on such behavioral intentions as performance, effort, and social influence. These findings have implications when introducing new technologies into organizations. Figure 12.14 shows the extended TAM model.

The organizational variables such as age and gender affect acceptance and therefore should be considered in design and implementation. Recall the case of recommendations in GSS communicated with knowledge-based explanations. It appears that novices more readily adopt recommendations of GSS in comparison to experts (Nah & Benbasat, 2004). This is because experts are more confident of their opinions and more critical of others' opinions. Knowing characteristics of users is therefore important in designing systems to increase the likelihood of acceptance.

## ▶ 8. E-COMMERCE: LINKING THE CUSTOMER TO THE ENTERPRISE

Trust seems to be essential to the success of e-commerce transactions. Online consumers must be confident that transactions are executed completely and accurately. Furthermore, they are concerned about the privacy and safety of transaction details such as credit card numbers.

The importance of trust suggests that design aspects of the e-commerce transaction interface must be executed with trust issues in mind. One of the signals of secure transactions is a pop-up dialog box that alerts the user when he or she is about to enter or leave a secure transaction environment. Allowing the user control over entering and leaving the environment with a click on an OK button also supports the perception of trust.

Another design aspect that has been shown to enhance trust in online auctions is a mechanism such as eBay's Feedback Forum (Ba & Pavlou, 2002). The forum allows buyers to report on specific sellers and their products. The inference is that disreputable

sellers will be exposed and eliminated from the site. Trust can mitigate information asymmetry by reducing transaction-specific risks, therefore generating price premiums for reputable sellers. In addition, the research also examines the role trust plays in mitigating the risks inherent in transactions that involve very expensive products.

A recent study of trust in e-commerce (Cheskin, 1999) concludes that a Web site's trustworthiness is a function of time and site characteristics. First, trust evolves in time from apparent chaos to trustworthiness. Second, the important site characteristics include effective navigation (elements of perceived ease of use) and perceived usefulness. Additionally, sites are more trusted when their brand is known and when they have recognized seals of security approval and evidence of use of recognized security technologies. Third, these characteristics can complement one another (e.g., lesser-known brand must have quality navigation).

## 8.1 Trust and TAM in Online Shopping

Gefen, Karahanna, and Straub (2003) explore the issues of trust and TAM in the online shopping experience. Online shopping consists of a separate and distinct interaction with an e-vendor and with its e-transaction interface. Research conducted on experienced, repeat online shoppers demonstrates that consumer trust is as important to online commerce as the widely accepted TAM use antecedents, which are perceived usefulness and perceived ease of use. Together, these variable sets are related to consumer intention to buy. The study also purports that online trust is composed of (1) a belief that the vendor has nothing to gain by cheating, (2) a belief that there are safety mechanisms built into the Web site, and (3) the existence of a standard interface.

Items 1 and 2 are directly related to interface design issues. The overarching rule of interface consistency is once again shown to be important. Experienced e-shoppers have come to expect a familiar or standard look and feel for e-transactions. They are expecting shopping cart–type interfaces and pop-up dialog boxes that alert them when they are entering or leaving a secure environment (see Figure 12.15). The e'Gourmet running case also illustrates a number of standard Web-based transaction screens.

Increasingly e-commerce crosses national cultures, so it is important to know whether the same site characteristics are perceived to be trustworthy in different cultures. We previously noted the dimensions of cultural differences, including individualistic versus collectivist cultures. Individualists are usually characterized by a utilitarian perspective and are expected to engage in calculative processes to form trust. They therefore rely on information about actual cases and willie usually trust the system until they are let down by it. In contrast, collectivists are characterized by an interdependent perspective and are more likely to base their trust on known relationships. They will usually engage in transference processes based on the recommendation of trustworthy friends. Collectivists, in comparison, will be more influenced by reputation.

Unfortunately, there is very little empirical support for such assertions. Jarvenpaa and Tractinsky (2000) could not identify strong cultural differences as hypothesized above (they compared Australians, who are high on ndividualism, with Israelis, who are low on individualism). However, the authors suggest that we need to be sensitive to cultural differences in trust formation, particularly in e-commerce environmnts.

## 8.2 Consumer Behavior Models

How do e-shoppers determine which products to purchase once they develop a sense of trust and technology acceptance? One theory that purports to explain choice and pre-

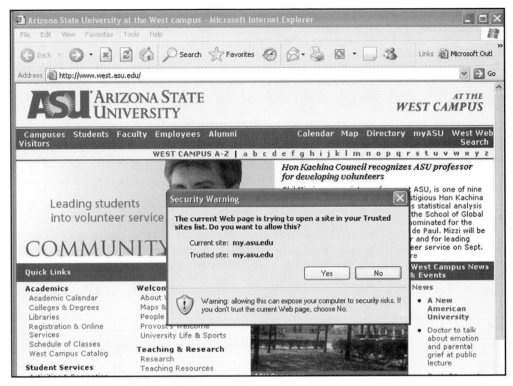

**Figure 12.15** Security Alert dialog box promoting trust.

choice behavior is put forth by Beach (1993). Beach's theory posits that decision makers use a series of discrete steps in narrowing their consideration sets to arrive at their final choice. Beach (1993) and Beach and Potter (1992) demonstrate that the screening of choice options (the initial stage) is qualitatively different from choosing the best option (the final stage). The image theory view of decision making is a two-stage process where screening is followed by choice.

> **Beach's Image Theory of Screening:** States that decision making is a two-stage process; screening is the first stage, followed by choice.

Understanding the way in which e-shoppers make purchase decisions is important to interface design. Interfaces may be designed to support a rational decision process. The field of visualization may inform HCI design. Such interface controls as filters based on decision criterion ranges could be built into the screening process to come up with a set of acceptable products and then the final choice.

A popular model of consumer behavior is the Engel, Blackwell, and Miniard (1995) model of the consumer decision process (referred to as the EBM model). The authors identify five steps in the decision process: need recognition, information search, alternative evaluation, purchase, and post-purchase evaluation. Applying ideas similar to TAM's perceived usefulness and ease of use, Teo and Yeong (2003) show how EBM can be used to explain the impact of e-store design on consumers' willingness to buy. For instance, when the users perceive higher benefits of information search (e.g., expect to find price reductions), they will pay more attention and invest more effort in using the system to search for information, which will eventually increase their intention to purchase. By the same token, increasing support for information search (e.g., making it easier to define a query) will also lead to actual information search and thereby increase the consumer's willingness to purchase.

**Table 12.2**  Steps in the Consumer Decision Process (EBM)

| Step | Example Operations |
| --- | --- |
| Recognize need | Identify needs by organizing display consistent with the way products are organized in private context or by reminding consumer of needs on the basis of user's history. |
| Search information | Easy navigation in e-store by consistent and known structures. Providing personalized information that eliminates irrelevant information. |
| Evaluate alternatives | Easy evaluation by attributes or aspects (such as price) defined to be important to the particular consumer. Easy access to objective evaluations. |
| Purchase | Make purchasing attractive by stimulating positive affect (pleasant music and colors). Make purchasing easy by providing a shopping cart to easily manage the products purchased or by adding a "product on sale" before payment. Build trust in the system (e.g., secure payment). |
| Evaluate after purchase | Provide post-sale support such as tracking orders and online help and repair service. |

More generally, we can construct a list of operations (functionality) to support the steps in the EBM model. Table 12.2 shows the five steps of online purchasing behavior and corresponding examples of operations to support each step and lead to a higher propensity to buy.

Table 12.2 can be regarded as a template with examples for a task analysis of online purchasing. The principles of design based on physical, cognitive, and affective engineering should be applied to each step separately and to the process as a whole. For instance, for certain physical products, such as handheld devices, only 3-D product visuals can enable accurate comparisons of the devices. As we examine these steps in more depth, we will need to rely more heavily on consumer behavior models. For example, consumers are influenced by visual primes in the way they attend to information (e.g., early signals of money may bias the consumer toward information about prices). In an experiment that compared different Web site backgrounds for an e-store that sells sofas or cars, consumers were primed by either signals of money (dollar signs on the screen background) or signals of quality (cloudy background that signals comfort). As expected, consumers primed with money chose the cheaper but lower-quality products and those primed with quality chose the reverse (Mandel & Johnson, 2002). Finally, pleasant colors or "elevator" music can create a more complying attitude and higher readiness to purchase (see Chapter 6 on affective engineering).

## ▷ 9. SUMMARY

This chapter presents the foundational models and frameworks for interpersonal relationships within the organizational context. Trust is discussed as a construct that is important to relationships between two entities. Various models that help us to understand the work group level and the organizational level are presented. The last section presents two consumer models from the marketing literature, both of which have implications for human–computer interactions in Web site interactions.

It is clear that human–computer interaction (HCI) takes place within an organizational context and that context impacts HCI in many ways. Such performance variables as productivity, user satisfaction, time to complete tasks, quality of decision making, and others are all impacted by organizational context. The converse is also true; computer usage and information systems have an impact on organizations. Organizational structure, centrality, power bases, innovation, reengineering, and other characteristics are all heavily influenced by information systems and human–computer interaction.

In both directions, the impact may be positive or negative. For the most part, the quantitative outcome variables are positively influenced by human–computer interaction (although measurement of white-collar productivity is difficult and current methods do not seem to capture the level of productivity increase that we intuitively believe is there). Further research is needed to provide empirical evidence of these generalizations. The philosophy of the authors of this book is that, whenever possible, human–computer interaction should add to the richness and quality of work life rather than detract from it.

## ▷ 10. SUMMARY OF CONCEPTS AND TERMS

| | |
|---|---|
| Anthony's Triangle | Beach's Image Theory of Screening |
| Collaboration software | Hofstede's Model of Cultural Differentiation |
| Innovation diffusion theory | Social identity and de-individuation processes |
| | Trust |

## ▷ 11. BIBLIOGRAPHY

Anthony, R. (1965). Planning and control systems: A framework for analysis, Cambridge. Boston, MA: Harvard University Graduate School, Business Administration.

Ba, S., & Pavlou, P. A. (2002). Evidence of the effect of trust building technology in electronic markets: Price premiums and buyer behavior. *MIS Quarterly, 26*(3), 243–268.

Beranek, P. M., Broder, J., Reinig, B. A., Romano, N. C., & Sump, S. (2005). Management of virtual project teams: Guidelines for team leaders. *Communications of the AIS, 16,* 247–259.

Beach, L. R. (1993). Broadening the definition of decision-making: The role of pre-choice screening of options. *Psychological Science, 4*(4), 215–220.

Beach, L. R., & Potter, R. E. (1992). The pre-choice screening of alternatives. *Acta Psychologica, 81,* 115–126.

Beath, C. M., & Ives, B. (1989). The information technology champion: Aiding and abetting, care and feeding. In P. Gray, W. R. King, E. R. McLean, & H. J. Watson (Eds.), *The management of information systems.* Chicago: Dryden Press.

Bjorn-Andersen, N., Eason, K., & Robey, D. (1986). *Managing computer impact: An international study of management and organizations.* Norwood, NJ: Ablex.

Boland, R., Tenkasi, R., & Te'eni, D. (1994). Designing information technology to support distributed cognition. *Organization Science, 5*(3), 456–475.

Briggs, R. O., Nunamaker, J. F., & Sprague, R. H. (1997/98). 1001 unanswered research questions in GSS. *Journal of Management Information Systems, 14*(2), 3–21.

Connolly, T., Jessup, L. M., & Valacich, J. S. (1990). The effects of anonymity and evaluative tone on idea generation. *Management Science, 36*(6), 689–703.

Cramton, C. D. (2001). The mutual knowledge problem and its consequences for dispersed collaboration. *Organization Science, 12*(3), 346–371.

Daft, R. L., & Macintosh, N. B. (1981). A tentative exploration into the amount and equivocality of information processing in organizational work units. *Administrative Science Quarterly, 25*, 207–224.

Davis, F. (1989). Perceived usefulness, perceived ease of use, and user acceptance of information technology. *MIS Quarterly, 13*(3), 319–340.

Diehl, M., & Stroebe, W. (1987). Productivity loss in brainstorming groups: Toward the solution of a riddle. *Journal of Personality and Social Psychology, 53*(3), 497–509.

Engel, J. F., Blackwell, R. D., & Miniard, P. W. (1995). *Consumer behaviour* (8th ed.). Fort Worth: Dryden Press.

Gefen, D., Karahanna, E., & Straub, D. W. (2003). Trust and TAM in online shopping: An integrated model. *MIS Quarterly, 27*(1), 51–90.

Hofstede, G. (1991). *Cultures and organizations.* New York: McGraw-Hill.

Jarvenpaa, S. L., Tractinsky, N., & Vitale, M. (2000). Consumer trust in an Internet store. *Information Technology and Management, 1*, 45–71.

Kanter, R. M. (1985). Innovation—The only hope for times ahead. In *The Best of MIT's Sloan Management Review.* Boston, MA: The Sloan School, MIT.

Komiak, S. X., & Benbasat, I. (2004). Understanding customer trust in agent-mediated electronic commerce, web-mediated electronic commerce and traditional commerce. *Information Technology and Management, 5*(1&2).

Kracher, B., Corritore, C. L., & Wiedenbeck, S. (2005). A foundation for understanding online trust in electronic commerce. *Information Communication & Ethics in Society, 3*(3), 131–141.

Lim, L. H., Raman, K. S., & Wei, K. K. (1994). Interacting effects of GDSS and leadership. *Decision Support Systems, 12*(3), 199–211.

Majchrzak, A., Rice, R. E., Malhotra, A., & King, N. (2000). Technology adaptation: The case of a computer-supported inter-organizational virtual team. *MIS Quarterly, 24*(4), 569–600.

Mandel, N., & Johnson, E. J. (2002). When Web pages influence choice: Effects of visual primes on experts and novices. *Journal of Consumer Research, 29*(2), 235–245.

McGrath, J. E. (1984). *Groups: Interaction and performance.* Englewood Cliffs, NJ: Prentice-Hall.

Mejias, R. J., Lazeneo, L., Rico, A., Torres, A., Vogel, D. R., & Shepherd, M. (1996). *A cross-cultural comparison of GSS and non-GSS consensus and satisfaction levels within and between the U.S. and Mexico.* Paper read at Hawaii International Conference on Systems Science.

Moorman, C., Deshpande, R., & Zaltman, G. (1993). Factors affecting trust in market research relationships. *Journal of Marketing, 57*(1), 81–101.

Morgan, R. M., & Hunt, S. D. (1994). The commitment-trust theory of relationship marketing. *Journal of Marketing, 58*(8), 20–38.

Nah, F. F., & Benbasat, I. (2004). Knowledge-based support in a group decision making context: An expert-novice comparison. *Journal of the AIS, 5*(3), 125–150.

Parent, M., & Gallupe, R. B. (2001). The role of leadership in group support systems failure. *Group Decision and Negotiation, 10*, 405–422.

Phillips, L. A., Calantone, R., & Lee, M. T. (1994). International technology adoption: Behavior structure, demand certainty and culture. *The Journal of Business & Industrial Marketing, 9*(4), 16–25.

Potter, R. E., & Balthazard, P. A. (2002). Understanding human interaction and performance in the virtual team. *The Journal of Information Technology Theory & Application, 4*(1), 1–25.

Rogers, E. (1983). *Diffusion of innovations* (3rd ed.). New York: The Free Press.

Schwartz, D., & Te'eni, D. (2000). Tying knowledge to action with kMail. *IEEE Intelligent Systems, 15*(3), 33–39.

Sengupta, K., & Te'eni, D. (1993). Feedback in GDSS: Enhancing control and reducing conflict. *MIS Quarterly, 17*, 87–109.

Siegal, J., Dubrovsky, V., Kiesler, S., & McGuire, T. W. (1986). Group processes in computer mediated communication. *Organizational Behavior and Human Decision Processes, 37*, 177–187.

Social software. (2005). *Wikipedia*. Retrieved from http://en.wikipedia.org/wiki/Social_software.

Spears, R., & Lee, M. (1992). Social influence and the influence of the "social" in computer mediated communication. In M. Lea (Ed.), *Contexts of computer mediated communication*. Hemel Hempstead: Harvester Wheatsheaf.

Tan, B. C. Y., Watson, R. T., & Wei, K. K. (1995). National culture and group support systems: Filtering communication to dampen power differentials. *European Journal of Information Systems, 4*(2), 82–92.

Te'eni, D. (2001). A cognitive-affective model of organizational communication for designing IT. *MIS Quarterly, 25*(2), 251–312.

Te'eni, D., & Schwarz, A. (2004). Communication in the IS community: A call for research and design. *Communications of AIS, 13*, 520–543.

Teo, T. S. H., & Yeong, Y. D. (2003). Assessing the consumer decision process in the digital marketplace. *Omega, 31*, 349–363.

Venkatesh, V., Morris, M. G., Davis, G. B., & Davis, F. D. (2003). User acceptance of information technology: Toward a unified view. *MIS Quarterly, 27*(3), 425–478.

Watson, H., Rainer, R. K., & Koh, C. E. (1991). Executive Information Systems: A framework for development and a survey of current practices. *MIS Quarterly, 15*(1).

Watson, R. T., Ho, T. H., & Raman, K. S. (1994). Culture: A fourth dimension of group support systems. *Communications of the ACM, 37*(10), 44–55.

Wagner, C. (2004). Wiki: A technology for conversational knowledge management and group collaboration. *Communication of the Association for Information Systems, 13*, 265–289.

## ▶ 12. EXERCISES

Ex. 1. Think about e-mail versus face-to-face communication. What are the benefits and drawbacks of each?

Ex. 2. What is IM (instant messaging)? Compare and contrast IM with phone conversations and e-mail.

Ex. 3. Do you make purchases over the Internet? What concerns do you have about purchasing online? Do you trust all Web sites? What are the Web site characteristics that would make you fear entering your personal information?

Ex. 4. Figure 12.7 shows a Wikipedia entry on its Usability Group and its call to redesign the Wikipedia entry. Propose a new design of the main Wikipedia page based on a task analysis of what you consider are the main tasks accomplished by students using Wikipedia for their course work.

# 13

# SOCIAL AND GLOBAL ISSUES

## CONTEXT AND PREVIEW

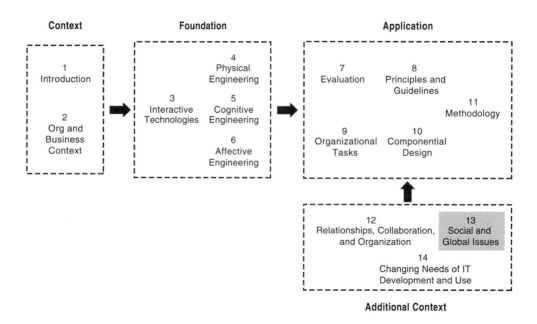

Chapter 12 provided the organizational context for HCI, exploring the nature of relationships between individuals, group, and organizational systems and work. The current chapter provides the larger social, ethical, and global context for HCI. This chapter presents some of the negative impacts that information systems bring to humankind and encourages a role of active advocacy for HCI practitioners. It is important to consider the larger consequences of information systems and in particular how human–computer interfaces may moderate those negative impacts. HCI designers are encouraged to think about the consequences of their work and to look beyond the immediate context. The chapter also explores the development of global software and the impact of the Internet on both social and global issues.

This chapter examines the social, ethical, and global context within which HCI design and development takes place. The social issues discussed in this chapter include anxiety, alienation, potency of the individual, speed and complexity, societal and organizational dependence, unemployment and displacement, and valuing of human diversity. Each social issue is presented and discussed along with the relevant HCI implications. Table 13.2 (see section 3.1 for a more complete explanation of this table) adds the ethical implications and global issues to these social issues. The ethical implications of information systems include accessibility, privacy, accountability, and property. Additionally software globalization and localization are discussed as well as the social and global impact of the Internet.

## LEARNING OBJECTIVES

Upon completion of this chapter, students should understand and be able to apply the following concepts:

- Define and discuss the nature of the social context of HCI development
- Define and discuss the nature of the global context of HCI development
- Understand and discuss the following social aspects of information systems and how HCI can ameliorate these aspects:
  - Anxiety
  - Alienation
  - Potency and impotency of the individual
  - Complexity and speed
  - Organizational and societal dependence
  - Unemployment and displacement
  - Valuing human diversity
- Understand and discuss the following ethical aspects of information systems and how HCI can ameliorate these aspects:
  - Accessibility
  - Accountability
  - Privacy
  - Property
- Understand how to utilize computers to support social responsibility
- Understand and apply the software globalization process
- Understand and apply the software localization process
- Understand and discuss the social and global impacts of the Internet

## ▷ 1.  INTRODUCTION

Chapter 12 looks at the organizational context within which human–computer interaction occurs. This chapter looks at the larger social and global context within which human–computer interaction occurs. This context extends beyond the boundaries of the organization into the private homes of individuals and into public places such as universities, libraries, and government agencies. This larger context cuts across all aspects of computer usage. We are concerned with two aspects of the social and global contexts: the impact of using information systems on society for which we, as developers, share the responsibility, and the impact of the context on the way we design information systems.

All the previous chapters are very analytical and focus on theory and the application of theory to create sound design. This chapter has a different focus. In this chapter we raise social and ethical issues surrounding information systems, relate them to the human concerns of HCI, and urge HCI professionals to take actions that address these issues.

The prevailing philosophy expounded here is one of active individual initiative regarding social responsibility. Computer specialists who are designing and building interfaces for information systems usually leave these issues to others. We agree with Ben Shneiderman (1990), who suggests that professionals who are developing information systems ask themselves the following basic questions:

- Have I considered individual differences among users in the design of my system?
- Have I considered the social and global context of users?
- Have I arranged for adequate participation of users in the design process?
- Have I considered how my design empowers users?

Additionally we add the question:

Have I considered the social responsibility impact of my design and of the resultant information system?

Positive answers to all these questions should result in a system that has been designed with the user in mind. The resultant systems should have a positive or at least a neutral impact on the quality of the user's life and perhaps society in general rather than a negative impact.

## ▶ 2. SOCIAL CONTEXT

This section explores potential negative impacts of information systems (Shneiderman, 1998; Shneiderman & Plaisant, 2005) and makes suggestions for HCI designers and developers for combating these problems. Table 13.1 lists each of the various social issues addressed in this section, the main human (primarily affective) concern for each issue, and the design implications raised by each issue.

### 2.1 Anxiety

Many people are afraid of computers. They are afraid to use them at all and afraid of the consequence of their use. As computers become more and more pervasive in our society, there is a feeling that computer phobia is less of a problem. That may be a fallacy. Perhaps a smaller proportion of the general population feel anxious about computers and their use, but those who experience anxiety are probably even more anxious than they were before when they were part of a majority rather than a minority. When most of the other people around are comfortable with computers, one must feel like an outsider.

What can designers do to alleviate the anxiety that inexperienced users may feel about the use of computers? The key lies in ease of use. Natural user interfaces that reinforce work processes, direct manipulation techniques such as touch screen and voice input, forgiving systems that trap errors and explain how to correct the errors, and systems that allow the user to feel in control rather than being controlled by the computer can all contribute to a lessening of anxiety.

What about those people who have never had the opportunity to use a computer? They probably not only experience anxiety but also must experience a sense of exclusion from experiences that many others share. How can we give this group access to positive computer experiences that will alleviate their anxiety and give them a positive attitude toward computers? A study by Carey-Young, Skelly, and Pitts (1983) found that usage

**Table 13.1**  Summary of Social Issues and Their Impacts on HCI

| Social Issues | Human Concern (Primarily Affective) | Implications for Design |
|---|---|---|
| Anxiety | Fear of computers | Design for ease of use and ease of learning<br>Standardization is critical |
| Alienation | Feelings of separation and disenfranchisement | Design to enrich computer-mediated interactions (i.e., add emotional indicators) |
| Potency and impotency of the individual | Feelings of powerlessness | Design to support empowerment (i.e., internal locus of control) |
| Complexity and speed | Feelings of bewilderment and confusion | Design to reduce complexity and give user control over rates of speed |
| Organizational and societal dependence | Feelings of helplessness and inability to perform | Design for reliability and human backup |
| Unemployment and displacement | Fear of financial incapacity | Design for job enrichment<br>Design retraining systems |
| Valuing human diversity | Feelings of belongingness and fit | Understand diverse user populations and design to fit |

of a system was the strongest predictor of positive attitude. The simple act of use can have a strong impact on attitude. Therefore, providing public access to computer-based systems should help lessen anxiety. In Hong Kong, for example, terminals that provide free access to the Internet can be found not only in shops and cafés but also in public services such as airports. More generally, such systems as computerized card catalogs at public libraries, ATMs (automatic teller machines), information kiosks at public malls and other public dwellings, walk-up computerized video games at arcades, and survey-gathering computers at public parks and recreation areas, to name a few, all provide opportunities for people to have initial contact with computers.

These initial contacts should be positive and not frustrating. We can all think of times when we have been frustrated with these very contacts. Many of these frustrations can be avoided by following the design principles and guidelines discussed in Chapter 8. However, the ubiquity of human–computer interaction in our daily lives intensifies some of the design issues raised. For example, anxiety due to inconsistent human–computer interfaces is a major source of frustration. Switching from one ATM to another, for instance, may cause us to encounter a very different interface. It would seem that standardizing the ATM interface across all machines would go a long way toward alleviating frustration. Computerized card catalogs often have specialized keys that must be pressed in order to take desired actions. Wouldn't it be better to use a standardized keyboard in combination with a touch screen or single-digit action? Since these design choices need to be made as universally as possible across multiple systems, good choices must be coordinated and agreed upon by groups of people who generally see themselves in competition with each other instead of choosing to collaborate on design standards. International standards bodies such as ANSI (American National Standards Institute) and ISI (International

Standards Institute) have formed groups to work on some of these issues. It is important for HCI designers to become familiar with the work of these standardization bodies. The presence of HCI designers in the membership of these bodies would likely advance the usability of the systems and technologies that are the focus of standardization. The first row in Table 13.1 relates to the social issue of anxiety (that is, fear of computers) and indicates that HCI designers can help to alleviate fear of computers by focusing on ease of use and ease of learning and by following international standards.

## 2.2 Alienation

Computers can contribute to feelings of alienation in society. Consider, for example, the changing nature of white-collar work in large organizations. In the past, workers would write memos, call on the telephone, or simply walk down the hall when they needed to communicate with others in the organization. Most of these face-to-face or at least voice-to-voice communications have been replaced with electronic mail, voice mail, or instance messaging. It is possible to have long, ongoing dialogues between people who never see each other or make direct phone contact.

For most of us, we view these computer-based electronic channels as time-saving and effective. However, we seldom think about the implications of going without direct human contact for long periods of time. We bank with machines, buy gas with machines, and do our work with machines, and many of us get much of our entertainment from machines. What does this replacement of human contact with machine contact mean to our quality of life and ability to get along in society? Are we creating a generation of people who cannot relate well to other humans and are also dependent on machines for stimulation and support?

What can designers and implementers of computer-based systems and social-technical engineers do to combat this potential alienation that is an unintended outcome of computer use? Chapter 6 discussed affective aspects of computing and the need to provide means for expressing emotions, not only factual content. The problem of alienation reinforces this need and prescribes it as an essential requirement of design even though it may not surface explicitly in the requirement analysis. Potential users are often not sensitive or do not even recognize many of the social problems mentioned in this chapter. For example, potential users of a communication support system may not be aware of the alienation problem until they experience it after months or years of interaction with the system. Designers must therefore be socially active and take the initiative to include the appropriate measures. Indeed, more and more communication support systems have emotion indicators that can be used to express feelings. Users have found adaptive ways in which to express their emotions. In graphic-based systems, users may express feelings through smiley faces that can be changed to express no emotion, anger, sadness, and so on (see Figure 13.1). In text-based systems, the user can use various "emoticons" to suggest mood (see Figure 13.2). The addition of multimedia to a communication system can add the actual voice or video of the persons communicating. These additions may serve to make the user feel more like she or he is communicating with a live person rather than some anonymous being at the other end of a linked machine. The promise of virtual reality also has the potential to make even long-distance, machine-based communication seem like "virtual" face-to-face

**Figure 13.1**  Assorted smiley faces.

| | |
|---|---|
| :) | classic smile |
| :-* | kiss |
| :-@ | screaming |
| :-< | very sad |
| :-c | very unhappy |
| :-] | tongue in cheek |
| ]:-> | devil |
| \|-o | Yawn |
| ':-) | raised eyebrow |

**Figure 13.2**  Emoticons (turn sideways to read).

communication. All of these ideas may serve to enrich the communication potential of the computer.

On the positive side, computers can also allow communication linkages between people who would otherwise be unable to communicate. The Internet has marvelous potential to link people to people and people to information across the world, to make the "global village" a reality. Computers with communication capabilities (bulletin boards and special interest groups) have been used to link caretakers of terminally ill patients with other caretakers to provide them with contact and support during this trying and very isolating activity (Brennen, 1993). Computers could also act as linkages to community for people physically isolated from each other because of location in geographically remote areas. Forest rangers in fire towers, scientists in remote areas, indigenous peoples in remote areas, and others all could benefit from connectivity to others via computers. Shortwave radios often support communication for these people now, but computers could support different-time, different-place communication while not requiring a "live" person at the other end at the exact time of communication.

Computer system designers and implementers must be proactive in finding positive uses for computer capabilities. Organizations that have a high-tech profile should take on socially responsible activities and support such positive endeavors. Academic researchers in the area of computer use should lend their expertise to find the "best practices" for such outreach efforts and work toward reducing the feelings of alienation that often accompany computer use. The second row in Table 13.1 relates to the social issue of alienation (i.e., feelings of separation and disenfranchisement) and suggests that HCI designers can help to alleviate alienation by focusing on the enrichment of computer-based interactions.

## 2.3 Potency and Impotency of the Individual

Modern life with its huge bureaucracies and rules and regulations already creates a feeling of impotence on the part of the individual. We often feel powerless as we go about our daily lives. The prevalence of computer-based systems as interfaces between people and organizations can add to our feelings of impotence. When a seemingly simple task, such as correcting a mistake in a bill, puts us in contact with a computer rather than another human we may feel powerless and frustrated. Designers and implementers of computer-based systems must build user interfaces that support internal locus of control. Internal locus of control means that an individual feels that he or she is in control of his or her environment. External locus of control may cause a perception that the external environment is in control of the individual. People with external locus of control may feel a lack of empowerment, behave less proactively, and take less responsibility for their own actions. All of these manifestations are less desirable than the opposite outcomes that are associated with internal locus of control. Therefore, designers should be aware of locus of control and try to design systems that support the internal locus of control. Design aspects that support internal locus of control include, but are not limited to, confirmation of user actions, choices for interaction (such as shortcut keys versus mouse clicks), text-only interfaces for persons with sight disabilities, context-sensitive help, navigation aids and clues, informative error messages that offer remedial options, and others.

On the other hand, using computers to accomplish work tasks can increase human potency. There is evidence from industry that computer usage enables people to be highly effective in accomplishing work tasks. Therefore, computers may empower people. Computers can also alleviate some of the more mundane tasks that people must perform and thereby allow them to focus on more important and critical tasks. Computers also increase the span of control of managers. In other words, one manager can manage more people with the support of the computer; thereby allowing subordinates to be more autonomous. All of these aspects are positive. Designers that develop user interfaces that help enfranchise and validate humans can help to dispel the feeling of impotence that often comes with computer usage. For example, a busy working mom may not have time to register to vote in person. Providing an online voter registration site may give this mom a feeling of empowerment and enfranchisement. The user interface is critical to the support of this task. A confusing and slow interface that does not give confirmation that the registration task has been completed may further frustrate and diminish the feeling of potency for the individual.

HCI professionals must be able to distinguish between aspects of systems and interfaces that reduce feelings of human potency and those that are empowering and then strive to design and implement those empowering aspects. The third row in Table 13.1 relates to the social issue of individual potency or feelings of powerless and suggests that HCI designers can help to alleviate it by focusing on the support of internal locus of control.

## 2.4 Complexity and Speed

Computers allow us to accomplish more tasks in less time. The interjection of computers into our daily lives increases the complexity and speed of our experiences. How can we reverse this trend? Should we reverse this trend?

Perhaps we should respond to this challenge by trying to make conscious decisions to slow down and simplify those activities that cause us to become anxious. For example, we may suffer "information overload" because of the thousands of chunks of information that are available to us in our workplace. We are buried under both a paper and electronic flurry of information. This overload causes us stress as we try to filter out that information that is irrelevant or at least less relevant to us so that we can attend to the information that we need to consider. Computer-based artificial intelligence systems have been and can be designed to act as a filter for us, thereby reducing the information load. We must remember that filtering systems may accidentally filter out information we really need, so periodic checks are needed to fine-tune the filtering system. Embedded models and heuristics and also profiles of individual "need to know" can be used to search for and filter information as it comes into or gets circulated around an organization. Intelligent agents have been incorporated into various systems to help us achieve our goals. For example, when we are trying to find a cheaper airline ticket or mortgage rate on the Internet, intelligent agents may be at work behind the scenes searching for the best options for us.

What about speed—can we do anything about the speed at which things happen and require responses that make us feel bewildered? This is perhaps a more difficult question. It does not make any intuitive sense to slow down computer-based processes. So perhaps the answer to this question lies in elimination of activities that require human intervention, thereby reducing both the perceived complexity and speed of the particular task. For example, a decision support system may require the user to select a particular mathematical model and specify data as inputs to the model. The human may make mistakes in the selection process that subsequently result in an incorrect decision. A well-designed user interface may use an intelligent question-and-answer format to support the model and data-selection processes and thus simplify the complexity from the user's perspective. In some cases, the designer can hide the processes that appear to be too fast and thus confusing by putting them in the background and then just alerting the user when the processes have been completed. That way, the user doesn't have to try to comprehend the intermediate steps but only the final solution.

Designers should take the issues of speed and complexity into consideration when they propose a new system or when they reengineer a current system. As designers, we often take steps to speed up processes and therefore it is somewhat difficult to think about slowing down processes. Think about the time it takes to download graphics when browsing the Internet. We recommend that graphic file size should be limited to support faster download time. However, we seldom think about slowing down other processes to allow for reflection. Sometimes slowing down or more preferably allowing the user to control the speed of the processes is an appropriate goal.

Combating complexity is a more natural goal for HCI designers than reducing speed. There is already a trend to simplify Web-based interfaces. Although portal sites like Yahoo and AOL have densely populated interfaces with flash and animated gifs and banners, most e-commerce sites have simplified the look and feelof their sites. This is in line with the design principles to improve performance, reduce effort, and value simplicity in design (see Chapter 8). Figures 13.3 and 13.4 illustrate the differences between a clean and simple well-designed e-commerce site and a complex and confusing site (also see figures in Chapter 1).

The fourth row in Table 13.1 relates to the social issue of complexity and speed, which may create feelings of bewilderment and confusion, and indicates that HCI designers can help to alleviate these feelings by focusing on simplicity of design and giving control of the rate of speed to the user.

## 2.5 Organizational and Societal Dependence

Societal dependence on computer-based systems means that if these systems break down, the society or organization breaks down. This possibility contributes again to a feeling of helplessness and reliance on machines. Recently, a light-emitting diode (LED) on a control panel in a nuclear plant burned out and caused a short in the wiring. From that simple act, the problem fanned out until that entire plant was shut down. Is this bad or good? From an efficiency point of view, this was bad since it cost a great deal of money to start up again, to say nothing of the cost due to loss of generating power. From an effectiveness point of view, that is what fail-safe systems are intended to do. Wouldn't it have been worse for the problem to go undetected and put the plant and surrounding area in jeopardy?

The key is for computers to behave reliably. They should shut down only as a result of a control action, not because of failure. Designers should design fail-safe systems that

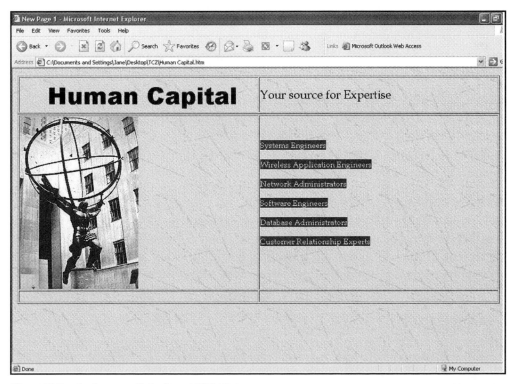

**Figure 13.3**  A clean, well-designed Web site.

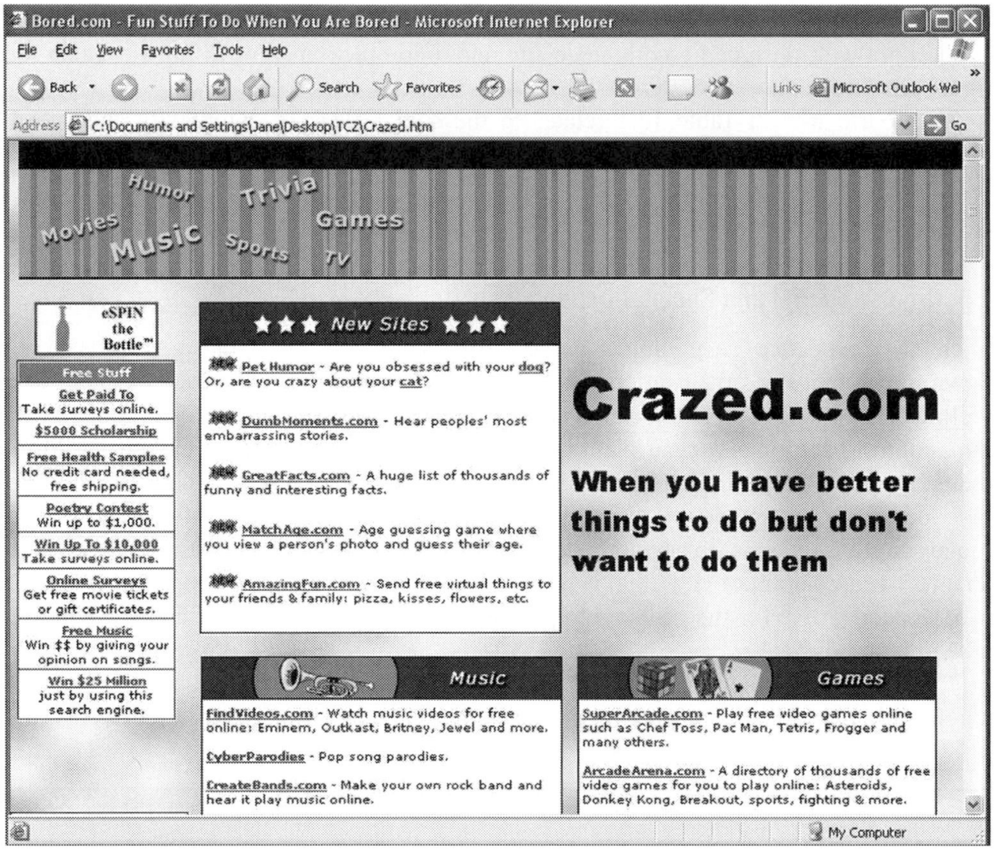

**Figure 13.4**  Too much complexity on a Web site. Although difficult to illustrate, there are three flashing graphics, multiple fonts, and several pop-up windows on this site.

are robust and not likely to break down. Breakdowns may be due to human errors; in those cases, systems should be designed to be forgiving, trapping human errors and correcting problems before they occur. Reliability is directly connected with careful design and thorough testing. New systems should be thoroughly tested before they are implemented. In cases where shutdown is due to hardware problems, backup systems should be available wherever possible and feasible. In all cases, manual override or backup should be provided. If the system breaks down, the whole organization should not have to come to a standstill. Good design and thorough testing can go far to combat this problem. The fifth row in Table 13.1 relates to the social issue of organizational and societal dependence, which gives users a feeling of helplessness and an inability to perform when the computer system is down or unavailable, and indicates that HCI designers can help to alleviate this feeling by focusing on reliability and human-based backup options.

## 2.6 Unemployment and Displacement

Reengineering and automation of work processes often leads to job displacement. Overall, when the economy is expanding, new jobs are being created, and the overall effect is one of stability in the unemployment figures; however, many individuals suffer short-term job displacement as a direct result of computer-based changes to work processes.

The amelioration of this problem cannot be the direct responsibility of systems designers since their job is to build efficient and effective systems. It is the responsibility of an organization to anticipate these changes and offer retraining and other jobs within the organization. Information systems professionals can urge their organizations to value the contributions of their workers and understand that overall employee morale and productivity can be directly affected by short-term job displacement. Policies that deal with this problem require farsighted organizations that are concerned with long-term environmental and societal impacts. We must all work to create a climate where the individual is valued and retained within the organization whenever possible. In today's world of software development, many programmer and technician jobs are being outsourced to offshore locations. Bangalore, India, is a center of IT job outsourcing. However, the PRC (Peoples' Republic of China) is now attracting some outsourced jobs away from India. There is a role for HCI in this complex issue. The authors believe that although it may be easy enough to outsource programming logic, usability testing and interface design and development do not lend themselves well to outsourcing. We believe that as the trend to outsource programming tasks increases, the roles of analysis and design will increase in importance and remain within organizations. HCI skills and experience will be more and more valued in this setting. See Chapter 14 for more information on this issue. The sixth row in Table 13.1 relates to the social issue of unemployment and displacement caused by information systems and indicates that HCI designers can help to alleviate the fear of financial incapacity by focusing on job enrichment and well-designed retraining systems for those persons who are displaced.

## 2.7 Valuing Human Diversity

What can computer-based systems do to increase the perception that humans, of diverse backgrounds and skills, are valued? The most obvious suggestion is to design interfaces that take human diversity into consideration. This is the last design principle described in Chapter 8. Interfaces should be flexible and adaptable for individuals with physical and learning disabilities. Interfaces should not reflect ethnocentric, sexist, age-related, religious, sexual orientation, or any other biases that may be present in human interaction. Designers should make clear design choices that reflect a neutral, unbiased interaction. Simplicity is important and also universality. In short, we must pay attention to good HCI design by applying the design guidelines outlined in Chapter 8.

Designers should not build interfaces that "talk down" to the users or make them feel powerless or stupid. The computer should be perceived as a tool to accomplish work, not as an anthropomorphic being that brings human prejudices with its interactions. Creating usable interfaces that are acceptable to all audiences should be the overarching goal of HCI work. The seventh row in Table 13.1 relates to the social issue of valuing human diversity and indicates that HCI designers can help to strengthen the feelings of belongingness and fit by understanding diverse user populations and designing to accommodate these users.

## ▷ 3. ETHICAL CONSIDERATIONS

### 3.1 Accessibility

As computers become more and more prevalent in our society, the consequences of the gap between those who have access to computers and those who do not become greater and greater. The old adage "knowledge is power" is very relevant to this problem. Consider the poor child in an urban neighborhood in pre-computer days. If she knew how to read, and experienced some triggering event that led her to explore the public library, the world of knowledge was nearly as accessible to her as it was to the richest citizen. Now, computer skills may be required to even gain access to the books in the public library and certainly to explore the online and offline databases that contain much of the reference material that was previously stored in hard copy form.

Computer literacy in the United States and most Western cultures is becoming more and more important to "full" citizenship. Those members of the information-poor minority are being victimized by their lack of access to computers and more importantly the information to which they provide linkages. More and more, students at universities need their own computers to facilitate their learning experiences. Scholarships are needed to provide those students who cannot afford computers with equal access. How can we provide access to those people who cannot afford computers? How can we provide usable access—and just as important, training—to these information-poor members of our society? One way is to provide computers and Internet access at public libraries and public schools. Training should also be provided. Grants to support this type of access should be part of the expenditures made to make the "information superhighway" a reality. It is up to those of us who are professionals in the information field to urge these measures and funds as a part of the planning process. To do that, we have to make our voices heard by writing or lobbying our legislators and influencing our international standards bodies.

What about the vast majority of the world's population that does not have computer access? The gap between the "have" and "have-not" countries in the information realm is growing more rapidly than the intracountry gap just discussed. The solutions are much more complex and require more than just money. The information infrastructure needed to link countries to countries and people to information does not exist in the majority of countries in the world. How can we afford to ameliorate these problematic gaps even if the will to do so exists? These are important problems that such bodies as the United Nations must deal with. From an information professional point of view, perhaps we can both urge progress along these lines and donate technical expertise via professional societies.

From an HCI point of view, we must make sure that the user interfaces that exist on public-access computers in public schools and public libraries (among other places) are as easy to use as possible. New and intermittent users should be able to use public-access computers without help and with a feeling of competence. As with the previous discussion of social issues, ethical issues reinforce the importance of the design guidelines described earlier. In particular, the digital divide calls for a widespread effort, perhaps enforced by international standards, to support diverse populations of users and require minimal skills to operate the systems.

Table 13.2 builds on Table 13.1 by adding a fourth column that links ethical implications to the social and global issues. For example, in the first row, last column, the ethical issue of accessibility is very important and is associated with five of the seven social issues, including anxiety, alienation, potency of the individual, complexity and speed,

**Ethical considerations:** The four main ethical considerations for information systems include accessibility, privacy, accountability, and property.

**Access:** Providing access to information via information systems and technologies is critical to full societal participation. HCI can play a role in breaking through barriers to access.

and valuing human diversity. Accessibility is also related to both globalization and localization of global software development.

**Table 13.2  Summary of Social Issue and Implications for HCI and Ethics**

| Social Issues | Human Concern (Primarily Affective) | Implications for Design | Ethical Implications |
|---|---|---|---|
| Anxiety | Fear of computers | Design for ease of use and ease of learning Standardization is critical | Accessibility, privacy, education, and training |
| Alienation | Feelings of separation and disenfranchisement | Design to enrich computer-mediated interactions (i.e., add emotional indicators) | Accessibility and accountability |
| Potency and impotency of the individual | Feelings of powerlessness | Design to support empowerment (i.e., internal locus of control) | Privacy and accessibility |
| Complexity and speed | Feelings of bewilderment and confusion | Design to reduce complexity and give user control over rates of speed | Accessibility and privacy |
| Organizational and societal dependence | Feelings of helplessness and inability to perform | Design for reliability and human backup | Accountability |
| Unemployment and displacement | Fear of financial incapacity | Design for job enrichment Design retraining systems | Job security and intellectual property |
| Valuing human diversity | Feelings of belongingness and fit | Understand diverse user populations and design to fit | Accessibility |

| Global Issues | Human Concern | Implications for Design | Ethical Implications |
|---|---|---|---|
| Globalization | Usefulness | Simplify functionality | Accessibility |
| Localization | Affective: cultural acceptance | Language and culturally specific icons | Accessibility |

## 3.2  Privacy

Computers provide information about individuals in ways we can only begin to understand. Credit bureaus in the United States such as Equifax and TRW have computerized data about almost all Americans. Holland is experimenting with a unified medical record that could be shared by all medical institutions and certain government agencies but at the same time preserve the patient's right to confidentiality and knowledge of the content of personal records. In many countries, government databases that are cross-indexed also contain information about individuals that should be private, not public. Unfortunately, firms such as TRW sell lists of individuals for marketing purposes. Much of the junk mail and telemarketing phone calls that arrive in our homes are due to the purchasing of these lists. Not only do the junk mail and annoying phone calls represent an invasion of our privacy, but they also represent a waste of natural resources such as trees (that produce the paper). More laws and regulations must be passed to protect our right to privacy. Junk mail and telemarketing are merely annoyances; what about the use of these databases to make decisions about employment or extending loans? Suppose that TRW has data about the medical history of an individual who is vying for a job? The human resources department in the hiring firm obtains this data and determines that the individual has a medical precondition that may cost the organization money in increased insurance premiums. Is it ethical, moral, or legal to use this information in the hiring decision?

**Privacy:** Protecting against public access to personal information about individuals.

In many countries, citizens have a constitutional or legal right to privacy. The laws are fairly clear on this. However, the entry of the computer and databases into this issue has created some gray areas that need more specific legislation. Until the legislation catches up with the computerized reality, it is up to socially responsible organizations to consider each release of data about employees, customers, and other constituencies in light of impact on personal privacy. Table 13.3 provides links to privacy principles (reported by third parties) in the United States, Canada, European Union, Brazil, and China.

As HCI practitioners, it is our ethical and moral duty to create interfaces that expose privacy infringements that underlie some applications. An example that comes to mind is the "cookies" that are stored on client machines when browsing some Web sites via the Internet. Users should be alerted to the fact that "cookies" are being created and they should be given the option to accept the "cookies" or not. Some applications inform the user that they must be able to accept cookies to effectively utilize a site. What is really needed is an alert box that allows the user to choose to accept the "cookie" or not. Table 13.2 links the ethical issue of privacy to the social issues of anxiety and potency of the individual.

**Table 13.3**  Privacy Principles in Various Countries

| | |
|---|---|
| **U.S.** | http://www.cdt.org/privacy/guide/basic/generic.html |
| **Canada** | http://canada.justice.gc.ca/en/news/nr/1998/attback2.html |
| **European Union** | http://www.cdt.org/privacy/guide/basic/generic.html |
| **Multiple countries** | http://www.privacyinternational.org/survey/phr2000/countriesag.html |
| **China** | http://www.privacyinternational.org/survey/phr2003/countries/china.htm |

### 3.3  Accountability

**Accountability:** Understanding who shares responsibility for the outcomes and impact of information systems.

It is tempting for information systems designers and users to put responsibility for ethical, social, and moral behavior onto the computer rather than accepting that responsibility themselves. Consider, for example, an expert system that makes suggestions for investment decisions. Who is responsible for loss of money if the system does not work due to system failure or bad advice? The designer? The user? The computer? The knowledge engineer? The expert from whom the investment rules were extracted? The placing of responsibility in this case is less clear than if a human investment counselor makes a recommendation. It is important that organizations set written policies that articulate responsibility and codes of conduct. The culture of an organization determines, to a great degree, what values and behaviors are acceptable. IS professionals should have their own universal codes of conduct that may serve to provide norms when organizations choose not to articulate their own norms. Table 13.2 links the ethical issue of accountability with the social issues of alienation and organizational and societal dependence on computer-mediated systems.

### 3.4 Intellectual Property

Intellectual property rights are complex and have economic and ethical implications. The origination of intellectual property can be extremely costly. However, once collected, it is easy to replicate and distribute. Since it is frequently in electronic, intangible form, it may be extremely difficult to safeguard.

> **Intellectual property:** An intellectual property is any product of the human intellect that is unique, is novel, and has some value in the marketplace. Electronic form of intellectual property is difficult to safeguard.

Consider the issue of software, music, and other types of intellectual property. People copy various forms of intellectual property for themselves and others with little regard for the loss of revenue for the creator or owner of these works. It is easy to forget that this act is really one of theft and is illegal as well as unethical. The "free" culture of the Internet has contributed to the felt norm that downloading and sharing of images, music, software, movies, and other files is not really a bad thing. Besides, users may think to themselves, everyone else is doing it and if I stop, the problem will not be solved. There are lawsuits in the courts today where music corporations are suing individuals who have shared music. It is a little too early to know if this approach will change the behaviors of those who view downloading as a right, not an illegal act.

What role can HCI play in the issue of intellectual property protection? Organizations such as SIGHCI (Special Interest Group on Human Computer Interaction in the Association of Information Systems) and SIGCHI (Special Interest Group on Computer Human Interaction of the Association of Computing Machinery) would be well served to think deeply about these issues and try to come up with codes of ethics or other options that would elevate the understanding of these issues in the public consciousness. Table 13.2 links the ethical issue of intellectual property with the social issue of unemployment and displacement.

### 3.5 Using Computers to Support Social Responsibility

Health care and education are two of our most pressing social issues. What can the information systems profession contribute to these issues while remaining within the economic constraints of profitability?

The health-care industry, in general, has been relatively slow to take advantage of computer-based technology to improve productivity and profitability. In recent times, however, the health-care industry has been automating such important activities as medication allocation and tracking, laboratory outcomes, scheduling for surgery, supplies inventory processing, and others. Of course, billing and accounts receivables have been in place for quite some time. However, many of the existing health-care systems lack integration and are basically stand-alone systems. The potential for great strides exists through integration and linking hospitals to pharmaceutical companies, insurance companies, patients, physicians, laboratories, and so on.

The possibility of a national health-care database also presents great opportunities for information systems' contributions to streamlining many health-care-related processes. Networks that link medical histories, drug availability, organ availability, and expertise all contribute to higher-quality care and more efficient processes. Streamlining the paperwork associated with hospital services is one of the important goals. A national network linking patients, hospitals, doctors, and pharmacies should cut down on the paperwork required to complete medical procedures. Imagine a national data bank with the medical records of all U.S. citizens. Legions of medical support staff persons would be freed up to do more direct care of patients. Of course, as we develop a national medical database, legal and ethical rules must be put in place to safeguard access and use of this critical personal information.

The Internet has changed the landscape of kindergarten through 12th grade public education in the United States and other countries. However, teachers often complain about the paperwork burden. The management overhead for running a classroom is very time-consuming. Class attendance management, student evaluation and performance, lesson planning, responding to outcomes assessment, managing student records, scheduling, testing, duplicating and developing course materials, finding instructional references and resources, and so on are all required and pull the teacher away from the direct teaching of students. Classroom information management systems that are integrated with central offices and perhaps state networks are urgently needed.

Public and private school systems' resources have been stretched to the limit. Perhaps the government needs to invest in the development of generic teaching management information systems to be distributed to classroom teachers in public school environments to help them cope with the demands of modern education. It may be possible that if an effective system did exist, schools would find the money to invest in it. A good system should pay off in the short and long term. Every classroom teacher would need a workstation at his or her desk that would be networked to a building local area network and linked via gateways to the Internet. The Internet has wonderful potential for knowledge exploration and linking of students with other students and expertise. The profitability in the education arena is less likely than in the health-care industry; however, the potential for social improvement is great. The possibilities are endless. The potential for profitability for the IS industry is also great. All of this work would be compensated. It would be a positive symbiotic relationship for both the medical field and the IS profession. The feeling of contributing to the well-being of the nation would be an aspect of compensation that is certainly not present in much that we undertake at this time. As HCI designers, our role in such a widely distributed system is to create usable user interfaces. HCI practitioners could be a strong component of the design and implementation of a successful system.

## ▷ 4. GLOBAL CONTEXT

### 4.1 Software Globalization

**Software globalization:** Creating a "generic" and functional version of software that is devoid of cultural context. The focus is on functionality and not packaging.

Software globalization is the process of extracting the domestic, cultural context from a package. The goal is to end up with a sort of generic product with an appendix or attachment that contains all the culturally specific items. In other words, it is the separation of product elements into culturally dependent and culturally independent parts. Localization is the opposite of globalization. Localization takes a generic product and adds features and elements to fit the target culture and market (Carey, 1998; Taylor, 1992).

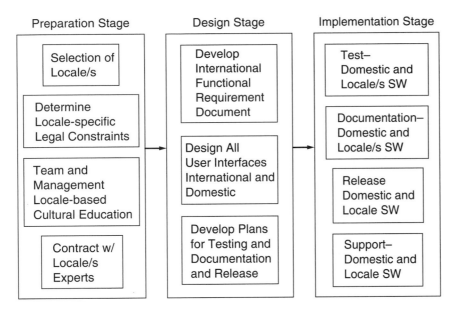

**Figure 13.5** Global software development process.

Both globalization and localization require that the programmers be aware of their own culture, language, social values, and expectations so that they understand how to recognize the culturally appropriate aspects to be implemented in the localization process and eliminated in the globalization process.

Globalization creates a framework and structure in which localization can take place. This framework (1) enables a software product to be sold worldwide, (2) allows for a more efficient development of the localized product, (3) encourages faster time to market, (4) consumes fewer resources, and (5) involves easier and less expensive maintenance, because single sourcing of code is possible (Luong, Lok, Taylor, & Driscoll, 1995).

Figure 13.5 depicts the stages in global software development. The overall structure follows the normal traditional development life cycle and includes the three stages of preparation (analysis), design, and implementation. However, within each stage, the specific steps are very different from the traditional development cycle. The key issues in global software development include translation issues, localization, cultural issues, and interface design issues.

Designers should consider form (user interface) and function (capabilities) when designing for an international market (del Galdo & Nielsen, 1990). To do this effectively, the issues of translation and local conventions should be taken into consideration early in the design stage. Such issues as character sets, collating sequence, numeric format, time and date formats, currency, and even telephone numbers vary from country to country.

Developers in the field of artificial intelligence have long been trying to build language translators, with limited success. Languages are enormously complex constructs. Alphabets and symbols vary from country to country. English is a type of Roman-based language that is considered a simple writing system since it is confined to 26 alphabetic characters. But even other languages in the Roman-based group have differing diacritical marks and hyphenation conventions than the English language. Simple writing systems include Roman, Greek, Cyrillic, Armenian, Ethiopian, and Georgian.

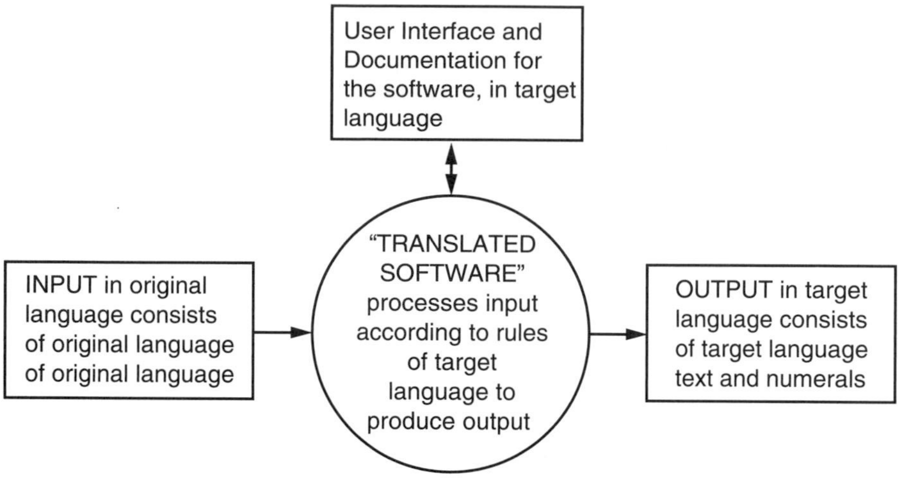

**Figure 13.6**  Translation process.

Large writing systems include Chinese, Japanese, Korean, Hebrew, Arabic, Thai, Burmese, Mongolian, and Tibetan. There are three input methods for Chinese alone: (1) phonetic (enter Pinyin, the computer displays a number of choices, the user selects one and returns), (2) stroke-definition input method (called bixing), and (3) code input method (user looks up character code and types it in). All of these input methods are more burdensome for the user than any of the simple writing systems. Figure 13.6 illustrates the translation process of software development. Essentially, components of the system that require language translation and the original language of the system are inputs to the translation process. The translation process occurs and the output is the interface components in the target language. Figure 13.6 is adapted from Luong et al. (1995).

Table 13.2 illustrates the relationship between software globalization and the ethical issue of accessibility.

## 4.2  Software Localization

Software localization is the process of adding back into the generic or "globalized" software locale-specific features of the target country. Software localization requires sophisticated HCI knowledge.

Locales are the features of the user's environment that are dependent on language, country, and cultural conventions. The choice of locale determines conventions such as sort order, keyboard layout, and date, time, number, and currency formats. *Locale-sensitive* means exhibiting different behavior or returning different data, depending on the locale. For example, sorting functions return different results depending on the parameter sent to each function.

In order to localize software, the following are required:

- A set of international APIs (Application Program Interfaces) for switching from one locale to another
- A locale definition for each locale you would want to support
- A locale compiler to make the locale information accessible to your program

**Software localization:**
Adding the cultural and locale-specific distinctiveness to globalized or generic software.

There are various levels of localization that determine both the cost of the process and the level of risk involved.

Full localization has the benefits of addressing a broader audience and making the software more accessible, easier to use, better accepted, and easier to support. The end result is that full localization allows for more sales and the ability to charge more. In addition to these benefits, some government agencies will only buy fully localized software (e.g., Spain).

What is a full localization? It includes the entire user interface including menus, dialogs, title bars, status messages, error messages, icons, bitmaps, online help, computer-based training materials, documentation, sample programs or files, and a translated macro language. Under some conditions, it may be reasonable to partially localize. However, if the product is targeted to the end-user rather than the programmer-developer market, then it should be fully localized.

Some markets in various countries—Sweden, for example—may tolerate an English version of the product. The Japanese will not, nor will the French. If the size of the market is quite small, it may be better to test a niche with a partial localization or leave out certain modules such as the network system. Ultimately, the decision is a monetary one and depends on the level of investment the company is willing to make.

Another decision point is to determine whether to localize in-house or through outsourcing. If the company is planning to localize on a frequent basis and quality is important, then the talent and capability to localize should be developed in-house. If the need for localization is infrequent and quality is not a necessity, then outsourcing may be a reasonable option.

Translation may be done by a target country subsidiary or by a translation agency. Either way, testing the localized version is very important. The timing of the localization is important. The key aspect is whether the company wants simultaneous shipment of the domestic product with the localized version or delivery of the localized version after the domestic release (Luong et al., 1995).

Uren, Howard, and Perinotti (1993) say there is no choice, that creating world-ready software is an imperative, not an option. The software market is global; software must be designed for worldwide customers, and quality standards are high around the world. Building an application and then retrofitting it to the world market is too slow and too vulnerable to low quality.

Figure 13.7 graphically depicts the software localization process. It is adapted from Kano (1995).

Not only is language translation an important part of the localization process, but also the cultural aspects of the interface deserve to have attention. It is not enough to translate the software from one language to another; it is equally important that the icons, symbols, and other cultural conventions feel comfortable and recognizable to the user. Culture is learned behavior consisting of thoughts, feelings, and actions. A cultural model compares the similarities and differences between two or more cultures by using international variables to organize cultural data (Hoft, 1996).

How do we come to grips with designing for other cultures (del Galdo & Nielsen, 1990)? We must educate ourselves on the cultural aspects of the use population. We must change design practices to ensure that these cultural aspects are taken into account. We must also ensure that we hire some team members who have been born and raised in the target culture. In today's international market, a lack of cultural insight may result in the death of the product.

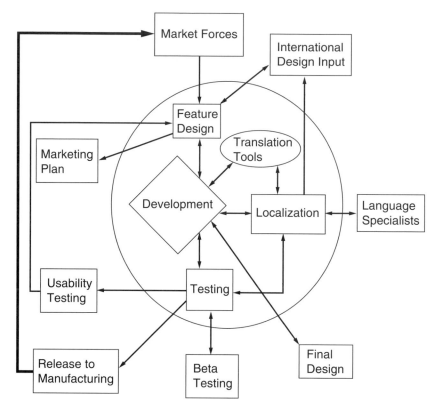

**Figure 13.7** The software localization process.

Ito and Nakakoji (1996) have explored the impact of user interface design in the global context. They call the information presented from computer to user the "Listening Mode." There are three phases in this mode, including perception, semantic association (sometimes referred to as anchoring), and logical reasoning. Each successive phase is subject to greater and greater cultural impact. The logical name for the mode in which information travels from user to computer is called the "Speaking Mode." There are four phases in this mode, including affordance perception (what is the purpose), applicability check (users validate their choice of actions), enactment with expectations (like a mouse click), and confirmation (it performed as expected). As with the "Listening Mode," the cultural impact goes up with each phase.

It is important to understand the target culture (Dray & Mzarek, 1996). There are several strategies that a software company can undertake to achieve this understanding. One is to hire an outside consultant who already understands the culture (it is reasonable to insist that the consultant be fluent in both the language of the country in which the original software was developed and the language of the target culture). Another strategy is to do a cultural study by sending human factors experts from the company to the target culture. The third strategy is to hire members of the target culture to become permanent members of the company or perhaps a subsidiary.

If a company decides to do a cultural study from within the company, to gain understanding of a target culture, the first step is to go to the target culture and establish a rapport. Once a rapport is established, some initial activities can be undertaken to customize the cultural study to the particular culture, and then formal data collection occurs. This data collection is most effective if a cross-cultural observation team is put together with members from the original culture and members from the target culture. Once the data is collected, there should be a wrap-up or debriefing in which preliminary findings are discussed. Then the team either returns to the original culture and applies the knowledge from the study or continues to stay in the target culture, refining the product and testing it using subjects from the target culture in the actual target environments.

The most effective process for creating localized products takes international considerations into account at the beginning of the product cycle and throughout development and expedites the shipping of multiple language editions (Kano, 1995). There are two basic rules for designing a user interface that is internationally acceptable and easy to localize: (1) use simple, generic graphics, and (2) avoid crowding those graphics. When English is translated into any other language, including other Roman-based scripts, the translation always takes up more room than the English version. This is especially true when translating to the large writing systems such as Chinese.

Bitmaps, icons, and sounds should be kept simple. It is best to avoid sounds and never use the first letters of commands as shortcuts. Menus and dialog translations are often longer than the English versions. To allow room for growth, you should use dialog tab controls to split up long menus.

HCI designers working on software globalization processes must remember to apply the guidelines articulated in Chapter 8. These guidelines are universal in nature and serve to enhance systems regardless of the target culture of use. Table 13.2 illustrates the relationship between software localization and the ethical issue of accessibility.

## ► 5. THE SOCIAL AND GLOBAL ASPECTS OF THE INTERNET

The widespread global diffusion of the Internet impacts global society. The ease of use, freedom of navigation, and graphic nature of the Internet also impact HCI design expectations on the part of users. The Internet has also shifted the locus of control from the organizations and providers of software to the users of software. The future holds more promise for end-user options and in turn poses changes and challenges for HCI. The authors have chosen to create a separate section in this chapter that explores the interaction of social and global contexts with the Internet.

### 5.1 Social Impact of the Internet

The Internet has created opportunities for people to connect with each other. Even before the Internet came onto the scene, there were text-based communities created by bulletin board systems, Listservs, news services, and so on. Blogs (Web logs) allow people to express their opinions, share their written artistic expression, and rally people to take action. People with common experiences, problems, illnesses, and challenges have multiple Web sites that can suggest answers and provide support. Singles can find partners. Adoptive children can find birth parents. People can find long-lost friends and relatives. Cancer sufferers can find treatments. Cancer survivors can find hope. Those who have lost a loved one to cancer can find comfort. People are able to reach out to others who share almost every human condition. Sometimes the relationships we form on the Internet are more intimate (in an anonymous way) than those relationships we have with the people living in our own homes.

**Internet:** A global network of networks that follows certain standards and protocols in order to support access, communication, and connectivity.

**Blogs:** Short for *Weblogs*, which are online journals accessible to Internet-enabled users.

Citizens can register to vote, renew their driver's licenses, pay taxes, write to their representatives, and even vote via the Internet. The Internet is influencing public opinion and even giving rise to candidates themselves. The candidacy of Howard Dean for the U.S. presidency in 2003 and 2004 was driven by grassroots Internet-based support. In early 2004, Dean's site had an average of 500,000 hits per month, while the other Democratic candidates together had an average of 200,000 hits per month (Cone, 2003). The use of the Internet for these previously time-consuming and often frustrating tasks has saved time and energy for citizens and a great deal of money for the government.

The availability of the Internet for various tasks (public and business-related) has resulted in a shift of responsibility to individuals. It is empowering to be able to order your airline e-tickets online and not be subject to the travel agents' hours of business and other constraints. However, as consumers and citizens complete more and more tasks, the responsibility for performance is shifting to the user via the Internet.

The Internet has had a tremendous impact on education in the United States and many other countries. Students can virtually visit places and interact with students from other cultures. They can watch NASA expeditions in near real time. They can experience cultural activities through Webcasts. Parents and students can interact with teachers via e-mail and instant messaging. Students can work in "virtual teams" to accomplish group work. They can conduct Internet-based "research" through a search engine like Google.

**Instant Messaging (IM):** allows one-to-one "real time" interactions via typed text.

Of course, in the field of education, the Internet has some drawbacks. Plagiarism seems to be more of a problem. At the college level, students can purchase papers rather than write them. Accidental or purposeful access to pornography both at home and at school sites requires filtering and human monitoring. The safeguarding of intellectual property is a difficult problem on the Internet. The laws are still being formulated around this thorny issue. Peer-to-peer sharing of music, books, and movies has cut into the profits of these important industries.

The invasion of privacy is also a problem. "Cookies" are left on users' machines when they visit commercial and other sites. These cookies contain information that may be shared and used in ways that the owners do not want or may not even be aware of.

**Negative social impacts:** Include anxiety, alienation, potency of the individual, speed and complexity, societal and organizational dependence, unemployment and displacement, and valuing of human diversity.

The Internet impacts work life. More and more people are able to telecommute because they can read their e-mail and instant message with those who are physically located anywhere. They store their documents in databases that can be accessed through the Internet. The Internet enables offshore outsourcing of work (especially software programming and development). Coordination of large multinational projects is greatly enhanced by the Internet.

There is a whole alternative trading system that has been enabled by C2C (consumer-to-consumer) e-commerce. EBay has created a nontaxable exchange of both new and used goods that supports many sellers and provides cheap alternative products to many buyers.

These examples are but a few of the many ways in which the Internet has positively and negatively impacted society. Most futurists believe that we are just beginning to see the potential of the Internet come to fruition.

## 5.2 Global Impact of the Internet

E-commerce in all of its forms (B2B, B2C, C2C) is having a tremendous impact on the nature of global business. While the Internet has the potential to reduce the costs associated with doing business globally, it also increases the likelihood that international competition will increase. Global suppliers and customers are connected to each other in a cheap, easy, and dependable way.

**Figure 13.8** Hebrew Web site for *Haaretz* newspaper (http://www.haaretz.com/).

The global digital divide is just as important as domestic access issues. How can countries where the telecommunications infrastructure cannot support Internet access compete? The Internet has exacerbated the gap between the "have" and "have-not" nations.

The virtual communities discussed in the previous section are also global in nature. Refugees and expatriates can stay connected to their families and countries via the Internet. Communities can exist across national boundaries. Language may be a problem, but translation interfaces that allow interactions to occur are improving all the time. Figures 13.8 to 13.13 are various Web sites in Hebrew, Spanish, Arabic, Romanian, and Chinese languages. Notice the language and cultural differences and how they impact the overall effect of the Web site. All of these sites have toggles to English versions. It is interesting to explore the differences between the native-language version and the English version. Figures 13.12 and 13.13 are the Chinese and English versions of the same Web site.

Global cultural differences can be shared and understood by interacting through the Internet. However, there is some fear that the dominance of the American and Western culture will serve to homogenize the global culture. This is sometimes referred to as the "McDonaldization" effect.

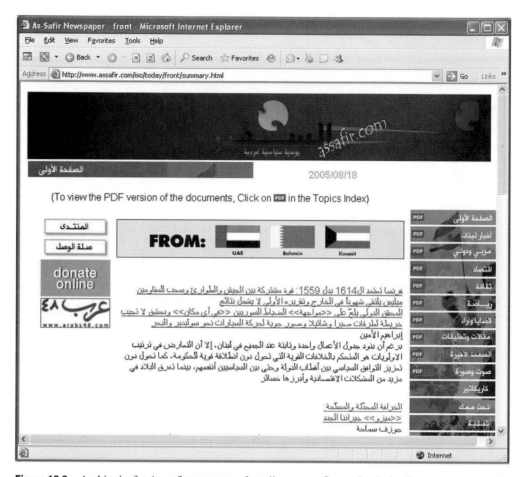

**Figure 13.9** Arabic site for *As-safir* newspaper (http://www.assafir.com/iso/today/front/summary.html).

## ▷ 6. SUMMARY

This chapter explores the social and global contexts within which human–computer interaction takes place. The authors recommend an active individual initiative regarding social responsibility. Computer specialists who are designing and building interfaces for information systems should take an active role in leading the world toward a better quality of life through integrated systems that promote social well-being and also combat the problems associated with the information age. Such issues as anxiety, alienation, the impotence of the individual, bewildering complexity and speed, organizational fragility, unemployment and displacement, and the undermining of human value (Shneiderman, 1998; Shneiderman & Plaisant, 2005) are all defined and discussed with recommendations for improvement. Table 13.1 serves to summarize the various social issues and related HCI design implications.

Four major areas of ethical issues are presented in this chapter. They include accessibility, privacy, accountability, and property. Table 13.2 summarizes the relationships between the ethical issues, the social issues, and the HCI implications.

The chapter presents two issues for the future attention of socially responsible IS professionals. These two issues are important to the quality of life in the future and have potential for increasing the profitability of those organizations involved in IS technology.

**Figure 13.10**  Spanish edition of *El Universal* newspaper (http://estadis.eluniversal.com.mx/ ol_nacion.html).

These issues are health care and education. Both of these areas have been slow to become automated. Attention to the information needs and potential IS advances for health-care organizations and educational institutions could reap great benefits for all citizens.

The globalization of business has had a tremendous impact on human–computer interaction. Today's software is being developed for international markets. Software globalization and localization require an alternative approach to the design and development of software that is quite different from the standard development life cycle that is appropriate for a domestic (U.S.) market.

Language, culture, symbols, customs, and other aspects of cultural interaction must be taken into consideration when designing interfaces and other human–computer interactions. The Internet, with its global reach, has also changed human–computer interaction expectations and has had a tremendous impact on society and the world. Table 13.2 includes both software globalization and localization and related ethical issues and HCI implications.

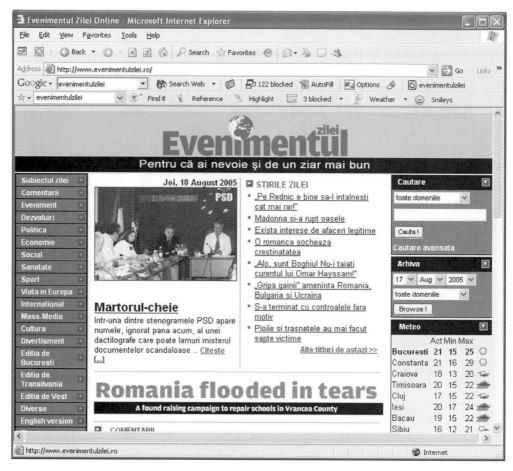

**Figure 13.11**   Romanian version of *Evenimentul Zilei* newspaper (http://www.expres.ro/topstory/ ?news_id=145710).

## ▶ 7.  SUMMARY OF CONCEPTS AND TERMS

Access

Ethical considerations

Internet

Software globalization

Accountability and accuracy

Instant messaging (IM)

Negative social impacts

Software localization

Blogs

Intellectual property

Privacy

## ▶ 8.  BIBLIOGRAPHY AND ADDITIONAL READINGS

Brennen, P. (1993). *Introducing caregivers to computer-based systems.* Paper read at the Fifth Symposium on Human Factors in Information Systems, Cleveland, OH.

Carey, J. M. (1998). Creating global software: A conspectus and review. *Interacting with Computers, 8*(4), 437–450.

Carey-Young, J., Skelly, G. U., & Pitts, R. E. (1983). *Acceptance of change—A management information systems model.* Paper read at Southwest American Institute of Decision Sciences, Houston, TX.

Cone, E. (2003). The marketing of the president 2004. *Baseline.* Retrieved from http:// www.baselinemag.com/print_article2/0,2533,a=114332,00.asp

**Figure 13.12** Chinese version of *China Today* (http://www.china.com/chinese/index.htm).

del Galdo, E. M., & Nielsen, J. (Eds.). (1990). *International user interfaces.* New York: John Wiley & Sons.

Dray, S., & Mzarek, D. (1996). A day in the life: Studying context across cultures. In E. M. del Galdo & J. Nielsen (Eds.), *International user interfaces.* New York: John Wiley and Sons.

Hoft, N. (1996). Developing a cultural model. In E. M. del Galdo & J. Nielsen (Eds.), *International user interfaces.* New York: John Wiley and Sons.

Ito, M., & Nakakoji, K. (1996). Impact of culture on user interface design. In E. M. del Galdo & J. Nielsen (Eds.), *International user interfaces.* New York: John Wiley and Sons.

Kano, N. (1995). *Developing international software: For Windows 95 and Windows NT.* Redmond, WA: Microsoft Press.

Luong, T. V., Lok, J. S. H., Taylor, D., & Driscoll, K. (1995). *Internationalization: Developing software for global markets.* New York: John Wiley & Sons.

Shneiderman, B. (1990). *Human values and the future of technology: A declaration of responsibility.* Paper read at the Third Symposium on Human Factors in Information Systems, Norman, OK.

Shneiderman, B. (1998). *Designing the user interface—Strategies for effective human-computer interaction* (3rd ed.). New York: Addison-Wesley.

Shneiderman, B., & Plaisant, C. (2005). *Designing the user interface: Strategies for effective human-computer interaction.* New York: Addison-Wesley.

Taylor, D. (1992). *Global software.* New York: Springer Verlag.

**Figure 13.13**  English version of *China Today* (http://www.china.com/English/index.htm).

Uren, E., Howard, R., & Perinotti, T. (1993). *Software internationalization and localization.* New York: Van Nostrand.

## ▷ 9. CASE STUDY

Lance Redux knows that customers are often reluctant to enter their personal information on Web sites. In order to promote trust, Lance has created a privacy policy that is linked to each of the pages via the navigation bars. The privacy policy is stated below.

Thank you for visiting the World Gourmet Web site. Please be assured that the privacy of our visitors is of utmost importance to us. **We collect no personally identifiable information about you when you visit our site unless you choose to provide that information to us. If you do choose to provide us with your personal information, please be assured that we do not share your information with any other parties.**

Some of our Web pages contain links to other Web sites. Please be aware that when you follow a link to another site, you are then subject to the privacy policies of the new site.

**Your Rights under the Privacy Act:** Information concerning the Privacy Act can be found on the following Web site: http://www.cftc.gov/foia/foiprivacyact.htm

## ▶ 10. EXERCISES

Ex. 1. Cartwright school district is located in a poor section of the city. Funding from the state has been way below the amount needed. There is only one outdated computer lab. Devise a plan for procuring hardware and software for the lab without spending any money. Start by designing the space and determining the number and type of computers, networking, and so on. The primary goal is to find creative ways to fund or solicit used computers.

Ex. 2. Use the Internet to determine the diffusion rate of the Internet in various countries. One of the countries should be the United States. Pick one country each in Africa, Asia, and Europe. What do these rates say about these various countries?

# 14

# MEETING THE CHANGING NEEDS OF IT DEVELOPMENT AND USE

## CONTEXT AND PREVIEW

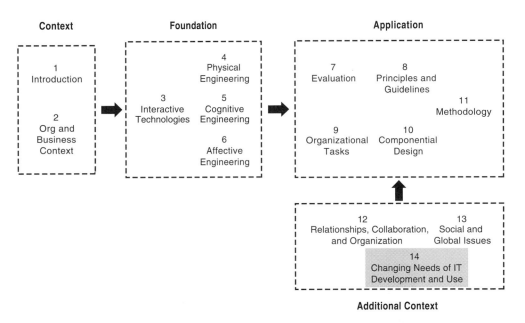

This chapter addresses some emerging changes (paradigm shifts and trends) both in using IT and in developing IT, and their impacts and implications on existing HCI development practice and methodologies. The chapter examines several rather drastic changes and illustrates how these changes affect HCI development. Specific challenges associated with these changes are highlighted and suggestions are given to cope with the changes. These discussions tie back to the HCI development methodology we introduced in Chapter 11. The discussions also prompt a forward look at the field in terms of potential technology development and subsequent use and impact on individuals, groups, organizations, and society. Such a forward-looking perspective reinforces our understanding of the ultimate goals and concerns of human interaction with technology, which we discussed in Chapter 7.

## LEARNING OBJECTIVES

Upon completion of this chapter, students should be able to do the following:

- Understand recent changes in IT use and their impact
- Understand recent trends in IT development
- Understand the potential challenges these changes and trends may present for HCI development

## ▷ 1. INTRODUCTION

From a historical perspective, computing devices have evolved from vacuum tubes and later transistors to silicon chips. At the same time, computer size has grown smaller and computer speed has grown faster. In the early days of computing, mainframes were the sole option; we then saw a shift to minicomputers, then to personal computers, then to mobile devices and information appliances, and finally to ubiquitous computers that exist in our environment without our awareness. Associated with this evolution are the ways in which computing devices are used via user interfaces, which have undergone a similar evolution. Consequently, the uses of these devices have challenged and changed many aspects of our work, our lives, and even our values. The globe has become much smaller. Our interactions with computers may not be apparent. We may not realize or sense that there is a computer in our environment even though we rely on this computer for some specific need.

As the penetration of computers into various aspects of our lives gets deeper, the definition of "user" is evolving as well. "A paradox of our time is that computers have become at once personal and communal, less visible yet ubiquitous, mobile yet entrenched in the dense fabric of information and communications technologies that permeate our lives. At the interface between human and computer, this paradox unfurls in an ongoing transformation of computer 'user' from a single person to an interacting group, from a group of people to an entire firm or other organization, and from an organization to a diffuse community with dynamic membership and purpose" (DeSanctis, 2006).

Another association with the computing device evolution is how the systems, especially the software systems, are being developed. Today, open-source software and reusable components are just some examples of how software can be put together. In addition, outsourcing—especially offshore outsourcing—has challenged many aspects of software development and related issues.

The result of all these advancements is a profound expansion in the scope of human–computer interaction (HCI) development and an explosion in the mandate for HCI research (DeSanctis, 2006). It is hard to predict what the new devices might be and what these devices will be able to do for humans in the next five or ten years. For example, in a short 10-year history, the Internet has created new ways to do personal things and conduct business that were not even imaginable before. It is also unimaginable what devices and associated software systems will be developed in the next 10 years. Yet, by examining some of the recent trends and analyzing the challenges of these changes on HCI development, we may learn the specific aspects that may help us to cope with future changes. This is the main goal of this chapter. We consider several radical changes both in the use and impact aspect and in the development of IT aspect and discuss the implications of these changes on HCI development. We do not have answers for all the challenges because some of these developments and challenges are still relatively new. They still need to be explored through academic research and industry practice.

## ▶ 2. EMERGING IT USE CHANGES AND THE IMPACTS

In this section, we briefly examine three categories of recent developments and trends in IT use and impacts: ubiquitous computing, social computing, and value-sensitive design. These developments in IT use have changed the ways we do things, including personal activities, job-related tasks, commerce, communication, community forming, and many more. The challenges and concerns involve more than just adapting to new ways but also how to reserve and implement our values by using technology. HCI is central in all of these developments.

### 2.1 Ubiquitous Computing (Ubicomp)

#### 2.1.1 What Is Ubicomp?

Broadly speaking, there are two views of ubiquitous computing (also know as ubicomp). The convergent device (one-does-all) view posits the computer as a tool through which anything, and indeed everything, can be done (Licklider, Taylor, & Herbert, 1978). The divergent device (many-do-all) view, by contrast, offers a world where microprocessors are embedded in everything and communicating with one another (Weiser, 1991). Both streams of technology are likely to coexist (Stanton, 2001).

> **Ubiquitous computing:** Integrating computation into the environment instead of having computers as distinct objects.

Licklider (1960) proposed a partnership between humans and computers, a sort of cognitive cyborg, to suggest that human thought augmented (externally) by computers could lead to a higher level of insight that could not be gained by either working alone. For this to be achieved, he argued that an intimate association between the person and the computer would need to be established. One proposition was to have natural language communication between humans and computers, which has been a holy grail of computing ever since (Stanton, 2001). Licklider and colleagues (1978) foresaw the advent of the Internet and the videoconference, and they speculated that this would be the end of business travel for meetings and presumably the end of academics traveling to conferences. Although we know that this has not happened yet, the other prediction about the use of the PC as a device for communicating and performing all manner of other tasks (such as an index, encyclopedia, and entertainment) has certainly come true (Stanton, 2001).

Weiser (1991) envisioned that technology would weave itself into the very fabric of everyday life and that it would be distributed in the environment (ubiquitous) yet be invisible or transparent; thus it would be impossible to define the boundaries of computing technology. Weiser's argument was that we need to get rid of the box to see a truly seamless integration of computing in people's working, domestic, and leisure lives. He put forward the view that ubiquity will have been achieved only when computing has become invisible (i.e., when microprocessors are embedded in the everyday objects we use but we are largely unaware of them) and there is "intelligent" communication between the objects that "anticipate" our next move (Stanton, 2001).

Integrating computers into the environment instead of having computers as distinct objects has the advantage of enabling people to move around and interact with computers more naturally than they normally do. Ubicomp slowly moves into our lives and becomes reality. Ubicomp, also called "pervasive computing," represents a major evolutionary step in computing work. For the past decade, ubicomp researchers have attempted to realize Weiser's and Licklider's views with the implicit goal of assisting everyday life and not overwhelming it.

"Ubiquitous computing is roughly the opposite of virtual reality. Where virtual reality puts people inside a computer-generated world, ubiquitous computing forces the computer to live in the world with people. Virtual reality is primarily a horsepower problem; ubiquitous computing is a very difficult integration of human factors, computer science, engineering, and social sciences" (http://www.ubiq.com/hypertext/ weiser/UbiHome.html).

Examples of ubicomp include applications of microprocessors embedded into a cooker timing and menu system, cars, conference rooms and classrooms, and wearable computers (small PCs, information appliances, and clothing that contain microprocessors, sensors, and displays). An example of information appliances is a device for fitness assessment that collects related data on muscle strength, aerobic endurance, flexibility, and motor ability and thus can replace the pen-and-paper method. Other examples of ubicomp include context-sensitive audio-based personal memory aids that can help users quickly retrieve forgotten information, and remote collaboration on problem visualization and intervention across a wide range of application areas, including the office, the home, and mobile environments.

### 2.1.2 Challenges for HCI Design and Evaluation

There are obviously several challenges. Here we focus on some issues that are closely related to HCI, including broad impact.

*Design Space.* New concepts for HCI have to be developed to fully realize ubicomp scenarios. Instead of a single screen-based user interface (UI), humans will interact with a number of devices that are distributed and interconnected. These computers range from highly personal and mobile appliances to systems that are integrated in everyday environments and are more or less invisible. When all the potential components are considered together, the design space for the UI becomes much larger than with conventional personal computers. In the process of designing UIs, decisions on the distribution of the input as well as the output through both space and time are needed. This also raises questions on how to deal with alternative, multiple input options, redundant output opportunities, and the fact that many of these UIs cannot expect to have people's attention for a long time (Dey, Ljungstrand, & Schmidt, 2001).

*User Experience.* Unlike just a few years ago, when we had at most one computer per person, many of us now routinely carry several "intelligent" devices. These may include PDAs, cell phones, laptop computers, portable digital music players, and so on. Additionally, our daily environments are often inhabited by digital devices such as computer display projectors and computer-augmented whiteboards. Increasingly, these devices have the ability to interconnect with one another, whether through short-range, proximity-based transports such as infrared or Bluetooth, via longer-range wireless technology, or through "traditional" wired networks. As we carry with us and are surrounded by increasing numbers of interconnectable devices—as well as rapidly proliferating interconnected software services—we are confronted with the question of how we will understand, make sense of, and ultimately use the functionality around us (Edwards, Newman, & Sedivy, 2001). Understanding and exploring user experiences in a ubicomp context is one area that yet needs to be researched so that better ubicomp can be developed and eventually adopted.

*Task-Centric Evaluation Techniques May Be Inappropriate.* The majority of usability techniques are task-centric. If the user's tasks are known, then an evaluation is performed to determine the fitness of the system and its interface for completing that task. It is not at all clear how to apply task-centric evaluation techniques to ubiquitous computing, where tasks are less clear or continuous without beginning or ending (Abowd & Mynatt, 2000). This notion goes with the task-centric HCI design method. New approaches are needed when tasks are less obvious and continuous.

*Social Implications.* Ubicomp can sense, understand, and react to phenomena in the physical world and can record those phenomena. These technologies carry with them numerous dangers, for example, making it too easy for people to build systems that effectively spy on others without any controlling authority (Abowd & Mynatt, 2000). Security, privacy, control, and visibility are among the important social issues. Although they cannot be addressed by merely technical means, any ubicomp designers should understand these issues and work together toward technological, design, social, and policy solutions to address these concerns.

## 2.2 Social Computing and Communityware

Owing to the fast development of the Internet, ubiquitous computing and mobile computing, new types of computing have emerged and have attracted researchers' attention. One of these is social computing, also called community computing or online community. For example, the first international conference on online communities and social computing was held July 22–27, 2004, in Las Vegas. The key ideas can be represented by the term *communityware*, among other terms. Communityware is software that allows large decentralized groups of people to form communities, share preferences and knowledge, and perform social activities (Ishida, Nishida, & Hattori, 1998). Unlike previous research on groupware, which has mainly supported the collaborative work of already-organized people with shared goals, communityware is for more diverse and amorphous groups of people sharing interests and preferences without obvious goals (Sumi & Mase, 2002). In communityware, the objectives and benefits of an activity are not centralized but rather distributed. The essence of the activities changes from finding solutions to finding issues to be solved. The interests and volunteering mind-sets of the participants empower these activities, not a sense of duty or direct rewards (Sumi & Mase, 2002).

Communityware has been developed for various purposes or applications. Here we introduce two examples to illustrate the variety of potential social computing applications. Sumi and Mase (2002) described communityware for providing digital assistants to support participants at an academic conference. The aim was to enhance communication among the conference participants. The events of various societies such as annual conferences give society members an attractive opportunity to experience new encounters and face-to-face knowledge exchanges and enable them to become informants as

> **Communityware:**
> Software that allows large decentralized groups of people to form communities, share preferences and knowledge, and perform social activities.

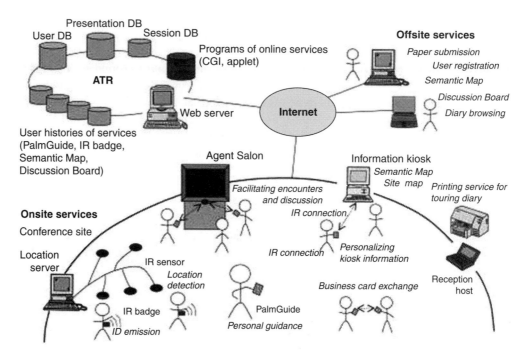

**Figure 14.1**  Overview of communityware for conference participants.

well as audience members. However, it is unexpectedly difficult to efficiently exploit this opportunity within the period of a conference: we tend to miss meeting other participants who have shared interests or fail to attend noteworthy presentations. In addition, even if we could meet and have fruitful discussions with other participants at the site of a conference, these relationships would likely terminate after the conference. The communityware designed for academic conferences comes with mobile and ubiquitous computing technologies, combines mobile assistant services with services on kiosk terminals located at the conference site, and integrates online services via the Web, which can be accessed before and after the conference. The principle of the system design is a mutual augmentation between online services via the Web and the services provided at the conference site. The online services are expected to reinforce tours at the conference site, and conversely, tours at the conference site are expected to provide users with motivation and focal points for communication beyond the existing temporal and spatial restrictions. Figure 14.1 is the overview of the system.

The second example of communityware is "Babble," a system that can support communication and collaboration among large groups of people over computing networks (Erickson & Kellogg, 2000). Specifically, Babble is for knowledge communities to support the creation, management, and reuse of knowledge in a social context. In designing Babble, researchers began by asking what properties of the physical world support graceful human–human communication in face-to-face situations; they argue that it is possible to design digital systems that support coherent behavior by making participants and their activities visible to one another. The main idea for designing Babble is based on the observation that social information in our lives provides the basis for interferences, planning, and coordination of activities: wrapping up a talk when the audience starts fidgeting, deciding to forgo grocery shopping because the parking lot is jammed, deciding to grab a particular type of wine when we see others do so, or approaching a group of gathered people when we recognize someone gesturing excitedly as others listen intently. Ironically, in the digital world, we are almost socially blind. Most of our knowledge about people, most of our attunement to their interactions, and most of our facility for improvising in a changing situation go unused. Babble is an attempt to address this blindness. With a social translucence approach, Babble is designed to have three characteristics: visibility, awareness, and accountability, which enable people to draw upon their experience and expertise to structure their interactions with one another.

## 2.3 Value-Sensitive Design (VSD)

### 2.3.1 What Is VSD?

Value-sensitive design (VSD) is a theoretically grounded approach to the design of technology that accounts for human values in a principled and comprehensive manner throughout the design process (Friedman, Kahn, & Borning, 2006). There has been a long-standing interest in designing information and computational systems that support enduring human values. The previous chapter examined several ethical issues, including accessibility, privacy, accountability, and intellectual property. We also saw how social consequences of technology, such as the impotency of individuals, displacement, and the digital divide, affect people's feelings, attitudes, trust, and overall well-being. VSD offers an overarching theoretical and methodological framework with which to handle the value dimensions of design work. This section is based primarily on the work of Friedman, Kahn, and Borning (2006) from the University of Washington.

> **Value-sensitive design:** A theoretically grounded approach to the design of technology that accounts for human values in a principled and comprehensive manner throughout the design process.

What is a value? In a narrow sense, the word *value* refers simply to the economic worth of an object. For example, the value of a computer could be said to be two thousand dollars. A broader meaning of the term *value* refers to what a person or group of people consider important in life. In this sense, people find many things of value, both lofty and mundane: their children, friendship, morning tea, education, art, a walk in the woods, nice manners, good science, a wise leader, and clean air. It is usually agreed that values should not be conflated with facts (the "fact/value distinction") especially insofar as facts do not logically entail value. In other words, "is" does not imply "ought." In this way, values cannot be motivated only by an empirical account of the external world but depend substantively on the interests and desires of human beings within a cultural milieu.

> **Value:** An object's property that has economic worth or is regarded as being important in the life of someone or a group.

VSD emphasizes human values with ethical import. Friedman and colleagues (2006) suggest a list of values that should be considered in the investigation of IT design (see Table 14.1). This list includes several terms that we regard as social and ethical issues and design criteria in our discussions earlier in the book. Here we present the list in its entirety to convey the very broad approach adopted in VSD.

Below we present two case studies to illustrate value-sensitive design. One involves HDTV display technology in an office environment, and the second involves user interactions and interface for an integrated land use, transportation, and environmental simulation.

### 2.3.2 Case 1: Room with a View: Using Plasma Displays in Interior Offices

> Janice is in her office, writing a report. She's trying to conceptualize the report's higher-level structure, but her ideas won't quite take form. Then she looks up from her desk and rests her eyes on the fountain and plaza area outside her building. She notices the water bursting upward and sees

a small group of people gathering by the water's edge. She rests her eyes on the surrounding pool of calm water. Her eyes then lift toward the clouds and the streaking sunshine. Twenty seconds later she returns to her writing task at hand, slightly refreshed, and with an idea taking shape.

What's particularly novel about this workplace scenario is that Janice works in an interior office. Instead of a real window looking out onto the plaza, Janice has a large-screen video plasma display that continuously displays the local outdoor scene in real time. Realistic? Beneficial? This design space is currently being researched by Kahn, Friedman, and their colleagues, using the framework of value-sensitive design.

In Kahn and colleagues' initial conceptual investigation of this design space, they drew on the psychological literature that suggests that interaction with real nature can garner physiological and psychological benefits. For example, one study found that post-operative recovery improved when patients were assigned to a room with a view of a natural setting (a small stand of deciduous trees) versus a view of a brown brick wall.

**Table 14.1**  Frequently Studied Human Values with Ethical Import

| Human Value | Definition |
| --- | --- |
| Human welfare | Refers to people's physical, material, and psychological well-being |
| Ownership and property | Refers to a right to possess an object (or information), use it, manage it, derive income from it, and bequeath it |
| Privacy | Refers to a claim, an entitlement, or a right of an individual to determine what information about himself or herself can be communicated to others |
| Freedom from bias | Refers to systematic unfairness perpetrated on individuals or groups, including preexisting social bias, technical bias, and emergent social bias |
| Universal usability | Refers to making all people successful users of information technology |
| Trust | Refers to expectations that exist between people who can experience goodwill, extend goodwill toward others, feel vulnerable, and experience betrayal |
| Autonomy | Refers to people's ability to decide, plan, and act in ways that they believe will help them to achieve their goals |
| Informed consent | Refers to garnering people's agreement, encompassing criteria of disclosure and comprehension (for "informed") and voluntariness, competence, and agreement (for "consent") |
| Accountability | Refers to the properties that ensure that the actions of a person, people, or institution may be traced uniquely to the person, people, or institution |
| Courtesy | Refers to treating people with politeness and consideration |
| Identity | Refers to people's understanding of who they are over time, embracing both continuity and discontinuity over time |
| Calmness | Refers to a peaceful and composed psychological state |
| Environmental sustainability | Refers to sustaining ecosystems such that they meet the needs of the present without compromising future generations |

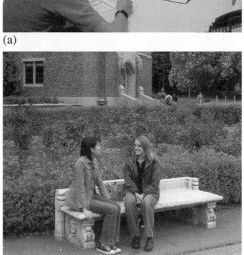

**Figure 14.2**   Plasma displays in interior offices. (a) The "Watcher." (b) The HDTV camera. (c) The "Watched." See also color plate VIII.

More generally, studies have shown that even minimal connection with nature—such as looking at a natural landscape—can reduce immediate and long-term stress, reduce sickness of prisoners, and calm patients before and during surgery. Thus Kahn and colleagues hypothesized that an "augmented window" of nature could render benefits in a work environment in terms of the human values of physical health, emotional well-being, and creativity.

   To investigate this question in a laboratory context, Kahn and colleagues compared the short-term benefits of working in an office with a view out the window of a beautiful nature scene versus an identical view (in real time) shown on a large video plasma display that covers the window in the same office (Figure 14.2a). In this latter condition, they employed a high-definition TV (HDTV) camera (Figure 14.2b) to capture real-time local images. The control condition involved a blank covering over the window. Their measures entailed (1) physiological data (heart rate), (2) performance data (on cognitive and creativity tasks), (3) video data that captured each subject's eye gaze on a second-by-second level, with time synchronized with the physiological equipment so that analyses can determine whether physiological benefits accrued immediately following an eye gaze onto the plasma screen, and (4) social-cognitive data (based on a 50-minute interview with each subject at the conclusion of the experimental condition wherein they garnered each subject's reasoned perspective on the experience). Preliminary results show the following trends. First, participants looked out the plasma screen just as frequently as they did the real window, and more frequently than they stared at the blank wall. In this sense, the plasma display window was functioning like a real window. But, when participants gazed for 30 seconds or more, the real window provided greater physiological recovery from low-level stress as compared to the plasma display window.

There are five aspects of this particular VSD that deserve discussion.

1. *Multiple Empirical Methods.* Under the rubric of empirical investigations, VSD supports and encourages multiple empirical methods to be used in concert to address the question at hand. As noted above, for example, this study employed physiological data (heart rate), two types of performance data (on cognitive and creativity tasks), behavioral data (eye gaze), and reasoning data (the social-cognitive interview).

2. *Direct and Indirect Stakeholders.* In their initial conceptual investigation of the values implicated in this study, Kahn and colleagues sought to identify not only direct but also indirect stakeholders affected by such display technology. An important class of indirect stakeholders (and their respective values) needed to be included, namely, the individuals who, by virtue of walking through the fountain scene, unknowingly had their images displayed on the video plasma display in the "inside" office (Figure 14.2c). In other words, if this application of projection technology were to come into widespread use (as Web cams and surveillance cameras have begun to), then it would potentially encroach on the privacy of individuals in public spaces—an issue that has been receiving increasing attention in the field of computer ethics and public discourse. Thus, in addition to the experimental laboratory study, Kahn and colleagues initiated two additional but complementary empirical investigations with indirect stakeholders: (1) a survey of 750 people walking through the public plaza, and (2) in-depth social-cognitive interviews with 30 individuals walking through the public plaza. Both investigations focused on indirect stakeholders' judgments of privacy in public space, and in particular having their real-time images captured and displayed on plasma screens in nearby and distant offices. The importance of such indirect stakeholder investigations is being borne out by the results. For example, significant gender differences were found in their survey data: more women than men expressed concern about the invasion of privacy through Web cameras in public places. This finding held whether their image was to be displayed locally or in another city (Tokyo) or viewed by one person, thousands, or millions. One implication of this finding is that future technical designs and implementations of such display technologies need to be responsive to ways in which men and women might perceive potential harms differently.

3. *Coordinated Empirical Investigations.* Once Kahn and colleagues identified an important group of indirect stakeholders and decided to undertake empirical investigations with this group, they coordinated these empirical investigations with the

initial (direct stakeholder) study. Specifically, a subset of identical questions was asked of both the direct stakeholders (the "Watchers") and the indirect stakeholders (the "Watched"). Results show some interesting differences. For example, more men in the "Watched" condition expressed concerns that people's images might be displayed locally, nationally, or internationally than men in the "Plasma Display Watcher" condition. No differences were found between women in the "Watcher Plasma Display Condition" and women in the "Watched" condition. Thus, the VSD methodology helps to bring to the forefront values that matter not only to the direct stakeholders of a technology (such as physical health, emotional well-being, and creativity) but also to the indirect stakeholders (such as privacy, informed consent, trust, and physical safety). Moreover, from the standpoint of VSD, the above study highlights how investigations of indirect stakeholders can be woven into the core structure of the experimental design with direct stakeholders.

4. *Multiplicity of and Potential Conflicts among Human Values.* VSD can help researchers uncover the multiplicity of and potential conflicts among human values implicated in technological implementations. In the above design space, for example, values of physical health, emotional well-being, and creativity appear to partially conflict with other values of privacy, civil rights, trust, and security.

5. *Technical Investigations.* Conceptual and empirical investigations can help to shape future technological investigations, particularly in terms of how nature (as a source of information) can be embedded in the design of display technologies to further human well-being. One obvious design space involves buildings. For example, if Kahn and colleagues' empirical results continue to emerge in line with their initial results, then one possible design guideline is as follows: we need to design buildings with nature in mind and within view. In other words, we cannot with psychological impunity digitize nature and display the digitized version as a substitute for the real thing (and worse, then destroy the original). At the same time, it is possible that technological representations of nature can garner some psychological benefits, especially when (as in an inside office) direct access to nature is otherwise unavailable.

In summary, this case study demonstrates the values of privacy in public spaces and human physical and psychological well-being.

### 2.3.3 Case 2: UrbanSim: Integrated Land Use, Transportation, and Environmental Simulation

In many regions in the United States (and globally), there is increasing concern about pollution, traffic jams, resource consumption, loss of open space, loss of coherent community, lack of sustainability, and unchecked sprawl. Elected officials, planners, and citizens in urban areas grapple with these difficult issues as they develop and evaluate alternatives for such decisions as building a new rail line or freeway, establishing an urban growth boundary, or changing incentives or taxes. These decisions interact in complex ways, and, in particular, transportation and land use decisions interact strongly with each other. There are both legal and commonsense reasons to try to understand the long-term consequences of these interactions and decisions. Unfortunately, the need for this understanding far outstrips the capability of the analytic tools used in current practice.

In response to this need, Waddell, Borning, and their colleagues have been developing UrbanSim, a large simulation package for predicting patterns of urban development for periods of 20 years or more, under different possible scenarios. Its primary purpose is to provide urban planners and other stakeholders with tools to aid in more informed decision making, with a secondary goal to support further democratization of the planning process. When provided with different scenarios—packages of possible policies and investments—UrbanSim models the resulting patterns of urban growth and redevelopment, of transportation usage, and of resource consumption and other environmental impacts. To date, UrbanSim has been applied in the metropolitan regions around Eugene/Springfield, Oregon, Honolulu, Hawaii, Salt Lake City, Utah, and Houston, Texas, with application to the Puget Sound region in Washington State under way. UrbanSim is undergoing significant redevelopment and extension in terms of its underlying architecture, interface, and social goals.

UrbanSim illustrates important aspects of value-sensitive design in addition to those described in the previous case study:

1. *Distinguishing Explicitly Supported Values from Stakeholder Values.* There is a distinction between explicitly supported values (i.e., ones that they explicitly want to embed in the simulation) and stakeholder values (i.e., ones that are important to some but not necessarily all of the stakeholders). In addition, there are three specific moral values to be supported explicitly. One is fairness, and more specifically freedom from bias. The simulation should not discriminate unfairly against any group of stakeholders or privilege one mode of transportation or policy over another. A second is accountability. Insofar as possible, stakeholders should be able to confirm that their values are reflected in the simulation, evaluate and judge its validity, and develop an appropriate level of confidence in its output. The third is democracy. The simulation should support the democratic process in the context of land use, transportation, and environmental planning. In turn, as part of supporting the democratic process, Borning and colleagues decided that the model should not a priori favor or rule out any given set of stakeholder values but instead should allow different stakeholders to articulate the values that are most important to them and then evaluate the alternatives in light of these values.

2. *Handling Widely Divergent and Potentially Conflicting Stakeholder Values.* The research team cannot focus on a few key values, as occurred in the "Room with a View" project (e.g., the values of privacy in public spaces and physical and psychological well-being). Rather, disputing stakeholders bring to the table widely divergent values about environmental, political, moral, and personal issues. Examples of stakeholder values are environmental sustainability, walkable neighborhoods, space for business expansion, affordable housing, freight mobility, minimal government intervention, minimal commute time, open space preservation, property rights, and environmental justice. How does one characterize the wide-ranging and deeply held values of diverse stakeholders, both present and future? Moreover, how does one prioritize the values implicated in the decisions? And how can one move from values to measurable outputs from the simulation to allow stakeholders to compare alternative scenarios?

3. *Designing for Credibility, Openness, and Accountability.* Credibility of the system is of great importance, particularly when the system is being used in a politically charged situation and is thus the subject of intense scrutiny. The research group has undertaken a variety of activities to help foster credibility, including using behaviorally transparent simulation techniques and performing sensitivity analyses

and a historical validation. In addition, techniques for fostering openness and accountability are also intended to support credibility. These include using open-source software (releasing the source code along with the executable), writing the code in as clear and understandable a fashion as possible, using a rigorous and extensive testing methodology, and complementing the open-source software with an open process that makes the state of our development visible to anyone interested. Similarly, the bug reports, feature requests, and plans are all on the Urban-Sim project Web site as well.

In summary, this case study demonstrates using value-sensitive design to investigate how a technology—an integrated land use, transportation, and environmental computer simulation—affects human values on both the individual and organizational levels and how human values can continue to drive the technical investigations, including refining the simulation, data, and interaction model.

### 2.3.4 VSD and HCI Development

VSD is a great effort to reflect what we as humans consider important in our lives. This is very much in line with the various concerns of HCI, although VSD is more sensitive to ethical or moral values. Moral values refer to issues that pertain to fairness, justice, human welfare, and virtue, encompassing within moral philosophical theory deontology, consequentialism, and virtue. VSD also accounts for conventions (e.g., standardization of protocols) and personal values (e.g., color preferences within a graphical user interface). On the other hand, the holistic human experience can be considered more general. It should consider both ethical and nonethical related values that we human beings regard as important. It can also refer to high-level human goals and individual realizations, as those specified by Maslow. These high-level goals and realizations can be considered high-level human values that may reflect more on the self than others. Overall, the HCI concerns and VSD are very much consistent with each other. These can be further demonstrated by the several features of VSD that tie closely with the HCI development philosophy, strategies, and concerns.

1. VSD seeks to be proactive: to influence the design of technology early in and throughout the design process. Starting early and working throughout the entire process has been the focus of the HCI development philosophy and methodology.

2. VSD enlarges the arena in which values arise to include not only the workplace but also education, the home, commerce, online communities, and public life. Early in the book, we discussed different HCI concerns and goals. The focus lies beyond the interface level and beyond usability, encompassing the broad organizational, social, cultural, and holistic human experiences.

3. VSD contributes a unique methodology that employs conceptual, empirical, and technical investigations, applied iteratively and integratively. This is very consistent with the iterative nature of HCI development.

4. VSD enlarges the scope of human values beyond those of cooperation, participation, and democracy to include all values, especially those with moral import. VSD also accounts for conventions and personal values.

5. VSD distinguishes between usability and human values with ethical import. Usability refers to characteristics of a system that make it work in a functional

sense (e.g., it is easy to use, easy to learn, and consistent, and it recovers easily from errors). However, not all highly usable systems support ethical values.

6. VSD identifies and takes seriously two classes of stakeholders: direct and indirect. Direct stakeholders refer to parties—individuals or organizations—who interact directly with the computer system or its output. Indirect stakeholders refer to all other parties who are affected by the use of the system. Often, indirect stakeholders are ignored in the design process. For example, computerized medical records systems have often been designed with many of the direct stakeholders in mind (e.g., insurance companies, hospitals, doctors, and nurses) but with too little regard for the values, such as the value of privacy, of a rather important group of indirect stakeholders: the patients.

7. VSD is an interactional theory: values are viewed neither as inscribed into technology (an endogenous theory) nor as simply transmitted by social forces (an exogenous theory). Rather, the interactional position holds that while the features or properties that people design into technologies more readily support certain values and hinder others, the technology's actual use depends on the goals of the people interacting with it.

8. VSD builds from the psychological proposition that certain values are universally held, although how such values play out in a particular culture at a particular point in time can vary considerably. Generally, the more concretely (act-based) one conceptualizes a value, the more one will be led to recognizing cultural variation; conversely, the more abstractly one conceptualizes a value, the more one will be led to recognizing universals. VSD seeks to work at both levels, the concrete and the abstract, depending on the design problem at hand. Note that this is an empirical proposition, based on a large amount of psychological and anthropological data, not a philosophical one. We also make this claim only for certain values, not all—there are clearly some values that are culture-specific.

## ▶ 3. EMERGING IT DEVELOPMENT CHANGES

In this section, we introduce three main emerging changes that fundamentally challenged the ways IT is developed: open source, component-based software development (CBSD), and outsourcing, especially offshore outsourcing. In each case, we discuss the challenges of these new development changes on HCI design and evaluation.

### 3.1 Open Source

#### 3.1.1 What Is Open Source?

Open source is a work methodology that fits the Open Source Definition. In general, open source is any computer software whose source code is either in the public domain or, more commonly, is copyrighted by one or more persons/entities and distributed under an open-source license. The Open Source Definition determines whether or not a software license can be considered open source. According to Wikipedia, the following conditions must be met:

- Free Redistribution: The software can be freely given away or sold.
- Source Code: The source code must either be included or be freely obtainable.

- Derived Works: Redistribution of modifications must be allowed.
- Integrity of the Author's Source Code: Licenses may require that modifications are redistributed only as patches.
- No Discrimination against Persons or Groups: No one can be locked out.
- No Discrimination against Fields of Endeavor: Commercial users cannot be excluded.
- Distribution of License: Rights must apply to everyone who receives the program.
- License Must Not Be Specific to a Product: The program cannot be licensed only as part of a larger distribution.
- License Must Not Restrict Other Software: The license cannot insist that any other software it is distributed with must also be open source.
- License Must Be Technology-Neutral: No click-wrap licenses or other medium-specific ways of accepting the license must be required.

> **Open source:** The same appearance, meaning, and operation hold true for all the user's interactions within the same application.
>
> **Open Source Definition:** Determines whether a piece of software can be regarded as open-source software by listing 10 conditions.

Open source is different from "free software." The latter can mean either software that can be used, copied, studied, modified, and redistributed by the user, or software that may be copied and used without payment (thus also referred to as "freeware" or "gratis software").

The open-source movement is a large movement of programmers and other computer users that advocates unrestricted access to the source code of software. Open-source advocates point out that as of the early 2000s, at least 90 percent of computer programmers are employed not to produce software for direct sale but rather to design and customize software for other purposes, such as in-house applications. According to advocates, this statistic implies that the value of software lies primarily in its usefulness to the developer or developing organization, rather than in its potential sale value, and that consequently there is usually no compelling economic reason to keep source code secret from competitors. Open-source advocates further argue that corporations frequently overprotect software in ways actually damaging to their own interests, for reasons ranging from mere institutional habit through reflexive territoriality to a rational but incorrect evaluation of the trade-offs between collecting secrecy rent and the quality and market payoff of openness.

As one can imagine, there are various debates over open source vs. closed source (also called proprietary development). One is about intellectual property rights. Some software development companies do use the copyright and patent rights provided for software developers as their primary source of income. By keeping their software source code hidden, they can demand fees for its use. While most software is written for internal use, the fees from the sale and license of commercial software are the primary source of income for companies that do sell software. Additionally, many companies with large research and development teams often develop extensive patent portfolios. These companies charge money for the use of their patents in software, but having software be open source means that there is a potential to have a nearly infinite number of derived works using patented technology, unbeknownst to the patent holder.

Another common argument, one that is more difficult for open-source advocates to contradict with hard facts, is that closed-source development allows more control over the final product. The theory behind this argument involves the incentives of producing the software. Open-source software is primarily a volunteer effort, while closed-source development is typically a salary-driven effort. By having the monetary resources to fund developers and management, and the ability to force development in a given direction, closed-source proponents argue that development can be more efficient and more focused.

### 3.1.2  Challenges for HCI Design and Evaluation

The decentralized and engineering-driven approach of open-source projects can be at odds with corporate processes and usability engineering methodologies. There is a common notion that open-source systems have poor user interfaces. Often they are created by engineers for engineers. The feedback cycle with real users does not exist because there are few usability experts participating in open-source development processes (Benson, Muller-Prove, & Mzourek, 2004).

Providing usability know-how that leads to usable and useful products is a win-win situation for developers, the corporations, and—most importantly—the users (Benson, Muller-Prove, & Mzourek, 2004). Efforts have been made to increase the likelihood that usability will become a core value in open-source software development (Frishberg, Dirks, Benson, Nickell, & Smith, 2002). Below we present three examples of open-source projects by Sun Microsystems to demonstrate how usability issues are handled in open-source projects. These cases are from a CHI'04 conference proceedings report (Benson, Muller-Prove, & Mzourek, 2004).

NetBeans is an integrated development environment that provides the foundations for Sun's Java development tools. It was one of the first open-source projects started at Sun in June 2000. Sun is the main contributor to NetBeans and the only HCI contributor. The biggest accomplishment of the NetBeans HCI group has been establishing a user interface specification document as part of the development process. Such documents now describe the detailed interaction and visual design of the majority of new features. The HCI group performs regular usability studies of NetBeans and publicizes results. Usability issues are given equal importance to functionality bugs and are tracked in the same database. Graphics such as splash screens, icons, and other artwork form a large part of the project and are contributed exclusively by Sun's designers under an open-source license. Sun's user experience contribution also includes accessibility, localization into Japanese and Simplified Chinese, and documentation.

GNOME is a free, cross-platform desktop environment. Sun has contributed usability resources to GNOME since August 2000. Sun's first major input was a usability study of GNOME 1.2. This offered the first feedback that many developers had received from real users, and the impact was profound. Consequently, the community formed the GNOME Usability Project (GUP), a cross-community group of HCI practitioners and students. Four of Sun's usability staff have served in this group, one role of which is to publish the GNOME Human Interface Guidelines. Developers have been quick to adopt these guidelines, partly due to the GNOME Release Team's decision not to ship applications with too many open usability bugs. Sun designed the GNOME accessibility framework on which several innovative assistive technologies are now being built. Finally, Sun has written or improved much of the GNOME user documentation, translated it into several languages, and returned the results to the community.

OpenOffice.org is the leading office application on Linux and the main competitor to Microsoft Office. The project was open-sourced by Sun in October 2000. The User Experience Team includes professionals from all fields of HCI: GUI and interaction design, usability engineering, linguistics, accessibility, and globalization. The latter is especially important, as OpenOffice.org is localized into more than 30 languages. The

User Experience Team plays a major role in the next design phase: writing specifications. These describe in detail the features and design changes for the user interface. As with source code, these documents are contributed back to the community. The design process is supported by internal Sun usability studies and external studies conducted by, for example, HCI students.

To conclude, although usability is still a relatively new concept for open-source projects, it is starting to exert some influence, for example, in the form of studies and guidelines. It is believed that integrating a suitable usability methodology into open-source processes is the first priority (Frishberg et al., 2002).

## 3.2 Component-Based Software Development (CBSD)

### 3.2.1 What Is CBSD?

Reuse of knowledge and artifacts from existing information systems to build new ones can be a very attractive way of saving software development time and cost and increasing product quality. Software components (also called software "building blocks") are becoming increasingly popular design and implementation technologies and have played important roles in the overall IS strategies of many organizations. There have been many reported successes by companies that reuse software components to build new ones. In general, component-based software development (CBSD) represents a paradigm that aims at leveraging software artifacts across numerous implementations.

With components, developers can encapsulate pieces of a system, which can be developed individually. Other developers making use of these components only need to know the external interface of the component to be able to use its functionality. The component's internal details are hidden. This makes it possible for components to be replaced by other components as long as they provide the same external interface (Brinkman, Haakma, & Bouwhuis, 2001).

Components have to be logically distinct elements. Components in a software product may be distinct user interface elements (for example, tools that provide different views of and interfaces to the same application data). They may have distinct users or functional characteristics (such as runtime libraries or class libraries in a Java or C++ development environment) (Green, 1999).

Components can be plugged and played to provide user-enhanceable software (Grundy & Hosking, 2002). While the traditional reuse paradigm allows changes to the code that is to be reused (white-box reuse), component-based software development advocates that components are reused as is (black-box reuse). Developers and sometimes end users compose or assemble applications from often stand-alone components in flexible ways to achieve a desired set of functionality. This requires components to have two main qualities: reusable in diverse situations without code modifications, and extendable and configurable via plug-and-play.

### 3.2.2 Challenges in HCI Design and Evaluation

Developing software components with user interfaces that can be adapted to diverse reuse situations is challenging, as are the planning and conducting of usability and user experience evaluations when the potential users, user tasks, and use context are unknown ahead of time when the components are built. Typically, many of the components used to build and/or extend an application have been developed separately, with no

**Component-based software development:** Using or reusing existing software components to build new software applications.

knowledge of the user interfaces of other components that may be composed with them. This can result in component-based applications with inappropriate and inconsistent interfaces (Grundy & Hosking, 2002). For example, composed components may provide inconsistent interface metaphors (e.g., menu items vs. buttons); they may show unsuitable interfaces or parts of interfaces to a user due to the user's level of expertise, the task or role being performed, or the user's preferences. As developers and end users reconfigure their applications, they may add new components with user interfaces that introduce further complications or inconsistencies to the overall application interface (Grundy & Hosking, 2002).

To address these challenges, researchers have been exploring different strategies and methods. One method to deal with the issues involved in user interface design and evaluation concerns in CBSD is to utilize layered protocols (Fearrell, Hollands, Taylor, & Gamble, 1999). The basic idea is that user–system interaction is portrayed on different layers. User–system interaction on the highest level is established by mediation of user–system interaction on lower levels. The interaction on each level may follow a different protocol (Brinkman, Haakma, & Bouwhuis, 2001).

Another method considers evaluating the individual component's usability from the user interface perspective. At the component level, components that hamper the overall interaction could be pinpointed and replaced by more usable ones. Ready-made usable components could be made for a specified user group to achieve a specified goal within a specified context of use (Brinkman, Haakma, & Bouwhuis, 2001). Then these components can be tested for the goals and use context. The usability and user experience of the composited user interface can be tested again after reusing and assembling various components.

In general, usability and user experience evaluation should occur at both the component level and the complete user interface level. More research and practice are needed in this area. The heavy analysis focus of the human-centered HCI development methodology still needs to be tested to determine its applicability to CBSD.

### 3.3 Outsourcing, Offshore Outsourcing, and Freelancing

*Outsourcing* became a popular buzzword in the 1990s and is especially popular today, although the concept started in the 1960s. Of considerable interest and concern to many IT-related professions is the outsourcing of professional jobs from the West to India, China, and other countries in Asia and South America. Outsourcing has been discussed frequently in almost every major news publication. Many local and small news channels also constantly report related news and debates. This is because it is widely acknowledged that outsourcing, especially offshore outsourcing, has affected many businesses and people and will continue to do so.

The driving factor behind this development has been the need to cut costs, while the enabling factor has been the global electronic network that allows digital data to be accessed and shipped instantly from and to anywhere in the world.

**Offshore outsourcing:** The practice of hiring an external business to perform some or all business functions in a country other than the one where the product will be sold or consumed.

#### 3.3.1 What Are Outsourcing, Offshore Outsourcing, and Freelancing?
The concept of outsourcing was first made popular by Ross Perot when he founded Electronic Data Systems (EDS) in 1962. EDS would say to a potential client, "You are good at designing and manufacturing widgets, but we are skilled with managing information technology. We will sell you the IT services that you require, and you can pay us periodically with a minimum commitment of two years."

In general, outsourcing involves turning over a segment of business (client) to another business (supplier). The segment can be either production or service. It involves transferring a significant amount of management control to the supplier. That is, outsourcing requires the turning over of management responsibilities for running a section of business from the requesting organization to the supplier. Thus outsourcing always involves a considerable degree of two-way information exchange, coordination, and trust between the two parties. Normally, the outsourcing business possesses the expertise inherent to the core of the outsourced business segment that the client organization does not have or does not plan to have.

Offshoring is the relocation of business processes to a lower-cost location. Similar to outsourcing, it can be either production/manufacturing offshoring or service offshoring. The offshored unit usually is part of the same organization. For example, a big company may build a manufacturing site in China and move certain parts of its business to this new location.

Offshore outsourcing is the practice of hiring an external organization to perform some or all business functions in a country other than the one where the product will be sold or consumed. Opponents argue that this sends work overseas, thereby reducing domestic employment. Many jobs in the infotech sectors—such as IT, data entry, and customer support—have been or are potentially affected. *Global sourcing* is a recent term for outsourcing the production of IT hardware, software, and services to other U.S. firms and to firms in other countries (Mann, 2004). It emphasizes the globalization of the offshore outsourcing practice.

> **Global sourcing:** Outsourcing to firms in other countries.

The general criteria for a job to be offshore-able are as follows:

- The job does not require direct customer interaction.
- The job can be teleworked.
- The work has a high information content.
- The work is easy to set up.
- There is a high wage difference between the original and offshore countries.
- The work is repeatable.

Freelancing on the Internet is an alternative to big companies' outsourcing or offshoring. This kind of Internet-based outsourcing can be thought of as a small-business variant of the wider business practice of offshoring. Whereas larger corporations may set up their own subsidiaries in cheaper-rate countries, small businesses as well as individual developers, whether employees or themselves freelancers, find it convenient to look for opportunities to get projects done through Internet freelancing sites. A typical project price, as of 2004, is several hundred U.S. dollars, well within reach of an individual or a small company in the United States. Freelancing can be best utilized for all Web-related work, where communication distance is virtually zero. Freelancing on the Internet has opened doors for many people to use their brain and earn money from any part of the world.

> **Freelancer:** A self-employed person working in a profession or trade in which full-time employment by a single employer is also common.
>
> **Freelancing:** Using freelancers to obtain outsourcing result.

The advent of the Internet has enabled individuals and small businesses to contract freelancers from all over the world to get projects done at a minimum cost. This trend runs in parallel with the tendency toward big corporations' outsourcing and may in the future serve to strengthen small businesses' capacity to compete with their bigger competitors capable of setting up offshore locations or of arriving at major contracts with offshore companies.

So what might be the impact of offshore outsourcing on the U.S. economy, IT workers, IT jobs, IT skills, and specifically HCI development and practice? A little bit of historical perspective can provide some insight and predictions.

There have been two waves of offshore outsourcing or global sourcing (Mann, 2004). The first one was the wave of hardware global sourcing that took place during the 1990s. By reducing the price of IT hardware, this global sourcing yielded increased investment in IT and more jobs for U.S. workers with IT skills. Global production and sourcing reduced the price of IT hardware some 20 percent below what it would have been without global sourcing. Lower prices encouraged disproportionately greater investment in IT throughout the overall U.S. economy. IT investment and IT jobs go hand in hand. By 2002, over 67 percent of the people employed in IT jobs in the United States did not work in the IT sector (Mann, 2004).

The second is the recent wave of software and IT service global sourcing. As hardware prices fell, the importance of software and IT services rose in proportion to the spending on the total IT hardware package. The spending ratio on software and services changed from $1.40 per $1 on hardware (1993) to $2.20 per $1 on hardware (2000) (Mann, 2004). The global sourcing of software and IT services will continue to reduce the overall price of IT products. This will help diffuse IT into the lagging sectors that did not use IT very intensively, such as health services, education, and many small and medium-size enterprises. This, in turn, will increase demand for workers with IT skills. Technological changes in IT development (such as open-source and component-based development) can modularize and decompose the functions into design, coding, maintenance, and user interface.

There are several other types of outsourcing, to make the list more comprehensive. "Onshore outsourcing" suggests that businesses such as IT work should be outsourced to smaller U.S. cities. There are lower-cost regions in the country where the customers live; thus this type of outsourcing can still be cheap and meanwhile help workers of the same country. "Nearshoring" or "nearshore outsourcing" is a type of outsourcing in which business processes relocate to cheaper locations that are geographically nearer. Nearshoring can be contrasted with offshoring.

### 3.3.2 Challenges in HCI Design and Evaluation

It is widely believed that analysis and design must be done together with the customer, while coding, IT documentation, IT maintenance, and other "back-end" tasks do not require close proximity with customers and can be done by less costly programmers abroad (Mann, 2004). Thus the higher-wage jobs, involving design and interface, must still be performed in the United States. Overall, the second wave of global sourcing will yield a further increase in jobs demanding IT knowledge and skills, especially for design, user interface, customization, and utilization of IT applications (Mann, 2004). From this perspective, many HCI concerns and issues discussed in this book are still relevant and important. Many methods and techniques can still be applied. The HCI methodology as a higher-level guideline is still valid.

- However, some recent evidence proves that higher-value "front-end" tasks are also being taken over by some offshore businesses in China and India (Marcus, 2004). These front-end jobs include user-experience development tasks such as the associated technology research, usability analysis, and evaluation, including testing, conceptual design, and even detailed visual design. A report in 2003 indicates that although it is accepted that Indian programmers are skilled, it is questionable whether users would say that the best interfaces come from India. Hardly any center of learning in India offers a significant course in HCI or usability. Most of the technically savvy programmers are unaware of principles and techniques of good design. Many software companies in these countries are well behind on HCI and usability expertise and considerations (see the box below for reality reflections on this). Further, myths that impede good design are rampant (Henry, 2003). Strategies and techniques need to be developed to address the following potential difficulties in offshore outsourcing IT development (Henry, 2003):

- Lack of usability professionals

- Local users are not representative

- Separation of usability professionals from users

Reality
Reflections

Software engineering has been a major strength in the Indian IT industry. However, expertise in HCI has been lagging behind other countries (Joshi, 2004). The usability maturity model is a method for measuring progress of usability and human–computer interaction (HCI) design in a company. There are six levels in the usability maturity model. A company is considered to be at the *unrecognized* level if people in the company believe that there are no problems related to the usability of its products. The next level is called *recognized* and is usually accompanied by the initial awareness that there is a problem (often through negative customer feedback). The third level is the *considered* level, which is generally accompanied by financial investment in HCI consultants and/or HCI training. Companies move to the fourth level or *implemented* level when they set up a specialized group to handle "user interface design." The fifth level is the *integrated* level where HCI design activities become routine. The goal is to become *institutionalized,* which occurs when the company starts considering itself a human-centered solutions company rather than a technology company and produces consistently usable products. Joshi contends that the majority of Indian companies are at the *considered* level and will not attain *institutionalized* status until 2009. Joshi (2004) believes that in 2009 the top 25 percent of Indian companies will be fully integrated, most of the remaining companies will be at the implemented level, and only a fringe 10 percent will be at the unrecognized level.

Another report in 2004 shows that many Asian countries have demonstrated remarkable progress in acquiring Western usability-oriented design and analysis skills (Marcus, 2004). That is, the first difficulty mentioned above is being addressed locally at the offshore firms. In general, user interface design and usability analysis/evaluation professions are also growing in these countries. Professionals are being produced in universities in these countries. Some Indian and Chinese firms started to take on the new development of products and services, indicating their ability to cover the entire spectrum of the IT development process—not merely a back-end engine (Marcus, 2004). This new phenomenon goes beyond just the impact on HCI practice. It creates a new competition between the West and these growing so-called offshore firms. Interestingly, some U.S.-based usability firms have started to take steps to grow their service engines in these offshore countries. Human Factors International, based in the United States, now has 60 people in Mumbai and expects to hire many more in the coming years. Their services will be primarily oriented to serving clients in North America and Europe (Marcus, 2004).

Based on the aforementioned new evidence and challenges, numerous debates have been triggered and solutions suggested. For example, one potential position involves mentoring, training, and relating to the offshore providers of services. Many professionals know how important this kind of project management is for large, complex, multilocation projects, in which teams must be coordinated to maintain close attention to client and user needs. Given the great geographic and cultural differences involved, this task will be very important (Marcus, 2004). In addition, providing a local face to project teams in the West and contact with key corporate customers is an important role that is unlikely to disappear. Local customers in the West want to have people on-site who understand their context and objectives, as well as their language and culture (Marcus, 2004).

These new strategies and techniques (such as a local face in the West) are very important when considering the multiple types of HCI concerns (see Chapter 9 on evaluation).

## ▷ 4. SUMMARY

In this chapter, we take a forward-looking perspective and examine a number of recent radical changes in technology development and use, as well as the corresponding challenges these changes bring to HCI researchers and professionals. Specifically, we review technology development in ubiquitous computing, social computing, and value-sensitive design and the use of these technologies in our daily lives for work or leisure. We also examine several new ways of developing applications such as open source, component-based systems development, and outsourcing. Among all these new developments and uses, some traditional HCI concerns and methods are still applicable, and some others are yet to be tested. Most importantly, there are challenges for the new development of HCI concerns and techniques. Most of these changes are relatively new and more practice and research are needed. We do not intend to provide answers to all challenges but wish to provide opportunities for discussion and more exploration. The new challenges require new solutions, which rely on the new generations of HCI students, designers, methodologists, practitioners, and visionaries.

## ▷ 5. SUMMARY OF CONCEPTS AND TERMS

| | | |
|---|---|---|
| Ubiquitous computing | Mobile computing | Social computing |
| Value-sensitive design | Open source | Component-based development |
| Outsourcing | Offshoring | Offshore outsourcing |

## ▷ 6. BIBLIOGRAPHY AND ADDITIONAL READINGS

Abowd, G. D., & Mynatt, E. D. (2000). Charting past, present, and future research in ubiquitous computing. *ACM Transactions on Computer-Human Interaction, 7*(1), 29–58.

Benson, C., Muller-Prove, M., & Mzourek, J. (2004). *Professional usability in open source projects: GNOME, OpenOffice.org, NetBeans.* Paper read at CHI, April 24–29, 2004, Vienna, Austria.

Brinkman, W. P., Haakma, R., & Bouwhuis, D. G. (2001). *Usability evaluation of component-based user interfaces.* Paper read at IFIP INTERACT'01: Human-Computer Interaction.

DeSanctis, G. (2006). Who is the user? Individuals, groups, communities. In P. Zhang & D. Galletta (Eds.), *Human-computer interaction and management information systems: Foundations.* Armonk, NY: M.E. Sharpe.

Dey, A. K., Ljungstrand, P., & Schmidt, A. (2001). *Distributed and disappearing user interfaces in ubiquitous computing.* Paper read at ACM CHI 2001 Conference on Human Factors in Computing Systems.

Edwards, W. K., Newman, M. W., & Sedivy, J. Z. (2001). *Building the ubiquitous computing user experience.* Paper read at ACM CHI 2001 Conference on Human Factors in Computing Systems.

Erickson, T., & Kellogg, W. A. (2000). Social translucence: An approach to designing systems that support social processes. *ACM Transactions on Computer-Human Interaction, 7*(1), 59–83.

Fearrell, P. S. E., Hollands, J. G., Taylor, M. M., & Gamble, H. D. (1999). Perceptual control and layered protocols in interface design: I. Fundamental concepts. *International Journal of Human-Computer Studies, 50*(6), 489–520.

Friedman, B., Kahn, P. H., & Borning, A. (2006). Value sensitive design and information systems. In P. Zhang & D. Galletta (Eds.), *Human-computer interaction and management information systems: Foundations.* Armonk, NY: M. E. Sharpe.

Frishberg, N., Dirks, A. M., Benson, C., Nickell, S., & Smith, S. (2002). *Getting to know you: Open source development meets usability.* Paper read at CHI 2002 Conference on Human Factors in Computing Systems.

Green, R. (1999). *Component-based software development: Implications for documentation.* Paper read at ACM 17th International Conference on Systems Documentation.

Grundy, J., & Hosking, J. (2002). Developing adaptable user interfaces for component-based systems. *Interacting with Computers, 14,* 175–194.

Henry, P. (2003). Advancing UCD while facing challenges working from offshore. *Interactions: New Visions of Human-Computer Interaction,* 38–47.

Ishida, T., Nishida, T., & Hattori, F. (1998). Overview of community computing. In T. Ishida (Ed.), *Community computing: Collaboration over global information networks.* New York: Wiley.

Joshi, A. (2004). *Institutionalizing HCI, the challenges in India.* Paper read at the 39th Annual National Convention of the Computer Society of India, December 3, 2004, Taj Lands End, Mumbai.

Licklider, J. C. R. (1960). Man-computer symbiosis. *IRE Transactions on Human Factors in Electronics, HFE-1,* 4–11.

Licklider, J. C. R., Taylor, R. W., & Herbert, E. (1978). The computer as a communication device. *International Science and Technology,* 21–31.

Mann, C. L. (2004). What global sourcing means for U.S. IT workers and for the U.S. economy. *Communication of the ACM, 47*(7), 33–35.

Marcus, A. (2004). Insights on outsourcing—What's in it for us? For them? Where are we headed? *Interactions: New Visions of Human-Computer Interaction, XI*(4), 12–17.

Stanton, N. A. (2001). Introduction: Ubiquitous computing: Anytime, anyplace, anywhere? *International Journal of Human-Computer Interaction, 13*(2), 107–111.

Sumi, Y., & Mase, K. (2002). Conference assistant system for supporting knowledge sharing in academic communities. *Interacting with Computers, 14,* 713–737.

Weiser, M. (1991). The computer for the 21st century. *Scientific American.*

## ▶ 7. CASE STUDY

Lance Redux is designing an e-commerce Web site for World Gourmet, an international food sales outlet. Once the traditional Web site is designed and implemented, he is going to build a site that will accommodate cell phones and PDA wireless media. This technology is known as WAP (short for Wireless Application Protocol), a secure specification that allows users to access information instantly via handheld wireless devices such as mobile phones, pagers, two-way radios, smart-phones, and communicators.

WAP supports most wireless networks. WAP is supported by all operating systems. WAPs that use displays and access the Internet run what are called microbrowsers— browsers with small file sizes that can accommodate the low-memory constraints of handheld devices and the low-bandwidth constraints of a wireless handheld network.

Although WAP supports HTML and XML, the WML language (an XML application) is specifically devised for small screens and one-hand navigation without a keyboard. WML is scalable from two-line text displays up through graphic screens found on items such as smart phones and communicators. WAP also supports WMLScript. It is similar to JavaScript but makes minimal demands on memory and CPU power because it does not contain many of the unnecessary functions found in other scripting languages.

For more information, see http://www.webopedia.com/TERM/W/WAP.html.

## ▶ 8. EXERCISES

Ex. 1.  Ubiquitous computing

Find some examples of ubiquitous computing. Discuss HCI concerns of these examples and how these concerns are addressed by the final products.

Ex. 2.  Mobile computing

Examine your or your friend's cell phone. List the main functions of the cell phone. List the main HCI issues and concerns. Provide a wish list for both better functions and better HCI features.

Ex. 3.  Social computing

List the online communities you belong to. What are your roles in these communities (leader, moderator, active contributor, lurker, etc.)? How do you benefit from these communities? Do you think these are important in people's lives? Why or why not?

Ex. 4.  Value-sensitive design

List a few key values of your own. Find some example applications (or their features) that are either supportive of your values or against your values.

Ex. 5.  Open source

Do some research to find out several popular open-source applications. Identify the main contributors. Are usability or HCI concerns addressed in these applications?

Ex. 6.  Component-based systems development

Do a search on the Internet to find out several popular component-based applications. Are usability or HCI concerns addressed in these applications?

Ex. 7.  Outsourcing

Do some research to find answers to the following questions:

Which country is the largest offshore outsourcing country?

What types of computer software applications are often outsourced offshore?

# Glossary

**Access:** Providing access to information via information systems and technologies is critical to full societal participation. HCI can play a role in breaking through barriers to access.

**Accountability:** Understanding who shares responsibility for the outcomes and impact of information systems.

**Affect:** A general term for a set of psychological processes and states including emotions, moods, affective impressions, and attitudes.

**Affective impression:** The user's appraisal of the affective qualities of the HCI.

**Affective quality:** The object's ability to cause a change in the user's core affect.

**Affordance:** The aspects of an object that the user perceives as indicating how to use the object (e.g., the handle of a teapot).

**Analogical consistency:** The correspondence between the system's representation and the real-world phenomenon in terms of appearance, meaning, and operation.

**Analysis:** Studies the current system and proposes alternative systems.

**Anthony's Triangle:** Classifies the levels of information systems and the levels of managerial users of these systems.

**Anthropomorphic design:** Resembles human beings.

**Attitude:** Represents a summary evaluation of an object.

**Audition:** The human process of hearing and comprehending sound.

**Auditory nonspeech output:** Any sound that is output by a computer device that is not speech-related.

**Automatic behavior:** Behavior characterized by cognitive processes that are fast and cognitively undemanding.

**Beach's Image Theory of Screening:** States that decision making is a two-stage process; screening is the first stage, followed by choice.

**Blogs:** Short for *Web logs*, which are online journals accessible to Internet-enabled users.

**Brightness:** The shades of gray increasing from white through gray to black.

**Chernoff faces:** Graphics constructed as facial expressions to represent quantitative information.

**Cognitive-affective mode of communication (Te'eni):** Explains how effective communicators adapt their behavior to reduce complexity.

**Cognitive fit:** The state in which the system's representation of the problem supports the user's strategies for performing the task.

**Cognitive performance:** The speed and accuracy of the information-processing task.

**Collaboration software:** Allows people to work together and includes groupware, e-mail, instant messaging, data conferencing, and videoconferencing, among others.

**Color:** Defined by hue, saturation, and brightness.

**Color wheel:** A spatial representation of colors as a circle, where each color corresponds to a light wavelength.

**Common Industry Format (CIF):** A standard method for reporting summative usability test findings.

**Communityware:** Software that allows large decentralized groups of people to form communities, share preferences and knowledge, and perform social activities.

**Complexity of HCI:** The amount of human resources needed for interacting with the computer to accomplish the task.

**Component-based software development:** Using or reusing existing software components to build new software applications.

**Componential design:** The process of selecting or adapting the appropriate component to fit the user and the user's task.

**Components:** The building blocks with which we construct the human–computer interface.

**Composite graphics (of quantitative information):** Meaningful arrangements of labels and spatial elements that represent characteristics or relationships of the data.

**Computer anxiety:** Emotions about the implications of using a computer such as the loss of important data.

**Context of HCI:** The situation and the physical and social factors in the environment that affect and give meaning to HCI.

**Controlled behavior:** Behavior characterized by cognitive processes that are relatively slow and cognitively demanding.

**Core affect (or feeling):** A neurophysiological state that integrates two dimensions: pleasure-displeasure and activated-nonactivated.

**Customer Account Management systems:** These systems support the management of customer accounts. They may be purchased as part of an "off-the-shelf" system.

**Customer Relationship Management (CRM) systems:** These systems enable organizations to better serve their customers via software. The term CRM can be used to describe either the software itself or the whole business strategy.

**Data entry systems:** Systems used to support the manual processes of data entry. These systems are generally proprietary and developed in-house specifically to accomplish data entry tasks.

**Data input:** Enables the user to input data to the computer by generating values or selecting from predefined values.

**Decision support systems:** Single-user systems designed to support decision making. DSS components include database, model-base, and user interface. The user interface is critical to the success of a DSS.

**Design:** To create the system according to the analysis results.

**Design guidelines:** Specific and usually context-dependent rules for designers to follow in order to achieve the design principles.

**Design principles:** High-level and largely context-free design goals based on theories of human–computer interaction.

**Dialogue design:** Focuses on how information is provided to and captured from users during a specific task.

**Direct manipulation:** An interaction style in which objects are represented and manipulated in a manner analogous to the real world (e.g., by directly pointing at an object and dragging it to a location rather than issuing logical instructions to bring about the same effect).

**Document preparation systems:** Office automation systems that are designed to support document preparation such as word processors, presentation software, publication software, and others.

**Emissions:** Electronic radiation waves emitted by visual display terminals.

**Emotion:** A core affect that is intentional and directed toward a certain object.

**Enterprise communication systems:** Systems designed to support enterprise-level communications including e-mail systems and conferencing systems.

**Enterprise Resource Planning (ERP) systems:** Systems designed to support all the functions and activities of an organization including marketing, production management, order fulfillment, accounting, personnel management, and financial management.

**Ergonomics:** The physical fit between human and machine.

**Errors:** Deviations from intentional behavior that is either skill-, rule-, or knowledge-based.

**Ethical considerations:** The four main ethical considerations for information systems include accessibility, privacy, accountability, and property.

**Evaluation:** The determination of the significance, worth, condition, or value by careful appraisal and study.

**Executive support systems:** Strategic systems designed to support executives. These systems give executives the capability of viewing data from an aggregate level and allow "drill down" to the more detailed level of data to help executives understand the nature of the aggregate level of data.

**External consistency:** The same appearance, meaning, and operation holds true for the user's interactions across applications.

**Fit:** The match between the computer design, the user, and the task so as to minimize the human resources needed to accomplish the task.

**Fitts' law:** Measures the time it takes for a human to move a certain distance.

**Flow:** The user's optimal experience of control, focus of attention, curiosity, and intrinsic interest.

**Form fill-in:** Enables the user to input information about some entity as a spatially organized set of data input widgets.

**Formative evaluation:** Conducted during the development of a product in order to form or influence design decisions.

**Freelancer:** A self-employed person working in a profession or trade in which full-time employment by a single employer is also common.

**Freelancing:** Using freelancers to obtain outsourcing result.

**Functionality:** The collection of system operations or services available to the users for their use.

**Functions:** The component's services to the user.

**Global sourcing:** Outsourcing to firms in other countries.

**GOMS:** Goals, Operators, Methods, and Selection rules are the elements of a model that describes purposeful HCI.

**Group support systems:** Systems designed to support group processes including decision making, communication, meetings, document control, calendaring, and others.

**Gulf of evaluation:** The gap between the computerized implementation of the user's goal and its evaluation by the user.

**Gulf of execution:** The gap between the user's goal and its computerized implementation.

**Haptic devices:** Generate sensation to the skin and muscles through touch, weight, and rigidity.

**HCSDLC:** A human-centered systems development methodology where organizational needs and human needs are considered together throughout the systems development life cycle.

**HCSDLC philosophy:** Information systems development should meet both organizational and individual needs; thus all relevant human factors should be incorporated into the SDLC as early as possible.

**Heuristic evaluation:** A group of experts, guided by a set of higher-level design principles or heuristics, evaluate whether interface elements conform to the principles.

**Heuristics:** Rules of thumb to perform a task that depend heavily on the content and context of the task.

**Hofstede's Model of Cultural Differentiation:** Includes four dimensions including power-distance, uncertainty avoidance, individualistic-collectivistic, and masculinity-femininity.

**Hue:** Corresponds to the normal meaning of color—changes in wavelength.

**Human concerns of HCI:** Physical, cognitive, affective, and usefulness.

**Human resources in HCI:** The physical and psychological resources needed for user activity.

**Innovation Diffusion Theory:** Explains the way in which organizations implement innovations.

**Input device:** Any machine that feeds data into a computer.

**Instant messaging (IM):** Allows one-to-one real-time interactions via typed text.

**Intellectual property:** An intellectual property is any product of the human intellect that is unique, is novel, and has some value in the marketplace. Electronic form of intellectual property is difficult to safeguard.

**Internal consistency:** The same appearance, meaning, and operation hold true for all the user's interactions within the same application.

**Internet:** A global network of networks that follows certain standards and protocols in order to support access, communication, and connectivity.

**Interorganizational systems:** Those systems that link companies with external organizations (not individual customers). Usually this link is a B2B (business-to-business) link between suppliers and business customers.

**Keyboard:** The set of typewriter-like keys that enable the user to enter data into the computer.

**Knowledge-based behavior:** Highly controlled behavior that requires assessment and generation of new rules of behavior and is demanding of cognitive resources.

**Knowledge work systems:** Single-user systems designed to support knowledge creation activities. KWS components include diagram support, stress and capacity testing, simulations, and prototyping tools.

**Leadership style:** Impacts the effectiveness of group systems.

**Lexical level:** Describes the way specific computer devices are used to implement the syntactic level.

**Media design:** Is concerned with the selection of certain media types to meet the specific needs.

**Mental model:** A representation of the conceptual structure of a device or a system.

**Metaphor:** A cognitive process in which an experience is related to an already familiar concept.

**Metaphor design:** Concerned with finding or inventing a metaphor or analogue to help the users develop a mental model of the system.

**Moods:** Nonintentional core affects that exist within a person independently of external objects.

**Multilayer activity (TSSL model):** A model of user activity that includes four levels: task, semantics, syntax, and lexicon.

**Muscular problems:** Sore and damaged muscles brought on by frequent use of computers.

**Navigation:** Enables the user to control the intersystem and intrasystem flow of activities and the user's navigation of the system.

**Negative social impacts:** Include anxiety, alienation, potency of the individual, speed and complexity, societal and organizational dependence, unemployment and displacement, and valuing of human diversity.

**Non-structured task:** Task that is ill-defined, has ambiguous goals (if it has any at all), and has no explicit procedures that can ensure successful completion of the task.

**Office automation systems:** Systems designed to automate and support the work of white-collar support staff members. Interface consistency is critical to the success of these systems.

**Offshore outsourcing:** The practice of hiring an external business to perform some or all business functions in a country other than the one where the product will be sold or consumed.

**Offshoring:** Relocation of business processes (including production/manufacturing) to a lower-cost location.

**Open source:** Any software whose source code is in the public domain or distributed under an open-source license.

**Organizational level:** These systems are designed to support the entire organizational entity and include communications, personnel management, and organizational learning.

**Organizational-level task:** A worker's designed effort to accomplish an organizational demand.

**Output device:** A machine capable of representing data from a computer.

**Outsourcing:** Turning over a segment of business to another business.

**Perceived ease of use:** The users' belief that using a particular system would be free of effort.

**Perceived enjoyment:** The extent to which fun can be derived from using the system as such.

**Perceived usefulness:** The users' belief that using the system will enhance their performance.

**Performance:** Reflects both the efficiency of performing the task and the quality of the task product.

**Physical engineering:** The science of human engineering, which combines the study of human body mechanics and physical limitations with industrial psychology.

**Physical human limitations:** Include such aspects as levels of hearing, arm reach, muscular strength, visual distance, and others.

**Pointing device:** Controls the movement of the cursor on a display screen.

**Presentation design:** Concerns the decisions on display layout and incorporation of metaphors, media, and dialogue designs with the rest of the displays.

**Privacy:** Protecting against public access to personal information about individuals.

**Processing of images:** Processing characterized as spatial, graphic, and holistic.

**Processing of verbal information:** Processing characterized as sequential, linguistic, and procedural.

**Project management systems:** Systems designed to support the management of projects. These systems include mechanisms for decomposing large tasks into smaller, more manageable subtasks. They also include modules that help to manage resources including time, labor, and money.

**Project selection and planning:** The first phase in SDLC where an organization's total information systems needs are analyzed and arranged, a potential information systems project is identified, and an argument for continuing or not continuing with the project is presented.

**Prototype:** A proof-of-concept representation of a design.

**Prototyping:** The process of quickly putting together a prototype.

**Repetitive-motion problems:** Physical discomfort and inflammation of tendons and tendon sheaths caused by frequent use of keyboards and other input devices.

**Representation:** A simplified depiction of a real-world phenomenon constructed to support some activity.

**Rule-based behavior:** Controlled behavior that relies on predefined rules of behavior that are contingent on the particular situation encountered.

**Satisfaction:** A positive affect resulting from the evaluation of the use of the computer system based on a comparison of expectations versus experience.

**Saturation:** The relative amount of pure light that must be mixed with the white light to produce the perceived color.

**SDLC:** A commonly used methodology for information systems development that breaks the whole systems development process into manageable phases.

**Semantic level:** Pertains to the set of objects and operations through which the computer becomes meaningful to the user.

**Skill-based behavior:** Automatic behavior that is predefined and requires minimal cognitive resources.

**Social identity and de-individuation processes:** Processes, such as e-mail, that reduce the impact of social norms and constraints.

**Software globalization:** Creating a "generic" and functional version of software that is devoid of cultural context. The focus is on functionality and not packaging.

**Software localization:** Adding the cultural and locale-specific distinctiveness to globalize or generic software.

**Speech recognition:** The ability of the computer to recognize and understand human speech.

**Standards:** Are concerned with prescribed ways of discussing, presenting, or doing things to achieve consistency across same type of products.

**Structured task:** Task that is well defined, has clear and explicit goals, and can be accomplished by following predefined procedures.

**Summative evaluation:** Conducted after the product is finished to ensure that it possesses a certain level of quality, meets certain standards, or satisfies certain requirements set by the sponsors or other agencies.

**Support for the physically impaired:** Software and hardware design that accommodates physically disabled users.

**Syntactic level:** Dictates the rules of combining the semantic objects and operations into correct instructions.

**System development methodology:** A standardized development process that defines a set of activities, methods and techniques, best practices, deliverables, and automated tools that systems developers and project managers are to use to develop and continuously improve information systems.

**System development philosophy:** Follow formal scientific and engineering practice, yet make room for a strong creative element.

**Task analysis:** Studies what users do to reach their goals, how they do it, and what they think and feel during this process.

**Task evaluation metrics:** Specify the expected human–computer interaction goals of the system being designed. There are four types of HCI goals.

**Task level:** Pertains to the information requirements that have to be met.

**Technical support for the hearing-impaired:** Software and hardware design that accommodates hearing-impaired users.

**Technical support for the visually impaired:** Software and hardware design that accommodates visually impaired users.

**Touch:** The human process of sensing environment objects and conditions such as temperature through skin as a sensory organ.

**Trust:** The willingness to rely on an exchange partner due to confidence that the partner will fulfill obligations.

**Ubiquitous computing:** Integrating computation into the environment instead of having computers as distinct objects.

**Usability:** The extent to which a system with given functionality can be used efficiently, effectively, and satisfactorily by specified users to achieve specified goals in a specified context of use.

**Usability engineering:** A process through which usability characteristics are specified, quantitatively and early in the development process, and measured throughout the process.

**Use and impact evaluation:** Conducted during the actual use of the product by real users in real context.

**User activity:** The physical and psychological aspects of the user's interaction with the computer to accomplish a task.

**User analysis:** Identifies the target users of the system and their characteristics.

**User-needs test:** A test during the analysis stage using simple mock-ups to assess the likelihood of the system's functionalities being accepted by its potential users.

**Value:** An object's property that has economic worth or is regarded as being important in the life of someone or a group.

**Value-sensitive design:** A theoretically grounded approach to the design of technology that accounts for human values in a principled and comprehensive manner throughout the design process.

**Virtual devices:** Those that support virtual reality interaction. Virtual reality is an artificial environment that is computer-generated and simulates a real but limited environment.

**Vision:** The human process of seeing and comprehending objects

**Vision problems:** Blurred visions and degraded ability to see brought on by frequent use of computers.

**Visual display:** An output device that is capable of rendering data from a computer. Data may take the form of graphic, tabular, text, or other.

**Well-being:** Reflects an overall concern with the user's physical and psychological welfare.

**Wireless devices:** Devices that are connected to networks and other devices through nonwire media such as infrared signals.

**Work flow management systems:** Systems that are designed to manage the flow of work. These systems include routing information (the path that work follows from person to person or from department to department). Other components of work flow systems include version control and work specification.

**Work group level:** Groups of people who work together, such as departments and project teams.

# Bibliography

Abbas, J. J., & Chizek, H. J. (1991). Feedback control of cornal plane hip angle in paraplegic subjects using functional neuromuscular stimulation. *IEEE Transactions on Biomedical Engineering, 38,* 687–698.

Abowd, G. D., & Mynatt, E. D. (2000). Charting past, present, and future research in ubiquitous computing. *ACM Transactions on Computer-Human Interaction, 7*(1), 29–58.

Agarwal, R., & Karahanna, E. (2000). Time flies when you're having fun: Cognitive absorption and beliefs about information technology usage. *MIS Quarterly, 24*(4), 665–694.

Ajzen, I. (1991). The theory of planned behavior. *Organizational Behavior & Human Decision Processes, 50*(2), 179–211.

Ajzen, I. (2001). Nature and operation of attitudes. *Annual Review of Psychology, 52,* 27–58.

Anthony, R. (1965). *Planning and control systems: A framework for analysis, Cambridge.* Boston, MA: Harvard University Graduate School, Business Administration.

Ba, S., & Pavlou, P. A. (2002). Evidence of the effect of trust building technology in electronic markets: Price premiums and buyer behavior. *MIS Quarterly, 26*(3), 243–268.

Baecker, R., Grudin, J., Buxton, W., & Greenberg, S. (1995). *Readings in human-computer interaction: Toward the year 2000* (2nd ed.). San Francisco, CA: Morgan Kaufmann Publishers, Inc.

Bailey, R. W. (1982). *Human performance engineering: A guide for system designers.* Englewood Cliffs, NJ: Prentice-Hall.

Beach, L. R. (1993). Broadening the definition of decision-making: The role of pre-choice screening of options. *Psychological Science, 4*(4), 215–220.

Beach, L. R., & Potter, R. E. (1992). The pre-choice screening of alternatives. *Acta Psychologica, 81,* 115–126.

Beath, C. M., & Ives, B. (1989). The information technology champion: Aiding and abetting, care and feeding. In P. Gray, W. R. King, E. R. McLean, & H. J. Watson (Eds.), *The management of information systems.* Chicago: Dryden Press.

Beck, K. (2000). *eXtreme programming eXplained.* Upper Saddle River, NJ: Addison-Wesley.

Benbasat, I., Dexter, S. S., & Todd, P. (1986). An experimental program investigating color-enhanced and graphical information presentation: An integration of the findings. *Communications of the ACM, 29*(11), 1094–1105.

Benson, C., Muller-Prove, M., & Mzourek, J. (2004). *Professional usability in open source projects: GNOME, OpenOffice.org, NetBeans.* Paper read at CHI 2004 Conference on Human Factors in Computing Systems, April 24–29, 2004, Vienna, Austria.

Bevan, N. (2001). International standards for HCI and usability. *International Journal of Human-Computer Studies, 55*(4), 533–552.

Bevan, N., Claridge, N., Athousaki, M., & Maguire, M. (2002). *Guide to specifying and evaluating usability as part of a contract.* Retrieved from http://www.usability.serco.com/prue/

Beyer, H., & Holtzblatt, K. (1998). *Contextual design: Defining customer-centered systems.* San Diego: Academic Press.

Bhattacherjee, A. (2001). Understanding information systems continuance: An expectation-confirmation model. *MIS Quarterly, 25*(3), 351–370.

Bjorn-Andersen, N., Eason, K., & Robey, D. (1986). *Managing computer impact: An international study of management and organizations.* Norwood, NJ: Ablex.

Blattner, M. M., Sumikawa, D. A., & Greenberg, R. M. (1989). Earcons and icons: Their structure and common design principles. *Human Computer Interaction, 4*(1), 11–44.

Boland, R., Tenkasi, R., & Te'eni, D. (1994). Designing information technology to support distributed cognition. *Organization Science, 5*(3), 456–475.

Booth, P. A. (1989). *An introduction to human-computer interaction.* Hove & London, UK: Lawrence Erlbaum Assoc.

Bosman, J. S. (1990). Macs talk to visually impaired. *Computerworld, 17.*

Brave, S., & Nass, C. (2003). Emotion in human-computer interaction. In J. Jacko & A. Sears (Eds.), *The human-computer interaction handbook.* Mahwah, NJ: Lawrence Erlbaum Associates, Inc.

Brennen, P. (1993). *Introducing caregivers to computer-based systems.* Paper read at the Fifth Symposium on Human Factors in Information Systems, Cleveland, OH.

Bretz, E. A. (2002). When work is fun and games. *IEEE Online.* Retrieved from http://www.spectrum.ieee.org/WEBONLY/resource/dec02/tool.html

Brewster, S. (2003). Non-speech auditory output. In J. A. Jacko & A. Sears (Eds.), *The human-computer interaction handbook: Fundamentals, evolving technologies, and emerging applications.* Mahwah, NJ: Lawrence Erlbaum Associates, Inc.

Briggs, R. O., Nunamaker, J. F., & Sprague, R. H. (1997/98). 1001 unanswered research questions in GSS. *Journal of Management Information Systems, 14*(2), 3–21.

Brinkman, W. P., Haakma, R., & Bouwhuis, D. G. (2001). *Usability evaluation of component-based user interfaces.* Paper read at IFIP INTERACT'01: Human-Computer Interaction.

Brown, C. (1992). Assistive technology: Computers and persons with disabilities. *Communications of the ACM, 35*(5), 36–45.

Bullinger, H. J. (1988). Principles and illustrations of dialogue design. In H. J. Bullinger & R. Gunzenhauser (Eds.), *Software ergonomics: Advances and applications.* Chichester, UK: Ellis Horwood.

Card, S., Moran, T. P., & Newell, A. (1983). *The psychology of human-computer interaction.* Hillsdale, NJ: Lawrence Erlbaum Associates.

Card, S. K., English, W. K., & Burr, B. J. (1978). Evaluation of mouse, rate-controlled isometric joystick, step keys, and text keys for text selection on a CRT. *Ergonomics, 21,* 601–613.

Carey, J. M. (1998). Creating global software: A conspectus and review. *Interacting with Computers, 8*(4), 437–450.

Carey, J., Galletta, D., Kim, J., Te'eni, D., Wildermuth, B., & Zhang, P. (2004). The role of HCI in IS curricula: A call to action. *Communication of the AIS, 13*(23), 357–379.

Carey-Young, J., Skelly, G. U., & Pitts, R. E. (1983). *Acceptance of change—A management information systems model.* Paper read at Southwest American Institute of Decision Sciences, Houston, TX.

Carroll, J. M., Mack, R. L., & Kellogg, W. A. (1988). Interface metaphors and user interface design. In M. Helander (Ed.), *Handbook of human-computer interaction.* Amsterdam: Elsevier.

Chapanis, A. (1965). *Man machine engineering.* Belmont, CA: Wadsworth.

Chen, H., Wigand, R. T., & Nilan, M. S. (1999). Exploring web users' optimal flow experiences. *Information Technology and People.*

Chernoff, H. (1973). Using faces to represent points in k-dimensional space graphically. *Journal of American Statistical Association, 68,* 361–368.

Cheung, W., Chang, M. K., & Lai, V. S. (2000). Prediction of Internet and World Wide Web usage at work: A test of an extended Triandis model. *Decision Support Systems, 30*(1), 83–100.

Compeau, D. R., & Higgins, C. A. (1995). Computer self efficacy: Development of a measure and initial test. *MIS Quarterly, 19*(2), 189–211.

Cone, E. (2003). The marketing of the president 2004. *Baseline*. Retrieved from http://www.baselinemag.com/print_article2/0,2533,a=114332,00.asp

Csikszentmihalyi, M. (1975). Play and intrinsic rewards. *Humanistic Psychology, 15*, 41–63.

Csikszentmihalyi, M. (1990). *Flow: The psychology of optimal experience*. New York: Harpers Perennial.

Daft, R. L., & Macintosh, N. B. (1981). A tentative exploration into the amount and equivocality of information processing in organizational work units. *Administrative Science Quarterly, 25*, 207–224.

Davis, F. (1989). Perceived usefulness, perceived ease of use, and user acceptance of information technology. *MIS Quarterly, 13*(3), 319–340.

Davis, F. D., Bagozzi, R. P., & Warshaw, P. R. (1989). User acceptance of computer technology: A comparison of two theoretical models. *Management Science, 35*(8), 982–1003.

del Galdo, E. M., & Nielsen, J. (Eds.). (1990). *International user interfaces*. New York: John Wiley & Sons.

Dennis, A. R., & Carte, T. A. (1998). Using geographical information systems for decision making: Extending cognitive fit theory to map-based presentations. *Information Systems Research, 9*(2), 194–203.

DeSanctis, G. (2006). Who is the user? Individuals, groups, communities. In P. Zhang & D. Galletta (Eds.), *Human-computer interaction and management information systems: Foundations*. Armonk, NY: M.E. Sharpe.

DeSanctis, G., & Poole, M. S. (1994). Capturing the complexity in advanced technology use: Adaptive Structuration Theory. *Organization Science, 5*(2), 121–147.

Dey, A. K., Ljungstrand, P., & Schmidt, A. (2001). *Distributed and disappearing user interfaces in ubiquitous computing*. Paper read at ACM CHI 2001 Conference on Human Factors in Computing Systems.

Diaper, D., & Stanton, N. A. (Eds.). (2004). *The handbook of task analysis for human-computer interaction*. Mahwah, NJ: Lawrence Erlbaum Associates.

Didio, L. (1988). Deaf students talk over 10NET LANs. *Network World, 5*(14), 79–81.

Diehl, M., & Stroebe, W. (1987). Productivity loss in brainstorming groups: Toward the solution of a riddle. *Journal of Personality and Social Psychology, 53*(3), 497–509.

Doll, W. J., & Torkzadeh, G. (1988). The measurement of end-user computing satisfaction. *MIS Quarterly, 12*(2), 259–274.

Dowell, J., & Long, J. (1989). Towards a conception for an engineering discipline of human factors. *Ergonomics, 32*, 1513–1535.

Dray, S., & Mzarek, D. (1996). A day in the life: Studying context across cultures. In E. M. del Galdo & J. Nielsen (Eds.), *International user interfaces*. New York: John Wiley and Sons.

Edwards, W. K., Newman, M. W., & Sedivy, J. Z. (2001). *Building the ubiquitous computing user experience*. Paper read at ACM CHI 2001 Conference on Human Factors in Computing Systems.

Elwart Keys, M., Halonen, D., Horton, M., Kass, R., & Scott, P. (1990). *User interface requirements for face to face groupware*. Paper read at Human Factors in Computing Systems, CHI'90.

Erickson, T. D. (1980). Working with interface metaphors. In Lakoff & Johnson (Eds.), *Metaphors we live by*. Chicago: University of Chicago Press.

Erickson, T., & Kellogg, W. A. (2000). Social translucence: An approach to designing systems that support social processes. *ACM Transactions on Computer-Human Interaction, 7*(1), 59–83.

ERP's second wave: Post-implementation best practices. (2002). *Government Finance Review, 18*(1), 48–49.

Fearrell, P. S. E., Hollands, J. G., Taylor, M. M., & Gamble, H. D. (1999). Perceptual control and layered protocols in interface design: I. Fundamental concepts. *International Journal of Human-Computer Studies, 50*(6), 489–520.

Finneran, C. M., & Zhang, P. (2003). A person-artefact-task (PAT) model of flow antecedents in computer-mediated environments. *International Journal of Human-Computer Studies, 59*(4), 475–496.

Fogg, B. J., & Tseng, H. (1999). *The elements of computer credibility.* Paper read at Human Factors in Computing Systems (CHI).

Forgas, J. P. (1995). Mood and judgment: The Affect Infusion Model (AIM). *Psychological Bulletin, 117*(1), 39–66.

Fowler, M., & Highsmith, J. (2001). *The Agile Manifesto.* Retrieved August 18, 2004, from http://www.sdmagazine.com

Friedman, B., Kahn, P. H., & Borning, A. (2006). Value sensitive design and information systems. In P. Zhang & D. Galletta (Eds.), *Human-computer interaction and management information systems: Foundations.* Armonk, NY: M. E. Sharpe.

Frishberg, N., Dirks, A. M., Benson, C., Nickell, S., & Smith, S. (2002). *Getting to know you: Open source development meets usability.* Paper read at CHI 2002 Conference on Human Factors in Computing Systems.

Gale, S. F. (2002). For ERP success, create a culture change. *Workforce, 81*(9), 88–94.

Gaver, W. W. (1991). *Technology affordances.* Paper read at Human Factors in Computing Systems (CHI).

Gaver, W. W. (1997). Auditory interfaces. In M. G. Helander, T. K. Landauer, & P. Prabhu (Eds.), *Handbook of human-computer interaction.* Amsterdam: Elsevier Science.

Ghani, J. (1995). Flow in human computer interactions: Test of a model. In J. Carey (Ed.), *Human factors in information systems: Emerging theoretical bases.* New Jersey: Ablex Publishing Corp.

Gibbs, W. W. (1997). Taking computers to task. *Scientific American*, July, 82–89.

Ginzberg, M. J. (1981). Early diagnosis of MIS implementation failure: Promising results and unanswered questions. *Management Science, 27*(4), 459–479.

Goodhue, D. L., & Thompson, R. L. (1995). Task-technology fit and individual performance. *MIS Quarterly, 19*(2), 213–236.

Gorn, G. J., Chattopadhyay, A., Yi, T., & Dahl, D. W. (1997). Effects of color as an executional cue in advertising: They're in the shade. *Management Science, 43*(10), 1387–1400.

Gould, J. D., & Lewis, C. (1985). Designing for usability: Key principles and what designers think. *Communications of the ACM, 28*(3), 300–311.

Grandjean, E. (1987). *Ergonomics in computerized offices.* London: Taylor and Francis.

Gray, P., Mandviwalla, M., Olfman, L., & Satzinger, J. (1993). The user interface in group support systems. In L. M. Jessup & J. S. Valacich (Eds.), *Group support systems—New perspectives.* New York: Macmillan Publishing Company.

Green, R. (1999). *Component-based software development: Implications for documentation.* Paper read at ACM 17th International Conference on Systems Documentation.

Greenstein, J. S. (1997). Pointing devices. In M. G. Helander, T. K. Landauer, & P. Prabhu (Eds.), *Handbook of human-computer interaction.* Amsterdam: Elsevier Science.

Grefen, P., Aberer, K., Hoffner, Y., & Ludwig, H. (2000). CrossFlow: Cross-organizational workflow management in dynamic virtual organizations. *International Journal of Computer Systems Science and Engineering, 15*(5), 277–290.

Grudin, J. (1989). The case against user interface consistency. *Communications of the ACM, 32*(10), 1164–1173.

Grudin, J. (1992). Utility and usability: Research issues and development contexts. *Interacting with Computers, 4*(2), 209–217.

Grudin, J. (1996). The organizational contexts of development and use. *ACM Computing Surveys, 28*(1), 169–171.

Grundy, J., & Hosking, J. (2002). Developing adaptable user interfaces for component-based systems. *Interacting with Computers, 14*, 175–194.

Hammond, N., & Barnard, P. (1984). Dialogue design: Characteristics of user knowledge. In A. Monk (Ed.), *Fundamentals of human-computer interaction*. London: Academic Press.

Hartson, H. R., & Hix, D. (1989). Toward empirically derived methodologies and tools for HCI development. *International Journal of Man-Machine Studies, 31*, 477–494.

Hassenzahl, M., Beu, A., & Burmester, M. (2001). Engineering joy. *IEEE Software* (January/February), 70–76.

Hefley, W. E., et. al. (1995). Integrating human factors with software engineering practices. In G. Perlman, G. K. Green, & M. S. Wogalter (Eds.), *Human factors perspectives on human-computer interaction: Selections from the Human Factors & Ergonomics Society Annual Meetings 1983-1994*. Santa Monica, CA: Human Factors and Ergonomics Society. (Original edition, *HFES Proceedings 1994*, pp. 315–319.)

Henry, P. (2003). Advancing UCD while facing challenges working from offshore. *Interactions: New Visions of Human-Computer Interaction, 10*(2), 38–47.

Hix, D., & Hartson, H. R. (1993). *Developing user interfaces: Ensuring usability through product and process*. New York: John Wiley.

Hoadley, E. D. (1990). Investigating the effects of color. *Communications of the ACM, 33*(2), 120–125.

Hoffer, J. A., George, J. F., & Valacich, J. S. (2005). *Modern systems analysis and design* (4th ed.). Upper Saddle River, NJ: Prentice Hall.

Hoffman, D. L., Novak, T. P., & Peralta, M. (1999). Building consumer trust online. *Communications of the ACM, 42*(4), 80–85.

Hofstede, G. (1991). *Cultures and organizations*. New York: McGraw-Hill.

Hoft, N. (1996). Developing a cultural model. In E. M. del Galdo & J. Nielsen (Eds.), *International user interfaces*. New York: John Wiley and Sons.

Hogarth, R. M. (1987). *Judgment and choice* (2nd ed.). Chichester: John Wiley & Sons.

Hong, K. K., & Kim, Y. G. (2002). The critical success factors for ERP implementation: An organizational fit perspective. *Information and Management, 40*(1), 25–40.

Hudlicka, E. (2003). To feel or not to feel: The role of affect in human-computer interaction. *International Journal of Human-Computer Studies, 59*(1–2), 1–32.

Hussain, D., & Hussain, K. M. (1984). *Information resource management*. Homewood, IL: Irwin.

Hutchines, E. L., Hollan, J. D., & Norman, D. A. (1986). Direct manipulation interfaces. In D. A. Norman & S. W. Draper (Eds.), *User centered systems design: New perspectives on human-computer interaction*. New Jersey: Lawrence Erlbaum Associates.

Igbaria, M., Parasuraman, S., & Baroudi, J. J. (1996). A motivational model of microcomputer usage. *Journal of Management Information Systems, 13*(1), 127.

Ishida, T., Nishida, T., & Hattori, F. (1998). Overview of community computing. In T. Ishida (Ed.), *Community computing: Collaboration over global information networks*. New York: Wiley.

Ishii, H. (1990). *Teamworkstation: Towards a seamless shared workspace*. Paper read at Computer Supported Cooperative Work.

Ishii, H., Kobayashi, M., & Grudin, J. (1992). *Integration of interpersonal space and shared workspaces*. Paper read at Computer Supported Cooperative Work.

Ito, M., & Nakakoji, K. (1996). Impact of culture on user interface design. In E. M. del Galdo & J. Nielsen (Eds.), *International user interfaces*. New York: John Wiley and Sons.

Iwata, H. (2003). Haptic interfaces. In J. A. Jacko & A. Sears (Eds.), *The human-computer interaction handbook: Fundamentals, evolving technologies, and emerging applications.* Mahwah, NJ: Lawrence Erlbaum Associates, Inc.

Jarvenpaa, S. L., & Dickson, G. W. (1988). Graphics and managerial decision making: Research-based guidelines. *Communications of the ACM, 31*(6), 764–774.

Jessup, L. M., & Valacich, J. S. (1993). Future directions and challenges in the evolution of group systems. In L. M. Jessup & J. S. Valacich (Eds.), *Group support systems—New perspectives.* New York: Macmillan Publishing Company.

Joshi, A. (2004). *Institutionalizing HCI, the challenges in India.* Paper read at the 39th Annual National Convention of the Computer Society of India, December 3, 2004, Taj Lands End, Mumbai.

Kano, N. (1995). *Developing international software: For Windows 95 and Windows NT.* Redmond, WA: Microsoft Press.

Kanter, R. M. (1985). Innovation—The only hope for times ahead. In *The best of MIT's Sloan Management Review.* Boston, MA: The Sloan School, MIT.

Karat, C. M., Vergo, J., & Nahamoo, D. (2003). Conversational interface technologies. In J. A. Jacko & A. Sears (Eds.), *The human-computer interaction handbook: Fundamentals, evolving technologies, and emerging applications.* Mahwah, NJ: Lawrence Erlbaum Associates, Inc.

Keeney, R. L. (1999). The value of Internet commerce to the customer. *Management Science, 44*(4), 533–542.

Kehoe, C., Pitkow, J., Sutton, K., Aggarwal, G., & Rogers, J. D. (1999). Results of GVU's Tenth World Wide Web User Survey: Graphics Visualization and Usability Center, Georgia Institute of Technology. Retrieved from http://www.gvu.gatech.edu/user_surveys

Kelley, C. L., & Charness, N. (1995). Issues in training older adults to use computers. *Behaviour and Information Technology, 14*(2), 107–120.

Kennedy, M., Te'eni, D., & Treleaven, J. (1998). Impacts of decision task, data and display on strategies for extracting information. *International Journal of Human Computer Studies, 48*, 159–180.

Kieras, D. E. (1988). Towards a practical GOMS model methodology for user interface design. In M. Helander (Ed.), *Handbook of human-computer interaction.* Amsterdam: Elsevier Science Publishers.

Kieras, D. E., & Polson, P. G. (1985). An approach to the formal analysis of user complexity. *International Journal of Man-Machine Studies, 22*(4), 365–394.

Kim, J., Lee, J., & Choi, D. (2003). Designing emotionally evocative homepages: An empirical study of the quantitative relations between design factors and emotional dimensions. *International Journal of Human-Computer Studies, 59*(6), 899–940.

Kumar, N., & Benbasat, I. (2004). The effect of anchoring and encoding on information representation: A comparison of 2D and 3D graphs. *MIS Quarterly, 28*(2), 255–281.

Kurke, L. B., & Aldrich, H. E. (1983). Mintzberg was right! A replication and extension of The Nature of Managerial Work. *Management Science, 29*, 975–984.

Labar, G. (1997). Ergonomics for the virtual office. *Managing-Office-Technology, 42*(10), 22–24.

Lavie, T., & Tractinsky, N. (2004). Assessing dimensions of perceived visual aesthetics of web sites. *International Journal of Human-Computer Studies, 60*(3), 269–298.

Lawrence, P. (Ed.). (1997). *Workflow handbook.* New York: John Wiley & Sons.

Legare, T. E. (2002). The role of organizational factors in realizing ERP benefits. *Information Systems Management, 19*(4), 21–42.

Lewis, J. D., & Weigert, A. (1985). Trust as a social reality. *Social Forces, 63*(4), 967–985.

Lewis, J. R., Potosnak, K. M., & Magyar, R. L. (1997). Keys and keyboards. In M. G. Helander, T. K. Landauer, & P. Prabhu (Eds.), *Handbook of human-computer interaction.* Amsterdam: Elsevier Science.

Licklider, J. C. R., & Taylor, R. W. (1968). The computer as a communication device. *Science and Technology,* 21–31.

Lim, L. H., Raman, K. S., & Wei, K. K. (1994). Interacting effects of GDSS and leadership. *Decision Support Systems, 12*(3), 199–211.

Lindsey, E. (1999). Keying in on computer problems. *Business-Insurance, 33*(37), 3–10.

Luong, T. V., Lok, J. S. H., Taylor, D., & Driscoll, K. (1995). *Internationalization: Developing software for global markets.* New York: John Wiley & Sons.

Mann, C. L. (2004). What global sourcing means for U.S. IT workers and for the U.S. economy. *Communication of the ACM, 47*(7), 33–35.

Mantei, M., & Teorey, T. (1989). Incorporating behavioral techniques into the system development life cycle. *MIS Quarterly, 13*(3), 257–274.

Marcus, A. (2004). Insights on outsourcing—What's in it for us? For them? Where are we headed? *Interactions: New Visions of Human-Computer Interaction, XI*(4), 12–17.

Maxwell, K. (2002). The maturation of HCI: Moving beyond usability toward holistic interaction. In J. M. Carroll (Ed.), *Human-computer interaction in the new millennium.* New York: Addison-Wesley.

Mayhew, D. J. (1999). *The usability engineering lifecycle—A practitioner's handbook for user interface design.* San Francisco, CA: Morgan Kaufmann Publishers, Inc.

Mehlenbacher, B. (2003). Documentation: Not yet implemented, but coming soon! In J. A. Jacko & A. Sears (Eds.), *The human-computer interaction handbook: Fundamentals, evolving technologies and emerging applications.* Mahwah, NJ: Lawrence Erlbaum Associates, Publishers.

Mejias, R. J., Lazeneo, L., Rico, A., Torres, A., Vogel, D. R., & Shepherd, M. (1996). *A cross-cultural comparison of GSS and non-GSS consensus and satisfaction levels within and between the U.S. and Mexico.* Paper read at Hawaii International Conference on Systems Science.

Mintzberg, H. (1973). *The nature of managerial work.* New York: Harper and Row.

Moon, J. Y., & Kim, J. (2003). Can interfaces affect users' feeling? *A model of the impact of the customer interface on the shopping experience.* Working paper.

Moorman, C., Deshpande, R., & Zaltman, G. (1993). Factors affecting trust in market research relationships. *Journal of Marketing, 57*(1), 81–101.

Moran, T. P. (1981). The command language grammar: A representation for the user interface of interactive computer systems. *International Journal of Man-Machine Studies, 15*(1), 3–50.

Morgan, R. M., & Hunt, S. D. (1994). The commitment-trust theory of relationship marketing. *Journal of Marketing, 58*(8), 20–38.

Murata, A. (1991). An experimental evaluation of mouse, joystick, joycard, lightpen, trackball, and touchscreen for pointing. In H.-J. Bullinger (Ed.), *Human aspects in computing: Design and use of interactive systems and work with computers.* Amsterdam: Elsevier.

Nelson, S. (2000). From e-commerce to CRM: The database as core system. Research report from the Gartner Group. Retrieved from http://www.ncr.com/repositor//research_reports/pdf/gartner_dbcore.pdf

Ngo, D. C. L., & Byrne, J. G. (2001). Application of an aesthetic evaluation model to data entry screens. *Computers in Human Behavior, 17*(2), 149–185.

Nielsen, J. (1993). *Usability engineering.* New York: AP Professional.

Nielsen, J. (2000). *Designing Web usability.* Indianapolis, IN: New Riders.

Nielsen, J., & Mack, R. L. (1994). *Usability inspection methods.* New York: John Wiley & Sons.

Norman, D. (1986). Cognitive engineering. In D. Norman & S. Draper (Eds.), *User centered design: New perspectives on human-computer interaction.* Hillsdale, NJ: Lawrence Erlbaum.

Norman, D. A. (1983). Design rules based on analyses of human error. *Communications of the ACM, 26*(4), 254–258.

Norman, D. A. (1988). *The design of everyday things.* New York: Doubleday.

Norman, D. A. (2002). Emotion and design: Attractive things work better. *Interactions: New Visions of Human-Computer Interaction, IX*(4), 36–42.

Norman, D. A. (2004). *Emotional design: Why we love (or hate) everyday things.* Cambridge, MA: Basic Books.

Olson, J., & Nilsen, E. (1988). Analysis of the cognition involved in spreadsheet software interaction. *Human-Computer Interaction, 3*, 309–349.

Parent, M., & Gallupe, R. B. (2001). The role of leadership in group support systems failure. *Group Decision and Negotiation, 10*, 405–422.

Pavett, C. M., & Lau, A. W. (1983). Managerial work: The influence of hierarchical level and functional specialty. *Academy of Management Journal, 26*, 170–177.

Phillips, L. A., Calantone, R., & Lee, M. T. (1994). International technology adoption: Behavior structure, demand certainty and culture. *The Journal of Business & Industrial Marketing, 9*(4), 16–25.

Picard, R. W. (1997). *Affective computing.* Cambridge, MA: MIT Press.

Post, D. L. (1997). Color and human-computer interaction. In M. G. Helander, T. K. Landauer, & P. V. Prabhu (Eds.), *Handbook of human-computer interaction.* Amsterdam: Elsevier.

Potter, R. E., & Balthazard, P. A. (2002). Understanding human interaction and performance in the virtual team. *The Journal of Information Technology Theory & Application, 4*(1), 1–25.

Preece, J., Rogers, Y., & Sharp, H. (2002). *Interaction design: Beyond human-computer interaction.* New York: John Wiley & Sons.

Preece, J., Rogers, Y., Sharp, H., Benyon, D., Holland, S., & Carey, T. (1994). *Human-computer interaction.* Reading, MA: Addison-Wesley.

QUIS. Retrieved from http://www.lap.umd.edu/QUIS/index.html

Rasmussen, J. (1986). *Information processing and human-machine interaction.* Amsterdam: North Holland.

Raymond, D. N., Niekerk, V., & Berthon, J. P. (1999). Going with the flow: Web sites and customer involvement. *Internet Research, 9*(2), 109–116.

Reason, J. (1990). *Human error.* Cambridge: Cambridge University Press.

Reeve, J. (2005). *Understanding motivation and emotion* (4th ed.). New York: John Wiley & Sons, Inc.

Reeves, B., & Nass, C. I. (1996). *The media equation: How people treat computers, televisions, and new media as real people and places.* New York: Cambridge University Press.

Robson, C. (2002). *Real world research: A resource for social scientists and practitioner-researchers.* Oxford, UK: Blackwell.

Rogers, E. (1983). *Diffusion of innovations* (3rd ed.). New York: The Free Press.

Rosson, M. B., & Carroll, J. M. (2002). *Usability engineering: Scenario-based development of human-computer interaction.* New York: Morgan Kaufmann Publishers.

Russell, J. A. (2003). Core affect and the psychological construction of emotion. *Psychological Review, 110*(1), 145–172.

Schenkman, B. N., & Jonsson, F. U. (2000). Aesthetics and preferences of Web pages. *Behaviour & Information Technology, 19*(5), 367–377.

Schwartz, D., & Te'eni, D. (2000). Tying knowledge to action with kMail. *IEEE Intelligent Systems, 15*(3), 33–39.

Shay, S. (1998). The eyes have it. *CIO, 11*(9), 18.

Shen, H., & Dewan, P. (1992). *Access for collaborative environments.* Paper read at Computer Supported Cooperative Work, New York.

Shneiderman, B. (1987). *Designing the user interface: Strategies for effective human-computer interaction*. Reading, MA: Addison-Wesley.

Shneiderman, B. (1990). *Human values and the future of technology: A declaration of responsibility*. Paper read at the Third Symposium on Human Factors in Information Systems, Norman, OK.

Shneiderman, B. (1998). *Designing the user interface—Strategies for effective human-computer interaction* (3rd ed.). Reading, MA: Addison-Wesley.

Shneiderman, B. (2000a). Creating creativity: User interfaces for supporting innovation. *ACM Transactions on Computer-Human Interaction, 7*(1), 114–138.

Shneiderman, B. (2000b). Universal usability. *Communication of the ACM, 43*(5), 84–91.

Shneiderman, B. (2002). *Leonardo's laptop: Human needs and the new computing technologies*. Cambridge, MA: MIT Press.

Shneiderman, B., & Plaisant, C. (2005). *Designing the user interface: Strategies for effective human-computer interaction*. New York: Addison-Wesley.

Sia, S. K., Tang, M., Soh, C., & Boh, W. F. (2002). Enterprise Resource Planning (ERP) systems as a technology of power: Empowerment or panoptic control? *Database for Advances in Information Systems, 33*(1), 23–37.

Siegal, J., Dubrovsky, V., Kiesler, S., & McGuire, T. W. (1986). Group processes in computer mediated communication. *Organizational Behavior and Human Decision Processes, 37*, 177–187.

Siemens. (2002). Webzine. Retrieved from http://w4.siemens.de/Ful/en/archiv/pof/heft2_02/artikle13/

Silver, M. S. (1991). *Systems that support decision makers: Description and analysis*. Chichester: John Wiley & Sons.

Smith, S. L., & Mosier, J. N. (1984). *Design guidelines for user-system interface software*. Hanscom Air Force Base, USAF Electronic Systems Division.

Spears, R., & Lee, M. (1992). Social influence and the influence of the "social" in computer mediated communication. In M. Lea (Ed.), *Contexts of computer mediated communication*. Hemel Hempstead: Harvester Wheatsheaf.

Sprague, R. H., Jr., & Mcnurlin, B. C. (1993). *Information systems management in practice* (3rd ed.). Englewood Cliffs, NJ: Prentice-Hall.

Stanton, N. A. (2001). Introduction: Ubiquitous computing: Anytime, anyplace, anywhere? *International Journal of Human-Computer Interaction, 13*(2), 107–111.

Sterman, J. D. (1989). Modeling managerial behavior: Misperceptions of feedback in a dynamic decision making experiment. *Management Science, 35*, 321–339.

Steuer, J. (1992). Defining virtual reality: Dimensions determining telepresence. *Journal of Communication, 42*(4), 73–93.

Sumi, Y., & Mase, K. (2002). Conference assistant system for supporting knowledge sharing in academic communities. *Interacting with Computers, 14*, 713–737.

Summerhoff, E. W. (1999). Positioning laptops for future use. *Facilities-Design-and-Management, 18*(6), 34.

Sun, H., & Zhang, P. (2006). The role of affect in IS research: A critical survey and a research model. In P. Zhang & D. Galletta (Eds.), *Human-computer interaction and management information systems: Foundations*. Armonk, NY: M.E. Sharpe.

Sutcliffe, A. (1997). Task-related information analysis. *International Journal of Human-Computer Studies, 47*, 223–257.

Sutcliffe, A. (2000). On the effective use and reuse of HCI knowledge. *ACM Transactions on Computer-Human Interaction, 7*(2).

Tan, B. C. Y., Watson, R. T., & Wei, K. K. (1995). National culture and group support systems: Filtering communication to dampen power differentials. *European Journal of Information Systems, 4*(2), 82–92.

Taylor, D. (1992). *Global software*. New York: Springer Verlag.

Te'eni, D. (1989). Determinants and consequences of perceived complexity in human-computer interaction. *Decision Sciences, 20*, 166–181.

Te'eni, D. (1991). Feedback in DSS: Experiments with the timing of feedback. *Decision Sciences, 22*, 597–609.

Te'eni, D. (1992). Process feedback in DSS. *Accounting, Management and Information Technology, 2*(1), 1–18.

Te'eni, D. (2001). A cognitive-affective model of organizational communication for designing IT. *MIS Quarterly, 25*(2), 251–312.

Te'eni, D. (2006). Designs that fit: An overview of fit conceptualizations in HCI. In P. Zhang & D. Galletta (Eds.), *Human-computer interaction and management information systems: Foundations*. Armonk, NY: M.E. Sharpe.

Tero, A., & Briggs, P. (1994). Consistency versus compatibility: A question of levels? *International Journal of Man-Machine Studies, 40*(5), 879–894.

Thatcher, J. B., & Perrewe, P. L. (2002). An empirical examination of individual traits as antecedents to computer anxiety and computer self-efficacy. *MIS Quarterly, 26*(4), 381–396.

Tichauer, E. R. (1978). *The mechanical basis of ergonomics*. New York: John Wiley.

Todd, P., & Benbasat, I. (1992). An experimental investigation of the impact of computer based decision aids on processing effort. *Management Information Systems Quarterly, 16*(2), 373–393.

Todd, P., & Benbasat, I. (2000). Decision aids and compensatory information processing. *Journal of Behavioral Decision Making, 13*(1), 91–106.

Tognazzini, B. (1990). Consistency. In B. Laurel (Ed.), *The art of human-computer interface design*. Reading, MA: Addison-Wesley.

Tractinsky, N., Katz, A. S., & Ikar, D. (2000). What is beautiful is usable. *Interacting with Computers, 13*, 127–145.

Trevino, L. K., & Webster, J. (1992). Flow in computer-mediated communication. *Communication Research, 19*(5), 539–573.

Tullis, T. S. (1997). Screen design. In M. Helander, T. Landauer, & P. Prabhu (Eds.), *Handbook of human-computer interaction*. Amsterdam: North-Holland.

Tversky, A., & Kahneman, D. (1974). Judgment under uncertainty: Heuristics and biases. *Science, 185*, 1124–1130.

Uren, E., Howard, R., & Perinotti, T. (1993). *Software internationalization and localization*. New York: Van Nostrand.

Valacich, J. S., George, J. M., & Hoffer, J. A. (2004). *Essentials of systems analysis and design* (2nd ed.). Upper Saddle River, NJ: Prentice Hall.

Vandenbosch, B., & Huff, S. L. (1997). Searching and scanning: How executives obtain information from executive information systems. *MIS Quarterly, 21*(1), 81–107.

Venkatesh, V., Morris, M. G., Davis, G. B., & Davis, F. D. (2003). User acceptance of information technology: Toward a unified view. *MIS Quarterly, 27*(3), 425–478.

Vessey, I. (1991). Cognitive fit: A theory-based analysis of the graphs versus tables literature. *Decision Sciences, 22*, 219–240.

Vessey, I., & Galletta, D. F. (1991). Cognitive fit: An empirical study of information acquisition. *Information Systems Research, 2*(1), 63–84.

Vredenburg, K., Mao, J., Smith, P. W., & Carey, T. (2002). *A survey of user-centered design practice*. Paper read at Computer Human Interaction (CHI).

Wagner, C. G. (1992). Enabling the "disabled." *Futurist, 26*(3), 29–32.

Waldrop, J. (1990). From handicap to advantage. *American Demographics, 12*(4), 32–35.

Watson, H., Rainer, R. K., & Koh, C. E. (1991). Executive Information Systems: A framework for development and a survey of current practices. *MIS Quarterly, 15*(1).

Watson, R. T., Ho, T. H., & Raman, K. S. (1994). Culture: A fourth dimension of group support systems. *Communications of the ACM, 37*(10), 44–55.

Webster, J., & Martocchio, J. J. (1992). Microcomputer playfulness: Development of a measure with workplace implications. *MIS Quarterly, 16*(1).

Webster, J., Trevino, L. K., & Ryan, L. (1993). The dimensionality and correlates of flow in human-computer interactions. *Computers in Human Behavior, 9*(4), 411–426.

Weiser, M. (1991). The computer for the 21st century. *Scientific American.*

Whitten, J., Bentley, L., & Dittman, K. (2004). *Systems analysis and design methods* (6th ed.). Boston: McGraw-Hill Irwin.

Williams, C. M. (1973). System response time: A study of users' tolerance. IBM Technical Report.

Woodson, W. E. (1981). *Human factors design handbook: Information and guidelines for the design of systems, facilities, equipment, and products for human use.* New York: McGraw Hill.

Zachary, W. W. (1988). Decision Support Systems: Designing to extend the cognitive limits. In M. Helander (Ed.), *Handbook of human-computer interaction.* Amsterdam: Elsevier.

Zelazny, G. (1999). *Say it with presentations: How to design and deliver successful business presentations* (3rd ed.). New York: McGraw-Hill.

Zhang, P., Benbasat, I., Carey, J., Davis, F., Galletta, D., & Strong, D. (2002). Human-computer interaction research in the MIS discipline. *Communications of the AIS, 9*(20), 334–355.

Zhang, P., Carey, J., Te'eni, D., & Tremaine, M. (2005). Integrating human-computer interaction development into the systems development life cycle: A methodology. *Communications of the AIS, 15*, 512–543.

Zhang, P., & Li, N. (2004a). An assessment of human-computer interaction research in management information systems: Topics and methods. *Computers in Human Behavior, 20*(2), 125–147.

Zhang, P., & Li, N. (2004b). *Love at first sight or sustained effect? The role of perceived affective quality on users' cognitive reactions to IT.* Paper read at International Conference on Information Systems (ICIS'04), Washington, DC.

Zhang, P., & Li, N. (2005). The importance of affective quality. *Communications of the ACM, 48*(9), 105–108.

Zhang, P., von Dran, G., Blake, P., & Pipithsuksunt, V. (2001). Important design features in different website domains: An empirical study of user perceptions. *e-Service Journal, 1*(1), 77–91.

Zviran, M., Te'eni, D., & Gross, Y. (2005). Colored e-mail is cheap, but does it make a difference? *Communication of the ACM,* in press.

# Index